D0295618

4£6 28/05/04

LIBRARY
Tel: 01244 375444 Ext: 3301

This book is to be returned on or before the last date stamped below. Overdue charges will be incurred by the late return of books.

CHESTER COLLEGE

CANCELLED

1 3 DEC 2004

CANCELLED
23 MAR 2005

CANCELLED
- 2 OCT 2006

UNDERSTANDING MOTOR DEVELOPMENT

Fifth Edition

UNDERSTANDING MOTOR DEVELOPMENT

Infants, Children, Adolescents, Adults

David L. Gallahue
Indiana University

John C. Ozmun
Indiana State University

Boston   Burr Ridge, IL   Dubuque, IA   Madison, WI   New York   San Francisco   St. Louis
Bangkok   Bogotá   Caracas   Kuala Lumpur   Lisbon   London   Madrid   Mexico City
Milan   Montreal   New Delhi   Santiago   Seoul   Singapore   Sydney   Taipei   Toronto

McGraw-Hill Higher Education

*A Division of The **McGraw-Hill** Companies*

UNDERSTANDING MOTOR DEVELOPMENT: INFANTS, CHILDREN, ADOLESCENTS, ADULTS, FIFTH EDITION

Published by McGraw-Hill, a business unit of The McGraw-Hill Companies, Inc., 1221 Avenue of the Americas, New York, NY 10020. Copyright © 2002, 1998, 1995, 1989 by The McGraw-Hill Companies, Inc. All rights reserved. No part of this publication may be reproduced or distributed in any form or by any means, or stored in a database or retrieval system, without the prior written consent of The McGraw-Hill Companies, Inc., including, but not limited to, in any network or other electronic storage or transmission, or broadcast for distance learning.

Some ancillaries, including electronic and print components, may not be available to customers outside the United States.

This book is printed on acid-free paper.

International   1 2 3 4 5 6 7 8 9 0 QPF/QPF 0 9 8 7 6 5 4 3 2 1
Domestic   2 3 4 5 6 7 8 9 0 QPF/QPF 0 9 8 7 6 5 4 3 2

ISBN 0-07-235366-X
ISBN 0-07-112198-6 (ISE)

Vice president and editor-in-chief: *Thalia Dorwick*
Executive editor: *Vicki Malinee*
Developmental editor: *Carlotta Seely*
Senior marketing manager: *Pamela S. Cooper*
Project manager: *Richard H. Hecker*
Production supervisor: *Enboge Chong*
Coordinator of freelance design: *Michelle D. Whitaker*
Cover designer: *Joshua Van Drake*
Cover images: *Runner and Swimmer images/PhotoDisc, Baby and Senior Citizen images/Stone*
Senior photo research coordinator: *Lori Hancock*
Supplement producer: *Brenda A. Ernzen*
Media technology producer: *Judi David*
Compositor: *Interactive Composition Corporation*
Typeface: *10/12 Minion*
Printer: *Quebecor World Fairfield, PA*

Unit opener 1: © PhotoDisc/Volume 58; Unit opener 3: © PhotoDisc/Volume 45;
Unit opener 4: ©: PhotoDisc/Volume 51; Unit opener 5: © PhotoDisc/Volume 51.

Library of Congress Cataloging-in-Publication Data

Gallahue, David L.
   Understanding motor development : infants, children, adolescents, adults / David L. Gallahue, John C. Ozmun. — 5th ed.
      p. cm.
   Includes bibliographical references and index.
   ISBN 0-07-235366-X — ISBN 0-07-112198-6 (ISE)
   1. Motor ability in children. 2. Motor ability. 3. Physical education for children.
I. Ozmun, John C., 1958-. II. Title.

RJ133 .G344   2002   2001044178
152.3—dc21   CIP

The Internet addresses listed in the text were accurate at the time of publication. The inclusion of a website does not indicate an endorsement by the authors or McGraw-Hill, and McGraw-Hill does not guarantee the accuracy of the information presented at these sites.

INTERNATIONAL EDITION ISBN 0-07-112198-6

Copyright © 2002. Exclusive rights by The McGraw-Hill Companies, Inc., for manufacture and export. This book cannot be re-exported from the country to which it is sold by McGraw-Hill. The International Edition is not available in North America.

www.mhhe.com

As always, *To the Sunshine of My Life:*
Ellie, David Lee, Jennifer, and Dan
DAVID L. GALLAHUE

To *the Treasures of My Heart:*
Ruth, Chet, Gus, Johnny, and Ray
JOHN C. OZMUN

BRIEF CONTENTS

CONTENTS

PREFACE

AUDIENCE

Understanding Motor Development is written for students taking a first course in motor development. It is presented in an easy-to-understand and easy-to-use manner to be of significant value to educators from a variety of disciplines, including kinesiology, physical and occupational therapy, special education, early childhood education, and elementary and secondary education. This text provides both descriptive and explanatory profiles of the individual from conception through adulthood.

APPROACH

Development is a process that begins at conception and continues throughout life. This text discusses motor development from conception through adulthood. Also, we have chosen to include primary cognitive and affective markers that affect motor development during each of these periods and have expanded coverage of these topics. By incorporating dynamic systems theory along with the hourglass model of the phases and stages of motor development we provide the reader with both an explanatory and descriptive basis for the processes and products of motor development.

CONTENT

Organization

Unit I: Background, provides the reader with essential introductory information on the study of motor development. Chapter 1, "Understanding Motor Development: An Overview," examines the history, methods of study, research problems, and terminology used in the study of motor development. Chapter 2, "Models of Human Development," offers a discussion of developmental models of child development. Particular attention is given to dynamic systems theory as well as the works of Jean Piaget, Erik Erikson, and Urie Bronfenbrenner and the implications of each for motor development. In chapter 3, "Motor Development: A Theoretical Model," a theoretical framework for studying the process of motor development is presented. The phases and stages of this life span model, as well as the subsystems of the task, the individual, and the environment serve as the organizational framework for the remainder of the text. In chapter 4, "Selected Factors Affecting Motor Development," there is an important discussion of critical factors within the individual, environment, and movement tasks that influence the process of development throughout life.

Unit II: Infancy, deals with a variety of important developmental topics of infancy.

Chapter 5, "Prenatal Factors Affecting Development," is devoted to discussion of those factors prior to birth that may affect later motor development. "Prenatal and Infant Growth" is the topic of chapter 6. This chapter provides the reader with a descriptive profile of early growth processes. Chapter 7 examines "Infant Reflexes and Rhythmical Stereotypies" in the neonate and young infant. Particular attention is given to the integration of both into the expanding movement repertoire of the young child. Chapter 8, "Rudimentary Movement Abilities," discusses the rapidly expanding movement repertoire of infants. The major stability, locomotor, and manipulative tasks of this period are outlined and summarized. An extensive discussion of "Infant Perception" in chapter 9 concludes the section on infancy. This chapter relates perceptual development to the motor behavior of infants.

Unit III: Childhood, provides the reader with a wealth of important information about childhood motor development. Chapter 10, "Childhood Growth and Development," offers a general overview of cognitive, affective, and motor characteristics during early and later childhood. This sets the stage for the three chapters that follow. Chapter 11, "Fundamental Movement Abilities," provides a practical, easy-to-use, three-stage approach (initial, elementary, mature) to observing and assessing the fundamental movement patterns of childhood. Mechanically correct line drawings provide a visual description that coincides with a brief verbal description of each stage, along with frequently encountered developmental difficulties. "Physical Development of Children" is the topic of chapter 12. A review of the latest information on children's health-related fitness and motor fitness is presented along with information on fitness training for children. "Childhood Perception and Perceptual-Motor Development" is the topic of chapter 13. Important information on both of these topics is reviewed and synthesized with a view toward their complex interaction with the motor behavior of the individual. Chapter 14 concludes the section on childhood with a discussion of "Childhood Self-Concept Development." The

latest information on self-esteem is reviewed along with the role of movement as an important facilitator of a positive self-concept.

Unit IV: Adolescence, examines a number of important topics. Chapter 15, "Adolescent Growth, Puberty, and Reproductive Maturity," opens this section with a wealth of important and useful information about physical change during this critical developmental period. Chapter 16, "Specialized Movement Abilities," centers on the topics of specialized movement skill development, fostering improvement, and the developmental sequence of specialized movement skills. This is followed by a discussion of the "Fitness Changes During Adolescence" in chapter 17 with a view toward their rapidly changing health-related and performance-related fitness. Chapter 18 concludes the section on adolescence with a discussion of "Adolescent Socialization." Particular attention is given to the role of physical activity in the process of positive socialization.

Unit V: Adulthood, provides the latest information available on the rapidly developing area of adult motor development. Chapter 19, "Physiological Changes in Adults," attempts to answer the question: Why do we age? A lively discussion is offered concerning changes in the adult musculoskeletal system, central nervous system, circulatory and respiratory systems, and sensory systems. Chapter 20, "Motor Performance in Adults," examines reaction time, balance and postural control, falls, gait, activities for daily living, and the elite performer. Chapter 21, "Psychosocial Development in Adults," examines a variety of psychological and social factors that influence and are influenced by the motor development and movement abilities of the aging adult.

Unit VI: Programming, synthesizes information from the preceding sections. Chapter 22, "Assessing Motor Behavior," takes a critical look at selected motor assessment instruments for infants and children, adolescents, and adults with a view to their utility in a variety of settings. It is important for the reader to appreciate that all developmentally based programming begins with assessment as a means of ensuring individually appropriate educational experiences. Chapter 23, "Programming for Developmental Physical Activity," may be the most important to the field professional. This chapter presents a developmental approach to systematic movement skill acquisition throughout life. Numerous diagrams are used to synthesize the concepts presented in this chapter. This practical application chapter forms the basis for a companion text, *Developmental Physical Education For Today's Children* (Gallahue and Cleland, 2003), which puts the concepts and principles described here to practical use through the implementation of developmentally appropriate movement programs.

NEW TO THIS EDITION

Expert Commentaries

Introducing the units on infancy, childhood, adolescence, and adulthood, the Expert Commentaries highlight key questions related to motor development at each of these periods of growth. Experts in the field offer thought-provoking answers to questions such as:

- Why is it valuable to study infant motor development?
- What is one of the most important findings related to childhood motor development?
- Recent studies suggest that puberty is beginning earlier among children than in past years. How does this affect motor development?
- What do you expect to be notable future research directions in the area of adult development and aging?

Web Resources

Each chapter includes Web Resources, a listing of websites that students can explore to find chapter-related information on the Internet. This feature allows students to expand their knowledge according to their abilities and goals and offers a springboard for independent learning.

New or Expanded Topics

This new edition has been significantly revised and updated. The following list is a sampling of topics that are either new to this edition or greatly expanded since the last edition.

Chapter 1: Understanding Motor Development: An Overview
- One- and two-dimensional means of classifying movement skills
- Environmental aspects of movement

Chapter 2: Models of Human Development
- "Defining events" related to Erikson's stages of psychosocial development and Piaget's phases of cognitive development
- Updated references and readings

Chapter 3: Motor Development: A Theoretical Model
- General updating of chapter content
- Updated references and readings

Chapter 4: Selected Factors Affecting Motor Development
- Infant bonding, stimulation and deprivation, prematurity and low birth weight, and eating disorders
- Risk factors associated with overweight and obesity and with eating disorders

Chapter 5: Prenatal Factors Affecting Development
- Prepregnancy visit with health care provider
- Factors influencing the prenatal environment

Chapter 6: Prenatal and Infant Growth
- New Centers for Disease Control (CDC) figures on stature for age and weight for age in boys and girls during infant and toddler years
- Characteristic changes during the neonatal period

Chapter 7: Infant Reflexes and Rhythmical Stereotypes

- Dynamic systems approach
- Primary stepping reflex

Chapter 8: Rudimentary Movement Abilities

- Programming for developmentally delayed or at-risk infants and toddlers
- Recommendations for infant aquatic programs

Chapter 9: Infant Perception

- Perceptual and motor development
- Updated references and readings

Chapter 10: Childhood Growth and Development

- New CDC figures on stature for age and weight for age in both boys and girls during childhood
- Dietary deficiencies and excesses

Chapter 11: Fundamental Movement Abilities

- Recent research in fundamental movements
- Environmental and task constraints
- Future of fundamental movement research
- Updated theoretical and application-oriented critical readings

Chapter 12: Physical Development of Children

- Use of accelerometers for assessing physical activity levels
- "Trigger hypothesis" for aerobic trainability in children

Chapter 13: Childhood Perception and Perceptual-Motor Development

- New figures and tables to enhance learning
- Increased attention to practical application
- Present and future state of perceptual-motor programming
- Updated theoretical and application-oriented critical readings

Chapter 14: Childhood Self-Concept Development

- Self-concept and peer relationships in youth sports
- Updated theoretical and application-oriented critical readings

Chapter 15: Adolescent Growth, Puberty, and Reproductive Maturity

- Early puberty in females
- Distinction between puberty and reproductive maturity

Chapter 16: Specialized Movement Abilities

- Levels and stages of movement skill learning focusing on the Fitts and Posner, Gentile, and combined models
- Cognitive state of the learner, learner's goals, and role of instructor at each level and stage of learning a new movement skill

Chapter 17: Fitness Changes During Adolescence

- Completely updated research
- Health-related fitness
- Comparison of abdominal strength in females and males
- Body-fat changes in females and males

Chapter 18: Adolescent Socialization

- Values formation and moral growth through physical activity during adolescence
- Exploration and experimentation as lifelong influencing factors
- Connection between self-esteem and achievement

Chapter 19: Physiological Changes in Adults

- Aging theories and strategies to slow the aging process
- New population figures and discussion
- Updated theoretical and application-oriented critical readings

Chapter 20: Motor Performance in Adults

- Multiple aspects of motor performance factors in adults
- Environmental and task factors
- Instructional strategies for teaching older adults new skills
- Updated theoretical and application-oriented critical readings

Chapter 21: Psychosocial Development in Adults

- Influence of exercise and physical activity on various psychological factors
- Ageism
- Successful aging
- Future needs in aging research
- Updated theoretical and application-oriented critical readings

Chapter 22: Assessing Motor Behavior

- New approach to existing testing instruments
- New assessment tools

Chapter 23: Programming for Developmental Physical Activity

- Completely rewritten chapter content
- Critical thinking core of developmental program
- Instructor's role in facilitating learning
- Revised developmental program models
- New revisions of assessment instruments
- Updated theoretical and application-oriented critical readings

SUCCESSFUL FEATURES

Throughout the text, you will find numerous pedagogical aids that enhance application and understanding of the content:

- **Chapter Competencies** begin each chapter and outline what students should master by the conclusion of the chapter.
- A list of **Key Terms** at the beginning of each chapter provides a convenient reference of important terms used in the chapter.

- A brief **Introduction** highlights the chapter's content and sets the stage for an up-to-date research-based discussion.
- **Key Concepts** appear throughout the text and are identified by the key icon. These help the reader focus more clearly on the key issues being discussed and reinforce the importance of obtaining a conceptual grasp of the process of motor development.
- The **Summary** found at the end of each chapter provides the reader with a concise overview and delineation of the major points discussed.
- **Critical Readings** conclude each chapter and refer the reader to additional sources of up-to-date information.
- A comprehensive **Bibliography** is found at the end of the text.
- A **Glossary of Terms** at the end of the book aids the reader in understanding important terms.
- Each chapter contains a wealth of **Tables, Figures, and Line Drawings** designed to synthesize information and provide the reader with a clear understanding of the topic being discussed.

ANCILLARIES

Brownstone's Diploma/Exam IV Computerized Testing

Brownstone's Diploma Computerized Testing is the most flexible, powerful, easy-to-use electronic testing program available in higher education. The Diploma system allows the test maker to create a print version, an online version (to be delivered to a computer lab), or an Internet version of each test. Diploma includes a built-in instructor gradebook, into which student rosters and files can generally be imported. Diploma is for Windows users, and the CD-ROM includes a separate testing program, Exam IV, for Macintosh users. This computerized testing is available for use with this edition of *Understanding Motor Development*.

PowerWeb

This edition of *Understanding Motor Development* has been packaged with PowerWeb, a valuable learning tool. PowerWeb is an easy-to-use online resource from McGraw-Hill that provides current articles, curriculum-based materials, weekly updates with assessment, informative and timely world news, related web links, research tools, student study tools, interactive tools, and more.

Access to PowerWeb also offers these resources:

- Study tips with self-quizzes
- Links to related sites
- Weekly updates
- Current news
- Daily newsfeed of related topics
- Web research guide

PowerWeb is a password-protected website. Your McGraw-Hill sales representative can guide you in creating a student package with PowerWeb. Preview this website at: www.dushkin.com/powerweb.

ACKNOWLEDGMENTS

Numerous people should be thanked for their contributions, both direct and indirect, to this edition. We would like to especially acknowledge the following:

Our Professional Colleagues: for their diligence and persistence in the pursuit and acquisition of knowledge. We would also like to thank those reviewers who provided us with valuable feedback as we prepared this revision:

Geffrey Colon	*Eastern Michigan University*
Anne Farrell	*California State Univesity-Bakersfield*
John Fizpatrick	*Chicago State University*
Jere Gallagher	*University of Pittsburgh*
David Kinnunen	*Southwest Missouri State University*
Lynda Reeves	*East Tennessee State University*
Steven Snowden	*Midwestern State University*

Our Students: for their enthusiasm, inquisitive minds, and dedication to personal as well as professional excellence.

Our Publisher and Editor: for their confidence in our abilities.

Our Families: for their support, patience, acceptance, love and prayers.

Our God: for a constant presence and the knowledge that in God and through God all things are possible.

David L. Gallahue
Bloomington, IN

John C. Ozmun
Terre Haute, IN

Background

With Chiselled touch
The stone unhewn and cold
Becomes a living mould.
The more the marble wastes,
The more the statue grows.
                    —Michelangelo

UNDERSTANDING MOTOR DEVELOPMENT: AN OVERVIEW

KEY TERMS

Longitudinal method
Cross-sectional method
Mixed-longitudinal method
Biological age
Growth
Development
Maturation
Experience
Motor
Learning
Motor learning
Motor behavior
Motor control
Motor development
Movement
Movement pattern
Fundamental movement pattern
Movement skill
Sport skill
Environmental context

CHAPTER COMPETENCIES

Upon completion of this chapter you should be able to:

- Be familiar with the research of several historical and contemporary scholars in motor development
- Compare and contrast motor development with other studies in motor behavior (motor learning and motor control)
- Demonstrate knowledge of the various forms of analysis used in the study of motor development
- Discuss advantages and shortcomings of the major methodologies associated with the study of change
- Identify key methods of assessing biological maturity
- Describe common problems associated with the study of motor development
- List the chronological age classifications of human development across the life span
- Define terms unique to physical growth and biological maturation
- Discuss the advantages and shortcomings of various methods of classifying movement skills

KEY CONCEPT

Motor development is continuous change in motor behavior throughout the life cycle, brought about by interaction among the requirements of the movement task, the biology of the individual, and the conditions of the environment.

The study of human development has been of keen interest to scholars and educators for many years. Knowledge of the processes of development lies at the core of education whether it be in the classroom, the gymnasium, or on the playing field. Without sound knowledge of the developmental aspects of human behavior, we can only guess at appropriate educational techniques and intervention procedures. Developmentally based instruction incorporates learning experiences that are appropriate not only for the chronological ages but also, and more importantly, for the developmental levels of the individuals being taught. Developmentally based field professionals recognize that although instruction is an important aspect of the teaching-learning process, instruction does not explain learning, development does.

CONCEPT 1.1

Instruction does not explain learning, development does.

Considerable research has been conducted and a number of texts have been written on the process of development. The research conducted on the developmental aspects of movement behavior has, in the past, been more limited in scope and magnitude than that conducted on the cognitive and affective processes of development. Historically, developmental psychologists tended to be only marginally interested in motor development, and

then frequently only as a visual indicator of cognitive functioning. Likewise, social psychologists interested in the process of affective development gave only fleeting attention to movement and its influence on the social and emotional development of the individual. The primary thrust of motor development research has come from the many branches of psychology, so it is natural that motor development has frequently been viewed through its potential influences on other areas of behavior, and as a convenient and readily observable means of studying behavior, rather than a phenomenon worthy of study for its own sake.

CONCEPT 1.2

The study of motor development in the past was overshadowed by interest in the cognitive and affective processes of development.

The study of motor development as a specialized field of scholarly inquiry by kinesiologists did not gain real impetus until the 1970s. Motor development is a legitimate area of study that cuts across the fields of exercise physiology, biomechanics, motor learning, and motor control, as well as the fields of developmental psychology and social psychology. The quest for understanding progressed at a slow but steady pace in the 1960s, and then began to escalate in the 1970s as developmental kinesiologists and psychologists shifted their focus away from a normative-descriptive approach back to the study of the underlying developmental processes.

During the 1980s an ever-expanding body of research by a new generation of scholars heightened interest in the study of motor development. An unprecedented amount of theory-based research has been conducted since the 1980s with developmentalists from a variety of fields interfacing with motor development scholars. The study of motor development has taken its place as a

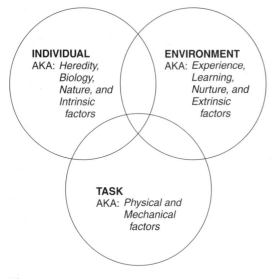

Figure 1.1
A transactional view of causation in motor development.

legitimate area of scientific inquiry within the fields of kinesiology and developmental psychology. Scholars are studying the underlying processes of development and its many and varied products.

Motor developmentalists recognize that the specific physical and mechanical demands of a movement task transact with the individual (biological factors) and the environment (experience or learning factors). Transactional models like the one depicted in figure 1.1 imply that factors within the task, the individual, and the environment are not only influenced by one another (interaction) but also may be modified (transaction) by one another.

The information contained here is not the last word on the process of motor development, but it is an honest attempt to be the latest word. Because research and study in this area are expanding rapidly, it is difficult to encompass all that is happening in this unfolding field; much that you read here is in danger of being obsolete in a few years. If it is to be of any real value to the field professional, the study of motor development must not focus only on the skilled performer in controlled laboratory settings. It must also analyze and document

what individuals of all ages can do under both normal and augmented circumstances. Our knowledge base is constantly growing, and even as this text is being written new hypotheses are being formulated and new conclusions being drawn from the excellent research being conducted throughout the world.

LIFE SPAN STUDY OF THE DEVELOPMENTAL PROCESS

Development is a continuous process beginning at conception and ceasing only at death. Development encompasses all aspects of human behavior and as a result may only be artificially separated into "domains," "stages," or "age periods." The growing acceptance of the concept of "life span" development is important to keep in mind. As study of the skilled athlete during adolescence and adulthood is important, so also is the study of movement during infancy, childhood, and later life. Much can be gained by learning about motor development at all ages and by viewing it as a lifelong process.

CONCEPT 1.3

Development is a lifelong process beginning at conception and ceasing only at death.

A life span perspective does not view development as domain-specific, stagelike, or age-dependent. Instead, the life span perspective suggests that *some* aspects of one's development can be conceptualized into domains, as being stagelike or age-related, whereas others cannot. Furthermore, the concept of life span development encompasses all developmental change—the positive changes generally associated with childhood and adolescence as well as the changes that take place with the regressive aging process.

Motor development is highly specific. The once commonly accepted notion of *general* motor ability has been disproved to the satisfaction of most scholars in the field. Superior ability in one area does not guarantee similar ability in others. The outmoded concept that one either possesses or does not possess ability in movement situations has been replaced by the concept that each person has specific capabilities within each of the many performance areas. Various factors involving movement abilities and physical performance interact in complex ways with cognitive and affective development. Each of these factors is in turn affected by a wide variety of biological, environmental, and specific task-related demands.

The process of development, and more specifically the process of motor development, should constantly remind us of the individuality of the learner. Each individual has a unique timetable for the acquisition and development of movement abilities. Although the "biological clock" is rather specific when it comes to the sequence of movement skill acquisition, the rate and extent of development is individually determined and dramatically influenced by the performance demands of the task. Typical age periods of development are just that: typical, and no more. Age periods merely represent approximate time ranges during which certain behaviors may be observed. Overreliance on these periods would negate the concepts of continuity, specificity, and the individuality of the developmental process.

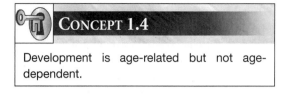

CONCEPT 1.4

Development is age-related but not age-dependent.

The study of motor development dates back only to the early part of the twentieth century. A number of methods of study have evolved, and a variety of problems have influenced both the quantity and quality of information available. The following sections briefly review the history, methods of study, and problems encountered in the study of motor development.

History of Motor Development

The first serious attempts at the study of motor development were from a maturational perspective, led by Arnold Gesell (1928) and Myrtle McGraw (1935). The maturationalists contended that development is a function of inborn biological processes that result in a universal sequence in infant movement skill acquisition. Since these early pioneering efforts Gesell's and McGraw's names have become legend in motor development research. Much of what we know about the sequence of infant movement skill acquisition is based on the descriptive work of Gesell and McGraw as well as that of Mary Shirley (1931) and Nancy Bayley (1935). The surge of research that these scholars brought about was largely motivated by their interest in the relationship of maturation and learning processes to cognitive development. In their separate but remarkably similar studies, these early researchers chronicled the well-known sequences of motor development during infancy. Their naturalistic observations of children provided a great deal of information about the sequential progression of normal development from the acquisition of early rudimentary movements to mature patterns of behavior. Although the rate at which children acquired selected movement abilities varied somewhat, these investigations revealed that the sequence of acquisition was universal and generally invariant.

The studies of Gesell and Thompson (1929, 1934) and McGraw (1935, 1940) are classics in the use of the co-twin control method of studying development. Their research provided considerable insight into the influence of augmented and restricted practice on the acquisition of various movement abilities and raised numerous questions concerning the effects of early practice. Monica Wild's study of throwing behavior (1938) was the first inquiry into developmental movement patterns in school-aged children. Unfortunately, after her study, outstanding in depth and completeness, there was little interest in exploring the various aspects of motor development until the end of World War II.

After World War II a new breed of motor developmentalists emerged. Led by Anna Espenschade, Ruth Glassow, and G. Lawrence Rarick (as cited in Rarick 1981), these individuals focused on describing the motor performance capabilities of children. All three were physical educators and as such were interested in understanding the outcomes of motor development for its own sake. Furthermore, their work focused on movement skill acquisition in school-aged youth rather than on infant motor performance. Although the extent of research during this period was limited and the pace slow, the work of these three early leaders did much to keep motor development alive as a legitimate field of scholarly inquiry. Clark and Whitall (1989) credit Espenschade, Glassow, and Rarick for motor development's emergence as a separate field of study within the physical education (kinesiology) profession.

Since 1960 the knowledge base in the study of motor development has grown steadily. The work of Lolas Halverson (1966) and several of her graduate students at the University of Wisconsin (Halverson and Roberton, 1966; Halverson, Roberton, and Harper, 1973; Halverson and Williams, 1985) on the acquisition of mature fundamental movement patterns did much to revive interest in children's research because of its emphasis on identifying the mechanisms behind the acquisition of skill rather than the final skill. *Fundamental Motor Patterns* (1983) by Ralph Wickstrom and the research conducted by Vern Seefeldt (1972) and his associates (Branta, Haubenstricker, and Seefeldt, 1984; Seefeldt and Haubenstricker, 1982) at Michigan State University on fundamental movement skill acquisition set the stage for the exciting research of the 1980s and beyond.

During the 1980s and 1990s, the emphasis of study in motor development again shifted dramatically. Instead of focusing on the product of development as with the normative/descriptive approaches of the preceding three decades, emphasis shifted back to understanding the underlying processes involved in motor development. Researchers led by the seminal work of Kugler, Kelso, and Turvey (1980) formulated new theoretical frameworks for the control and development of motor behavior. Since then the work of Esther Thelen and her colleagues (1986a, 1986b, 1987a, 1987b, 1991, 1994), Jane Clark and her colleagues (1988, 1989), and others led to the formulation of a dynamic systems theory of motor development, guiding much of the research being conducted at the present time.

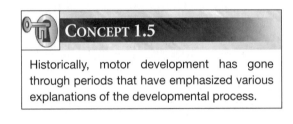

CONCEPT 1.5

Historically, motor development has gone through periods that have emphasized various explanations of the developmental process.

In summary, the years from about 1930 through World War II could be characterized as the "maturational period" and those from 1946 through the 1970s as the "normative/descriptive period" for the study of motor development. The time from the 1980s to the present may be described as the "process-oriented period" (Clark and Whitall, 1989). The study of motor development began with a process orientation (i.e., studying the underlying biological processes governing maturation), then shifted to a product orientation (i.e., describing the mechanics of various stages of movement skill acquisition, and developing normative criteria for a variety of motor performance measures), and moved back to a process orientation (i.e., explaining the processes causing change in motor behavior over time). Important research is now being conducted throughout much of the world on the critically important topic of motor development from infancy through adulthood.

Methods of Studying Development

Motor development is studied in three ways: the longitudinal method, the cross-sectional method, and the mixed-longitudinal method. Because motor development research involves the study of changes that occur in motor behavior over time, the longitudinal method of study is ideal and the only true means of studying development.

The **longitudinal method** of data collection attempts to explain behavior changes over time (i.e., developmental time) and involves charting various aspects of an individual's motor behavior for several years. The longitudinal approach allows one to observe changes in selected variables over time and, although time consuming, treats the study of motor development as a function of developmental time rather than age (i.e., real time). The longitudinal method involves study of a single group of individuals, all at the same age, over several years. The major purpose of the longitudinal study is to measure age-related *changes* in behavior. It does not, however, permit measurement of age *differences* in development. In short, the longitudinal method permits study of intraindividual change over time.

The Medford Boys Growth Study conducted by H. Harrison Clarke (1971) from 1956 to 1968 is one of the most complete longitudinal studies of growth ever carried out. The motor development study, beginning in 1966 by Vern Seefeldt at Michigan State University and continuing for over thirty years, collected extensive anthropometric data as well as thousands of feet of film footage on children performing selected fundamental movement skills. The treadmill stepping research of Beverly and Dale Ulrich at Indiana University (1995) has collected extensive data on the onset of quality walking in infants with Down syndrome. All are fine examples of longitudinal studies of growth and motor development.

The longitudinal method of data collection is time consuming. Additionally, the dropout rate is often great because participants move or become ill or disabled. Therefore, large numbers of participants need to be tested to retain a representative sample at the end of the five- to ten-year study period. Problems in methodology and design are also likely to creep into the longitudinal study. Varying levels of reliability and objectivity in testers over the course of the study period may cause problems in data interpretation. The potential accrued learning effects from repeated performances on the

measured items have also proven troublesome. These difficulties have prompted many researchers to opt for the cross-sectional approach.

The **cross-sectional method** of study permits the researcher to collect data on different groups of people at varying age levels at the same point in time. The major purpose of the cross-sectional study is to measure age-related differences in behavior. This method does not permit measurement of age-related *change* and has attracted controversy. The cross-sectional method yields only average *differences* in groups across real time and not individual changes across developmental time. The basic assumption behind the cross-sectional study has been that random selection of research participants will provide a representative sample of the population for each age group tested. It is questionable, however, that this assumption can be met in most cases. In reality, cross-sectional studies, although simple and direct, can only describe typical behaviors at the specific ages studied. As a result, they are not considered by most authorities to be true developmental studies. The problem is that historically the vast majority of motor development research has used the cross-sectional approach.

To overcome the glaring weakness of the cross-sectional technique, developmental psychologists and motor development researchers have begun to look more closely at combining the cross-sectional and longitudinal research designs in individual research investigations. This sequential method of studying development, or **mixed-longitudinal method,** combines the best aspects of the cross-sectional and longitudinal methods. It covers all of the possible data points necessary for describing and/or explaining both differences and change over time as functions of development as well as functions of age. Research participants are selected and studied cross-sectionally, but they also are followed longitudinally for several years. This permits comparison of cross-sectional data results with longitudinal results and serves as a means of validating or refuting age-related changes with true developmental changes. It also gives the researcher an opportunity to analyze and report on preliminary data early in the investigation rather than waiting five or more years.

 CONCEPT 1.6

Whereas age-related changes in motor behavior can be studied through cross-sectional research designs, true developmental change can only be studied through longitudinal and mixed-longitudinal designs.

The longitudinal, cross-sectional, and mixed-longitudinal methods of study may be applied to a variety of research formats. An investigation may take the form of an experimental study, the most powerful method because of the rigid controls required, or it may be cross-cultural, involving naturalistic observation, surveys, interviews, case history reports, or a combination of these techniques. Table 1.1 provides a brief overview of these formats for studying development.

As noted earlier, there has been a shift in the study of motor development from process to product and now back to process again. The early researchers emphasized the importance of *process-oriented research*, that is, form and function. H. M. Halverson (1931, 1937), Shirley (1931), and Wild (1938) all focused on the sequential acquisition

of movement patterns. Their suggestions for studying the process of motor skill development went largely unheeded until the 1980s, when interest in such study was revived; since then, it has been a focus of motor development research. The use of cinematography, electrogoniometry, and electromyographic techniques in conjunction with computer analysis has enhanced our knowledge of the process of movement, its underlying motor mechanisms, and resulting influence on the movement product (Roberton and Konczak, 2001).

Product-oriented research, or research on the performance capabilities of individuals, has been conducted for many years. This type of research is concerned typically with the outcome of the individual's performance. The distance a ball travels, the velocity with which it can be kicked, or how far one can jump are examples of motor performance scores. Strength, endurance, power, balance, and flexibility as measured by a particular battery of tests are examples of fitness performance scores.

CONCEPT 1.7

Motor development may be studied from either a process or a product orientation.

TABLE 1.1 | **Primary Methods of Studying Motor Development**

Longitudinal study: The same individuals are studied over a five- to ten-year period

Cross-sectional study: Different individuals representing a variety of ages are studied at the same point in time

Mixed-longitudinal study: A sequential method of studying development that combines essential elements of both the longitudinal and cross-sectional methods

Experimental method: Random selection and/or assignment of participants to treatment conditions. Rigid control of influencing variables

Cross-cultural: May or may not use an experimental design. Comparison of various factors across different cultures

Naturalistic observation: Nonobtrusive observation of behavior in the natural environment

Survey: Group or personal interviews on a series of selected topics to reveal attitudes, opinions

Case history: Report on individual participants providing a variety of detailed background information

Problems in Studying Motor Development

Data collection, whether it be product- or process-oriented, can be difficult when infants, children, adolescents, and adults are being studied. Problems in data collection are the chief cause of the scarcity of motor development research information on infants and children.

Infants and preschoolers tend to be challenging research participants unless procedures that accommodate their natural independent natures are adopted. The two primary problems associated with good data collection are inhibited or exaggerated performance and inconsistency in performance. Special precautions must be taken to eliminate, as far as possible, the potential bias of the data caused by these factors. Time-consuming orientation periods and modified data collection procedures that simulate a more naturalistic setting are frequently employed to put a child at ease. This still will not ensure consistency in performance.

For example, when a young child is asked to "throw the ball overhand as far as you can," he or she may throw first with the right hand and then casually begin throwing with the left. Some throws may be overhand, others sidearm or underhand, even after precise instructions on the overhand technique. Some throws may go several yards, others only a few feet. Some throws may closely approximate mature patterns of action while others may look like shot-put attempts or grenade-tossing exercises. The researcher must exercise considerable patience and work with the child until he or she has demonstrated what the researcher judges to be a maximum or representative effort using the most characteristic pattern of movement. The potential problems are serious. Learning and fatigue factors may contaminate the data, as may errors in experimenter judgment.

CONCEPT 1.8

Developmental data collection, for many reasons, is often a difficult and time-consuming process.

Another problem that plagues the developmental researcher is interrater reliability. It is crucial, for example, that observational assessment be systematically analyzed and that observers be carefully trained in how to observe and what to look for. Still another problem, and potentially the most serious one facing the researcher, involves the reliability and validity of the measuring instrument. A variety of motor development assessment devices are available. Some have been meticulously designed; others represent a combination of measures of unproven reliability and validity.

The benefits to be gained from motor development research far outweigh the problems and pitfalls. As information gradually accumulates and is replicated, we gain a more accurate picture of the processes involved in motor development. Efforts that employ sound research designs and recognize the need for patient, unbiased data collection are increasing our understanding of motor development across the life span.

AGE CLASSIFICATIONS OF DEVELOPMENT

Developmental levels may be classified in a variety of ways. The most popular method, but often the least accurate, is classification by chronological age. *Chronological age,* or one's age in months and/or years, enjoys universal use and represents a constant. By knowing one's birth date we can easily calculate age in years, months, and days. Table 1.2 provides a conventional chronological classification of age from conception through older adulthood. Although chronological ages are highly specific during the early years, they become increasingly more general throughout life. As you review this table keep in mind that although development is age-related, it is not age-dependent. Chronological age merely provides a rough estimate of one's developmental level, which may be more accurately determined through other means.

The **biological age** of an individual provides a record of his or her rate of progress toward maturity. It is a variable age that corresponds only

TABLE 1.2	Conventional Chronological Classifications of Age
Period	**Approximate Age Range**
I Prenatal Life	(Conception to Birth)
A. Period of the zygote	Conception–1 week
B. Embryonic period	2 weeks–8 weeks
C. Fetal period	8 weeks–Birth
II Infancy	(Birth to 24 Months)
A. Neonatal period	Birth–1 month
B. Early infancy	1–12 months
C. Later infancy	12–24 months
III Childhood	(2 Years to 10 Years)
A. Toddler period	24–36 months
B. Early childhood	3–5 years
C. Middle/later childhood	6–10 years
IV Adolescence	(10–20 Years)
A. Prepubescence	10–12 years (F)
	11–13 years (M)
B. Postpubescence	12–18 years (F)
	14–20 years (M)
V Young Adulthood	(20–40 Years)
A. Novice period	20–30 years
B. Settling period	30–40 years
VI Middle Adulthood	(40–60 Years)
A. Midlife transition	40–45 years
B. Middle age	45–60 years
VII Older Adulthood	(60+ Years)
A. Young old	60–70 years
B. Middle old	70–80 years
C. Oldest old	80+ years

roughly to chronological age and may be determined by measures of: (1) morphological age, (2) skeletal age, (3) dental age, or (4) sexual age.

Morphological age is a comparison of one's attained size (height and weight) to normative standards. Normative size was first determined by Wetzel (1948) and others through exhaustive charting of heights and weights of thousands of individuals. The Wetzel Grid was used for many years by most pediatricians as the primary means of determining the morphological age of their patients. Although not used today due to secular changes (i.e., generational changes) in height and weight,

the Wetzel Grid was at one time the most popular method of determining morphological age. Today, pediatricians use the physical growth charts developed by the National Center for Health Statistics (2000). Copies of these charts are located in chapter 6 (birth to 36 months) and chapter 10 (ages 2–20) and can be found online at *cdc.gov/nchs/*.

Skeletal age provides one with a record of the biological age of the developing skeleton. Skeletal age can be accurately determined by x-ray of the carpal bones of the hand and wrist. Skeletal age is used as a laboratory research tool and in cases where growth is either extremely delayed or accelerated. It is rarely used as a measure of biological age outside laboratory or clinical settings because of cost, inconvenience, and the accumulative effects of radiation.

Dental age is another accurate but infrequently used means of determining biological age. The sequence of tooth development from first appearance of the cusp to root closure provides a measure of calcification age. Eruption age may also be determined by charting the progressive emergence of the teeth.

Sexual age is a fourth method of determining biological age. Sexual maturation is determined by the variable attainment of primary and secondary sexual characteristics. The Tanner maturity scale (Tanner, 1962) is an accurate means of assessing sexual maturity. It is described in chapter 15. This method is used infrequently because of social and cultural constraints.

Several other methods of classifying one's age exist. They include measurements of: (1) emotional age, (2) mental age, (3) self-concept age, and (4) perceptual age. *Emotional age* is a measure of socialization and ability to function within a particular social/cultural milieu. *Mental age* is a complex measure of an individual's mental potential as a function of both learning and of self-perception. It often fluctuates within one's lifetime. *Self-concept age* is a measure of an individual's personal assessment of his or her value or worth. *Perceptual age* is an assessment of the rate and extent of one's perceptual development.

CONCEPT 1.9

Although chronological age is the most commonly used means of age classification, it is frequently the least valid.

All measures of maturity are variable. They are related to chronological age but are not dependent upon it. Therefore, anyone who works with infants, children, adolescents, or adults must avoid overreliance on a chronological classification of age simply because of its ease and convenience.

TERMINOLOGY USED IN MOTOR DEVELOPMENT

Gaining a working knowledge of the terms commonly used in any area of study is important. Whether it is medicine or law, special education or economics, there is jargon typical to each field, and motor development is no exception. A variety of terms that have come into common use are presented in this section. As with the jargon in most areas of study, agreement on the meaning of each term is not universal. We must strive for greater consistency. With this concept in mind, the following definitions are presented.

CONCEPT 1.10

Terms convey critical concepts essential to understanding motor development.

Growth and Development

The terms **growth** and **development** are often used interchangeably, but each implies a difference in emphasis. In its purest sense, *physical growth* refers to an increase in the size of an individual's body or its parts during maturation. In other words, physical growth is an increase in the structure of the body brought about by the multiplication or enlargement of cells. The term *growth,* however, is often used to refer to the totality of physical change, and as a result it becomes more inclusive and takes on the same meaning as development. In our discussion of growth through this text, we will adopt the former.

Development, in its purest sense, refers to changes in an individual's level of functioning over time. Keogh and Sugden (1985) defined development as "adaptive change toward competence" (p. 6). Such a definition implies that throughout the life span one is required to adjust, compensate, or change to gain or maintain competence. For example, the infant learning to walk needs to compensate for changes in his or her base of support and center of gravity. So, too, the adult needs to compensate for the diminution and regression in walking competency frequently brought about by arthritis and reduced joint flexibility. We will adopt Keogh and Sugden's definition throughout the text, because it clearly and succinctly states that development is a lifelong process of change.

Although development is most frequently viewed as an emerging and broadening of one's ability to function on a higher level, we must recognize that the concept of development is much broader, and that it is a lifelong process. The study of development is concerned with what occurs and how it occurs in the human organism in its journey from conception through maturity to death. Development is a continuous process encompassing all the interrelated dimensions of our existence, and care must be taken not to consider these dimensions as autonomous or limited to the growing years of childhood. Adults are as involved in the developmental process as are young children.

The interwoven elements of maturation and experience play key roles in the developmental process. **Maturation** refers to qualitative changes that enable one to progress to higher levels of functioning. Maturation, when viewed from a biological perspective, is primarily innate; that is, it is genetically determined and resistant to external or environmental influences. Maturation is characterized by a fixed order of progression in which the pace may vary but the sequence of appearance of characteristics generally does not. For example, the progression and approximate ages at which an infant learns to sit, stand, and walk are highly influenced by maturation. The sequence of appearance of these abilities is generally fixed and resistant to change, with only the rate of appearance being altered by the environmental influences of learning and experience.

Experience refers to factors within the environment that may alter the appearance of various developmental characteristics through the process of learning. A child's experiences may affect the rate of onset of certain patterns of behavior.

The developmental aspects of both maturation and experience are interwoven. Determining the separate contribution of each of these processes is impossible. A heated debate in the literature over the relative importance of the two raged for well over a century. As a result, the term *adaptation* has come into vogue and is often used to refer to the complex interplay between forces within the individual and the environment.

Domains of Behavior

The classification of human responses into *domains of behavior* was first popularized by Bloom and his associates (1956) and Krathwohl, Bloom, and Masia (1964) in their pioneering attempts to establish a taxonomy of educational objectives. Unfortunately, their separation of behavior into psychomotor (motor behavior), cognitive (intellectual behavior), and affective (social-emotional behavior) domains has caused many to deal with each domain as an independent entity of human development. We must not lose sight of the interrelated nature of development and the three domains of human behavior even though we tend to separate them for convenience in our discussion and study of human development.

The *psychomotor domain* includes the processes of change, stabilization, and regression in physical structure and neuromuscular function. In the psychomotor domain, movement may be the result of cognitively mediated processes in higher brain centers (motor cortex), reflexive activity in lower brain centers, or automatic responses in the central nervous system. The psychomotor domain encompasses all physical and physiological change throughout the life span. As a result, the psychomotor domain may be categorized into the study of motor performance and the study of movement abilities.

Motor performance is the term frequently used to lump together the various components of health-related fitness (muscular strength, muscular endurance, aerobic endurance, joint flexibility, and body composition) and performance-related fitness (speed of movement, agility, coordination, balance, and power) together. Motor performance is associated with the capacity to perform movement tasks, and its study is product-based in how far, how fast, and how many.

Movement abilities is a comprehensive term grouping the three categories of movement (locomotion, manipulation, and stability). The study of movement abilities is process-oriented and involves observing the mechanics of movement and trying to understand the underlying causes for change. Thus, one may be interested in an aspect of the psychomotor domain as it relates to understanding motor performance and as it applies to the performance of a variety of movement abilities across age, gender, or social class.

The *cognitive domain* as applied to the study of movement behavior involves the functional relationship between mind and body. The reciprocal interaction of mind and body has been explored by observers ranging from Socrates and Plato to the developmental theorists of the twentieth century. Jean Piaget, known for his theory of cognitive development, is an example of a theorist who recognized the important role of movement, particularly during the early years of life. Piaget's work has done much to spread the notions that perceptual-motor development and academic concept readiness can be enhanced through the medium of movement.

The term *perceptual-motor* came into vogue in the 1960s and 1970s to signify the important influence that sensory cues and the perceptual process have on motor activity. In its broadest sense a perceptual-motor act is any voluntary movement that relies on sensory data to process information used in the performance of that act. In other words, all voluntary movement may be viewed as perceptual-motor in nature. Movements that are subcortically controlled (reflexes) are the only forms of movement of the skeletal muscles that do not require some element of perception.

The *affective domain* as related to the study of human movement involves feelings and emotions as applied to self and others through movement. Movement confidence, self-concept, and cultural socialization are areas of interest to students of motor development. *Movement confidence* is an individual's belief in his or her ability to satisfy the

demands of various movement tasks. *Self-concept* is one's personal assessment of self-worth. It is influenced by a variety of factors, one of which is movement. *Cultural socialization* is the level of social interaction evidenced by an individual. Play behavior has a developmental base that manifests in changing peer relations and more sophisticated levels of functioning. Playfulness is viewed by biologists as well as an activity vital to brain development (Fagen, 1992).

CONCEPT 1.11

Human behavior may be classified into three domains: psychomotor, cognitive, and affective.

These definitions of the psychomotor, cognitive, and affective domains as they influence, and are influenced by, developmental processes permit us to clarify a variety of terms that contain the words *motor* or *movement* (see table 1.3). What follows is not a mere exercise in semantics. Words reflect concepts and convey ideas. It is important that we impose similar meanings on them because even subtle differences in definitions can lead to confusion and lack of clarity.

Motor Development

The term **motor** when used by itself refers to the underlying biological and mechanical factors that influence movement. The term, however, is rarely used alone but serves as a suffix or prefix in such words as: *psychomotor, perceptual-motor, sensorimotor, motor learning, motor control,* and *motor development.* The terms *psychomotor, perceptual-motor,* and *sensorimotor* have gained popularity in the jargon of psychologists and educators. Kinesiologists, on the other hand, have tended to limit use of the prefixes of these words to discussions that focus on specific aspects of the motor process. In other words, the term *motor* is used as a prefix to describe specific areas of study. The following is a

TABLE 1.3 The Interrelated Nature of Terms Commonly Used in Motor Development

Motor behavior: Study of change in motor learning, motor control, and motor development brought about by the interaction of learning and biological processes

Motor control: Underlying changes in the performance of isolated tasks

Motor learning: Underlying changes involved in movement performance

Motor development: Progressive change in motor behavior throughout the life cycle brought about by interaction among the requirements of the task, the biology of the individual, and the conditions of the environment

Motor: Underlying factors affecting movement

Movement: The observable act of moving

Motor pattern: Common underlying biological and mechanical processes

Movement pattern: An organized series of related movements (e.g., a sidearm pattern)

Fundamental motor pattern: Common underlying process of basic movements

Fundamental movement pattern: An organized series of basic movements (e.g., striking)

Motor skill: Common underlying process of control in movement

Specialized movement skill: Form, accuracy, and control in performance of a movement (e.g., striking an oncoming object or splitting wood)

Sport skill: The combination of a fundamental movement pattern with form, accuracy, and control in the performance of a sport-related activity (e.g., batting in baseball or softball)

Movement education: The lifelong process of change in movement behavior brought about by motor learning, motor control, and motor development

brief description of several of these terms as they are commonly used.

Learning is an internal process that results in consistent changes in behavior seen as evidence of its occurrence. Learning is the result of experience, education, and training interacting with biological processes. It is shaped largely by an individual's state of development and is a function of practice. Learning is a phenomenon in which experience is prerequisite, whereas development is a process that may occur relatively independently of experience. **Motor learning,** then, is that aspect of learning in which movement plays a major part. Motor learning is a relatively permanent change in motor behavior resulting from practice or past experience.

Motor behavior is defined here as changes in motor learning and development that embody learning factors and maturational processes associated with movement performance. Motor behavior research is concerned with the study of motor learning, motor control, and motor development.

Motor control is that aspect of motor learning and development that deals with the study of isolated tasks under specific conditions. Research in this area looks at the underlying processes involved in the performance of a movement act consistent from trial to trial. Much of the current research in motor development, especially that conducted from a dynamic systems perspective approaches it from the standpoint of motor control.

Motor development is continuous change in motor behavior throughout the life cycle. It may be studied as a process and as a product. As a process, motor development involves the underlying biological, environmental, and task demands influencing both the motor performance and movement abilities of individuals from infancy through older adulthood. As a product, motor development may be regarded as descriptive or normative and is typically viewed in stages (infancy, childhood, adolescence, and adulthood) that reflect the particular interest of the investigator.

The terms *motor pattern, fundamental motor pattern, motor skill,* and *perceptual-motor skill* refer to the underlying sensory, integrative, and decision-making processes that precede the performance of an observable movement. Perception and cognition are important variables because they influence underlying motor processes. Underlying motor processes are involved in the performance of all voluntary movement.

CONCEPT 1.12

Motor behavior is an umbrella term encompassing the complementary but essentially different areas of study embodied by motor learning, motor control, and motor development.

Movement Forms

The term **movement** refers to observable change in the position of any part of the body. Movement is the culminating act of the underlying motor processes. The word *movement* is often linked with others to broaden or clarify its meaning, but in general it refers to the overt act of moving. The following is a brief description of some movement terms as they are commonly used.

A **movement pattern** is an organized series of related movements. More specifically, a movement pattern represents the performance of an isolated movement that in and of itself is too restricted to be classified as a fundamental movement pattern. For example, the sidearm, underarm, or overarm patterns of movement alone do not constitute the fundamental movements of throwing or striking but merely represent an organized series of movements.

A **fundamental movement pattern** refers to the observable performance of basic locomotor, manipulative, and stabilizing movements. Fundamental movement patterns involve the combination of movement patterns of two or more body segments. Running, jumping, striking, throwing, twisting, and turning are examples of fundamental movement patterns.

Although the terms *movement pattern* and *movement skill* are often used interchangeably, a **movement skill** is viewed here as a fundamental movement pattern performed with greater accuracy, precision, and control. In a movement skill, accuracy is stressed and extraneous movement is limited; in a fundamental movement pattern, movement is stressed but accuracy is limited and not necessarily seen as the goal.

A **sport skill** is the refinement or combination of fundamental movement patterns or movement skills to perform a sport-related activity. The fundamental movement patterns of twisting the body and striking may be developed to a high degree of precision and applied in a horizontal form to batting in the sport of baseball or in a vertical form to playing golf or serving a tennis ball. The performance of a sport skill requires making increasingly precise alterations in the basic patterns of movement to achieve higher levels of skill.

Movement education has been defined in a variety of ways, all of which seem somewhat restrictive and shortsighted. It has been defined as a method, as a process, and as an aspect of the physical education program generally limited to children. For the purpose of our discussion we will view movement education as the lifelong process of changes in motor behavior brought about by the processes of motor control, motor learning, and motor development. Input from qualified therapists, teachers, and coaches, positive motivation and reinforcement, appropriate facilities and equipment, and a positive environmental context facilitate the process of movement education.

CLASSIFYING MOVEMENT SKILLS

A variety of schemes exist for classifying movement skills. Traditionally, most have been one-dimensional. That is, they have accounted for only one aspect of movement skill along a broad spectrum. Two-dimensional taxonomies are a more comprehensive means for classifying movement skills. Both are discussed in the following sections.

CONCEPT 1.13

Although there are a variety of helpful one and two-dimensional schemes for classifying movement, all fall short in fully capturing the breadth, depth, and scope of human movement.

One-Dimensional Schemes

Four ways of classifying movement skills along a single dimension have gained popularity over the years: (1) muscular, (2) temporal, (3) environmental, and (4) functional. Each is briefly discussed in the following paragraphs and visually presented in table 1.4.

Muscular Aspects of Movement

There is not a clear delineation between the terms *gross* and *fine*, but movements are often classified as one or the other. A *gross motor movement* involves movement of the large muscles of the body. Most sport skills are classified as gross motor movements, with the exception perhaps of target shooting, archery, and a few others. A *fine motor movement* involves limited movements of parts of the body in the performance of precise movements. The manipulative movements of sewing, writing, and typing are generally thought of as fine motor movements. Physical therapists and physical education teachers are primarily concerned with the learning or relearning of gross motor skills, whereas occupational therapists and coaches are often more concerned with the fine motor aspects of skillful movement.

TABLE 1.4	**Popular One-Dimensional Models for Classifying Movement**		
Muscular Aspects of Movement (the size/extent of the movement)	**Temporal Aspects of Movement (the time series in which the movement occurs)**	**Environmental Aspects of Movement (the context in which the movement occurs)**	**Functional Aspects of Movement (the purpose of the movement)**
Gross Motor Skills: Use several large muscles to perform a movement task (running, jumping, throwing, catching)	*Discrete Motor Skills:* Have a clearly defined beginning and ending (hitting a pitched ball, flipping a switch)	*Open Motor Skills:* Occur in an unpredictable and constantly changing environment (wrestling, catching a fly ball, most computer games)	*Stability Tasks:* Place emphasis on gaining or maintaining balance in either static or dynamic movement situations (sitting, standing, balancing on one foot, walking on a narrow beam)
Fine Motor Skills: Use several small muscles to perform a movement task with precision (writing, typing, knitting, portrait painting)	*Serial Motor Skills:* Series of discrete skills performed in rapid succession (dribbling a basketball, opening a locked door)	*Closed Motor Skills:* Occur in a stable unchanging environment (putting in golf, word processing on a computer)	*Locomotor Tasks:* Transport the body from one point to another through space (crawling, running, performing the high jump in track)
	Continuous Motor Skills: Perform repeatedly for an arbitrary time (peddling a bicycle, swimming, playing a violin)		*Manipulative Tasks:* Impart force to an object or receive force from an object (striking, volleying, writing, knitting)

Temporal Aspects of Movement

On the basis of its temporal aspects, movement may also be classified as discrete, serial, or continuous. A *discrete movement* has a definite beginning and ending. Throwing, jumping, kicking, and striking a ball are examples of discrete movements. *Serial movements* involve the performance of a single, discrete movement several times in rapid succession. Rhythmical hopping, basketball dribbling, and volleying in soccer or volleyball are typical serial tasks. *Continuous movements* are movements repeated for a specified time. Running, swimming, and cycling are common continuous movements.

Environmental Aspects of Movement

Fundamental movement patterns and movement skills are often referred to as open motor tasks or closed motor tasks. An *open task* is one performed in an environment where the conditions are constantly changing. These changing conditions require the individual to make adjustments or modifications in the pattern of movement to suit the demands of the situation. Plasticity or flexibility in movement is required in the performance of an open skill. Most dual and group activities involve open skills that depend on external and internal feedback for their successful execution. For example, the child taking part in a typical game of tag, which requires running and dodging in varying directions, is never using the exact same patterns of movement during the game. The child is required to adapt to the demands of the activity through a variety of similar but different movements. Performance of an open movement task differs markedly from performance of a closed movement task.

A *closed task* is "a motor skill performed in a stable or predictable environment where the performer determines when to begin the action" (Magill, 2001, p. 7). A closed movement skill or fundamental movement pattern demands rigidity of performance. It depends on kinesthetic rather than visual and auditory feedback from the execution of the task. The child performing a headstand, throwing at a target, or doing a vertical jump is performing a closed movement task.

Intended Function of Movement

Movement skills may be classified on the basis of their intent. Although all movement tasks involve an element of balance, movements in which one's body orientation places a premium on gaining and/or maintaining a stable body orientation are called *stability tasks.* Sitting and standing, balancing on a narrow beam, body rolling, and dodging fit into this category, as do axial movements such as bending or stretching and twisting or turning. Movements for the purpose of transporting the body from one point to another such as walking, running, or performing the high jump or the hurdling event in track and field are *locomotor tasks.* Those that involve giving force to an object or receiving force from an object are *object manipulation tasks.* Throwing, catching, kicking a soccer ball, striking a baseball, and dribbling a basketball are common manipulative skills.

The reader is cautioned not to be arbitrary in the classification of movement into either one-dimensional or two-dimensional schemes. Distinct separation and classification of movements is not always possible or desirable. We are dynamic, moving beings, constantly responding to many subtle environmental factors and the demands of the movement task. The arbitrary classification of movement should serve only to focus attention on the specific aspect of movement under consideration.

Two-Dimensional Models

Two-dimensional models for classifying movement skills, although still descriptive, are somewhat more complete in recognizing the complexity of human movement. They offer a more sophisticated means for viewing movement as occurring along a continuum from simple to complex and from general to specific. The two-dimensional model proposed by Gentile (2000) is focused on the processes of motor skill learning. The one proposed by the senior author of this text (Gallahue, Werner, & Luedke, 1972, 1975; Gallahue, 1982) is focused on the products of motor development. Both are discussed briefly in the paragraphs that follow and are depicted in tables 1.5 and 1.6, respectively.

TABLE 1.5 An Adaptation of Gentile's (2000) Two-Dimensional Model for Classifying Movement with Examples Provided

Environmental Context of the Movement Task		Intended Function of the Movement Task			
		Stability without Manipulation	Stability with Manipulation	Locomotion without Manipulation	Locomotion with Manipulation
Stationary regulatory conditions*	No intertrial variability = Completely closed movement task	• Sitting in a chair • Standing in place	• Striking a ball off a tee • Kicking a stationary ball	• Walking on a flat surface • Jumping to a fixed height	• Walking with a suitcase • Rhythmically jumping a self-turned rope
Stationary regulatory conditions*	+Intertrial variability = Moderately closed movement task	• Sitting in chairs set at varying heights • Standing up from chairs set at varying heights	• Striking a ball off tees set at varying heights • Kicking different types of stationary balls	• Walking on a treadmill • Jumping upward to varying heights	• Walking on a slippery surface with a bag of groceries • Jumping a fixed distance to catch a self-tossed ball
In motion regulatory conditions**	No intertrial variability = Moderately open movement task	• Standing on a moving escalator • Sitting on a large exercise ball	• Striking a ball tossed from a pitching machine • Kicking a slow rolling ball on a smooth, flat surface	• Walking onto an escalator • Running and jumping up to a fixed height	• Performing the shot put event in track • Throwing the javelin from a run
In motion regulatory conditions**	Intertrial variability = Completely open movement task	• Standing on a moving escalator • Sitting on a large exercise ball with both feet raised	• Striking a pitched ball • Kicking a fast moving soccer football	• Walking across a swinging bridge • Running and then jumping up to varying heights	• Running to catch a fly ball • Jumping up to catch a rebounding ball

*The spatial aspects of the movement are controlled by the requirements of the task, but the temporal aspects of the task are controlled by the mover.

**Both the spatial and temporal aspects of the movement are controlled by the requirements of the task.

18

TABLE 1.6 Gallahue's Two-Dimensional Model for Classifying Movement with Examples Provided

Phases of Motor Development	Intended Function of the Movement Task		
	Stability (Emphasis is on body balance in static and dynamic movement situations)	Locomotion (Emphasis is on body transportation from point to point)	Manipulation (Emphasis is on imparting force to or receiving force from an object)
Reflexive Movement Phase: Involuntary subcortically controlled movements in utero and early infancy	• Labyrinthine righting reflex • Neck righting reflex • Body righting reflex	• Crawling reflex • Primary stepping reflex • Swimming reflex	• Palmer grasp reflex • Plantar grasp reflex • Pull-up reflex
Rudimentary Movement Phase: The maturationally influenced movements of infancy	• Control of head and neck • Control of trunk • Unsupported sitting • Standing	• Crawling • Creeping • Upright gait	• Reaching • Grasping • Releasing
Rudimentary Movement Phase: The basic movement skills of childhood	• Balancing on one foot • Walking on a low beam • Axial movements	• Walking • Running • Jumping • Hopping	• Throwing • Catching • Kicking • Striking
Specialized Movement Phase: The complex skills of later childhood and beyond	• Performing a balance beam routine in gymnastics • Defending a goal kick in soccer football	• Running the 100-meter dash or hurdles event in track • Walking on a crowded street	• Performing a goal kick in soccer or football • Striking a pitched ball

Gentile's Two-Dimensional Model

Gentile (2000) looked beyond the one-dimensional approaches for classifying movement skills. Her two-dimensional scheme takes into account: (1) the environmental context in which the movement task is to be performed, and (2) its intended function. Although the original intent of this taxonomy was to aid physical therapists in their rehabilitation efforts, it also provides a workable framework for setting up practice sessions and training routines for anyone interested in teaching movement skills.

The first dimension deals with the environmental context of the movement task to be performed. According to Gentile, the **environmental context** refers to having *regulatory conditions* that are either *stationary* or *in motion,* as well as having either *intertrial variability* or *no intertrial variability.* If the regulatory conditions during performance of a skill are stationary, then the environmental context is unchanging. There may be, however, either no intertrial variability, as in a completely closed movement task such as sitting down or standing up from a chair, or intertrial variability as in a moderately closed movement task such as sitting down or standing up from varying heights. On the other hand, if the regulatory conditions of the environment are in motion, they may also have either no intertrial variability, as in a moderately open movement skill such as sitting on a large exercise ball, or intertrial variability as in a completely open movement task such as sitting on a large exercise ball and balancing with the feet raised off the ground.

The second dimension of Gentile's two-dimensional scheme for classifying movement skills deals with the intended function of the movement task (i.e., category of movement). One's body orientation may focus on either stability or locomotion (Gentile uses the term "body transport") occurring either with or without object manipulation. Take a few minutes to study table 1.5 and the examples provided. There is a definite progression of difficulty running from left to right and from top to bottom in the movement exam-

ples provided. For example, the upper-left quadrant, the least complex, emphasizes body stability with no object manipulation and has stationary environmental regulatory conditions with no intertrial variability. Completely closed movement skills such as sitting and standing fit here. On the other hand, movement skills in the lower right-hand quadrant, the most complex, emphasize body transport (locomotion) while manipulating an object and have environmental regulatory conditions in motion as well the presence of intertrial variability. Completely open movement skills such as leaping to catch a ball in baseball or basketball or fielding a pass on the run in a game of soccer, are found in this part of the taxonomy.

Gentile's two-dimensional scheme for classifying movement skills solves many of the problems found in one-dimensional schemes. By identifying where the desired movement task is located on the sixteenth category continuum, the therapist or teacher can determine how well the learner performs the task by progressively altering the context of the environment. This then enables selection of the most appropriate learning progression based on where the learner is, rather than where she or he should be (Magill, 2001).

Gallahue's Two-Dimensional Scheme

The central theme of this text is based on the two-dimensional model originally proposed by the senior author (Gallahue, Werner, and Luedke 1972, 1975, Gallahue, 1982). It will be elaborated on more fully throughout the text and is only briefly discussed here. This descriptive two-dimensional model of motor development (see chapter 4) emphasizes: (1) the intended function of the movement task as expressed in the three movement categories of *stability, locomotion,* and *manipulation;* and (2) the phases of motor development as expressed by their complexity through the terms *reflexive, rudimentary, fundamental,* and *specialized movement phases.*

Briefly, *reflexive movements* are subcortically controlled and as a result, involuntary. Although we all possess a variety of primitive reflexes, they are of special importance in their postural form during early infancy. The postural reflexes are represented in their stability, locomotor and manipulative forms through involuntary actions such as the labyrinthine and body righting reflexes (stability), the primary stepping and crawling reflexes (locomotion), and the palmer and planter grasping reflexes (manipulation).

Rudimentary movements are voluntary movements typically mastered during infancy. They involve basic stability skills such as gaining control of the muscles of the head and trunk; manipulative skills such as reaching for and grasping and releasing objects; and locomotor skills such as crawling, creeping, and walking with support.

Fundamental movements are gross motor skills common to daily living and typically mastered during childhood. They include fundamental stability movements such as sitting, standing, bending, stretching, twisting, and turning. They also include fundamental locomotor actions such as running, jumping, hopping, and leaping and fundamental object manipulation tasks such as throwing, catching, kicking, and striking.

Specialized movements are fundamental movements that have been refined or combined with other movements into more complex forms. They are typically mastered during later childhood and beyond and may take the form of complex skills for daily living, recreational activities, and competitive sport. Walking on a slippery surface, downhill skiing, and performing a competitive gymnastics routine on the balance beam are examples of specialized stability skills. Specialized locomotor and manipulative skills are found in the daily living activities of carrying a suitcase up a flight of stairs or stepping onto a moving escalator with a shopping bag full of purchases. They are also found in a recreational game of golf or tennis and the competitive sports of soccer, football, and basketball.

Take a few minutes to study table 1.6. It sets the stage for the sections that follow on understanding motor development among infants, children, adolescents, and adults.

SUMMARY

This chapter has focused on a variety of general topics to provide you with a brief overview of the field of motor development. The study of human development may take many forms, one form being the study of motor development. In turn, motor development may be studied in a variety of ways. The field has gone through a rather interesting history in its move from a process-oriented maturational approach, to a product-oriented normative/descriptive approach, and now back to a process approach examining underlying mechanisms of motor development.

Research designs and problems in the study of motor development were discussed as they relate to the longitudinal, mixed-longitudinal, and the cross-sectional approaches to study. The advantages and limitations of each were discussed, with the caveat that only the longitudinal and mixed-longitudinal designs are true studies of development. These research designs look at change in "developmental time" rather than "real time" as in the cross-sectional study.

Various age classifications of development were examined with the intent of conveying the concept that although development is age-related, it is not age-dependent. Chronological age is the most frequently used and most convenient indicator of change, but it is the least accurate indicator of development. Age does not generate or cause development; it is merely an indicator of what has transpired because of the developmental process.

The chapter concluded with a discussion of terminology commonly used in the study of motor development techniques for classifying movement skills. The intent of this discussion was to help you the reader and us the authors proceed through the text using a common language to maximize understanding of the important topics and concepts to follow.

CRITICAL READINGS

Clark, J. E., & Whitall, J. (1989). What is motor development? The lessons of history. *Quest, 41,* 183–202.

Corbin, C., Dale, D., & Pangazi, R. (1999). Promoting physically active lifestyles among youths. *JOPERD, 70(6),* 26–28.

Gentile, A. M. (2000). Skill acquisition: Action, movement, and neuromotor processes. In J. Carr & R. Sheperd (Eds.), *Movement Science: Foundations for Physical Therapy in Rehabilitation.* 2nd ed. (pp. 111–187). Gaithersburg, MD: Aspen.

Keogh, J., & Sugden, D. (1985). *Movement Skill Development* (Chapter 1). New York: Macmillan.

Lefrancois, G. (1993). *The Lifespan* (Chapter 1). Belmont, CA: Wadsworth.

Magill, R. A. (2001). *Motor Learning: Concepts and Applications* (Chapter 1). Boston, MA: McGraw Hill.

Roberton, M., & Konczak, J. (2001). Predicting children's overarm throw ball velocities from their developmental levels in throwing. *Research Quarterly for Exercise and Sport, 72,* 91–103.

Smoll, F. L. (1982). Developmental kinesiology: Toward a subdiscipline focusing on motor development. In J. A. S. Kelso & J. E. Clark (Eds.), *The Development of Movement Control and Co-ordination* (pp. 319–354). New York: Wiley.

Thomas, J. R., & Thomas, K. T. (1989). What is motor development: Where does it belong? *Quest, 41,* 203–212.

 ## WEB RESOURCES

Background information on Myrtle McGraw
www.webster.edu/~woolflm/mcgraw.html

Esther Thelen's Motor Development
Laboratory at Indiana University
http://php.indiana.edu/~gormleyf

Homepage for the journal *Human Development*
www.karger.ch/journals/hde/hde_jh.htm

MODELS OF HUMAN DEVELOPMENT

KEY TERMS

Phase-stage theory
Developmental task
Developmental milestone
Ecological theory
Dynamic systems theory
Affordances
Rate limiters
Behavior setting theory
Adaptation
Accommodation
Assimilation
Schema

CHAPTER COMPETENCIES

Upon completion of this chapter you should be able to:

- Compare and contrast maturational, environmental, interactionist, and transactional views of causation in motor development
- Demonstrate familiarity with a variety of theoretical models of human development
- Discuss changes in cognition as a developing process
- Classify theories of development into various conceptual viewpoints
- Analyze changes in psychosocial development across the life span
- Identify the major developmental tasks across the life span

> **KEY CONCEPT**
>
> Human development may be studied from a variety of theoretical frameworks, each of which has implications for the motor development and movement education of infants, children, adolescents, and adults.

During the past century, several developmental theorists have closely studied the phenomenon of human development. Sigmund Freud (1856–1939), Erik Erikson (1902–1994), Arnold Gesell (1880–1947), Robert Havighurst (1900–1991), and Jean Piaget (1896–1980), among others, have made valuable contributions to our knowledge of human development. Each has constructed theoretical models that depict the developmental process and form a basis for much of today's work.

This chapter takes a brief look at the models of development proposed by these theorists. As a basis for a more detailed study of motor development, we also examine characteristic ways in which theorists view the phenomenon of human development with particular attention given to ecological theories. We finish the chapter by examining three popular theories of development in particular, those of Erik Erikson, Jean Piaget, and Robert Havighurst.

THEORETICAL MODELS OF HUMAN DEVELOPMENT

Austrian psychiatrist Sigmund Freud's (1927) *psychoanalytic theory* of human behavior may be viewed, in part, as one of the first models of human development, even though his work centered around personality and abnormal functioning. Freud's famous psychosexual stages of development reflected various zones of the body with which the individual seeks gratification of the *id* (the unconscious source of motives, desires, passions, and pleasure seeking) at certain general age periods.

The *ego* mediates between the pleasure-seeking behavior of the id and the *superego* (common sense, reason, and conscience). Freud's *oral, anal, phallic, latency,* and *genital* stages of personality development represent the terms applied to the pleasure-seeking zones of the body that come into play at different age periods. Each stage relies heavily on physical sensations and motor activity.

Freud's psychoanalytic theory has received its share of criticism primarily due to the inability to scientifically objectify, quantify, and validate its concepts. It has, however, stimulated considerable research and study and served as the basis for the notable works of his German-born student Erik Erikson (1963).

Erik Erikson (1963, 1980) focused on the influence of society, rather than sex, on development. His *psychosocial theory* describes eight stages of the human life cycle and puts them on a continuum, emphasizing factors in the environment, not heredity, as facilitators of change. Erikson's view of human development acknowledges factors within the individual's experiential background as having a primary role in development. His view of the importance of motor development is more implicit than explicit, but he clearly points out the importance of success-oriented movement experiences as a means of reconciling the developmental crises that each individual passes through.

> **CONCEPT 2.1**
>
> There are numerous models of human development, each of which reflects its originator's knowledge, interests, and biases.

Arnold Gesell's (1928, 1954) *maturational theory* of growth and development emphasizes maturation of the nervous system as the principal driver of the physical and motor aspects of human behavior. Gesell documented and described general age periods for the acquisition of a wide variety of rudimentary movement abilities during infancy and viewed these maturation-based tasks as important indicators of social and emotional growth.

Gesell also described various ages when children are in "nodal" periods or when they are "out of focus" with their environment. A nodal stage is a maturational period during which the child exhibits a high degree of mastery over situations in the immediate environment, is balanced in behavior, and generally pleasant. Being out of focus is the opposite; the child exhibits a low degree of mastery over situations in the immediate environment, is unbalanced or troubled in behavior, and generally unpleasant. Maturational theory is not widely accepted today, but it played a significant role in the evolution of child development as an area of study.

A fourth developmental model, that of Robert Havighurst (1972), views development as an interplay between biological, social, and cultural forces through which individuals are continually enhancing their abilities to function effectively in society. Havighurst's *environmental theory* views development as a series of tasks that must be achieved within a certain time frame to ensure the proper developmental progression of the individual. According to Havighurst's model, there are teachable moments when the body is ready and when society requires successful completion of a task. As with the other models discussed, the tasks described by Havighurst rely heavily on movement, play, and physical activity for their development, particularly during infancy and childhood.

 CONCEPT 2.2

No one theory is complete or totally accurate in describing or explaining human development, and, as a result, all break down at some point.

A fifth developmental theory popular among educators is that of Swiss psychologist Jean Piaget (1969). Piaget's *cognitive development theory* places primary emphasis on the acquisition of cognitive thought processes. He gained insight into the development of cognitive structures through careful observation of infants and children. The genius in Piaget's work lies in his uncanny ability to pick out subtle clues in children's behavior that give us indications of their cognitive functioning. Piaget viewed these subtle indicators as milestones in the hierarchy of cognitive development. Movement is emphasized as a primary agent in the acquisition of increased cognitive structures, particularly during infancy and the preschool years. Piaget used chronological age only as a broad and general indicator of cognitive functioning and relied instead on observed behaviors. These observed behaviors served for Piaget as the primary indicators of the child's ever-increasing complexity in cognitive development. Piaget identified these developmental phases as *sensorimotor* (birth to 2 years), *preoperational* (2 to 7 years), *concrete operations* (7 to 11 years), and *formal operations* (12 years and over). Piaget did not directly concern himself with development beyond about age 15 because he believed that highly sophisticated intellectual capabilities were developed by this time.

All theorists look at human development from somewhat different points of view, but close inspection reveals remarkable similarities. Each theorist emphasizes movement and play as important facilitators of enhanced functioning. Also, each tends to be more descriptive than explanatory. In other words, they tell us "what" is happening in the normal process of development, rather than "why" it is happening.

CONCEPTUAL VIEWPOINTS OF DEVELOPMENT

Close inspection of the five models of development outlined, as well as the study of others, reveals a distinct tendency for each model to group around one of four conceptual frameworks. These frameworks are classified here as (1) phase-stage, (2) developmental task, (3) developmental milestone, and (4) ecological theories of human development (table 2.1). We will take a brief look at each, with particular attention given to the newer ecological theories.

TABLE 2.1	Conceptual Approaches to the Study of Human Development	
Conceptual Approach	**Representative Theorists**	**Research Focus**
Phase-Stage Theory	Sigmund Freud	Study of psychosexual development from birth through childhood
	Erik Erikson	Study of life span psychosocial development
	Arnold Gesell	Study of maturational processes in central nervous system development from birth through childhood ("ontogeny recapitulates phylogeny")
Developmental Task Theory	Robert Havighurst	Study of the interaction of biology and society on developmental maturity from infancy through old age
Developmental Milestone Theory	Jean Piaget	Study of cognitive development as an interactive process between biology and the environment from infancy through childhood
Ecological Theory (Dynamical Systems branch)	Nicholas Bernstein; Kugler, Kelso, and Turvey	Study of development as a discontinuous, self-organizing, transactional process among the task, individual, and environment throughout life
Ecological Theory (Behavior Setting branch)	Roger Barker; Urie Bronfenbrenner	Study of development as a function of the individual's interpretation of specific environmental settings transacting with the sociocultural and historical milieu

CONCEPT 2.3

Theories of development may be studied from distinct conceptual viewpoints.

Phase-Stage Theory

The **phase-stage** approach to developmental theory is the oldest of the conceptual viewpoints. All classical developmental theorists (i.e., stage theorists), whether they are studying cognitive, moral, personality, or motor development, contend that there are universal age periods characterized by certain types of behavior. These behaviors occur in phases or stages, last for arbitrary lengths of time, and are invariant. In other words, stages are

sequential and cannot be reordered, but one or more stages may be skipped. Furthermore, stage theory focuses on broad-based changes rather than narrow or isolated behaviors.

Each phase (i.e., typical behavior) generally covers a period of one year or more and may be accompanied by one or more other stages. Some theorists subdivide particular phases into smaller stages. Others prefer to look at one phase typifying one particular period. Most theorists who propose a phase-stage scheme have divided childhood, or even the entire life cycle, into ten periods or less. The phase-stage concept is probably the most popular among parents and educators and is often reflected in our thinking and speech when we say, "She is just going through a stage" or "I will be happy when he is out of that phase." Freud, Erikson, and Gesell each viewed child development as a phase-stage–related process.

Stages have been proposed for several fundamental movement tasks. The viability of a rigid stage theory of motor development is questionable. More flexible stage models based on the components of a movement rather than on the total body configuration hold greater promise. Any phase-stage theory describes only general (i.e., group or normative) developmental characteristics for a generic (average) individual postulated to be common to all people. Phase-stage theory gives us a view of the "big picture" but does not accommodate the details.

Developmental Task Theory

A second conceptual viewpoint of development is the **developmental task** approach. A developmental task is an important accomplishment that individuals must achieve by a certain time if they are to function effectively and meet the demands placed on them by society. Proponents of developmental task theory view the accomplishment of particular tasks within a certain time span as prerequisite to smooth progression to higher levels of functioning. This concept of development differs from the phase-stage view in that it is predictive of later success or failure based on the individual's performance at an earlier stage and does not merely attempt to describe typical behavior at a particular age. Havighurst's view of development uses the developmental task concept to both describe and predict behavior from infancy through adolescence (Havighurst and Levine, 1979). The hemispherical dominance theory and treatment techniques for individuals with learning disorders as proposed by Delacato (1966) also follow a developmental task approach. Although developmental task theories claim predictability, little has been done to test their assertions. Hence, there is considerable question as to their validity.

Developmental Milestone Theory

The **developmental milestone** approach is a third conceptual framework from which development is viewed. Developmental milestones are similar to

developmental tasks except for their emphasis. Instead of referring to accomplishments that take place if the individual is to adapt to the environment, this approach refers to strategic indicators of how far development has progressed. The accomplishment of a developmental milestone may or may not in itself be crucial to adjustment in the world as it is with a developmental task. Milestones are merely convenient guidelines by which the rate and extent of development can be gauged. As with phase-stage theories, the developmental milestone theories are more descriptive than predictive, but unlike stage theories, they view development as a continual unfolding and intertwining of developmental processes, not as a neat transition from one stage to another. Piaget's cognitive development theory is generally considered to be a developmental milestone theory, as is the dynamical systems theory of motor development.

Recognition that most models of human development tend to fall under one of these three concepts enables us to view the phenomena of growth and development more objectively. Each concept has merit and operates to a certain degree throughout the developmental process. The years of infancy and early childhood do require the achievement of certain important tasks such as learning to walk, talk, and take solid foods by a specific age for normal functioning to be established. These years also encompass a variety of stages that children pass through at more or less the same age, in addition to a variety of milestones achieved as subtle indicators of how far development has progressed.

Ecological Theory

It is important to know about the products of development in terms of *what* people are typically like during particular phases and stages, developmental milestones, and developmental tasks (description). It is equally important, however, to know *why* these changes occur (explanation). To this end many developmentalists are looking at explanatory models in an attempt to understand more about the underlying processes that actually development.

Ecological theory, or contextual theory as it is sometimes called, attempts to be of practical benefit, by being both descriptive and explanatory. **Ecological theory,** or "contextual theory" as it is sometimes called, views development occurring as a function of the environmental "context" and historical time frame in which one lives. The study of human ecology from a developmental perspective is a matter of studying the relationship of individuals to their environment and to one another. Two ecological approaches popular among motor developmentalists are dynamic systems theory and behavior setting theory.

Dynamic Systems Branch

Dynamic systems theory is popular among many developmentalists (Alexander et al., 1993; Caldwell and Clark, 1990; Kamm et al., 1990; Thelen, 1989; Thomas, 2000). It is based largely on the work of the Russian physiologist Nicholas Bernstein (1967) and has been expanded by Kugler, Kelso, and Turvey (1982). The word *dynamic* conveys the concept that developmental change is nonlinear and discontinuous. Because development is viewed as nonlinear, it is seen as a discontinuous process. That is, individual change over time is not necessarily smooth and hierarchical and does not necessarily involve moving toward ever higher levels of complexity and competence in the motor system. Individuals, particularly those with disabling impairments, may be impeded in their motor development. For example, children with spastic cerebral palsy are frequently delayed in learning to walk independently. When independent walking is achieved, their gait patterns will be individualized and achieved when appropriate for each child. Although, by definition, development is a continuous process, it is also a discontinuous process when viewed from a dynamical perspective. In other words, development is a "continuous-discontinuous" process.

The dynamics of change occur over time, but in a highly individual manner influenced by a variety of critical factors within the system. These factors are termed **affordances** and **rate limiters.** *Affordances* tend to promote or encourage developmental change. *Rate limiters* are constraints that serve to impede or retard development. For children with cerebral palsy, for example, these constraints are neurological and biomechanical. Affordances may include assisted support, handholds, encouragement, and guided instruction.

The word *systems* conveys the concept that the human organism is self-organizing and composed of several subsystems. It is *self-organizing* in that humans, by nature, are inclined to strive for motor control and movement competence. Systems derived from the task, the individual, and the environment operate separately and in concert to determine the rate, sequence, and extent of development. Coordination and control of movement is the result of several systems working dynamically together in a cooperative manner. No one factor is more important than the other. All systems interact in a manner that causes motor behavior to emerge independent of any one system (Alexander et al., 1993). Children with spastic cerebral palsy, as self-organizing systems, develop individually unique gait patterns in response to their capabilities for meeting the achievement demands of the walking task. Preferred patterns of movement behavior develop in response to unique factors within the individual, the task, and the environment. These movement patterns are the result of the most efficient interaction of systems and the least amount of energy required. Although preferred patterns of movement behavior do exist (chapters 8, 11, and 16), they are altered when the demands of the system dictate change.

Viewed from a systems perspective, numerous elements can change as one grows and develops. Bernstein (1967) referred to these as *degrees of freedom.* The performance of a movement task includes neuromotor as well as biomechanical degrees of freedom. The number of degrees of freedom are, however, constrained through the individual gaining motor control and movement coordination of the movement task, thereby resulting in the formation of movement patterns. The individual develops preferred patterns of movement, but these preferred patterns may be reorganized through control parameters. *Control parameters* are "those variables that provide a condition for a pattern change. Control parameters do not dictate what change will occur, but when they reach a critical value, they act as an agent for reorganization of the motor pattern" (Alexander et al., 1993, p. 3).

Transition from one pattern of movement to another is called a *phase shift*. Phase shifts are plentiful among infants when moving from one form of locomotion (crawling to creeping) to another (creeping to walking). During this time the baby is in a state of instability, shifting from one pattern to the other until a new preferred pattern is firmly established.

Dynamic systems theory attempts to answer the "why" or process questions that result in the observable product of motor development. Much of the work to date has centered on infant motor development, but an increasing amount of research is focusing on dynamical explanations of motor development among children, adolescents, and adults in populations of both typically and atypically developing individuals.

For years developmentalists have recognized the interactive role of two primary systems on the developmental process: heredity and environment. Many now, however, have taken this view one step farther in recognizing that the specific demands of the movement task transact with the individual (i.e., hereditary or biological factors) and the environment (i.e., experience or learning factors) in the development of stability, locomotor, and manipulative movement abilities. Such a transactional model implies that systems within the task, the individual, and the environment not only interact but also have the potential for modifying and being modified by the other as one strives to gain motor control and movement competence (figure 2.1).

Both the processes and the products of motor development should remind us of the individuality of the learner. Each individual has his or her unique timetable for the development of abilities. Although our "biological clock" is rather specific

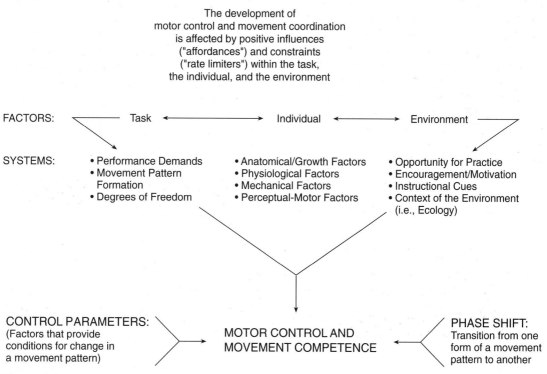

Figure 2.1
Development from a dynamical systems perspective.

when it comes to the sequence of movement skill acquisition, the rate and extent of development is individually determined and dramatically influenced by the specific performance demands of the individual task.

Typical age periods of development are just that: typical, and nothing more. Age periods merely represent approximate time ranges during which certain behaviors may be observed for the mythical "average" individual. Overreliance on these time periods would negate the concepts of continuity, specificity, and individuality in the developmental process and are of little practical value when working with individuals from a developmental perspective.

Behavior Setting Branch

Behavior setting theory is a branch of ecological psychology that has its roots in the work of Kurt Lewin in the 1930s to 1940s and his colleague Roger Barker in the 1950s to 1970s (Thomas, 2000). Lewin is credited with developing a branch of Gestalt psychology known as *topological psychology,* a term taken from mathematics where "topology" is the study of geometric properties that remain unchanged even when under distortion. Lewin used the term *life space* to account for all that influences a child's behavior at a given time.

Barker (1978) extended Lewin's thinking with the notion that the *behavior setting,* that is, the specific environmental conditions of the child's life space, account for a large portion of the individual variation among children. His concept of *standing patterns of behavior* (i.e., typical ways in which people act) explains why different settings evoke different responses. For example, we can predict that if a typical second grader is outside for recess, her behavior will be active, energetic, and noisy. When in the classroom, however, her predicted standing pattern of behavior will be the opposite. If a teenager is hanging out at the mall, his predicted behavior is considerably different from that expected in the marching band.

Furthermore, the milieu in which these events occur, according to Barker, encompasses the expected actions of people in a specific behavior setting. To that extent Barker felt that the "physical

setting" and the "time boundaries" of a behavior setting are instrumental in shaping the expected behavior. Take, for example, our abrupt change in behavior when sitting in a theater several minutes before a play begins, and when the lights dim and the first act begins. The physical setting of the brightly lit theater encourages talking and looking about the auditorium. On the other hand, when the lights dim and the actors come on stage, talk abruptly ceases and the audience settles into their seats to watch the play. If the play is relatively short, the time boundaries are acceptable to most and full attention is given to the actors on stage. But if the play is long and continues on and on, the standing patterns of behavior begin to change as a function of the time boundaries of the play. People begin to fidget, whisper, and otherwise divert their attention to something other than the play. Wise playwrights, therefore, divide their plays into two or three acts, thus allowing for a brief intermission between acts, which will restore the pattern of behavior expected from the audience.

The work of Urie Bronfenbrenner in the 1970s to 1990s is an extension of Barker's. It places strong emphasis on factors within the environment as being key to development. Bronfenbrenner (1979) defined the ecology of human development as:

> the scientific study of the progressive, mutual accommodation between an active, growing human being and the changing properties of the immediate settings in which the developing person lives, as this process is affected by relations between those settings, and by the larger contexts in which the settings are embedded. (p. 21)

Bronfenbrenner's ecological theory, however, is based on the premise that it is not the behavior setting that predicts behavior, but the individual's interpretation of the setting in both time and space. That is, the *meaning* attached to the environment, not the environment, guides behavior. Bronfenbrenner argues that it is nonsense to try to understand behavior from the objective reality of the environment without also learning what the environment means to the individual. As a result, he places considerable importance on one's perceptions of the activities, roles, and interpersonal relations typically displayed in a behavior setting. *Activities* are what people are doing. *Roles* are the expected behaviors in that setting for a given position in society—parent, teacher, adolescent, coach, and so forth. *Interpersonal relations* are the ways in which people treat each other by what they say and what they do, in that setting.

Development occurs within a broad range of environmental contexts. Bronfenbrenner terms these settings the *microsystem* (one's family, school,

neighborhood, and peers), the *mesosystem* (the interaction among various settings within the microsystems), the *exosystem* (social settings in which the individual does not play an active role but is affected by its decisions), the *macrosystem* (the culture in which one exists), and the *chronosystem* (the sociohistorical events of one's lifetime). Figure 2.2 illustrates the microsystems of the family, school, neighborhood, and peer group influencing an individual based on his or her perceived notion of appropriate activities, roles, and interpersonal relations within the context of each. In our

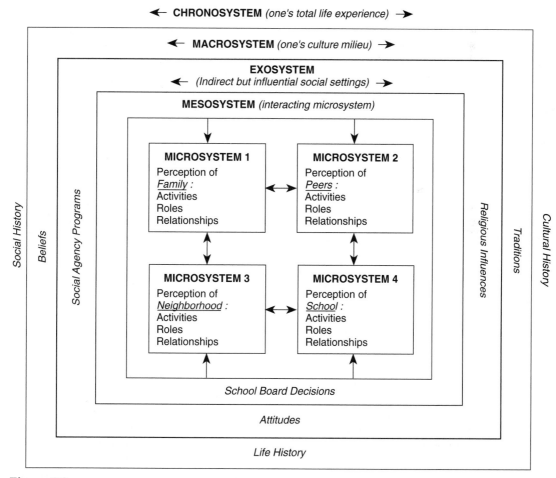

Figure 2.2

A conceptualization of Bronfenbrenner's ecological theory of development as influenced by one's perceptions of his or her behavior settings.

example, the mesosystem is composed of the interaction patterns among these four microsystems. The exosystems in our hypothetical example are settings that do not directly involve the individual but affect, or are affected by, what happens in a behavior setting. The macrosystem is the cultural milieu in which the individual exists and is composed of such things as beliefs, traditions, attitudes, and practices shared throughout one's immediate culture. Finally, the chronosystem involves the pattern of events over one's life span.

THREE LEADING THEORIES OF HUMAN DEVELOPMENT

In this section, summaries of three theories, each representing a different conceptual point of view, are presented. The phase-stage theory of Erik Erikson, the developmental milestone theory of Jean Piaget, and the developmental task theory of Robert Havighurst have been selected because of their thoroughness, popularity, and important implications for motor development. Ecological theories were discussed in the preceding paragraphs.

Erik Erikson

The psychosocial theory of Erik Erikson (1963, 1980) adheres to the phase-stage approach to studying human development. It is an experience-based theory widely acclaimed by educators and psychologists. The following overview of Erikson's stage theory is presented for clarity and ease of understanding. See table 2.2 for an outline of Erikson's stages and the approximate age periods when they appear. Note the numerous implications for movement throughout the theory.

CONCEPT 2.4

Individuals' psychosocial development is influenced by their motor development and movement education throughout the life span.

A. Acquiring a Sense of Basic Trust Versus Mistrust (Infancy)

According to Erikson, bodily experiences provide the basis for a psychological state of *trust versus mistrust*. The infant learns to trust "mother," oneself, and the environment through mother's perception of the infant's needs and demands. Mutual trust and a willingness to face situations together is established between mother and child. For the neonate, trust requires a feeling of physical comfort and a minimum of fear and uncertainty. A sense of basic trust helps an individual to be receptive to new experiences willingly.

Movement is an essential ingredient of the reciprocal relationship between parent and child. The rhythmical rocking, bathing, and general play behaviors between parent and baby provide a natural means, through movement, for establishing a sense of trust. Mistrust arises out of uncertainty; insecurity; and failure to respond to baby's needs for comfort, attention, and mutual play dialogue.

B. Acquiring a Sense of Autonomy Versus Doubt and Shame (Toddler)

During the stage in which the toddler is establishing a sense of *autonomy versus doubt and shame*, Erikson believed that continued dependency creates a sense of doubt and shame about one's capabilities. It is therefore critical that the young child assert autonomy as a normal stage of psychosocial development. Children are bombarded by the conflicting pulls of asserting their autonomy and of denying themselves the right and capacity to make this assertion. During this period they need guidance and support as they strive for autonomy, lest they find themselves at a loss and are forced to turn against themselves with shame and doubt. At this stage of development, children are typically eager to explore and accomplish new feats. During this period it is essential that proper development of the ego occurs, thereby permitting awareness of oneself as an autonomous whole.

Active play is particularly important during this stage because it allows children to develop autonomy within their own boundaries. A child's

TABLE 2.2 Erik Erikson's Stages of Psychosocial Development

Stage	Characteristics	Approximate Age Period	Defining Event
I Trust vs. Mistrust	Trust during infancy is achieved by having basic needs met by responsive, sensitive caregivers. Mistrust is developed through uncertainty about the future and inconsistent meeting of basic needs.	Infancy	Mutual affirmation
II Autonomy vs. Doubt and Shame	Autonomy is developed as a toddler by being permitted to assert one's will and establish a rudimentary sense of independence. Doubt and shame develop out of overly harsh and inconsistent discipline and "smothering" behaviors by caregivers.	Toddler	"Terrible two's"
III Initiative vs. Guilt	Initiative is established during the early childhood years when children are challenged to engage in more purposeful and responsible socialized behaviors. Guilt feelings develop from excessive anxiety arising out of irresponsible behavior.	Preschool	Play age
IV Industry vs. Inferiority	Industry is maximized during the exuberant years of childhood when children direct their energies to mastering the new cognitive and physical skills of their rapidly expanding world. Inferiority develops from feelings of incompetence and failure to achieve expectation levels.	School Age	Learning new skills
V Identity vs. Role Confusion	Identity is achieved by adolescents finding out who they are and what they are about and exploring alternative solutions to life's problems. Role confusion is likely among those stifled in this quest.	Early Adolescence	Fidelity and devotion to friends and causes
VI Intimacy vs. Isolation	Intimacy is achieved during young adulthood by forming long-term, close, personal ties with significant others. Isolation occurs among those unable to reveal themselves in intimate relationships.	Late Adolescence	Mutually satisfying love and affiliation
VII Generativity vs. Self-Absorption	The mature adult who has achieved generativity is genuinely interested in helping others, especially the younger generation, lead productive lives. Those more concerned about their own wants and needs than those of others are self-absorbed.	Adulthood	Resolves "midlife crisis"
VIII Integrity vs. Despair	Older adults who look back over their life and positively evaluate what they have done with it are individuals with integrity. Those who lament the past and the decisions of a lifetime do so with despair.	Old Age	Wisdom, reflection, and a sense of fulfillment

autonomy emerges from the realization that the environment and the self can be controlled. During this stage children frequently violate the mutual trust established with others in order to establish autonomy in distinct areas.

C. Acquiring a Sense of Initiative Versus Guilt (Preschool)

During this stage in which the child establishes a sense of *initiative versus guilt,* avid curiosity and enthusiasm or feelings of guilt and anxiety develop. According to Erikson, the conscience is established during this stage. Specific tasks are mastered, and children assume responsibility for themselves and their world. They realize that life has a purpose. Children discover that with their greater mobility they are not unlike the adults in their environment. They begin to incorporate into their consciences who their parents are as people, and not merely what their parents try to teach them. With improvements in their use of language, children can expand their fields of activity and imagination. Awareness of sex differences also develops at this stage.

During this period children find pleasurable accomplishment in manipulating meaningful toys. Fundamental movement skills are being mastered, influencing children's success in the game activities of their culture. Successful play and game experiences contribute to a sense of initiative. Unsuccessful experiences promote feelings of doubt and shame. In the normal scheme of things a sense of accomplishment in other areas quickly compensates for most guilt and failure. For the child, the future tends to absolve the past.

D. Acquiring a Sense of Industry Versus Inferiority (School Age)

Acquiring a sense of *industry versus inferiority* is marked by the development of the skills necessary for life in general and preparation for adulthood. During this phase Erikson believed that children should be finding places among their peers instead of among adults. They need to work on mastering social skills and becoming competent and self-striving. They need feelings of accomplishment for

having done well. Failure during this stage is difficult to accept, and the child has a distinct tendency to ward off failure at any price. During this period children begin to recognize that they must eventually break with accustomed family life. Dependence on parents begins to shift to reliance on social institutions such as the school, the team, or the gang.

Play activities during this phase tend to reflect competition through organized games and sports. Boys and girls generally play separately. Play for its own sake begins to lose importance at the end of this stage. In conjunction with puberty, involvement in play merges into semiplayful and, eventually, real involvement in work.

E. Acquiring a Sense of Identity Versus Role Confusion (Early Adolescence)

When acquiring a sense of *identity versus role confusion* there is rapid body growth and sexual maturation. Masculine or feminine identity develops. Feelings of acceptance or rejection by peers are important. Conflicts frequently arise when peers say one thing and society says another. Identity is essential for making adult decisions about vocation and family life. Youth select people who mean the most to them as significant adults. These role models may be family members, friends, sports heroes, or other accomplished individuals in their lives. During this stage of development, the individual slowly moves into society as an interdependent and contributing member. A sense of identity assures the individual a definite place within his or her corner of society.

Organized sports help many youth acquire a sense of identity. Skill proficiency, team membership, and competitive victories contribute to a sense of identity. Failure and unsuccessful experiences, on the other hand, contribute to a sense of role confusion.

F. Acquiring a Sense of Intimacy Versus Isolation (Late Adolescence)

Erikson believed that in acquiring a sense of *intimacy versus isolation* that an individual accepts himself or herself and goes on to accept others by fusing his or her personality with others. Childhood and youth are at an end. The individual settles down to the task of full participation in the community and begins to enjoy life with adult responsibilities as well as adult liberties. At this stage the individual shows readiness and ability to share mutual trust and to regulate cycles of work, procreation, and recreation.

Play through the games, sports, and recreational activities of adulthood serves as one important medium for fostering a sense of intimacy with same-sex and opposite-sex teammates. Efforts on behalf of a team, whether in a competitive or recreational setting, reflect a level of intimacy due to the need for cooperative behaviors and teamwork. Failure to develop and refine game and sport skills, to at least a recreational level, can lead to a sense of isolation from a team or social group.

G. Acquiring a Sense of Generativity Versus Self-Absorption (Adulthood)

Generativity versus self-absorption, according to Erikson, refers to the course an individual pursues in society to provide the next generation with the hope, virtues, and wisdom he or she has accumulated. It also includes parental responsibility to uphold society's interests in child care, education, the arts and sciences, and cultural traditions. This stage is manifested when an individual shows more interest in the next generation than in his or her problems.

In a movement sense, generativity may be viewed as wanting to pass on the joys and values of play, games, and sport activities to the next generation for their enjoyment and self-fulfillment. Failure during this stage involves self-absorbed disappointment and the inability to accept one's waning capabilities as middle age approaches.

H. Acquiring a Sense of Integrity Versus Despair (Mature Adult, and Old Age)

During this final stage, in which the mature adult acquires a sense of *integrity versus despair,* Erikson believed that the individual accomplishes the fullest sense of trust as the assured reliance on the integrity of significant others. A different love of

one's parents is established. Parents are seen as individuals with weaknesses as well as strengths, and deserving of love for who they are and not what they are. Integrity provides a successful solution to an opposing sense of despair. Fulfillment of this stage involves a sense of wisdom and a philosophy of life that often extends beyond the life cycle of the individual and relates directly to the future of new developmental cycles. Successfully meeting the challenge of this stage enables one to look back on his or her life with all of its successes and failures, good times and bad times, and to do so with integrity. Failure to meet the challenges of this stage causes one to look back with remorse, and to look forward in despair.

Movement in the form of active play, games, recreational sport, and general mobility is of real importance during this stage. During this period, successful movement, whether it involves walking, driving a car, or swimming laps, means independence. Movement at this stage means freedom and life. Looking back upon one's movement accomplishments, and forward at declining capabilities, does not cause despair in the individual who meets the challenges of this stage. Instead, movement helps one to maintain competence and accept physical changes.

Jean Piaget

The developmental milestone theory of Jean Piaget (1952, 1954, 1969, 1974) is among the most popular of the theories postulated by experts in the field of child development because of its clarity and insight into and understanding of the development of cognition. Table 2.3 outlines Piaget's phases of cognitive development. Cognitive development, according to Piaget, occurs through the process of adaptation. **Adaptation** requires one to make adjustments to environmental conditions and intellectualize these adjustments through the complementary processes of accommodation and assimilation (figure 2.3).

Accommodation is adaptation that the child must make to the environment when new and incongruent information is added to his or her

TABLE 2.3   Jean Piaget's Phases of Cognitive Development

Phase	Characteristics	Approximate Age-Period	Defining Event
I Sensorimotor	The infant constructs meaning of her world by coordinating sensory experiences with movement.	Birth to 2 years	Basic assimilation and schema formation through movement
II Preoperational Thought	The young child displays increased symbolic thinking by linking his world with words and images.	2 to 7 years	Advanced assimilation by using physical activity to perform cognitive processes
III Concrete Operations	The child reasons logically about concrete events and can classify objects in her world into various sets.	7 to 11 years	Reversibility with intellectual experimentation through active play
IV Formal Operations	The adolescent is capable of reasoning more logically and in abstract and idealistic ways.	11 years onward	Deductive reasoning through abstract hypothesis formulation

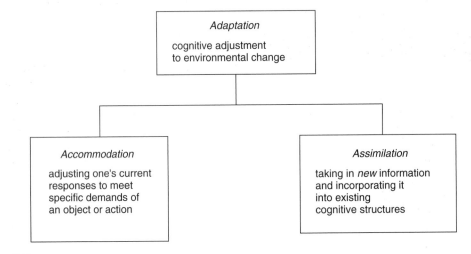

Figure 2.3
Piaget's view was that adaptation occurs through the complementary processes of accommodation and assimilation.

repertoire of possible responses. The individual adjusts the response to meet the demands of the specific challenge. Accommodation is a process that reaches outward toward reality and results in a visible change in behavior. For example, when playing in the shallow water of a bathtub or wading pool, a child learns to take into account many of the physical properties and realities of the water.

However, when trying to swim in deep water, the child will have to go through a series of new actions (e.g., not being able to touch the bottom, letting go, floating, and breath holding) to accommodate to the new reality of deep water.

Assimilation, on the other hand, is Piaget's term for the interpretation of new information based on present interpretations. Assimilation involves taking in information from the environment and incorporating it into the individual's existing cognitive structures. If this information cannot be incorporated into existing structures because of small variations, accommodation will occur. However, if the information is too different from the existing structures, it will not be assimilated or accommodated. For example, giving a toddler a ball to toss may be a new experience, but after a series of accommodations (i.e., adjustments), the child may attempt to play catch. You would not, however, expect the child to challenge you to a game of basketball. Although basketball playing involves various forms of ball tossing, it is too different from playing toss and catch to be assimilated (i.e., incorporated) by the child.

A summary of Piaget's theory follows. Note the numerous implications for movement throughout Piaget's phases of cognitive development.

CONCEPT 2.5

Higher cognitive structures are formulated through the processes of accommodation and assimilation, both of which rely on self-discovery through play and movement activity.

A.   Sensorimotor Phase (Birth to 2 Years)

The *sensorimotor phase* is the period during which children learn to differentiate themselves from objects and others. Motor activity is critical because the child learns through his or her physical interactions with the world. During the sensorimotor phase of development, the major developmental tasks of infancy are coordination of the infant's actions or movement activities and his or her perceptions into a tenuous whole. The sensorimotor phase is composed of several overlapping stages.

1. *Use of reflexes* (birth to 1 month): Piaget believed that there is a continuation of prenatal reflexes for the purpose of enabling the infant to gain additional information about his or her world. Reflexes are spontaneous repetitions caused by internal and external stimulation. Through reflexes and stereotypical behaviors, rhythm is established through practice, and habits are formed that later emerge as voluntary movements.

2. *Primary circular reactions* (1 to 3 months): Primary circular reactions refer to the assimilation of a previous experience and the recognition of the stimulus that triggered the reaction required to generate the experience. At this point in the infant's development, new or past experiences have no meaning unless they become part of the infant's primary circular reaction pattern. During this period, reflexive movement is gradually replaced with voluntary movement, but neurological maturity must be reached before sensations can be understood. What previously had been automatic behavior for the infant is now repeated voluntarily, and more than one sensory modality can be used at a time. Accidentally acquired responses become new sensorimotor habits.

3. *Secondary circular reactions* (3 to 9 months): During this stage, the infant tries to make events last and tries to make them occur. Secondary circular reactions mean that the focus of the infant is on retention, not repetition, as in the previous stage. The infant now tries to create a state of permanency by repeating and prolonging primary circular reactions with secondary reactions. During this stage, two or more sensorimotor experiences are related to one experiential sequence or schema. **Schema,** as used here, is Piaget's term for a pattern of physical or motor action occurring in early infancy. It should not be confused with Schmidt and Lee's (2000) use of the word "Schema," in which they are referring to later motor skills. For the infant at the secondary circular reactions stage, vision is the prime coordinator of behavior. The other sensory modalities are used to a lesser degree. This is the stage, according to Piaget, where

imagination, play, and emotion begin to appear.

4. *Application of the secondary schemata to new situations* (8 to 12 months): Piaget viewed this stage as being characterized by the child's ability to distinguish means from ends; that is, being able to produce the same result in more than one way. During this period, children use previous behavioral achievements primarily as the basis for adding new achievements to their expanding repertoire. As a result, there is increased exploration in which ends and means are differentiated through experimentation. Accommodation occurs as the result of experimentation, and the infant can now experience action by observation.

5. *Tertiary circular reactions* (12 to 18 months): Tertiary circular reactions is Piaget's term for the infant's discovery of new means through active experimentation. During this period, curiosity and novelty-seeking behavior are developing. Fundamental reasoning comes into play and is developed. As a result, failure to remember is seen as failure to understand. The infant begins to develop spatial relationships upon discovering objects as objects. Imitation develops and play is important because the child repeats the action phase, linking cognitive processes to movement processes.

6. *Invention of new means through mental combinations* (12 to 24 months): During this stage, Piaget recognized a shift from sensorimotor experiences to increased reflection about these experiences. This represents the stepping-stone to the next phase, a more advanced level of intellectual behavior. Children at this stage are capable of discerning themselves as one object among many. Therefore, they tend to perceive and use objects for their intrinsic qualities. Additionally, they begin to relate objects to new actions without perceiving all of the actions. Sensorimotor patterns are slowly

replaced by semimental functioning. Imitation copies the action or the symbol of the action. Parallel play appears, and identification, as a mental process, becomes evident by the end of this phase, depending on the level of the child's intellectual development. Furthermore, this period is characterized by the creation of means and not merely the discovery of means. The rudiments of insight begin to develop.

B. Preoperational Thought Phase (2 to 7 Years)

During the *preoperational thought phase,* the first real beginnings of cognition occur. It is "preoperational" because the child is not yet capable of mentally manipulating objects and must rely on physical activity to do so. Additionally, the preoperational thought phase is a period of transition from self-satisfying behavior to rudimentary socialized behavior in young children. As a result, children attempt to adjust new experiences to previous patterns of thinking. Continuous investigation of one's world develops, but the child knows the world only as he or she sees it. Assimilation (i.e., interpreting new information based on present interpretations) is the paramount task of the child. During this phase, emphasis on "why" and "how" becomes a primary tool for adaptation to occur. Conservation of quantity, involving such things as object permanence and conservation of volume, must be mastered before a concept of numbers can be developed.

Language begins to replace sensorimotor activity as a primary facilitator of learning and as the preferred mode of expressing thoughts. Additionally, events are judged by outward appearance regardless of their objective logic. The child responds to either the qualitative aspects of an event or its quantitative aspects, but not both simultaneously. As a result, the child is unable to merge concepts of objects, space, and causality into interrelationships with a concept of time. Time is a nebulous concept that eludes the child in this phase of development.

The child, according to Piaget, is egocentric (i.e., self-centered) in his or her relationship to the world rather than autistic (i.e., nonrelating) as in the sensorimotor phase. Play serves as an important means of assimilation and occupies most of the child's waking hours. Imaginary play and parallel play are important tools for learning. Play also serves to enact the rules and values of one's elders. Characteristic of the preoperational thought phase is the child's widening of social interest in his or her world. As a result, egocentricity is reduced and social participation increases. The child begins to exhibit interest in relationships between people. Understanding the social roles of "mother," "father," "sister," and "brother" and their relationship to one another is important to the child at this phase.

C. Concrete Operations Phase (7 to 11 Years)

During the *concrete operations phase* of development, the child becomes aware of alternative solutions, uses rules in thinking, and is able to differentiate between appearance and reality. It is called "concrete" because the child's mental actions (i.e., "operations") are still tied to concrete objects.

The concept of reversibility becomes established during this phase. Reversibility refers to the capacity of the child to understand that any change of shape, order, position, number, and so forth can be mentally reversed and returned to its original shape, order, position, or number. Reversibility enables the child to relate an event or thought to a total system of interrelated parts and to consider the event or thought from beginning to end or from end to beginning. This form of operational thought enhances the child's mental capacity to order and relate experiences to an organized whole.

The concrete operational thought level presupposes that mental experimentation still depends on perception. At this phase perceptions are more accurate, and the child applies his or her interpretation of these environmental perceptions knowingly. The child examines the parts to gain knowledge of the whole and establishes means of classification for organizing parts into a hierarchical system.

The child uses play during this phase to understand his or her physical and social world. Rules

and regulations are of interest to the child when applied to play. Play, however, loses its assimilative characteristics and becomes a balanced subordinate process of cognitive thought. As a result, curiosity finds expression in intellectual experimentation instead of active play alone.

D. Formal Operations Phase (11 Onward)

During the *formal operations phase*, childhood ends and youth begins as the individual enters the world of ideas. In this fourth and final phase of cognitive development, a systematic approach to problem solving appears. Logical deduction by implication develops, and the individual is capable of thinking vertically; that is, beyond the present. At this level the individual can dream and does not need concrete reality. Deduction by hypothesis and judgment by implication enable one to reason beyond cause and effect.

Robert Havighurst

The theory of Robert Havighurst (1953, 1972; Havighurst and Levine, 1979) is based on the concept that successful achievement of developmental tasks leads to happiness and success with later tasks, whereas failure leads to unhappiness, social disapproval, and difficulty with later tasks. Havighurst disagreed with any theory that proposes an innate basis of growth and development. He believed that living is learning and growing is learning. Development, then, according to Havighurst, is the process of learning one's way through life. Havighurst conceived of successful development as requiring mastery of a series of tasks. At each level of development the child encounters new social demands. These demands, or tasks, arise out of three sources. First, tasks arise from physical maturation. Such tasks as learning to walk, talk, and get along with one's age-mates are maturation-based. Second, tasks arise out of the cultural pressures of society, such as learning how to read and learning to be a responsible citizen. The third source of tasks is oneself. Tasks arise out of the maturing personality and the individual's values and unique aspirations.

Havighurst's theory has implications for all age levels. His theory is of particular importance to educators because it describes teachable moments in which a person's body and self are ready to achieve a certain task. Educators can better time their efforts at teaching by identifying the tasks suitable for a particular level of development, being fully aware that a child's level of readiness is influenced by biological, cultural, and self factors interacting with one another.

CONCEPT 2.6

Numerous developmental tasks must be achieved for the normal process of development to proceed unencumbered.

Havighurst has suggested six major periods of development: infancy and early childhood (birth through 5 years), middle childhood (6 through 12 years), adolescence (13 through 18 years), early adulthood (19 through 29 years), middle adulthood (30 through 60 years), and later maturity (60 years and up). A summary of Havighurst's developmental tasks in outline form follows. The reader is cautioned to be flexible in the interpretation of these tasks with respect to age. Ages are only convenient approximations and should not be viewed as rigid time frames. However, significant delay beyond these age boundaries would, according to Havighurst, represent failure in a developmental task, with resulting unhappiness and great difficulty with future tasks.

A. Infancy and early childhood (birth to 5 years)
   1. Learning to walk.
   2. Learning to take solid foods.
   3. Learning to talk.
   4. Learning to control the elimination of bodily wastes.
   5. Learning sex differences and sexual modesty.
   6. Acquiring concepts and language to describe social and physical reality.
   7. Readiness for reading.
   8. Learning to distinguish right from wrong and developing a conscience.

B. Middle childhood (6 to 12 years)
   1. Learning physical skills necessary for ordinary games.
   2. Building a wholesome attitude toward oneself.
   3. Learning to get along with age-mates.
   4. Learning an appropriate sex role.
   5. Developing fundamental skills in reading, writing, and calculating.
   6. Developing concepts necessary for everyday living.
   7. Developing a conscience, morality, and a scale of values.
   8. Achieving personal independence.
   9. Developing acceptable attitudes toward society.

C. Adolescence (13 to 18 years)
   1. Achieving mature relations with both sexes.
   2. Achieving a masculine or feminine social role.
   3. Accepting one's physique.
   4. Achieving emotional independence of adults.
   5. Preparing for marriage and family life.
   6. Preparing for an economic career.
   7. Acquiring values and an ethical system to guide behavior.
   8. Desiring and achieving socially responsible behavior.

D. Early adulthood (19 to 29 years)
   1. Selecting a mate.
   2. Learning to live with a partner.
   3. Starting a family.
   4. Rearing children.
   5. Managing a home.
   6. Starting an occupation.
   7. Assuming civic responsibility.

E. Middle adulthood (30 to 60 years)
   1. Helping teenage children to become happy and responsible adults.
   2. Achieving adult social and civic responsibility.

3. Satisfactory career achievement.
4. Developing adult leisure-time activities.
5. Relating to one's spouse as a person.
6. Accepting the physiological changes of middle age.
7. Adjusting to aging parents.

F. Later maturity (60 years and up)
1. Adjusting to decreasing strength and health.

2. Adjusting to retirement and reduced income.
3. Adjusting to death of spouse.
4. Establishing relations with one's age group.
5. Meeting social and civic obligations.
6. Establishing satisfactory living quarters.

SUMMARY

The process of development is commonly viewed as hierarchical. That is, the individual proceeds from general to specific, and from simple to complex, in gaining mastery and control over his or her environment. Erik Erikson's phase-stage theory, Jean Piaget's developmental milestone theory, and Robert Havighurst's developmental task theory make it obvious that the human organism throughout all aspects of its development is moving from comparatively simple forms of existence to more complex and sophisticated levels of development. Until recently, these levels of development have been expressed primarily in terms of the cognitive and affective behaviors of the individual, with only indirect attention given to motor development. Ecological theories, particularly dynamic systems theory and behavior setting theory, offer newer perspectives on development and are particularly relevant to the study of motor behavior.

Although the theoretical formulations of Erikson, Piaget, and Havighurst are of value, none adequately address motor development. It is appropriate, therefore, that a theoretical model of motor development that integrates elements from each, plus a dynamic systems and behavior setting perspective, be put forth in order that we may describe and explain this important aspect of human development. Chapter 3, "Motor Development: A Theoretical Model," is dedicated to this end.

CRITICAL READINGS

Anderson, A. (1997). Learning strategies in physical education: Self-talk, imagery, and goal setting. *JOPERD, 68(1)*, 30–35.

Bongaart, R., & Meijer, O. G. (2000). Bernstein's theory of motor behavior: Historical development and contemporary relevance. *Journal of Motor Behavior, 32*, 57–71.

Erikson, E. (1980). *Identity and the Life Cycle.* New York: W. W. Norton.

Kamm, K., et al. (1990). A dynamical systems approach to motor development. *Physical Therapy, 70*, 763–774.

Kamii, C. K., & DeVries, R. (1993). *Physical Knowledge in Preschool Education: Implications of Piaget's Theory.* New York: Teachers College Press. (Foreword by Jean Piaget).

Lefrancois, G. (1999). *The Lifespan.* Belmont, CA: Wadsworth.

Peterson, R., & Felton-Collins, V. (1986). *The Piaget Handbook for Teachers and Parents: Children in the Age of Discovery, Preschool–Third Grade.* New York: Teachers College Press.

Schmidt, R. A., & Lee, T. D. (2000). *Motor Control and Learning: A Behavioral Emphasis* (Chapter 1). Champaign, IL: Human Kinetics.

Sherman, C. (1999). Integrating mental management skills into the physical education curriculum. *JOPERD, 70(5)*, 25–30.

Sinclair, G., & Sinclair, D. (1994). Developing reflective performers by integrating mental management skills with the learning process. *The Sport Psychologist, 8*, 13–27.

Thelen, E., & Ulrich, B. D. (1991). Hidden skills. *Monographs of the Society for Research in Child Development, No. 223, 65,* 1.

Thomas, R. M. (2000). *Comparing Theories of Child Development.* Belmont, CA: Wadsworth.

 WEB RESOURCES

Background information on Urie Bronfenbrenner
www.people.cornell.edu/pages/ub11

Highlights of Erik Erikson's stages of psychosocial development
http://snycorva.cortland.edu/~ANDERSMD/ERIK/welcome.HTML

Highlights of Jean Piaget and his theory of cognitive development
www.unige.ch/piaget

Homepage for the Jean Piaget Society
www.piaget.org

MOTOR DEVELOPMENT: A THEORETICAL MODEL

KEY TERMS

Descriptive theory
Explanatory theory
Phases of motor development
Inductive theory formulation
Deductive theory formulation
Category of movement
Reflexes
Rudimentary movement abilities
Fundamental movement abilities
Specialized movement abilities
Heuristic
Algorithm
Hourglass heuristic

CHAPTER COMPETENCIES

Upon completion of this chapter you should be able to:

- Define life span motor development
- View an individual's motor behavior as "more" or "less" advanced on a developmental continuum rather than as "good" or "bad"
- Demonstrate an understanding of neural, physiological, perceptual, and cognitive changes across the life span
- Distinguish between inductive and deductive theory formulation
- Describe the phases of motor development
- List and describe the stages within the phases of motor development

> ### KEY CONCEPT
>
> Motor development may be conceptualized, using an hourglass heuristic, as a discontinuous and overlapping phase-stage process.

A major function of theory is to integrate existing facts, to organize them in such a way as to give them meaning. Theories of development take existing facts about the human organism and provide a developmental model congruent with these facts. Therefore, theory formulation serves as a basis for fact testing and vice versa. Facts are important, but they alone do not constitute a science. The development of a science depends on the advancement of theory as well as on the accumulation of facts. In the study of human behavior, especially in the areas of cognitive and affective development, theory formulation has gained increased importance over the past several years. Theory has played a critical dual role in both of these areas; namely, it has served and continues to serve as an integrator of existing facts and as a basis for the derivation of new facts (Bigge and Shermis, 1999; Learner, 1986).

DESCRIBING AND EXPLAINING MOTOR DEVELOPMENT

Until relatively recently, interest in motor development had been concerned primarily with describing and cataloging data, with little interest in developmental models leading to theoretical explanations of behavior across the life span. This research was necessary and important to our knowledge base. But it did little to help us answer the critically important questions of what lies underneath the process of motor development and how the process occurs. Only a limited number of comprehensive models of motor development exist, and there are few comprehensive theories of motor development. Now, however, scholars in motor development are reexamining their work with a view toward more carefully thought out

research grounded in sound theoretical frameworks. The intent of this chapter is to present a comprehensive model of motor development, based on specific theoretical viewpoints, in an effort to both describe and explain development and to serve as a basis for generating new facts about this important aspect of human behavior.

> ### CONCEPT 3.1
>
> Few comprehensive theoretical models of motor development exist.

The first function of a theoretical model of motor development should be to integrate the existing facts encompassed by the area of study. The second function should be to serve as a basis for the generation of new facts. One might argue that the facts could be interpreted in more than one way, that is, from different theoretical perspectives. This is entirely possible and desirable. Different viewpoints generate theoretical arguments and debates, the spark for research to shed new light on differing theoretical interpretations. Even if theoretical differences do not exist, research should be undertaken to determine whether the hypotheses derived from the theory can be both experimentally and ecologically supported.

Theory should undergird all research and science, and the study of motor development is no exception. Developmental theory must be both **descriptive** and **explanatory**. In other words, the developmentalist is interested in what people are typically like at particular age periods (description) and why these characteristics occur (explanation). Without a theoretical base of operation, research in motor development, or any other area, tends to yield little more than isolated facts. However, without an existing body of knowledge (facts), we cannot formulate theory, and without the formulation and constant testing of theory, we cannot hope for a higher level of understanding and awareness of the phenomenon that we call motor development.

CONCEPT 3.2

Theoretical models attempt to describe and explain behavior and may be inductive or deductive.

A theory is a group of statements, concepts, or principles that integrate existing facts and lead to the generation of new facts. The model of the **phases of motor development** presented in this chapter is not based solely on the accumulation of facts. Such a model would result from using an **inductive method** of theory formulation. In the inductive method the investigator first starts with a set of facts and then tries to find a conceptual framework around which to organize and explain them. The **deductive method** of theory formulation, as used here, is based on inference and has three primary qualifications. First, the theory should integrate existing facts and account for existing empirical evidence that bears on the content of the theory. Second, the theory should lend itself to the formulation of testable hypotheses in the form of: If _____ , then _____ statements. Third, the theory should meet the empirical test; that is, experimentally tested hypotheses should yield results that lend further support to the theory.

The use of a deductive, rather than an inductive, model enables us to see how well-accumulated facts fit together into a cohesive, understandable whole. It also enables us to identify the information needed to fill in gaps in the theory or to clarify or refine it. The phases of motor development outlined here are deductively based and serve as a model for theory formulation. In subsequent sections of the text each phase will be explored in greater detail.

THE PHASES OF MOTOR DEVELOPMENT

The process of motor development reveals itself primarily through changes in movement behavior. All of us, infants, children, adolescents, and adults, are involved in the lifelong process of learning how to move with control and competence in response to challenges we face daily in a constantly changing world. We are able to observe developmental differences in movement behavior, brought about by factors within the individual (biology), the environment (experience), and the task (physical/mechanical). We can do this through observation of changes in process (form) and product (performance). Therefore, a primary means by which the process of motor development may be observed is through studying changes in movement behavior throughout the life cycle. In other words, a "window" to the process of motor development is provided through an individual's observable movement behavior, which provides us with clues to underlying motor processes.

CONCEPT 3.3

The process of motor development may be viewed as phaselike and stagelike.

Observable movement may be grouped into three functional categories according to their purpose: stabilizing movement tasks, locomotor movement tasks, and manipulative movement tasks, or combinations of the three. In the broadest sense, a stability movement is any movement in which some degree of balance is required (i.e., virtually all gross motor activity). In a narrower sense, a stability movement is one that is both nonlocomotor and nonmanipulative. The category conveniently encompasses movements such as twisting, turning, pushing, and pulling that cannot be classified as locomotor or manipulative. In this book, stability, as a **category of movement,** is viewed as more than a convenient catchall term, but as less than a global term applicable to all movement. *Stability* refers to any movement that places a premium on gaining and maintaining one's equilibrium in relation to the force of gravity. Thus, axial movements (another term sometimes used for nonlocomotor movements) as well as inverted and body rolling postures are considered here as stability movements.

The *locomotor movement* category refers to movements that involve a change in location of the body relative to a fixed point on the surface. To walk, run, jump, hop, skip, or leap is to perform a locomotor task. In our use of the term, such activities as the forward roll and backward roll may be considered both locomotor and stability movements—locomotor because the body is moving from point to point, stability because of the premium placed on maintaining equilibrium in an unusual balancing situation.

The *manipulative movement* category refers to both gross and fine motor manipulation. Gross motor manipulation involves imparting force to, or receiving force from, objects. The tasks of throwing, catching, kicking, and striking an object, as well as trapping and volleying, are gross motor manipulative movements. Fine motor manipulation involves intricate use of the muscles of the

hand and wrist. Sewing, cutting with scissors, and typing are fine motor manipulative movements. A large number of movements involve a combination of stability, locomotor, and/or manipulative movements. For example, jumping rope involves locomotion (jumping), manipulation (turning the rope), and stability (maintaining balance). Likewise, playing soccer involves locomotor skills (running and jumping), manipulative skills (dribbling, passing, kicking, and heading), and stability skills (dodging, reaching, turning, and twisting).

In summary, if movement serves as a window to the process of motor development, then one way of studying this process is through examining the sequential progression of movement abilities throughout the entire life span. The following phases of motor development and the developmental stages within each phase are designed to serve as a model for this study. (See figure 3.1 for a

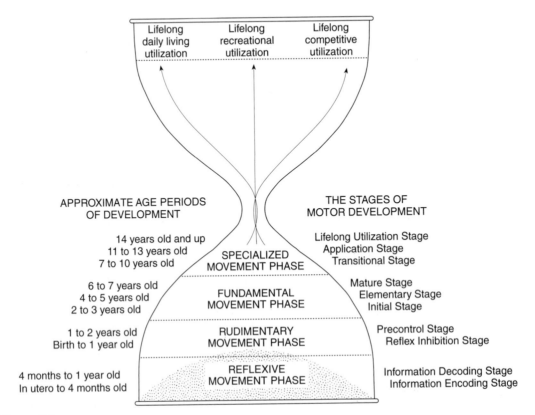

Figure 3.1
The phases of motor development.

visual representation of the four phases and their corresponding stages.)

Reflexive Movement Phase

The first movements the fetus makes are reflexive. **Reflexes** are involuntary, subcortically controlled movements that form the basis for the phases of motor development. Through reflex activity the infant gains information about the immediate environment. The infant's reactions to touch, light, sounds, and changes in pressure trigger involuntary movement activity. These involuntary movements, coupled with increasing cortical sophistication in the early months of postnatal life, play an important role in helping the child learn more about his or her body and the outside world.

Primitive reflexes may be classified as information-gathering, nourishment-seeking, and protective responses. They are information gathering in that they help stimulate cortical activity and development. They are nourishment seeking and protective because there is considerable evidence that they are phylogenetic in nature. Primitive reflexes such as the rooting and sucking reflexes are thought to be primitive survival mechanisms. Without them, the newborn would be unable to obtain nourishment.

Postural reflexes are the second form of involuntary movement. They are remarkably similar in appearance to later voluntary behaviors but are entirely involuntary. These reflexes seem to serve as neuromotor testing devices for stability, locomotor, and manipulative mechanisms that will be used later with conscious control. The primary stepping reflex and the crawling reflex, for example, closely resemble later voluntary walking and crawling behaviors. The palmar grasping reflex is closely related to later voluntary grasping and releasing behaviors. The labyrinthine righting reflex and the propping reflexes are related to later balancing abilities. The reflexive phase of motor development may be divided into two overlapping stages.

CONCEPT 3.4

Reflexes are the first forms of human movement.

Information Encoding Stage

The information encoding (gathering) stage of the reflexive movement phase is characterized by observable involuntary movement activity during the fetal period until about the fourth month of infancy. During this stage lower brain centers are more highly developed than the motor cortex and are essentially in command of fetal and neonatal movement. These brain centers are capable of causing involuntary reactions to a variety of stimuli of varying intensity and duration. Reflexes now serve as the primary means by which the infant is able to gather information, seek nourishment, and find protection through movement.

Information Decoding Stage

The information decoding (processing) stage of the reflex phase begins around the fourth month. During this time there is a gradual inhibition of many reflexes as higher brain centers continue to develop. Lower brain centers gradually relinquish control over skeletal movements and are replaced by voluntary movement activity mediated by the motor area of the cerebral cortex. The decoding stage replaces sensorimotor activity with perceptual-motor ability. That is, the infant's development of voluntary control of skeletal movements involves processing sensory stimuli with stored information, not merely reacting to stimuli.

Chapter 7 focuses on the primitive and postural reflexes of infancy as they relate to the information encoding and decoding stages. Special attention is given to the relationship between the reflexive phase of development and voluntary movement.

Rudimentary Movement Phase

The first forms of voluntary movement are rudimentary movements. They are seen in the infant beginning at birth to about age 2. Rudimentary movements are maturationally determined and are characterized by a highly predictable sequence of appearance. This sequence is resistant to change under normal conditions. The rate at which these abilities appear will vary from child to child, however, and depends on biological, environmental, and task factors. The **rudimentary movement abilities** of the infant represent the basic forms of voluntary movement required for survival. They involve stability movements such as gaining control of the head, neck, and trunk muscles; the manipulative tasks of reaching, grasping, and releasing; and the locomotor movements of creeping, crawling, and walking. The rudimentary movement phase of development may be subdivided into two stages that represent progressively higher orders of motor control.

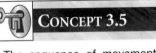

CONCEPT 3.5

The sequence of movement skill acquisition during the rudimentary movement phase is generally fixed, but the rate is variable.

Reflex Inhibition Stage

The reflex inhibition stage of the rudimentary movement phase may be thought of as beginning at birth. At birth, reflexes dominate the infant's movement repertoire. From then on, however, the infant's movements are increasingly influenced by the developing cortex. Development of the cortex, and lessening of certain environmental constraints, causes several reflexes to be inhibited and gradually disappear. Primitive and postural reflexes are replaced by voluntary movement behaviors. At the reflex inhibition level, voluntary movement is poorly differentiated and integrated because the neuromotor apparatus of the infant is still at a rudimentary stage of development. Movements, though purposeful, appear uncontrolled and unrefined. If the infant wishes to make contact with an object, there will be global activity of the entire hand, wrist, arm, shoulder, and even trunk. The process of moving the hand into contact with the object, although voluntary, lacks control.

Precontrol Stage

Around 1 year of age, children begin to bring greater precision and control to their movements. The process of differentiating between sensory and motor systems and integrating perceptual and motor information into a more meaningful and congruent whole takes place. The rapid development of higher cognitive processes and motor processes encourages rapid gains in rudimentary movement abilities during this stage. During the precontrol stage, children learn to gain and maintain their equilibrium, to manipulate objects, and to locomote throughout the environment with an amazing degree of proficiency and control considering the short time they have had to develop these abilities. The maturational process may partially explain the rapidity and extent of development of movement control during this phase, but the growth of motor proficiency is no less amazing.

Chapter 8 provides a detailed explanation of the development of rudimentary movement abilities. Particular attention is paid to the interrelationship between the stages within this phase and the stages within the reflexive phase of development. Attention is also focused on the critical function that the rudimentary movement phase serves in preparing the child for the development of fundamental movement abilities.

Fundamental Movement Phase

The **fundamental movement abilities** of early childhood are an outgrowth of the rudimentary movement phase of infancy. This phase of motor development represents a time in which young children are actively involved in exploring and experimenting with the movement capabilities of their bodies. It is a time for discovering how to perform a variety of stabilizing, locomotor, and manipulative movements, first in isolation and then in combination with one another. Children developing fundamental patterns of movement are learning how to respond with motor control and movement competence to a variety of stimuli. They are gaining increased control in the performance of discrete, serial, and continuous movements as evidenced by their ability to accept changes in the task requirements. Fundamental movement patterns are basic observable patterns of behavior. Locomotor activities such as running and jumping, manipulative activities such as throwing and catching, and stability activities such as the beam walk and one-foot balance are examples of fundamental movements that should be developed during the early childhood years.

A major misconception about the developmental concept of the fundamental movement phase is the notion that these abilities are maturationally determined and are little influenced by task demands and environmental factors. Some child development experts (not in the motor development area) have written repeatedly about the "natural" unfolding of the child's movement and play skills and the idea that children develop these abilities merely by growing older (maturation). Although maturation does play a role in the development of fundamental movement patterns, it should not be viewed as the only influence. The conditions of the environment—namely, opportunities for practice, encouragement, instruction, and the ecology (context) of the environment—play important roles in the degree to which fundamental movement patterns develop.

CONCEPT 3.6

Affordances and constraints contained within the movement task, biology of the individual, and the conditions of the learning environment have a profound effect on the acquisition of mature fundamental movement skills.

Several researchers and assessment instrument developers have attempted to subdivide fundamental movements into a series of identifiable sequential stages. For the purposes of our model we will view the entire fundamental movement phase as having three separate but often overlapping stages: the initial, elementary, and mature. These stages are described briefly here and in greater detail in chapter 11.

Initial Stage

The initial stage of a fundamental movement phase represents the child's first goal-oriented attempts at performing a fundamental skill. Movement is

characterized by missing or improperly sequenced parts, markedly restricted or exaggerated use of the body, and poor rhythmical flow and coordination. The spatial and temporal integration of movement is poor. Typically, the locomotor, manipulative, and stability movements of the 2-year-old are at the initial level. Some children may be beyond this level in the performance of some patterns of movement, but most are at the initial stage.

Elementary Stage

The elementary stage involves greater control and better rhythmical coordination of fundamental movements. The synchronization of the temporal and spatial elements of movement are improved, but patterns of movement at this stage are still generally restricted or exaggerated, although better coordinated. Children of normal intelligence and physical functioning tend to advance to the elementary stage primarily through the process of maturation. Observation of the typical 3- or 4-year-old child reveals a variety of fundamental movements at the elementary stage. Many individuals, adults as well as children, fail to get beyond the elementary stage in many patterns of movement.

Mature Stage

The mature stage within the fundamental movement phase is characterized by mechanically efficient, coordinated, and controlled performances. The majority of available data on the acquisition of fundamental movement skills suggests that children can and should be at the mature stage by age 5 or 6 in most fundamental skills. Manipulative skills that require visually tracking and intercepting moving objects (catching, striking, volleying) develop somewhat later because of the sophisticated visual-motor requirements of these tasks. Even a casual glance at the movements of children and adults reveals that a great many have not developed their fundamental movement skills to the mature level. Although some children may reach this stage primarily through maturation and with a minimum of environmental influences, the vast majority require opportunities for practice, encouragement, and instruction in an environment that fosters learning. Failure to offer such opportunities makes it nearly impossible for an individual to achieve the mature stage of a skill within this phase and will inhibit further application and development in the next phase.

Specialized Movement Phase

Specialized movement abilities are an outgrowth of the fundamental movement phase. During the specialized phase, movement becomes a tool applied to a variety of complex movement activities for daily living, recreation, and sport pursuits. This is a period when fundamental stability, locomotor, and manipulative skills are progressively refined, combined, and elaborated upon for use in increasingly demanding situations. The fundamental movements of hopping and jumping, for example, may now be applied to rope-jumping activities, to performing folk dances, and to performing the triple jump (hop-step-jump) in track and field.

The onset and extent of skill development within the specialized movement phase depends on a variety of task, individual, and environmental factors. Reaction time and movement speed, coordination, body type, height and weight, customs, peer pressure, and emotional makeup are but a few of these factors. The specialized movement phase has three stages.

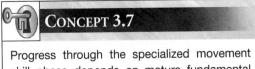

CONCEPT 3.7

Progress through the specialized movement skill phase depends on mature fundamental movement skill development.

Transitional Stage

Somewhere around their seventh or eighth year, children commonly enter a transitional movement skill stage (Haubenstricker and Seefeldt, 1986). During the transitional period, the individual begins to combine and apply fundamental movement skills to the performance of specialized skills in sport and recreational settings. Walking on a rope bridge, jumping rope, and playing kickball are examples of common transitional skills. Transitional movement skills contain the same elements as fundamental movements with greater form, accuracy, and control. Fundamental movement skills developed and refined during the previous stage are applied to play, game, and daily living situations. Transitional skills are applications of fundamental movement patterns in somewhat more complex and specific forms.

The transitional stage is an exciting time for the parent and the teacher as well as for the child. Children are actively involved in discovering and combining numerous movement patterns and are often elated by their rapidly expanding movement abilities. The goal of concerned parents, teachers, and youth sport coaches during this stage should be to help children increase their motor control and movement competence in a wide variety of activities. Care must be taken not to cause the child to specialize or restrict his or her activity involvement. A narrow focus on skills during this stage is likely to have undesirable effects on the last two stages of the specialized movement phase.

Application Stage

From about age 11 to age 13 (the middle school years) interesting changes take place in the skill development of the individual. During the previous stage, the child's limited cognitive abilities, affective abilities, and experiences, combined with a natural eagerness to be active, caused the normal focus (without adult interference) on movement to be broad and generalized to "all" activity. In the application stage, increased cognitive sophistication and a broadened experience base enable the individual to make numerous learning and participation decisions based on a variety of task, individual, and environmental factors. For example, the 5-feet, 10-inch (179 cm) 12-year-old who likes team activities and applying strategy to games, who has reasonably good coordination and agility, and who lives in Indiana may choose to specialize in the development of his or her basketball playing abilities. A similarly built child who does not really enjoy team efforts may choose to specialize in a variety of track and field activities. The individual begins to make conscious decisions for or against participation in certain activities. These decisions are based, in large measure, on how he or she perceives the extent to which factors within the task, himself or herself, and the environment either enhance or inhibit chances for enjoyment and success. This self-examination of strengths and weaknesses, opportunities and restrictions, narrows the choices.

During the application stage, individuals begin to seek out or to avoid participation in specific activities. Increased emphasis is placed on form, skill, accuracy, and the quantitative aspects of movement performance. This is a time for more complex skills to be refined and used in advanced games, lead-up activities, and selected sports.

Lifelong Utilization Stage

The lifelong utilization stage of the specialized phase of motor development begins around age 14 and continues through adulthood. The lifelong utilization stage represents the pinnacle of the process of motor development and is characterized by the use of one's acquired movement repertoire throughout life. The interests, competencies, and choices made during the previous stage are carried over; further refined; and applied to a lifetime of daily living, recreational, and sports-related activities. Factors such as available time and money, equipment and facilities, and physical and mental limitations affect this stage. Among other things, one's level of activity participation will depend on talent, opportunities, physical condition, and personal motivation. An individual's lifetime performance level may range anywhere from professional status and the Olympics; to intercollegiate and interscholastic competition; to participation in organized or unorganized, competitive or cooperative, recreational sports and simple daily living skills.

In essence, the lifelong utilization stage represents a culmination of all preceding stages and phases. It should, however, be viewed as a continuation of a lifetime process. One of the primary goals of education is to help individuals to become

happy, healthy, contributing members of society. We must not lose sight of this lofty but worthy goal. We must view the hierarchical development of movement abilities as stepping-stones to the specialized movement skill level. We must cease in viewing children as miniature adults who can be programmed to perform in such potentially high-pressure, physiologically and psychologically questionable activities as Little League Baseball and Pee Wee Football. We must view children as developmentally immature individuals and structure meaningful movement experiences appropriate for their particular developmental levels. When we recognize that the progressive acquisition of movement skills in a developmentally appropriate manner is imperative to the balanced motor development of infants, children, adolescents, and adults, we begin making real contributions to their total development. Specialized skill development can and should play a role in our lives, but it is unfair to require children to specialize in one or two skill areas at the expense of developing their abilities in and appreciation for many other areas.

CONCEPT 3.8

The primary goal of a person's motor development and movement education is to accept the challenge of change in the continuous process of gaining and maintaining motor control and movement competence throughout a lifetime.

THE HOURGLASS: A LIFE SPAN MODEL

The age ranges for each phase of motor development should be viewed as general guidelines, illustrative only of the broad concept of age appropriateness. Individuals often function at different phases depending on their experiential backgrounds and genetic makeups. For example, it is entirely possible for a 10-year-old to function in the specialized movement phase at the lifelong utilization stage in stability activities involving gymnastic movements, but only at the elementary stage of the fundamental movement phase in manipulative and locomotor skills such as throwing, catching, or running. Although we should encourage this precocious behavior in gymnastics, we should also help the child catch up to his or her age-mates in the other areas and develop acceptable levels of proficiency in them as well.

It is important to gather facts about the process of motor development. Throughout this text we discuss study after study, but if we fail to provide you with a theoretical framework and a conceptual grasp of the process of motor development, we will have presented isolated facts that tell you little about their implications for successful developmental teaching, therapy, and parenting. Therefore, we would like to propose a theoretical model for the process of motor development and work through this model with you. This model as presented is not a comprehensive theory of motor development. It is a **heuristic** device, that is, a conceptual representation, or model, of motor development, that provides us with general guidelines for describing and explaining motor behavior. Heuristics differ from algorithms in one important way. Whereas an **algorithm** is a procedure or set of rules guaranteed, if followed, to lead to solution of a given kind of problem, heuristics are rules of thumb giving one clues for how to search for answers to given problems. In the study of development, many theories use heuristic devices that researchers hope will eventually lead to algorithms.

CONCEPT 3.9

The hourglass model is a helpful heuristic device for conceptualizing and explaining the process of motor development.

To understand this model, picture yourself as an hourglass (figure 3.2). Into your hourglass we need to place the stuff of life: "sand." Sand gets into your hourglass from two different containers. One is your hereditary container and the other your

environmental container. The hereditary container has a lid. At conception our genetic makeup is determined and the amount of sand in the container is fixed. However, the environmental container has no lid. Sand may be added to the container and to your hourglass. We could reach down into the "sand pile" (i.e., the environment) and get more sand to put into your hourglass.

The two buckets of sand signify that both the environment and heredity influence the process of development. The relative contributions of each have been a volatile topic of debate for years. Arguing the importance of each is a meaningless exercise because sand is funneled from *both* containers into your hourglass. In the final analysis it does not really matter if your hourglass is filled with hereditary sand or environmental sand. What is important is that somehow sand gets into your hourglass and that this stuff of life is the product of *both* heredity and the environment.

Now, what do we know about motor development during the early phases of life? When we look at the reflexive and rudimentary phases of motor development, we know that sand pours into the hourglass primarily, but not exclusively, from the hereditary container. The sequential progression of motor development during the first few years of life is rigid and resistant to change except under environmental extremes. Therefore, we know in the first two phases of motor development that the developmental sequence is highly predictable. For example, children all over the world learn how to sit before they stand, how to stand before they walk, and how to walk before they run. However, we do see considerable variability in the rates at which the very young acquire their rudimentary movement abilities. This is something in which researchers and program developers have become increasingly interested over the past few years. We have seen a rapid rise in the number of infant stimulation programs and infant-toddler movement programs. Some make elaborate claims about the worth of these programs and their ultimate importance to the child. Unfortunately, we have little hard evidence at this juncture to either support or refute these claims. The rate of movement skill

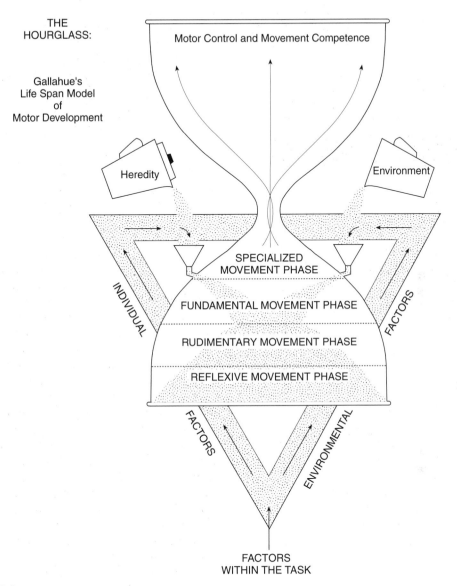

THE HOURGLASS:

Gallahue's Life Span Model of Motor Development

Motor Control and Movement Competence

Heredity

Environment

INDIVIDUAL

SPECIALIZED MOVEMENT PHASE

FUNDAMENTAL MOVEMENT PHASE

RUDIMENTARY MOVEMENT PHASE

REFLEXIVE MOVEMENT PHASE

FACTORS

FACTORS

ENVIRONMENTAL

FACTORS WITHIN THE TASK

Figure 3.2
Filling the hourglass with "sand" (i.e., the stuff of life).

acquisition is variable from infancy throughout life. If an infant, child, adolescent, or adult receives additional opportunities for practice, encouragement, and instruction in an environment conducive to learning, movement skill acquisition will be promoted. The absence of these environmental

affordances (i.e., enabling factors) will constrain movement skill acquisition. Furthermore, the acquisition rate will vary depending on the mechanical and physical requirements of each task. If an infant does not have sufficient handholds (an affordance) in her environment to enable her to pull herself up to a stand, she will have to wait until sufficient balance (a mechanical task factor) and strength in the legs (a physical task factor) have developed, before she is able to bring herself to a standing position unaided.

In the fundamental movement phase, boys and girls are beginning to develop a whole host of basic movement abilities—running, hopping, jumping, throwing, catching, kicking, and trapping. Unfortunately, many still have the notion that children somehow "automatically" learn how to perform these fundamental movements. Many naively think that children at this phase of development will, through the process of maturation, develop mature fundamental movement skills. This is not true for the vast majority of children. Most children must have some combination of opportunities for practice, encouragement, and instruction in an ecologically sound environment. These conditions are crucial to helping them through each of the stages within the fundamental movement phase. Furthermore, as the task requirements of a fundamental movement skill change, so too will the process and the product. For example, the perceptual requirements of hitting a pitched ball are considerably more sophisticated than those required to strike a stationary ball or to perform a striking pattern without making contact with another object. Teachers of individuals at the fundamental movement phase must learn to recognize and analyze the task requirements of movement skills to maximize learner success. Teachers who overlook these duties erect proficiency barriers at the specialized movement skill phase.

At the specialized movement skill phase, successful performance of the mechanics of movement depends on mature fundamental movements. After the transitional stage we progress to the final stages in which specialized movement skills are applied to daily living, recreational, and sport experiences.

At some point, the hourglass turns over (figure 3.3). The timing of this occurrence is variable and depends more on social and cultural factors than on physical and mechanical factors. For most individuals, the hourglass turns over and the

"sand" begins to pour out during the late teens and early 20s. This is a time in which many individuals enter the adult world of work, car payments, mortgages, family responsibilities, and a host of other time-consuming tasks. Time restrictions limit the pursuit of new movement skills and the maintenance of skills mastered during childhood and adolescence.

There are several interesting features in the overturned hourglass that we need to consider. The sand falls through two different filters. One is the *hereditary filter* with which we can do very little. For example, an individual may have inherited a predisposition toward longevity or coronary heart disease. The hereditary filter is going to be either dense, causing the sand to filter through slowly, or easy to penetrate, allowing the sand to flow through more rapidly. Sand that has fallen through the hereditary filter cannot be recovered, but it must pass through a second, or final, filter called the lifestyle filter.

The density of the *lifestyle filter* is determined by such things as physical fitness, nutritional status, diet, exercise, the ability to handle stress, and social and spiritual well-being. The lifestyle filter is environmentally based, and we have a good deal of control over the rate at which sand falls through this filter. Although we can never stop sand from flowing to the bottom of the hourglass, we can slow down the rate at which it falls. A former surgeon general of the United States, Dr. C. Everett Koop, once stated that although we cannot stop the aging process, we can control it by up to 40 percent. We can directly influence how fast sand falls through our hourglasses. As teachers, coaches, therapists, and parents we have the wonderful opportunity to shovel "sand" into many "hourglasses." We also have the privilege and the obligation to help others develop "lifestyle filters" that will slow the rates at which sand falls in their hourglasses. Sand can still be added even when hourglasses are overturned and the sand is falling to the bottom. Each of us has *lifelong opportunities for learning*. By taking advantage of the numerous opportunities for continued development and physical activity, we can add more sand. We cannot add sand faster than it is

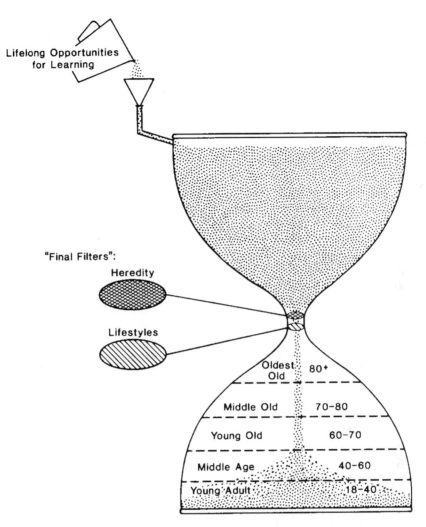

Lifelong Opportunities
for Learning

"Final Filters":

Heredity

Lifestyles

Oldest Old · 80+

Middle Old · 70-80

Young Old · 60-70

Middle Age · 40-60

Young Adult · 18-40

Figure 3.3
Emptying the overturned hourglass of life.

falling and claim immortality. We can, however, extend and improve the quality of life.

The **hourglass heuristic** device as described to this point gives the impression that development is an orderly and continuous process. Note, however, that the sand at the bottom of the hourglass in both figures 3.2 and 3.3 is distributed in a bell-shaped curve. The shape of this curve implies that there is a distribution of movement skills among the categories of movement (locomotion, manipulation, and stability), and within the various movement tasks. For example, one may be at the elementary stage in some skills, the mature stage in others, and at a sport skill level in still others. Additionally, one may be at different stages of development within the same skill. For example, when children and adults perform the overhand throw, they are often at the initial stage in their trunk action, the elementary stage in their arm action, and at the mature stage in their leg action.

Motor development in the hourglass model, therefore, is a *discontinuous process;* that is, a process that, although phaselike and stagelike in a general sense, is highly variable in a specific sense. Motor development when viewed as discontinuous is in effect a *dynamic* (i.e., nonlinear) process occurring within a self-organizing system (i.e., the "hourglass").

 CONCEPT 3.10

Motor development is a discontinuous process occurring within a self-organizing system.

The hourglass model of motor development is not one-dimensional, that is, unaffected by the cognitive and affective domains of human behavior. Unlike the two-dimensional representation of the hourglass in figures 3.2 and 3.3, "real" hourglasses are present only in three-dimensional space. As a result, real hourglasses have height, width, and depth and must be supported if they are to remain upright. Visualize, if you will, an individual's hourglass as being supported by a cognitive pillar, an affective pillar, and a motor pillar. The hourglass is multidimensional; thus, there is a triple interaction among the cognitive, affective, and motor domains. In other words, the hourglass model is

more than a motor model. It is a model of motor development that influences, and is influenced by, a wide variety of cognitive and affective factors operating within both the individual and the environment.

You may find it helpful to visualize the hourglass heuristic device as you proceed through the following sections dealing with motor development during infancy, childhood, adolescence, and adulthood. Remember, however, that it is not important that you accept this model as proposed. Theoretical models are just that—"models." As such they are incomplete, inexact, and subject to verification and further refinement. What is important is that you visualize how the process of motor development occurs. Remember, understanding motor development helps to explain how learning occurs. Both are crucial to the creation of effective, developmentally appropriate instruction.

CONCEPT 3.11

Understanding the process of motor development helps explain how movement skill learning occurs, which is crucial to developmentally appropriate instruction.

SUMMARY

The acquisition of competency in movement is an extensive process beginning with the early reflexive movements of the newborn and continuing throughout life. The process by which an individual progresses from the reflexive movement phase, through the rudimentary and fundamental movement phases, and finally to the specialized movements skill phase of development is influenced by factors within tasks, the individual, and the environment.

Reflexes and rudimentary movement abilities are largely based on maturation. Reflexes appear and disappear in a fairly rigid sequence. Rudimentary movements form the important base upon which fundamental movement abilities are developed.

Fundamental movement abilities are basic movement patterns that begin developing around the same time that a child is able to walk independently and move freely through his or her environment. These basic locomotor, manipulative, and stability abilities go through a definite, observable process from immaturity to maturity. Stages within this phase include the initial, elementary, and mature stages. Attainment of the mature stage is influenced greatly by opportunities for practice, encouragement, and instruction in an environment that fosters learning. Under the proper circumstances, children are capable of performing at the mature stage in the vast majority of fundamental movement patterns by age 6. The fundamental movement skills of children entering school are too often incompletely developed. Therefore, the primary grades offer an excellent opportunity to develop fundamental movement skills to their mature levels. These same fundamental skills will be enhanced and refined to form the specialized movement abilities so highly valued for recreational, competitive, and daily living tasks.

The specialized movement skill phase of development is in essence an elaboration of the fundamental phase. Specialized skills are more precise than fundamental skills. They often involve a combination of fundamental movement abilities and require a greater degree of precision. Specialized skills involve three related stages. The transitional stage is typically the level of the child in grades three through five. At this level, children are involved in their first real applications of fundamental movements to sport. If the fundamental abilities used in a particular sport activity are not at the mature level, the child will resort to less mature or elementary

patterns of movement. Involving children in sport skill refinement before they reach mature levels of ability in prerequisite fundamentals is unwise. When this happens, the immature movements found in the basic patterns are carried over to the related sport skills. The child will regress to his or her characteristic pattern. It is important that sensitive teaching and coaching be incorporated at this point.

When we look at the process of motor development, we need to look at it first from a theoretical perspective. Each of us needs to have a theoretical framework to use as the basis for our actions. It is not important that you agree with the theoretical framework presented here. The hourglass model is our way of viewing the process of motor development and its implications for life. What is your theoretical framework? How does it influence your teaching, coaching, therapy, or parenting, and how does it influence you personally?

CRITICAL READINGS

Bigge, M. L., & Shermis, S. S. (1999). *Learning Theories for Teachers*. New York: Longman.

Gallahue, D. L. (2000). Motor development. In J. Winnick (Ed.), *Adapted Physical Education and Sports*. Champaign, IL: Human Kinetics.

Kamm, K., Thelen, E., & Jensen, J. (1990). A dynamical systems approach to motor development. *Physical Therapy, 70*, 763–775.

Seefeldt, V., & Haubenstricker, J. (1982). Patterns, phases, or stages: An analytic model for the study of developmental movement. In J. A. S. Kelso, & J. E. Clark (Eds.), *The Development of Movement Control and Coordination* (pp. 309–318). New York: Wiley.

 ## WEB RESOURCES

Homepage for the National Institute on Aging
www.nih.gov/nia

International Society on Infant Studies
www.isisweb.org

Journal of Adolescence
www.academicpress.com/adolescence

Society for Research in Child Development
www.srcd.org

CHAPTER

4 SELECTED FACTORS AFFECTING MOTOR DEVELOPMENT

KEY TERMS

Developmental direction
Growth rate
Reciprocal interweaving
Readiness
Sensitive period
Phylogenetic skills
Ontogenetic skills
Bonding
Premature
Very low birth weight
Low birth weight
Young-for-date
Obesity
Binge eating disorder
Anorexia nervosa
Bulimia nervosa
Physical fitness
Force
Law of inertia
Law of acceleration
Law of action and reaction

CHAPTER COMPETENCIES

Upon completion of this chapter you should be able to:

- Identify genetic and environmental factors influencing growth and biological maturation
- Derive principles of motor development and apply these principles to teaching/learning situations at various points in the life span
- Describe "catch-up" growth and the factors affecting this phenomenon
- Analyze relationships among growth, biological maturation, and physiological changes in motor skill development
- Discuss the effects of environmental deprivation on life span motor development
- Discuss the effects of enrichment, special practice, and teaching on life span motor development
- Define and discuss the concepts of critical and sensitive periods, phylogenetic and ontogenetic skills, and co-twin control
- Identify and order from simple to complex the environmental variables that may influence developmental levels
- Explain the similarities and differences between bonding and imprinting
- Hypothesize about the impact of temperament on the interactive process of development
- Describe differences and similarities implied by the terms "low birth weight" and "young-for-date"

58

KEY CONCEPT

Both the process and products of motor development are influenced by a wide variety of factors operating in isolation and in conjunction with one another.

The development and refinement of movement patterns and movement skills are influenced in complex ways. Both the process and products of movement are rooted in one's unique heredity and background of experiences, coupled with the specific demands of the movement task. Any study of motor development would be incomplete without a discussion of several of these influencing factors. This chapter focuses on factors within the individual, the environment, and the task that influence the process of development throughout the life cycle.

FACTORS WITHIN THE INDIVIDUAL

The unique genetic inheritance that accounts for our individuality can also account for our similarity in many ways. One similarity is the trend for human development to proceed in an orderly, predictable fashion. A number of biological factors affecting motor development seem to emerge from this predictable pattern.

Developmental Direction

The principle of **developmental direction** was first formulated by Gesell (1954) as a means of explaining increased coordination and motor control as a function of the maturing nervous system. Through observations, Gesell noted that an orderly, predictable sequence of physical development proceeds from the head to the feet (cephalocaudal) and from the center of the body to its periphery (proximodistal). The principle of developmental direction has encountered criticism during the last few years, however, and should not be viewed as operational at all levels of development or in all

individuals. It may be that the observation of tendencies toward distinct developmental directions is not exclusively a function of the maturing nervous system, as originally hypothesized by Gesell, but is due, in part, to the demands of the specific task. For example, the task demands of independent walking are considerably greater than those for crawling or creeping. There is less margin for error in independent walking than there is in creeping and, in turn, crawling. In other words, it is mechanically easier to crawl than it is to creep and to creep than it is to walk. Therefore, the apparent cephalocaudal progression in development may not be due to maturation of the nervous system, but also to the performance demands of the task. Care, therefore, should be taken when interpreting the concept of developmental direction, particularly during the period of infancy.

 CONCEPT 4.1

Neuromotor maturation principles may be used to explain, in part, both the sequence and rate of motor development throughout the life cycle.

The *cephalocaudal* aspect of developmental direction refers specifically to the gradual progression of increased control over the musculature, moving from the head to the feet. It may be witnessed in the prenatal stages of fetal development as well as in later postnatal development. In the developing fetus, for example, the head forms first, and the arms form prior to the legs. Likewise, infants exhibit sequential control over the musculature of the head, neck, and trunk, prior to gaining control over the legs and feet. Young children are often clumsy and exhibit poor motor control over their lower extremities. This may be due to incomplete cephalocaudal development and to the complexity of the task demands of independent walking.

The second aspect of developmental direction, known as *proximodistal* development, refers specifically to the child's progression in control of the musculature from the center of the body to its most distant parts. As with cephalocaudal development, the proximodistal concept applies to both growth processes and the acquisition of movement skills. For example, with regard to growth, the trunk and shoulder girdle grow prior to arms and legs, which grow prior to the fingers and toes. In skill acquisition, the young child is able to control the muscles of the trunk and shoulder girdle prior to the muscles of the wrist, hand, and fingers. This principle of development is frequently used in the primary grades when children are taught the less refined elements of manuscript writing before they learn the more complex and refined movements of cursive writing.

The cephalocaudal and proximodistal process is operational throughout life and has a tendency to reverse itself as one ages. Actions of the lower body and extremities are the first to regress. Certainly, however, older individuals can forestall and reduce such regression by staying active throughout life.

Rate of Growth

One's **growth rate** follows a characteristic pattern universal for all and resistant to external influence. A minor interruption of the normal pace of growth is compensated for by a still unexplained process of *self-regulatory fluctuation* (Gesell, 1954) that enables a child to catch up to his or her age-mates. This *developmental plasticity* occurs, for example, when a severe illness limits a child's normal gains in height, weight, and movement ability, but upon recovery the child tends to catch up. The same phenomenon is seen with low-birth-weight infants. Despite low weights at birth, most of these babies catch up to the characteristic growth rates of their age-mates in a few years. Conditions surrounding the causes of low birth weight, such as inadequate nutrition, must not persist. Appropriate intervention must occur early on for this developmental plasticity process to fully manifest in the growing infant. Measures of height, weight, and motor development taken prior to age 2 are generally meaningless for predicting later growth and development.

The self-regulatory process of growth will compensate for relatively minor deviations in the growth pattern, but it is frequently unable to make up for major deviations, especially during infancy and childhood. For example, low-birth-weight infants under three pounds, and children experiencing severe and prolonged nutritional deficiencies, frequently suffer permanent deficits in height and weight, as well as in their cognitive and motor development.

CONCEPT 4.2

The permanency of growth retardation is particularly devastating during the first two years of life.

Severe and prolonged restricted opportunities for movement and deprivation of experience have been shown repeatedly to interfere with children's abilities to perform movement tasks characteristic of their age levels. The effects of sensory and motor experience deprivation can sometimes be overcome when nearly optimal conditions are established for a child. The extent to which the child will be able to catch up to his or her peers, however, depends on the duration and severity of deprivation, the age of the child, and the child's genetic growth potential.

Reciprocal Interweaving

The coordinated and progressive intricate interweaving of neural mechanisms of opposing muscle systems into an increasingly mature relationship, termed **reciprocal interweaving** by Gesell (1954), is characteristic of the developing child's motor behavior. Two different but related processes are associated with this increase of functional complexity: differentiation and integration.

CONCEPT 4.3

Neuromotor maturation is evidenced through increased ability to differentiate and integrate motor and sensory mechanisms.

Differentiation is associated with the gradual progression from the gross globular (overall) movement patterns of infants to the more refined and functional movements of children and adolescents. For example, the manipulative behaviors of the newborn for reaching, grasping, and releasing objects is poor; there is little control of movement. But as the child develops, the control improves. The child is able to differentiate among various muscle groups and begins to establish control. Control continues to improve with practice until we see the precise movements of block building, cutting with scissors, cursive writing, and violin playing.

Integration refers to bringing various opposing muscle and sensory systems into coordinated interaction with one another. For example, the young child gradually progresses from ill-defined corralling movements when attempting to grasp an object to more mature and visually guided reaching and grasping behaviors. The differentiation of movements of the arms, hands, and fingers, followed by the integration of the use of the eyes with the movements of the hand to perform eye-hand coordination tasks, is crucial to normal development.

Differentiation and integration tend to be reversible with aging. As one ages and movement abilities begin to regress, the coordinated interaction of sensory and motor mechanisms frequently becomes inhibited. The extent to which one's coordinated movement abilities regress is not merely a function of age, but is influenced greatly by activity levels and attitude.

There is little doubt that the processes of differentiation and integration operate simultaneously. The complex abilities of the adult cannot be explained merely as a process of integration of simpler responses. What occurs, instead, is a constant interlacing of both processes.

Readiness

E. L. Thorndike (1913), the "grandfather" of learning theory, first proposed the principle of readiness primarily in reference to emotional responses to actions or expected actions. According to his concept, readiness depended on the biological maturation model, which was popular at the turn of the century. Today's concept of readiness, however, is much broader and refers to readiness for learning. **Readiness** may be defined as convergence of the requirements of the task, the biology of the individual, and the conditions of the environment that make mastery of a particular skill appropriate. The concept of readiness, as used today, extends beyond biological maturation and includes consideration of factors that can be modified or manipulated to encourage or promote learning. Several related factors combine to promote readiness. Physical and mental maturation, interacting with motivation, prerequisite learning, and an enriching environment all influence readiness. At this juncture we do not know how to pinpoint exactly when someone is ready to learn a new movement skill. However, research suggests that early experience in a movement activity before the individual is ready is likely to have minimal benefits.

CONCEPT 4.4

Readiness for learning depends on convergence of biological, environmental, and physical factors.

In recent years a great deal of attention has been focused on developing reading readiness through appropriate types of preschool and primary grade experiences. Entire educational programs have been built around the notion that children must achieve a certain level of development before they are ready to pursue intellectual tasks such as reading and writing (Bergen et al., 2001; Bredenkamp and Rosengrant, 1995), and mathematics (Kamii and Housman, 2000), as well as movement tasks involving locomotion, manipulation, and stability (Gallahue and Cleland, 2003). Readiness training is a part of many preschool and primary grade educational programs. An integral part of these readiness programs has been the use of movement as a means of enhancing basic perceptual-motor qualities. Although it has not been conclusively documented that perceptual-motor experiences have a direct effect on the attainment of specific cognitive readiness skills, it is safe to assume that they have at least an indirect influence because they encourage a child's self-esteem and a positive "Yes I can" approach to learning.

The concept of readiness, whether for the learning of cognitive skills or motor skills, is probably best summed up in Bruner's (1965) statement that "the foundation of any subject may be taught to anybody at any age in some form" (p. 12). In other words, the burden of being "ready" is as much the instructor's responsibility in recognizing it, as it is the student's. Readiness, a combination of maturational "ripeness," environmental openness, and caregiver sensitivity, has numerous implications for lifelong learning opportunities.

Critical and Sensitive Learning Periods

The concept of *critical* and *sensitive learning periods* is closely aligned to readiness and revolves around the observation that an individual is more sensitive to certain kinds of stimulation at certain times. Normal development in later periods may be hindered if a child fails to receive the proper stimulation during a critical period. For example, inadequate nutrition, prolonged stress, inconsistent nurturing, or a lack of appropriate learning experiences may have a more negative impact on development if they occur early in life rather than at a later age. The concept of critical periods also has a positive side. It suggests that appropriate intervention during a specific period tends to facilitate more positive forms of development at later stages than if the same intervention occurs at another time.

One should recognize that the tendency of a child to follow a critical period pattern is closely linked to the theory of developmental tasks and to a lesser degree linked to the milestone and phase-stage views. Robert Havighurst's theoretical framework of development (as reviewed in chapter 2) is a critical period hypothesis, applied from the perspective of education.

The notion of critical periods of development has been so pervasive in education that an entire federally funded educational program was established on this premise. Operation Head Start, begun in the 1960s and continued today throughout the United States, viewed the age period of 3 to 5 years as critical to children's intellectual development. It was hypothesized that if given a "head start" through a carefully structured environment designed to develop school-oriented skills, deprived children would be able to begin school on nearly the same level as their nondeprived counterparts. The results of Head Start programs did not entirely bear out the critical period hypothesis. This was probably due to the existence of more than one critical period for intellectual development. In addition, the age period of 3 to 5 years may not be as pivotal as originally assumed. Current views of the critical period hypothesis reject the notion that one must develop motor skills within highly specific time frames.

CONCEPT 4.5

There are broadly defined sensitive periods during which individuals can learn new tasks most efficiently and effectively.

It is safe to assume, however, that there are **sensitive periods,** or broad time frames, for development. Critical or sensitive periods should not be too narrowly defined. Failure to account for individual differences and for special environmental circumstances will lead one to conclude that a sensitive period is a universal point in time. Instead, a notion of sensitive periods as broad, general guidelines susceptible to modification should be adopted. Learning is a phenomenon that continues throughout life. As scientists learn more about the aging brain and the aging motor system, they continually demonstrate this important concept (Hinton, 1992; Selkoe, 1992). Learning can be a lifelong process, and the effects of aging can be slowed and reduced through continual use of the brain and motor system.

Individual Differences

The tendency to exhibit *individual differences* is crucial. Each person is unique with his or her timetable for development. This timetable is a combination of an individual's heredity and environmental influences. Although the sequence of appearance of developmental characteristics is predictable, the rate of appearance may be variable. Therefore, strict adherence to a chronological classification of development by age is without support or justification.

> ## CONCEPT 4.6
> Interindividual and intraindividual variation are the key concepts upon which developmental education is based.

The "average" ages for the acquisition of all sorts of developmental tasks, ranging from learning how to walk (the major developmental task of infancy) to gaining bowel and bladder control (the first restrictions of a civilized society on the child) have been bandied about in the professional literature and the daily conversation of parents and teachers for years. It must be remembered that these average ages are just that and nothing more—mere approximations that serve as convenient indicators of developmentally appropriate behaviors. It is common to see deviations from the mean of as much as six months to one year in the appearance of numerous movement skills. The tendency to exhibit individual differences is closely linked to the concept of readiness and helps to explain why some individuals are ready to learn new skills when others are not.

Phylogeny and Ontogeny

Many of the rudimentary abilities of the infant and the fundamental movement abilities of the young child, when viewed from the maturation perspective proposed by Gesell (1954), are considered to be phylogenetic; that is, they tend to appear automatically and in a predictable sequence within the maturing child. **Phylogenetic skills** are resistant to external environmental influences. Movement skills such as the rudimentary manipulative tasks of reaching, grasping, and releasing objects; the stability tasks of gaining control of the gross musculature of the body; and the fundamental locomotor abilities of walking, jumping, and running are examples of what may be viewed as phylogenetic skills. **Ontogenetic skills,** on the other hand, depend primarily on learning and environmental opportunities. Such skills as swimming, bicycling, and ice skating are considered ontogenetic because they do not appear automatically within individuals but require a period of practice and experience and are influenced by one's culture. The entire concept of phylogeny and ontogeny needs to be reevaluated in that many skills heretofore considered phylogenetic can be influenced by environmental interaction.

> ## CONCEPT 4.7
> Several types of movement patterns may have their basis in phylogeny (biology), but ontogenetic (environmental) conditions shape the rate and extent to which the patterns are acquired.

Although there may be a biological tendency for the development of certain abilities due to phylogenetic processes, it is simplistic to assume that maturation alone will account for motor development. The extent or level to which any voluntary movement ability is mastered depends, in part, on ontogeny, or the environment. In other words, opportunities for practice, encouragement, and instruction, and the ecology, or conditions, of the environment contribute significantly to movement skill development throughout life. Little solid support exists for Gesell's notion that "ontogeny recapitulates phylogeny," although some phylogenetic behaviors may be present in humankind.

Factors in the Environment

Over the past several years considerable speculation and research has focused on the effects of parenting behaviors during infancy and early childhood as they influence the subsequent functioning of children. Because of the extreme dependence of human infants on their caregivers and because of the length of this period of dependence, a variety of parental care factors influence later development. Among the most crucial are the effects of environmental stimulation and deprivation, and the bonding that occurs between parent and child during the early months following birth.

Bonding

The study of parent-to-infant attachment, or **bonding,** has its roots in the early imprinting (i.e., attachment) studies conducted by Lorenz (1966), Hess (1959), and others on birds, ducks, and other animals. These experiments with animals revealed that the degree to which the newborn imprinted on its mother was directly related to their contact time. Human infants do not imprint in the narrow sense of the word as animals do, but it is commonly believed by many that there is a broad "sensitive" period in which parent-to-infant attachment occurs during the early months of postnatal life. Popular culture has speculated that if this sensitive period is missed, the parent and child may fail to bond. Compelling new evidence places the validity of this belief in jeopardy (Eyer, 1994; Lewis, 1998). Experiences such as the death of a family member, divorce, accidents, and severe and prolonged disease are far more important to the long term development of children and youth than the early maternal bond.

Concept 4.8

The reciprocal interaction between parent and child influences both the rate and extent of development.

Bonding is a strong emotional attachment that endures over time, distance, hardship, and desirability. This emotional bond begins developing at birth and may be incompletely established with early separation. The leading factors contributing to initial separation are prematurity and low birth weight, which result in the incubation of the newborn and mild or severe neonatal problems at birth.

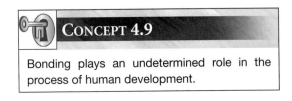

Concept 4.9

Bonding plays an undetermined role in the process of human development.

Early attachment between parent and child may influence some aspects of development, but it is fair to question whether bonding is essential to the welfare of the child. Generations of adopted children will attest to the success of their development even though bonding with "mother" was delayed by weeks, months, or even years. The reciprocal interaction between parent and child creates a mutually satisfying and rewarding relationship, the importance of which cannot be minimized. Care must be taken, however, not to define the concept of bonding too narrowly or to overemphasize its importance. Further research is necessary to clearly establish its link to the process of development. The reader is referred to the excellent discussions on infant-mother attachment by Eyer (1994), Lamb et al. (1985), and Lewis (1998).

Stimulation and Deprivation

A great deal of study has been done over the years to determine the relative effects of *stimulation* and *deprivation* on the learning of a variety of skills. There has been considerable controversy among hereditarians and environmentalists over the issue during the past 100 years. Numerous textbooks have recorded the nature versus nurture debates, but little has been settled in the attempt to categorize the effects of each on development. The current trend has been to respect the individual importance of both nature and nurture and to recognize the complexly intertwined influences of maturation and experience.

CONCEPT 4.10

Both stimulation and deprivation of experiences have potential for influencing the rate of development.

Students of motor development have recognized the futility of debating the separate merits of maturation and experience and have instead concentrated their research on three major questions. The first of these questions deals with the approximate ages at which various skills can be learned most effectively. The research of Bayley (1935), Shirley (1931), and Wellman (1937) represented the first serious attempts to describe the age at which many of the rudimentary and fundamental movement abilities appear. Each of these researchers reported a somewhat different timetable for the rate of appearance of numerous rudimentary movement skills acquired during infancy. They did, however, show amazing consistency in the sequential order of appearance of these abilities. This factor illustrates the combined effects of both intrinsic, or maturationally determined, influences on the sequence of development and extrinsic, or environmentally influenced, behaviors on the rate of development.

Until recently, little has been done to more clearly ascertain the ages at which fundamental movement skills can be learned most effectively. The principle of readiness has been viewed as a cornerstone of our educational system, but little more than lip service has been paid to its importance, particularly with regard to developing fundamental movement abilities. We know now that children can develop many movement skills early in life and that they have the developmental potential to be fit the mature stage in most fundamental movements by age 6 or 7.

The second question deals with the effects of special training on the learning of motor skills. A number of co-twin control studies have been conducted to ascertain the influence of special practice on early learning. The use of identical twins enables the researcher to ensure identical hereditary backgrounds and characteristics of the research participants. One twin is given advanced opportunities for practice while the other is restricted from practicing the same skills over a prescribed time. The famous studies of Gesell and Thompson (1929), Hilgard (1932), and McGraw (1935, 1939) demonstrated the inability of early training to hasten development to an appreciable degree. However, follow-up studies of the co-twin control experiments of both Gesell and McGraw showed that the trained participants exhibited greater confidence and assurance in the activities in which they had received special training. In other words, special attention and training may not influence the quantitative aspects of the movement skills learned as much as the qualitative aspects. Again, we see the complex interrelationship between maturation and experience.

With the advent of neonatal and infant intensive care units in the 1970s, the survival rate for preterm and low-birth-weight infants has risen dramatically. Parents, physicians, and researchers have wondered about the effects of infant stimulation programs on the subsequent development of these high-risk infants. Ulrich (1984) in her comprehensive review of the research concluded: "Despite difficulties in comparing studies due to the variability of subjects used, and type, intensity, and duration of treatment, the overwhelming evidence indicates beneficial effects" (p. 68). Such a conclusion is encouraging and leads one to consider the timing and duration of special training or stimulation. Is there a "sensitive period" beyond which the benefits of stimulation are minimally beneficial?

From the 1980s until the present, there has been a tremendous surge of interest in stimulation programs for infants, toddlers, and preschoolers. Structured swim and gym programs have sprung up all across North America and beyond. There have been considerable claims and counterclaims about the supposed benefits of these programs. There is, however, little solid evidence that structured stimulation programs provide any long-term benefits in advancing motor skills. The American Academy of Pediatrics in a 1988 policy statement reaffirmed in 1994, specifically recommended that: (1) structured infant exercise programs not be promoted as being therapeutically beneficial for the development of healthy infants and (2) parents be encouraged to provide a safe, nuturing, and minimally structured play environment for their infant (www.aap.org/policy/02223.html).

The third question concerns the effect of limited or restricted opportunities for practice on the acquisition of motor skills. Studies of this nature have centered generally on experimentally induced environmental deprivation in animals. Only a few studies have been reported in which children have been observed in environments where unusual restrictions of movement or experience have existed.

An investigation conducted by Dennis (1960) examined infants reared at three separate institutions in Iran. The infants in two of the institutions were found to be severely retarded in their motor development. In the third there was little motor retardation. The discrepancy led Dennis to investigate the lifestyles of the children in each institution. The results of his investigation led to the conclusion that lack of handling, blandness of surroundings, and general absence of movement opportunity or experience were causes of motor retardation in the first two institutions. Another investigation, by Dennis and Najarian (1957), revealed similar findings in a smaller number of creche infants reared in Beirut, Lebanon. Both investigations lend support to the hypothesis that behavioral development cannot be fully attributed to the maturation hypothesis.

Due to cultural mores, the humanitarian virtues of most investigators, and concerned parents, there are few experiments in which the environmental circumstances of infants or young children have been intentionally altered to determine whether serious malfunctioning or atypical behavior will result. The general consensus

of the research that does exist is that severe restrictions and lack of experience can delay normal development.

To understand the influence of experience on development, we need only to look as far as the school playground and observe many girls jumping rope expertly and many boys throwing and catching balls with great skill. When asked to reverse the activities, however, each group tends to revert to less mature patterns of movement. Factors within our culture, unfortunately, often predetermine the types of movement experiences in which boys and girls engage (Gallahue et al., 1994). Additionally, the gross motor development of blind children, as well as children confined in their early weeks and months of postnatal life, to the neonatal intensive care unit, have repeatedly been shown to be behind their age-mates on standardized measures of gross motor behavior as well as classroom behavior (Hack et al., 1994; Islebanov et al., 1994). Furthermore, very low birth weight babies (<1500 g) as well as blind children, have been shown to acquire some rudimentary movement skills out of the normally expected sequence.

CONCEPT 4.11

Extreme conditions of environmental deprivation may disrupt both the sequence and rate of movement skill acquisition.

In summary, both maturation and learning play important roles in the acquisition of movement abilities. Although experience seems to have little influence on the sequence of their emergence, it does affect the time of appearance of certain movements and the extent of their development. One of the greatest needs of children is to practice skills at a time when they are developmentally ready to benefit the most from such skills. Special practice prior to maturational readiness is of dubious benefit. The key is to be able to accurately judge the time at which each individual is "ripe" for learning and then to provide a series of educationally sound and effective movement experiences. However, all indications are that young children are generally capable of more than we have suspected, and many of the traditional readiness signposts that we have used may be incorrect.

> ### CONCEPT 4.12
>
> The extent to which environmental stimulation may affect development is as yet unknown.

PHYSICAL TASK FACTORS

A number of additional factors affect motor development. The influence of social class (Malina and Bouchard, 1991), gender (Branta et al., 1987), and ethnic and cultural background (Bril, 1985; Gallahue et al., 1996; Krebs, 1995) all have an impact on growth and motor development. Motor development is not a static process. It is not only the product of biological factors but is also influenced by environmental conditions and physical laws. The interaction of both environmental and biological factors modifies the course of motor development during infancy, childhood, adolescence, and adulthood. Premature birth, eating disorders, fitness levels, and biomechanical factors, as well as the physiological changes associated with aging and lifestyle choice, all influence the lifelong process of motor development in important ways.

Prematurity

The normal birth weight of an infant is about 3,300 grams (about 7 pounds). Formerly, any infant weighing under 2,500 grams (about 5.5 pounds) was classified as **premature.** Today, however, 1,500–2,500 grams (about 3.35 pounds to 5.56 pounds) is used as the standard, unless there is evidence that the gestation period was less than 37 weeks. Infants born under 1,500 grams are considered to be **very low birth weight** (VLBW) babies (D'Agostino and Clifford, 1998). The practice of labeling a newborn as premature based on gestation period or weight

alone is no longer used for two reasons. First, it is often difficult to accurately determine the gestational age of the infant, and, second, the highest mortality and morbidity rates are present for infants of the very lowest birth weights. As a result, the terms *low birth weight* and *young-for-date* have emerged as more accurate indicators of prematurity in the true sense of the word. Prematurity is of major concern because it is closely associated with physical and mental retardation, hyperactivity, and infant death. Prevention is considered to be the most important factor in improving infant health and survival rates.

> ### CONCEPT 4.13
>
> Prematurity puts the newborn at risk and frequently undermines the process of motor development.

Low Birth Weight

Low-birth-weight (LBW) infants weigh less than expected for their gestational age. Two standard deviations below the mean for a given gestational age is the generally accepted criterion for **low birth weight.** Therefore, a LBW infant may be one born at term (40 weeks) or preterm (37 weeks or under). Low-birth-weight infants have experienced "intrauterine growth retardation" and are generally called "small-for-date." A variety of prenatal maternal factors have been implicated, including diet, drugs, smoking, infections, and disease (Kopp and Kaler, 1989). Other factors such as social class, multiple births, and geographic locale have been shown to influence birth weight (Mason, 1991). The long-term effects of low birth weight are directly related to the degree of intrauterine growth retardation and gestational age of the child. An encouraging finding in outcome studies of LBW infants is that the majority survive with little or no disability. However, babies classified as VLBW experience a much higher incidence of major disability (D'Agostino and Clifford, 1998; Lemons, et al., 2001).

Young-for-Date

Children born at the expected birth weight (less than two standard deviations below the mean) for their gestational age but before full term (37 weeks or less) are called **young-for-date,** or *preterm infants*. There is little agreement on the exact causes of preterm birth, but a number of factors have been shown to contribute, including drug use, smoking, maternal age, excessive weight gain, and adverse social and economic conditions. Until recent years the prognosis for young-for-date infants who were either small-for-date or normal-weight-for-date was bleak. Their morbidity and mortality rates were abnormally high when compared with normal-term infants. Bennett (1997) reported that the lower the gestational age the higher the incidence of major disability.

The preterm infant is still likely to have more learning difficulties, language and social interaction disadvantages, and motor coordination problems than his or her full-term counterpart. For some unknown reason, boys seem to be more severely affected than girls. The usual treatment of hospital-born premature infants is to put them in a sterile isolette, where temperature, humidity, and oxygen can be precisely controlled. It has been suggested that the absence of normal stimulation from the mother and the surrounding environment contributes to these deficits.

Long-Term Effects of Prematurity

The data are clear that VLBW babies are more likely to die in the first few weeks following birth than are normal-weight babies. Preterm LBW babies, however, have a much brighter prognosis. Tremendous strides have been made in reducing the overall infant mortality rate with about 7.2 per 1,000 live births in the United States in 1998, as compared to about 165 per 1,000 live births in 1900 (National Center for Health Statistics, 2000). Preterm LBW, however, ranks second behind congenital anomalies as the leading cause of infant death in the United States. The United States currently ranks a dismal twenty-sixth in international Rankings for Infant Mortality (NCHS-FASTATS, 2000). Figure 4.1 depicts the estimated mortality risk for female and for males based on birth weight and gestational age. Note that as both gestational age and weight increase, mortality correspondingly decreases.

The long-term effects of premature birth are not as clear as are the short-term consequences. In recent years, Neonatal Intensive Care Units have been implicated in long-term developmental problems of some premature babies. The effects of noise, light, and the absence of pleasurable touch on the developing neurologic system have been studied. The encouraging news is that the majority survive with little or no disability. But as the age of viability (i.e., the lowest gestational age possible for survival) continues to decrease with medical advances, and the survival rate of VLBW babies increases, there has been a greater incidence of both minor and major developmental disabilities (Saigal et al., 1994; Lemons et al., 2001; Tommiska et al., 2001).

Eating Disorders

North Americans live in a world far different from that of their ancestors. Vigorous physical exertion is not a necessary part of the daily life pattern of most people. Today, most exercise, if it occurs, is planned and is not an integral part of one's existence. In addition, many, for the present, have an abundance of food. It is possible for an individual to consume a large amount of food and use up little of the energy contained in that food. The maintenance of body weight is relatively simple. It requires maintaining a balance between caloric intake and caloric expenditure. If more calories are consumed than are burned over a time, obesity is the eventual result. On the other hand, if fewer calories are consumed than expended, weight loss will result over time. Weight loss caused by a long-term aversion to food (anorexia nervosa) or repeated binging and purging (bulimia) is of growing concern and must be considered in any discussion of eating disorders.

CONCEPT 4.14

Eating disorders among children, adolescents, and adults dramatically affect their growth and motor development.

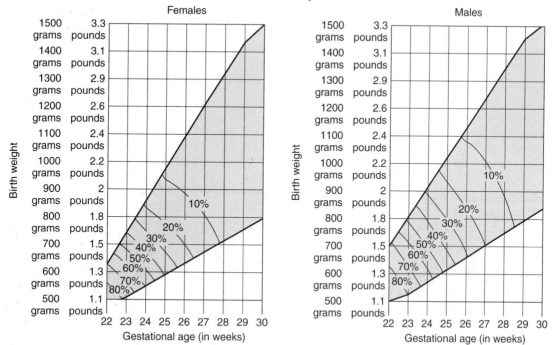

Figure 4.1

Estimated mortality risk for females and males based on birth weight and gestational age.

Adapted from: Lemons, et al. (2001). Very low birth weight outcomes of the Neonatal Institute of Child Health and Human Development Neonatal Research Network. *Pediatrics, 107 (1)*. Online: www.pediatrics.org/cgi/content/full/107/1/e1

Obesity

Obesity, or any excessive increase in the amount of stored body fat, is considered to be the most prevalent chronic nutritional disease in North America. Obesity and overweight occur in over 20 percent of children, and 55 percent of adults in the United States. Today, obesity is considered to be the second leading cause of unnecessary death of over 300,000 Americans each year (American Obesity Association, 2000).

Fat has a number of constructive functions. It is a reserve source of energy; it is a vehicle for fat-soluble vitamins; it provides protection and support to the body parts, insulating the body from the cold; and in proper proportion, it enhances the appearance of the body. However, to serve these functions, the proportion of fat desired in adults is about 15 to 18 percent for males and 20 to 25 percent for females.

The full-term infant has about 12 to 16 percent fat, much of which develops during the last two months of the gestation period. By the sixth month following birth body fat percentages have increased to about 25 percent, declining thereafter through childhood to about 15 to 18 percent. During the preadolescent period, fat deposits increase in girls, but not in boys. There is a small but significant decrease in the percentage of body fat among males (Fomon et al., 1982). Ideally, the percentage of body fat in proportion to total body weight changes little from late adolescence through adulthood. However, the percentage of body fat may range from a low of about 8 percent (typical of the long-distance, ectomorphic runner) to as high as 50 percent (characteristic of the very obese).

Millions of Americans are overweight. The prevalence of obesity has been estimated at 14 to 20 percent in different regions of the United States

TABLE 4.1   **Body Mass Index Chart**

Height (inches)	Body Weight (pounds)																
	19	20	21	22	23	24	25	26	27	28	29	30	31	32	33	34	35
58	91	96	100	105	110	115	119	124	129	134	138	143	148	153	158	162	167
59	94	99	104	109	114	119	124	128	133	138	143	148	153	158	163	168	173
60	97	102	107	112	118	123	128	133	138	143	148	153	158	163	168	174	179
61	100	106	111	116	122	127	132	137	143	148	153	158	164	169	174	180	185
62	104	109	115	120	126	131	136	142	147	153	158	164	169	175	180	186	191
63	107	113	118	124	130	135	141	146	152	158	163	169	175	180	186	191	197
64	110	116	122	128	134	140	145	151	157	163	169	174	180	186	192	197	204
65	114	120	126	132	138	144	150	156	162	168	174	180	186	192	198	204	210
66	118	124	130	136	142	148	155	161	167	173	179	186	192	198	204	210	216
67	121	127	134	140	146	153	159	166	172	178	185	191	198	204	211	217	223
68	125	131	138	144	151	158	164	171	177	184	190	197	203	210	216	223	230
69	128	135	142	149	155	162	169	176	182	189	196	203	209	216	223	230	236
70	132	139	146	153	160	167	174	181	188	195	202	209	216	222	229	236	243
71	136	143	150	157	165	172	179	186	193	200	208	215	222	229	236	243	250
72	140	147	154	162	169	177	184	191	199	206	213	221	228	235	242	250	258
73	144	151	159	166	174	182	189	197	204	212	219	227	235	242	250	257	265
74	148	155	163	171	179	186	194	202	210	218	225	233	241	249	256	264	272
75	152	160	168	176	184	192	200	208	216	224	232	240	248	256	264	272	279
76	156	164	172	180	189	197	205	213	221	230	238	246	254	263	271	279	287

Data from: *Clinical Guidelines on the Identification, Evaluation, and Treatment of Overweight and Obesity in Adults,* National Institutes of Health, National Heart, Lung, and Blood Institute, June 1998.

(AOA, 2000). It is estimated that obese children who have not slimmed down by age 14 have a 70 percent risk of remaining obese as adults (AOA, 2000).

In North America the percentage of lean body mass tends to decrease with age. The percentage of body fat is the most important determiner of obesity. A person's weight is less crucial than the ratio of fat to lean tissue. Body composition is a valid criterion for determining obesity. Body composition is determined by calculating one's body mass index (BMI). To calculate your BMI use the following formula: weight (in pounds)____ + height (in inches)^2 × 704.5 = BMI. Worldwide, a BMI of 30 or greater is considered obese. A BMI from 25.0–29.9 is considered overweight (WHO, 1998) (or go to table 4.1 where it has been calculated for you).

Among adults, the evidence is clear; there has been a substantial increase in the incidence of overweight in the United States, particularly in the last decade. A growing body of evidence has impli-

cated obesity as a major contributing factor in a wide variety of negative health outcomes several of which are depicted in table 4.2. Obesity places additional stress on the circulatory, respiratory, and metabolic systems and may cause, or intensify, disorders in these systems. Obese adults have a well-established increased risk of cardiovascular morbidity and mortality independent of age, cholesterol level, blood pressure, smoking, and glucose intolerance. In addition, obese children and adults frequently suffer ridicule from their peers, poor academic performance, poor self-image, and persistent concern with dieting.

The primary environmentally based causes of obesity in individuals with normal hormonal balances are excessive eating and lack of exercise, or a combination of both. Poor eating and exercise habits are formed in childhood and carried on into adult life. The child urged to clean the plate at every meal but not encouraged to exercise regularly has the potential for a serious weight problem.

TABLE 4.2 **Overweight and Obesity Increase the Risk of Several Diseases and Is Associated with Numerous Negative Health Conditions**

Overweight and Obesity Are Known Risk Factors for:	Overweight and Obesity Is Associated with:
Type 2 Diabetes	Elevated Cholesterol
Heart Disease	Complications During Pregnancy
Stroke	Menstrual Irregularities
Hypertension	Excessive Body and Facial Hair
Rheumatoid Arthritis	Birth Defects (neural tube defects)
Osteoarthritis (especially of the knees, hips, back, and hands)	Carpal Tunnel Syndrome
Sleep Apnea	Daytime Sleepiness
Some Forms of Cancer (breast, uterine, colorectal, kidney, and gallbladder)	Gout
Gallbladder Disease	Impaired Immune Response
Heat Disorders	Impaired Respiratory Function

Data from: American Obesity Association. (2000). *The Facts About . . . Health Effects of Obesity.* Washington, DC: Author; National Institute of Diabetes and Digestive and Kidney Diseases (NIDDK). (1998). *Statistics Related to Overweight and Obesity.* Online at: www.niddk.nih.gov/health/nutrition/pubs/statobes.htm.

An area of interest to many who study obesity is the activity levels of obese children. Physical inactivity appears to contribute to obesity, as indicated by studies linking television watching to the prevalence of childhood obesity. Bar-Or and Baranowski (1994) noted in a review paper of physical activity and obesity among adolescents several studies that clearly indicate that the intensity of physical activity is significantly lower in obese children and adolescents. Although increased levels of physical activity coupled with moderation in caloric intake may be the keys to reducing the trend toward increased fatness, Bar-Or and Baranowski concluded that of the many physical intervention programs studied there was only a small (1–3 percent body fat) reduction in adiposity among adolescents. Dieting does not appear to be the complete, or the best, solution to behaviorally based obesity in children. Their food intake may be normal, so dieting may cause serious deficiencies in the nutrients required for proper growth and health. A major cause of obesity in children is lack of activity, therefore long-term increases in this area may be the best and most healthful solution (AOA, 2000; Rickard et al., 1996).

CONCEPT 4.15

Both genetic and environmental factors contribute to the onset and extent of obesity.

The etiology of obesity in most children is unknown, but genetic as well as environmental factors appear to be involved. Obesity appears to be highly familial with either a hereditary or environmental basis or a combination of both. Obesity occurs at higher rates in African Americans (30.2 percent and Mexican Americans (28.4 percent) than their white counterparts (21.2 percent) (Elegal et al., 1998). Twin studies support the concept that genetic factors play a major role in obesity (Stunkard et al., 1986, 1990). Additionally, obesity among children after 10 years of age appears to be strongly genetic with about two-thirds of the variability in body weight attributable to genetic factors (Malina and Bouchard, 1991). Although both hereditary and environmental factors play a role, regular, vigorous physical activity may be the most important variable in preventing obesity.

Binge Eating Disorder

Binge eating disorder is relatively uncommon in the general population but common among the obese, occurring in 20 percent or more (Marcus, 1993). Although the causes are yet unknown, binge eating disorder includes up to 50 percent with a history of depression. Negative emotions such as anger, anxiety, sadness, and boredom may trigger episodes of binge eating. Individuals with a binge eating disorder consume large amounts of food in binges but do not engage in the purging or fasting behaviors typical of individuals with bulimia or anorexia (Yanovski Zelitch, 1993). An individual with **binge eating disorder** is characterized as having reoccurring episodes of binge eating (without purging) within any two-hour period, at least two days per week for a period of at least six months. Furthermore, binge eaters typically eat much more rapidly than usual; eat until feeling uncomfortably full; eat large quantities of food when not feeling hungry; eat alone because of embarrassment about how much they eat; and feel guilty, depressed, or disgusted with themselves after overeating (Spritzer et al., 1993).

Anorexia Nervosa/Bulimia Nervosa

A problem as perplexing and potentially as dangerous as obesity is **anorexia nervosa,** characterized by an aversion to the consumption of food and an obsession with being "too fat," even when the person is clearly underweight. These self-starvers can lose 25 to 50 percent of their normal body weights in the pursuit of thinness. They start dieting and, although emaciated, continue to refuse food because they see themselves as fat. **Bulimia nervosa,** another severe eating disorder, is similar to anorexia in terms of results. Persons with bulimia have the same "need" for thinness but use a binge-purge process. Individuals with bulimia often eat large quantities of food and then force themselves to vomit. It is estimated that anorexia and bulimia occurs in 3 to 4 percent of the female population, with 90 percent of all cases being female (NIMH, 2000). Both disorders have major long-term health consequences and are related to amenorrhea during the childbearing years and osteoporosis during the postmenopausal years.

Characteristically, in both anorexia nervosa and bulimia, there is no true loss of appetite or awareness of hunger pains corresponding to the body's need for food. Some individuals brainwash themselves into believing that the pain feels good. In about 25 percent of the cases, food refusal alternates with eating binges followed by forced vomiting and/or the use of laxatives, enemas, and diuretics (bulimia).

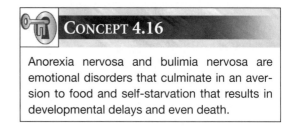

CONCEPT 4.16

Anorexia nervosa and bulimia nervosa are emotional disorders that culminate in an aversion to food and self-starvation that results in developmental delays and even death.

Individuals with anorexia or bulimia often pursue their goal of thinness not only through food restriction but also through exhausting exercise. Exercise becomes a way to burn off calories. Despite their weakness due to extreme loss of weight, many with anorexia display incredible energy. The longer it is left undiagnosed, the more difficult it is to treat. To help those with eating disorders and the underlying emotional issues, psychotherapy is generally recommended. Antidepressant medication is frequently prescribed. Some early warning signals of binge eating disorder, anorexia nervosa, and bulimia nervosa are listed in table 4.3.

Society is partly to blame for the increase in eating disorders in North America. The lean, slender form is glorified by society, which propagates the idea that being thin symbolizes beauty, desirability, and self-control and is a magic key to a happier life. Educators may be among the first to recognize eating disorders. They should be able to recognize the early stages of either illness while it is still relatively easy to reverse.

Fitness Levels

A wide variety of factors from all three domains of human behavior (cognitive, affective, and psy-

TABLE 4.3	Early Warning Signs of Eating Disorders	
Binge Eating Disorder	**Anorexia Nervosa**	**Bulimia Nervosa**
1. Eating binges without purging 2. Irregular weight loss 3. Frequently obese 4. Difficulty losing weight and keeping it off 5. Obsessed with food 6. Frequent among people on a medically supervised weight-control program 7. Disgusted with self after a binging episode 8. Frequent history of depression 9. Eating binges triggered by extreme negative emotions	1. Over identification with a doctor-prescribed weight-control program 2. Obsession with dieting and talk of food 3. Social isolation accompanying slimness (loner) 4. No participation in the courting behavior of classmates 5. Sudden increased involvement in athletics, usually of a solitary nature 6. Exaggerated concern with achieving high academic grades 7. Overconcern with weight 8. Failure to consume food 9. Denial of hunger 10. Obsession with exercise	1. Eating binges followed by purging 2. Irregular weight loss 3. Long periods in the bathroom after meals 4. Variable performance 5. Loss of tooth enamel 6. Fear of gaining weight 7. Prolonged/extreme exercise 8. Emotional instability and impulsivity 9. Depression and frequent mood swings 10. Throat, esophagus, stomach, or colon problems

chomotor) influence development, as well as factors within the individual, the environment, and the task. Task factors within the psychomotor domain are termed *physical* and *mechanical* factors. These factors have a profound impact on the acquisition, maintenance, and diminution of our movement abilities throughout life. Our level of physical fitness coupled with the mechanical requirements of a task greatly influence our ability to move with control, skill, and confidence. Figure 4.2 illustrates this important concept.

The interaction among physical activity, genetics, and nutrition suggests the upper and lower limits of physical fitness that can be reasonably expected of an individual. Nutritional status can greatly inhibit or enhance one's level of physical functioning (Meredith and Dwyer, 1991; Rickard et al., 1996), and genetic structure determines the ultimate level of fitness that can be attained (Malina and Bouchard, 1991). Therefore, for the purposes of this text, **physical fitness** is defined as a set of attributes that one possesses related to the ability to perform physical activity, coupled with one's genetic makeup, and the maintenance of nutritional adequacy. Physical fitness may be subdi-

vided into health-related and performance-related components.

Health-Related Fitness

Muscular strength, muscular endurance, aerobic endurance, joint flexibility, and body composition are usually considered the components of health-related fitness. The extent to which each of these factors is possessed will influence an individual's performance capabilities in movement. For example, how far a person can run or ride a bicycle is related to his or her level of muscular strength, muscular endurance, and aerobic endurance.

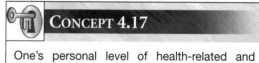

CONCEPT 4.17

One's personal level of health-related and performance-related fitness influences motor development in many ways.

Performance-Related Fitness

Performance-related fitness, also widely known as motor fitness, is the performance aspect of physical

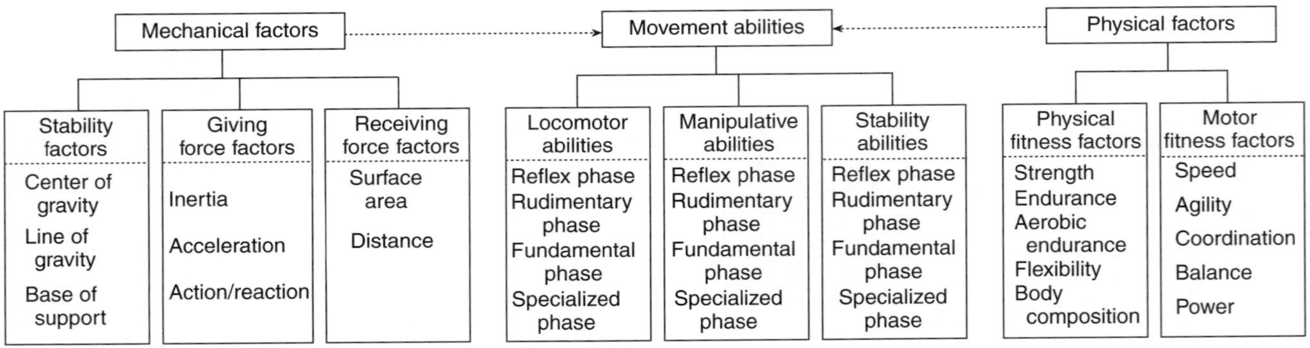

Figure 4.2
Physical and mechanical factors affect the development of movement abilities at all phases of motor development.

fitness. *Motor fitness* is generally thought of as one's current performance level as influenced by factors such as movement, speed, agility, balance, coordination, and power.

The generality and specificity of motor fitness have been debated and researched for years, with the bulk of research evidence in favor of its specificity (Magill, 2001). For years it was thought that motor fitness was general; as a result, the term *general motor ability* came into vogue. It was often assumed that if an individual excelled in a certain sport, that corresponding ability would automatically carry over to other activities. Although this often occurs, it is probably due to the individual's personal motivation, numerous activity experiences, and several specific sport aptitudes, not to a transfer or carryover of skills from one activity to another. One's motor fitness has a definite effect on the performance of any movement activity that requires quick reactions, speed of movement, agility and coordination of movement, explosive power, and balance.

Biomechanics

Before embarking on a detailed discussion of motor development, it will be useful to review some mechanical principles of movement as they relate to stability, locomotion, and manipulation. The human body is capable of moving in numerous ways. Learning all of the skills involved in the performance of children's game, sport, and dance activities may appear to be an impossible task. Closer inspection of the total spectrum of movement will reveal, however, that fundamental mechanical laws affect all human movement. Selected mechanical principles are considered here to serve as basic preparation for the chapters that follow.

> ### CONCEPT 4.18
> All movement is governed by fundamental mechanical laws.

Balance

All masses within the gravitational pull of the earth are subjected to the force of gravity. The three pri-

mary factors of concern in the study of balance principles are (1) center of gravity, (2) line of gravity, and (3) base of support.

A *center of gravity* exists within all objects. In geometric shapes, it is located in the exact center of the object. In asymmetrical objects (e.g., human bodies), it is constantly changing during movement. The center of gravity of our bodies always shifts in the direction of the movement or the additional weight (figure 4.3). The center of gravity of a child standing in an erect position is approximately at the top of the hips between the front and the back of the trunk. Activities in which the center of gravity remains in a stable position, such as standing on one foot or performing a headstand, are known as static balance activities. If the center of gravity is constantly shifting, as in jumping rope, walking, or doing a forward roll, the activities are dynamic balance movements.

The *line of gravity* is an imaginary line that extends vertically through the center of gravity to the center of the earth. The interrelationship of the center of gravity and the line of gravity to the base of support determines the degree of stability of the body (figure 4.4).

The *base of support* is the part of the body that comes into contact with the supporting surface. If the line of gravity falls within the base of support, the body will be in balance. If it falls outside the base, it is out of balance. The wider the base of support, the greater the stability, as can be seen when one balances on two feet rather than on one foot. The nearer the base of support to the center of gravity, the greater the stability. Someone standing erect may be pushed off balance more easily than someone in a lineman's stance with the feet spread and the body slightly forward. The nearer the center of gravity to the center of the base of support, the greater the stability. A foot position that allows for a larger base of support in the direction of the movement gives additional stability. This principle is illustrated by the foot position of a runner attempting to stop or of a catcher trying to receive and control a heavy object.

Giving Force

Force is one of the basic concepts of movement and body mechanics. **Force** is the instigator of all

Figure 4.3
The center of gravity shifts as the body changes position.

Figure 4.4
The body remains in balance when the center of gravity and line of gravity fall within the base of support.

movement and may be defined as the effort that one mass exerts on another. The result may be (1) movement, (2) cessation of movement, or (3) resistance of one body against another. There may be force without motion, as is seen in isometric activities, but motion is impossible without the application of some form of force. Three forces relative to the human body are of concern to us: (1) force produced by muscles, (2) force produced by the gravitational pull of the earth, and (3) momentum. The entire science of force is based on Newton's three laws of motion, namely, the law of inertia, the law of acceleration, and the law of action and reaction.

The **law of inertia** states that a body at rest will remain at rest and a body in motion will remain in motion at the same speed in a straight line unless acted upon by an outside force. For movement to occur, a force must act upon a body sufficiently to overcome that object's inertia. If the applied force is less than the resistance offered by the object, motion will not occur. Large muscles can produce more force than small muscles. Once an object is in motion, it takes less force to maintain its speed and direction (i.e., momentum) than it does to stop it. This may be readily observed in snow skiing, the glide in swimming, or rolling a ball. The heavier the object and the faster its speed, the more force required to overcome its moving inertia or to absorb its momentum. It is harder to catch a heavy object than it is to catch a light object.

The **law of acceleration** states that the change in the velocity of an object is directly proportional to the force producing the velocity and inversely proportional to the object's mass. The heavier an object, the more force is needed to accelerate or decelerate it. This may be observed when a heavy object (shot put) and a light object (softball) are thrown a given distance. An increase in speed is proportional to the amount of force that is applied. The greater the amount of force imparted to an object, the higher the speed at which the object will travel. If the same amount of force is exerted on two bodies with a different mass, greater acceleration will be produced on the lighter or less massive object. The heavier object, however, will have greater momentum once inertia is overcome and will exert a greater force than the lighter object on something that it contacts.

The **law of action and reaction** states that for every action there is an equal and opposite reaction. This principle of counterforce is the basis for all locomotion and is evident when one leaves footprints in the sand. This principle applies to both linear and angular motion. Its application requires that adjustments be made by an individual to sustain the primary forces in any movement. For example, the use of opposition in the running pattern counters the action of one part of the body with that of another.

Receiving Force

To stop ourselves or a moving object, we absorb force over the greatest distance possible and with the largest surface area possible. The greater the distance over which the force is absorbed, the less the impact on whatever receives the force. This may be demonstrated by catching a ball with the arms straight out in front of the body and then catching again with the arms bent. The same thing may be observed when landing from a jump with the legs bent as opposed to landing with the legs straight. Forces should be absorbed over as large a surface area as possible. The impact is reduced in proportion to the size of the surface area, and the likelihood of injury is diminished. For example, trying to absorb the shock of a fall with the hands and arms extended will probably result in injury because the small surface area of the hand must receive the entire impact. It is far better to let as much of the body as possible absorb the impact.

The final direction of a moving object depends on the magnitude and the direction of all of the forces that have been applied. Therefore, whenever we kick, strike, or throw an object, its accuracy and the distance depend on the forces acting on it. If we are performing a vertical jump, we must work for a summation of forces in a vertical direction, whereas a good performance in the long jump requires a summation of horizontal and vertical forces so that the takeoff is at the appropriate angle.

Separate discussion of the principles of balance, giving force, and receiving forces should not be taken to mean that one is used in the absence of the others. Most of our movements combine all three. An element of balance is involved in almost all of our movements, and we give and receive force whenever we perform any locomotor or manipulative movement. A gymnast, for example, must maintain his or her equilibrium when performing a tumbling trick, such as a front flip, and also must absorb force from the body (on the landing). A tennis player must move to a position of readiness (giving to and receiving force from the body), contact the ball (giving force to an object), and maintain balance. Although each of the movement patterns and skills discussed in the chapters that follow involve a specific sequence of movements, all incorporate the basic mechanics discussed here because these mechanical principles are common to all movement situations.

SUMMARY

Motor development represents one aspect of the total developmental process. It is intricately interrelated with the cognitive and affective domains of human behavior and is influenced by a variety of factors. The importance of optimal motor development must not be minimized or regarded as secondary in relation to other developmental areas. Common factors affecting motor development emerge. These factors illustrate the gradual progression from relatively simple levels of functioning to more complex levels. Biological, experiential, and physical factors influence the process and the products of motor development. Each individual is unique in his or her development and will progress at a rate determined by environmental and biological circumstances in conjunction with the specific requirements of the movement task.

CRITICAL READINGS

American Obesity Association. (2000). *Facts about Obesity*. Washington, DC: Author.

Booth, M. (2000). Assessment of physical activity: An international perspective. *Research Quarterly for Exercicise and Sport, 71,* 114–120.

Eyer, D. E. (1994). *Infant Bonding: A Scientific Fiction*. New Haven, CT: Yale University Press.

Lemons, J. A. et al. (2001). Very low birth weight outcomes of the neonatal institute of child health and human development neonatal research network. *Pediatrics, 107,* Electronic text: www.pediatrics.org/cgi/content/full/107/1/e1.

Malina, R. M., & Bouchard, C. (1991). *Growth, Maturation and Physical Activity* (Chapter 24). Champaign, IL: Human Kinetics.

Thomas, J. R. (2000). 1999 C. H. McCloy Research Lecture: Children's control, learning and performance of motor skills. *Research Quarterly for Exercicise and Sport, 71,* 1–9.

Tommiska, V. et al. (2001). A national short-term follow-up study of extremely low birth weight infants born in 1996–1997. *Pediatrics, 104,* Electronic text: www.pediatrics.org/cgi/content/full/107/1/e2.

Troiano, R. P. et al. (1995). Overweight prevalence and trends for children and adolescents. *Archives of Pediatric & Adolescent Medicine, 149,* 1085–1091.

Trost, S. G. (2000). Children's understanding of the concept of physical activity. *Pediatric Exercise Science, 12,* 293–299.

WEB RESOURCES

American Academy of Pediatrics policy statement on structured infant exercise programs www.aap.org/policy//02223.html

Homepage for the National Association of Anorexia Nervosa and Associated Disorders www.anad.org

Homepage for the National Institute of Child Health and Human Development www.nichd.nih.gov

Information on obesity from the Centers for Disease Control and Prevention www.cdc.gov/health/obesity.htm

Infancy

. . . for I am fearfully and wonderfully made . . .

—Psalm 139:14

INFANCY

Beverly D. Ulrich

Beverly D. Ulrich, Ph.D., is Dean of the Division of Kinesiology at the University of Michigan, Ann Arbor. She has held an endowed professorship in child development at Indiana University. Dr. Ulrich has served as president of the North American Society for the Psychology of Sport and Physical Activity and as chair of the Motor Development Academy of the American Alliance for Health, Physical Education, Recreation and Dance. Her research has been published in Developmental Medicine and Child Neurology, Child Development, Physical Therapy, Journal of Motor Behavior, *and* Human Movement Science.

Why do you believe it is valuable to study infant motor development?

Aristotle reportedly said, "He who sees things from their beginning will have the finest view of them." I believe Aristotle was right. We can understand better how motor skills emerge if we observe them from their very beginning, that is, *before* and *as* they emerge. We can learn a lot by examining infants' spontaneous actions and early attempts to perform a new motor task in context and in relation to other factors that may impact their development. Infancy is a particularly informative period because many new skills emerge quickly during the first months of life, and infants are born with a relatively small repertoire of skills that they can control voluntarily. Observations enable us to gain insight into factors that may be important to the process of change. Then, we can test these ideas by designing experiments. One goal of motor development research is to explain the process by which skills emerge. Ultimately, these explanations should lead us to interventions, ways to help infants and children with motor problems learn to move more easily. Research clearly shows that early intervention is important in maximizing the potential for infants at risk for developmental delay. Therefore, I believe that for theoretical and practical reasons it is important to study infant motor development.

What has been one of the most interesting projects related to infant motor development with which you have had the opportunity to be involved?

The most interesting project I've been part of was the one in which my husband, Dale Ulrich, and I and several of our students tested the effect of a treadmill intervention on the onset of walking in infants with Down syndrome. That was interesting for several reasons. First, we demonstrated that we could help babies with Down syndrome learn to walk earlier than they normally would. We gave parents small, motorized treadmills and showed them how to use them to help their babies practice stepping. We believe that the practice helped babies increase their leg and trunk strength and control. Second, because this was a longitudinal study and we saw them every two weeks for approximately nine to eighteen months, we got to know the families and infants very well. We felt like part of their extended families, enjoying birthdays and milestones in their lives with them. Third, the results of this study were not only clinically relevant but also theoretically significant. Our data showed that the onset of walking, often referred to as a phylogenetic skill, does not simply wait for the nervous system to mature but is, in fact, quite significantly affected by external factors, such as practice. This provides hope for more intervention efforts to help infants and young children learn functional skills as well as skills for recreation and fitness.

What is your current research focus in the area of infant development?

Recently I began a collaborative effort with Dr. Mijna Hadders-Algra, a physician and researcher from The Netherlands. We are studying the emergence of spontaneous leg movements, the infant stepping response, and treadmill stepping patterns in infants with spina bifida and in a control group of infants. We believe this approach will lead to a better understanding of the impact that spinal and peripheral factors have on the development of stepping and walking. We also hope this information will lead us to ways we can help infants with spina bifida learn to walk earlier and more efficiently.

CHAPTER

5

PRENATAL FACTORS AFFECTING DEVELOPMENT

KEY TERMS

High-risk pregnancy

Teratogen

Malnourishment

Illicit drugs

Fetal alcohol syndrome

Down syndrome

Genetic defects

Chemical pollutants

Sexually transmitted diseases

Obstetrical medication

CHAPTER COMPETENCIES

Upon completion of this chapter you should be able to:

- Describe the influence of maternal nutrition on later development
- Critically analyze the impact of maternal chemical intake on fetal development
- List and discuss factors to be considered when determining the influence of a drug on an unborn child
- Distinguish between chromosome-based disorders and gene-based disorders
- List and describe the causes and effects of several chromosome- and gene-based disorders
- Describe the potential effects of radiation and chemical pollutants on later development
- List and discuss several maternal and fetal medical problems that may affect later development
- Describe the influence of maternal exercise during pregnancy on fetal development
- Demonstrate knowledge of birth process factors that may affect later development
- Critically analyze the prenatal period and describe the interrelated nature of a variety of factors that may influence later development

KEY CONCEPT

A number of prenatal factors, many of which can be controlled, affect motor development during infancy and beyond.

Among the most positive contributions of medical technology are advances that have been made in reducing infant mortality. Infant mortality rates have dropped significantly in most categories of death causations in the last two decades (table 5.1). Not long ago prenatal and neonatal illness and death were common in North America. One need, however, only look at less-advanced cultures throughout the world, and among the poor, deprived, and neglected in our society, to see that the threat of severely disabling conditions resulting from a variety of prenatal factors still exists. The current leading cause of severe impairment, among rich and poor, stems from prenatal factors. Birth defects refer to abnormal conditions such as heart defects, skeletal deformities, and body chemistry imbalances present at birth. Birth defects can range from mild to severe and may result in a physical or mental disability, debilitating disease, or early death. An estimated one of every 28 babies born in the United States experience some form of birth defect (March of Dimes Perinatal Data Center, 1997). In the United States, a country in which the population is estimated to be in excess of 280 million (U.S. Bureau of the Census, 2000) it is essential to identify and eliminate prenatal factors that adversely affect later growth and development. It is staggering to contemplate that more than 2 million Americans have severe afflictions because of conditions over which they had no control. It is doubly staggering when we speculate on the number of individuals who have been only moderately or slightly affected by these conditions.

A number of birth defects are associated with high-risk pregnancies. A **high-risk pregnancy** represents a situation when the expectant mother has a condition before or during pregnancy that increases her unborn child's chances of experiencing either prenatal or postnatal problems. Table 5.2 presents a list of conditions that may put a mother-to-be in the high-risk category. Several of these are described in further detail throughout this chapter.

While it is important to recognize the severity of the consequences of birth defects, it is even more important to understand that many birth defects can be prevented or their impact greatly reduced by the expectant mother practicing some simple yet extremely effective behaviors. Of primary importance is the scheduling of regular appointments with her health care provider prior to and during her pregnancy. The medical professional will be able to discuss the anticipating mother's health and lifestyle and guide her in maintaining beneficial behaviors and eliminating or reducing unhealthy ones. Table 5.3 lists several measures that should be addressed with a health care specialist prior to or during the early stages of pregnancy.

NUTRITIONAL AND CHEMICAL FACTORS

Whatever the expectant mother ingests will affect the unborn child in some way. Whether these effects are harmful and will have lasting consequences depends on a variety of circumstances. The condition of the fetus, degree of nutritional or chemical abuse, amount or dosage, period of pregnancy, and presence of other influencing factors are a few of the circumstances that influence the probability of teratogenic effects. A **teratogen** is any substance that may cause the unborn child to develop in an abnormal manner. The fetus is "at risk" when any one or more of the following nutritional or chemical factors are present.

Prenatal Malnutrition

Prenatal malnutrition is a common cause of later developmental difficulties throughout the world. *Prenatal malnutrition* may result from one or more of the following three factors: (1) placental factors, (2) fetal factors, and (3) maternal factors.

TABLE 5.1 Ten Leading Causes for Under 1-Year-Old Infant Deaths and Mortality Rates per 100,000 Live U.S. Births by Cause of Death Including Percentages and Percent Changes from 1979 to 1998

Cause of Death	Number (1998)	Percent of Total Deaths	Rate per 100,000 Live Births	Percent Change from 1979–1998
ALL RACES, ALL CAUSES	28,371	100	719.8	−44.9
1. Congenital anomalies	6,212	21.9	157.6	−38.3
2. Disorders relating to short gestation and unspecified low birth weight	4,101	14.5	104.0	4.0
3. Sudden infant death syndrome	2,822	9.9	71.6	−52.6
4. Newborn affected by maternal complications of pregnancy	1,343	4.7	34.1	−26.5
5. Respiratory distress syndrome	1,295	4.6	32.9	−78.9
6. Newborn affected complications of placenta, cord, and membranes	961	3.4	24.4	−12.2
7. Infections specific to the perinatal period	815	2.9	20.7	−26.3
8. Accidents and adverse effects	754	2.7	19.1	−38.2
9. Intrauterine hypoxia and birth asphyxia	461	1.6	11.7	−70.7
10. Pneumonia and influenza	441	1.6	11.2	−65.3

Data from: Murphy, S. L. (2000). Deaths: Final data for 1998. National Vital Statistics Reports, Centers for Disease Control and Prevention, Vol. 48, No. 11, p. 89.

TABLE 5.2 Conditions That May Result in High-Risk Pregnancy

Medical Conditions	Exposure to	Use of	History
Asthma	Certain medications	Alcohol	Age ($<16, >35$)
Cancer	Chemical pollutants	Illicit drugs	Bleeding
Diabetes	Cytomegalovirus	Tobacco	Heredity
Hypertension	Excessive radiation		Nutritional inadequacy
Heart disease	Rubella		Previous miscarriage
Kidney disease	Toxoplasmosis		Seriously overweight
Liver disease			or underweight
Maternal stress			Poverty
Thyroid disorders			
Sexually transmitted diseases			

TABLE 5.3 Factors to be Discussed During a Prepregnancy Visit with a Health Care Provider

- Maternal nutrition and nutritional supplementation
  - Necessity of the B-vitamin folic acid
- Smoking abstinence
- Alcohol consumption abstinence
- Exercise/physical activity
- Recreational drugs abstinence
- Prescription drugs monitoring
- Over-the-counter drugs monitoring
- Currency of rubella and chicken pox inoculations
- Rh incompatibility potential
- Conditions/diseases that run in mother's and father's families
- Specific maternal conditions/diseases
  - Epilepsy
  - Diabetes
  - Hypertension

Placental malnutrition arises out of problems associated with the supply and transport of nutrients from the placenta to the fetus. The fetus depends on the mother's blood supply and the osmotic action of the placenta and umbilical cord for its nutrients.

Fetal malnutrition is associated with the inability on the part of the developing fetus to use the nutrients available to it. This generally is due to complications in the metabolism of the fetus that interrupt or prevent the normal use of available nutrients.

Maternal malnutrition is associated with inadequacies in the expectant mother's current nutritional intake as well as her general level of nutrition. Because of this, deficiencies in the mother's diet both prior to and during pregnancy can have a harmful effect on the child. A sound, nutritious diet is absolutely essential for the mother's health and the health of her unborn child.

Placental, fetal, and maternal malnutrition negatively influence human development throughout the world.

Malnourishment is of concern to nutritionists and specialists in child development in the West, where most people enjoy an abundance of food. Millions of women of childbearing age are malnourished worldwide. They are not receiving the proper nutrients through their normal daily intake of food. The reasons for maternal malnourishment range from poor eating habits to poverty, low socioeconomic class, anxiety, stress, and trauma.

Maternal malnutrition may result in inadequacies of certain nutrients that not only contribute to the overall health of the mother and unborn baby, but in some cases prevent birth defects. In recent years it has been demonstrated that the B-vitamin folic acid can help reduce neural tube defects (i.e., spina bifida) when taken prior to and during pregnancy (Locksmith and Duff, 1998). Because of the potential for unplanned pregnancies, it is generally recommended that all females of childbearing age should consume 400 micrograms of folic acid daily in addition to maintaining a healthy diet (American Academy of Pediatrics, 1999; Centers for Disease Control and Prevention, 1999).

Inadequate maternal nutrition often results in low birth weight. About 1 in every 14 infants born in the United States is of low birth weight, that is being born with a gestational weight under 1,500 grams or 3.3 pounds. Fifty to 60 percent of all infant deaths are related to very low birth weight (Lemons et al., 2001; Tommiska et al., 2001). Low birth weight can classified by the time of delivery. If a low birth weight infant is born before the thirty-seventh week of pregnancy, he or

she is considered "preterm." A "small-for-date" classification, however, is when the baby is born full-term but is underweight (March of Dimes, 1999). Figure 5.1 depicts the percentage of incidents of low birth weight over the last three decades.

The amount of weight gained by the expectant mother, in the absence of other complications, may serve as a general indicator of the unborn child's nutritional status. Maternal weight gain of 20 to 28 pounds is generally recommended. Table 5.4 lists the proportions of average weight gain during pregnancy.

Common Maternal Drugs

The wall of the placenta is porous, and chemicals may penetrate it with tragic results to the unborn child. The drugs found in the average person's medicine cabinet are potentially destructive to the fetus. Every drug has side effects, whether it is a prescription or nonprescription substance. Even if the drug has been given during pregnancy to other women without serious side effects, it cannot be regarded as safe for all unborn children. The following factors need to be considered whenever the influence of a drug on an unborn child is evaluated.

1. The time of pregnancy during which the drug is taken
2. The dosage of the drug
3. The length of time the drug is taken
4. The genetic predisposition of the fetus
5. How these four factors interact

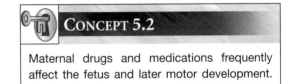

CONCEPT 5.2

Maternal drugs and medications frequently affect the fetus and later motor development.

A drug may affect the unborn child in various ways. Drugs may interfere with organ growth or cell differentiation and result in deviations from

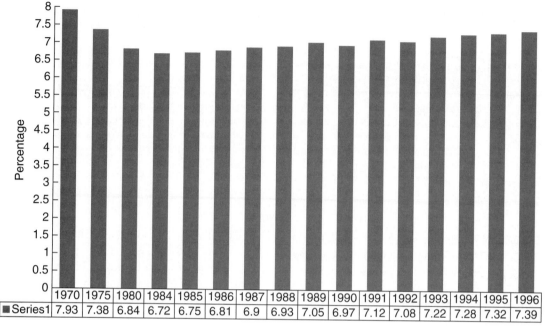

Series1: 1970: 7.93, 1975: 7.38, 1980: 6.84, 1984: 6.72, 1985: 6.75, 1986: 6.81, 1987: 6.9, 1988: 6.93, 1989: 7.05, 1990: 6.97, 1991: 7.12, 1992: 7.08, 1993: 7.22, 1994: 7.28, 1995: 7.32, 1996: 7.39

Years/Percentage

Figure 5.1

Percentage of low birth weight live births from 1970–1996.

Data from National Center for Health Statistics. (1998). Health, United States, 1998 with Socioeconomic Status and Health Chartbook. Hyattsville, Maryland: Public Health Service, p. 181.

TABLE 5.4	Distribution of Maternal Weight Gain During Pregnancy
	Weight Averages (in pounds/kg)
Fetus	7.5/3.4
Placenta	1.0/.45
Amniotic fluid	2.0/.91
Increase in uterus's weight	2.5/1.1
Increase in breasts' weight	3.0/1.4
Increase in the mother's fat	4–8/1.8–3.6
	20–28 pounds/9.1–12.7 kilograms

normal development. The penetrability of the placenta may be altered and reduce the flow of oxygen and nutrients or magnify the drug concentration flowing to the fetus. Drugs may impair development and functioning of the fetus's liver, which balances blood waste products called *bilirubin*. The inability of the biliary ducts to excrete bilirubin efficiently results in *jaundice*. Excessive jaundice results in a condition called *kernicterus*. Kernicterus can result in permanent and devastating brain

TABLE 5.5	The Effects of Common Drugs on the Unborn Child	
Drug	**Use**	**Possible Effects**
Coumadin	An anticoagulant used for blood clots	May cause bleeding before or during birth, resulting in brain damage
Diuretics	To treat toxemia, particularly water retention	Water and salt imbalance. An electrolyte imbalance may result in brain damage
Streptomycin	To treat infection in the mother	Impairment of kidneys, hearing, and balance
Aspirin	For aches, pain, fever. Almost 80 percent of over-the-counter drugs contain aspirin	Death; congenital deformities; bleeding under the skull, causing brain damage; hemorrhaging during birth
Tetracyclines	For acne	Stunts bone and teeth growth

damage. Table 5.5 provides a few examples of common drugs taken during pregnancy and their associated risk factors.

"Necessary" Maternal Drugs

During pregnancy the expectant mother may be under the care of a physician because of an illness or disease. Good, consistent medical care is doubly important because the developing fetus inside a mother with a special medical condition may also have special needs. The medications prescribed for the mother may have to be modified to protect her unborn child. A mother being treated for epilepsy, for example, should avoid the use of Dilantin and phenobarbital and other drugs used for seizure control. Although she may not be able to discontinue the use of medication completely, the drug should not be taken automatically and the dosage may need modification under medical supervision.

The expectant mother with cancer is at risk when chemotherapy is used to decrease the rate of malignant cell growth, particularly during the first three months of pregnancy. The use of progesterone to correct menstrual cycle abnormalities and to prevent miscarriage should be avoided in expectant mothers because of the potentially harmful effects on the newborn.

One of the most notorious teratogens is the drug thalidomide. Thalidomide was given in the late fifties and early sixties as a sedative primarily in several non-U.S. countries. Thalidomide was shown to cause severe limb malformations. Although the drug was banned or highly restricted, it was approved in 1998 by the U.S. Food and Drug Administration for use with conditions related to leprosy and AIDS. Groups such as the American Academy of Pediatrics were alarmed that an increase in thalidomide-related birth defects would occur (Hanson, 1997).

CONCEPT 5.3

Many over-the-counter and prescription medications have the potential to impair fetal development.

The unborn child of a diabetic mother-to-be is particularly vulnerable. The severity of the disease and whether the mother is insulin-dependent has a great deal to do with possible problems. Prior to the development of insulin, diabetic women did not have children. After insulin became available (about 1922) more diabetic women were able to give birth. However, the prenatal mortality rate was over 50 percent, and many of the children who survived had serious congenital deformities. Today, with careful management of the diabetes, use of special tests to monitor fetal well-being, and excellent medical care, the fetal mortality rate has

TABLE 5.6 Common Drugs for Medical Conditions During Pregnancy and the Possible Effects on the Unborn Child

Maternal Condition	Drug	Possible Effects
Hypertension	Resperine	Choking, gasping, nasal congestion at birth
Thyroid	Thiouracile Iodides Radioactive iodine	Thyroid abnormalities in child: cretinism (hypothyroidism)
Diabetes	Insulin	Excessive birth weight, prematurity, heart defects, jaundice, low blood sugar, convulsions, mental and physical retardation, deformities
Menstrual abnormality	Progesterone	Gross deformities, masculinization of female organs
Allergy or cold	Antihistamines	Deformities (in animal studies)
Epilepsy	Seizure control drugs	Cleft palate and other malformations

been sharply reduced (American Diabetes Association, 2000). Approximately one in every 100 women of childbearing age has diabetes prior to becoming pregnant with another 2 to 5 percent developing diabetes during pregnancy. It is critical in both cases to monitor blood sugar levels. Poorly controlled diabetes can result in serious birth problems such as heart defects and neural tube defects (NTD—birth defect of the brain or spinal cord). They also have an increased risk of miscarriage and stillbirth.

Table 5.6 summarizes some common medical conditions, treatments, and possible effects on the fetus.

CONCEPT 5.4

The use of illicit drugs by the expectant mother may cause devastating damage to her unborn child.

Despite decades of educational efforts by government and social service agencies, the use of **illicit drugs** by women of childbearing age is alarmingly high. It is estimated that over 5 percent of infants born each year in the United States were delivered

from mothers who had used illicit drugs sometime during their pregnancies (National Institute on Drug Abuse, 1995). The use of opiates (opium, heroin), amphetamines (speed), lysergic acid diethylamide (LSD), and cannabis (hashish, marijuana) is of great concern to those interested in the well-being of unborn children. Pregnant drug users are at an increased risk for miscarriages and stillbirths while their newborn babies have higher incidents of low birth weight and smaller head sizes than those born to nondrug users.

The use of cocaine by pregnant women has received a great deal of attention due to its triple properties of being addictive, toxic, and teratogenic. In teratogenic effects, research data as well as clinical observation clearly indicate that cocaine-exposed infants are at risk of increased mortality, morbidity, and problems in development and long-term behavior. Such problems include low birth weight, withdrawal symptoms, hypertension, mental disabilities, cerebral palsy, and malformation of the urinary tract (March of Dimes, 1999a). As prenatally exposed children grow older, they have been shown to have deficits in both gross and fine motor development, in particular balance and eye-hand coordination (Arendt et al., 1999).

Table 5.7 provides an overview of the possible effects of some mind-altering drugs on the newborn child.

TABLE 5.7	Possible Effects of Illicit Drugs on Development of the Unborn Child
Drug	**Possible Effects**

Heroin and morphine	Irritable. Sleeps poorly. High-pitched cry
	Vomiting and diarrhea
	Marked physiological withdrawal symptoms
	Decreased oxygen in the blood tissues
	Hepatitis from unclean needle
	Susceptible to infection
	Complications:
	  1. Toxemia
	  2. Breech birth
	  3. Prematurity
	  4. Small for date of birth
	  5. Premature separation of the placenta
	Complications if not treated:
	  1. Dehydration
	  2. Respiratory distress
	  3. Shock
	  4. Coma
	  5. Death

Amphetamines and barbiturates	Miscarriage Birth defects
Tranquilizers	Such drugs as Sominex,® Nytol,® Sleep-Eze,® and Compoz® contain two antihistamines that have produced congenital deformities in animals
LSD (lysergic acid diethylamide)	May cause chromosome damage Sometimes contaminated with quinine or other materials that may harm the unborn child. A few surveys have found a higher incidence of congenital defects in children of LSD users
Cocaine	Physiological withdrawal Hypertension Poor thermal regulation Low birth weight Learning disabilities Behavioral problems Increased mortality

Alcohol and Tobacco

Although alcohol and tobacco are considered by many to be mind- or mood-altering drugs, we are treating them separately because of the frequency of their use and to amplify their potential hazards. It has been variously reported that there are more than 1 million alcoholics of childbearing age. The fetus is affected twice as fast as the mother by her alcohol consumption and at the same level of concentration. At one time, the widespread myth that the fetus takes what it needs from its mother and is uninfluenced by her consumption of foods and beverages caused expectant mothers to be unconcerned about their alcohol consumption. The potential dangers of alcohol to the unborn child were recognized, however, as far back as the Greek era, when newly married couples were forbidden to consume alcohol in order to prevent conception while intoxicated.

In the 1890s William Sullivan, a physician at a Liverpool, England, prison for women, was the first to carefully document the effects of chronic alcoholism on the offspring of 120 alcoholic inmates. This early study revealed a significantly greater mortality rate among the 600 offspring and a much higher number of developmental difficulties in the infants (Rosett and Sander, 1979). Further research into the effects of maternal alcoholism lagged in the United States and Great Britain after 1920, following the enactment of Prohibition, although some research continued in France and Germany. It was not until 1970 that the "discovery" and labeling of **fetal alcohol syndrome** (FAS) took place (Witti, 1978).

CONCEPT 5.5

Although completely preventable, alcohol use is a leading cause of birth defects in the United States.

Alcohol consumption by an expectant mother is one of the most common causes of birth defects. Each year in the United States approximately 50,000 infants are born with some degree of alcohol-related damage with somewhere between 2,000 and 12,000 born with fetal alcohol syndrome (March of Dimes, 1999b). Fetal alcohol syndrome, and its less dramatic counterpart fetal alcohol effects (FAE), are preventable birth defects. Up to 40 percent of infants born to mothers who are chronic alcohol consumers, considered alcoholic, or who go on drinking binges will have fully expressed FAS. Children with FAS are born with mental retardation and marked physical defects. As they age, deficits in a number of psychomotor characteristics are observed as well (Larroque et al., 1995). On the other hand, children with FAE are often at additional risk because they appear to be normal and frequently do not receive the attention

TABLE 5.8	Characteristics of Fetal Alcohol Syndrome
Growth	Growth failure before birth
	Growth failure after birth
	Small head circumference
	Small in length compared to weight
Eyes	Lesions in the eyelids
	Fold of skin in corner of the eye
	Perceptual problems
	Narrow eyes
Face	Flat midface
	Low nasal bridge
	Short, upturned nose
	Minor outer ear deformity
	Underdevelopment of jaw
	Thin upper lip
Other	Heart defects
	Hip dislocation
	Skeletal defects
	Decrease in joint mobility
	Motor development delay
	Abnormal creases in the palm of the hand
	Female genital defects
Behavior	Jittery
	Hyperactive
	Poor coordination
	Poor sucking
	Irregular sleeping
	Self-stimulator
Intelligence	Mental retardation borderline to moderate

they need during the crucial early years to help them reach their full potential. Table 5.8 summarizes some of the potential characteristics of FAS.

Alcohol in the mother's blood passes directly through the placenta to the fetus. The fetus does not have any ethanol-oxidizing or alcohol dehydrogenasic abilities; therefore, the alcohol is fed directly into its system. Evidence is unclear on the exact amounts of alcohol harmful to the fetus and on the critical periods during which it should be avoided. However, a review of the research on fetal alcohol syndrome clearly reveals that consumption of large quantities of alcohol is likely to result in central nervous system damage, growth and mental retardation, and distinct facial abnormalities, while moderate to small doses of alcohol may have similar results. Such results have led some of the premiere health advocacy groups such as the March of Dimes (1999b) and the American Academy of Pediatrics (2000) to recommend abstinence from all alcohol consumption for women who are pregnant or who are planning a pregnancy.

CONCEPT 5.6

Smoking by the expectant mother has been shown to have negative effects on fetal development.

It has been estimated that about 13 percent of pregnant women smoke during their pregnancy. It is further estimated that 12 percent of infants born to mothers who smoked while pregnant were classified as low birth weight. Smoking has been implicated in numerous studies as a cause of low birth weight in infants and increased risk of preterm delivery (March of Dimes, 2000a). Additional conditions such as cleft lip and/or palate and mental retardation have been associated with maternal smoking as well (Drews et al., 1996). Postnatal exposure to environmental tobacco smoke has also been associated with lower respiratory illness, serious infectious diseases, asthma, and sudden infant death syndrome (American Academy of Pediatrics, 1997). The cessation of smoking by women who are planning a pregnancy or who are pregnant results in significantly positive health benefits for both the baby and the mother.

HEREDITARY FACTORS

Until relatively recently the study of heredity through the science of genetics was only a matter of theory and speculation. Today, however, with the initiation of the Human Genome Project in 1990, funded by the U.S. Department of Energy and the National Institutes of Health, our knowledge of genetics and heredity has increased dramatically. It is impossible to discuss it in detail within the confines of this chapter, so we will concern ourselves with the potential impact of various hereditary factors on later development.

The union of a sperm with an egg begins the process of development. The sperm carries 23 chromosomes, which contain all of the father's hereditary material. The egg also contains 23 chromosomes, the mother's contribution to the child's heredity. The new embryo, therefore, contains a total of 46 chromosomes (23 pairs). Each chromosome, by the process of cell division (*mitosis*), has a replica in every cell of the body. Genes are found on each chromosome. It has been estimated that each chromosome may contain up to 20,000 genes. The genes determine the vast variety of individual characteristics such as gender, hair and eye color, body size, and physical structure.

CONCEPT 5.7

The genetic inheritance of the fetus will control the upper and the lower limits of its functioning.

Under most conditions the chromosomes and genes remain unaltered throughout the prenatal period. (There is growing speculation that certain chemical substances may contribute to chromosomal damage after conception.) However, a variety of genetic factors prior to conception have been shown to alter the normal process of development.

Chromosome-Based Disorders

It has been estimated that 15 to 50 percent of pregnancies are terminated by spontaneous abortion, usually during the first trimester. Most of these spontaneous abortions are the result of chromosomal abnormalities (Malina and Bouchard, 1991; Santrock, 2001). Most chromosome variations are so potent that they are rarely seen in surviving newborns, but 1 percent of live infants show evidence of chromosomal damage.

Probably the most common chromosomal alteration is that of **Down syndrome.** The most common type of Down syndrome is the result of an error in which 47 chromosomes are present rather than the standard 46. This cause of Down syndrome is called trisomy 21 because of the presence of three #21 chromosomes. Trisomy 21 accounts for the majority of Down syndrome cases and occurs in approximately 1 in 800 to 1,000 births (March of Dimes, 2000). The rate of incidence seems to be age-related and shows dramatic increases as women give birth at older ages. According to the National Down Syndrome Society (2001) a pregnant mother who is 35 years of age has a 1 in 400 chance of conceiving a child with Down syndrome. This chance increases gradually until age 40 where she has a 1 in 110 chance. At age 45 the incidence becomes approximately 1 in 35.

Children with Down syndrome are often born prematurely. Their rate of growth is slower than normal, often resulting in shorter stature. The nose, chin, and ears tend to be small; the teeth are poorly developed; and the eyesight is weak. Poor balance, hypotonus, short arms and legs, and nonelastic skin are other characteristics of the child with Down syndrome. Cardiovascular defects resulting in frequent respiratory ailments are common, along with limited intellectual functioning. Language and conceptualization skills are generally poor. Motor development appears to proceed in sequence as in the normal infant, but at a substantially slower rate.

The major findings of studies describing the motor development of infants with Down syndrome include: (1) delays in the emergence and inhibition of primitive and postural reflexes, (2) hypotonia and hyperflexia, and (3) substantial delays in the attainment of motor milestones. Elementary school–aged children with Down syndrome display levels of motor development consistently behind their nondisabled peers. Furthermore, they tend to fall farther and farther behind as they grow older (Henderson, 1985; Block, 1991).

This, however, is linked more closely to insufficient environmental stimulation than to identifiable biological factors. Early identification and intervention programs appear to be successful in improving the motor functioning of infants and young children with Down syndrome (Ulrich, 1997, 1998). Activities to improve reflexive behavior and to facilitate the acquisition of rudimentary movement skills such as independent sitting, standing, and walking should be provided during the crucial early years. As children with the condition mature, additional opportunities and assistance with fundamental movement skill development should be provided (Gallahue, 1993, 2000). Developmentally appropriate activities should serve as the basis for teaching fundamental movement skills. If and when appropriate, basic sport skills may be introduced.

Chromosome-linked disorders other than Down syndrome sometimes occur. Fortunately, conditions such as Patau's syndrome and Edward's syndrome are rare. Little is known about them other than that they are also associated with an extra chromosome and that they result in severe deformities, retardation, and early mortality.

CONCEPT 5.8

Chromosome-based and gene-linked abnormalities will have an impact, ranging from mild to severe to catastrophic, on later development.

Gene-Based Disorders

Genetic defects vary widely in their consequences. The severity of the defect depends on whether the mutant gene is on an autosomal or on a sex-linked chromosome and whether it is on a single gene or also on its mate. Delay and retardation in motor and cognitive functioning are not usually present in autosomal dominant mutations. Autosomal recessive mutations, however, are often associated with mental retardation and problems in motor development. Among the more common autosomal mutations that affect later motor development are talipes, sickle cell disease, Tay-Sachs disease, phenylketonuria (PKU), and spina bifida.

Talipes, often referred to as clubfoot, is one of the most common of all birth defects and historically has been one of the major orthopedic problems of children. About 1 in 700 babies born in the United States each year has a severe form of talipes,

and boys are twice as likely to have this condition as girls (March of Dimes, 1997). There are three major forms of talipes: equinovarus, calcaneal valgus, and metatarsus varus (figure 5.2). With *equinovarus* the foot is twisted inward and downward. The Achilles tendon is generally very tight, making it impossible to bring the foot into normal alignment. *Calcaneal valgus* is the most common

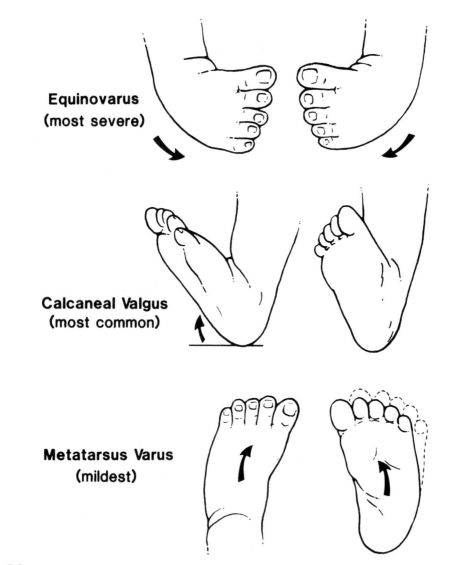

Equinovarus (most severe)

Calcaneal Valgus (most common)

Metatarsus Varus (mildest)

Figure 5.2
Three forms of talipes.

form of talipes. The foot is sharply angled at the heel, with the foot pointing up and outward. This condition is less severe than equinovarus and easier to correct. *Metatarsus varus* is the mildest form of talipes. The front part of the foot is turned inward and is often not diagnosed until the baby is a few months old. With all forms of talipes, early, persistent treatment will maximize the chances for normal lives. Left untreated until too late in childhood, talipes will be a major limiting factor in normal upright locomotion.

Sickle cell disease is an inherited blood disease. It is a relatively common gene-based disorder occurring in approximately 1 in every 400 African Americans. It can also occur in people of Hispanic, Arabian, Greek, Italian, and southern Asian ancestry. One in 12 blacks carry the sickle cell gene, and there is a 1-in-4 chance that a child of a gene carrier will develop the disease (March of Dimes, 1999). The effects of the disease vary greatly from person to person—anemia, pain, damage to vital organs, and death in childhood or early adulthood are possible. The growth and motor development of individuals with sickle cell disease are often impaired. Also, patients tend to tire easily and are frequently short of breath. The sickle cell trait or disease can be easily detected through a blood test called hemoglobin electrophoresis. A prenatal test to determine whether the fetus will carry the trait, be normal, or will develop the disease is also available.

Tay-Sachs disease is a gene-based disorder typical of descendants of Central and Eastern European Jews known as Ashkenazim. Nearly 1 out of every 30 American Jews carries the Tay-Sachs gene. Another group with similar risk is non-Jewish individuals of French-Canadian ancestry, including the Cajun population in Louisiana (March of Dimes, 2000b). If both parents carry the Tay-Sachs gene, there is a 1-in-4 chance that any of their children will develop Tay-Sachs disease or become carriers. If only one parent carries the gene, none of their children can have the disease, but the chance of becoming a carrier is 1 in 2. There is no known cure for Tay-Sachs disease, and it is always fatal. It first appears in infancy with the baby losing

motor control. Blindness and paralysis follow, with death by age 5. Tay-Sachs disease can be diagnosed through amniocentesis prior to birth. A simple blood test prior to pregnancy will determine if one is a carrier.

Phenylketonuria (PKU) is the only gene-based disorder completely treatable if detected early enough. PKU, a metabolic disorder, is the result of a recessive gene that inhibits production of phenylalanine hydroxylase, necessary to convert the amino acid phenylalanine to tyrosine. Without this enzyme the child is unable to digest many foods, including dairy products. Identification is done through a routine blood test at birth, required in every state in the United States. Treatment consists of following a scientifically controlled diet that eliminates foods containing phenylalanine. The can of diet cola you may consume periodically probably contains phenylalanine with a warning on the label. Left untreated PKU will result in severe mental retardation. However, if PKU is detected (about one week after birth), the devastating results can be entirely avoided with proper dietary precautions. This dietary control should be maintained throughout the individual's life (American Academy of Pediatrics, 1996).

Spina bifida is a birth defect of the spinal column, caused by a weakened or absent formation of the vertebral arch. According to the March of Dimes Birth Defects Foundation (1999), about 1 in every 2,000 babies born each year has spina bifida ("open spine"). Spina bifida follows no particular law of inheritance, although it does appear to run in certain families. Families with one affected child have about a 1-in-40 chance of having a second with spina bifida. Families with two affected children have about a 1-in-20 chance of having a third child with the condition. Spina bifida may take three forms. The first may be so slight that only an X ray of the spinal column will detect its presence. This form rarely bothers the child. In the second form, a lump or cyst that contains the spinal cord pokes through the open part of the spine. The lump may be surgically removed, permitting the baby to grow normally. In the third and most severe form of spina bifida, the cyst holds deeper

TABLE 5.9	Common Gene-Based Birth Defects
Genetic Defect	**Condition**
Talipes (Clubfoot)	Equinovarus Calcaneal Valgus Metatarsus Varus
Sickle Cell Disease	Anemia, pain, damage to vital organs, slow growth and motor development, possible death
Tay-Sachs Disease	Loss of motor control, blindness, paralysis, certain death
Phenylketonuria (PKU)	Severe mental retardation
Spina Bifida	Paralysis in legs, poor bladder and bowel control

nerve roots of the spinal cord. Little or no skin protects the lump and spinal fluid may leak out. The site of this cyst is generally in the lower spine, resulting in paralysis and loss of sensation to the legs, a permanent condition. Spina bifida can be detected during pregnancy through a combination of blood screening, ultrasound, and amniocentesis techniques. As mentioned earlier in this chapter, recent findings have indicated that the consumption of recommended amounts of folic acid by females of childbearing age can greatly reduce the incidence of spina bifida. It is estimated that through the addition of this supplement the risk of spina bifida and other neural tube defects can be reduced by 50 percent (American Academy of Pediatrics, 1999).

Table 5.9 summarizes a variety of gene-based birth defects.

ENVIRONMENTAL FACTORS

For sometime the effects of the general environment on prenatal development have attracted attention. The influence of radiation and chemical pollutants are areas of particular concern to parents of unborn children.

Radiation

The environment's influence on development is evident in the effects of high doses of radiation. Radiation dosage is measured in units called *rads*. An exposure to the developing fetus of more than 25 rads would be considered a high dosage. The fetus is most vulnerable during the first trimester of pregnancy. Excessive radiation has been implicated in *microcephaly* (small head and brain) and mental retardation. Therefore, exposure to X rays early in pregnancy, especially repeated X rays of the pelvic region, may put the developing fetus at risk. Radiation prior to pregnancy is also an area of concern. A few studies have suggested a relationship between ovarian radiation and chromosomal defects and between the buildup of rads over the years and genetic damage.

CONCEPT 5.9

A variety of environmental factors have been shown to affect later development of the fetus.

Chemical Pollutants

It is difficult to establish a direct causal link between **chemical pollutants,** the pregnant mother, and later developmental abnormalities in her offspring. A number of other variables may account for, or interact with, chemical pollutants to cause birth defects. Lead and mercury, however, have been conclusively linked to birth defects in humans

(March of Dimes, 1999; American Academy of Pediatrics, 1998). Additional substances shown to have an adverse effect on a developing fetus include PCB and high levels of vitamin A.

MEDICAL PROBLEMS

The causes and effects of developmental difficulties in the offspring of mothers with various sexually transmitted diseases, infections, hormonal and chemical imbalances, Rh incompatibility, and severe stress are continually being investigated. These conditions play a significant role in placing the unborn child at risk.

CONCEPT 5.10

A number of maternal medical conditions may contribute to developmental difficulties in offspring.

Sexually Transmitted Diseases

Over the last two decades there has been a growing awareness and concern over a variety of **sexually transmitted diseases (STDs)**. The ravages of genital herpes, chlamydia, gonorrhea, syphilis, and HIV/AIDS (human immunodeficiency virus/ acquired immunodeficiency syndrome) are a direct threat to the unborn child. A mother's STD can be passed on to her child before birth, during delivery, or through her breast milk. STDs such as syphilis cross the placenta and infect the baby in utero. Gonorrhea, chlamydia, and genital herpes can be transmitted to the newborn baby at the time of delivery as the infant passes through the birth canal. HIV infection can be transmitted in utero, during the delivery, and from breast feeding. The consequences of STDs can be devastating to both mother and child. It is imperative that women planning a pregnancy or who are already pregnant be tested for STDs by a health care professional.

Genital herpes has become a serious health problem with an estimated 45 million sufferers in the United States (March of Dimes, 1999). A pregnant woman with an active case of genital herpes may infect her baby, resulting in permanent brain damage or death. The baby may be protected through a cesarean delivery.

Chlamydia is a highly contagious sexually transmitted disease that has been significantly underreported. In 1999, only about 600,000 cases were reported, but it is estimated that around 3 million U.S. citizens have contracted the disease (Centers for Disease Control and Prevention, 1999). Although curable with certain antibiotics, it is difficult to diagnose. If left untreated, chlamydia may result in sterility or premature births and stillbirths as well as infant pneumonia, eye infections, and blindness.

Gonorrhea is a common sexually transmitted disease contracted by approximately 650,000 people in the United States each year (Centers for Disease Control and Prevention, 2000). Although curable with antibiotics, some strains of the bacteria have become resistant to treatment. Gonorrhea may result in ectopic pregnancies and eye damage to the newborn.

Maternal syphilis is easily cured with antibiotics if detected in the early stage. The newborn with congenital syphilis is likely to be stillborn or display severe illnesses. The long-term effects of maternal syphilis are still unclear, but preliminary data indicate a greater incidence of prematurity and later motor, sensory, and cognitive disabilities.

HIV/AIDS is the newest and most deadly of the various sexually transmitted diseases. HIV is the virus that causes AIDS. A person with AIDS cannot resist other diseases and is at a greater risk for infections, cancer, and other serious problems that are life-threatening or fatal. HIV is transmitted through sexual contact, contaminated needles, and transfusions. Mothers with HIV/AIDS are at risk of transmitting the virus during pregnancy, childbirth, or breast feeding. This maternal-child transmission is referred to as *perinatal HIV infection*. It is estimated that the majority of the approximately 15,000 children in the United States

TABLE 5.10   Sexually Transmitted Diseases and Their Possible Effects

Sexually Transmitted Disease	Possible Effects on the Newborn Child
Acquired Immunodeficiency Syndrome (AIDS)	Fever, weight loss, lethargy, diarrhea, pneumonia, death
Chlamydia	Prematurity, stillbirths, pneumonia, eye infections, blindness
Genital Herpes	Brain damage, death
Gonorrhea	Ectopic pregnancies, eye damage
Syphilis	Severe illnesses, nervous system damage, death

(under 13 years of age) who have HIV contracted the disease at birth (March of Dimes, 1999e).

Table 5.10 summarizes the possible effects of sexually transmitted diseases.

Maternal Infections

Perhaps the most significant diseases contracted by the mother that adversely affect her fetus are cytomegalovirus (CMV) and rubella contracted during the first trimester of pregnancy. Both of these diseases pass through the placenta to the fetus and can have serious debilitating effects.

CMV is a common infectious cause of birth defects, including blindness, deafness, and mental retardation. Little is known about this virus and its effects. It is still unclear whether the virus is introduced into the fetus by a primary infection to the mother during pregnancy or whether it may already be present genetically but in latent form. About 4 percent of pregnant women secrete the virus, but 95 percent of infected infants are asymptomatic. The remaining 5 percent will suffer a range of developmental difficulties ranging from mild to severe motor retardation in the form of speech and problems in gross and fine motor coordination.

Rubella, sometimes called the "three-day measles," is caused by a mild, contagious virus. It is not the same as regular measles, called rubeola. Vaccination against rubella has been possible since 1969 and has greatly reduced the incidence of birth

defects due to this virus, to the point that no cases were reported in 1994 (figure 5.3). However, those who received the vaccine during the late 1960s and early 1970s need to be retested for immunity, because not all vaccines were found to be lifelong. Vaccination should occur during childhood and not during pregnancy. A blood test called a "rubella titer" is available to determine whether a person has had rubella or is immune. The child born of a mother who has had rubella during the first trimester of pregnancy is likely to be deaf, blind, or mentally retarded due to interference with sensory and/or cognitive development during the embryonic or early fetal period.

Hormonal and Chemical Imbalances

An inadequate hormonal or chemical environment in the thyroid patient can result in congenital hypothyroidism and cretinism in the infant due to a lack of thyroxine in the mother's blood during the early months of pregnancy. Diabetes in the expectant mother is a chronic chemical imbalance that may adversely affect a child's later development. The inadequate production of insulin prevents the proper metabolizing of sugar and other carbohydrates. Untreated diabetes can result in mental retardation, circulatory and respiratory problems in the infant, or even death. Many women are diabetic only during pregnancy. As a result it is prudent for all expectant mothers to be regularly checked.

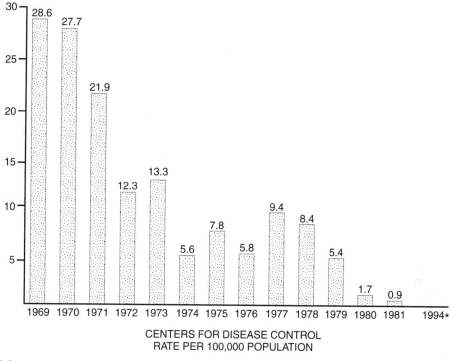

Figure 5.3

Incidence of infectious rubella in the United States.

*1994 = zero cases

Source: Data from Centers for Disease Control and Prevention, U.S. Department of Health and Human Services.

Rh Incompatibility

Rh incompatibility results from the incompatibility of blood types between mother and child. Although the bloodstream of the infant and that of the mother have no direct link, some seepage of blood from the fetus to the mother may occur during the later stages of pregnancy. If an expectant Rh negative mother is carrying her first Rh positive child, this seepage will cause the mother to produce antibodies in her blood. The production of antibodies generally has no effect on the first child. The time lag between the first and subsequent children, however, provides ample opportunity for the production of antibodies in the mother. These antibodies may have a devastating effect on future pregnancies by destroying the fetal red corpuscles of Rh positive babies.

Erythroblastosis fetalis is the name given to this condition, characterized by anemia and jaundice. Rh incompatibility occurs only in cases where the father is Rh positive and the mother is Rh negative. Routine blood tests and a *rhogam* injection immediately after birth of the first child will prevent the formation of antibodies. Rhogam is the gamma globulin component of blood obtained from an Rh negative person previously sensitized to the Rh factor. The rhogam neutralizes the Rh factor in the mother and prevents the buildup of antibodies. A rhogam injection must be given with each Rh positive pregnancy.

Maternal Emotional Stress

The effects of severe prolonged maternal emotional stress on the unborn child are another concern.

Severe stress factors such as death of a loved one and marital problems have been associated with complications during pregnancy and fetal abnormalities. Although there is no direct link between the nervous system of the mother and the fetus, the mother's emotional state may influence development. Because the nervous system and the endocrine system communicate through the blood, the emotional trauma experienced by the mother is transferred from her cerebral cortex to the thalamus and hypothalamus. The autonomic nervous system acts on the endocrine system, which empties into the bloodstream. The mother's bloodstream then transports the endocrine secretions to the placenta through which some are passed into the fetal bloodstream and finally to its nervous system. This hypothesis is speculative, but it is clear that prolonged maternal stress may have detrimental effects. Children born of emotionally stressed mothers tend to be vulnerable to a variety of illnesses and physical problems throughout life (March of Dimes, 1999).

Teenage Pregnancy

In the United States more than a half million girls give birth each year. Babies born to teen mothers have a much higher risk of serious health problems than do children born to a fully mature mother. Teenage mothers as a group are more likely to have children born small-for-date or young-for-date. Low-birth-weight babies are statistically more likely to suffer from a variety of developmental abnormalities, including mental retardation, immature organ systems, thermoregulatory difficulties, learning difficulties, respiratory problems, and death. Furthermore, the maternal death rate from complications in pregnancy is much higher among girls under age 15 who give birth than among older mothers.

Additional risk factors often found in teenage pregnancies include psychological stress, low socioeconomic status, inadequate parenting behaviors, maternal drug and alcohol abuse, and poor or nonexistent medical care. The complex risks involved in teenage pregnancies need further investigation so that appropriate intervention strategies may be devised.

Toxoplasmosis

In addition to the infections, diseases, and special conditions already discussed as high-risk considerations, expectant parents need to be aware of *toxoplasmosis* so that they can protect their unborn children against the offending protozoan. Toxoplasmosis is amazingly prevalent. It has been estimated that 1 in every 1,000 infants is infected (March of Dimes, 2000). Infected children, although often small-for-date at birth, may appear normal at birth and even into their 20s. But, the toxoplasma cysts may rupture at any time, releasing thousands of parasites that attack the eyes, heart, other internal organs, and central nervous system.

The natural reservoir of the *Toxoplasma gondii sporozoan* is the mouse, and most cats come in contact with mice. The spores passed in the feces of infected cats can be inhaled or ingested. The symptoms of infection in humans are similar to the flu, but many times there are no symptoms. Persons who have been infected carry antibodies against toxoplasmosis. However, the fetus does not have the ability to make such antibodies and takes the effects of the infection full force. About 10 percent of the 3,000 infants infected with toxoplasmosis each year are severely brain damaged and suffer a variety of sensory and motor disabilities.

Toxoplasmosis is a more prevalent health problem than either rubella or PKU, but its devastation to the unborn child has had little publicity. However, the parents of an unborn child can do some specific things to protect their child from this infection. All beef, pork, and lamb should be cooked until well done because the protozoan cysts exist in the muscle of meat. Because the toxoplasma organisms are transmitted through cat feces, it is wise to avoid contact with cats during pregnancy.

PRENATAL DIAGNOSIS AND TREATMENT

A variety of prenatal diagnostic procedures have become available and are frequently used to detect the presence of fetal developmental abnormalities. Among the most recognized diagnostic techniques are amniocentesis, chorionic villus sampling, ultrasound, and fetoscopy.

CONCEPT 5.11

Prenatal diagnostic techniques are valuable tools for determining the status of the developing fetus.

Amniocentesis is a technique whereby a hollow needle is inserted into the pregnant woman's abdomen. It is an almost painless procedure that sounds much worse than it feels. A small amount of amniotic fluid is withdrawn through the needle and analyzed. Fetal cells are contained within the amniotic fluid and can be analyzed to detect any form of chromosomal abnormality, nearly 100 metabolic disorders, and some structural defects.

Amniocentesis is generally performed between the sixteenth and eighteenth weeks of pregnancy. It can, however, be performed late in the pregnancy as a means of determining fetal maturity and the severity of Rh disease. Amniocentesis is an invasive procedure known to cause miscarriages in a small but significant number of cases. Therefore, it should only be used for specific medical purposes and not for determining gender or for routine examination of the developing fetus.

Chorionic villus sampling (CVS) is a similar procedure to amniocentesis but instead of amniotic fluid being removed and analyzed, chorionic villi fragments from the developing placenta are extracted. The primary advantage of CVS over amniocentesis is that laboratory results can be obtained much earlier in the pregnancy.

Ultrasound, which uses high-frequency sound waves, is another prenatal diagnostic technique to determine the size and structure of the fetus. It also provides visual information about the fetus's position in the womb. Ultrasound is used in conjunction with amniocentesis as a means of guiding the physician when inserting the needle through the abdomen and into the uterus.

Fetoscopy involves the insertion of a fine caliper scope into the uterus to observe fetal devel-opment. It is a procedure that initially offered promising benefits but due to the risk of spontaneous abortions, it is rarely used.

Additional methods of screening for prenatal conditions include *magnetic resonance imaging (MRI), fetal echocardiography,* and *maternal serum screening* (American Academy of Pediatrics, 1994).

Open fetal surgery represents a unique and amazing form of treating certain types of prenatal conditions. Although first performed in 1981 on an unborn baby to correct a urinary obstruction, it is a procedure that has been conducted numerous times since to correct birth defects in utero. Many have been performed for the condition spina bifida. The procedure involves surgically extracting the mother's uterus, which is opened to work on the unborn child. It can be risky due to blood loss, potential infections, and preterm labor and delivery, but has tremendous potential for the future.

VIGOROUS ACTIVITY DURING PREGNANCY

Fundamental societal changes regarding vigorous exercise and the continual quest for fitness have prompted important questions concerning vigorous physical activity during pregnancy. Among them are: How will maternal exercise affect fetal development? Will maternal exercise help or hinder delivery? Will maternal exercise influence infant development? Conclusive answers to each of these questions are still being determined, but a growing body of research has begun to shed some light on the topic.

A number of studies were conducted in the 1990s and summarized in various reviews (Bell and O'Neill, 1994; Clapp, 2000; Wolfe et al., 1994). It appears that there is strong support for exercise during pregnancy as long as the type, intensity, frequency, and duration of the exercise is monitored. Benefits for the mother include the maintenance or improvement of cardiovascular fitness, limited weight gain, lower fat retention, easier labor, and an improvement in a number of psychological and emotional factors. Benefits to the unborn baby include a decrease in fat and an improved stress tolerance. Long-term benefits for the child include leaner body composition during the early childhood years.

There are certainly some concerns regarding exercise during pregnancy when the mother has one or more conditions that place her pregnancy at high risk. Some of these conditions include persistent vaginal bleeding, incomplete cervix, ruptured membranes, and if the mother has experienced preterm labor in a previous pregnancy.

For pregnant women who are sedentary but have no medical contraindications, it is recommended that they participate in some daily physical activity such as walking, housework, or gardening for 30 minutes or several times a day in 10-minute bouts. Women who are expecting and exercised regularly prior to their pregnancy should be encouraged to maintain their prepregnancy activity level (Clapp, 2000; March of Dimes, 1997b).

CONCEPT 5.12

Mothers-to-be may continue to exercise throughout their pregnancies with the guidance of their physicians and careful self-monitoring.

BIRTH PROCESS FACTORS

The average length of intrauterine life is 279 days from the day of conception to the day of birth. Two-thirds of expectant mothers give birth within 279 days, plus or minus a two-week period. The beginning of labor is marked by the passage of blood and amniotic fluid from the ruptured amniotic sac through the vagina and the onset of labor pains. There are three distinguishable stages of labor. In the first stage the neck of the uterus (the cervix) dilates to about 4 centimeters in diameter. Dilation is responsible for labor pains and may last for only one or two hours or up to eighteen to twenty-four hours. Labor is generally longer with the first child (*primiparas*) than for subsequent children (*multiparas*). When the cervix reaches 2 centimeters, full labor begins. It is at this point that the amniotic sac breaks and the fluid flows out of the mother.

Complete dilation to about 10 centimeters marks the onset of the second stage of labor: the expulsion stage. During this stage the baby, through the continued increase in uterine pressure, is forced down the birth canal. This phase takes an average of ninety minutes for the first child and about half as long for subsequent children. The third stage of labor begins after the baby has emerged and continues until after the umbilical cord and placenta (afterbirth) have been delivered. During any stage of the birth process a number of obstetrical medications and obstetrical procedures may influence later development of the child.

CONCEPT 5.13

Obstetrical medications and birthing procedures have an impact on the later development of the child.

Obstetrical Medication

A controversial issue among obstetricians and infant researchers involves the effects of **obstetrical medication** commonly used during the birth process. Several years ago Brackbill (1979) argued that drugs given during childbirth will impair the newborn and its subsequent development because of the structural and functional immaturity of the infant's nervous system at birth and because of the rapid absorption rate across the placenta. Table 5.11 lists common types of predelivery, general, and local anesthetics used during delivery. These medications are used to initiate or augment labor (*oxytocics*), relieve pain (*analgesics*), and relieve anxiety (*sedatives*).

Earlier studies have indicated a relationship between drug use during labor and motor and cognitive development (Brackbill, 1970; Conway and Brackbill, 1970; Goldstein et al., 1976; Muller et al., 1971). Currently, an increase in the knowledge of drug dosage and the development and administration of new medication such as *prostaglandins* decreases the possibility of problems during delivery.

TABLE 5.11 Function of Common Types of Predelivery and Delivery Drugs

Predelivery Drugs	Delivery Drugs
Oxytocics (premedication agents)	*General Analgesics* (inhalants, intravenous injections)
Induce labor	Relieve fetal distress
Augment labor	Speed up delivery
Increase uterine tonus	Mother emotionally unsuited to remain awake
Sedatives (Demerol, meperidine)	Multiple births
Reduce anxiety	*Local Analgesics* (caudal, lumbar, spinal)
Reduce excitement	Pain relief
Slow down labor	Relaxation

Birth Entry

A variety of birth entry factors also have been shown to put the infant at risk. Among them are malpresentation, the use of forceps, and cesarean section. About 4 in every 100 babies are born buttocks first or feet first (*breech birth*) and 1 out of 100 are in a crosswise position (*transverse presentation*). Breech or transverse fetal presentations are found in one-third to one-half of infants delivered at less than 1,500 grams. These presentations can sometimes be altered by the attending physician or midwife. The danger in malpresentation, as with drug-assisted labor and umbilical cord difficulties, is anoxia. Anoxia is generally considered to be the major cause of perinatal death and has been implicated as the cause of mental retardation, learning disabilities, and cerebral palsy.

Forceps are occasionally used to withdraw the baby from the birth canal. Today, the use of forceps is limited largely to emergency situations, but they were used routinely in obstetrics until the 1940s. Forceps are now used to speed delivery when the mother is displaying uncontrollable pushing, when the infant has a weak heartbeat, when the umbilical cord emerges before the head and endangers the baby's oxygen supply, or when there is a premature separation of the placenta. Forceps play a vital role in obstetrics as a lifesaving device, but their overuse and misuse have had debilitating and lethal effects on both mothers and children.

From 1970 until 1990 the number of *cesarean* deliveries increased dramatically. Over the last decade, however, that number has experienced a slight but steady decline (figure 5.4). Some of the reasons for the initial increases in the procedure included the ability to plan the exact delivery date, avoidance of pain (a general anesthetic is usually given), the advent of newer incision techniques leaving a smaller and less noticeable scar, and the desire to spare the fetus any distress. A cesarean delivery, however, is a major operation and in the past was considered only in cases of malpresentation, fetal distress, and failed use of forceps. The decline in the procedure over recent years may be due to the recommendation by most obstetricians and medical societies that it be used only when there are extenuating circumstances.

CONCEPT 5.14

Both mother- and father-to-be have an obligation to their unborn child to ensure its optimal development by monitoring those factors over which they can exercise control.

The birth process is an important beginning in the three-way bonding among mother, infant, and father. Because of this, parents frequently choose the method in which they wish to introduce their offspring into the world. The Lamaze and the Leboyer methods of childbirth are two procedures from which prospective parents can choose. The Lamaze method centers on the mother and father. It uses

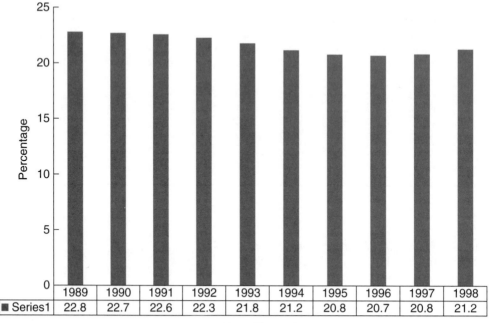

■ Series1	1989	1990	1991	1992	1993	1994	1995	1996	1997	1998
	22.8	22.7	22.6	22.3	21.8	21.2	20.8	20.7	20.8	21.2

Years/Percentage

Figure 5.4

Percentage of cesarean deliveries from 1989–1998.
Data from Ventura, S. J., Martin, J. A., Curtin, S. C., Mathews, T. J., and Park, M. M. (2000).
Births: Final data for 1998. National Vital Statistics Reports, Centers for Disease Control and Prevention, National Center for Health Statistics, 48, 13.

conscious relaxation techniques that incorporate rhythmical breathing to block the sensations of pain. It relies on the mother's complete knowledge of what to expect during labor and delivery (Lamaze, 1976). The Leboyer method focuses almost entirely on the infant. The aim is to simulate the conditions of the womb as closely as possible. Delivery occurs in a dimly lit room without loud noises. The baby is immediately immersed in a warm fluid solution and gradually, but gently, introduced into the world. Many hospitals have made dramatic changes in their delivery procedures. Birthing rooms, birthing chairs, and rooming-in are widely popular procedures that reflect greater concern for the health and comfort of both mother and child.

SUMMARY

This chapter discussed a wide variety of prenatal factors that impact on later development in general and motor development in particular. There is growing realization among many prospective parents that they can do something to reduce the chances of putting their offspring at risk. Many now understand that poor choices in what expectant mothers ingest in the way of nutrients, alcohol, tobacco, drugs, and medications can be devastating to unborn children. Many are now sensitive to the possible harmful effects of caffeine, certain food additives, overexposure to radiation, noxious chemicals, and obstetrical medications. As a result there has been a resurgence of interest in "natural" childbirth techniques, rooming-in, and home births and a return by many to a more responsible attitude about giving birth. More mothers are asserting their rights for drug-free pregnancies and are working knowledgeably with concerned obstetricians to produce the healthiest offspring possible.

The prenatal period is too important to be left to chance. An "intelligent" pregnancy and delivery, although not a guarantee, can do much to reduce the risk of problems for both mother and child.

CRITICAL READINGS

American Academy of Pediatric. (1999). Folic acid for the prevention of neural tube defects. Policy statement by the Committee on Genetics. *Pediatrics, 104,* 325–327.

The American College of Obstetricians and Gynecologists. (2000). *Planning Your Pregnancy and Birth.* 3rd ed. Washington DC: The American College of Obstetricians and Gynecologist.

Arendt, R., Angelopoulos, J., Salvator, A., & Singer, L. (1999). Motor development of cocaine-exposed children at age two years. *Pediatrics, 103,* 86–92.

Clapp, J. F. (2000). Exercise during pregnancy: A clinical update. *Clinical Sports Medicine, 19,* 273–286.

Santrock, J. W. (2001). *Child Development* (Chapter 4). 9th ed. St. Louis: McGraw-Hill.

WEB RESOURCES

American Academy of Pediatricians
www.aap.org

American College of Obstetricians and Gynecologists
www.acog.org

Centers for Disease Control and Prevention
www.cdc.gov

Human Genome Project
www.ornl.gov/hgmis

March of Dimes
www.modimes.org

Teratology Society
www.teratology.org

PRENATAL AND INFANT GROWTH

KEY TERMS

Zygote

Mitosis

Embryo

Ectoderm

Mesoderm

Endoderm

Congenital malformations

Fetus

CHAPTER COMPETENCIES

Upon completion of this chapter you should be able to:

- Discuss embryonic and fetal growth and biological maturation
- Describe and interpret the normal displacement and velocity graphs of infant growth
- Discuss proportional changes in segmental length from birth through childhood
- Speculate on prenatal periods critical to normal growth
- Describe the process of prenatal growth from conception to birth

> **KEY CONCEPT**
>
> The rate of growth from conception through infancy is unsurpassed throughout the rest of life.

This chapter focuses on the process of normal growth from conception through the period of infancy. It is important for the student of motor development to have a reference point from which to view the normal growth process. The approach taken here provides that reference point from the standpoint of the mythical "average" child. In other words, heights, weights, and other growth statistics are presented in averages. There may be considerable normal variation from these figures as a result of the interaction between biological and environmental processes.

PRENATAL GROWTH

Growth begins at the moment of conception and follows an orderly sequence throughout the prenatal period. Prechtl's (1986) studies of the motor development of the fetus demonstrated that prenatal movement and growth patterns are as predictable during the fetal period as they are throughout infancy. The uniting of a mature sperm and ovum marks the beginning of this process. The ovum is one of the largest cells in the female body. It is about 0.004 of an inch (.01 mm) in diameter and is barely visible to the naked eye. The sperm, on the other hand, is microscopic and one of the smallest cells in the male body. Fertilization occurs if one of the approximately 20 million sperm released from the male during intercourse meets and penetrates the ovum in the fallopian tube. Fertilization may also occur through an in vitro process. Once the sperm cell penetrates the outer membrane of the egg, fertilization occurs. Each parent contributes twenty-three chromosomes (barlike structures in cells that carry all of a person's genetic information). The two cell nuclei lie side by side for a few hours before they merge to form a **zygote** (the fertilized egg with forty-six chromosomes). It is at

this instant that one's genetic potential is determined. Realization of this potential will depend on many environmental as well as hereditary factors. The genetic inheritances of both mother and father are transferred to this single cell. The pattern for a variety of traits is now established, including eye and hair color, general body shape, and complexion.

During the germinal period, the zygote splits into two cells through a process called **mitosis.** The two cells form four cells, and the four cells form eight. Three days after conception the zygote has grown into thirty-two cells, and after four days it consists of about ninety cells. Because all cells have the same genetic arrangement except for sex cells, the division of cells is not simultaneous, and stages in early embryonic life have been observed in which there is an odd number of cells. After the first three or four days of mitotic cell division, the zygote travels down the fallopian tube to the uterus, where it attaches to the uterine wall. This implantation process marks the true onset of pregnancy, although the days of pregnancy are counted from the first day of the last menstrual bleeding. The ovum is normally fertilized within a day of ovulation, near the fourteenth day of the menstrual cycle. Therefore, during the first two weeks of what is considered pregnancy, the woman is not pregnant. Implantation generally occurs by the end of the first week after fertilization.

> **CONCEPT 6.1**
>
> The union of ovum and sperm marks the point of conception and the determination of one's genetic inheritance.

Zygotic Period (Conception–1st Week)

During the first week (period of the zygote), the fertilized egg remains practically unchanged in size. It lives off its yoke and receives little outside nourishment. By the end of the first week, the zygote is only a small round disk about 0.01 of an inch (2.5 mm) wide. The situation for the zygote is especially precarious during this time. Although the mother-to-be may not be aware that she is pregnant, her system will automatically attempt to slough off this foreign body, as it would any foreign matter. The expectant mother may continue to ingest a variety of chemical substances, drugs, alcohol, and tobacco that could prove damaging, if not lethal, to the zygote. Malina and Bouchard (1991) estimate that, for a variety of reasons, approximately 50 percent of fertilized eggs spontaneously abort during the first trimester. Although this statistic may appear alarmingly high, this process of spontaneous abortion helps to ensure that only the fittest of zygotes survive.

CONCEPT 6.2

Pregnancy does not begin until the zygote is implanted on the uterine wall.

Embryonic Period (2nd Week–2nd Month)

The differentiation of embryonic cells into layers marks the end of the period of the zygote and the beginning of the period of the **embryo.** By the end of the first month there is a definite formation of three layers of cells. The **ectoderm,** from which the sense organs and nervous system develop, begins to form. The **mesoderm** accounts for the formation of the muscular, skeletal, and circulatory systems. The **endoderm** eventually accounts for the formation of the digestive and glandular systems (table 6.1). Every part of the body develops from these three kinds of cells and is formed in rudimentary structure by the end of the embryonic period. Special cells form the *placenta*, through which nutritive substances will be carried and wastes removed. Another special layer of cells begins formation of the *amnion*, which will enclose the embryo except at the umbilical cord throughout the prenatal period.

The embryonic period is an especially important time in the formation of all of the body systems and, as such, is a highly sensitive period for

TABLE 6.1	Systems That Develop from Three Layers of Cells
Layer	**Systems**
Endoderm (inner layer)	Digestive system Respiratory system Glandular system
Mesoderm (middle layer)	Muscular system Skeletal system Circulatory system Reproductive system
Ectoderm (outer covering)	Central nervous system Sensory end-organs Peripheral nervous system Skin, hair, nails

susceptibility to **congenital malformations.** Congenital malformation refers to a condition with which the infant is born but does not refer to the specific defect. The risk of congenital malformations is greatest during the embryonic period. This period of rapid cell division is vulnerable to changes in the sequence, rate, and timing of events. A wide variety of environmental factors (see chapter 5 for a complete discussion) as well as the embryo's specific genetic composition determine its susceptibility to congenital malformations.

CONCEPT 6.3

The cell layers that will eventually form the various systems of the body are differentiated during the embryonic period.

By the end of the first month the embryo is about $\frac{1}{4}$ of an inch (6 mm) long and weighs about 1 ounce (28 g). It is crescent shaped, with small bumps on its sides (limb buds). It has a tail and tiny ridges along the neck. These gill-like ridges mark the beginning of a primitive mouth opening, heart, face, and throat. By the end of the first month the embryo has a rudimentary circulatory system, and the heart begins to beat. Growth accelerates toward

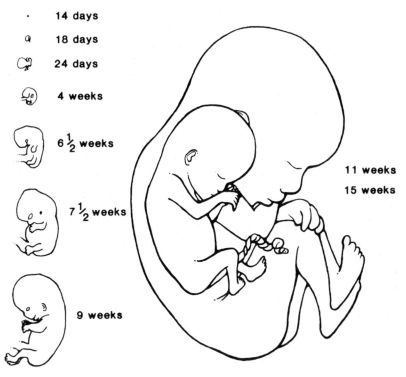

14 days
18 days
24 days
4 weeks
$6\frac{1}{2}$ weeks
$7\frac{1}{2}$ weeks
9 weeks
11 weeks
15 weeks

Figure 6.1
Embryos drawn to actual size.

the end of the first month. The organism grows about $\frac{1}{4}$ of an inch (6 mm) each week. By the end of the second month the embryo is about $1\frac{1}{2}$ inches (4 cm) long. The beginnings of the face, neck, fingers, and toes develop, and the embryo starts to take on a more human appearance. The limb buds lengthen, the muscles enlarge, and the sex organs begin to form. Brain development is rapid, and the head is large in comparison to the rest of the body. The embryo is now firmly implanted in the uterine wall and receiving nourishment through the placenta and the umbilical cord. This marks the end of the embryonic period and the beginning of the fetal period of prenatal life (figure 6.1).

Early Fetal Period (3rd–6th Month)

The period of the **fetus** begins around the third month and continues until delivery. Although no new anatomical features appear during this period,

this critical time for the fetus is easily influenced by a variety of factors over which it has no control. During the third month the fetus continues to grow rapidly. It is about 3 inches (8 cm) long by the end of the third month. Sexual differentiation continues, buds for the teeth emerge, the stomach and kidneys begin to function, and the vocal cords appear. By the beginning of the third month the first reflex actions are felt. The fetus opens and closes its mouth, swallows, clenches its fist, and can even reflexively suck its thumb. The growth rate during the fourth month is the most rapid for the fetus. It doubles in length to about 6 to 8 inches (15–20 cm) and weighs about 6 ounces (171 g). The hands are fully shaped, and the transparent cartilaginous skeleton begins to turn into bony tissue, starting in the middle of each skeletal bone and progressing toward the ends. The lower limbs, which lagged behind in their initial development, now catch up with the rest of the body.

By the beginning of the fifth month the fetus has reached half of its birth length but only 10 percent of its birth weight. The fetus is now sloughing off skin and respiratory cells and replacing them with new ones. Sloughed off cells remain in the amniotic fluid, providing a basis for amniocentesis (refer to chapter 5 for a brief discussion of this technique).

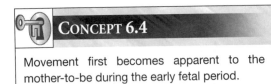

Concept 6.4

Movement first becomes apparent to the mother-to-be during the early fetal period.

At the beginning of the fifth month the fetus is about 8 to 10 inches (20–26 cm) long and weighs about $\frac{1}{2}$ pound (227 g). Skin, hair, and nails appear. The internal organs continue to grow and assume their proper anatomical positions. The entire body of the fetus is temporarily covered with a very fine soft hair called *lanugo*. The lanugo on the head and eyebrows becomes more marked by the end of the fifth month and is replaced by pigmented hair. The lanugo is generally shed before birth, although some may still remain. The larger size and cramped quarters of the rapidly developing fetus generally result in considerable reflexive movement during the fifth month.

By the sixth month the fetus is about 13 inches (33 cm) long and weighs about a pound (.45 kg). During this month the eyelids, which have been fused shut since the third month, reopen and are completed. The *vernix caseosa* forms from skin cells. It is a fatty secretion that protects the thin and delicate skin of the fetus. There is little in the way of subcutaneous fat at this point, and the fetus appears red and wrinkled and resembles an old and frail individual. An infant born prematurely during the sixth month has a very poor chance of survival even with the most sophisticated technology available. Although it can cry weakly and move about, it cannot perform the more basic functions of spontaneous breathing

and temperature regulation. By the end of the sixth month, the fetus weighs approximately 2 pounds (.9 kg) and is about 14 inches (36 cm) long. It is structurally complete but needs additional time for the various systems of the body to become functionally mature.

Later Fetal Period (7th–9th Month)

From the seventh month to term the fetus triples its weight (figure 6.2). A layer of adipose tissue begins to form under the skin and serves as both an insulator and food supplier. The lanugo hair is shed, along with much of the vernix fluid, and the nails often grow beyond the ends of the fingers and toes, necessitating an immediate manicure after birth to prevent scratching. During the seventh month the fetus is often quiet for long periods as if resting up for the "big event." The fetal brain becomes more active and assumes increasing control over the body systems. The majority of fetuses born at the end of the seventh month survive, although many require special handling during the early weeks after birth.

Concept 6.5

The last two months of fetal life are a time for filling out in preparation for birth.

During the eighth and ninth months the fetus becomes more active. The cramped quarters result in frequent changes in position, kicking, and thrusting of the legs and arms. The skin's red coloration disappears as fatty deposits become more evenly distributed in these last two months. The birth process is initiated by the placenta and contraction of the uterine musculature and not the fetus. Birth generally occurs after about 40 weeks of gestation. Normal variation in gestational age ranges from 38 to 42 weeks. At birth the normal-term infant is about 19 to 21 inches (48–53 cm) long and weighs between 6 and 8 pounds (3–4 kg).

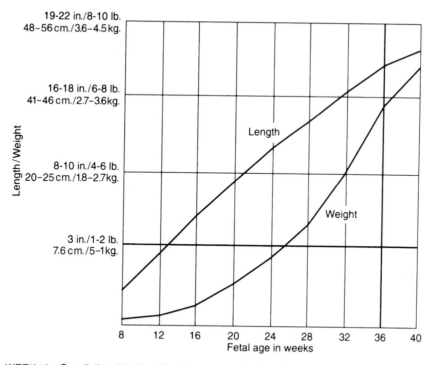

WEEK 12: Sex distinguishable. Eyelids sealed shut. Buds for deciduous teeth. Vocal cords. Digestive tract. Kidneys and liver secrete.

WEEK 16: Head about one third of total length. Nose plugged. Lips visible. Fine hair on body. Pads on hands and feet. Skin dark red, loose, wrinkled.

WEEK 20: Body axis straightens. Vernix caseosa covers skin as skin glands develop. Internal organs move toward mature positions.

WEEK 24-28: Eyes open. Taste buds present. If born, can breathe, cry, and live for a few hours without life support.

WEEK 28-40: Fat deposited. Rapid brain growth. Nails develop. Testes descend. Becomes viable.

Figure 6.2
Summary of development during the fetal period.

Table 6.2 includes a summary of development during the fetal period.

INFANT GROWTH

The growth process during the first two years after birth is truly amazing. The infant progresses from a tiny, helpless, horizontal, relatively sedentary creature to a considerably larger, autonomous, vertical, active child. The physical growth of the infant has a definite influence on its motor development. The size of the head, for example, will influence the child's developing balance abilities. Hand size will influence the mode of contact with different-size objects, and strength development will influence the onset of locomotion.

TABLE 6.2 **Highlights of Prenatal Growth and Development**

Age	Length	Weight	Major Events
Conception	1 cell	Less than 0.03 oz/1 g	Genetic inheritance determined
1 week	0.01 in./.25 mm	Less than 0.03 oz/1 g	Germinal period, period of rapid cell differentiation
2 weeks	0.05 in./1.3 mm	0.05 oz/1.5 g	Implantation in the uterus
1 month	0.25 in./6.4 mm	1 oz/29 g	Endoderm, mesoderm, and ectoderm formed; growth organized and differentiated
2 months	1.5 in./4 cm	2 oz/57 g	Rapid growth period, begins to take on human form; weak reflex activity
3 months	3 in./7.6 cm	3 oz/86 g	Sexual differentiation; stomach and kidney function; eyelids fuse shut
4 months	6–8 in./15–20 cm	6 oz/171 g	Rapid growth period, first reflexive movements felt; bone formation begins
5 months	8–10 in./20–25 cm	8 oz/228 g	Half birth height; internal organ completion; hair over entire body
6 months	13–15 in./33–38 cm	1–2 lb/0.45–0.9 kg	Eyes reopen; vernix caseosa forms; structurally complete but functionally immature
7 months	14–16 in./36–41 cm	2–4 lb/0.9–1.8 kg	Rapid weight gain, adipose tissue deposited
8 months	16–18 in./41–46 cm	4–6 lb/1.8–2.7 kg	Active period, fatty deposits distributed
9 months	19–21 in./48–53 cm	6–8 lb/2.7–3.6 kg	Uterine contractions, labor and delivery

CONCEPT 6.6

Increases in body proportions are uneven and influenced by the principles of proximodistal and cephalocaudal development.

Neonatal Period (Birth–4 Weeks)

The neonatal period is generally considered to comprise the first two to four weeks of postnatal life. The typical full-term newborn is 19 to 21 inches (48–53 cm) long, but the head accounts for fully one-fourth of that length. The proportionately large head size makes it difficult for the baby to gain and maintain equilibrium. The remaining body length is taken up with a 4-to-3 ratio of trunk to lower-limb length. The eyes are about half their adult size, and the body is about one-twentieth its eventual adult dimension (figure 6.3).

There is considerable normal variation in the weight of newborns, which may be attributed to a variety of environmental and hereditary factors. Birth weight is closely related to the socioeconomic and nutritional status of the mother. The birth weight of male infants is about 4 percent higher than that of females. Optimal growth requires proper nutrition, a positive state of health, and a nurturing environment. However, low-birth-weight babies and young-for-date babies tend to catch up to their age-mates if their deficiencies are not too severe and corrective intervention strategies have been implemented. J. M. Tanner (1978), a physician, has devoted much time to the study of the growth characteristics of the infant. He noted that an individual's ultimate growth potential seemed to

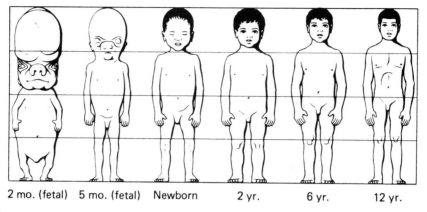

2 mo. (fetal)   5 mo. (fetal)   Newborn   2 yr.   6 yr.   12 yr.

Figure 6.3
Changes in body form and proportion before and after birth.

be determined early in life and could be amended under limited conditions if prematurity, illness, or malnutrition deflected the child from his or her normal growth curve. If an infant is moderately malnourished or ill, the growth rate will slow and then accelerate (or catch up) to the normal trajectory with an adequate diet or the termination of the illness. The rate will then slow down again. Under most conditions we see infants and children fitting into broadly determined ranges for height and weight, with little in the way of extremes at either end of the developmental continuum. Although the trajectory approximates the normal curve, low-birth-weight children usually remain somewhat smaller than full-term children throughout life.

Figures 6.4 through 6.7 provide graphic representations of changes in body length and weight of both boys and girls from birth to age 3. *Body length* is the term used when it is measured from a recumbent position, the commonly accepted means of measurement from birth to age 2 or 3. After that an erect standing measure is taken and referred to as *height*. They are the result of data collection that involved infants and children of various ethnic and racial backgrounds and reflect a combination of breast-fed and bottle-fed subjects. Previous growth curves represented a more narrow sample of the U.S. population. Thus, greater generalizability can be achieved through these most recent growth curves (National Center for Health Statistics, 2000).

Early Infancy (4 Weeks–1 Year)

During the child's first year there are rapid gains in both weight and length. In the first six months, growth is mainly a process of "filling out," with only slight changes in body proportions. In fact, the "newborns" often pictured in advertisements are actually 2 or 3 months old, displaying a chubby look rather than the wrinkled look of the actual newborn.

Birth weight is doubled by the fifth month, almost tripled by the end of the first year, and quadrupled by 30 months of age. Length increases to around 30 inches (76 cm) by the first birthday. After 6 months of age, the thoracic region is larger than the head in normal children and increases with age. Infants suffering from malnutrition will have a weight deficit but generally have head sizes larger than the thoracic regions.

CONCEPT 6.7

Early infancy is characterized by rapid growth in length and substantial increases in subcutaneous tissue.

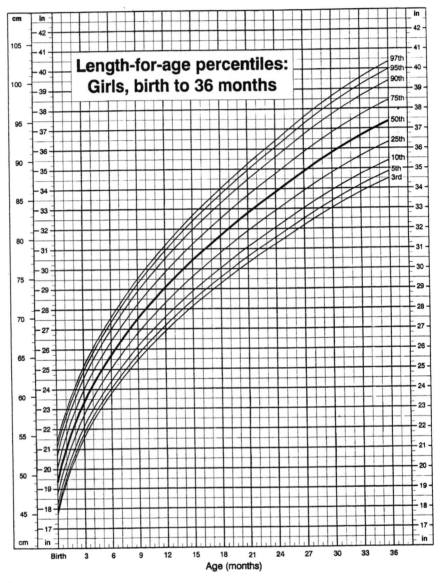

Length-for-age percentiles: Girls, birth to 36 months

Figure 6.4

U.S. female length-for-age percentiles: Girls, birth to 36 months.

Data from National Center for Health Statistics (2000).

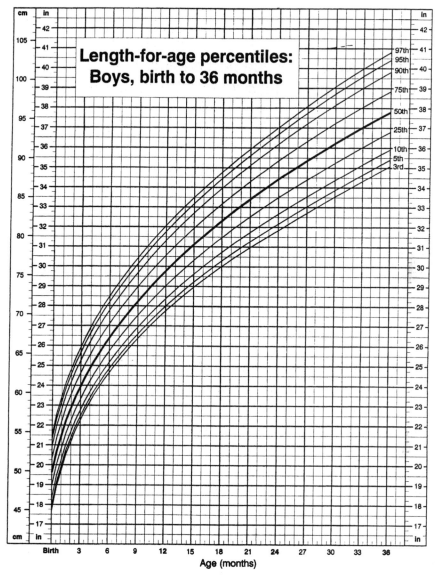

Length-for-age percentiles: Boys, birth to 36 months

Figure 6.5

U.S. male length-for-age percentiles: Boys, birth to 36 months.
Data from National Center for Health Statistics (2000).

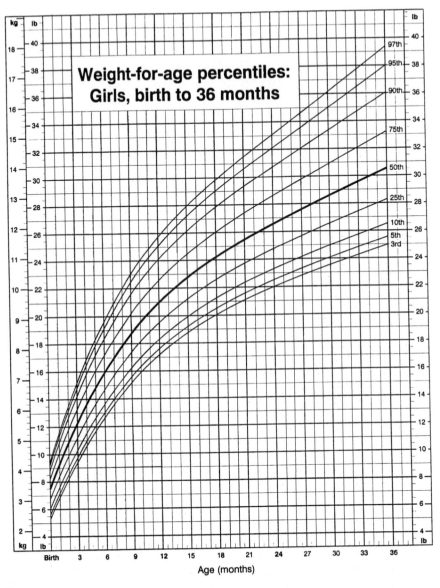

Weight-for-age percentiles:
Girls, birth to 36 months

Figure 6.6

U.S. female weight-for-age percentiles: Girls, birth to 36 months.
Data from National Center for Health Statistics (2000).

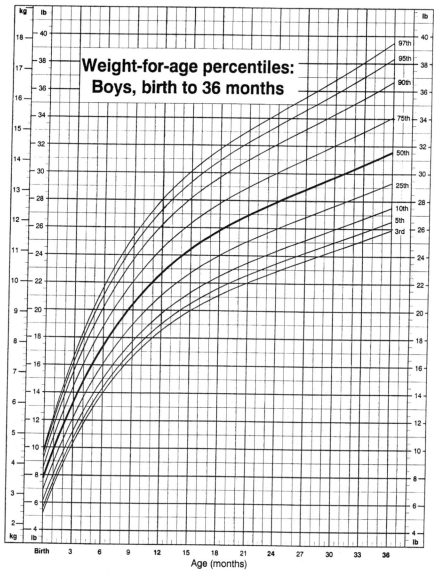

Weight-for-age percentiles:
Boys, birth to 36 months

Figure 6.7

U.S. male weight-for-age percentiles: Boys, birth to 36 months.
Data from National Center for Health Statistics (2000).

Later Infancy (1 Year–2 Years)

Physical growth during the second year continues at a rapid pace but at a slower rate than the first year. By age 2 the height of the average boy is about 35 inches (89 cm). Girls are about 34 inches (86 cm) tall and weigh about 26 pounds (12 kg), whereas boys average 28 pounds (12.7 kg). Height and weight have about a .60 correlation, showing a moderate degree of relationship between these two indices of physique. Because growth follows a directional trend (i.e., proximodistal and cephalocaudal), increase in size of the body parts is uneven. Upper arm growth precedes lower arm growth and hand growth. Therefore, from infancy to puberty the greatest amount of growth takes place in the distal portions of the limbs. Head growth slows from infancy onward, trunk growth proceeds at a moderate rate, limb growth is faster, and growth of the hands and feet is most rapid.

SUMMARY

Throughout the prenatal period a variety of environmental factors may influence and dramatically alter later development. The relationship between the unborn child and the mother is essentially one of parasite and host. The fetus uses the mother to supply all of its vital needs, including the intake of oxygen and nutrients and the expulsion of carbon dioxide and other wastes. These nutrients are "screened" by the mother in her bloodstream. The condition and content of the circulatory systems of both mother and fetus are crucial to future growth and development.

The normal process of prenatal and infant growth is crucial to the motor development of the child. The length, weight, physique, and maturational level of the child plays an important role in his or her acquisition and performance of rudimentary movement patterns. The prenatal period and infancy set the stage for what is to come in the development of the young child's repertoire of fundamental movement and physical abilities.

CRITICAL READINGS

Crawford, S. M. (1996). Anthropometry. In D. Docherty (Ed.), *Measurement in Pediatric Exercise Science.* Canadian Society for Exercise Physiology. Champaign, IL: Human Kinetics.

Malina, R. M., & Bouchard, C. (1991). *Growth, Maturation, and Physical Activity* (Chapter 3). Champaign, IL: Human Kinetics.

Pařízková, J. (1996). *Nutrition, Physical Activity, and Health in Early Life* (Chapter 1). Boca Raton, FL: CRC Press.

Rowland, T. W. (1996). *Developmental Exercise Physiology* (Chapter 1). Champaign, IL: Human Kinetics.

Santrock, J. W. (2001). *Child Development* (Chapter 5). 9th ed. St. Louis: McGraw-Hill.

WEB RESOURCES

American Academy of Pediatrics
www.aap.org

Centers for Disease Control and Prevention
www.cdc.gov

World Health Organization: Global database on child growth and malnutrition
www.who.int/nutgrowthdb

CHAPTER

7

INFANT REFLEXES AND RHYTHMICAL STEREOTYPIES

KEY TERMS

Primitive survival reflexes
Primitive postural reflexes
Encoding stage
Decoding stage
Neuromaturational theory
Dynamic systems theory
Rhythmical stereotypies

CHAPTER COMPETENCIES

Upon completion of this chapter you should be able to:

- Describe primitive and postural reflexes that appear before birth or during the first year, and explain the neural development that occurs with these changes
- Relate inhibition of specific reflexes and appearance of specific reactions to development of particular voluntary motor skills
- Distinguish between "primitive reflexes" and "postural reflexes"
- Speculate on the relationship of reflexes and rhythmical stereotypies to later voluntary movement behavior
- Identify and discuss several rhythmical stereotypies present in the human infant
- Speculate on the purpose and role of rhythmical stereotypies
- Devise an infant reflex/stereotypy observational assessment instrument

KEY CONCEPT

The study of infant reflexes and stereotypical patterns of behavior yields useful information for understanding the process of motor development.

Reflex movements are evident in all fetuses, neonates, and infants to greater or lesser degrees, depending on their ages and neurological makeups. Reflex movements are involuntary reactions of the body to various forms of external stimulation. Most reflexes are subcortical in that they are controlled by the lower brain centers, which are also responsible for numerous involuntary life-sustaining processes such as breathing. Although not the topic of this chapter, equilibrium reflexes are mediated by the cerebral cortex. Voluntary motor control in the normal child is a function of the maturing cerebral cortex. Consciously controlled movements result from nerve impulses transmitted from the cerebral cortex along motor neurons.

Many early reflexes are related to infant survival (**primitive survival reflexes**), whereas others are precursors of voluntary movements that will appear between the ninth and fifteenth months after birth (**primitive postural reflexes**). Reflexive walking, swimming, crawling, and climbing movements were reported by Shirley (1931), McGraw (1939), and Ames (1937). These reflexes are inhibited prior to the appearance of their voluntary counterparts, but their mere presence is an indication of how deeply locomotor activities are rooted within the nervous system.

CONCEPT 7.1

Reflexes are the first forms of human movement and provide interesting insights into the process of motor development.

From about the fourth month of fetal life until the fourth month of infancy, most of a baby's movements are reflexive. Involuntary reactions result from changes in pressure, sight, sound, and tactile stimulation. These stimuli and the responses form the basis for the *information-gathering stage*, or **encoding stage**, of the reflexive movement phase. Reflexes, at this point in the child's life, serve as a primary information-gathering device for information storage in the developing cortex. As higher brain centers gain greater control of the sensorimotor apparatus, the infant is able to process information more efficiently. This *information-processing stage*, or **decoding stage**, parallels Piaget's first three stages within his sensorimotor phase of development, namely, the use of reflexes, primary circular reactions, and secondary circular reactions.

CONCEPT 7.2

Infant reflexive behaviors serve as a primary information-gathering source during the neonatal period.

REFLEXIVE BEHAVIOR AND VOLUNTARY MOVEMENT

Two main functions of the primitive survival reflexes are to seek nourishment and to seek protection. Several primitive reflexes during early infancy resemble later voluntary movements. These postural reflexes, as they are sometimes called, have been subjected to considerable debate over the past several years. Over the last few decades it has been hypothesized and demonstrated that these reflex movements form the basis for later voluntary movement (Bower, 1976; McGraw, 1954; Thelen, 1980; Zelazo, 1976). As the cortex gradually matures, it assumes control over the postural reflexes of stepping, crawling, and swimming. Over twenty-five years ago, Zelazo questioned the dualistic position of the anatomists in favor of a hierarchical view, stating,

> Indeed, current behavioral and neurological research with infants challenges the validity and generality of the hypothesized independence

between early reflexive and later instrumental behavior. An alternative hypothesis holds that the newborn's reflexes do not disappear but retain their identity within a hierarchy of controlled behavior (p. 88).

Anatomists and neurologists, on the other hand, argued that a recognizable gap of up to several months occurs between the inhibition of a postural reflex and the onset of voluntary movement (Kessen et al., 1970; Pontius, 1973; Prechtl and Beintema, 1964; Wyke, 1975). This time lag, they contended, clearly indicated that there was no direct link between postural reflexes and later voluntary movement. Therefore, Zelazo's view was heavily criticized. Furthermore, anatomists and neurologists argued that the performance of reflexive movements and voluntary movements was controlled by entirely different brain centers. Bower (1976), however, contended that "such results pointed to the possibility that the reason abilities disappear is that they are not exercised" (p. 40).

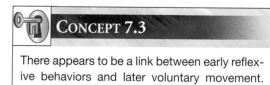

CONCEPT 7.3

There appears to be a link between early reflexive behaviors and later voluntary movement.

From the anatomist's theoretical point of view it was perceived that there was little basis for assuming that the infant's first reflexive movements prepared him or her for later voluntary movement in a direct way. By the mid-1970s it proposed that the results of early reflexive activity of the infant were internalized and that this information was stored for future use (Zelazo, 1976). Thelen (1985) further argued that studies demonstrate continuity between reflexive and voluntary walking. She contended, as did Bower (1976), that the period of inhibition disappears if the reflex is exercised. Thelen argued that the reflex disappears because leg mass increases. Preservation of the reflex strengthens the leg and lower body, thus permitting the infant to continue the movement with little or no lag between the locomotor reflex and its voluntary counterpart. Explanations such as this account for

at least an indirect link between the infant's postural reflexes and later voluntary movement.

Anyone interested in the study of movement must have a clearer understanding of the first forms of movement behavior. Two theories that attempt to bring clarification to this area are the neuromaturational theory and the dynamic systems theory.

The **neuromaturational theory** of motor development (Eckert, 1987) holds that as the cortex develops it inhibits some of the functions of the subcortical layers and assumes ever-increasing neuromuscular control. The cortex joins in its ability to store information received by way of sensory neurons. This phenomenon is evidenced in the phasing out of reflex behaviors and the assumption of voluntary movements by the infant. Concurrent formation of myelin prepares the body for the mature neuromuscular state. Movements become more localized as functional neural pathways serve isolated regions of the body with greater precision and accuracy.

More recently, the **dynamic systems theory** contends that neuromaturation serves as a constraint to development and is only one of many rate limiters influencing the emergence of controlled voluntary movement (Thelen, 1986; Thelen et al., 1987; Thelen and Ulrich, 1991). The dynamics of the system shape movement, and a *rate limiter* is something in the individual, task, and/or environment that constrains or restricts coordinated movement from occurring with little central input. Such things as body proportions, insufficient myelination, body weight, muscular strength, or a host of environmental conditions inhibit or promote progress from the reflexive to the rudimentary movement phase of development.

DIAGNOSING CENTRAL NERVOUS SYSTEM DISORDERS

It is common for a pediatrician to attempt to elicit primitive and postural reflexes in the neonate and young infant. If a reflex is absent, irregular, or uneven in strength, neurological dysfunction is suspected. The absence of normal reflexive movements or the prolonged continuation of various reflexes beyond their normal periods may also cause the physician to suspect neurological impairment.

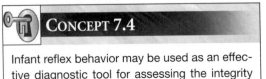

CONCEPT 7.4

Infant reflex behavior may be used as an effective diagnostic tool for assessing the integrity of the central nervous system.

The use of developmental reflexes as a tool for diagnosing central nervous system disorders has been widespread. Over the years, scientists have compiled an approximate timetable for the appearance and inhibition of neonatal and infant behaviors. For example, the resting posture of the newborn tends to be the flexed position. The flexors are dominant over the extensors in the early part of infancy. Shortly, however, increased cortical control permits the normal neonate to raise its head from the prone position. An absence of the head-lifting response in the first week or two following birth may suggest the possibility of neurological abnormalities.

Several other meaningful examples of this principle exist. The *doll-eye* movements of the neonate permit it to maintain constancy of the retinal image. When the head is tilted back, the eyes look down toward the chin, and when the head is tilted forward, the eyes look up toward the forehead. This response is almost always seen in premature infants and during the first day following birth in the normal neonate, after which it is replaced by voluntary eye movements. Perseveration of this reflex could indicate delayed cortical maturation.

One means of diagnosing possible central nervous system disorders, therefore, is through perseverating reflexes. Complete absence of a reflex is usually less significant than a reflex that remains too long. Other evidence of possible damage may be reflected in a reflex that is too strong or too weak. A reflex that elicits a stronger response on one side of the body than on the other may also indicate central nervous system dysfunction. An asymmetrical tonic neck reflex, for example, which shows full arm extension on one side of the body

and only weak extensor tone when the other side is stimulated, may also provide evidence of damage.

Only a trained examiner should inspect and evaluate reflexive behaviors in the neonate. The examinations provide physicians with a primary means of diagnosing central nervous system integrity in full-term, premature, and at-risk infants. Furthermore, they serve as a basis for intervention by physical and occupational therapists working with individuals displaying pathological reflexive behaviors beyond their expected periods of inhibition. Neurological dysfunction may be suspected when any one of the following conditions appear:

1. Perseveration of a reflex beyond the age at which it should have been inhibited by cortical control
2. Complete absence of a reflex
3. Unequal bilateral reflex responses
4. Responses that are too strong or too weak

CONCEPT 7.5

Infant reflexes appear and are inhibited on a predictable schedule of rate and sequence.

PRIMITIVE REFLEXES

Primitive reflexes are closely associated with the obtainment of nourishment and the protection of the infant. They first appear during fetal life and persist well into the first year. The following is a partial list of the numerous primitive reflexes exhibited by the fetus and the neonate. Their approximate times of appearance and inhibition are found in table 7.1, which also includes information about postural reflexes.

Moro and Startle Reflexes

The Moro and startle reflexes may be elicited by placing the infant in a supine position and tapping on the abdomen or by producing a feeling of insecurity of support (for instance, allowing the head to drop suddenly backward a short distance). It may even be self-induced by a loud noise or the

TABLE 7.1	Developmental Sequence and Approximate Rate for Appearance and Inhibition of Selected Primitive and Postural Reflexes

								Month						
Primitive Reflexes	0	1	2	3	4	5	6	7	8	9	10	11	12
Moro	×	×	×	×	×	×	×						
Startle								×	×	×	×		
Search	×	×	×	×	×	×	×	×	×	×	×	×	
Sucking	×	×	×	×									
Palmar-mental	×	×	×										
Palmar-mandibular	×	×	×	×									
Palmar grasping	×	×	×	×	×								
Babinski	×	×	×	×									
Plantar grasp					×	×	×	×	×	×	×	×	×
Tonic neck	×	×	×	×	×	×	×						
Postural Reflexes													
Labyrinthine righting			×	×	×	×	×						
Optical righting							×	×	×	×	×	×	×
Pull-up			×	×	×	×	×	×	×	×	×	×	
Parachute and propping					×	×	×	×	×	×	×	×	×
Neck righting	×	×	×	×	×	×	×						
Body righting							×	×	×	×	×	×	×
Crawling	×	×	×	×									
Stepping	×	×	×	×	×								
Swimming	×	×	×	×	×								

infant's cough or sneeze. In the Moro reflex, there is a sudden extension and bowing of the arms and spreading of the fingers. The legs and toes perform the same actions, but less vigorously. The limbs then return to a normal flexed position against the body (figure 7.1). The startle reflex is similar in all ways to the Moro reflex except that it involves flexion of the limbs without prior extension.

The Moro reflex is present at birth and during the following six months. The Moro reflex has been one of the most widely used tools in the neurological examination of the young infant. The reaction is most pronounced during the infant's first few weeks. The intensity of the response gradually decreases until it is finally characterized by a jerking motion of the body in response to the stimulus (startle reflex). Persistence of the reflex beyond the sixth month may be an indication of neurological

dysfunction. An asymmetrical Moro reflex may indicate Erb's palsy or an injury to a limb.

Search and Sucking Reflexes

The search, or rooting, and sucking reflexes enable the newborn to obtain nourishment from its mother. Stimulation of the area around the mouth (search reflex) will result in the infant's turning its head toward the source of stimulation. The search reflex is strongest during the first three weeks and gradually gives way to a directed head turning response that becomes refined and appears to be a purposeful behavior to bring the mouth into contact with the stimulus. The search reflex is most easily obtained when the infant is hungry, sleeping, or in his or her normal feeding position. Stimulation of the lips, gums, tongue, or hard palate will

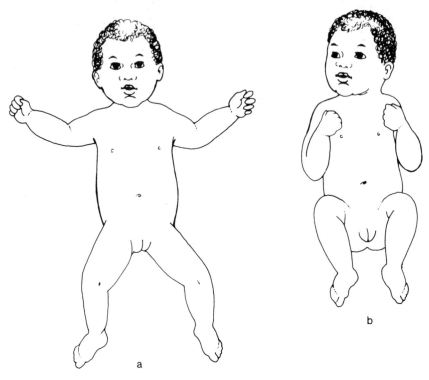

Figure 7.1
The Moro reflex: (a) extension phase, (b) flexion phase.

cause a sucking motion (sucking reflex) in an attempt to ingest nourishment. The sucking action is usually rhythmically repetitive. If it isn't, gentle movement of the object within the mouth will produce sucking. The sucking reflex has two phases, the expressive phase and the suction phase.

During the *expressive phase* of sucking, the nipple is squeezed between the tongue and palate. During the *suction phase,* negative pressure is produced in the mouth cavity. This reflex is elicited daily during the feeding times of a healthy neonate. Additionally, when high-risk newborns are stimulated to elicit the sucking and swallowing reflexes, it has been beneficial in reducing the need for intravenous feeding.

Both of these reflexes are present in all normal newborns. The search reflex may persist until the end of the first year; the sucking movement generally disappears as a reflex by the end of the third month but persists as a voluntary response.

Hand-Mouth Reflexes

Two hand-mouth reflexes are found in the newborn. The *palmar-mental reflex,* elicited by scratching the base of the palm, causes contraction of the chin muscles, which lift the chin up. This reflex has been observed in newborns but disappears relatively early.

The *palmar-mandibular reflex,* or *Babkin reflex,* as it is sometimes called, is elicited by applying pressure to the palms of both hands. The responses usually include mouth opening, closing of eyes, and flexing the head forward. This reflex begins decreasing during the first month after birth and usually is not visible after the third month.

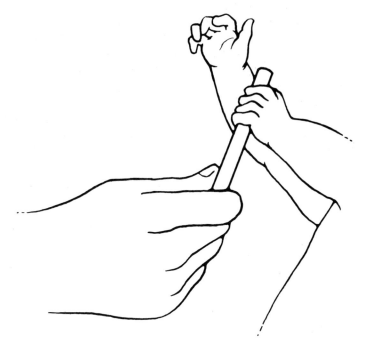

Figure 7.2
The palmar grasping reflex.

Palmar Grasping Reflex

During the first two months, the infant usually has its hands closed tightly. Upon stimulation of the palm, the hand will close strongly around the object without use of the thumb. The grip tightens when force is exerted against the encircling fingers. The grip is often so strong that the infant is able to support his or her weight when suspended (figure 7.2).

The grasping reflex is normally present at birth and persists during the first four months. The intensity of the response tends to increase during the first month and slowly diminish after that. Weak grasping or persistence of the reflex after the first year may be a sign of delay in motor development or of hemiplegia, if it occurs on only one side.

Babinski and Plantar Grasping Reflexes

In the newborn the Babinski reflex is elicited by a stroke on the sole of the foot. The pressure causes an extension of the toes. As the neuromuscular system matures, the Babinski reflex gives way to the plantar reflex, a contraction of the toes upon stimulation of the sole of the foot (figure 7.3).

The Babinski reflex is normally present at birth but gives way around the fourth month to the plantar grasp reflex, which may persist until about the twelfth month. The plantar grasp reflex may be most easily elicited by pressing the thumbs against the ball of the infant's foot. Persistence of the Babinski reflex beyond the sixth month may be an indication of a developmental lag.

Asymmetrical and Symmetrical Tonic Neck Reflexes

The asymmetrical tonic neck reflex is probably the most widely researched reflex in the therapeutic literature. To elicit it, the infant is placed by a trained examiner in a supine position, and the neck is turned so that the head is facing toward either side. The arms assume a position similar to

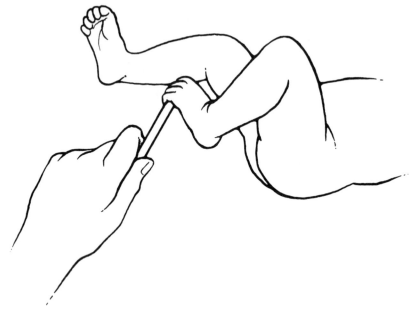

Figure 7.3
The plantar grasping reflex.

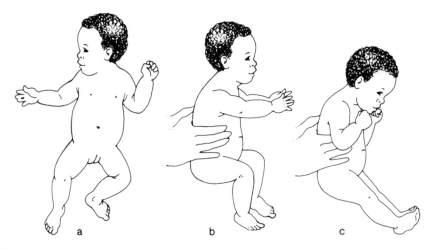

Figure 7.4
(a) The asymmetrical tonic neck reflex and (b & c) the symmetrical tonic neck reflex.

the fencer's "en garde." That is, the arm extends on the side of the body toward which the head is turned, and the other arm assumes an acute flexed position. The lower limbs assume a position similar to the arms. The symmetrical tonic neck reflex may be elicited from a supported sitting position. Extension of the head and neck will produce extension of the arm and flexion of the legs. If the head and neck are flexed, the arms flex and the legs extend (figure 7.4).

Both tonic neck reflexes may be observed in most premature infants, but they are not an obligatory response in newborns (i.e., they do not occur each time the infant's head is turned). However, the 3- or 4-month-old infant assumes the asymmetrical position about 50 percent of the time and then this response gradually fades away. Persistence beyond the sixth month may be an indication of lack of control over lower brain centers by higher ones.

Persistence of the asymmetrical tonic neck reflex into the early childhood years can prevent the child from developing motor tasks such as body rolling, body midline crossing, eye-hand coordination, and various swim strokes. Children and adults with severe cerebral palsy often exhibit a persistent asymmetrical tonic neck reflex (Sherrill, 1998).

POSTURAL REFLEXES

Postural reflexes resemble later voluntary movements. Postural reflexes automatically provide for an individual's maintenance of an upright position in relation to his or her environment. They are found in all normal infants during the early postnatal months of life and may, in a few cases, persist through the first year. The following sections discuss postural reflexes of particular interest to the student of motor development. These reflexes are

associated with later voluntary movement behavior and should be carefully studied by all concerned with the development of voluntary patterns of movement. (The approximate times of appearance and inhibition of these reflexes are also found in table 7.1.)

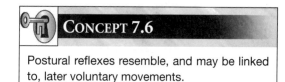

CONCEPT 7.6

Postural reflexes resemble, and may be linked to, later voluntary movements.

Labyrinthine and Optical Righting Reflexes

The labyrinthine and the optical righting reflexes may be elicited when the infant is held in an upright position and is tilted forward, backward, or to the side. The child will respond by attempting to maintain the upright position of the head by moving it in the direction opposite to the one in which its trunk is moved. For example, if the baby is held in a prone position and tilted downward, it will respond by raising the head upward (figure 7.5). The optical righting reflex is the same as the labyrinthine reflex except that the eyes can be observed to follow the upward lead of the head. In the labyrinthine righting reflex, impulses arising in the otolith of the labyrinth cause the infant to

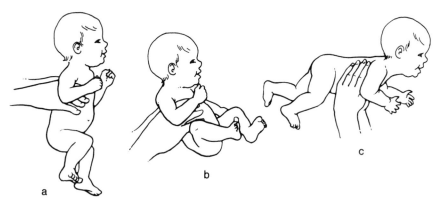

Figure 7.5

The labyrinthine righting reflexes from three positions: (a) upright, (b) tilted backward, and (c) prone.

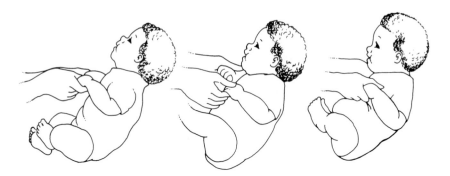

Figure 7.6
The pull-up reflex.

maintain its head in proper alignment to the environment even when other sensory channels (i.e., vision or touch) are excluded. The labyrinthine righting reflex makes its first appearance around the second month and persists to about the sixth month, when vision generally becomes an important factor. The reflex continues into the first year as the optical righting reflex. The optical righting reflex, and its more primitive cousin, the labyrinthine righting reflex, help the infant achieve and maintain an upright head and body posture, and contribute to the infant's forward movement around the end of the first year.

Pull-Up Reflex

The pull-up reflex of the arms is an involuntary attempt on the part of the infant to maintain an upright position. When the infant is in an upright sitting position and held by one or both hands, it will flex its arms in an attempt to remain upright when tipped backward. It will do the same thing when tipped forward. The reflexive pull-up reaction of the arms usually appears around the third or fourth month and often continues through the first year (figure 7.6).

Parachute and Propping Reflexes

Parachute and propping reactions are protective movements of the limbs in the direction of the displacing force. These reflexive movements occur in response to a sudden displacing force or when balance can no longer be maintained. Protective reflexes depend on visual stimulation and thus do not occur in the dark. They may be a form of a startle reflex.

The forward parachute reaction may be observed when the infant is held vertically in the air and then tilted toward the ground. The infant extends the arms downward in an apparent attempt to cushion the anticipated fall (figure 7.7). The downward parachute reactions may be observed when the baby is held in an upright position and rapidly lowered toward the ground. The lower limbs extend, tense, and abduct. Propping reflexes may be elicited by pushing the infant off balance from a sitting position either forward or backward. The forward and downward parachute reactions begin to occur around the fourth month. The sideways propping reaction is first elicited around the sixth month. The backward reaction is first seen between the tenth and twelfth months. Each of these reactions tends to persist beyond the first year and are necessary before the infant can learn to walk.

Neck and Body Righting Reflexes

The neck righting reflex can be observed when the infant is placed in a supine position with the head turned to one side. The remainder of the body

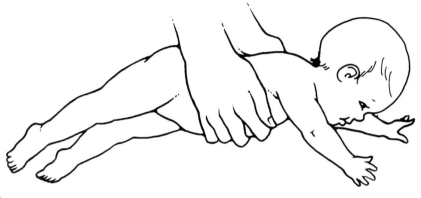

Figure 7.7
The parachute reflex.

moves reflexively in the same direction of the head. First the hips and legs turn into alignment, followed by the trunk. In the body righting reflex the reverse occurs. When tested from a side-lying position with the legs and trunk turned in one direction, the baby will turn its head reflexively in the same direction and right the body in alignment with the head (figure 7.8). The neck righting reflex disappears around 6 months of age. The body righting reflex emerges around the sixth month and persists to about 18 months of age. The body righting reflex forms the basis for voluntary rolling that occurs from the end of the fifth month onward.

Crawling Reflex

The crawling reflex can be seen when the infant is placed in a prone position and pressure is applied to the sole of one foot. It will reflexively crawl, using both its upper and lower limbs. Pressure on the soles of both feet will elicit a return of pressure by the infant. Pressure on the sole of one foot will produce returned pressure and an extensor thrust of the opposite leg (figure 7.9).

The crawling reflex is generally present at birth and disappears around the third or fourth month. There is a lag between reflexive crawling

and voluntary crawling, which appears around the seventh month.

Primary Stepping Reflex

When the infant is held erect, with its body weight placed forward on a flat surface, it will respond by "walking" forward. This walking movement involves the legs only (figure 7.10). The primary stepping reflex is normally present during the first six weeks and disappears by the fifth month. Zelazo (1976) and Bower (1976) studied how early and persistent practice of the primary stepping reflex affects the onset of voluntary walking behavior. The results of these investigations revealed that the age of independent walking was accelerated through conditioning of the stepping reflex in the experimental group; the control group did not show accelerated development. Building on these findings, Thelen (1986a) was able to elicit a stepping reflex in infants several months after it should have been inhibited but prior to the onset of voluntary walking. She suggested that the conditioning of the reflex improves the strength in the limbs exercised, thus becoming a key to early voluntary walking. Several investigations have used this seminal work to explore the facilitation of voluntary walking in infants with Down syndrome (Ulrich and Ulrich, 1995; Ulrich et al., 1995; Ulrich et al., 1997).

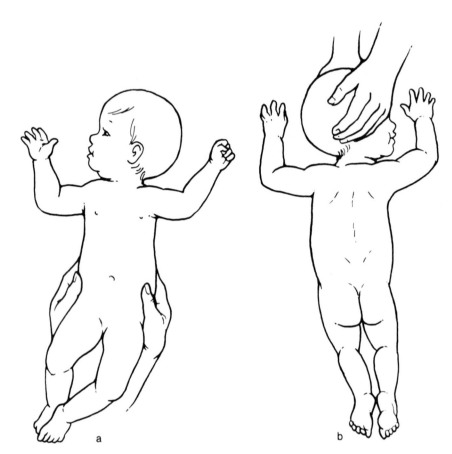

Figure 7.8
(a) The neck righting reflex and (b) the body righting reflex.

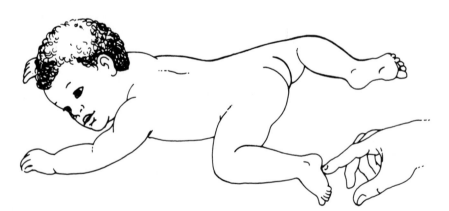

Figure 7.9
The crawling reflex.

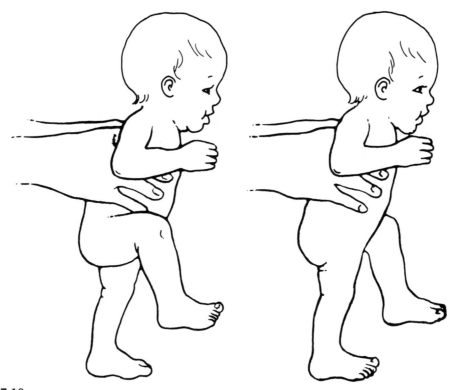

Figure 7.10
The primary stepping reflex.

Swimming Reflex

When placed in a prone position in or over water, the infant will exhibit rhythmical extensor and flexor swimming movements of the arms and legs. The movements are well organized and appear more advanced than any of the other locomotor reflexes. McGraw (1939) filmed reflexive swimming movements in the human infant as early as the eleventh day following birth. These involuntary movements generally disappear around the fourth month. McGraw discovered that a breath-holding reflex is elicited when the infant's face is placed in the water and that the swimming movements are more pronounced from this position. McGraw (1954) has since speculated on the theory that the infant's swimming reflex is a precursor to walking. "Basically the neuromuscular mechanisms which

mediate the reflexive swimming movements may be essentially the same as those activated in the reflexive crawling and stepping movements of the infant" (p. 360). It is interesting to reflect on the relationship among the crawling, stepping, and swimming reflexes.

RHYTHMICAL STEREOTYPIES

Researchers have been interested in the many intriguing questions concerning infant reflexes for several decades. This research has important implications for the diagnosis of central nervous system disorders and for the physical and occupational therapist working with individuals who display various pathological conditions. Furthermore, the study of the origin of reflexes and their relationship to later voluntary behaviors is forging new inroads into learning theory and how the human being organizes itself for the learning of new movement skills.

 CONCEPT 7.7

Infant rhythmical stereotypies provide evidence that human motor development is a self-organizing system that strives for increased motor control.

Only in the last two decades have investigators gone beyond cataloging and describing infant reflexive behaviors to attempt to examine the underlying mechanisms. Esther Thelen is among the first to attempt to answer the many questions raised by the stereotypical behaviors of the infant. She studied **rhythmical stereotypies** in normal human infants to classify these movements and explain their occurrences. (*Stereotypies* are rhythmical behaviors performed over and over for their own sakes.) In children and adults, stereotypies are regarded as evidence of abnormal behavior, but in infants they are normal.

Thelen (1979, 1981, 1996) observed and cataloged the rhythmical stereotypies of normal infants from 4 weeks to 1 year of age. Her observations revealed forty-seven stereotypical behaviors, which have been subdivided into four groups: (1) movements of the legs and feet; (2) movements of the torso; (3) movements of the arms, hands, and fingers; and (4) movements of the head and face. According to Thelen (1979), "These behaviors showed developmental regularities as well as constancy of form and distribution. Groups of stereotypies involving particular parts of the body or postures had characteristic ages of onset, peak performance, and decline" (p. 699).

Rhythmic movements of given body systems tended to increase just before the infant gained voluntary control of that system. Therefore, the maturational level of the infant appears to control rhythmical stereotypies. Thelen and her colleagues (Thelen et al., 1985; Thelen et al., 1987) have argued that the presence of stereotypical behaviors in normal human infants is evidence of a self-organizing central motor program in control of infant motor development.

Legs and Feet

Thelen (1979, 1985) found that rhythmical kicking movements of the legs and feet were the earliest stereotypies observed. The majority of rhythmical kicking took place when infants were in either prone or supine positions. The supine position afforded infants the greatest amount of freedom with flexibility at both the hip and knee joints. When kicking from this back-lying position, the babies' legs were bent slightly at the hips, knees, and ankles with moderate outward rotation at the hips. From this position the infants could alternately kick the legs in what resembled a "bicycling" action. From the prone position alternate leg kicking was more restricted and occurred only from the knee joint. Thelen noted that stereotypies of the legs and feet began around 4 weeks of age, earlier than for arms, and reached their peak occurrence between 24 and 32 months of age. Other forms of kicking discovered were foot rubbing from a related position and single leg kicking from both prone and supine positions.

Torso

Thelen (1979) also observed several rhythmical stereotypies of the torso. The most common was from a prone position. The infant arched the back, lifted the arms and legs from the supporting surface, and rhythmically rocked back and forth in an airplanelike position. Another frequently observed stereotypy of the torso occurred from a hands-and-knee prone creeping position. From this position the infant moved the body forward by extending the upper position of the leg and keeping the lower leg stationary. The arms remained extended throughout but moved forward on the backward thrust of the legs.

Other common, but less frequently observed, rhythmical stereotypies of the torso included rhythmical actions from sitting, kneeling, and standing postures. From either a supported or unsupported sitting position, the infant rhythmically rocked the torso forward and back. Rhythmical stereotypies from a kneeling position included rocking back and forth, side to side, and up and down. Standing stereotypies were common and generally occurred from a support-standing position. The infant bent at the knees and performed a rhythmical up-and-down bouncing movement. Infants might also rhythmically rock forward and back and from side to side.

Arms, Hands, and Fingers

Rhythmical stereotypies of the arms, hands, and fingers were observed in all of the infants sampled by Thelen. Waving (actions without an object) and banging (actions with an object in the infant's grasp) were the most frequently observed. Both were the same motor pattern and involved rhythmical movement in a vertical action from the shoulder. Banging differed from waving only in that the infant made contact with the surface on the downward action. Rhythmical clapping of the hands in front of the body was another common stereotypy, as in arm sway. The arm sway stereotypy is elicited, however, only when the infant is grasping an object and involves shoulder-initiated action across the front of the body.

Head and Face

Rhythmical stereotypies of the head and face, according to Thelen (1979), are much less frequent. They involve actions such as rhythmical head shaking from side to side ("no") and up and down ("yes"). Rhythmical sticking out of the tongue and drawing it back was routinely observed, along with nonnutritive sucking behaviors.

Of the forty-seven rhythmical stereotypies observed by Thelen, movements of the legs and feet were the most common, began the earliest, and peaked between 24 and 32 weeks of age. Arm and hand stereotypies are also common but peaked somewhat later, between 34 and 42 weeks. Torso stereotypies, although common, are less frequent than movements of the legs and feet and the hands and arms. Furthermore, torso stereotypies from sitting, kneeling, or standing positions tend to peak later than the others.

SUMMARY

Primitive reflexes, under the control of subcortical brain layers, are observed in the fetus from about the eighteenth week of gestation. Generally, reflexes serve the double function of helping the neonate to secure nourishment and protection. Many of the movements represent initial methods of gaining information about the infant's environment.

As neurological development proceeds in the normal fetus, and later in the normal neonate, reflexes appear and disappear on a fairly standard, though informal, schedule. The presence of a primitive or postural reflex is evidence of subcortical control over some neuromuscular functions. Although cortical control soon dominates, the function of the subcortex is never completely inhibited. Throughout life, it maintains control over such activities as coughing, sneezing, and yawning, as well as over the involuntary life processes. The cortex mediates more purposeful behavior, whereas subcortical behavior is limited and stereotyped.

Although it is not yet possible to determine whether a direct relationship between reflexive behavior and later voluntary movement exists, it is safe to assume that there is at least an indirect link. This link may be associated with the ability of the developing cortex to store information received from the sensory end-organs regarding the performance of the involuntary movement. Or it may be due to improved strength in the involuntarily (reflexively) exercised body part.

CRITICAL READINGS

Sherrill, C. (1998). *Adapted Physical Activity, Recreation and Sport: Crossdisciplinary and Lifespan* (Chapter 10). 5th ed. St. Louis: McGraw-Hill.

Snow, C. W. (1998). *Infant Development.* 2nd ed. Upper Saddle River, NJ: Prentice-Hall.

Thelen, E. (1986). Treadmill-elicited stepping in seven-month-old infants. *Child Development, 57,* 1498–1506.

Thelen, E. (1996). Normal infant stereotypies: A dynamic systems approach. In R. L. Sprague & K. M. Newell (Eds.), *Stereotyped Movements: Brain and Behavior Relationships* (pp. 139–165). Washington DC: American Psychological Association.

Thelen, E., Kelso, J. A. S., & Fogel, A. (1987). Self-organizing systems and infant motor development. *Developmental Review, 7,* 39–65.

Zelazo, P. (1976). From reflexive to instrumental behavior. In L. P. Lipsett (Ed.), *Developmental Psychobiology—The Significance of Infancy.* Hillsdale, NJ: Lawrence Erlbaum.

 ## WEB RESOURCES

American Physical Therapy Association
www.apta.org

International Society on Infant Studies
www.isisweb.org

Physical Therapist Online
www.physicaltherapist.com

Vanderbilt Medical Center Pediatric Interactive Digital Library
www.mc.vanderbilt.edu/peds/pidl

RUDIMENTARY MOVEMENT ABILITIES

KEY TERMS

Reflex inhibition stage

Precontrol stage

Stability

Locomotion

Manipulation

Crawling

Homolateral pattern

Creeping

Contralateral pattern

Early intervention

Hyponatremia

Giardia

CHAPTER COMPETENCIES

Upon completion of this chapter you should be able to:

- Describe intertask "motor milestones" that lead to upright locomotion and visually guided reaching
- Distinguish between the reflex inhibition and the precontrol stages within the rudimentary movement phase of development
- Discuss historical and contemporary study of infant motor development
- List and describe the developmental sequence of acquisition of rudimentary stability, locomotor, and manipulative abilities
- Distinguish between *creeping* and *crawling* and describe the developmental process of each
- Discuss the interaction between maturation and experience on the acquisition of rudimentary movement abilities
- Devise your rudimentary movement infant observational assessment instrument

> **KEY CONCEPT**
>
> Mastery of the rudimentary movement abilities of infancy is a reflection of increased motor control and movement competence, brought about by factors within the task and the environment, as well as within the individual.

We are all products of specific genetic structures, and the total of the experiences we have had since conception. As such, a child is not a blank slate, ready to be molded and shaped to our whims or a precut pattern. Research has made it abundantly clear that infants are able to process a great deal more information than we suspected. Infants think and use movement as a purposeful, though initially imprecise, way of gaining information about their environments. Each child is an individual, and no two individuals will respond in exactly the same manner. The child's hereditary and experiential background, as well as the specific demands of the movement tasks, have a profound effect on the rate of attainment of the rudimentary movement abilities of infancy.

It is important to study motor development, beginning with the early movement experiences of infancy, to gain a better understanding of the development that takes place before children enter school and to learn more about the developmental concept of how humans learn to move.

Gaining control over musculature, learning to cope with the force of gravity, and moving in a controlled manner through space are major developmental tasks facing the infant. During the neonatal period, movement is ill defined and poorly controlled. Reflexes are gradually inhibited and the **reflex inhibition stage** begins (see figure 3.1, p. 46). This period stretches throughout most of the infant's first year. The infant gradually moves toward controlled rudimentary movement that represents a monumental accomplishment in suppressing reflexes and integrating the sensory and motor systems into controlled purposeful movement.

As the primitive and postural reflexes of the previous phase begin to fade, higher brain centers take over many of the skeletal muscle functions of lower brain centers. The reflex inhibition stage essentially begins at birth. From the moment of birth the newborn is bombarded by sight, sound, smell, tactile, and kinesthetic stimulation. The task is to bring order to this sensory stimulation. Initial reflexive responses are inhibited throughout the first year until around the first birthday, when the infant displays remarkable progress in bringing a semblance of control to his or her movement.

The period from about 12 months to between 18 and 24 months represents a time for practice and mastery of the many rudimentary tasks initiated during the first year. The infant begins to bring his or her movements under control during this precontrol period. The **precontrol stage** spans roughly the period between the first and second birthdays. During this stage the infant begins to gain greater control and precision in movement. Differentiation and integration of sensory and motor processes become more highly developed, and the rate limiters of early infancy become less pronounced.

As the infant makes crude but purposeful attempts at a variety of movement tasks, he or she should be encouraged. An environment that provides sufficient stimulation through abundant opportunities for practice and positive encouragement may prove beneficial in hastening development of the rudimentary stability, locomotor, and manipulative tasks that follow. The question, however, should be asked: What are the benefits of early motor skill acquisition? The answer is becoming more clear, and it is possible to build a strong case for encouraging early motor skill acquisition in normally developing infants (Nash, 1997) as well as in infants with developmental disabilities (Greenspan, 1997).

STUDY OF INFANT MOTOR DEVELOPMENT

The study of the rudimentary movement abilities of infancy received its impetus in the 1930s and 1940s, when a wealth of information was obtained from the observations of developmental psychologists. Many of these studies have become classics and have withstood the tests of time because of their careful controls and thoroughness. The works of H. M. Halverson, Mary Shirley, Nancy Bayley, and Arnold Gesell are particularly noteworthy.

The work of H. M. Halverson (1937) is probably the most comprehensive on the sequence of the emergence of voluntary grasping behavior during infancy. Through film analysis of infants from 16 to 52 weeks of age, he described three distinct stages of approach toward a cube and the development of the use of fingers-thumb opposition in grasping behavior.

Mary Shirley's (1931) pioneering study of twenty-five infants from birth to age 2 enabled her to describe a sequential developmental progression of activities leading to upright posture and a walking gait. She noted that "each separate stage was a fundamental step in development and that every baby advanced from stage to stage in the same order" (p. 98). She also noted that although the sequence was fixed, individual differences were expressed in variations in the rates of development between infants.

Nancy Bayley (1935) conducted an extensive study similar to that of Shirley. As a result of her observations of infants, she was able to describe a series of emerging locomotor abilities progressing from reflexive crawling to walking down a flight of stairs using an alternate foot pattern. Based on this information Bayley developed a cumulative scale of infant motor development that has been widely used as a diagnostic tool to determine an infant's developmental status.

Arnold Gesell (1945) conducted extensive studies of infant motor development. He viewed posture (i.e., stability) as the basis of all forms of movement. Therefore, according to Gesell, any form of locomotion or infant manipulation is a closely related series of sequential postural adjustments. The sequence of motor development is predetermined by innate biological factors that cut across all social, cultural, ethnic, and racial boundaries. This common base of motor development during the early years of life has caused many

experts to speculate that some voluntary movements (particularly locomotor movements) are phylogenetic (Eckert, 1973) and that, because these movements are maturationally based, they are not under voluntary developmental control (Hellebrandt et al., 1961). This view has often led to the erroneous assumption that infants and particularly young children acquire their movement abilities at about the same chronological age solely by the action of neural maturation and with little dependence on experience.

CONCEPT 8.1

The sequence of infant motor development is predictable, but the rate is variable.

Although the sequence of skill acquisition is generally invariant during infancy and childhood, the rate of acquisition differs from child to child. This causes one to hypothesize that early motor development is not only a function of neurological maturation but also a function of a self-organizing system involving the task, the environment, and the individual. As with the reflexive phase, neural maturation may only be one of a number of factors influencing the developmental rate of children's rudimentary movement abilities. In accordance with the hourglass model of motor development presented in chapter 3, it is time to look beyond neural maturation as the sole means of explaining infant motor development. Researchers are now looking more closely at the transactional processes embodied in the task, the individual, and the environment through a self-organizing dynamical systems perspective (Alexander et al., 1993; Newell, 1992; Thelen et al., 1987).

From the moment of birth the infant is in a constant struggle to gain mastery over the environment to survive. During the earliest stages of development, the infant's primary interaction with the environment is through the medium of movement. The infant must begin to master three primary categories of movement for survival and effective and efficient interaction with the world. First, the infant must establish and maintain the relationship of the body to the force of gravity to achieve an upright sitting posture and an erect standing posture (**stability**). Second, the child must develop basic abilities to move through the environment (**locomotion**). Third, the infant must develop the rudimentary abilities of reach, grasp, and release to make meaningful contact with objects (**manipulation**).

 CONCEPT 8.2

Variations in the rate of infant motor development lend support to the proposition that development is a dynamic process within a self-organizing system.

The rudimentary movement abilities in the infant are the building blocks for more extensive development of the fundamental movement abilities in early childhood and the specialized movement skills of later childhood and beyond. These so-called rudimentary movement abilities are highly involved tasks for the infant. The importance of their development must not be overlooked or minimized. The question that arises is: Can factors in the environment enhance the development of those movement abilities? The answer is an unqualified yes. Rudimentary movement abilities are not genetically determined to the point where they are not susceptible to modification. Early enrichment does seem to influence later development, but further information is needed about the type, timing, degree, and duration.

STABILITY

The infant is in a constant struggle against the force of gravity to achieve and maintain an upright posture. Establishing control over the musculature in opposition to gravity is a process that follows a predictable sequence in all infants. The events leading to an erect standing posture begin with gaining control over the head and neck and proceed

down to the trunk and the legs. Operation of the cephalocaudal principle of development is generally apparent in the infant's sequential progress from a lying position to a sitting posture and eventually to an erect standing posture. Table 8.1 provides a summary of the developmental sequence and the approximate age of onset of selected rudimentary stability abilities.

CONCEPT 8.3

Stability is the most basic of the three categories of movement because all voluntary movement involves an element of stability.

Control of the Head and the Neck

At birth the infant has little control over the head and neck muscles. If the infant is held erect at the trunk, the head will drop forward. Around the end of the first month, the infant gains control over these muscles and is able to hold the head erect when supported at the base of the neck. By the end of the first month, the infant should be able to lift the chin off the crib mattress when lying in a prone position. By the fifth month the infant should be able to lift the head off the crib mattress when lying in a supine position.

Control of the Trunk

After infants have gained mastery of the head and neck muscles, they begin to gain control of the muscles in the thoracic and lumbar regions of the trunk. The development of trunk control begins around the second month. Control of the trunk muscles may be observed if you hold the infant off the ground by the waist and note the ability to make postural adjustments necessary to maintain an erect position.

By the end of the second month, the infant should be capable of lifting the chest off the floor when placed in a prone position. After the infant can lift the chest, he or she begins to draw the knees up toward the chest and then kick them out

TABLE 8.1	Developmental Sequence and Approximate Age of Onset of Rudimentary Stability Abilities	
Stability Tasks	**Selected Abilities**	**Approximate Age of Onset**
Control of head and neck	Turns to one side	Birth
	Turns to both sides	1 week
	Held with support	First month
	Chin off contact surface	Second month
	Good prone control	Third month
	Good supine control	Fifth month
Control of trunk	Lifts head and chest	Second month
	Attempts supine-to-prone position	Third month
	Success in supine-to-prone roll	Sixth month
	Prone-to-supine roll	Eighth month
Sitting	Sits with support	Third month
	Sits with self-support	Sixth month
	Sits alone	Eighth month
	Stands with support	Sixth month
Standing	Supports with handholds	Tenth month
	Pulls to supported stand	Eleventh month
	Stands alone	Twelfth month

suddenly as if swimming. This usually occurs by the sixth month. Another indication of increasing control over the trunk muscles is the ability to turn over from a supine to a prone position. This is generally accomplished around the sixth month and is easily done by flexing the hips and stretching the legs out at right angles to the trunk. Mastery of the roll from a prone to a supine position usually occurs somewhat later.

Sitting

Sitting alone is an accomplishment that requires complete control over the entire trunk. The infant of 4 months is generally able to sit with support in the lumbar region. The infant has control over the upper trunk but not the lower portion. During the next month or two the infant gradually gains control over the lower trunk. The first efforts at sitting alone are characterized by an exaggerated forward lean to gain added support for the lumbar region.

Gradually, the ability to sit erect with a limited amount of support develops. By the seventh month, the infant is generally able to sit alone completely unsupported. At this juncture he or she has now gained control over the upper half of the body (figure 8.1). At the same time that the infant is learning to sit alone, he or she is developing control over the arms and hands—a further example of the cephalocaudal and proximodistal principles of development in operation described in chapter 4 (described earlier in the text).

Standing

Achievement of an erect standing posture represents a developmental milestone in the infant's quest for stability. It is an indication that control over the musculature has been gained to the extent that the force of gravity can no longer place such demanding restraints on movement. The infant is now on the verge of achieving upright locomotion

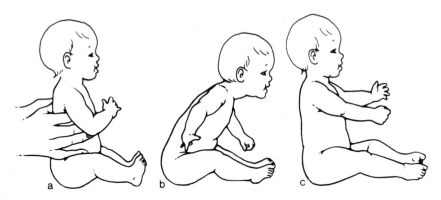

Figure 8.1
Three stages in achieving independent sitting: (a) third month, (b) sixth month, and (c) eighth month.

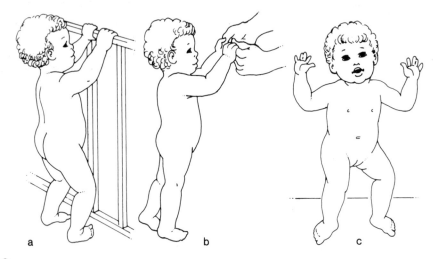

Figure 8.2
Three stages in gaining a standing posture: (a) sixth month, (b) tenth month, and (c) twelfth month.

(walking), a feat heralded by parents and pediatricians as the infant's most spectacular task of motor development.

The first voluntary attempts at standing occur around the fifth month. When held under the armpits and brought in contact with a supporting surface, the infant will voluntarily extend at the hip, straighten and tense the muscles of the legs, and maintain a standing position with considerable outside support. Around the ninth or tenth month, infants are able to stand beside furniture and support themselves for a considerable time.

Gradually, the infant begins to lean less heavily on the supporting object and can often be seen testing balance completely unsupported for a brief instant. Between the eleventh and twelfth months the infant learns to pull to a stand by first getting to the knees and then pushing with the legs while the upward extended arms pull down. Standing alone for extended periods generally takes place with walking alone and does not appear separately in most babies. The onset of an erect standing posture normally occurs somewhere between 11 and 13 months (figure 8.2). At this point the

TABLE 8.2	Developmental Sequence and Approximate Age of Onset of Rudimentary Locomotor Abilities	
Locomotor Tasks	**Selected Abilities**	**Approximate Age of Onset**
Horizontal movements	Scooting	Third month
	Crawling	Sixth month
	Creeping	Ninth month
	Walking on all fours	Eleventh month
Upright gait	Walks with support	Sixth month
	Walks with handholds	Tenth month
	Walks with lead	Eleventh month
	Walks alone (hands high)	Twelfth month
	Walks alone (hands low)	Thirteenth month

infant has gained considerable control over the musculature and can accomplish the difficult task of rising from a lying position to a standing position completely unaided.

From a developmental perspective it is important to note that movement patterns demonstrated by infants and toddlers when moving from a supine to a standing position do change as the child grows older (Marsala and VanSant, 1998).

LOCOMOTION

The infant's movement through space depends on emerging abilities to cope with the force of gravity. Locomotion does not develop independently of stability; it relies heavily on it. The infant will not be able to move about freely until the rudimentary developmental tasks of stability are mastered. The following are discussions of the most frequent forms of locomotion engaged in by the infant while learning how to cope with the force of gravity. These forms of locomotion are also summarized in table 8.2.

CONCEPT 8.4

Development of rudimentary locomotor abilities provides the infant with a means for exploring a rapidly expanding world.

Crawling

The crawling movements of the infant are the first attempts at purposeful locomotion. **Crawling** evolves as the infant gains control of the muscles of the head, neck, and trunk. In a prone position and using a **homolateral pattern,** the infant may reach for an object in front of her, raising her head and chest off the floor. On coming back down, the outstretched arms pull her back toward the feet. The result of this combined effort is a slight sliding movement forward (figure 8.3). The legs are usually not used in these early attempts at crawling. Crawling generally appears in the infant by the sixth month but may appear as early as the fourth month.

Creeping

Creeping evolves from crawling and often develops into a highly efficient form of locomotion for the infant. Creeping differs from crawling in that the legs and arms are used in opposition to one another. The infant's first attempts at creeping are characterized by deliberate movements of one limb at a time. As the infant's proficiency increases, movements become synchronous and more rapid. Most efficient creepers use a **contralateral pattern** (right arm and left leg). There is some evidence that suggests that infants who had skipped crawling and moved directly to creeping were less efficient

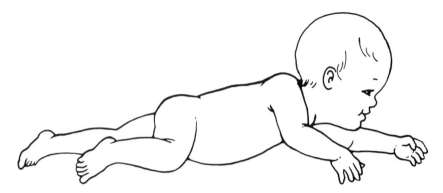

Figure 8.3
Crawling.

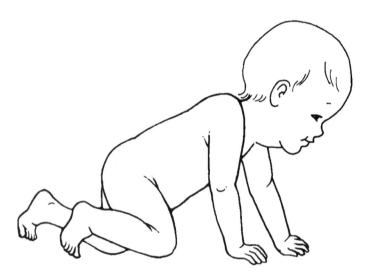

Figure 8.4
Creeping.

in their creeping movements than those who experienced crawling initially (Adolph, Vereijken, and Denny, 1998). See figure 8.4 for a visual representation of contralateral creeping.

There has been considerable speculation about the importance of creeping in the infant's motor development and the "proper" method of creeping. The neurological organization rationale of Carl Delacato (1966), often referred to as neurological

patterning, placed great importance on proper creeping and crawling techniques as a necessary stage in achieving cortical hemispherical dominance. Dominance of one side of the cortex is necessary, according to Delacato, for proper neurological organization. Faulty organization, it is hypothesized, will lead to motor, perceptual, and language problems in the child and adult. This hypothesis has been attacked by neurologists, pediatricians, and researchers in the area of child development. In 1982 and again in 1999 the American Academy of Pediatrics stated that neurological patterning treatment programs offer no special merit and the claims of its proponents remain unproven (American Academy of Pediatrics, 1982, 1999).

Upright Gait

The achievement of upright gait or walking depends on the infant's stability. The infant must first be able to control the body in a standing position before tackling the dynamic postural shifts required of upright locomotion. The infant's first attempts at independent walking generally occur somewhere between the tenth and fifteenth months and are characterized by a wide base of support, the feet turned outward, and the knees slightly flexed. These first walking movements are not synchronous and fluid. They are irregular, hesitant, and unaccompanied by reciprocal arm movements. While central nervous system maturation is extremely important to the advent of walking, other individual-oriented factors such as the elastic qualities of the muscles, anatomical properties of the bones and joints, and the energy delivered to the moving limbs serve as critical interactive systems (Thelen, 1992). Additional environmental factors such as parental encouragement and assistance and availability of furniture handholds may contribute to the timing of when independent walking appears.

Shirley (1931) identified four stages that the infant passes through in learning how to walk unaided: "(a) an early period of stepping in which slight forward progress is made (3–6 months); (b) a period of standing with help (6–10 months); (c) a period of walking when led (9–12 months); (d) a period of walking alone (12–15 months)" (p. 18). As the infant passes through each of these stages and progresses toward a mature walking pattern, several changes occur. First, the speed of walking accelerates and length of the step increases. Second, the width of the step increases until independent walking is well established, and then decreases slightly. Third, the eversion of the foot

gradually decreases until the feet are pointing straight ahead. Fourth, the upright walking gait gradually smooths out, the length of the step becomes regular, and the movements of the body become synchronous. Shortly after independent walking has been achieved, the toddler will experiment with walking sideways, backward (Eckert, 1973), and on tiptoes (Bayley, 1935).

MANIPULATION

As with stability and locomotion, the manipulative abilities of the infant evolve through a series of stages. In this section, only the most basic aspects of manipulation—reaching, grasping, and releasing—will be considered. As with the sections on stability and locomotion, the manipulative abilities of the infant may be susceptible to early appearance even though the process is influenced greatly by maturation. If the child is maturationally ready, she will benefit from early opportunities to practice and perfect rudimentary manipulative abilities.

The following are the three general steps in which the infant engages during the acquisition of rudimentary manipulative abilities. Table 8.3 provides a summary of the developmental sequence and approximate age of onset of rudimentary manipulative abilities.

CONCEPT 8.5

The emergence of rudimentary manipulative abilities provides the developing infant with the first meaningful contact with objects in the immediate environment.

Reaching

During the first 4 months, the infant does not make definite reaching movements toward objects, although she may attend closely to them visually and make globular encircling motions in the general direction of the object. Around the fourth

TABLE 8.3   Developmental Sequence and Approximate Age of Onset of Rudimentary Manipulative Abilities

Manipulative Tasks	Selected Abilities	Approximate Age of Onset
Reaching	Globular ineffective reach	First to third month
	Definite corralling reach	Fourth month
	Controlled reach	Sixth month
Grasping	Reflexive grasp	Birth
	Voluntary grasp	Third month
	Two-hand palmar grasp	Third month
	One-hand palmar grasp	Fifth month
	Pincer grasp	Ninth month
	Controlled grasp	Fourteenth month
	Eats without assistance	Eighteenth month
Releasing	Basic release	Twelfth to fourteenth month
	Controlled release	Eighteenth month

month she begins to make the fine eye and hand adjustments necessary for contact with the object. Often the infant can be observed making alternating glances between the object and the hand. The movements are slow and awkward, involving primarily the shoulder and elbow. Later the wrist and the hand become more directly involved. By the end of the fifth month, the child's aim is nearly perfect, and she is now able to reach for and make tactual contact with objects in the environment. This accomplishment is necessary before she can take hold of the object and grasp it in the hand. Some factors demonstrated to influence the accuracy of infant reaching including the speed of the movement (Thelen, Corbetta, and Spencer, 1996) and the position of the infant's body when reaching (i.e., vertical, reclined, or supine) (Savelsbergh and Kamp, 1994).

Grasping

The newborn will grasp an object when it is placed in the palm of the hand. This action, however, is entirely reflexive until about the fourth month. Voluntary grasping must wait until the sensorimotor mechanism has developed to the extent that

efficient reaching and meaningful contact can take place. Halverson (1937) identified several stages in the development of prehension. In the first stage, a 4-month-old infant makes no real voluntary effort at tactual contact with object. In the second stage, the 5-month-old infant is capable of reaching for and making contact with the object. He is able to grasp the object with the entire hand, but not firmly. In the third stage, the child's movements are gradually refined so that by the seventh month the palm and fingers are coordinated. The child is still unable to effectively use the thumb and fingers. In the fourth stage, at about 9 months of age, the child begins use of the forefinger in grasping. At 10 months of age reaching and grasping are coordinated into one continuous movement. In the fifth stage, efficient use of the thumb and forefinger comes into play at around 12 months of age. In the sixth stage, when the child is 14 months old, prehension abilities are much like those of adults. Environmental factors that appear to influence the quality of the grasping movement include the size, weight, texture, and shape of the object being held (Case-Smith, Bigsby, and Clutter, 1998; Siddiqui, 1995).

The developmental progression of reaching and grasping is complex. Landreth (1958) stated

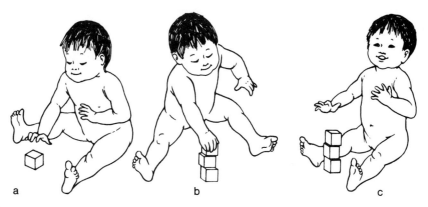

a   b   c

Figure 8.5
Rudimentary (a) reaching, (b) grasping, and (c) releasing.

that six component coordinates appear to be involved in the development of prehension. Eckert (1987) neatly summed up these six developmental acts in the following statement:

> These acts involve transitions and include: (1) the transition from visually locating an object to attempting to reach for the object. Other transitions involve: (2) simple eye-hand coordination, to progressive independence of visual effort with its ultimate expression in activities such as piano playing and typing; (3) initial maximal involvement of body musculature to a minimum involvement and greater economy of effort; (4) proximal large muscle activity of the arms and shoulders to distal fine muscle activity of the fingers; (5) early crude raking movements in manipulating objects with the hands to the later pincer-like precision of control with the opposing thumb and forefinger; and (6) initial bilateral reaching and manipulation to ultimate use of the preferred hand. (pp. 122–123)

Releasing

The frantic shaking of a rattle is a familiar sight when observing a 6-month-old infant at play. This is a learning activity usually accompanied by a great deal of smiling, babbling, and obvious glee. Minutes later, however, the same infant may be observed shaking the rattle with obvious frustration

and apparent rage. The reason for this abrupt shift in moods may be that at 6 months of age the infant has yet to master the art of releasing an object from the grasp. The child has succeeded in reaching for and grasping the handle of the rattle but is not maturationally able to command the flexor muscles of the fingers to relax their grip on the object on command. Learning to fill a bottle with stones, building a block tower, hurling a ball, and turning the pages of a book are seemingly simple examples of a young child's attempts to learn to release, but when compared with earlier attempts at reaching and grasping, these are indeed remarkable advances. By the time the child is 14 months old, she has mastered the rudimentary elements of releasing objects from her grasp. The 18-month-old has well-coordinated control of all aspects of reach, grasp, and release (Halverson, 1937).

As the infant's mastery of the rudimentary abilities of manipulation (reach, grasp, and release) are developing, the reasons for handling objects are revised. Instead of manipulating objects simply to touch, feel, or mouth them, the child now becomes involved in the process of manipulating objects to learn more about the world in which he lives. The manipulation of objects becomes directed by appropriate perceptions to achieve meaningful goals (figure 8.5).

The development of locomotor, stability, and manipulative movement abilities in infants is influenced by both maturation and learning. These two facets of development are interrelated, and it is through this interaction that the infant develops and refines rudimentary movement abilities. These movement abilities are necessary stepping-stones to the development of fundamental movement patterns and specialized movement abilities.

SPECIAL PROGRAMS FOR INFANTS

For years parents, pediatricians, therapists, and educators have recognized the importance of providing infants with a stimulating and enriching environment in which to grow and develop. This is particularly evident with developmentally delayed or at-risk infants (Ramey and Ramey, 1994). This awareness led to the passage of Public Law 99-457 in 1986 and its reauthorization in Public Law 105-17 in 1997, which mandated **early intervention** services for infants and toddlers with disabilities. One of the stipulations of this legal action is that an individualized family service plan (IFSP) is devised by a multidisciplinary team to provide structure and evaluation to a strategy for facilitating healthy development and reducing or eliminating the potential for developmental delays. Successful implementation of such plans is contingent on the intensity and quality of the intervention program (Ramey and Ramey, 1998). Additionally, the theoretical foundation on which the intervention activities are based should be well developed (Palmer, 1992).

Enriching movement experiences are often a major part of the IFSP of an infant at-risk. Moving about and interacting with the environment is one of the primary means by which infants develop cognitively. A recent and unique early intervention strategy on the horizon is the facilitation of independent walking in infants with developmental delays using a treadmill training paradigm. Based on the theoretical studies of Esther Thelen (1985, 1986), Beverly and Dale Ulrich have pursued a line of research that has resulted in a procedure that can facilitate the onset of independent walking in infants with Down syndrome (Ulrich and Ulrich, 1995; Ulrich, Ulrich, and Collier, 1992; Ulrich, Ulrich, Collier, and Cole, 1995). Their technique

involves supporting the infant upright on a small, motorized treadmill. As the belt begins to move, the infants display a well-coordinated, alternating stepping pattern even though they are unable to walk independently. As a result of stepping practice sessions on the treadmill, infants with Down syndrome walked independently months sooner than their counterparts who did not have practice. These findings may be the result of a number of factors including the strengthening and stabilizing of the walking movement pattern, an increase in leg strength, and the improvement of body mechanisms associated with balance and posture (Ulrich and Ulrich, 1999). While progress is still being made in the treadmill design and procedures, treadmill training represents an early intervention strategy that shows great promise for infants with Down syndrome or other developmental delays.

Another body of research that has emerged over the last ten years is the area of enhancing brain development or recovering from brain injury by attempting complex motor tasks in environmentally enriched settings (Ivanco and Greenough, 2000; Jones and Greenough, 1996; Jones, Klintsova, Kilman, Sirevaag, and Greenough, 1997; Kleim, Pipitone, Czerlanis, and Greenough, 1998). While these studies involved the use of rats as subjects, they lay the groundwork for later theoretical and application research with human beings. This represents the potential for exciting outcomes with not only infants but across the lifespan.

CONCEPT 8.6

Developmental stimulation programs for at-risk infants have the potential for enhancing later development.

Infant Aquatic Programs

Infant aquatic programs are a popular activity in the United States. Most communities with swimming facilities offer some form of aquatics for babies. Parents enroll their children in infant swimming programs for varying reasons. Some want to "drownproof" their children. Others want babies to learn how to swim in the belief that this is a "critical period" for developing swimming skills. Still others enroll their babies for the sheer pleasure of interacting in a different medium and enhancing the bonding process. Although each of these reasons may have merit, aquatic programs for infants should be approached with caution.

CONCEPT 8.7

Infant aquatic programs may be beneficial in providing additional stimulation and promoting parent-child interaction, but they involve potential dangers that must be acknowledged.

Langendorfer (1987) points out that "regardless of age or skill, *no* person is completely water safe!" (p. 3). Parents who attempt to drownproof their children need to be alerted that this is not possible and that constant vigilance is necessary when children are near the water. Langendorfer further indicated that there is no evidence to suggest that infant swimming enhances later development. The notion of a narrowly defined critical period for learning how to swim is not supported by available research.

Other problems associated with infant swim programs are hyponatremia (or infant water intoxication) and Giardia. **Hyponatremia** is a rare but serious condition activated by swallowing excessive amounts of water, which reduces the body's serum sodium level. Symptoms include lethargy, disorientation, weakness, nausea, vomiting, seizures, coma, and death. **Giardia,** a problem much more common to infant swimming classes, is an intestinal parasite that may be transmitted between infants. It causes severe and prolonged diarrhea.

As a result of the misinformation about infant aquatics and potential problems, the American Academy of Pediatrics (2000) offers a series of recommendations, which include the following:

- Children are generally not developmentally ready for formal swimming lessons until after their fourth birthday.
- Aquatic programs for infants and toddlers should not be promoted as a way to decrease the risk of drowning.
- Parents should not feel secure that their child is safe in water or safe from drowning after participation in such programs.
- Whenever infants and toddlers are in or around water, an adult should be within an arm's length, providing "touch supervision."
- All aquatic programs should include information on the cognitive and motor limitations of infants and toddlers, the inherent risks of water, the strategies of prevention of drowning, and the role of adults in supervising and monitoring the safety of children in and around water.
- Hypothermia, water intoxication, and communicable diseases can be prevented by following existing medical guidelines and do not preclude infants and toddlers from participating in otherwise appropriate aquatic experience programs.

SUMMARY

During infancy the child's primary concerns are with self-gratification. Primitive reflexes serve the infant well in meeting basic survival needs, but as the child develops, other needs emerge. Among them is the characteristic need to "know." Development proceeds in a predictable sequence but at varying rates as control is gained first over head and trunk and then over the limbs. Sitting enables the infant to more effectively use the arms for exploration. Manipulative skills, including mouthing, allow use of the sensorimotor mechanisms to gain information. Movements become the symbols of the child's thought process because language is limited.

The motor achievements of the normal human infant are not only a function of neurological maturation but also a function of a self-organizing system. Biology plays an important role in the predictable sequence of motor development. There is, however, considerable normal variation in the rate of development. Although neuromuscular maturation must occur for the infant to progress to the next developmental level, several environmental and task demand factors determine the rate. Environments that provide stimulation and opportunities for exploration encourage early acquisition of rudimentary movement patterns. Crawling, for example, is often the outgrowth of an ocular following pattern, while standing and an upright gait are reinforced by the presence of handholds in the child's environment.

CRITICAL READINGS

Cowden, J. E., Sayers, K. L., & Torrey, C. C. (1998). *Pediatric Adapted Motor Development and Exercise: An Innovative, Multisystem Approach for Professionals and Families.* (1998). Springfield, IL: Charles C. Thomas.

Langendofer, S. J., & Bruya, L. D. (1995). *Aquatic Readiness.* Champaign, IL: Human Kinetics.

Ouden, L. D. et al. (1991). Is it correct to correct? Developmental milestones in 555 'normal' preterm infants compared with term infants. *Journal of Pediatrics, 118*(3), 399–404.

Ramey, C. T., & Ramey, S. L. (1998). Early intervention and early experiences. *The American Psychologist, 53,* 109–120.

Thelen, E. (1992). Development of locomotion from a dynamic systems approach. In H. Forssberg & H. Hirschfeld (Eds.), *Movement Disorders in Children, Medicine and Sport Science, Vol. 36.* Basel: Karger.

Ulrich, B. D., Ulrich, D. A., Collier, D. H., & Cole, E. (1995). Developmental shifts in the ability of infants with Down syndrome to produce treadmill steps. *Physical Theraapy, 75,* 14–21.

 ## WEB RESOURCES

Esther Thelen's Infant Motor Development Laboratory at Indiana University
http://php.indiana.edu/~gormleyf

Growing Child Newsletter–List of Developmental Milestones
www.growingchild.com/milestones.html

International Society on Infant Studies
www.isisweb.org

Society for Research in Child Development
www.srcd.org

CHAPTER 9

INFANT PERCEPTION

KEY TERMS

Perception

Sensations

Habituation

Dishabituation

Evoked potentials

Consensual pupillary reflex

Visual acuity

Accommodation (visual)

Peripheral vision

Binocular vision

Tracking

Bifoveal fixation

Fusion

Stereopsis

Saccades

Depth perception

Chromatic intensity

Color perception

Form perception

Auditory perception

Olfactory perception

Tactile perception

Gustatory perception

CHAPTER COMPETENCIES

Upon completion of this chapter you should be able to:

- Discuss changes in perceptual functioning during infancy
- Describe various methods of studying infant perception
- Discuss developmental aspects of infant visual perception
- Describe developmental changes in visual acuity, accommodation, and peripheral vision
- Distinguish between the terms *binocularity, fixation,* and *tracking*
- Discuss the visual-cliff experiments and draw conclusions about infant depth perception
- Debate the question concerning infants' perception of color
- Trace the developmental aspects of form perception
- Describe various aspects of infant auditory, olfactory, and gustatory perception

KEY CONCEPT

Perceptual development in infancy is intricately entwined with motor development, resulting in an interdependent system.

From the moment of birth, infants begin the process of learning how to interact with the environment. This interaction is a perceptual as well as a motor process. **Perception** refers to any process in which sensory information or sensations are interpreted or given meaning regarding what is occurring about ourselves. *Perceptual-motor* refers to the process of organizing incoming information with stored information that leads to an overt act or motor performance. All voluntary movement involves an element of perception. Students of motor development should be concerned with perceptual development because of the important link between perceptual and motor processes. Santrock (2001) points out that through a dynamic systems approach perceptual development and motor development "do not develop in isolation from one another but, rather, are coupled" (p. 158). Therefore people perceive in order to experience movement and move in order to experience perception.

To gain immediate information about the outside world, we must rely on our various senses. Newborns receive all sorts of stimulation (visual, auditory, olfactory, gustatory, tactile, and kinesthetic) through the various sense modalities. They make responses to these stimuli, but these responses have limited utility. Only when sensory stimuli can be integrated with stored information do these **sensations** take on meaning for the infant and truly warrant being called perceptions.

Newborns attach little meaning to sensory stimuli. For example, light rays impinging on the eyes register on the retinas and are transmitted to appropriate nerve centers in the sensory areas of the cortex. The newborn's reaction is simple (sensation)—if the light is dim the pupils dilate, and if the light is bright the pupils constrict and some of

the stimulation is obscured (*consensual pupillary reflex*). Soon the neonate blinks as the stimulus approaches. These simple reflex actions persist throughout life, but in a short time the infant begins to attach meaning to the visual stimuli received. Soon a certain face becomes "mother." An object is identified as having either three or four sides. The infant attends to certain stimuli and begins to apply basic meaning to them with the powers of visual perception.

CONCEPT 9.1

Development of the perceptual system is more rapid than that of the motor system during infancy.

As with the development of movement abilities in the infant, the development of perceptual skills is a matter of experience and maturation. Maturation plays an important role in the development of increased acuity of perception, but much improvement in acuity is due to experience. Learning opportunities afforded children and adults enhance the sophistication of their perceptual modalities. Similarly, only through experience will the infant be able to acquire many perception capabilities. The infant's perceptual development is basic to later functioning and, as we will see, is intricately intertwined with the motor system.

METHODS OF STUDYING INFANT PERCEPTION

In the study of infant perceptual abilities a number of techniques are used to determine infants' responses to various stimuli. Because they cannot verbalize or fill out questionnaires, indirect techniques of naturalistic observation are used as the primary means of determining what infants can see, hear, feel, and so forth. Each of these methods compares an infant's state prior to introduction of the stimulus with its state during or immediately following the stimulus. The difference between the two measures provides the researcher with an indication of the level and duration of the response to the stimulus. For example, if a uniformly moving pattern of some sort is passed across a neonate's visual field, repetitive following movements of the eyes occur (Atkinson and Braddick, 1982). The occurrence of these eye movements provides evidence that the moving pattern is perceived at some level by the newborn. Similarly, changes in the infant's general level of motor activity—turning the head, blinking the eyes, crying, and so forth—have been used by researchers as visual indicators of the infant's perceptual abilities.

Such techniques, however, have limitations. First, the observation may be unreliable in that two or more observers may not agree that the particular response occurred, or to what degree it occurred. Second, responses are difficult to quantify. Often the rapid and diffuse movements of the infant make it difficult to get an accurate record of the number of responses. The third, and most potent, limitation is that it is not possible to be certain that the infant's response was due to the stimulus presented or to a change from no stimulus to a stimulus. The infant may be responding to aspects of the stimulus different than those identified by the investigator. Therefore, when observational assessment is used as a technique for studying infant perceptual abilities, care must be taken not to overgeneralize from the data or to rely on one or two studies as conclusive evidence of a particular perceptual ability of the infant.

CONCEPT 9.2

It is unwise to generalize from conclusions reached in some observational studies of infant perceptual development, even though the study techniques are sophisticated.

Observational assessment techniques have become much more sophisticated, reducing the limitations just presented. Film analysis of the infant's responses, heart and respiration rate monitors, and nonnutritive sucking devices are used as effective tools in understanding infant perception. Film analysis permits researchers to carefully study the infant's responses over and over and in slow motion. Precise measurements can be made of the length and frequency of the infant's attention between two stimuli. Heart and respiration rate monitors provide the investigator with the number of heartbeats or breaths taken when a new stimuli is presented. Numerical increases are used as quantifiable indicators of heightened interest in the new stimulus. Increases in *nonnutritive sucking* were first used as an assessment measure by Siqueland and DeLucia (1969). They devised an apparatus that connected a baby's pacifier to a counting device. As stimuli were presented, changes in the infant's sucking behavior were recorded. Increases in the number of sucks were used as an indicator of the infant's attention to, or preference for, a given visual display.

Two additional techniques of studying infant perception have come into vogue: habituation-dishabituation and evoked potentials. In the *habituation-dishabituation* technique, a single stimulus is presented repeatedly to the infant until there is a measurable decline (**habituation**) in whatever attending behavior is being observed. At that point a new stimulus is presented, and any recovery (**dishabituation**) in responsiveness is recorded. If the infant fails to dishabituate and continues to show habituation with the new stimulus, it is assumed that the baby is unable to perceive the new stimulus as different. The habituation-dishabituation paradigm has been used most extensively with studies of auditory and olfactory perception in infants. **Evoked potentials** are electrical brain responses that may be related to a particular stimulus because of where they originate. Electrodes are attached to the infant's scalp. Changes in the electrical pattern of the brain indicates that the stimulus is getting through to the infant's central nervous system and eliciting some form of response.

Each of the preceding techniques provides the researcher with evidence that the infant can detect or discriminate between stimuli. With these sophisticated observational assessment and electrophysiological measures we know that the neonate of only a few days is far more perceptive than previously suspected. However, these measures are only "indirect" indicators of the infant's perceptual abilities. Rigid adherence to a chronological age classification of these abilities is unwise.

VISUAL PERCEPTION

At birth, the infant's eyes have all of the parts necessary for sight and are almost completely formed. The fovea is incompletely developed and the ocular muscles are immature. These two factors result in poor fixation, focusing, and coordination of eye movements. The blinking and lacrimal (tear formation) apparatuses are poorly developed at birth, and the neonate is unable to shed tears for one to seven weeks after birth. Also, it is debatable whether the newborn possesses color vision because of the amount of rhodopsin and iodopsin (visual purple) present in the rods and cones of the eye. Visual acuity, accommodation, peripheral vision, binocularity, fixation, tracking, color vision, and form perception develop rapidly during the early weeks and months following birth. Table 9.1 presents a list of the major developmental aspects of infant visual perception, along with the approximate age at which these abilities begin to emerge.

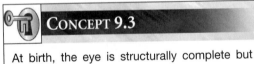

CONCEPT 9.3

At birth, the eye is structurally complete but functionally immature.

Contrast Sensitivity

The visual apparatus is anatomically complete at birth, although it may be functionally immature. Vision is first used by the newborn in responding to various light intensities. At birth the newborn exhibits a **consensual pupillary reflex** in which the pupils dilate or constrict in response to the intensity of a localized light source. Hershenson (1964) found that 2- to 4-day-old infants looked at medium-intensity lights longer than at dim or high-intensity lights. Peeples and Teller (1975)

found that 2-month-old infants could discriminate between bars of light against a black background almost as well as adults. The babies were able to detect differences in brightness of as little as 5 percent, whereas adults were able to make 1 percent discriminations. Additionally, it has frequently been observed that newborns tighten their eyelids when asleep in brightly lit rooms, and they tend to be more active in dim light than in bright. Perhaps this helps explain why infants are frequently more active at night than during the daylight hours.

CONCEPT 9.4

Visual perceptual abilities develop rapidly during the first six months following birth.

Visual Acuity, Accommodation, and Peripheral Vision

The eye grows and develops rapidly during the child's first two years. In the infant, the cornea is thinner and more spherical than in the adult. As a result, the cornea is more refractive and the infant tends to be slightly myopic at birth. Normal visual acuity is gradually achieved as the cornea rounds out and the lens flattens. The term **visual acuity** refers to the degree of detail that can be seen in an object. The newborn has a focal distance of about 4 to 10 inches (10.2–25.4 cm). The length of focus increases almost daily and is within the range of normal adult acuity by the time the infant is 6 to 12 months old (Aslin and Dumais, 1980; Cohen et al., 1979).

Accommodation, the ability of the lens of each eye to vary its curvature to bring the retinal image into sharp focus, improves with age. The study by Haynes et al. (1965) demonstrated that adultlike accommodation does not occur until around the fourth month. Banks (1980), in a replication of the Haynes study, found partial accommodation at one month and near adultlike focusing around the second month. These studies demonstrated that, until at least 2 months of age, infants are not able to bring objects into sharp focus.

TABLE 9.1 Developmental Aspects of Selected Infant Visual Perceptual Abilities

Visual Quality	Selected Abilities	Approximate Age of Onset
Sensitivity to Light The visual apparatus is complete in the newborn and is first put to use by adjusting to varying intensities of the light source.	Consensual pupillary reflex (contraction and dilation of the pupils) Strabismus Turns head toward light source Closes eyes if light is bright Tightens eyelids when asleep More active in dim light than in bright light	Birth 2 to 3 hours Birth to 14 days Birth Birth Birth Birth to 1 year
Visual Acuity The length of focus increases daily as the eye matures.	Organically complete visual apparatus Length of focus 4 to 10 in. (10.2–25.4 cm) Length of focus about 36 in. (91.4 cm) Length of focus about 100 ft. (30.5 m)	Birth Birth to 1 week 3 months 1 year
Accommodation Accommodation depends on functional maturity of the lens.	Poor Near adultlike	Birth to 2 months 2 to 4 months
Peripheral Vision Peripheral vision improves rapidly in a horizontal direction.	15 degrees from center 30 degrees from center 40 degrees from center	Birth to 2 weeks 1 to 2 months 5 months
Fixation Fixation is monocular and essentially reflexive during the first weeks.	Fixates one eye on bright objects Fixates both eyes on bright objects Turns head from one stationary bright surface to another Follows an object in motion, keeping the head stationary Directs eyes toward an object	Birth 2 to 3 days 11 days 23 days 10 weeks
Tracking Tracking is first saccadic and gradually smooths out. Develops far sooner than the motor component.	Horizontal Vertical Diagonal Circular	Saccadic pursuit begins at birth Smooth pursuits begin by 2 months Sequence is fixed
Depth Perception Monocular vision at birth soon gives way to binocular vision and perception of depth.	Monocular vision Binocular vision Depth perception	Birth 2 months 2 to 6 months
Color Discrimination and Preference Inconsistent evidence. Color vision may be present at birth depending on the amount of rhodopsin and iodopsin present.	Color vision Color perception Prefers shape to color Color discrimination	Birth? 10 weeks 15 days 3 months
Form Perception Discrimination begins early and develops rapidly in complexity. The human face is the favorite object.	Prefers patterned objects to plain Imitates facial gestures Prefers human face Size and shape constancy Discriminates between two- and three-dimensional figures	Neonate Neonate Neonate 2 months 3 months 6 months

Peripheral vision is the visual field that can be seen without a change in fixation of the eyes. Tronick's (1972) work suggests that the visual field of the 2-week-old is narrow (about 15 degrees from center), but expands to about 40 degrees from center by the fifth month. In line with Tronick (1972), Aslin and Salapatek (1975) found that 1- and 2-month-old infants had a visual field of about 30 degrees from center. Normal adult peripheral vision is about 90 degrees from center to either side.

CONCEPT 9.5

Although myopic at birth, with a short focal distance and limited peripheral vision, the neonate responds to various light intensities.

Cohen et al. (1979) reported that "by 6 months of age both the infant's central and peripheral systems are quite mature" (p. 404). It appears, therefore, that visual acuity, accommodation, and peripheral vision improve dramatically as the eyes mature during early infancy. The interaction between these three developing systems is, at present, unknown.

Binocularity, Fixation, and Tracking

The topics of infant binocularity, fixation, and tracking have interested researchers for years. Prerequisite to efficient fixation and tracking behaviors is binocular vision. **Binocular vision** requires that the eyes work together in visually attending to a stationary object *(fixation)* or to a moving object **(tracking)**.

Binocular vision, according to the theoretical framework originally presented by Worth in 1915 as discussed by Aslin and Dumais (1980), occurs at three levels: bifoveal fixation, fusion, and stereopsis. For **bifoveal fixation** to occur, the fovea of the two eyes must be aligned and directed at the same instant toward the object of visual regard. If bifoveal fixation is absent, then fusion and stereopsis cannot occur.

CONCEPT 9.6

Binocular vision occurs at three levels: bifoveal fixation, fusion, and stereopsis.

Fusion is the second level of binocular vision. Fusion is a process in which the images on the two retinas are combined into a single visual percept. When looking at an object, each eye sends information to the retina and on to the brain from a different orientation. The two eyes are about 6 centimeters apart, so a direct line from each eye to the object is different. Krieg (1978) noted that the interocular distance between the two eyes increases by about 50 percent from birth to adulthood. Limited data suggest that infants have fusion by the fourth to sixth month of postnatal life (Aslin, 1977). Fusion is required for stereopsis to occur.

Stereopsis is the third level of binocularity and enables one to detect depth. Stereopsis is based on the extent of retinal disparity, or mismatch, between the two eyes and has been demonstrated in infants 3 months and older (Fox et al., 1980). Aslin and Dumais (1980) stated that "the presence of bifoveal fixation in infants does not guarantee that fusion and stereopsis are present" (p. 60). Therefore, although it is possible that these three levels of binocularity are hierarchical, it is also possible that they exist as three parallel functions interdependent upon one another. The primary developmental determinants of binocular vision, which makes fixation and tracking possible, are visual acuity, contrast sensitivity, accommodation, and the distance between the eyes (Aslin and Dumais, 1980).

Visual fixation is monocular at birth, probably because of the infant's poor visual acuity and contrast sensitivity. Also, visual-motor control of the two eyes is immature. These conditions improve rapidly during the first 6 months, suggesting improvement in the infant's ability to binocularly fixate (Atkinson and Braddick, 1982).

CONCEPT 9.7

Saccadic eye movements govern visual tracking by the young infant.

CONCEPT 9.8

Perception of depth by the infant is a function of experience as well as maturation.

Binocular tracking is the most basic aspect of visual-motor pursuit. Tracking involves directing the eyes from one line of sight to another. These eye movements are either of a high velocity (saccadic) or slow velocity (smooth pursuit). **Saccades** are quick movements of the eyes that involve a redirection of focus from one object of regard to another. Saccadic eye movements govern the object tracking of the very young infant. A series of saccadic movements are made as the infant tracks an object across the visual field. A variety of hypotheses are available for this yet unexplained phenomenon (Aslin, 1984), but by the end of the second week of postnatal life the neonate is capable of making reliable saccadic tracking movements. Dayton and Jones (1964) were the first to demonstrate that the eye movements of the infant are totally saccadic until the end of the second month. However, Aslin (1981), using a very slow moving target, found evidence of smooth pursuits beginning by the sixth week of age. Although the exact timing of the onset of smooth pursuits is debatable, the sequence is clear. Smooth pursuits tracking behaviors first occur in a horizontal direction, followed by vertical, then diagonal, and finally circular (Field, 1976; Haith, 1966; Pratt, 1954).

Depth Perception

Perception of depth involves the ability to judge the distance of an object from oneself. Williams (1983) categorized **depth perception** into "static" and "dynamic" components. *Static depth perception* involves making depth or distance judgments with regard to stationary objects. *Dynamic depth perception* requires one to make distance judgments about moving objects.

Static depth perception has been extensively investigated in infants through the now classic *visual-cliff* experiments by Gibson and Walk (1960) and Walk (1966). In their research design, infants and animals capable of self-produced locomotion were encouraged to crawl across a thick sheet of glass that contained a variety of depth cues (figure 9.1). The experiments concluded that mobile infants, even when coaxed, would not crawl across the "deep end" to their mothers. Svejda and Schmidt (1979) assessed the cardiac responses of prelocomotor infants (mean age of 6.9 months) and locomotor infants (mean age of 7.1 months) as they were lowered to the shallow or to the deep side of the cliff. Prelocomotor infants exhibited little or no difference in heart rate levels when lowered to either side. However, locomotor infants showed significant increases in heart rate responses to both sides, but a "more marked acceleration" on the deep side. The results of this experiment tends to confirm the Held and Hein (1963) and Walk (1978) hypotheses that the development of depth perception is in part a function of experience. It also indicates that sensorimotor feedback through early locomotor experience is sufficient to account for a developmental shift on the visual cliff between prelocomotor and locomotor infants. Whether sensorimotor experiences are a necessary condition is still uncertain.

A number of investigations into dynamic depth perception have been conducted with infants in recent years. The reaching responses of young infants presented with moving stimuli have been carefully studied by von Hofsten (1979, 1982, 1986). The results of his investigations clearly demonstrated that infants as young as 5 days of age make what appear to be purposeful, but poorly controlled, reaching movements toward moving

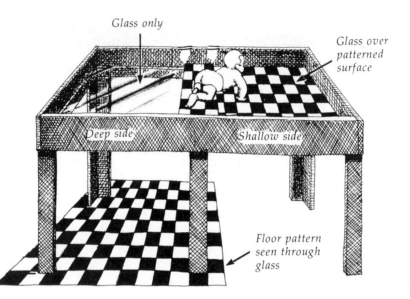

Glass only

Glass over patterned surface

Deep side

Shallow side

Floor pattern seen through glass

Figure 9.1
The visual cliff.

objects. Dynamic depth perception appears to be present in rather sophisticated form by the fourth month of postnatal life. von Hofsten (1986) stated that: "Thus it seems without doubt that shortly before four months of age the infant starts to be able to use also the purely visual mode of control whereby the seen position of the hand is related to the seen position of the object" (p. 174).

At this point the motor system lags behind the perceptual system. Movements toward an object, though purposeful, are crude, demonstrating poor integration between the visual and motor systems. Adultlike reaching behaviors do not appear until around the sixth month, when differentiation of muscle groups and integration with sensory systems begin to conjoin.

Color Perception

A large number of studies have been conducted over the years to determine if infants perceive color and are able to distinguish among different colors. Much of the experimentation prior to the 1960s yielded confusing and often conflicting results. Out of this research, however, came the realization that the infant responds to the brightness

(i.e., **chromatic intensity**) of the colors presented prior to responding to hue. Hershenson (1964) was the first to demonstrate this in infants, prompting a new wave of studies that attempted to control for the brightness factor. As cited by Cohen et al. (1979), Oster (1975) found that by 10 weeks of age infants perceive colors over a large portion of the visible color spectrum. Schaller (1975) also found similar results with 11- to 12-week-old infants. These two experiments clearly demonstrated that infants as young as 10 weeks of age have the ability to perceive color. We do not know if infants younger than 10 weeks perceive color. The amount of *rhodopsin* and *iodopsin* present in the rods and cones may be insufficient for color vision. Similarly, we do not know categorically if the **color perception** of the infant is identical to that of adults, but limited evidence favors this notion.

CONCEPT 9.9

Infants tend to respond more to the chromatic intensity of color than to the actual hue.

Bornstein et al. (1976) demonstrated that 4-month-old infants were capable of discriminating between blue, green, yellow, and red. Another experiment by Bornstein et al. (1976) with 3-month-olds yielded similar results. It appears, therefore, that infants as young as 3 months of age do have the ability to make adultlike color discriminations. The question concerning the "favorite" color of infants is open to further speculation and study. Spears (1964) noted that it is clear that babies as young as 15 days prefer colors to noncolors (i.e., unpatterned whites and grays), and that they prefer shape to color.

Form Perception

A number of investigators have examined **form perception** in infants. Form perception is the ability to distinguish between shapes and to discriminate among a variety of patterns. Haith (1980) found that newborns placed in a darkened room would look for subtle shadows and edges. Moreover, Kessen et al. (1972), in a similar experiment, reported that newborns responded only to vertical high-contrast edges. However, Haith found that they could also respond to horizontal lines. Fantz et al. (1975) reported that newborns were able to perceive form and preferred curved lines over straight lines.

Salapatek (1975) reported that other researchers examining neonatal responses to squares, circles, and triangles found that the infants tend to fixate on a single line or edge at 1 month of age but spent much more time scanning the figures at 2 months of age. Salapatek drew three important conclusions from the abundance of research on form perception in the newborn:

> First, before 2 months of age visual attention appears to be captured by a single or limited number of features of a figure or pattern. Second, before approximately 1 to 2 months of age there is little evidence that the arrangement or pattern of figural elements plays any role in visual selection or memory. Third, before 1 to 2 months, there is little evidence that the line of sight is attracted by anything more than the greatest number or size of visible contour elements per unit area, regardless of type or arrangement of elements. (p. 226)

CONCEPT 9.10

Complexity governs the infant's visual attending behaviors, in that the infant prefers shape to color and prefers complex shapes to simpler ones.

Infants over 3 months of age appear to exhibit a variety of sophisticated abilities with regard to form perception. Cohen et al. (1979) reported that several investigators have determined that infants can discriminate one pattern from another even when the pattern is placed in a variety of arrangements. Furthermore, "the evidence is reasonably convincing that at some point within the first 6 months following birth infants can perceive multiple forms and can respond to, and prefer, a change in pattern arrangement" (Cohen et al., p. 412). Fantz (1963) found that 2-month-old infants prefer looking at the human face over all other simple stimuli. Cohen et al. reported that by 6 months of age infants can distinguish among two-dimensional photographs of human faces. Clearly, the ability of the infant to discriminate between shapes and patterns develops rapidly during this period and has reached rather sophisticated levels by the end of the first 6 months of postnatal life.

AUDITORY, OLFACTORY, GUSTATORY, AND TACTILE PERCEPTION

Available research data concerning the development of **auditory, olfactory, gustatory,** and **tactile perception** in the human infant are much less complete than for the visual modality. As with vision, the auditory abilities do not unfold exclusively without the influences of the environment. Environmental conditions influence the extent of development of audition. The ear is structurally complete at birth, and the infant is capable of hearing as soon as the amniotic fluid drains (usually within a day or two after birth). The fetus responds to sound before birth (Bernard and Sontag, 1947). These reactions, however, may be in response to tactile sensations created by the vibrations produced (Aslin et al., 1983). At present we do not know if the fetus is capable of hearing sound.

CONCEPT 9.11

Although less widely studied, infant auditory, olfactory, and tactile-kinesthetic perceptions also influence the process of motor development.

Research indicates that the newborn is less sensitive to sound than adults. Aslin et al. (1983) reported that the difference is at least 10 decibels.

Sensitivity to sound improves with age, and infants as young as 6 months are more sensitive to high-frequency sounds than neonates (Trehub et al., 1980). Infant auditory perception may be adultlike by 2 years of age (Schneider et al., 1980). The infant can localize sounds at birth and reacts primarily to loudness and duration (Trehub et al., 1991). Crude pitch discriminations have been demonstrated by Leventhal and Lipsett (1964) as early as the first 4 days of postnatal life. Definite responses to tonal differences are seen around the third month, and the infant reacts with pleasure to a parent's voice by the fifth month (Leventhal and Lipsett, 1964).

TABLE 9.2 Developmental Aspect of Selected Infant Auditory, Olfactory, and Gustatory Abilities

Perceptual Quality	Selected Abilities	Approximate Age of Onset
Auditory Perception The ear is structurally complete at birth, and the newborn can respond to sound.	Responds to loud, sharp sounds	Prenatal
	Ability to localize sounds	Birth
	Reacts primarily to loudness and duration	Birth
	Crude pitch discrimination	1 to 4 days
	Responds to tonal differences	3 to 6 months
	Reacts with pleasure to parent's voice	5 to 6 months
	Adultlike	24 months
Olfactory Perception The olfactory mechanism is structurally complete at birth, and the newborn responds crudely to various odors.	Responds to odors	Birth
	Reduced sensitivity upon repeated application of the stimuli (habituation)	Neonate
	Distinguishes between pleasant and unpleasant odors	2–3 days
	Shows preference for mother's odor	2 weeks
	Discrimination abilities improve with practice	Infancy
Gustatory Perception The newborn reacts to variation in sweet, sour, and bitter tastes. Little research data are available on this modality.	Shows preference in tastes (prefers sweet to sour, sour to bitter)	Neonate
Tactile Perception The newborn reacts to a variety of tactile sensations by responding with reflexive movements.	Turns head when cheek is stroked, sucks when lips are stroked, curls fingers and toes when pressure is applied to those areas	Prenatal

The research on olfactory and gustatory perception is sparse. It is difficult to separate the developmental sequence of smell and taste because the nose and mouth are closely connected, and stimuli applied to one are likely to affect the other. The newborn does, however, appear to react to certain odors, although this may be due more to pain caused by the pungent odors than to smell. Lipsett et al. (1963) demonstrated that newborns less than 24 hours old made definite responses when exposed to a highly offensive odor. Engen and Lipsett (1965) showed that infants as young as 32 hours were able to discriminate between two different odors. McFarlane (1975) in studying infants less than a week old found that they could discriminate between the mother's breast pad and a clean pad, with a clear preference for mother's pad. Not one of the infants, however, could discriminate between his or her mother's breast pad and that of another. It may not be until the second week that recognition of mother's smell is developed. Newborns react to taste, preferring sweet tastes to sour ones and sour tastes to bitter ones.

Table 9.2 presents a summary of the major developmental aspects of infant auditory, gustatory, olfactory perception, and tactile.

SUMMARY

The study of infant perception has intrigued researchers for years. We now know that the newborn, neonate, and young infant are much more perceptually aware and capable than previously thought. Newer techniques for observing and recording infant responses to various stimuli have been responsible for a shift in our assumptions about the perceptual capabilities of the very young. Observational assessment techniques that use film analysis, heart and respiration monitors, nonnutritive sucking devices, and electrical brain impulse recorders are making new inroads into our understanding of the perceptual world of the infant.

The visual world of the infant has been the most extensively studied perceptual modality. The newborn's eyes are structurally complete, but functionally immature. Rapid progress is seen in the acquisition of a vast array of visual perceptual abilities. Although it is difficult to pinpoint when these abilities emerge, it is possible to chart the sequence of acquisition of many visual perceptual abilities. (Generalized application of observations to all infants should be avoided, however.) The motor developmentalist is especially interested in the visual modality because of its close, often essential, link to voluntary movement. Much movement behavior is governed by our perceptions. Although the visual perceptual world of the infant develops rapidly, the motor system tends to lag behind. It is not until later infancy that the motor system begins to catch up and a matching of perceptual and motor data occurs.

These other sensory modalities (auditory, gustatory, olfactory, and tactile), although important, are less clearly understood in the infant. Furthermore, their link to the motor system, although significant, is less crucial than vision. Therefore, the matching of perceptual and motor data in the infant and young child will probably continue to be a topic of keen interest to researchers and educators.

CRITICAL READINGS

Fantz, R. L. (1963). Pattern vision in newborn infants. *Science, 140,* 296–297.

Haith, M. M. (1980). *Rules that Babies Look By.* Hillsdale, NJ: Erlbaum.

Johnson, S. P., & Aslin, R. N. (1996). Perception of object unity in young infants: The roles of motion, depth, and orientation. *Cognitive Development, 11,* 161–180.

Lipsett, L. P. et al. (1963). Developmental changes in the olfactory threshold of the neonate. *Child Development, 34,* 371–376.

Magill, R. A. (2001). *Motor Learning: Concepts and Applications* (Chapter 6). 6th ed. St. Louis: McGraw-Hill.

Payne, V. G., & Isaacs, L. D. (2002). *Human Motor Development: A Lifespan Approach.* 4th ed. Mountain View, CA: Mayfield.

Santrock, J. W. (2001). *Child Development* (Chapter 5). 9th ed. St. Louis: McGraw-Hill.

Simons, K. (Ed.) (1993). *Early Visual Development: Normal and Abnormal.* New York: Oxford University Press.

Snow, C. W. (1997). *Infant Development.* 2nd ed. Simon & Schuster.

Snow, C. W. (1998). *Infant Development.* 2nd ed. Upper Saddle River, NJ: Prentice-Hall.

 WEB RESOURCES

The Consultative Group on Early Childhood Care and Development
www.ecdgroup.com/guestdoc/infancy.html

International Society on Infant Studies
www.isisweb.org

KidsHealth, a website devoted to the health and development of infants and children
http://kidshealth.org/parent/growth/senses/sensenewborn.html

Society for Research in Child Development
www.srcd.org

Childhood

The childhood shows the man, as the morning shows the day.

— *John Milton*

Childhood

Clersida Garcia

Clersida Garcia, Ph.D., is associate professor and director of the Motor Development Research Laboratory and Pedagogy Laboratory at Northern Illinois University in DeKalb, Illinois. She has served as chair of the Motor Development Academy of the American Alliance for Health, Physical Education, Recreation and Dance and chair of the Council of Physical Education of AAHPERD. Dr. Garcia has authored articles in several journals, including Research Quarterly for Exercise and Sport, Chronicle of Higher Education, *and* Journal of Teaching Elementary Physical Education.

Why did you find the study of childhood motor development interesting?

The study of childhood motor development is not only interesting but also fascinating. I am convinced that this age represents a window of opportunity for learning—particularly for learning to move and learning through movement. At this age, movement becomes one of the most important means for learning and a very important aspect of the child's life. This is the time when children begin exploring their environment and their body capabilities. This age represents the beginning of expressive learning and the emergence of the fundamental motor skills. You can observe learning and development in the most pure form—from no skill to acquiring and developing the skill or behavior.

Over my twenty-three years of teaching experience, sixteen years have been dedicated to understanding the learning and development of motor skills at the early childhood level. During this period of research studies and practical experiences, I have come to realize the significant importance and value of early movement experiences. Children at this age are developing the neural "architectural" structure of their brains—the communication network of their bodies with the outside world. The foundation of movement depends on the conduction of nerve impulses from the periphery of the body to the central nervous system and back to the muscles, thereby providing the potential for speedy, accurate, and sophisticated movement later in life. Early movement experiences are essential for the development of a sophisticated neural network of the brain, the basis for learning and development.

Another reason why this age is fascinating is because you learn something new every day. The plasticity and adaptability of young children and their unpredictable developmental strides in all areas of development, stimulate your inquiry on a daily basis. This age is also fascinating because you learn about the holiness of the body and its interrelated systems. All the areas of development become evident, and you realize the impact of your work on the children's development. Learning about childhood motor development is fun, exciting, and it never ends.

What do you believe is the one or two most important findings related to childhood motor development?

I personally believe that one of the most important findings related to childhood motor development is the concept of individual variability in the developmental process. Variability is now perceived as representing "soft assembly," or temporary assembly, of the coordinative structures intertwining a particular task. Thus, the dynamical system approach sees variability as part of the developmental process. Variability is not noise but, rather, important data that account for the overall formation of stable patterns of movement.

During early childhood, variability in performance is the most sure observation a practitioner will encounter. This variability can be due to single, multiple, or a combination of variables, although, as researchers, we have traditionally been trained to see variability as noise. In my research, variability is the way the system searches for and explores solutions to the presented task, within the given abilities or capabilities of the individual body system and the individual personal goal. I have come to the conclusion that when children are constantly varying their movements, they are actively searching for a new solution to a given motor problem, thus establishing different integrative neuronal communication. When children are showing some relative consistency, they are strengthening some functional-neural pathways that are actually allowing them to meet their goals at a given time. Both of these processes are highly important for development and learning.

10

CHILDHOOD GROWTH AND DEVELOPMENT

KEY TERMS

Myelination

Chronic malnutrition

Growth retardation

Hypertrophy

Atrophy

Endomorphic

Mesomorphic

Ectomorphic

Growth plate injuries

Bone mineralization

Secular trend

CHAPTER COMPETENCIES

Upon completion of this chapter you should be able to:

- Describe and interpret the normal curve and displacement and velocity graphs during childhood
- Discuss secular trends in physical size and biological maturation
- Discuss the influence of nutritional status on childhood growth processes
- Distinguish between *malnutrition* and *undernutrition* and discuss the causes and implications of each
- Describe the relative influences of exercise and injury on the childhood growth process
- List and describe several factors associated with influencing the childhood growth process
- List typical cognitive, affective, and motor development characteristics of the young child (ages 2 to 6) and discuss implications for the developmental movement program
- List typical cognitive, affective, and motor development characteristics of the older child (ages 6 to 10) and discuss implications for the developmental movement program

KEY CONCEPT

Development during the period of childhood is marked by steady, incremental changes in the cognitive, affective, and motor domains.

CONCEPT 10.1

The rate of growth decelerates throughout early childhood resulting in yearly average incremental gains in height and weight of about 2 inches (5.1 cm) and 5 pounds (2.3 kg), respectively.

The period of childhood is marked by steady increases in height, weight, and muscle mass. Growth is not as rapid during this period as it is during infancy, and it slows gradually throughout childhood until the adolescent growth spurt. Childhood is divided here into the early childhood period of 2 to 6 years of age and the later childhood period from about 6 to 10 years of age. Figures 10.1 through 10.4 present height (stature) and weight growth charts for males and females from 2 to 20 years of age (National Center for Health Statistics, 2000).

GROWTH IN EARLY CHILDHOOD

During the early childhood years, growth in height and weight is not as rapid as it is during infancy. The growth rate decelerates slowly. By 4 years of age, the child has doubled his or her birth length, which represents only about one-half the gain experienced during the first 2 years. The total amount of weight gained from 2 through 5 years of age is less than the amount gained during the first year of life. The growth process slows down after the first 2 years but maintains a constant rate until puberty. The annual height gain from the early childhood period to puberty is about 2 inches (5.1 cm) per year. Weight gains average 5 pounds (2.3 kg) per year. Early childhood, therefore, represents an ideal time for the child to develop and refine a wide variety of movement tasks ranging from the fundamental movements of early childhood to the sport skills of middle childhood.

Gender differences may be seen in height and weight, but they are minimal. The physiques of male and female preschoolers are remarkably similar when viewed from a posterior position, with boys being slightly taller and heavier. Boys have more muscle and bone mass than girls, and both show a gradual decrease in fatty tissue as they progress through the early childhood period. The proportion of muscle tissue remains fairly constant throughout early childhood at about 25 percent of total body weight.

Body proportions change markedly during early childhood because of the various growth rates of the body. The chest gradually becomes larger than the abdomen, and the stomach gradually protrudes less. By the time preschoolers reach first grade, their body proportions more closely resemble those of older children. Bone growth during early childhood is dynamic, and the skeletal system is particularly vulnerable to malnutrition, fatigue, and illness. The bones ossify at a rapid rate during early childhood and have been shown to be retarded by as much as three years in growth in deprived children.

The brain is about 75 percent of its adult weight by age 3 and almost 90 percent by age 6. The midbrain is almost fully developed at birth, but it is not until age 4 that the cerebral cortex is completely developed. The development of myelin around the neurons (**myelination**) permits the transmission of nerve impulses and is not complete at birth. At birth many nerves lack myelin, but greater amounts of myelin are laid down along nerve fibers as the child matures. Myelination is largely complete by the end of the early childhood period, allowing for the complete transference of

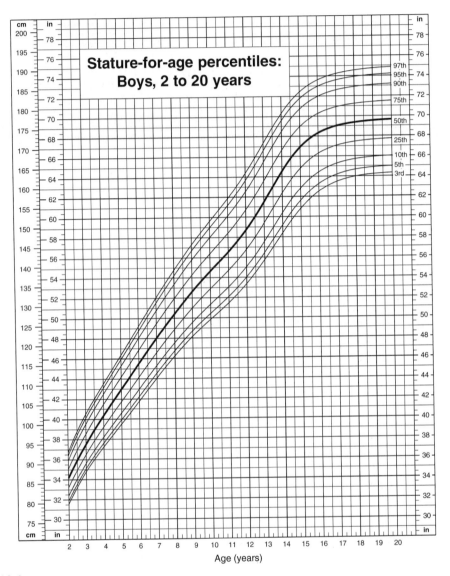

Figure 10.1
U.S. male stature-for-age percentiles: Boys, 2 to 20 years.
Data from National Center for Health Statistics (2000).

nerve impulses throughout the nervous system. A child's movement patterns are increasingly complex following myelination of the cerebellum.

The sensory apparatus is still developing during the preschool years. The eyeball does not reach its full size until about 12 years of age. Certain sections of the retina are not completely developed until around the sixth year, and the young child is generally farsighted. Preschool children have more taste buds than adults. They are generously

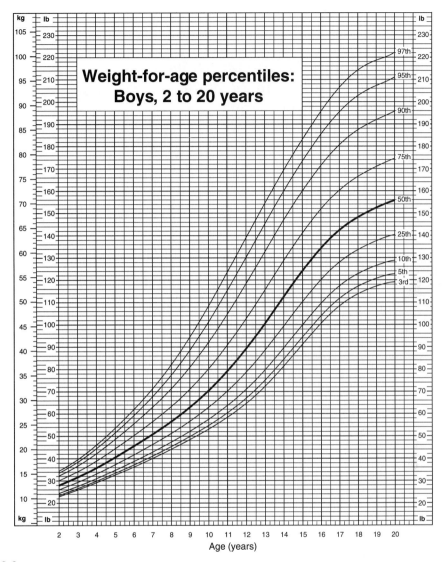

Weight-for-age percentiles: Boys, 2 to 20 years

Age (years)

Figure 10.2
U.S. male weight-for-age percentiles: Boys, 2 to 20 years.
Data from National Center for Health Statistics (2000).

distributed throughout the insides of the throat and cheeks as well as on the tongue, causing greater sensitivity to taste. The eustachian tube, which connects the middle ear with the throat, is shorter and flatter in the child, causing greater sensitivity to ear infections and fluid retention.

DEVELOPMENT IN EARLY CHILDHOOD

Play is what young children do when they are not eating, sleeping, or complying with the wishes of adults. Play occupies most of their waking hours, and it may literally be viewed as the child's

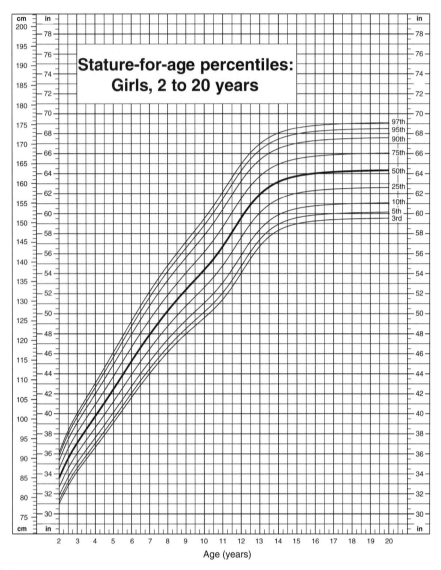

Stature-for-age percentiles: Girls, 2 to 20 years

Figure 10.3

U.S. female stature-for-age percentiles: Girls, 2 to 20 years.
Data from National Center for Health Statistics (2000).

equivalent of work. Children's play is the primary mode by which they learn about their bodies and movement capabilities. It also serves as an important facilitator of cognitive and affective growth in the young child, as well as an important means of developing both fine and gross motor skills.

Young children are actively involved in enhancing their cognitive skills in a variety of ways. These early years are a period of important cognitive development and have been termed the "preoperational thought phase" by Piaget. During this time children develop cognitive functions that will

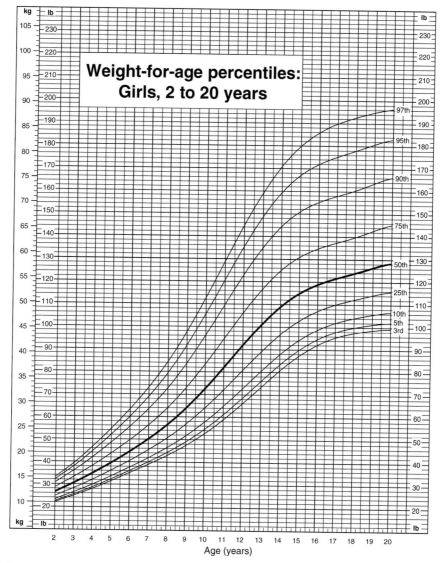

Figure 10.4

U.S. female weight-for-age percentiles: Girls, 2 to 20 years.
Data from National Center for Health Statistics (2000).

eventually result in logical thinking and concept formulation. Young children are not capable of thinking from any point of view other than their own. They are extremely egocentric and view almost everything in terms of themselves. The perceptions of preschoolers dominate their thinking, and what is experienced at a given moment has great influence on them. During this preconceptual phase of cognitive development, seeing is, literally, believing. In the thinking and logic of preschool children, their conclusions need no justifications. Children at this age are unable to reconstruct their thoughts and show others how they arrived at their conclusions. Play serves as a vital means by which higher cognitive structures are gradually developed. It provides a multitude of settings and variables for promoting cognitive growth.

CONCEPT 10.2

During early childhood, gender differences are minimal.

Affective development is also dramatic during the early childhood years. During this period children are involved in the two crucial social-emotional tasks of developing a sense of autonomy and a sense of initiative. Autonomy is expressed through a growing sense of independence, which may be seen in a child's delight in answering no to almost any direct question. For instance, even if a child wants to play outside, he or she will often refuse an invitation to do so. This may be viewed as an expression of a new sense of independence and an ability to manipulate some factors in the environment rather than as an expression of sheer disobedience. A way in which to avoid this natural autonomous reaction is to rephrase the question "Do you want to go outside?" to form a positive statement such as "Let's go play outdoors." In this way, the child is not confronted with a direct yes-or-no choice. Care must be taken, however, to give children abundant situations in which expressions of their autonomy are reasonable and proper.

A young child's expanding sense of initiative is seen in curiosity, exploration, and very active behavior. Children engage in new experiences, such as climbing, jumping, running, and throwing objects, for their own sake and for the sheer joy of sensing and knowing what they are capable of doing. Failure to develop initiative and autonomy leads to feelings of shame, worthlessness, and guilt. The establishment of a stable self-concept is crucial to proper affective development in a young child because it has an effect on cognitive and psychomotor functions.

Through the medium of play, young children develop a wide variety of fundamental locomotor, manipulative, and stability abilities. With a stable and positive self-concept, the gain in control over musculature is a smooth one. The timid, cautious, and measured movements of the 2- to 3-year-old gradually give way to the confident, eager, and often reckless abandon of the 4- and 5-year-old. Vivid imaginations make it possible for young children to jump from "great heights," climb "high mountains," leap over "raging rivers," and run "faster" than an assorted variety of "wild beasts."

Children of preschool age are rapidly expanding their horizons. They are asserting their personalities, developing their abilities, and testing their limits as well as the limits of their family and others around them. In short, they are pushing out into the world in many complex and wondrous ways. Caretakers must understand preschoolers' developmental characteristics, their limitations, and their potentials. Only in this way can we effectively structure developmental experiences that truly reflect children's needs and interests and are within their levels of ability.

The following developmental characteristics represent a synthesis of findings from a wide variety of sources and are presented here to provide a more complete view of a child during the early childhood years.

Physical and Motor Development Characteristics

1. Boys and girls range from about 33 to 47 inches (83.8–119.4 cm) in height and from 25 to 53 pounds (11.3–24.0 kg) in weight.
2. Perceptual-motor abilities are rapidly developing, but confusion often exists in body, directional, temporal, and spatial awareness.
3. Good bladder and bowel control are generally established by the end of this period, but accidents still occur.
4. Children during this period are rapidly developing fundamental movement abilities in a variety of motor skills. Bilateral movements such as skipping, however, often present more difficulty than unilateral movements.

5. Children are active and energetic and would often rather run than walk, but they still need frequent short rest periods.
6. Motor abilities are developed to the point that the children are beginning to learn how to dress themselves, although they may need help straightening and fastening articles of clothing.
7. The body functions and processes become well regulated. A state of physiological homeostasis (stability) becomes well established.
8. The body builds of both boys and girls are remarkably similar. A back view of boys and girls reveals no readily observable structural differences.
9. Fine motor control is not fully established, although gross motor control is developing rapidly.
10. The eyes are not generally ready for extended periods of close work due to farsightedness.

Cognitive Development Characteristics

1. There is constantly increasing ability to express thoughts and ideas verbally.
2. A fantastic imagination enables imitation of both actions and symbols with little concern for accuracy or the proper sequencing of events.
3. There is continuous investigation and discovery of new symbols that have a primarily personal reference.
4. The "how" and "why" of the child's actions are learned through almost constant play.
5. This is a preoperational thought phase of development, resulting in a period of transition from self-satisfying behavior to fundamental socialized behaviors.

Affective Development Characteristics

1. During this phase children are egocentric and assume that everyone thinks the way they do. As a result, they often seem to be quarrelsome and reluctant to share and get along with others.
2. They are often fearful of new situations, shy, self-conscious, and unwilling to leave the security of that which is familiar.
3. They are learning to distinguish right from wrong and are beginning to develop consciences.
4. Two- and 4-year-old children are often seen to be unusual and irregular in their behavior, whereas those who are 3 and 5 are often viewed as stable and conforming in their behavior.
5. Self-concept is rapidly developing. Wise guidance, success-oriented experiences, and positive reinforcement are especially important during these years.

Implications for the Developmental Movement Program

1. Plenty of opportunity for gross motor play must be offered in both undirected and directed settings.
2. Movement experiences should stress movement exploration and problem-solving activities to maximize the child's creativity and desire to explore.
3. The movement education program should include plenty of positive reinforcement to encourage the establishment of a healthy self-concept and to reduce the fear of failure.
4. Stress should be placed on developing a variety of fundamental locomotor, manipulative, and stability abilities, progressing from the simple to the complex as the child becomes "ready."
5. Interests and abilities of boys and girls are similar, with no need for separate activities during this period.
6. Plenty of activities designed specifically to enhance perceptual-motor functioning are necessary.
7. Advantage should be taken of the child's great imagination through the use of an assortment of activities, including drama and imagery.

8. Because of children's often awkward and inefficient movements, be sure to gear movement experiences to their maturity levels.

9. Provide a wide variety of activities that require object handling and eye-hand coordination.

10. Begin to incorporate bilateral and cross-lateral activities, such as galloping and skipping, after unilateral movements such as hopping have been fairly well established.

11. Encourage children—to help overcome tendencies to be shy and self-conscious—to take an active part in the movement education program by "showing" and "telling" others what they can do.

12. Activities should stress arm, shoulder, and upper body involvement.

13. Without emphasizing mechanics correct execution in a wide range of fundamental movements is the primary goal, without emphasis on standards of performance.

14. Do not stress coordination in conjunction with speed and agility.

15. Poor habits of posture are beginning. Reinforce good posture with positive statements.

16. Provide convenient access to toilet facilities and encourage the children to accept this responsibility on their own.

17. Provide for individual differences and allow for children to progress at their own rates.

18. Establish standards for acceptable behavior and abide by them. Provide wise guidance in the establishment of a sense of doing what is right and proper instead of what is wrong and unacceptable.

19. The developmental movement program should be prescriptive and based on each individual's developmental level.

20. A multisensory approach should be used; that is, one in which a wide variety of experiences are incorporated, using several sensory modalities.

GROWTH IN LATER CHILDHOOD

The period from the sixth through the tenth years of childhood is typified by slow but steady increases in height and weight and progress toward greater organization of the sensory and motor systems. Changes in body build are slight during these years. Childhood is more a time of lengthening and filling out prior to the prepubertal growth spurt that occurs around 11 years of age for girls and 13 years for boys. Although these years are characterized by gradual physical growth, the child makes rapid gains in learning and functions at increasingly mature levels in the performance of games and sports. This period of slow growth gives the child time to get used to his or her body and is an important factor in the typically dramatic improvement seen in coordination and motor control during the childhood years. The gradual change in size and the close relationship maintained between bone and tissue development may be important factors in increased levels of functioning.

Differences between the growth patterns of boys and girls are minimal during the middle years. Both have greater limb growth than trunk growth, but boys tend to have longer legs, arms, and standing heights during childhood. Likewise, girls tend to have greater hip widths and thigh sizes during this period. There is relatively little difference in physique or weight exhibited until the onset of the preadolescent period. Therefore, in most cases, girls and boys should be able to participate together in activities. During childhood there is slow growth in brain size. The size of the skull remains nearly the same although there is a broadening and a lengthening of the head toward the end of childhood.

CONCEPT 10.3

Growth in height and weight during later childhood is slow and steady, representing a time of lengthening and filling out prior to puberty.

Perceptual abilities during childhood become increasingly refined. The sensorimotor apparatus is working in ever greater harmony so that by the end of this period the child can perform numerous sophisticated skills. Striking of a pitched ball, for example, improves with age and practice due to improved visual acuity, tracking abilities, reaction and movement time, and sensorimotor integration. A key to maximum development of more mature growth patterns in the child is use. Practice and experimentation with the maturing perceptual abilities will enhance the process of integration with the motor structures. Failure to have the opportunity for practice, instruction, and encouragement during this period will prevent many individuals from acquiring the perceptual and motor information needed to perform skillful movement activities.

DEVELOPMENT IN LATER CHILDHOOD

Children in the elementary school years are generally happy, stable, eager, and able to assume responsibilities. They are able to cope with new situations and are anxious to learn more about themselves and their expanding world. Primary grade children take another big step when they enter first grade. Although first grade rarely represents a child's first separation from the home for a regularly scheduled, extended block of time, it is the first step out of the secure play environment of the home, nursery school, or day-care center into the world of older children and adults. Entering a school represents the first time that many children are placed in group situations in which they are not the center of attention. It is a time when sharing, concern for others, and respect for the rights and responsibilities of others are established. Kindergarten is a readiness time in which to make the gradual transition from an egocentric, child-centered play world to the group-oriented world of adult concepts and logic. In the first grade, the first formal demands for cognitive understanding are made. The major milestone of the first and second grader is learning how to read at a reasonable level. The 6-year-old is generally developmentally ready

for the important task of "breaking the code" and learning to read. The child is also developing the first real understanding of time, money, and numerous other cognitive concepts. By the second grade, children should be well able to meet and surmount the broader array of cognitive, affective, and psychomotor tasks placed before them.

The following is a listing of the general developmental characteristics of the child from about age 6 to 10. It is presented to provide a more complete view of the total child and represents a synthesis of current findings.

CONCEPT 10.4

Boys and girls are similar in their growth patterns, with limb growth being greater than trunk growth throughout childhood.

Physical and Motor Development Characteristics

1. Boys and girls range from about 44 to 60 inches (111.8–152.4 cm) in height and 44 to 90 pounds (20.0–40.8 kg) in weight.
2. Growth is slow, especially from age 8 to the end of this period. There is a slow but steady pace of increments, unlike the more rapid gains in height and weight during the preschool years.
3. The body begins to lengthen, with an annual gain in height of only 2 to 3 inches (5.1–7.6 cm) and an annual gain in weight of only 3 to 6 pounds (1.4–2.7 kg).
4. The cephalocaudal (head to toe) and proximodistal (center to periphery) principles of development, in which the large muscles of the body are considerably more developed than the small muscles, are apparent.
5. Girls are generally about a year ahead of boys in physiological development, and separate interests begin to emerge toward the end of this period.

6. Hand preference is firmly established with about 85 percent preferring the right hand and about 15 percent preferring the left.
7. Reaction time is slow, causing difficulty with eye-hand and eye-foot coordination at the beginning of this period. By the end they are generally well established.
8. Both boys and girls are full of energy but often possess low endurance levels and tire easily. Responsiveness to training, however, is great.
9. The visual perceptual mechanisms are fully established by the end of this period.
10. Children are often farsighted during this period and are not ready for extended periods of close work.
11. Most fundamental movement abilities have the potential to be well defined by the beginning of this period.
12. Basic skills necessary for successful play become well developed.
13. Activities involving the eyes and limbs develop slowly. Such activities as volleying or striking a pitched ball and throwing require considerable practice for mastery.
14. This period marks a transition from refining fundamental movement abilities to the establishment of transitional movement skills in lead-up games and athletic skills.

Cognitive Development Characteristics

1. Attention span is generally short at the beginning of this period but gradually extends. However, boys and girls of this age will often spend hours on activities that are of great interest to them.
2. They are eager to learn and to please adults but need assistance and guidance in making decisions.
3. Children have good imaginations and display extremely creative minds; however, self-consciousness seems to become a factor toward the end of this period.
4. They are often interested in television, computers, video games, and reading.

5. They are not capable of abstract thinking and deal best with concrete examples and situations during the beginning of this period. More abstract cognitive abilities are evident by the end of this period.
6. Children are intellectually curious and anxious to know "why."

Affective Development Characteristics

1. Interests of boys and girls are similar at the beginning of this period but soon begin to diverge.
2. The child is self-centered and plays poorly in large groups for extended periods of time during the primary years, although small-group situations are handled well.
3. The child is often aggressive, boastful, self-critical, overreactive, and accepts defeat and winning poorly.
4. There is an inconsistent level of maturity; the child is often less mature at home than in school.
5. The child is responsive to authority, "fair" punishment, discipline, and reinforcement.
6. Children are adventurous and eager to be involved with a friend or group of friends in "dangerous" or "secret" activities.
7. The child's self-concept becomes firmly established.

Implications for the Developmental Movement Program

1. There should be opportunities for children to refine fundamental movement abilities in the areas of locomotion, manipulation, and stability to a point where they are fluid and efficient.
2. Children need help in making the transition from the fundamental movement phase to the specialized movement phase.
3. Acceptance and affirmation tell children that they have stable and secure places in their schools and homes.
4. Abundant opportunities for encouragement and positive reinforcement from adults are

necessary to promote continued development of positive self-concepts.

5. Opportunities and encouragement to explore and experiment through movement with their bodies and objects in the environment enhance perceptual-motor efficiency.

6. There should be exposure to experiences in which progressively greater amounts of responsibility are introduced to promote self-reliance.

7. Children learn to adjust to the rougher ways of the playground and neighborhood without becoming rough or crude themselves.

8. Opportunities for gradual introduction to group and team activities should be provided at the proper time.

9. Imaginary and mimetic activities may be effectively incorporated into the program during the primary years because the children's imaginations are still vivid.

10. Activities that incorporate the use of music and rhythmics are enjoyable at this level and are valuable in enhancing fundamental movement abilities, creativity, and a basic understanding of the components of music and rhythm.

11. Children at this level learn best through active participation. Integration of academic concepts with movement activities provides an effective avenue for reinforcing critical thinking skills.

12. Activities that involve climbing and hanging are beneficial to develop the upper torso and should be included in the program.

13. Discuss play situations involving such topics as taking turns, fair play, not cheating, and other universal values as a means of establishing a more complete sense of right or wrong.

14. Begin to stress accuracy, form, and skill in the performance of movement skills.

15. Encourage children to think before they engage in an activity. Help them recognize potential hazards as a means of reducing their often reckless behavior.

16. Encourage small-group activities followed by larger-group activities and team sport experience.

17. Posture is important. Activities need to stress proper body alignment.

18. Use of rhythmic activities to refine coordination is desirable.

19. Specialized movement skills are developed and refined toward the end of this period. Plenty of opportunity for practice, encouragement, and selective instruction is important.

20. Participation in youth sport activities that are developmentally appropriate and geared to the needs and interests of children should be encouraged.

FACTORS AFFECTING CHILD GROWTH AND DEVELOPMENT

Growth is not an independent process. Although heredity sets the limits of growth, environmental factors play an important role in the extent to which these limits are reached. The degree to which these factors affect motor development is not clear and needs further study. Nutrition, exercise, and physical activity are major factors affecting growth.

Nutrition

The potentially harmful effects of poor nutrition during the prenatal period were highlighted earlier. Among the factors influencing physical development during the prenatal period, nutrition is the most important. Numerous investigations have provided clear evidence that dietary deficiencies can have harmful effects on growth during infancy and childhood. The extent of growth retardation obviously depends on the severity, duration, and time of onset of undernourishment. For example, if severe chronic malnutrition occurs during the child's first 4 years, there is little hope of catching up to one's age-mates in mental development, because the critical brain growth period has passed.

CONCEPT 10.5

Prolonged dietary deficiencies and excesses can have a serious impact on the growth patterns of children.

The physical growth process can be interrupted by malnutrition at any time between infancy and adolescence. Malnutrition may serve also as a mediating condition for certain diseases that affect physical growth. For example, lack of vitamin D in a diet can result in *rickets,* a softening and deformity of the bones that occurs as a result of lime salts in newly formed bones. Vitamin B_{12} deficiencies may cause *pellagra,* characterized by skin lesions, gastrointestinal problems, mitosal and neurological symptoms. Chronic lack of vitamin C may lead to *scurvy,* a disease characterized by loss of energy, joint pains, anemia, and a tendency toward epiphyseal fractures. All are relatively rare in most modern developed countries, but the effects of *kwashiorkor,* a debilitating disease, are seen in many parts of the world where there is a general lack of food and good nutrition. In the child with kwashiorkor, growth retardation can be expected as well as a large, puffed belly, sores on the body, and diarrhea.

Studies indicate that children suffering from **chronic malnutrition,** particularly during infancy and early childhood, never completely catch up to the growth norms for their age levels and suffer from **growth retardation.** This is apparent in developing nations where adult height and weight norms are considerably lower than those for industrialized nations. Nutritional status is linked to income level. Growth retardation can be found in all ethnic groups but its prevalence varies with sex, ethnic origin, and income level. Stunted growth in children due to malnutrition is evident worldwide. In some third world countries almost 50 percent of children experience growth retardation due to inadequate nutrition (Pařízková, 1996). Even in industrial developed countries growth deficiencies occur in many cases caused by poverty and parental ignorance of basic nutritional information. The Centers for Disease Control reported that iron deficiency resulting in anemia represents the most common known form of nutritional deficiency in the United States (1998). They state that anemic infants were significantly delayed in attaining the motor milestones typical of that age period. Several child health organizations, including the American Academy of Pediatrics (Barness, 1993), have issued guidelines for the prevention of such childhood nutritional concerns.

Dietary excesses also affect the growth of children. In affluent countries, obesity is a major problem. Research has proposed an interesting hypothesis linking obesity and its intractability to dietary habits established during infancy and the period of childhood. There is considerable concern among professionals over the high consumption of refined starches and sugars by children. The constant barrage of television commercials loudly extolling one junk food or another, the "fast food" addiction of millions, and the use of nonnutritive edibles as a reinforcer for good behavior all may have an effect on the nutritional status of children. The critical difference between adequate and inadequate nutrition has not been identified. The individual nature of the child, with his or her unique biochemical composition, makes it difficult to pinpoint where adequate nutrition ends and malnutrition begins. It is, however, a serious question that needs further exploration. The welfare of a vast number of children is at stake.

Exercise and Injury

One of the principles of physical activity is the concept of use and disuse. According to this principle, a muscle that is used will **hypertrophy** (i.e., increase in size) and a muscle that is not used will **atrophy** (i.e., decrease in size). Anyone who has had a limb placed in a cast for several weeks knows about atrophy. In children, activity definitely promotes muscle development. Although the number of muscle fibers does not increase, the size of the fibers does increase. Muscles respond and adapt to greater amounts of stress. Maturation alone will not account for increases in muscle mass. An environment that promotes vigorous physical activity on the part of the child will do much to promote muscle development. Active children have less body fat in proportion to lean body mass. They do not have more muscle fibers; they simply have more muscle mass per fiber and smaller fat cells.

CONCEPT 10.6

Physical activity generally has a positive effect on growth, except in cases of excessive levels of exercise.

Although it is doubtful that an individual's basic physique can be altered, it is certain that improvements within limits can be made. A popular method of classification of adult physique was developed by Sheldon et al. (1940) and later extended to children by Peterson (1967). This much-used system classifies individuals on the basis of fat, muscle, and bone length. An **endomorphic** physique is one that is soft and rounded in physical features (pear shape). The **mesomorphic** physique is well muscled, with broad shoulders, narrow waist, and thick chest (V shape). The **ectomorphic** physique is characterized by a tall, thin, lean look (angular shape).

Within each classification a person is rated on a scale of 1 to 7, with 1 representing the least amount of a characteristic and 7 the most of a characteristic. Therefore, the three-number sequence of 1-7-1 would represent a person very low on endomorphy, very high on mesomorphy, and very low on ectomorphy. A 2-3-6 would typify a person low on endomorphy, with some mesomorphic characteristics, and high on ectomorphy (perhaps a high jumper, or middle distance runner). Sheldon et al. (1954) found that males could typically be classified at the middle of the scale (i.e., 3-4-4 or 4-4-3) and females rated higher in endomorphy and lower in mesomorphy (i.e., 5-3-3).

Although physical activity generally has positive effects on the growth of children, it may have some negative effects if carried to the extreme. Malina (1994) indicated that several studies have reported reduced growth rates in the height and weight of young athletes involved in intensive training programs, but that in many cases the research

methodologies had limitations. He did point out the concern of **growth plate injuries** and their effect on bone growth. Certain sports lend themselves to the overuse of specific joints of a child's body. Overuse may result in epiphyseal injuries, and growth plate damage. Much more research needs to be conducted on the beneficial limits of strenuous physical activity during childhood. The critical point separating harmful and beneficial activity is not clear. The rapid rise of youth sports and the intensity of training leave many unanswered questions. We can, however, assume that strenuous activity carried out over an extended period may result in injury to muscle and bone tissue of the child. "Swimmer's shoulder," "tennis elbow," "runner's knees," and stress fractures are but a few of the ailments plaguing children who have exceeded their developmental limits. Exercise and activity programs for children must be supervised carefully. The potential benefits to the growth process are great, but individual limitations must be accommodated.

CONCEPT 10.7

The critical line between beneficial and harmful amounts of physical exertion is not clear.

In summary, little evidence exists to support the notion that regular exercise has a direct effect on the length of bone growth (Malina, 1994). Bone growth is a hormonal process unaffected by activity levels. Exercise does, however, increase bone width and promote **bone mineralization,** which make for stronger, less brittle bones. Stress within the limits of the particular individual is beneficial to the bones. Chronic inactivity, on the other hand, has harmful effects on bone growth and may result in growth retardation.

Physical activity stimulates bone mineralization and muscle development and helps retard the depositing of fat. The vast majority of physical activity and athletic programs for children, not including marathon running, wrestling, and other heavy strength and endurance activities, have beneficial effects. Injury, whether acute or chronic, may have negative effects on growth, depending on the severity and location. Refer to chapter 12, "Physical Development of Children," for a further discussion of health-related fitness training.

CONCEPT 10.8

Age of onset, duration, and severity determine how a variety of activity and nutrition factors influence later development.

Illness and Climate

A number of other factors influence the growth process, including illness and disease, climate, emotions, and disabling conditions.

The standard childhood illnesses (chicken pox, colds, measles, and mumps) do not have a marked effect on the growth of the child. The extent to which illnesses and diseases may retard growth depends on their duration, severity, and timing. Often, the interaction of malnutrition and illnesses in the child makes it difficult to accurately determine the specific cause of growth retardation. However, the combination of conditions puts the child at risk and greatly enhances the probability of measurable growth deficits.

A great deal of literature has reported the differences in height, weight, and onset of adolescence among individuals of varying climates. The interacting effects of nutrition and health as well as possible genetic differences (e.g., when comparing black Africans with white Americans) make it impossible to demonstrate a direct causal relationship between climate and physical growth. The available data suggest that American children born and raised in the tropics have more linear physiques, but grow and mature at a slower rate than American children raised in more temperate climates. It is difficult, however, to relate climatic conditions to specific factors of growth and maturation. As noted by Malina and Bouchard (1991):

> The effects of climate extend beyond temperature and include other components such as relative humidity, precipitation, and topography,

as well as the effects on food production, availability of suitable conditions for infectious and parasitic disease vectors, and so on. (p. 412)

Secular Trends

A positive **secular trend** reflects the tendency for children to be taller, heavier, and more mature at an earlier age than children one or more generations ago. The trend for secular increases is not universal. Increases in growth, maturation, and physical performance levels have been demonstrated in most developed countries. Developing nations throughout the world, however, have not demonstrated secular increases and in some cases have even shown decreases in stature. There may be many reasons for this, but it is largely a reflection of the limited improvements in lifestyle and nutritional habits from one generation to another.

Malina (1978) reported that secular changes in length and weight are slight at birth but become progressively more pronounced until puberty, when there is again a lessening of differences. The largest differences in height and weight are found from age 11 to 15 (the pubertal years) and are apparent across all socioeconomic classes and races in developed countries.

CONCEPT 10.9

Although secular trends appear to have ceased in North America, this is not a universal phenomena.

Children today mature more rapidly than they did a hundred years ago. The age at menarche, for example, decreased in European populations over the past century from an estimated range of 15.5 to 17.4 years to between 12.5 and 14 years (Eveleth and Tanner, 1976). Although secular trends in the maturation of boys are no doubt present, maturity data for them are lacking. However, the average age at which voices begin to change for members of boys' choirs today is considerably lower (about 13 years) than that estimated for boys performing in choirs more than a hundred years ago (about 18 years) (Daw, 1974).

Malina and Bouchard (1991) reported that the secular trend in size and maturation in the United States and many other developed nations has stopped. There have been few indications of secular trends in height, weight, and maturation in the past twenty years. This is probably due largely to the elimination of growth-inhibiting factors and a peaking of improved nutritional and health conditions.

SUMMARY

Growth during childhood decelerates from the rapid pace characteristic of the first 2 years. The slow but steady increases in height and weight during childhood provide the child with an opportunity to coordinate perceptual and motor information. The child has time to lengthen, fill out, and gain control over his or her world. Numerous factors, however, can interrupt the normal developmental process. Nutritional deficiencies and excesses may influence growth patterns and have lasting effects on the child, depending on the severity and duration of the poor nutrition. Severe and prolonged illness also interrupts the growth process.

The effects of acute and chronic exercise at low and high intensity levels is of great interest to researchers and youth sport coaches. Physical exercise has a positive influence on the growth process. Little evidence exists to support the claim that physical activity can be harmful to children, except in cases of extreme training requirements. The problem, however, is knowing when "extremes" have been reached for each child. Climatic factors have also been shown to accelerate or decelerate growth in children. North American children today are taller and heavier than their counterparts of a hundred years ago. Definite secular trends can be seen in many but not all cultures. Differences in lifestyle and dietary circumstances play an important role in the presence or absence of secular trends.

CRITICAL READINGS

American Academy of Pediatrics Committee on Sports Medicine and Fitness. (2000). Intensive training and sports specialization in young athletes. *Pediatrics, 106,* 154–157.

Eveleth, P. B., & Tanner, J. M. (1976). *Worldwide Variation in Human Growth.* Cambridge, MA: Cambridge University Press.

Gallahue, D. L., & Cleland, F. (2003). *Developmental Physical Education for Today's Children.* 4th ed. Champaign, IL: Human Kinetics.

Malina, R. M. (1994). Physical growth and biological maturation of young athletes. *Exercise and Sport Sciences Reviews, 22,* 389–434.

Pařízková, J. (1996). *Nutrition, Physical Activity, and Health in Early Life* (Chapter 7). Boca Raton, FL: CRC Press.

Sherrill, C. (1998). *Adapted Physical Activity, Recreation and Sport: Crossdisciplinary and Lifespan* (Chapter 24). 5th ed. St. Louis: McGraw-Hill.

WEB RESOURCES

American Academy of Pediatrics Committee on Nutrition
www.aap.org/visit/cmte25.htm

Centers for Disease Control and Prevention: National growth charts
www.cdc.gov/growthcharts

World Health Organization: Global database on child growth and malnutrition
www.who.int/nutgrowthdb

Fundamental Movement Abilities

KEY TERMS

Locomotion

Stability

Manipulation

Movement pattern

Fundamental movement

Qualitative change

Intraskill sequences

Segmental assessment approach

Total body assessment approach

Between-child differences

Between-pattern differences

Within-pattern differences

CHAPTER COMPETENCIES

Upon completion of this chapter you should be able to:

- Categorize performer's movement into developmental stages
- Demonstrate observational assessment skill in a variety of fundamental movement patterns
- Discuss the uses of a developmental sequence checklist for assessing motor development
- Identify motor behavior characteristics of children with developmental difficulties within specific skills
- Discuss the concept of a developmental sequence of fundamental movement skill acquisition
- Describe the meaning of the "initial," "elementary," and "mature" stages within the fundamental movement phase
- Distinguish between "between-child differences," "between-pattern differences," and "within-pattern differences" in movement skill acquisition
- Devise a fundamental movement observational assessment checklist as an individual or group evaluative tool
- Critically analyze the influences of opportunities for practice, encouragement, and instruction on the acquisition of fundamental movement abilities

KEY CONCEPT

Although age-related, the acquisition of mature fundamental movement skills is not age-dependent because of numerous factors within the task, the individual, and the environment.

As children approach their second birthdays, marked changes can be observed in how they relate to their surroundings. By the end of the second year, they have mastered the rudimentary movement abilities developed during infancy. These movement abilities form the basis on which each child develops or refines the fundamental movement patterns of early childhood and the specialized movement skills of later childhood and adolescence. Children are no longer immobilized by their basic inability to move about freely or by the confines of their cribs or playpens. They are now able to explore the movement potentials of their bodies as they move through space (**locomotion**). They no longer have to maintain a relentless struggle against the force of gravity but are gaining increased control over their musculature in opposition to gravity (**stability**). They no longer have to be content with the crude and ineffective reaching, grasping, and releasing of objects characteristic of infancy but are rapidly developing the ability to make controlled and precise contact with objects in their environment (**manipulation**).

Young children are involved in the process of developing and refining fundamental movement skills in a wide variety of stability, locomotor, and manipulative movements. This means that they should be involved in a series of coordinated and developmentally sound experiences designed to enhance knowledge of the body and its potential for movement. **Movement pattern** development is not specifically concerned with developing high degrees of skill in a limited number of movement situations, but rather with developing acceptable levels of proficiency and efficient body mechanics in a wide variety of movement situations. A **fundamental movement** involves the basic elements of that particular movement only. It does not include such things as the individual's style or personal peculiarities in performance. It does not emphasize the combining of a variety of fundamental movements into complex skills such as the layup shot in basketball or a floor exercise routine in gymnastics. Each movement pattern is first considered in relative isolation from all others, and then linked with others in a variety of combinations. The locomotor movements of running, jumping, and leaping, or the manipulative movements of throwing, catching, kicking, and trapping, are examples of fundamental movement abilities first mastered separately by the child. These movements are then gradually combined and enhanced in a variety of ways to become sport skills. The basic elements of a fundamental movement should be the same for all children.

The development of fundamental movement skills is basic to the motor development of children. A wide assortment of movement experiences provide them with a wealth of information on which to base their perceptions of themselves and the world.

DEVELOPMENTAL SEQUENCE OF FUNDAMENTAL MOVEMENTS

With the renewed interest in the study of motor development that began in the 1960s, several scales appeared that illustrated a relationship between age and motor performance. Johnson (1962), using a large sample of boys and girls from grades 1 through 6, found that the mean scores on a variety of motor performance items showed a definite upward trend until the fifth grade. Cratty and Martin (1969) presented age-related sequences of acquisition for a variety of locomotor, manipulative, and perceptual abilities of 365 children ranging in age from 4 to 12 years. Williams's (1970) summary of the movement abilities of children between 3 and 6 years old revealed more advanced forms of movement with increases in age. Sinclair (1973) studied the motor development of 2- to 6-year-old children. The results of her longitudinal film analysis of twenty-five movement tasks at six-month intervals lent further support to the basic assumption that movement skill acquisition is a developing process during the early childhood years.

CONCEPT 11.1

Children have the developmental potential to be at the mature stage of most fundamental movement skills by about age 6.

These normative studies of motor development are interesting and informative about the quantity or outcome of movement in that they tell "how far," "how fast," and "how many." They failed, however, to provide information about **qualitative change** that occurs as the child progresses toward a more mature form. As a result, a number of investigators, all using film and computer techniques to analyze the intraskill aspects of a variety of fundamental movement patterns, began to collect data leading to a stage concept of motor development during early childhood (Halverson and Roberton, 1966, 1979; Seefeldt, 1972; Wild, 1938). Seefeldt and Haubenstricker (1976) and several others conducted important investigations into the **intraskill sequences** of a variety of fundamental movement tasks. Out of these investigations have come three popular methods of charting the stage classification of children in observational settings. The systems devised by Roberton (1978), McClenaghan and Gallahue (1978b), and Seefeldt and Haubenstricker (1976) have been used successfully in observational assessment with young children. The Roberton method expands the stage theory to an analysis of the separate components of movement within a given pattern and is commonly referred to as a **segmental assessment approach.** The Seefeldt method assigns an overall stage classification score (stage 1 through stage 5) and is referred to as a **total body assessment approach.**

In the book *Developmental Physical Education for Today's Children* (2003) Gallahue and Cleland offer a practical, easy-to-use, and reliable system for classifying individuals at the initial, elementary,

mature, or sport skill stages, along with a wide variety of developmentally appropriate movement experiences for each stage in twenty-three fundamental movement skills. This method encourages use of both the total body configuration and segmental analysis approaches to informally assess fundamental movement pattern development for instructional purposes. (Note: This is not intended to be used as a research tool.) First, the examiner observes the movement task using a total body assessment approach. This provides a general picture of the stage at which the individual, group, or class is performing a specific movement skill. If the movement is observed to be at the mature stage, further diagnostic observational assessment is not necessary. If, however, the fundamental movement skill is observed to be at the initial or elementary stage in a general sense, then further assessment is warranted. At this time a segmental assessment is conducted to identify specifically those body parts that are lagging behind. This method recognizes the differential rates of development within fundamental movement patterns as well as the need for an easy-to-apply tool for daily teaching situations.

CONCEPT 11.2

Several effective techniques have been devised for observational assessment of fundamental movement patterns.

Not all movement patterns fit precisely into an arbitrary three-stage progression. The developmental aspects of some movements may be more completely described in four-, five-, or even eight-stage sequences, depending on the specific pattern and the level of sophistication of the observer. The three-stage approach is used in the following sections because it accurately and adequately fits the developmental sequence of most fundamental movement patterns and provides the basis for a reliable, easy-to-use, observational assessment instrument. Tables 11.1A–C provide a

TABLE 11.1A Sequence of Emergence of Selected Stability Abilities

Movement Pattern	Selected Abilities	Approximate Age of Onset
Dynamic Balance		
Dynamic balance involves maintaining one's equilibrium as the center of gravity shifts	Walks 1-inch (2.5 cm) straight line	3 years
	Walks 1-inch (2.5 cm) circular line	4 years
	Stands on low balance beam	2 years
	Walks on 4-inch (10 cm) wide beam for a short distance	3 years
	Walks on same beam, alternating feet	3–4 years
	Walks on 2- or 3-inch (5.1 or 7.6 cm) beam	4 years
	Performs basic forward roll	3–4 years
	Performs mature forward roll*	6–7 years
Static Balance		
Static balance involves maintaining one's equilibrium while the center of gravity remains stationary	Pulls to a standing position	10 months
	Stands without handholds	11 months
	Stands alone	12 months
	Balances on one foot 3–5 seconds	5 years
	Supports body in basic 3-point inverted positions	6 years
Axial Movements		
Axial movements are static postures that involve bending, stretching, twisting, turning, and the like	Axial movement abilities begin to develop early in infancy and are progressively refined to a point where they are included in the emerging manipulative patterns of throwing, catching, kicking, striking, trapping, and other activities	2 months–6 years

*The child has developmental "potential" to be at the mature stage. Attainment will depend on factors within the task, individual, and environment.

visual representation of the emergence sequence of selected fundamental stability, locomotor, and manipulative abilities.

MOVEMENT CONDITIONS

The fundamental movement phase of development has been extensively studied over the past several years. Most would agree that this phase follows a sequential progression that may be subdivided into stages. The normally developing child tends to progress from one stage to another in a sequential manner influenced by maturation and experience. Children cannot rely solely on maturation to attain the mature stage in their fundamental movement abilities. Environmental conditions that include opportunities for practice,

encouragement, and instruction are crucial to the development of mature patterns of fundamental movement. Miller (1978) investigated the facilitation of fundamental movement skill learning in children 3 to 5 years of age. She found that programs of instruction can increase fundamental movement pattern development beyond the level attained solely through maturation. She also found that an instructional program in skill development was more effective than a free-play program and that parents working under the direction of a trained specialist can be as effective as physical education teachers alone in developing fundamental movement skills. Luedke (1980) found similar results, using two different methods of instruction for the mature stage of throwing with fourth-grade boys and girls. Both instructional groups were more

TABLE 11.1B **Sequence of Emergence of Selected Locomotor Abilities**

Movement Pattern	Selected Abilities	Approximate Age of Onset
Walking Walking involves placing one foot in front of the other while maintaining contact with the supporting surface	Rudimentary upright unaided gait Walks sideways Walks backward Walks upstairs with help Walks upstairs alone—follow step Walks downstairs alone—follow step	13 months 16 months 17 months 20 months 24 months 25 months
Running Running involves a brief period of no contact with the supporting surface	Hurried walk (maintains contact) First true run (nonsupport phase) Efficient and refined run Speed of run increases, mature run*	18 months 2–3 years 4–5 years 5 years
Jumping Jumping takes three forms: (1) jumping for distance; (2) jumping for height; and (3) jumping from a height. It involves a one- or two-foot takeoff with a landing on both feet	Steps down from low objects Jumps down from object with one-foot lead Jumps off floor with both feet Jumps for distance (about 3 ft/1 m) Jumps for height (about 1 ft/30 cm) Mature jumping pattern*	18 months 2 years 28 months 5 years 5 years 6 years
Hopping Hopping involves a one-foot takeoff with a landing on the same foot	Hops up to 3 times on preferred foot Hops from 4 to 6 times on same foot Hops from 8 to 10 times on same foot Hops distance of 50 feet (15 m) in about 11 seconds Hops skillfully with rhythmical alteration, mature pattern*	3 years 4 years 5 years 5 years 6 years
Galloping The gallop combines a walk and a leap with the same foot leading throughout	Basic but inefficient gallop Gallops skillfully, mature pattern*	4 years 6 years
Skipping Skipping combines a step and a hop in rhythmic alteration	One-footed skip Skillful skipping (about 20 percent) Skillful skipping for most*	4 years 5 years 6 years

*The child has the developmental "potential" to be at the mature stage. Attainment will depend on factors within the task, individual, and environment.

TABLE 11.1C Sequence of Emergence of Selected Manipulative Abilities

Movement Pattern	Selected Abilities	Approximate Age of Onset
Reach, Grasp, Release		
Reaching, grasping, and releasing involve making successful contact with an object, retaining it in one's grasp, and releasing it at will	Primitive reaching behaviors	2–4 months
	Corralling of objects	2–4 months
	Palmar grasp	3–5 months
	Pincer grasp	8–10 months
	Controlled grasp	12–14 months
	Controlled release	14–18 months
Throwing		
Throwing involves imparting force to an object in the general direction of intent	Body faces target, feet remain stationary, ball thrown with forearm extension only	2–3 years
	Same as above but with body rotation added	$3\frac{1}{2}$–5 years
	Steps forward with leg on same side as the throwing arm	4–5 years
	Boys exhibit more mature pattern than girls	5 years and over
	Mature throwing pattern*	6 years
Catching		
Catching involves receiving force from an object with the hands, moving from large to progressively smaller balls	Chases ball; does not respond to aerial ball	2 years
	Responds to aerial ball with delayed arm movements	2–3 years
	Needs to be told how to position arms	2–3 years
	Basket catch using the body	3 years
	Fear reaction (turns head away)	3–4 years
	Catches using the hands only with a small ball	5 years
	Mature catching pattern*	6 years
Kicking		
Kicking involves imparting force to an object with the foot	Pushes against ball; does not actually kick it	18 months
	Kicks with leg straight and little body movement (kicks *at* the ball)	2–3 years
	Flexes lower leg on backward lift	3–4 years
	Greater backward and forward swing with definite arm opposition	4–5 years
	Mature pattern (kicks *through* the ball)*	5–6 years
Striking		
Striking involves sudden contact to objects in an overarm, sidearm, or underhand pattern	Faces object and swings in a vertical plane	2–3 years
	Swings in a horizontal plane and stands to the side of the object	4–5 years
	Rotates the trunk and hips and shifts body weight forward	5 years
	Mature horizontal pattern with stationary ball*	6–7 years

*The child has the developmental "potential" to be at the mature stage. Attainment will depend on factors within the task, individual, and environment.

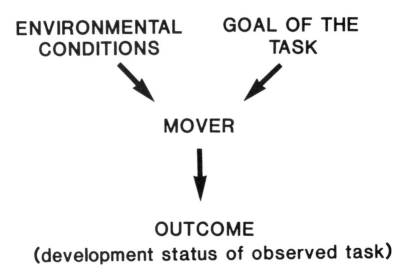

Figure 11.1
The interactions between the environmental conditions and the mover, and the goal of the task and the mover, will affect the apparent developmental maturity of a specific movement task.

proficient in form and performance than a noninstructed control group. The interactions of the environment and the mover, and the goal of the task and the mover, have a dramatic impact on the observed developmental maturity of a fundamental movement task (figure 11.1).

CONCEPT 11.3

Progression to the mature stage of a fundamental movement pattern depends on a variety of experiential factors, including opportunities for practice, encouragement, and instruction in an environment conducive to learning.

Natural conditions within the environment—such as temperature, lighting, surface area, and gravity—may influence the quantitative aspects of a movement task as well as its qualitative aspects. Similarly, artificial conditions such as the size, shape, color, and texture of objects may dramatically influence performance (Payne and Isaacs,

2002). Furthermore, conditions such as object velocity, trajectory, and weight may influence success in interceptions. The goal of the task is another important influencer of the observed developmental status of a fundamental movement task. If, for example, the focus is on accuracy in a throwing task, such as with the game of darts, then it is reasonable to assume that the pattern of movement will be different than if the goal of the task was throwing for distance. Langendorfer (1988) observed two groups of subjects (children and adults) performing an overhand throwing pattern under two different goal conditions (force and accuracy). The results of his investigation indicated that motor patterns are not absolute under all environmental circumstances. Some individuals can accommodate their movements to shifting environmental constraints, but others cannot. The degree to which a mover is able to make adjustments to an altered goal will be influenced by several factors within the mover as well as the degree to which the task demands have changed. For example, an individual with limited ability to increase throwing velocity (due to inefficient mechanics or lack of strength) will be able to make only minor adjustments when switching from an accuracy throwing task to a distance throwing task.

The link among the mover, the conditions of the environment, and the demands of the task is not completely understood. Many of the developmental descriptions of the fundamental movement patterns that follow are laboratory-generated; that is, they are hypothesized developmental sequences that are the products of research in artificial settings unlike the real world in which children move. Little is known, as yet, about the changing context of the environment and its influence on the observed developmental status of movement in children. As we turn to methods of analyzing children's movement in more natural settings we may find these hypothesized stages of development to be somewhat different. This point is echoed by Roberton (1987), who indicated that researchers have frequently been so concerned with describing changes in the movement characteristics of their research participants that they have often failed to consider the powerful influences of other elements (i.e., conditions of the environment and goal of the task) on the resulting observed developmental status of the fundamental movement pattern.

DEVELOPMENTAL DIFFERENCES

When observing and analyzing the fundamental movement abilities of children, it soon becomes apparent that there are various stages of development for each pattern of movement. Also, differences in abilities exist between children, between patterns, and within patterns.

CONCEPT 11.4

Although age-related, numerous differences are present between children, between patterns, and within patterns in the performance of fundamental movement tasks.

Between-child differences should remind us of the principle of individuality in all learning. The sequence of progression through the initial, elementary, and mature stages is the same for most children. The rate, however, will vary, depending on both environmental and hereditary factors. Whether a child reaches the mature stage depends primarily on instruction, encouragement, and opportunities for practice. When these are absent, normal differences between children will be magnified.

Between-pattern differences are seen in all children. A child may be at the initial stage in some movement tasks, the elementary in others, and the mature in still others. Children do not progress evenly in the development of their fundamental movement abilities. Play and instructional experiences will greatly influence the rate of development of locomotor, manipulative, and stability abilities.

Within-pattern differences are an interesting and often curious phenomenon. Within a given pattern, a child may exhibit a combination of initial, elementary, and mature elements. For example, in the throw, the arm action may be at the elementary stage while the leg action is at the mature stage and the trunk action at the initial stage. Developmental differences within patterns are common and usually the result of: (1) incomplete modeling of the movements of others, (2) initial success with the inappropriate action, (3) failure to require an all-out effort, (4) inappropriate or restricted learning opportunities, or (5) incomplete sensorimotor integration. Children exhibiting within-pattern differences should be assessed using the segmental analysis approach. This will permit the observer to accurately determine the stage of development of each body segment. With this knowledge, appropriate intervention strategies can be mapped out.

Creative, diagnostic teaching can do much to aid the child in the balanced development of his or her fundamental movement abilities. Observational assessment of the child's movement abilities will enable the teacher to plan experiences and instructional strategies that will help the child establish mature patterns of movement. Once movement control has been established, these mature patterns may be further refined in force production and accuracy in the specialized movement phase. Failure to achieve proficiency in a wide variety of fundamental movement skills will inhibit the development of efficient and effective patterns of movement that may be applied to the game, sport, and dance activities characteristic of a child's culture.

FUNDAMENTAL STABILITY MOVEMENTS

Stability is the most fundamental aspect of learning to move. It is through this dimension that children gain and maintain a point of origin for the explorations that they make in space. Stability involves the ability to maintain one's relationship to the force of gravity. This is true even though the nature of the application of the force may be altered as the requirements of the situation change, causing the general relationship of the body parts to the center of gravity to be altered. Movement experiences designed to enhance children's stability abilities enable them to develop flexibility in postural adjustments as they move in a variety of different and often unusual ways relative to their center of gravity, line of gravity, and base of support.

CONCEPT 11.5

Stability is the most fundamental aspect of learning to move, because all movement involves an element of stability.

The ability to sense a shift in the relationship of the body parts that alters one's balance is required for efficient stability. The ability to compensate rapidly and accurately for these changes with appropriate movements is also essential. These compensatory movements should ensure maintenance

of balance, but they should not be overdone. They should be made with only those parts of the body required for balance rather than with the entire body. Children's stability abilities should be flexible so that they may make all types of movements under all sorts of conditions and still maintain their fundamental relationship to the force of gravity.

Stability, as used in this text, goes beyond the catch-all terms of *nonlocomotor* or *nonmanipulative* movements sometimes used by other authors. The movement category of stability encompasses these terms but further implies maintenance of body control in movements that place a premium on balance. All movement involves an element of stability when viewed from the balance perspective. Therefore, strictly speaking, all locomotor and manipulative activities are, in part, stability movements. Certain fundamental movements may, however, be separated from all others that require the controlled maintenance of equilibrium. Table 11.2 summarizes the usual sequence of emergence of several fundamental stability abilities.

Axial movements and various static and dynamic balance postures are considered here as the major components of stability. Axial, or nonlocomotor, movements are orientation movements of the trunk or limbs while in a static position. Twisting, turning, bending, stretching, and swinging are axial movements. *Postures* are other body positions that place a premium on the maintenance of equilibrium while in a position of static or dynamic balance. Standing, sitting, inverted supports, rolling, stopping, dodging, and landing, as well as beam walking, stick balancing, and one-foot balances, are dynamic or static balance postures.

Axial Movements

Axial movements are movements of the trunk or limbs that orient the body while it remains in a stationary position. Bending, stretching, twisting, turning, swinging, swaying, reaching, lifting, pushing, and pulling are axial movements. They are often combined with other movements to create more elaborate movement skills. Skilled performances in diving, gymnastics, figure skating, and modern dance typically incorporate a variety of axial movements along with various locomotor movements. Axial movements are included with a variety of manipulative skills in soccer, baseball, football, and track and field.

Little is known about the developmental sequence of axial movements (figure 11.2). To date, few film analyses or observational studies have been conducted with children. Ozmun and Robertson (1992), however, completed a preliminary cross-sectional investigation of the total body pushing action with fifteen 3- to 7-year-olds. The results of their study identified a stage sequence of progression to the mature stage of pushing. The initial stage was identified as having the feet together and pushing from either an upright position or from a forward body lean. The elementary stage was identified as having the feet staggered with the front foot off the surface and the body leaning forward. The mature stage of the total body pushing action was identified as having the feet staggered with both feet on the surface with the legs bent and the body leaning forward.

The following discussion represents a proposed developmental sequence for axial movements in general. It is based on observation of numerous children and is subject to further verification and refinement.

Body Rolling

Body rolling postures, although locomotor, require inordinate amounts of balance control. Considerable disturbance of the fluid in the semicircular canals results from rolling actions; therefore, they are regarded as fundamental stability movements. Body rolling movements may involve rolling forward, sideways, or backward. In each, the body is momentarily inverted and must maintain positional control as it travels through space. The specialized skills of the forward and backward somersault are elaborations of the fundamental forward and backward rolling patterns. Walkovers

and handsprings are sophisticated combinations of rolling patterns combined with transitional inverted supports.

Developmental studies of body rolling are limited (Roberton and Halverson, 1984; Wickstrom, 1983; Williams, 1980). The proposed sequence in table 11.3 and figure 11.3 is based on these studies.

Dodging

Dodging is a fundamental stability pattern of movement that combines the locomotor movements of sliding with rapid changes in direction. Dodging involves rapid shifts in direction from side to side and requires good reaction time and speed of movement. Extensive developmental studies of dodging have not been conducted with children. However, observational assessment of children and the work of Roberton and Halverson (1984) does provide the basis for the sequence in table 11.4 and figure 11.4.

One-Foot Balance

The one-foot balance is probably the most common measure of static balance ability. Several investigators have studied the one-foot balance in research participants with their eyes open or closed and the arms at the sides, folded, or on the hips (Cratty, 1986; DeOreo, 1971, 1980; Eckert and Rarick, 1975). Performance trends for balancing on one foot are reported in a later chapter. Table 11.5 and figure 11.5 appear to be the developmental sequence gleaned from these performance investigations, but they are subject to verification and refinement.

Beam Walking

The beam walk is the most frequently measured fundamental dynamic balance ability. A variety of investigations have been conducted using walking boards that vary in length, width, and height

TABLE 11.2 **Developmental Sequence for Axial Movements**

I. Axial Movements
  A. Initial stage
    1. Exaggerated base of support
    2. Momentary loss of balance
    3. Visual monitoring of body and model when possible
    4. Combined movements appear jerky and segmented
    5. Lack of fluid transition from one level or plane to another
    6. Only one to two actions possible at a time
  B. Elementary stage
    1. Good balance
    2. Appropriate base of support
    3. Requires visual model
    4. Does not have to monitor own body
    5. Good coordination of similar movements
    6. Poor transition in dissimilar movements
    7. Can combine two to three actions into one fluid movement
  C. Mature stage
    1. Smooth, rhythmical flow
    2. Sequences several movements with ease
    3. Vision unimportant
    4. Appears totally in control
    5. Can combine four or more movements into one fluid movement
II. Developmental Difficulties
  A. Visually monitoring body
  B. Visually mimicking a model
  C. Poor rhythmical coordination
  D. Segmented combination of movements
  E. Loss of balance
  F. Lack of smooth transition in flow of movement
  G. Inability to perform at various tempos
  H. Inability to perform at different levels

from the supporting surface (DeOreo, 1971, 1980; Goetzinger, 1961; Seashore, 1949). Considerable information concerning the performance abilities of children from year to year is available, but little is known about the developmental sequence of the beam-walking process itself. The developmental sequences in table 11.6 and figure 11.6 are based on observational assessments of numerous children and are subject to refinement and verification.

Inverted Supports

Inverted supports involve postures in which the body assumes an upside-down position for a number of seconds before the movement is discontinued. Stabilization of the center of gravity and maintenance of the line of gravity within the base of support apply to the inverted posture as well as to the erect standing posture. An inverted supporting posture, however, uses either the head, hands,

INITIAL

ELEMENTARY

MATURE

Figure 11.2
Stages of axial movement development.

TABLE 11.3 **Developmental Sequence for Body Rolling**

I. Body Rolling
   A. Initial stage
      1. Head contacts surface
      2. Body curled in loose "C" position
      3. Inability to coordinate use of arms
      4. Cannot get over backward or sideways
      5. Uncurls to "L" position after rolling forward
   B. Elementary stage
      1. After rolling forward, actions appear segmented
      2. Head leads action instead of inhibiting it
      3. Top of head still touches surface
      4. Body curled in tight "C" position at onset of roll
      5. Uncurls at completion of roll to "L" position
      6. Hands and arms aid rolling action somewhat but supply little push-off
      7. Can perform only one roll at a time
   C. Mature stage
      1. Head leads action
      2. Back of head touches surface very lightly
      3. Body remains in tight "C" throughout
      4. Arms aid in force production
      5. Momentum returns child to starting position
      6. Can perform consecutive rolls in control
II. Developmental Difficulties
   A. Head forcefully touching surface
   B. Failure to curl body tightly
   C. Inability to push off with arms
   D. Pushing off with one arm
   E. Failure to remain in tucked position
   F. Inability to perform consecutive rolls
   G. Feeling dizzy
   H. Failure to roll in a straight line
   I. Lack of sufficient momentum to complete one revolution

forearms, or upper arms (or a combination) as the base of support. The shoulders are above the point of support. The tip-up, tripod, headstand, and handstand are examples of skills that incorporate the fundamental pattern of the inverted support.

To date, no developmental studies have been conducted with inverted supports. Table 11.7 and figure 11.7 represent a developmental sequence based on observation of numerous children and are subject to verification and refinement.

INITIAL

ELEMENTARY

MATURE

Figure 11.3
Stages of body rolling development.

TABLE 11.4 **Developmental Sequence for Dodging**

I. Dodging
  A. Initial stage
    1. Segmented movements
    2. Body appears stiff
    3. Minimal knee bend
    4. Weight is on one foot
    5. Feet generally cross
    6. No deception
  B. Elementary stage
    1. Movements coordinated but with little deception
    2. Performs better to one side than to the other
    3. Too much vertical lift
    4. Feet occasionally cross
    5. Little spring in movement
    6. Sometimes outsmarts self and becomes confused
  C. Mature stage
    1. Knees bent, slight trunk lean forward (ready position)
    2. Fluid directional changes
    3. Performs equally well in all directions
    4. Head and shoulder fake
    5. Good lateral movement
II. Developmental Difficulties
  A. Inability to shift body weight in a fluid manner in direction of dodge
  B. Slow change of direction
  C. Crossing feet
  D Hesitation
  E. Too much vertical lift
  F Total body lead
  G. Inability to perform several dodging actions in rapid succession
  H. Monitoring body
  I. Rigid posture

INITIAL

ELEMENTARY

MATURE

Figure 11.4
Stages of the dodging pattern.

TABLE 11.5 **Developmental Sequence for the One-Foot Balance**

I. One-foot Balance
   A. Initial stage
      1. Raises nonsupporting leg several inches so that thigh is nearly parallel with contact surface
      2. Either in or out of balance (no in-between)
      3. Overcompensates ("windmill" arms)
      4. Inconsistent leg preference
      5. Balances with outside support
      6. Only momentary balance without support
      7. Eyes directed at feet
   B. Elementary stage
      1. May lift nonsupporting leg to a tied-in position on support leg
      2. Cannot balance with eyes closed
      3. Uses arms for balance but may tie one arm to side of body
      4. Performs better on dominant leg
   C. Mature stage
      1. Can balance with eyes closed
      2. Uses arms and trunk as needed to maintain balance
      3. Lifts nonsupporting leg
      4. Focuses on external object while balancing
      5. Changes to nondominant leg without loss of balance
II. Developmental Difficulties
   A. Tying one arm to side
   B. No compensating movements
   C. Inappropriate compensation of arms
   D. Inability to use either leg
   E. Inability to vary body position with control
   F. Inability to balance while holding objects
   G. Visually monitoring support leg
   H. Overdependence on outside support

INITIAL

ELEMENTARY

MATURE

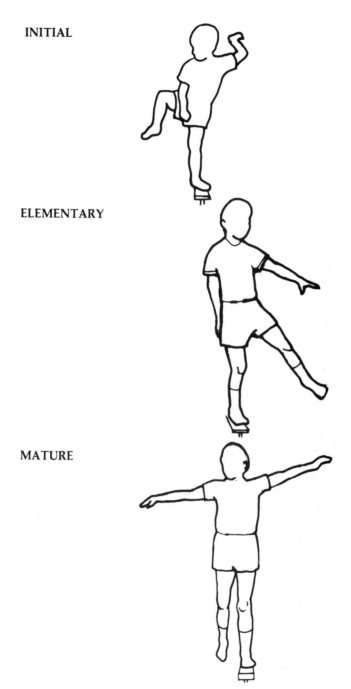

Figure 11.5
Stages of the one-foot balance.

TABLE 11.6 **Developmental Sequence for the Beam Walk**

I. Beam Walk
   A. Initial stage
      1. Balances with support
      2. Walks forward while holding on to a spotter for support
      3. Uses follow-step with dominant foot lead
      4. Eyes focus on feet
      5. Body rigid
      6. No compensating movements
   B. Elementary stage
      1. Can walk a 2-inch (5 cm) beam but not a 1-inch (2.5 cm) beam
      2. Uses a follow-step with dominant foot leading
      3. Eyes focus on beam
      4. May press one arm to trunk while trying to balance with the other
      5. Loses balance easily
      6. Limited compensating movements
      7. Can move forward, backward, and sideways but requires considerable concentration and effort
   C. Mature stage
      1. Can walk a 1-inch (2.5 cm) beam
      2. Uses alternate stepping action
      3. Eyes focus beyond beam
      4. Both arms used at will to aid balance
      5. Can move forward, backward, and sideways with assurance and ease
      6. Movements are fluid, relaxed, and in control
      7. May lose balance occasionally
II. Developmental Difficulties
   A. Overdependence on spotter
   B. Visually monitors stepping leg
   C. Tying one arm in
   D. Rigid, hesitant movement
   E. Failure to negotiate the problem of balance
   F. Inability to perform without holding on to a spotter
   G. Poor rhythmical coordination of both sides of body
   H. Overcompensating for loss of balance

INITIAL

ELEMENTARY

MATURE

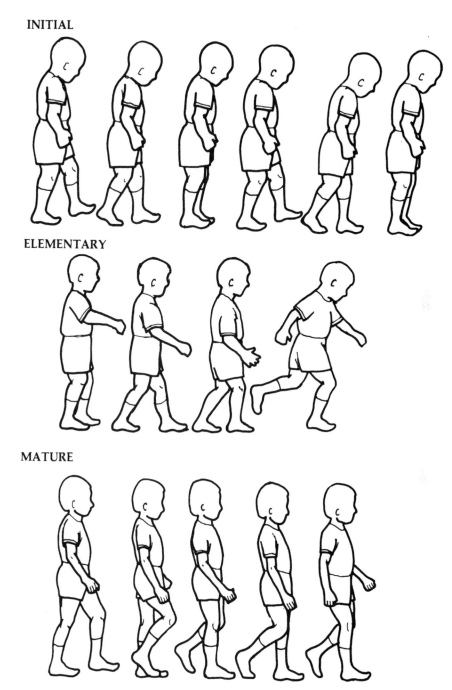

Figure 11.6
Stages of the beam walk.

TABLE 11.7 **Developmental Sequence for Inverted Supports**

I. Inverted Supports
  A. Initial stage
    1. Able to maintain triangular, low-level, three-point balance positions
    2. Able to assume inverted three-point postures for up to three seconds
    3. Poor kinesthetic feel for unseen body parts
    4. Minimal coordinated control of movements
  B. Elementary stage
    1. Can maintain controlled triangular three-point and low two-point contacts with surface
    2. Able to hold balance for three seconds or longer with frequent brief addition of another balance point
    3. Gradual improvement in monitoring of unseen body parts
  C. Mature stage
    1. Good surface contact position
    2. Good control of head and neck
    3. Good kinesthetic feel for body part location
    4. Appears to be in good control of body
    5. Maintains inverted low- and high-level two- and three-point balance positions for three or more seconds
    6. Comes out of static posture under control
II. Developmental Difficulties
  A. Inability to accurately sense location and position of body parts not visually monitored
  B. Inability to keep line of gravity within base of support
  C. Inadequate or exaggerated base of support
  D. Overbalancing by shifting the body's weight too far forward
  E. Inability to hold inverted balance position for three seconds or longer

FUNDAMENTAL LOCOMOTOR MOVEMENTS

Locomotion is a fundamental aspect of learning to move effectively and efficiently within one's environment. It involves projection of the body into external space by altering its location relative to fixed points on the surface. Activities such as walking, running, jumping, hopping, sliding, and skipping are considered fundamental locomotor movements. Performance of these movements must be sufficiently flexible so that they can be altered as the requirements of the environment demand without detracting from the purpose of the act. The child must be able to: (1) use any one of a number of types of movements to reach the goal, (2) shift from one type of movement to another when the situation demands, and (3) alter each movement as the conditions of the environment change. Throughout this process of alteration and modification, attention must not be diverted from the goal. For example, the locomotor pattern of walking may be used singularly, or it may be used in conjunction with manipulative or stability movements. The walking pattern can be elaborated upon by including object handling, such as bouncing a ball and walking on a balance beam. Development and refinement of the following locomotor patterns in children is essential because it is through these movements that they explore the world.

INITIAL

ELEMENTARY

MATURE

Figure 11.7
Stages of inverted support development.

TABLE 11.8 **Developmental Sequence for Walking**

I. Walking
  A. Initial stage
    1. Difficulty maintaining upright posture
    2. Unpredictable loss of balance
    3. Rigid, halting leg action
    4. Short steps
    5. Flat-footed contact
    6. Toes turn outward
    7. Wide base of support
    8. Flexed knee at contact followed by quick leg extension
  B. Elementary stage
    1. Gradual smoothing out of pattern
    2. Step length increased
    3. Heel-toe contact
    4. Arms down to sides with limited swing
    5. Base of support within the lateral dimensions of trunk
    6. Out-toeing reduced or eliminated
    7. Increased pelvic tilt
    8. Apparent vertical lift
  C. Mature stage
    1. Reflexive arm swing
    2. Narrow base of support
    3. Relaxed, elongated gait
    4. Minimal vertical lift
    5. Definite heel-toe contact
II. Developmental Difficulties
  A. Inhibited or exaggerated arm swing
  B. Arms crossing midline of body
  C. Improper foot placement
  D. Exaggerated forward trunk lean
  E. Arms flopping at sides or held out for balance
  F. Twisting of trunk
  G. Poor rhythmical action
  H. Landing flat-footed
  I. Flipping foot or lower leg in or out

CONCEPT 11.6

Fundamental locomotor movements involve projecting the body into space in a horizontal, vertical, or diagonal plane.

Walking

Walking has often been defined as the process of continually losing and regaining balance while moving forward in an upright position. The walking pattern has been extensively studied in infants, children, and adults. The onset of walking behavior in the infant depends primarily on maturation but is also influenced by the environmental factors such as the availability of handholds. Burnett and Johnson (1971) indicated that the average age for achieving independent walking is 12.5 months, with a range from 9 to 17 months. Once independent walking has been achieved, the child progresses

INITIAL

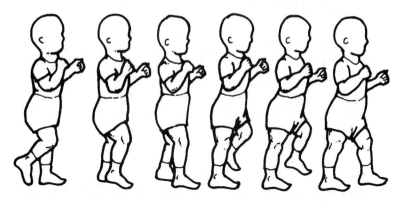

ELEMENTARY

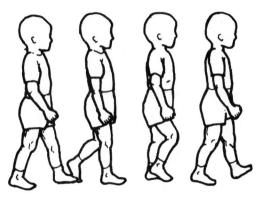

MATURE

Figure 11.8
Stages of the walking pattern.

TABLE 11.9 Developmental Sequence for Running

I. Running
   A. Initial stage
      1. Short, limited leg swing
      2. Stiff, uneven stride
      3. No observable flight phase
      4. Incomplete extension of support leg
      5. Stiff, short swing with varying degrees of elbow flexion
      6. Arms tend to swing outward horizontally
      7. Swinging leg rotates outward from hip
      8. Swinging foot toes outward
      9. Wide base of support
   B. Elementary stage
      1. Increase in length of stride, arm swing, and speed
      2. Limited but observable flight phase
      3. More complete extension of support leg at takeoff
      4. Arm swing increases
      5. Horizontal arm swing reduced on backswing
      6. Swinging foot crosses midline at height of recovery to rear
   C. Mature stage
      1. Stride length at maximum; stride speed fast
      2. Definite flight phase
      3. Complete extension of support leg
      4. Recovery thigh parallel to ground
      5. Arms swing vertically in opposition to legs
      6. Arms bent at approximate right angles
      7. Minimal rotary action of recovery leg and foot
II. Developmental Difficulties
    A. Inhibited or exaggerated arm swing
    B. Arms crossing the midline of the body
    C. Improper foot placement
    D. Exaggerated forward trunk lean
    E. Arms flopping at the sides or held out for balance
    F. Twisting of the trunk
    G. Poor rhythmical action
    H. Landing flat-footed
    I. Flipping the foot or lower leg in or out

rapidly to the elementary and mature stages. Several authors have described the walking pattern and indicated that mature walking is achieved sometime between the fourth and the seventh year (Eckert, 1987; Grieve and Gaer, 1966; Guttridge, 1939; Saunders et al., 1953; Wickstrom, 1983; Williams, 1983). Many subtle changes continue to occur in the walking pattern, but they are not ob-

servable through unaided visual assessment. Sophisticated film analysis and electromyography techniques must be used to detect progress in walking skill beyond this point (Wickstrom, 1983). Gad-Elmawla's 1980 dissertation is used as the basis for description of the developmental sequence in the walking pattern found in table 11.8 and figure 11.8.

INITIAL

ELEMENTARY

MATURE

Figure 11.9
Stages of the running pattern.

TABLE 11.10 Developmental Sequence for Jumping from a Height

I. Jumping from a Height
   A. Initial stage
      1. One foot leads on takeoff
      2. No flight phase
      3. Lead foot contacts lower surface prior to trailing foot leaving upper surface
      4. Exaggerated use of arms for balance
   B. Elementary stage
      1. Two-foot takeoff with one-foot lead
      2. Flight phase, but lacks control
      3. Arms used ineffectively for balance
      4. One-foot landing followed by immediate landing of trailing foot
      5. Inhibited or exaggerated flexion at knees and hip upon landing
   C. Mature stage
      1. Two-foot takeoff
      2. Controlled flight phase
      3. Both arms used efficiently out to sides to control balance as needed
      4. Feet contact lower surface simultaneously with toes touching first
      5. Feet land shoulder-width apart
      6. Flexion at knees and hip congruent with height of jump
II. Developmental Difficulties
   A. Inability to take off with both feet
   B. Twisting body to one side on takeoff
   C. Exaggerated or inhibited body lean
   D. Failure to coordinate use of both arms in the air
   E. Tying one arm to side while using the other
   F. Failure to land simultaneously on both feet
   G. Landing flat-footed
   H. Failure to flex knees sufficiently to absorb impact of landing
   I. Landing out of control

Running

Running is an exaggerated form of walking. It differs principally from the walk in that there is a brief flight phase during each step, in which the body is out of contact with the supporting surface. The flight phase is first seen around the second birthday. Prior to that the run appears as a fast walk with one foot always in contact with the supporting surface. The initial stage of the running pattern does not depend on mature walking (Broer and Zernicke, 1979). Many young children begin to run before they master the mature walking pattern. The mature running pattern is fundamental to successful participation in a variety of sport-related activities. The running pattern has been extensively studied by a number of investigators

(Roberton, 1985; Roberton and Halverson, 1984; Seefeldt, 1972; Wickstrom, 1983). The four-stage developmental sequence hypothesized by Roberton has been collapsed into three stages and is shown in table 11.9 and figure 11.9.

Jumping from a Height

The movements involved in jumping from a low height are somewhat similar to those found in the jump for distance and the jump for height, particularly at the initial stage. The jump from a low height has been studied by a few investigators (Bayley, 1935; McCaskill and Wellman, 1938) who have concentrated on the takeoff, flight phase, and landing aspects of the pattern. The description of stages in table 11.10 and figure 11.10 is based on this research

INITIAL

ELEMENTARY

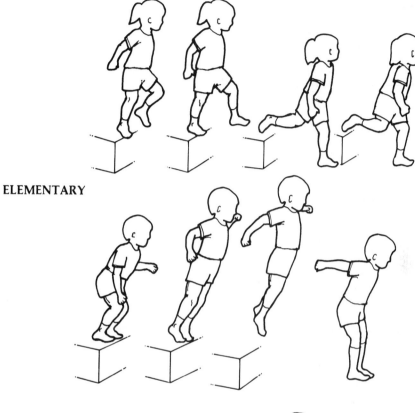

MATURE

Figure 11.10
Stages of the jump from a height.

TABLE 11.11   Developmental Sequence for Vertical Jumping

I. Vertical Jumping
   A. Initial stage
      1. Inconsistent preparatory crouch
      2. Difficulty in taking off with both feet
      3. Poor body extension on takeoff
      4. Little or no head lift
      5. Arms not coordinated with the trunk and leg action
      6. Little height achieved
   B. Elementary stage
      1. Knee flexion exceeds 90-degree angle on preparatory crouch
      2. Exaggerated forward lean during crouch
      3. Two-foot takeoff
      4. Entire body does not fully extend during flight phase
      5. Arms attempt to aid in flight (but often unequally) and balance
      6. Noticeable horizontal displacement on landing
   C. Mature stage
      1. Preparatory crouch with knee flexion from 60 to 90 degrees
      2. Forceful extension at hips, knees, and ankles
      3. Simultaneous coordinated upward arm lift
      4. Upward head tilt with eyes focused on target
      5. Full body extension
      6. Elevation of reaching arm by shoulder girdle tilt combined with downward thrust of nonreaching arm at peak of flight
      7. Controlled landing very close to point of takeoff
II. Developmental Difficulties
   A. Failure to become airborn
   B. Failure to take off with both feet simultaneously
   C. Failure to crouch at about a 90-degree angle
   D. Failure to extend body, legs, and arms forcefully
   E. Poor coordination of leg and arm actions
   F. Swinging of arms backward or to the side for balance
   G. Failure to lead with eyes and head
   H. One-foot landing
   I. Inhibited or exaggerated flexion of hips and knees on landing
   J. Marked horizontal displacement on landing

and on observation of numerous children. It is, therefore, subject to refinement and verification.

Vertical Jumping

Jumping for height, or the vertical jump, has been studied by several investigators (Martin and Stull, 1969; Myers et al., 1977; Poe, 1976; Wickstrom, 1983; Williams, 1983). The jump for height involves projecting the body vertically into the air from a one- or two-foot takeoff with a landing on both feet. The developmental sequence proposed by Myers et al. (1977), based on film analysis, is presented in table 11.11 and figure 11.11.

Horizontal Jumping

The jump for distance is an explosive movement requiring coordinated performance of all parts of the body. This is a complex movement pattern

INITIAL

ELEMENTARY

MATURE

Figure 11.11
Stages of the vertical jumping pattern.

TABLE 11.12 **Developmental Sequence for Horizontal Jumping**

I. Horizontal Jumping
   A. Initial stage
      1. Limited swing; arms do not initiate jumping action
      2. During flight, arms move sideward-downward or rearward-upward to maintain balance
      3. Trunk moves in vertical direction; little emphasis on length of jump
      4. Preparatory crouch inconsistent in leg flexion
      5. Difficulty in using both feet
      6. Limited extension of the ankles, knees, and hips at takeoff
      7. Body weight falls backward at landing
   B. Elementary stage
      1. Arms initiate jumping action
      2. Arms remain toward front of body during preparatory crouch
      3. Arms move out to side to maintain balance during flight
      4. Preparatory crouch deeper and more consistent
      5. Knee and hip extension more complete at takeoff
      6. Hips flexed during flight; thighs held in flexed position
   C. Mature stage
      1. Arms move high and to rear during preparatory crouch
      2. During takeoff, arms swing forward with force and reach high
      3. Arms held high throughout jumping action
      4. Trunk propelled at approximately 45-degree angle
      5. Major emphasis on horizontal distance
      6. Preparatory crouch deep, consistent
      7. Complete extension of ankles, knees, and hips at takeoff
      8. Thighs held parallel to ground during flight; lower leg hangs vertically
      9. Body weight forward at landing
II. Developmental Difficulties
   A. Improper use of arms (i.e., failure to use arms opposite the propelling leg in a down-up-down swing as leg flexes, extends, and flexes again)
   B. Twisting or jerking of body
   C. Inability to perform either a one-foot or a two-foot takeoff
   D. Poor preliminary crouch
   E. Restricted movements of arms or legs
   F. Poor angle of takeoff
   G. Failure to extend fully on takeoff
   H. Failure to extend legs forward on landing
   I. Falling backward on landing

in which it is difficult to inhibit the tendency to step forward on one foot. Instead the takeoff and landing must be with both feet. The horizontal jumping pattern has been extensively studied (Clark and Phillips, 1985; Roberton and Halverson, 1984; Seefeldt and Haubenstricker, 1976; Wickstrom, 1983). The developmental sequence proposed by McClenaghan (1976), based on film analysis, is used in table 11.12 and figure 11.12.

Hopping

Hopping is similar to the jump for distance and the vertical jump but both the takeoff and the landing

INITIAL

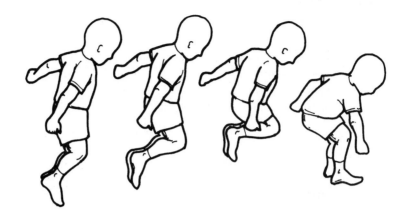

ELEMENTARY

MATURE

Figure 11.12
Stages of the horizontal jumping pattern.

TABLE 11.13 Developmental Sequence for Hopping

I. Hopping
  A. Initial stage
    1. Nonsupporting leg flexed 90 degrees or less
    2. Nonsupporting thigh roughly parallel to contact surface
    3. Body upright
    4. Arms flexed at elbows and held slightly to side
    5. Little height or distance generated in single hop
    6. Balance lost easily
    7. Limited to one or two hops
  B. Elementary stage
    1. Nonsupporting leg flexed
    2. Nonsupporting thigh at 45-degree angle to contact surface
    3. Slight forward lean, with trunk flexed at hip
    4. Nonsupporting thigh flexed and extended at hip to produce greater force
    5. Force absorbed on landing by flexing at hip and by supporting knee
    6. Arms move up and down vigorously and bilaterally
    7. Balance poorly controlled
    8. Generally limited in number of consecutive hops that can be performed
  C. Mature stage
    1. Nonsupporting leg flexed at 90 degrees or less
    2. Nonsupporting thigh lifts with vertical thrust of supporting foot
    3. Greater body lean
    4. Rhythmical action of nonsupporting leg (pendulum swing aiding in force production)
    5. Arms move together in rhythmical lifting as the supporting foot leaves the contact surface
    6. Arms not needed for balance but used for greater force production
II. Developmental Difficulties
  A. Hopping flat-footed
  B. Exaggerated movements of arms
  C. Exaggerated movement of nonsupporting leg
  D. Exaggerated forward lean
  E. Inability to maintain balance for five or more consecutive hops
  F. Lack of rhythmical fluidity of movement
  G. Inability to hop effectively on both left foot and right foot
  H. Inability to alternate hopping feet in a smooth, continuous manner
  I. Tying one arm to side of body

are on the same foot. The hop has been studied by Halverson and Williams (1985), Roberton and Halverson (1984), and Seefeldt and Haubenstricker (1976). The four-stage developmental sequence proposed by Halverson and Williams is summa-rized in table 11.13 and figure 11.13 and condensed into three stages.

Galloping and Sliding

Galloping and sliding involve the combination of two fundamental movements, the step and the

INITIAL

ELEMENTARY

MATURE

Figure 11.13
Stages of the hopping pattern.

TABLE 11.14 **Developmental Sequence for Galloping and Sliding**

I. Galloping and Sliding
  A. Initial stage
    1. Arrhythmical at fast pace
    2. Trailing leg often fails to remain behind and often contacts surface in front of lead leg
    3. Forty-five-degree flexion of trailing leg during flight phase
    4. Contact in a heel-toe combination
    5. Arms of little use in balance or force production
  B. Elementary stage
    1. Moderate tempo
    2. Appears choppy and stiff
    3. Trailing leg may lead during flight but lands adjacent to or behind lead leg
    4. Exaggerated vertical lift
    5. Feet contact in a heel-toe, or toe-toe, combination
    6. Arms slightly out to side to aid balance
  C. Mature stage
    1. Moderate tempo
    2. Smooth, rhythmical action
    3. Trailing leg lands adjacent to or behind lead leg
    4. Both legs flexed at 45-degree angles during flight
    5. Low flight pattern
    6. Heel-toe contact combination
    7. Arms not needed for balance; may be used for other purposes
II. Developmental Difficulties
  A. Choppy movements
  B. Keeping legs too straight
  C. Exaggerated forward trunk lean
  D. Overstepping with trailing leg
  E. Too much elevation on hop
  F. Inability to perform both forward and backward
  G. Inability to lead with nondominant foot
  H. Inability to perform to both left and right
  I. Undue concentration on task

leap, with the same foot always leading in the direction of movement. The movement is called a gallop when the person is moving forward or backward, and a slide when he or she is progressing sideward. Sapp (1980) and Williams (1983) described a developmental sequence for galloping that may also be applied to sliding. This sequence is shown in table 11.14 and figure 11.14.

Leaping

The leap is similar to the run in that there is a transference of weight from one foot to the other, but the loss of contact with the surface is sustained, with greater elevation and distance covered than in the run. Leaping involves using greater amounts of force to produce more height and to cover a greater distance than in a run. Biomechanical studies have been conducted on the hurdle event in track, but

INITIAL

ELEMENTARY

MATURE

Figure 11.14
Stages of the sliding pattern.

TABLE 11.15 Developmental Sequence for Leaping

I. Leaping
  A. Initial stage
    1. Child appears confused in attempts
    2. Inability to push off and gain distance and elevation
    3. Each attempt looks like another running step
    4. Inconsistent use of takeoff leg
    5. Arms ineffective
  B. Elementary stage
    1. Appears to be thinking through the action
    2. Attempt looks like an elongated run
    3. Little elevation above supporting surface
    4. Little forward trunk lean
    5. Stiff appearance in trunk
    6. Incomplete extension of legs during flight
    7. Arms used for balance, not as an aid in force production
  C. Mature stage
    1. Relaxed rhythmical action
    2. Forceful extension of takeoff leg
    3. Good summation of horizontal and vertical forces
    4. Definite forward trunk lean
    5. Definite arm opposition
    6. Full extension of legs during flight
II. Developmental Difficulties
  A. Failure to use arms in opposition to legs
  B. Inability to perform one-foot takeoff and land on opposite foot
  C. Restricted movements of arms or legs
  D. Lack of spring and elevation in push-off
  E. Landing flat-footed
  F. Exaggerated or inhibited body lean
  G. Failure to stretch and reach with legs

there is a dearth of information about the developmental aspects of the leaping pattern. The description of stages shown in table 11.15 and figure 11.15 is based on observational assessment of numerous children and is subject to refinement and verification.

Skipping

The skipping action puts two fundamental movement patterns, the step and the hop, together into a combined pattern of movement. Seefeldt and Haubenstricker (1976) as well as Halverson and Roberton (1979) have studied the skipping pattern and reported a three-stage developmental sequence, which serves as the basis of the description found in this text. The skip is a continuous flow of the step and hop involving rhythmical alteration of the leading foot. See table 11.16 and figure 11.16.

INITIAL

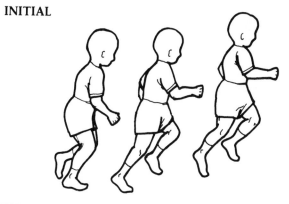

ELEMENTARY

MATURE

Figure 11.15
Stages of the leaping pattern.

TABLE 11.16 **Developmental Sequence for Skipping**

I. Skipping
   A. Initial stage
      1. One-footed skip
      2. Deliberate step-hop action
      3. Double hop or step sometimes occurs
      4. Exaggerated stepping action
      5. Arms of little use
      6. Action appears segmented
   B. Elementary stage
      1. Step and hop coordinated effectively
      2. Rhythmical use of arms to aid momentum
      3. Exaggerated vertical lift on hop
      4. Flat-footed landing
   C. Mature stage
      1. Rhythmical weight transfer throughout
      2. Rhythmical use of arms (reduced during time of weight transfer)
      3. Low vertical lift on hop
      4. Toe-first landing
II. Developmental Difficulties
   A. Segmented stepping and hopping action
   B. Poor rhythmical alteration
   C. Inability to use both sides of body
   D. Exaggerated movements
   E. Landing flat-footed
   F. Exaggerated, inhibited, or unilateral arm movements
   G. Inability to move in a straight line
   H. Inability to skip backward and to side

FUNDAMENTAL MANIPULATIVE MOVEMENTS

Gross motor manipulation involves an individual's relationship to objects and is characterized by giving force to objects and receiving force from them. Propulsive movements involve activities in which an object is moved away from the body. Fundamental movements such as throwing, kicking, striking, and rolling a ball are examples. Absorptive movements involve activities in which the body or a body part is positioned in the path of a moving object for the purpose of stopping or deflecting that object. Fundamental movements such as catching and trapping are examples. The essence of manipulative movements is that they combine two or more movements and are generally used in conjunction with other forms of movement. For example, propulsive movements are usually a composite of stepping, turning, swinging, and stretching. Absorptive movements generally consist of bending and stepping.

CONCEPT 11.7

Fundamental movements categorized as manipulative involve giving force to objects and/or receiving force from them.

Through the manipulation of objects children are able to explore the relationship of moving objects in space. These movements involve making estimates of the path, distance, rate of travel, accuracy, and mass of the moving object. At the point of contact a check on previous estimates is possible. Through such types of experimentation children learn the nature and effect of the movement of objects. Because manipula-

INITIAL

ELEMENTARY

MATURE

Figure 11.16
Stages of the skipping pattern.

TABLE 11.17 **Developmental Sequence for Ball Rolling**

I. Ball Rolling
  A. Initial stage
    1. Straddle stance
    2. Ball is held with hands on the sides, with palms facing each other
    3. Acute bend at waist, with backward pendulum motion of arms
    4. Eyes monitor ball
    5. Forward arm swing and trunk lift with release of ball
  B. Elementary stage
    1. Stride stance
    2. Ball held with one hand on bottom and the other on top
    3. Backward arm swing without weight transfer to the rear
    4. Limited knee bend
    5. Forward swing with limited follow-through
    6. Ball released between knee and waist level
    7. Eyes alternately monitor target and ball
  C. Mature stage
    1. Stride stance
    2. Ball held in hand corresponding to trailing leg
    3. Slight hip rotation and trunk lean forward
    4. Pronounced knee bend
    5. Forward swing with weight transference from rear to forward foot
    6. Release at knee level or below
    7. Eyes are on target throughout
II. Developmental Difficulties
  A. Failure to transfer body weight to rear foot during initial part of action
  B. Failure to place controlling hand directly under ball
  C. Releasing the ball above waist level
  D. Failure to release ball from a virtual pendular motion, causing it to veer to one side
  E. Lack of follow-through, resulting in a weak roll
  F. Swinging the arms too far backward or out from the body
  G. Failure to keep eyes on target
  H. Failure to step forward with foot opposite hand that holds ball
  I. Inability to bring ball to side of the body

tive patterns commonly combine both locomotor and stabilizing movements, efficient use of them should not be expected at the same time that locomotor and stability abilities are developing. Only after these patterns have been fairly well established do we begin to see the emergence of efficient manipulative movements. The following is a description of several manipulative patterns of movement.

Ball Rolling

Rolling an object is another fundamental movement pattern that has not been methodically studied. Ability in ball rolling has most often been assessed by accuracy in knocking down bowling pins rather than from the standpoint of form. Numerous sport and recreational activities use the fundamental patterns found in rolling. Bowling, curling, shuffleboard, and the underhand pitch in softball employ variations of the pattern found in mature rolling. The developmental sequence shown in table 11.17 and figure 11.17 is based on observational assessment of numerous children and is subject to verification and further refinement.

Overhand Throwing

The overhand throw has been studied extensively over the past several decades (Deach, 1951; Haubenstricker et al., 1983; McClenaghan and

INITIAL

ELEMENTARY

MATURE

Figure 11.17
Stages of the ball rolling pattern.

TABLE 11.18 **Developmental Sequence for Overhand Throwing**

I. Throwing
   A. Initial stage
      1. Action is mainly from elbow
      2. Elbow of throwing arm remains in front of body; action resembles a push
      3. Fingers spread at release
      4. Follow-through is forward and downward
      5. Trunk remains perpendicular to target
      6. Little rotary action during throw
      7. Body weight shifts slightly rearward to maintain balance
      8. Feet remain stationary
      9. There is often purposeless shifting of feet during preparation for throw
   B. Elementary stage
      1. In preparation, arm is swung upward, sideward, and backward to a position of elbow flexion
      2. Ball is held behind head
      3. Arm is swung forward, high over shoulder
      4. Trunk rotates toward throwing side during preparatory action
      5. Shoulders rotate toward throwing side
      6. Trunk flexes forward with forward motion of arm
      7. Definite forward shift of body weight
      8. Steps forward with leg on same side as throwing arm
   C. Mature stage
      1. Arm is swung backward in preparation
      2. Opposite elbow is raised for balance as a preparatory action in the throwing arm
      3. Throwing elbow moves forward horizontally as it extends
      4. Forearm rotates and thumb points downward
      5. Trunk markedly rotates to throwing side during preparatory action
      6. Throwing shoulder drops slightly
      7. Definite rotation through hips, legs, spine, and shoulders during throw
      8. Weight during preparatory movement is on rear foot
      9. As weight is shifted, there is a step with opposite foot
II. Developmental Difficulties
   A. Forward movement of foot on same side as throwing arm
   B. Inhibited backswing
   C. Failure to rotate hips as throwing arm is brought forward
   D. Failure to step out on leg opposite the throwing arm
   E. Poor rhythmical coordination of arm movement with body movement
   F. Inability to release ball at desired trajectory
   G. Loss of balance while throwing
   H. Upward rotation of arm

Gallahue, 1978a; Roberton, 1978, 1985, 2001; Seefeldt, 1972; Wild, 1938), with attention focused on form, accuracy, and distance. The components of the throw vary depending on which of these three factors the thrower is concentrating on and the starting position that is assumed. When viewing the overhand throw from the standpoint of the process or form, the developmental sequence depicted in table 11.18 and figure 11.18 is apparent. Variability is particularly evident in the early developmental stages of throwing, resulting in a high degree of inconsistency (Pascual and Grimshaw, 1998; Yan, Payne, and Thomas, 2000). In regard to task constraints, Manoel and Oliveira (2000) found that

INITIAL

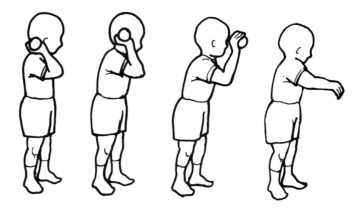

ELEMENTARY

MATURE

Figure 11.18
Stages of the overhand throwing pattern.

in a group of 7-year-old boys and girls, mature throwers threw farther than their initial and elementary-level counterparts. They did not, how-

ever, perform better on throwing for accuracy tasks. The size of the ball being thrown has also influenced the mechanics of the throwing pattern (Burton,

TABLE 11.19 **Developmental Sequence for Catching**

I. Catching
  A. Initial stage
    1. There is often an avoidance reaction of turning the face away or protecting the face with arms (avoidance reaction is learned and therefore may not be present)
    2. Arms are extended and held in front of body
    3. Body movement is limited until contact
    4. Catch resembles a scooping action
    5. Uses of body to trap ball
    6. Palms are held upward
    7. Fingers are extended and held tense
    8. Hands are not used in catching action
  B. Elementary stage
    1. Avoidance reaction is limited to eyes closing at contact with ball
    2. Elbows are held at sides with an approximately 90-degree bend
    3. Initial attempt at contact with child's hands is often unsuccessful, therefore, arms trap the ball
    4. Hands are held in opposition to each other; thumbs are held upward
    5. At contact, the hands attempt to squeeze ball in a poorly timed and uneven motion
  C. Mature stage
    1. No avoidance reaction
    2. Eyes follow ball into hands
    3. Arms are held relaxed at sides, and forearms are held in front of body
    4. Arms give on contact to absorb force of the ball
    5. Arms adjust to flight of ball
    6. Thumbs are held in opposition to each other
    7. Hands grasp ball in a well-timed, simultaneous motion
    8. Fingers grasp more effectively
II. Developmental Difficulties
  A. Failure to maintain control of object
  B. Failure to "give" with the catch
  C. Keeping fingers rigid and straight in the direction of object
  D. Failure to adjust hand position to the height and trajectory of object
  E. Inability to vary the catching pattern for objects of different weight and force
  F. Taking eyes off object
  G. Closing the eyes
  H. Inability to focus on, or track the ball
  I. Improper stance, causing loss of balance when catching a fast-moving object
  J. Closing hands either too early or too late
  K. Failure to keep body in line with the ball

Greer, and Wiese, 1992; Burton, Greer, and Wiese-Bjornstal, 1993). There is also some evidence that suggests boys throw with more mature kinematics than girls during the early elementary years (Raud-sepp and Paasuke, 1995).

Catching

The fundamental movement pattern of catching involves use of the hands to stop tossed objects. The elements of the underhand and overhand catch are essentially the same. The major difference is in the position of the hands upon impact with

INITIAL

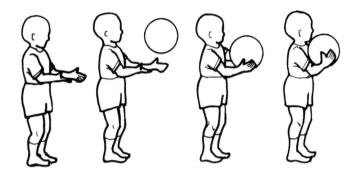

ELEMENTARY

MATURE

Figure 11.19
Stages of the catching pattern.

the object. The underhand catch is performed when the object to be caught is below the waist. The palms of the hands and the wrists are turned upward. When the object is above the waist, the palms face away from the individual in the direction of the flight of the object.

TABLE 11.20 **Developmental Sequence for Kicking**

I. Kicking
  A. Initial stage
    1. Movements are restricted during kicking action
    2. Trunk remains erect
    3. Arms are used to maintain balance
    4. Movement of kicking leg is limited in backswing
    5. Forward swing is short: there is little follow-through
    6. Child kicks "at" ball rather than kicking it squarely and following through
    7. A pushing rather than a striking action is predominant
  B. Elementary stage
    1. Preparatory backswing is centered at the knee
    2. Kicking leg tends to remain bent throughout the kick
    3. Follow-through is limited to forward movement of the knee
    4. One or more deliberate steps are taken toward the ball
  C. Mature stage
    1. Arms swing in opposition to each other during kicking action
    2. Trunk bends at waist during follow-through
    3. Movement of kicking leg is initiated at the hip
    4. Support leg bends slightly on contact
    5. Length of leg swing increases
    6. Follow-through is high; support foot rises to toes or leaves surface entirely
    7. Approach to the ball is from either a run or leap
II. Developmental Difficulties
  A. Restricted or absent backswing
  B. Failure to step forward with nonkicking leg
  C. Tendency to lose balance
  D. Inability to kick with either foot
  E. Inability to alter speed of kicked ball
  F. Jabbing at ball without follow-through
  G. Poor opposition of arms and legs
  H. Failure to use a summation of forces by the body to contribute to force of the kick
  I. Failure to contact ball squarely or missing it completely (eyes not focused on ball)
  J. Failure to get adequate distance (lack of follow-through and force production)

Several researchers have investigated the development of catching abilities in children (Guttridge, 1939; Haubenstricker et al., 1983; McClenaghan and Gallahue, 1978a; Roberton and Halverson, 1984). The developmental sequence of catching, shown in table 11.19 and figure 11.19, is based on these and McClenaghan's (1976) study. Recent investigations examining the developmental skill characteristics of catching have focused on various environmental constraints. Factors such as visual field restrictions and levels of illumination have been demonstrated to influence the kinematics of catching (Bennett, Button, Kingsbury, and Davids, 1999; Savelsbergh and van der Kamp, 2000).

Kicking

Kicking is a form of striking in which the foot is used to impart force to an object. Precise variations of the kicking action may be accomplished by making adjustments with the kicking leg and by bringing the arms and trunk into play.

INITIAL

ELEMENTARY

MATURE

Figure 11.20
Stages of the kicking pattern.

Table 11.21 Developmental Sequence for Trapping

I. Trapping
   A. Initial stage
      1. Trunk remains rigid
      2. No "give" with ball as it makes contact
      3. Inability to absorb force of the ball
      4. Difficulty getting in line with object
   B. Elementary stage
      1. Poor visual tracking
      2. "Gives" with the ball, but movements are poorly timed and sequenced
      3. Can trap a rolled ball with relative ease but cannot trap a tossed ball
      4. Appears uncertain of what body part to use
      5. Movements lack fluidity
   C. Mature stage
      1. Tracks ball throughout
      2. "Gives" with body upon contact
      3. Can trap both rolled and tossed balls
      4. Can trap balls approaching at a moderate velocity
      5. Moves with ease to intercept ball
II. Developmental Difficulties
   A. Failure to position body directly in path of ball
   B. Failure to keep eyes fixed on ball
   C. Failure to "give" as ball contacts body part
   D. Failure to angle an aerial ball downward toward feet
   E. Causing body to meet ball instead of letting ball meet body
   F. Inability to maintain body balance when trapping in unusual or awkward positions

The primary factors that influence the type of kick used are: (1) the desired trajectory of the ball and (2) the height of the ball when it is contacted. The fundamental kicking pattern for a stationary ground ball is the only common striking movement that does not use the arms and hands directly. The developmental aspects of kicking a stationary ball have been studied extensively by Deach (1951) and Seefeldt and Haubenstricker (1981). The developmental sequence shown in table 11.20 and figure 11.20 is based on these studies and the work of McClenaghan (1976).

Trapping

Trapping an object is a form of catching in which the feet or the body, instead of the hands

and arms, is used to absorb the force of the ball. Trapping is a skill that must be highly refined for an individual to successfully play soccer. With young children, however, trapping should be viewed very generally, that is, as the ability to stop a ball without use of the hands or arms. A developmental sequence for trapping in children is shown in table 11.21 and figure 11.21. It is based on observational assessment of numerous children and is subject to verification and further refinement.

Striking

The first striking movements (other than kicking) appear in young children whenever they hit objects

INITIAL

ELEMENTARY

MATURE

Figure 11.21
Stages of the trapping pattern.

TABLE 11.22 **Developmental Sequence for Striking**

I. Striking
  A. Initial stage
    1. Motion is from back to front
    2. Feet are stationary
    3. Trunk faces direction of tossed ball
    4. Elbow(s) fully flexed
    5. No trunk rotation
    6. Force comes from extension of flexed joints in a downward plane
  B. Elementary stage
    1. Trunk turned to side in anticipation of tossed ball
    2. Weight shifts to forward foot prior to ball contact
    3. Combined trunk and hip rotation
    4. Elbow(s) flexed at less acute angle
    5. Force comes from extension of flexed joints. Trunk rotation and forward movement are in an oblique plane
  C. Mature stage
    1. Trunk turns to side in anticipation of tossed ball
    2. Weight shifts to back foot
    3. Hips rotate
    4. Transfer of weight is in a contralateral pattern
    5. Weight shift to forward foot occurs while object is still moving backward
    6. Striking occurs in a long, full arc in a horizontal pattern
    7. Weight shifts to forward foot at contact
II. Developmental Difficulties
  A. Failure to focus on and track the ball
  B. Improper grip
  C. Failure to turn side of the body in direction of intended flight
  D. Inability to sequence movements in rapid succession in a coordinated manner
  E. Poor backswing
  F. "Chopping" swing

with implements. Swinging at a ball on the ground, on a batting tee, or in flight is a familiar act to most children. Only a limited amount of scientific investigation has been conducted on the developmental aspects of striking in children (Deach, 1951; Halverson and Roberton, 1966; Seefeldt and Haubenstricker, 1976). The developmental sequence proposed by Seefeldt and Haubenstricker is summarized in table 11.22 and figure 11.22.

Dribbling

Dribbling a ball with one hand is a fundamental movement pattern that has received attention in the literature on children (Payne and Isaacs, 2002; Wickstrom, 1983; Williams, 1983). Dribbling is a complicated task requiring precise judgment of an object's distance, force, and trajectory. Dribbling is preceded by ball bouncing and catching. Good figure-ground and depth perception are also required for efficient dribbling. The proposed developmental sequence shown in table 11.23 and figure 11.23 is based on Wickstrom's work and on observational assessment of numerous children. It is subject to further refinement.

INITIAL

ELEMENTARY

MATURE

Figure 11.22
Stages of the striking pattern.

TABLE 11.23 Developmental Sequence for Dribbling

I. Dribbling
   A. Initial stage
      1. Ball held with both hands
      2. Hands placed on sides of ball, with palms facing each other
      3. Downward thrusting action with both arms
      4. Ball contacts surface close to body, may contact foot
      5. Great variation in height of bounce
   B. Elementary stage
      1. Ball held with both hands, one on top and the other near the bottom
      2. Slight forward lean, with ball brought to chest level to begin the action
      3. Downward thrust with top hand and arm
      4. Force of downward thrust inconsistent
      5. Hand slaps at ball for subsequent bounces
      6. Wrist flexes and extends and palm of hand contacts ball on each bounce
      7. Visually monitors ball
      8. Limited control of ball while dribbling
   C. Mature stage
      1. Feet placed in narrow stride position, with foot opposite dribbling hand forward
      2. Slight forward trunk lean
      3. Ball held waist high
      4. Ball pushed toward ground, with follow-through of arm, wrist, and fingers
      5. Controlled force of downward thrust
      6. Repeated contact and pushing action initiated from fingertips
      7. Visual monitoring unnecessary
      8. Controlled directional dribbling
II. Developmental Difficulties
   A. Slapping at ball instead of pushing it downward
   B. Inconsistent force applied to downward thrust
   C. Failure to focus on and track ball efficiently
   D. Inability to dribble with both hands
   E. Inability to dribble without visually monitoring ball
   F. Insufficient follow-through
   G. Inability to move about under control while dribbling

INITIAL

ELEMENTARY

MATURE

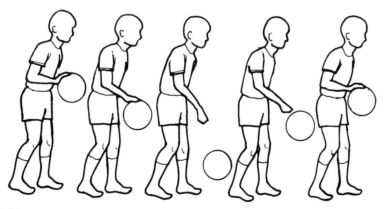

Figure 11.23
Stages of the dribbling pattern.

TABLE 11.24 Developmental Sequence for Volleying

I. Volleying
  A. Initial stage
    1. Inability to accurately judge path of ball or balloon
    2. Inability to get under the ball
    3. Inability to contact ball with both hands simultaneously
    4. Slaps at the ball from behind
  B. Elementary stage
    1. Failure to visually track ball
    2. Gets under the ball
    3. Slaps at ball
    4. Action mainly from hands and arms
    5. Little lift or follow-through with legs
    6. Unable to control direction or intended flight of ball
    7. Wrists relax and ball often travels backward
  C. Mature stage
    1. Gets under the ball
    2. Good contact with fingertips
    3. Wrists remain stiff and arms follow through
    4. Good summation of forces and use of arms and legs
    5. Able to control direction and intended flight of ball
II. Developmental Difficulties
  A. Failure to keep eyes on ball
  B. Inability to accurately judge flight of ball and to properly time movements of body
  C. Failure to keep fingers and wrists stiff
  D. Failure to extend all of the joints upon contacting ball (lack of follow-through)
  E. Inability to contact ball with both hands simultaneously
  F. Slapping at ball
  G. Poor positioning of body under ball

Volleying

Volleying is a form of striking in which an overhand pattern is used. It resembles the two-handed set shot that was once popular in basketball and is similar to the overhead set shot used in power volleyball. Use of balloons and beach balls for volleying practice prior to using volleyballs is recommended as a means of promoting success and proper body mechanics. The developmental sequence shown in table 11.24 and figure 11.24 is based on observation of children and is subject to verification and refinement.

FUTURE DIRECTIONS IN INVESTIGATING FUNDAMENTAL MOVEMENT PATTERNS

While the fundamental movement patterns of a wide variety of skills have been investigated for several decades, more recent studies have begun focusing on the influence of environmental and task constraints. Environmental factors, such as visual field restriction when the skill of catching is performed (Bennett et al., 1999), and task factors, such as throwing for distance and accuracy outcomes by initial, elementary, and mature throwers (Manoel and Oliveira, 2000), are some recent examples.

INITIAL

ELEMENTARY

MATURE

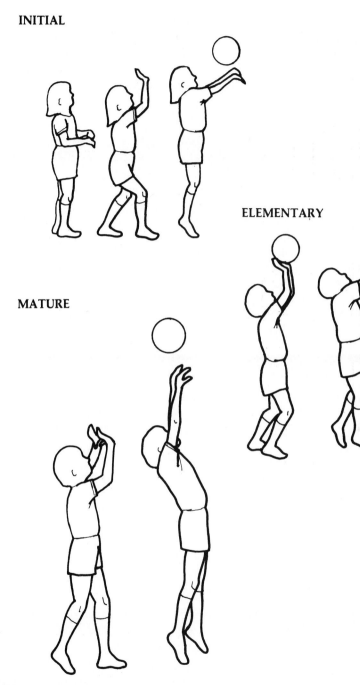

Figure 11.24
Stages of the volleying pattern.

The developmental sequence of new skills may emerge as well. For example, Fox and Tipps (1995) describe a developmental sequence for playground swinging. The investigation of new skills may be driven by the desire of parents of children with developmental delays to include their children in as many neighborhood activities as possible. The ability to swing at the playground or ride a tricycle with friends may be perceived as more beneficial to the overall development of a child with special needs than devoting time and energy on more traditional movement patterns.

SUMMARY

The fundamental movement pattern phase of development tends to follow a sequential progression. A child without developmental disabilities, under optimal circumstances, will progress through the initial, elementary, and mature stages in a sequential manner. Developmental sequences for several fundamental movements have been identified through biomechanical assessment of children at different age levels. Developmental sequences have also been proposed, based on film, videotape, and observational assessments of numerous children. The fundamental movement phase of development is greatly influenced by conditions within the environment and the goal of the task which create a variety of between-child, between-pattern, and within-pattern differences. Developmental sequences have been proposed and are at different levels of validation. Knowledge of these developmental sequences enables one to be more effective in diagnosing developmental disabilities and programming meaningful movement experiences.

CRITICAL READINGS

Clark, J. E. (1995). On becoming skillful: Patterns and constraints. *Research Quarterly for Exercise and Sport, 66*, 173–183.

Gallahue, D. L., & Cleland, F. (2003). *Developmental Physical Education for Today's Children.* 4th ed. Champaign, IL: Human Kinetics.

Payne, V. G., & Isaacs, L. D. (2002). *Human Motor Development: A Lifespan Approach* (Chapters 13–14). 4th ed. Mountain View, CA: Mayfield.

Roberton, M. A., & Konczak, J. (2001). Predicting children's overarm throw ball velocities from their developmental levels in throwing. *Research Quarterly for Exercise and Sport, 72*, 91–103.

Ulrich, B. D. (1997). Dynamic systems theory and skill development in infants and children. In K. Connolly & H. Forssberg (Eds.), *Neurophysiology and Psychology Motor Development* (pp. 319–345). London: Mac Keigh Press.

WEB RESOURCES

American Academy of Pediatrics Committee on Nutrition
www.aap.org/visit/cmte25.htm

Information Website for Physical Education Teachers
www.pecentral.org

Michigan State University Longitudinal Motor Performance Study
http://ed-web3.educ.msu.edu/KIN/Activities/mps.htm

Physical Education Information Website
www.pelinks4u.org

CHAPTER 12

PHYSICAL DEVELOPMENT OF CHILDREN

KEY TERMS

Gold standard
Health-related fitness
Aerobic endurance
Maximal oxygen consumption (VO_2 max)
Accelerometer
Muscular strength
Isometric
Isotonic
Isokinetic
Dynamometers
Muscular endurance
Joint flexibility
Static flexibility
Dynamic flexibility
Body composition
Hydrostatic weighing
Skinfold calipers
Anabolic hormones
Catabolic hormones
Testosterone
Neuromuscular adaptation
Growth plates
Motor fitness
Coordination
Balance
Speed
Agility
Power

CHAPTER COMPETENCIES

Upon completion of this chapter you should be able to:

- Demonstrate knowledge of data available on performance scores and motor pattern changes during childhood
- Describe gender differences and similarities in motor development
- Discuss changes in movement dimensions such as balance, timing, or force production/control
- Demonstrate knowledge of major changes in body composition and physiological functioning in males and females
- Discuss the effect of exercise on body systems and body composition such as bone and muscle development and cardiorespiratory capacity
- Draw conclusions concerning the merits and/or liabilities of strength and endurance training for prepubescent males and females
- Distinguish between health-related and performance-related fitness during childhood
- Interpret velocity curves on various parameters of children's fitness
- Identify gender differences and similarities in motor performance

KEY CONCEPT

The physical fitness of children has been assessed through a variety of laboratory and field-based measures and may be improved through the application of appropriate training techniques.

The health-related fitness and motor fitness of children should be of great concern to all—not only the physical educator, coach, and physician. For the past several decades the fitness levels of boys and girls in North America have received considerable attention in the professional and lay literature. The American Alliance for Health, Physical Education, Recreation, and Dance (AAHPERD) became a leader in surveying the fitness of American youth through the development and promotion of a national youth fitness test. This test, with revisions, became the basis for decade-by-decade comparisons in 1965, 1975, and 1985. The AAHPERD Youth Fitness Test (1980) and the AAHPERD Health-Related Physical Fitness Tests (1980) were probably the most widely used standardized physical fitness tests throughout the United States during the 1980s. A new generation of field-based fitness measures are now the nation's premier youth fitness test. *The President's Challenge* (President's Council on Physical Fitness and Sports, 2001) and *Fitnessgram* (American Fitness Alliance, 2000) have emerged as the two most popular fitness batteries available for use by field professionals in the United States.

CONCEPT 12.1

A variety of available field measures claim to measure various aspects of children's physical fitness.

Noted professionals as well as professional organizations report that a great many children are unfit (Baranowski et al., 1992; Kuntzleman and Reiff,

1992; Updyke, 1992). Moreover, the National Children and Youth Fitness Study (Ross and Gilbert, 1985) revealed that more than one-third of the children and youth tested (ages 10 to 18) were not sufficiently active in their daily lives for aerobic benefit. A second survey (National Center for Health Statistics, 2001) clearly reveals that children in the United States are heavier and fatter than their counterparts of twenty years ago.

Two primary factors seem to have contributed greatly to this state of affairs. First, the need to enhance fitness in the United States has centered on adults. Until recently, relatively little research has been focused on the physical activity needs of children. As a result, our knowledge of the fitness of children and their capacity for work has been limited.

CONCEPT 12.2

Conventional wisdom suggests that today's children are unfit, but little conclusive evidence exists to either support or deny this assertion.

A second assumption has been that children are naturally active and get plenty of vigorous physical activity as a normal part of their daily routines. However, apartment living, city dwelling, and the ubiquitous television set have created sedentary lifestyles for many children (DuRant et al., 1996). Blair (1992), however, takes exception to this position:

> Anyone who has taught or raised children should know that they are physically active. Nevertheless, we have been bombarded by propaganda over the past 35 years in both the professional and lay literature that deplores the status of youth fitness in the United States. (p. 120)

There are three primary reasons why it makes little sense to argue whether children are fit or unfit. First, we have not completely or adequately defined "physical fitness." As simple as this may seem, there has been considerable debate as to what constitutes physical fitness. Defining *fitness* is a necessary first step toward establishing children's fitness standards. Although we do not have universal agreement on the term **physical fitness,** we will use the following definition as our guide: "Physical fitness is a positive state of well-being influenced by regular physical activity, genetic makeup, and nutritional adequacy."

Second, there are few valid and reliable gold standards for assessing physical fitness in the laboratory. **Gold standard** is a term used to refer to an ultimate and universally accepted measure of a particular quality. To date, laboratory gold standards have not been established for most measures of physical fitness. This makes it difficult to conclusively establish the validity of common field measures of fitness. In their two recommendations for future research in physical activity and physical fitness, Baranowski et al. (1992) recommended that: (1) gold standard laboratory measures and corresponding valid field measures be developed and (2) valid measures of health-related fitness that are applicable to laboratory, field, and clinical settings be identified.

Third, specific criteria for determining who is "physically fit" or "physically unfit" have yet to be established. Classifying one as being fit or unfit is based more on supposition and hunches, rather than on scientifically determined standards. Specific numerical levels have been established as guidelines for determining mental retardation, high cholesterol, obesity, and a number of other educational and health issues. It follows then that criteria can and should be established for minimal physical fitness levels necessary for good health. "*Fitnessgram*" (American Fitness Alliance), a field-based fitness test, does that. It compares children's scores on six health-related fitness measures to carefully researched health standards rather than national norms.

With these concerns in mind we will now turn to a discussion about what we *do* know about the health-related and performance-related aspects of children's physical fitness. The information that follows is based on information gleaned from laboratory, field, and clinical settings.

HEALTH-RELATED FITNESS

Extensive studies in the area of physical fitness have been conducted over the past several years, and we are gradually piecing together what is known about the physical fitness of children. A review of the literature on fitness, however, reveals a marked lack of information on children under 6 years of age. The reasons for this are many. Most tests of physical fitness require the individual to go "all out" and perform at his or her maximum. Anyone familiar with young children will recognize the difficulty of this situation. The problems lie in: (1) being able to sufficiently motivate the youngster for maximal performance, (2) accurately determining whether a maximum effort has been achieved, and (3) overcoming the fears of anxious parents. Experts working with young children have fertile area for the study of physical fitness. Carefully controlled, patient research will yield much valuable information. Aerobic endurance, muscular strength, muscular endurance, joint flexibility, and body composition are the components of **health-related fitness.** Each of these components is discussed briefly in the following paragraphs regarding what is known at present.

Cardiovascular Aerobic Endurance

Aerobic endurance is an aspect of muscular endurance, specific to the heart, lungs, and vascular system. It refers to the ability to perform numerous repetitions of a stressful activity requiring considerable use of the circulatory and respiratory system. **Maximal oxygen consumption (VO$_2$ max)** refers to the largest quantity of oxygen an individual can consume during physical work while breathing air at sea level. It is a measure of one's maximum ability to transmit oxygen to the tissues of the body. An increase in one's aerobic capacity is an excellent indicator of a higher energy output. It is generally considered that up to a 20 percent improvement in VO$_2$ max is possible, because one's genetic inheritance plays a crucial role in the capacity to consume oxygen. Maximal oxygen consumption tends to improve as a function of age until about 18 to 20 in males, but tends to level off at about 14 in females (Armstrong and Welsman, 2000). Improvement thereafter is primarily a function of training. Due to size differences, females possess about 75 percent of the capacity of males to consume oxygen. More specifically, when comparing females and males at various age levels boys' values are about 12 percent higher than girls at age 10. Sex differences, however, become more dramatic during the teen years typically reaching 37 percent by age 16 (Armstrong and Welsman, 2000). The differences between males and females prior to puberty are largely unexplored. Oxygen consumption in children under 8 has been investigated by relatively few researchers, and the results have often been conflicting because of the questionable reliability and reproducibility of VO_2 max measures with this young age group. However, attempts are being made to develop and establish clinical guidelines for measuring aerobic factors with pediatric populations.

Maximal aerobic power as measured by maximal oxygen consumption is a universally accepted means of measuring status and change in cardiovascular fitness. It is not, however, universally accepted or understood how to express maximal aerobic ability in relation to body size. The literature concerning the aerobic capacity of children, particularly under the age of 8, is limited. Young children make difficult subjects, and the testing environment is restricted by the extent of their interest in putting forth a maximal effort. Knowing how maximal aerobic power relates to body mass and body size is important when dealing with children. The difficulty is in knowing if changes in aerobic capacity are a function of training or growth or if both play a role.

Over the years several laboratory studies have been conducted with children to determine their VO_2 max values. Pate and Blair (1978) in their review of two decades of studies concluded that values ranging from 45 to 55 milliliters of oxygen per kilogram of body weight (ml.kg) had been consistently reported in the United States. In a more recent review of twenty-nine longitudinal studies, Krahenbuhl et al. (1985) found similar mean values. Armstrong and Welsman (2000) noted that

VO_2 max relative to weight remains stable for males 8 to 18 years at about 48 to 50 ml.kg but declined for females from 45 to 35 ml.kg as they advanced in years. A minimum VO_2 max threshold value of 42 is generally recommended for adults, and according to Simons-Morton et al. (1987), in their review of children and fitness, "it appears that most children are well above this level" (p. 297).

Heart rate responses to exercise are sometimes used as crude measures of cardiovascular endurance in young children because of the difficulty in gathering accurate VO_2 max data. Normal resting heart rates in children range from approximately 60 to 80 beats per minute. Maximum exercise heart rates in children have been reported to range from about 150 to 230 beats per minute. Mrzena and Macuek (1978) in what should be considered a pioneering experiment because of its methodology, tested children 3 to 5 years old on the treadmill. Each subject was required to walk or run for 5 minutes at a level grade with the treadmill set at three different speeds (3, 4, and 5 km/h). The highest heart rates were recorded at 142 beats per minute. Another group performed the treadmill task at 4 km/h while the grade was increased from 5° to 10° to 15°. This group produced heart rates averaging 162 beats per minute. Investigators noted that when the treadmill speed was increased to 6 km/h and the inclination to 20°, "the children were not able to increase the step frequency and lost their balance" (p. 31). The average maximum aerobic capacity of preschool children is certainly greater than the scores obtained in this experiment, but maturity of movement as well as the psychological and emotional state of the young child determine the degree of cooperation and effort during testing.

In an investigation by Parizkova (1977), heart rates of 160 beats per minute were recorded in a bench-stepping task with 3-year-old children. The children had considerable difficulty maintaining the cadence of 30 steps per minute on the low bench without the investigator's assistance. The children in this investigation also had difficulty maintaining the task even though normal play heart rates of young children often exceed 200 beats per minute. Cumming and Hantiuk (1980) reported that normal maximal heart rates for children range from 180 to 234 beats per minute. This investigation again reminds us of the extreme difficulty in achieving a maximal effort for a sustained period with young children.

For years, researchers have used a variety of techniques to measure physical activity. *Activity self-reports* in which the subject completes a form designed to aid in recalling several days of physical activity have been used extensively. Although valid instruments with adolescents and adults, they are not recommended for research purposes with children under age 10 because of the inability of most boy and girls under this age to cognitively recall, in detail, their physical activity. *Heart rate monitors* have also been used extensively to measure daily physical activity. Once again, validity is doubtful, especially with children, because heart rates below 120 beats per minute are not valid predictors of exercise intensity (Rowlands, Eston, and InblePew 1997), and other factors, such as emotions, can elevate the heart rate. The use of *doubly labeled water*, which contains a stable isotope that can be accurately traced when excreted in the urine, and direct observation of physical activity, although valid for use with children, are unrealistic because of their expense.

As a result, *accelerometers* have emerged as a preferred means of assessing children's physical activity because it is valid and economical. An **accelerometer** is an electromechanical device worn by the subject that detects and records motion in a single plane or multiple planes. In a study by Ott and colleagues (2000) twenty-eight children 9 to 11 years of age wore accelerometers while engaged in a variety of physical activities. The results of this study revealed that average heart rates did

not differ significantly between girls and boys for seven activities (video game play, throw and catch, walking, bench stepping, basketball, aerobic dance, and running) of the eight (hop-scotch).

Muscular Strength

Muscular strength is the ability of the body to exert force. In its purest sense, it is the ability to exert one maximum effort. Children engaged in daily active play are enhancing their leg strength by running and bicycling. Their arm strength is developed through such activities as lifting, carrying objects, handling tools, and swinging on the monkey bars. Strength may be classified as **isometric, isotonic,** or **isokinetic.** *Isometric strength* involves exerting force on an immovable object. The muscle contracts, but there is little change in its length. *Isotonic strength* refers to the ability of a muscle to go through its full range of motion. The muscles involved contract, but they also shorten and lengthen during the activity. A barbell curl and a bench press are examples of isotonic strength activities. *Isokinetic strength* involves contracting a muscle and maintaining that contraction through its full range of motion. Isokinetic strength is measured by use of special machines that accommodate resistance at a set velocity as the muscle works.

In laboratory situations *strength* is commonly measured by using a dynamometer or tensiometer. These devices are highly reliable when used by trained personnel. **Dynamometers** are calibrated devices designed to measure grip strength, leg strength, and back strength. *Tensiometers* are more versatile than dynamometers in that they permit measurement of many different muscle groups. The classic longitudinal studies conducted by Clarke (1971) used eighteen different cable tensiometer tests and revealed yearly strength increments in boys between 7 and 17 years. Although information is limited on young children, Beunen and Thomis (2000) reported that from 3 to 6 years of age there are minimal sex differences and that strength gradually increases from year to year. These yearly increases are most closely associated

CONCEPT 12.3

Although a variety of instruments report to reliably measure children's physical activity levels, accelerometers have emerged as the most valid and economical field measure.

with size increases and improvement in fundamental movement abilities. In boys from age 6 onto the onset of puberty (generally around age 12) there is a gradual linear increase in strength, with dramatic acceleration to age 17 and beyond. In girls, we see linear strength increases until about age 15, followed by a pronounced plateauing and regression in the late teens and beyond.

> ## CONCEPT 12.4
>
> Although incremental, strength gains during childhood are not linear; therefore, estimating strength scores in later years based on scores achieved during childhood offers little in the way of predictive validity.

Relatively few longitudinal investigations have been conducted on the development of strength in children at all ages. However, the available information indicates consistency in the development of strength in children over time. Strength has been shown to increase more rapidly than muscle size during childhood (Beunen and Thomis, 2000). This is probably due to the improved skill and coordination with which maximal contractions may be performed. This indicates the interrelationship between strength, coordination, and motor performance in children.

Although strength is a relatively stable quality throughout childhood, predicting strength levels at later years from measures taken in childhood has met with little success. The "strong" child at age 8, for example, will not necessarily make the greatest gains in strength from childhood through adolescence. Neither will the "weak" child necessarily make the least gains in strength from childhood through adolescence. Rapid change in body size, positively correlated with strength, and individual variability of growth patterns make prediction a precarious venture.

Muscular Endurance

Muscular endurance is the ability of a muscle or a group of muscles to perform work repeatedly against moderate resistance. Muscular endurance is similar to muscular strength in the activities performed but it differs in emphasis. Strength-building activities require overloading the muscles to a greater extent than endurance activities. Endurance-building activities require less of an overload on the muscle but more repetitions. Therefore, endurance may be thought of as the ability to continue in strength performance. Children performing sit-ups, push-ups, and pull-ups are engaged in endurance activities, even though strength is required for any movement to begin. These three activities are among the most often used measures of muscular endurance and are among the best field measures available. There are, however, problems with pull-up measures because of body weight. The entire body weight must be lifted, and many children are unable to accomplish such a task. Therefore, a modified pull-up test is frequently used.

> ## CONCEPT 12.5
>
> Endurance levels of children approach and often exceed those of adults when adjusted for body weight.

The daily uninhibited play routines of young children are excellent examples of endurance that most adults would be unable to duplicate. *Relative endurance* refers to the child's endurance level adjusted to body weight. An adult's gross levels of endurance and fitness are generally greater than those of the child, but when body weight is factored into the total fitness score, the differences are less pronounced.

Throughout childhood both boys and girls tend to make steady year-to-year improvements on most measures of muscular endurance with boys only slightly outperforming girls prior to puberty. Girls reaching puberty ahead of their male counterparts (generally around age 10 or 11) often outperform them for a short period.

Joint Flexibility

Joint flexibility is the ability of the various joints of the body to move through their full range of motion. There are two types of flexibility: static and dynamic. **Static flexibility** is the range of motion achieved by a slow and steady stretch to the limits of the joints involved. **Dynamic flexibility** is the range of motion achieved when rapidly moving a body part to its limits.

Flexibility is joint specific and can be improved with practice. Dynamic flexibility in the shoulder, knee, and thigh joints tends to decrease with age among sedentary children. Clarke (1975) reviewed the research on flexibility and concluded that flexibility begins to decline in boys around age 10 and in girls around age 12.

CONCEPT 12.6

Activity levels offer a better guide to joint flexibility than chronological age, because of the highly specific nature of this fitness component.

The National Children and Youth Fitness Study II (1987) tested thousands of children 6 to 9 years of age for flexibility. A sit-and-reach test was used as a measure of joint flexibility in the lower back and hip area. Mean scores clearly favored the girls. They tended to be slightly more flexible than boys at all ages. Girls showed little improvement with age, but neither did they regress. The boys, however, were on the average slightly less flexible at age 9 than they were at age 6.

Body Composition

Body composition is defined as the proportion of lean body mass to fat body mass. Relative fatness can be determined through a variety of means. **Hydrostatic weighing** (underwater) techniques, although the most accurate, are seldom used in studying the body composition of children. Instead, **skinfold calipers** are the preferred method, even though the accuracy of measurement is sometimes questionable (Lohman, 1986). Measurement sites include the triceps, subscapular region, and

the medial portion of the calf. National surveys of body fatness have shown that children of all ages are fatter than they were twenty years ago. This trend toward increased fatness of American youth reflects dramatic changes in physical activity patterns and nutritional habits.

CONCEPT 12.7

Over the past twenty years, a number of factors have contributed to a secular trend toward higher body fat percentages among children living in the United States.

With regard to activity patterns, Parizkova (1972, 1973, 1977) demonstrated repeatedly that young athletes are less fat than their more sedentary age-mates. Conversely, it has been repeatedly documented that obese children are significantly less active than their lean peers (Bandini, 1987; Romanella et al., 1991; Rowland, 1991).

The reasons for adoption of a sedentary lifestyle among children are many, but the implications are clear. Lower activity levels result in increased body fat percentages, whereas higher activity levels tend to promote lower body fat levels. The activity habits of a lifetime are formed during childhood. Parents, teachers, and other significant individuals in a child's environment can make a difference in activity levels both by example and by positive encouragement. Ward and Bar-Or (1986) reported, after reviewing thirteen school-based obesity intervention programs, that the success of these programs was dependent upon the following elements:

1. Multidisciplinary, integrating behavior modification, nutrition education, and physical activity
2. Structured physical activity opportunities four to five times per week, with encouragement and incentives for after-school activities
3. Team approach, with the participation of the school nurse, guidance counselor, lunchroom supervisor, and physical education teacher

4. Parental involvement, in order to achieve continuity and to coordinate home support for the development of new behaviors (Bar-Or, 1987, p. 306)

Rickard and colleagues (1995) found that a multicomponent intervention program with obese children that used a play and a constructivist approach with young children could serve as a valuable means of reducing health risks associated with obesity. Parents, classroom teachers, health workers, and physical education teachers working as a team can play important roles in reversing the trend toward increased body fatness in children.

CHILDREN'S FITNESS TRAINING

During the last several years our knowledge base has expanded dramatically in the area of children's fitness training. Although we still have many unanswered questions, research shows that children are capable of much more in aerobic conditioning, strength and endurance enhancement, and flexibility improvement than previously thought. Although we do not have adequate information to clearly delineate the physical activity patterns of children, we do know that the active child can make significant health-related fitness gains.

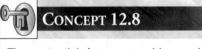

CONCEPT 12.8

The potential for measurable aerobic trainability in prepubescent children has yet to be conclusively documented.

Aerobic Training

An area of study that has received increased attention deals with the *aerobic trainability* of prepubescent children in their potential for making significant gains in VO_2 max scores. Because it has been widely documented that adults respond to training protocols, it is commonly believed that children can produce similar physiologically measurable training effects.

In 1983 Katch proposed what has become known as the *"trigger hypothesis"* for aerobic trainability. This hypothesis contends that with prepubertal children efforts to improve aerobic endurance are likely to be wasted largely due to their low levels of androgens and growth hormone, metabolism, and muscular development. Rowland (1997) reviewed Katch's 1983 hypothesis with the benefit of fourteen years of accumulated evidence on the topic and found little reason to refute his claim. In fact, the evidence leads us to conclude that children do not respond as predicted to aerobic training. A number of explanations have been proposed including: (1) the need for children to have a higher training intensity to demonstrate significant aerobic trainability, (2) that children are naturally more active and have higher fitness levels than adults resulting in the need for proportionally more activity to demonstrate a training effect, and (3) that children may be less motivated to train. All may have merit, but there is beginning to be an accumulation of evidence that "true biological differences may exist between children and adults that restrict improvement in aerobic fitness with training with immature compared to mature subjects" (Rowland, 1997).

In summary, a meta-analysis of the quantitative effects of aerobic training on the VO_2 max scores of children was completed by Payne and Morrow (1993). Their investigation, which included thirty studies that met inclusionary criteria, revealed that:

In the most rigorously controlled studies (pre/post test), subjects improved less than 2 ml.kg-1.min-1. When contrasting studies with "sufficient" and "insufficient" training protocols, significance was not achieved. These findings indicate that many current practices concerning children's fitness should be viewed with skepticism. (p. 3)

Many leading professionals and national professional associations endorse the practice of increasing the amount of a child's vigorous physical activity as a means of enhancing aerobic endurance. To date, the data do not conclusively support this hypothesis. Training protocols that produce significant training effects in children should be studied, and the specific attributes of those being trained must be identified.

Strength Training

In the past it was assumed that prepubescent children would not benefit significantly from a monitored strength-training program. (Please refer to table 12.1 for a description of common terms used in resistance training [National Strength and Conditioning Association, 1985; American Academy of Pediatrics, 2001].) Early negative findings led many people to believe that strength-training programs were ineffective because of low levels of circulating androgens (male sex hormones) in prepubescent boys and in females of all ages (Legwold, 1982, 1983; Vrijens, 1978). A 1983 position paper by the American Academy of Pediatrics concluded that prepubescent strength training, although acceptable if properly supervised, was largely ineffective. However, Bar-Or (1983) asked, if women, who have low levels of testosterone, are capable of making significant strength gains, then why can't prepubescent children make similar gains? A number of studies clearly point out that children are capable of making significant strength gains in properly conducted and supervised programs of sufficient duration and intensity (Duda, 1986; Sewell and Micheli, 1984). These investigations

and others prompted the American Academy of Pediatrics (2001) to regularly update their position statement to recognize the efficacy of prepubescent strength training.

With proper supervision, strength training can benefit prepubescent children in strength enhancement; injury reduction; and improved performance (Payne et al., 1997). However, strength training is different from weight lifting. *Strength training* involves the use of progressive resistance techniques using the body, weights, or machines to improve one's ability to exert or resist a force. *Weight lifting* is a sport in which one attempts to lift the maximum number of pounds possible. Weight lifting is not recommended for prepubescent children (American Acedemy of Pediatrics, 2001).

CONCEPT 12.9

Prepubescent children can, under certain conditions, make significant gains in muscular strength in properly designed and carefully supervised resistance-training programs.

Hormonal control of protein synthesis in muscle tissue involves the complex interaction of many **anabolic hormones** (muscle-enhancing) and **catabolic hormones** (muscle-destroying). One of the most important anabolic hormones is *growth hormone* (GH), found in prepubescent children. According to Bernuth et al. (1985): "Exercise has been

TABLE 12.1	Terms Commonly Used in Strength Training

Resistance training: Any method used to overcome or bear force.

Strength training: The use of resistance to increase the ability to exert or resist force. Various devices, including machines, weights, or one's body may be used as a means of increasing strength.

Weight training: The use of free weights (barbells, dumbbells), stationary weights, or machines to increase strength.

Weight lifting: A competitive sport sometimes referred to as "power lifting" that involves lifting the maximum weight possible in prescribed events ("snatch," "clean and jerk," "squat," "bench press," and "dead lift").

found to be the most potent stimulus for GH release in children" (p. 100). It seems, therefore, that children have at least some of the hormones necessary for muscle hypertrophy. Most studies examining prepubescent weight training, however, have found no evidence of muscle hypertrophy following a training program (Blimkie et al., 1989; Ozmun, Mikesky, and Surburg, 1994; Weltman et al., 1986). Only one investigation has claimed to have observed muscle hypertrophy in a prepubescent population (Mersch and Stoboy, 1989). These results, however, require verification as the research participants involved only two sets of identical twins.

Testosterone has been the primary sex hormone associated with the tremendous gains in muscular strength seen in adolescent males. Like growth hormone, testosterone is an anabolic hormone, but whether it enhances muscular development by direct action on muscle tissue or by an indirect inhibition of the catabolic action of other hormones is unclear. It is the combination of testosterone and growth hormone, however, that enhances protein synthesis and inhibits protein destruction in muscle tissue, contributing to an increase in muscle size and strength. Therefore, although females of all ages and prepubescent males have low levels of circulating androgens, they possess other anabolic hormones such as growth hormone that can facilitate protein synthesis and result in significant strength increases under sufficiently enhanced levels of training.

Prepubescent children can increase their strength through resistance training due to enhanced stimulation of the central nervous system beyond that which would occur with normal growth and maturation. The term **neuromuscular adaptation** is used for changes that result from training. When the body is subjected over time to significant amounts of anatomical or physiological stress, the natural reaction is to adapt to the new conditions. It has been demonstrated that a short-term weight-training program results in neuromuscular adaptations with prepubescent participants (Blimkie et al., 1989; Ozmun et al., 1994). There are, however, special considerations for the

preadolescent involved in a strength-training program.

The possibility that weight training harms the still-growing epiphyseal **growth plates** in young bones is a concern. Indeed, these cartilaginous structures, by their soft and spongy nature, are susceptible to injury, especially from excessive weight-bearing, shearing forces, and chronic stress. The potential vulnerability of the growth plates through excessive stress must not be minimized. A high correlation exists between damage to these areas and children involved in weight lifting (Gumbs et al., 1982). As a result, the National Strength and Conditioning Association (1985) and the American Academy of Pediatrics (2001) recommend that prepubescent athletes avoid the sport due to the immaturity of their bones.

Another prime cause of epiphyseal damage in children engaged in weight training and chronic stress activities is improper training techniques. In addition, some weight-training equipment may be unsuitable with or without proper technique. Most machine-type resistance equipment is made to adult body proportions, with little or no consideration given to youth proportions. Epiphyseal growth plate injuries due to overuse have also been reported in children participating in certain sports. Distance running, gymnastics, and distance swimming have the potential for causing overuse injuries in the prepubescent athlete. Overuse injuries are beginning to be reported in sports such as soccer as playing seasons continue to increase in length.

In summary, it appears that prepubescent strength training can, if properly supervised, produce significant strength gains in boys and girls. One must be careful, however, to use this information wisely. Damage to the epiphyseal growth end plates of the long bones may occur if the young body is pushed too far. At this juncture it is not possible to determine the extent to which any one individual may be pushed in training before damage is done. As a result, carefully supervised weight-training programs that emphasize proper technique and actively discourage maximal lifts are recommended. Programs should also use equipment adapted to the child's size and stress low resistance training. In no case should prepubescent athletes be encouraged or permitted to engage in weight lifting (i.e., "max-out").

Flexibility Training

Besides strength and endurance training, another key health-related fitness component considered essential to injury prevention is joint flexibility. Improving the range of motion about the various joints of the body plays an important role in enhancing movement performance. Historically, it was believed that any type of weight training would decrease an individual's flexibility by not allowing the muscle to work through the full range of motion. The isokinetic weight-training equipment of today is designed to solve this problem. With the principle of variable resistance, an intricate system of cams and pulleys compensates for the inherent weak areas in a joint's range of motion. Flexibility can be maintained or even augmented with proper technique and certain types of weight-training equipment.

CONCEPT 12.10

Children frequently exhibit decreased levels of joint flexibility during the prepubescent growth spurt because bone growth precedes muscle and tendon growth.

Micheli and Micheli (1985) reported less flexibility in males and females during the prepubescent growth spurt. The reason is that bone growth precedes muscle and tendon growth. As a result, musculotendinous units tighten. It is essential for the prepubescent athlete to engage in a good stretching program along with any form of strength or endurance training to help counter the tendency for reduced flexibility. Overuse injuries such as "swimmer's shoulder" are related to a lack of flexibility. Do not assume that endurance

activities such as running and swimming promote flexibility. The young performer must be encouraged to engage in a proper stretching program prior to and after any endurance workout to minimize the possibility of injury to the area around the joints.

HEALTH-RELATED FITNESS AND MOVEMENT ABILITIES

The interaction between the components of health-related fitness and physical activity is obvious. Performance of any movement task, whether it be at the rudimentary, fundamental, or sport skill level, requires varying degrees of cardiovascular fitness, muscular strength, muscular endurance, and joint flexibility. All movement involves exerting force to overcome inertia. To exert that force, one must possess some degree of muscular strength. If a movement task is to be performed repeatedly, as in dribbling a ball, muscular endurance is also required. If the action is to be repeated over an extended period at a rapid pace, as in dribbling a ball up and down a basketball court, both cardiovascular endurance and flexibility are required. Reciprocity in building the components of physical fitness is evident in that performance of movement activities maintains and develops higher levels of physical fitness. The components of physical fitness are inseparable from movement activity. Rarely, if ever, is a movement activity performed that does not involve some aspect of strength, muscular endurance, or flexibility.

CONCEPT 12.11

One's health-related fitness, motor fitness, and movement abilities are interrelated; each influences the other in the "real" world and operates in isolation only in the research laboratory.

It is not possible under normal conditions to isolate the basic components of skill performance. However, tests have been devised that require more of one component of fitness than of another. Through this indirect means of measuring health-related fitness we are able to determine estimates of one's functional health (table 12.2).

MOTOR FITNESS

Considerable research has been conducted on the motor skill performance of the adolescent, adult, and skilled performer. The literature is replete with

TABLE 12.2	Common Measures of Children's Health-Related Fitness and a Synthesis of Findings		
Health-Related Fitness Components	**Common Tests**	**Specific Aspect Measured**	**Synthesis of Findings**
Cardiovascular endurance	Step test Distance run Treadmill stress test Bicycle ergometer Heart rate monitor Accelerometer	Physical work capacity Aerobic endurance Max VO_2 Max VO_2 Heart rate Heart rate	VO_2 max estimates are tenuous with young children. Children can achieve maximum VO_2 values at or above adults when corrected for body weight. Maximal heart rates decrease with age. Trend for improved VO_2 max values in both boys and girls with age. Girls level off after age 12 or so. Boys continue to improve.
Muscular strength	Hand dynamometer Back and leg dynamometer Cable tensiometer	Isometric grip strength Isometric back and leg strength Isometric joint strength	Annual increase for boys from age 7 on. Girls tend to level off after age 12. Boys slow prior to puberty, then gain rapidly throughout adolescence. Boys superior to girls at all ages.
Muscular endurance	Push-ups Sit-ups Flexed arm hang Pull-ups	Isotonic upper body endurance Isotonic abdominal endurance Isometric upper body endurance Isotonic upper body endurance	Similar abilities throughout childhood slightly in favor of boys on most items. Lull in performance prior to age 12. Large increases in boys from 12 to 16, then a leveling off. Girls show no significant increases without special training after age 12.
Flexibility	Bend and reach Sit and reach	Hip joint flexibility Hip joint flexibility	Flexibility is joint specific. Girls tend to be more flexible than boys at all ages. Flexibility decreases with reduced activity levels.
Body composition	Hydrostatic weighing Skinfold calipers Body mass index Electrical impedance	Percent body fat Estimate of percent body fat Estimate of percent body fat Estimate of percent body fat	Children at all ages have higher percentages of fat than their age-mates of twenty years ago. Active children are leaner than obese children at all ages. Obese children are less active than nonobese children.

information dealing with their performance levels, biomechanics, and neurophysiological capabilities, but relatively little has been done with preschool and elementary school age children. The situation is much the same as with health-related fitness. Investigators have also begun to more closely analyze the motor fitness of children. Studies on the specific factors that make up the child's **motor fitness** indicate that a well-defined structure is present during early childhood but that these factors may differ somewhat from those of older age groups (Peterson et al., 1974; Seefeldt, 1980). There is a statistically determined structure of motor abilities in children generally consisting of four or five items depending on the age level investigated. *Movement control factors* of balance (both static and dynamic balance) and coordination (both gross motor and eye-hand coordination), coupled with the *force production factors* of speed, agility, and power, tend to emerge as the components that most influence motor performance. The movement control factors (balance and coordination) are of particular importance during early childhood when the child is gaining control of his or her fundamental movement abilities. The force production factors (speed, agility, and power) become more important after the child has gained control of his or her fundamental movements and passes into the specialized movement phase of later childhood.

Fjortoft (2000) studying 5 to 7-year-olds found differences in motor fitness to be dependent mainly on age and to a lesser extent on sex. Differences in height and weight at these ages do not seem to correlate with measures of motor fitness.

CONCEPT 12.12

The components of motor fitness may be grouped into movement control factors and force production factors.

As with the components of health-related fitness, one's motor fitness is intricately interrelated with

movement skill acquisition. One depends in large part on the other. Without adequate motor fitness, a child's level of skill acquisition will be limited, and without adequate skill acquisition, the level of motor fitness attainment will be impeded. The components of motor fitness are discussed here and synthesized in table 12.3.

Coordination

Coordination is the ability to integrate separate motor systems with varying sensory modalities into efficient patterns of movement. The more complicated the movement tasks, the greater the level of coordination necessary for efficient performance. Coordination is linked to the motor fitness components of balance, speed, and agility, but does not appear to be closely aligned with strength and endurance. Coordinated behavior requires the child to quickly and accurately perform specific movements in a series. Movement must be synchronous, rhythmical, and properly sequenced to be coordinated.

CONCEPT 12.13

Coordinated movement requires integration of sensory and motor systems into a congruent and harmonious action pattern.

Eye-hand and eye-foot coordination are characterized by integrating visual information with limb action. Movements must be visually controlled and precise to project, make contact with, or receive an external object. Bouncing, catching, throwing, kicking, and trapping all require considerable amounts of visual input integrated with motor output to achieve efficient coordinated movement.

Gross body coordination in children involves moving the body rapidly while performing various fundamental movement skills. Measures such as the shuttle run, 30-yard dash, various hopping

TABLE 12.3 Common Measures of Children's Performance-Related Fitness and a Synthesis of Findings

Motor Fitness Component	Common Tests	Specific Aspect Measured	Synthesis of Findings
Coordination	Cable jump	Gross body coordination	Year-by-year improvement with age in gross body coordination. Boys superior from age 6 on in eye-hand and eye-foot coordination.
	Hopping for accuracy	Gross body coordination	
	Skipping	Gross body coordination	
	Ball dribble	Eye-hand coordination	
	Foot dribble	Eye-foot coordination	
Balance	Beam walk	Dynamic balance	Year-by-year improvement with age. Girls often outperform boys, especially in dynamic balance activities, until about age 8. Abilities similar thereafter.
	Stick balance	Static balance	
	One-foot stand	Static balance	
	Flamingo stand	Static balance	
Speed	20-yard dash	Running speed	Year-by-year improvement with age. Boys and girls similar until age 6 or 7, at which time boys make more rapid improvements. Boys superior to girls at all ages.
	30-yard dash	Running speed	
Agility	Shuttle run	Running agility	Year-by-year improvement with age. Girls begin to level off after age 13. Boys continue to make improvements.
	Side straddle	Lateral agility	
Power	Vertical jump	Leg strength and speed	Year-by-year improvement with age. Boys outperform girls at all age levels.
	Standing long jump	Leg strength and speed	
	Distance throw	Upper-arm strength and speed	
	Velocity throw	Upper-arm strength and speed	

and skipping tests, and the standing long jump require high levels of gross body coordination. Gross body coordination and eye-hand and eye-foot coordination appear to improve with age in a roughly linear fashion. Also, boys tend to exhibit better coordination than girls throughout childhood (Frederick, 1977; Van Slooten, 1973).

Balance

Balance is the ability to maintain the equilibrium of one's body when it is placed in various posi-

tions. Balance is basic to all movement and is influenced by visual, tactile-kinesthetic, and vestibular stimulation. Vision plays an important role in balance with young children. Cratty and Martin (1969) found that boys and girls age 6 and under could not balance on one foot with their eyes closed. By age 7, however, they were able to maintain balance with their eyes closed, and balancing ability continued to improve with age. Use of the eyes enables the child to focus on a reference point to maintain balance. The eyes also enable the young child to visually monitor the body during a static or dynamic balance task.

CONCEPT 12.14

Balance is critical to all movement behavior and is influenced by a variety of sensory mechanisms.

Balance is profoundly influenced by the vestibular apparatus. The fluid contained in the *semicircular canals* and the *otolith* plays a key role in helping an individual maintain equilibrium. The receptors in the semicircular canal respond to changes in angular acceleration (dynamic and rotational balance), whereas the otolith receptors respond to linear accelerations (static balance). The movements of *macula* (hairs) in either the otolith or the semicircular canals trigger nerve impulses by changing the electrical potential of adjoining nerve cells. Movement of the body and gravity are sensed by these vestibular receptors to keep the individual aware of both static and dynamic postural changes and changes in acceleration. The vestibular apparatus coordinates with the visual, tactile, and kinesthetic systems in governing balance. It appears that vestibular development of balance occurs early in life and that the vestibular apparatus is structurally complete at birth. However, the body musculature and the other sensory modalities involved in maintaining balance must mature and be integrated with vestibular clues to be of any use to the child in maintaining either static or dynamic balance.

Balance is often defined as static or dynamic. *Static balance* refers to the ability of the body to maintain equilibrium in a stationary position. Balancing on one foot, standing on a balance board, and performing a stick balance are common means of assessing static balance abilities. Research on the static balance abilities of children shows a linear trend toward improved performance from ages 2 through 12 (DeOreo, 1971; Keogh, 1965; Van Slooten, 1973). Prior to age 2 children generally are not able to perform a one-foot static balance task, probably because of their still-developing abilities to maintain a controlled upright posture. DeOreo (1980) indicated that clear-cut boy-girl differences are not as apparent in static balance performance

tasks as they are with other motor performance tasks. Girls tend to be more proficient than boys until about age 7 or 8, whereupon the boys catch up. Both sexes level off in performance around age 8, prior to a surge in abilities from age 9 to age 12.

Dynamic balance refers to the ability to maintain equilibrium when moving from point to point. Balance beam walking tests are used most often as measures of dynamic balance in children. The available literature on dynamic balance indicates a trend similar to that for static balance. Girls are often more proficient than boys until age 8 or 9, whereupon they perform at similar levels. Both slow in their progress around age 9, before making rapid gains to age 12 (DeOreo, 1971; Frederick, 1977).

Speed

Speed is the ability to cover a short distance in as brief a time as possible. Speed is influenced by *reaction time* (the amount of elapsed time from the signal "go" to the first movements of the body) as well as *movement time* (the time elapsed from the initial movement to completion of the activity). Reaction time depends on the speed with which the initial stimulus is processed through the afferent and efferent neural pathways and is integrated with the initial response pattern. Reaction time improves in children as they get older.

Cratty (1986) reported that the information available on simple reaction time indicates that it is about twice as long in 5-year-olds as it is in adults for an identical task and that there is rapid improvement from age 3 to age 5. These developmental differences are probably due to neurological maturation, variations in the information-processing capabilities of children and adults, as well as to environmental and task considerations.

Speed of movement in children is most generally measured through various tests of running speed. Frederick (1977), who tested the running speeds of five groups of children 3 to 5 years of age on the 20-yard dash, found linear improvement with age but no gender differences. In a study of the running speed of elementary school children, Keogh (1965) found that boys and girls are similar in running speed at ages 6 and 7, but boys were superior from ages 8 to 12. Both boys and girls improve with age at a rate of about 1 foot per second per year from ages 6 to 11 (Cratty, 1986). Keogh also found similar improvements and boy-girl differences in the 50-foot hop for speed, although girls tended to perform better than boys on hopping and jumping tasks requiring greater precision and accuracy of movement.

Fifty-yard sprint run scores are recorded as part of the Amateur Athletic Union (AAU) Physical Fitness Program (1993). These data are viewed as highly representative of the running speed of children and adolescents because of the large sample size, geographical distribution, and randomization techniques used. Both boys and girls are reported to make annual incremental improvements with males slightly outperforming females at all ages. Similarity in performance on the sprint run does not appear to carry over into the adolescent years. Males continue to make dramatic improvements throughout the teen years, whereas females tend to regress slightly after age 14. Both factors are associated with pubescent male strength increases, limb length increases and body fat decreases, and female body fat increases.

Speed of movement generally improves until about age 13 in both boys and girls. After this, however, girls tend to level off and even regress, whereas boys tend to continue improving throughout the adolescent years. The movement speed of both boys and girls may be encouraged during childhood and beyond through vigorous physical activity that incorporates short bursts of speed.

> ## CONCEPT 12.15
>
> Reaction time and movement time influence movement speed, agility, and power, which tend to advance linearly during childhood but require special training afterward for continued improvement.

Agility

Agility is the ability to change the direction of the body rapidly and accurately. With agility, one can make quick and accurate shifts in body position during movement. An assortment of agility runs have been used as indirect measures of agility. Unfortunately, the wide variety of ways in which these scores have been obtained makes it impossible to compare studies. Scores from the 30-foot shuttle run are typically used as a measure of agility. Annual incremental improvements are seen throughout childhood with an edge given to boys at all ages.

Power

Power is the ability to perform a maximum effort in as short a period as possible. Power is sometimes referred to as "explosive strength" and represents the product of force divided by time. This combination of strength and speed is exhibited in children's activities that require jumping, striking, throwing for distance, and other maximum efforts. The speed of contraction of the muscles involved, as well as the strength and coordinated use of these muscles, determine the degree of power of the individual. It is difficult, if not impossible, to obtain a pure measure of this component because power involves a combination of motor abilities. The often-used throwing and jumping measures give only an indirect indication of power because of the skill required for both of these tasks. Frederick (1977), however, found significant yearly increments in vertical jump, standing long jump, and distance throwing tasks for children ages 3 through 5. The boys outperformed the girls on all measures at all age levels. The same results were found by Keogh (1965) for boys and girls from 6 to 12 years of age and by Van Slooten (1973) for children 6 to 9 years of age on the throw for distance, but with gender differences magnified beyond age 7. Luedke's (1980) excellent review of the literature on throwing supports these results.

Linear improvements and differences between boys and girls have been demonstrated in the standing long jump from age 3 through 5 (Frederick, 1977), from age 6 through 12 (Keogh, 1965), and from age 10 through 17 (Ross and Gilbert, 1985). Differences in throwing velocity based on age and gender have also been shown in samples of children from age 6 to 14 years old (Glassow and Kruse, 1960; Luedke, 1980). However, differences from age to age and between sexes are closely related to yearly strength and speed of movement increments as well as to the varying sociocultural influences on boys and girls.

SUMMARY

Although questions remain, there is general agreement regarding the advisability of vigorous physical activity in children. The growth patterns of almost all the internal organs are in proportion to the remainder of the body. Hence the lungs, heart, and so forth, are able to cope with the demands placed on them. Proportional to their mass, young children can transport and use oxygen volumes comparable to or above adults. There seems to be no appreciable difference in the fatigue patterns between children and high school youth and adults. The general consensus among researchers is that a sound heart cannot be injured by vigorous physical activity. Precautionary measures need to be taken for a child with a suspected or known cardiac and/or pulmonary dysfunction.

Muscular strength, muscular endurance, joint flexibility, and body composition are also components of health-related fitness. They affect one's state of health in much the same way as does aerobic endurance. Good levels of fitness tend to reduce vulnerability to numerous physical ailments. The components of health-related fitness improve with age but not always in a linear fashion. There is a strong tendency to make small gains during early and later childhood, followed by a lull during the preadolescent period. Throughout adolescence, boys often make rapid gains in all measures of fitness, whereas girls tend to level off and sometimes decline in their performance scores after midadolescence.

The motor fitness components of coordination and balance are closely aligned with the development of movement control during early childhood. Once good control has been established, the child is able to focus on improvement in the force components of motor fitness. Speed, agility, and power improve dramatically during later childhood, as balance and coordination improve during early childhood. There is a linear trend for improvement in all measures of motor fitness. The motor fitness levels of both boys and girls improve with age and effort, with boys outperforming girls at all levels except during the prepubescent period.

CRITICAL READINGS

American Academy of Pediatrics. (1990). Strength training, weight and power lifting, and body building by children and adolescents. *Pediatrics, 85,* 801–803.

American Academy of Pediatrics. (2001). Strength training by children and adolescents. *Pediatrics, 107,* 1470–1472.

Armstrong, N., & Welsman, J. R. (2000). Development of aerobic fitness during childhood and adolescence. *Pediatric Exercise Science, 12,* 128–149.

Baranowski, T. et al. (1992). Assessment, prevalence, and cardiovascular benefits of physical activity and fitness in youth. *Medicine and Science in Sports and Exercise, 24,* S237–S247.

Beunen, G., & Thomis, M. (2000). Muscular strength development in children and adolescents. *Pediatric Exercise Science, 12,* 174–197.

Blair, S. N. (1992). Are American children and youth fit? The need for better data. *Research Quarterly for Exercise and Sport, 63,* 120–123.

Corbin, C. B., & Pangrazi, R. P. (1992). Are American children and youth fit? *Research Quarterly for Exercise and Sport, 63,* 96–106.

Payne, V. G. et al. (1997). Resistance training in children and youth: A meta-analysis. *Research Quarterly for Exercise and Sport, 68,* 80–88.

Ross, J. G., & Pate, R. R. (1987). The national children and youth fitness study II. *Journal of Physical Education, Recreation and Dance, 58,* 49–96.

Rowland, T. W. (1997). The "trigger hypothesis" for aerobic training. *Pediatric Exercise Science, 9,* 1–9.

WEB RESOURCES

American Academy of Pediatrics
policy statement on strength training
www.aap.org/policy/re0048.html

Centers for Disease Control and Prevention
guidelines for school and community programs
promoting lifelong physical activity
www.cdc.gov/nccdphp/dash/phactaag.htm

Fitnessgram health-related
fitness test (2000).
www./americanfitness.net/fitnessgram/

Physical activity and health: A report of the
surgeon general
www.cdc.gov/nccdphp/sgr/sgr.htm

Prevalence of overweight among children and
adolescence
www.cdc.gov/nchs/products/pubs/pubd/hestats/
overweight99.htm

The President's challenge physical fitness program
packet (2000–2001).
www.fitness.gov/challenge.html

Various topics related to children's fitness
www.kidshealth.org/parent/nutrition_fit/fitness/
fitness_6_12.html

CHILDHOOD PERCEPTION AND PERCEPTUAL-MOTOR DEVELOPMENT

KEY TERMS

Visual acuity

Figure-ground perception

Depth perception

Visual-motor coordination

Perceptual-motor

Perception

Body awareness

Spatial awareness

Directional awareness

Temporal awareness

Rhythm

Perceptual-motor training

CHAPTER COMPETENCIES

Upon completion of this chapter you should be able to:

- Discuss changes in perceptual functioning during childhood
- Analyze the relationship and interaction between perceptual and motor development
- Identify motor behavioral characteristics of children with developmental lag
- Analyze the effect of cognitive processing differences within and across age groups on motor skill development and performance
- Evaluate cognitive processing demands on motor skill performance
- Discuss the developmental aspects of visual acuity, figure-ground perception, depth perception, and visual motor coordination, and their interaction with motor performance
- Demonstrate an understanding of perceptual training and its impact on the skill learning process
- Define the term *perceptual-motor* and diagram the perceptual-motor process
- Describe the perceptual-motor components and give examples of each
- Discuss the influence of the perceptual-motor process on cognitive development and academic achievement

KEY CONCEPT

All voluntary movement involves an element of perception; as such, childhood motor development is closely associated with perceptual-motor functioning.

Study of the perceptual process and perceptual-motor development attempts to answer the age-old question of how we come to know our world. The nature of the perceptual process and its impact on movement and cognition have been topics of considerable interest to researchers and educators for years. From the moment of birth, children begin to learn how to interact with their environment. This interaction is a perceptual as well as a motor process. As described earlier in this text perception takes place when sensory input

is monitored and interpreted. Perception takes place in various sections of the brain and allows a person to establish meaning to the sensory data (Winnick, 2000). Figure 13.1 illustrates the various locations of the brain where sensory information is processed.

This chapter focuses on various developmental aspects of perception, with particular emphasis on vision, and perceptual-motor behavior during childhood. The importance of developing both perceptual and perceptual-motor abilities is discussed along with factors that influence their emergence.

PERCEPTUAL DEVELOPMENT IN CHILDHOOD

By the time children reach 2 years of age, the ocular, or visual, apparatus is mature. The eyeball is near its adult size and weight. All anatomical and

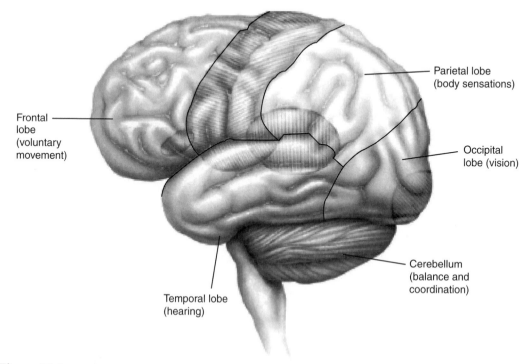

Figure 13.1
Processing locations of the brain.

physiological aspects of the eye are complete, but the perceptual abilities of young children are still incomplete. Although children are able to fixate on objects, track them, and make accurate judgments of size and shape, numerous refinements still need to be made. A young child is unable to intercept a tossed ball with any degree of control. Difficulty with letter and number reversals is common, and a child's perception of moving objects is poorly developed, as are figure-ground perceptual abilities, perception of distance, and anticipatory timing.

CONCEPT 13.1

Children's perceptual and motor abilities are influenced by one another even though they develop at different rates.

The extent to which movement plays a role in visual perceptual development is debatable. In the past, investigators have speculated on the importance of movement in the development and refinement of visual perceptual abilities (Held, 1963; Riesen and Aarons, 1959; Smith and Smith, 1966). These investigations were conducted based on the hypothesis that self-produced movement is both necessary and sufficient for *visual-motor adjustment* to occur within a visually altered environment. They contended that without movement, visual perceptual adjustments will not occur and that the muscles and the motor aspect of the nervous system are intimately involved with perception and are dependent on one another. The concept of a relationship between movement activity and perceptual development has also been indirectly supported by the decline in performance on perceptual and motor deprivation experiments (Hebb, 1949; Riesen and Aarons, 1959) and experiments testing visual perceptual adjustments to optically rearranged environments (Gallahue, 1982; Held and Blossom, 1961; Held and Mikaelian, 1964; Hoepner, 1967). The gist of this research has led to what Payne and Isaacs (2002) termed the *motion hypothesis,* which contends that to develop

a normal repertoire of visual-spatial skill, one must pay attention to objects that move.

CONCEPT 13.2

Movement has been shown to be a sufficient condition for the development of selected visual perceptual abilities, but it has not been demonstrated to be a necessary condition.

However, the results of each of these experiments are speculative at best when applied to the development of perceptual abilities in children. We still do not know the extent to which movement plays a role in perceptual development. It is probably safe to say, however, that movement is a "sufficient" condition for encouraging the development of perceptual abilities. Whether it is a "necessary" condition is doubtful.

Although it is doubtful that self-produced movement is a necessary condition for development of a child's visual perceptual abilities, there is little doubt that the developmental level of his or her visual perceptual abilities will affect the performance levels of movement skills. It is important that we become familiar with the child's developing perceptual abilities and understand the impact of perception on movement skill learning and refinement. Visual acuity, figure-ground perception, depth perception, and visual-motor coordination are important developmentally based visual qualities and influence movement performance. Table 13.1 provides a summary of these qualities and a hypothesized developmental sequence.

Visual Acuity

Visual acuity is the ability to distinguish detail in objects. The finer the details that can be distinguished, the better one's visual acuity, and vice versa. Visual acuity may be measured in both static and dynamic settings. *Static visual acuity* is the degree of distinguishable detail that one is able to detect when both the individual and the object of

TABLE 13.1	Selected Developmental Aspects of Children's Visual Perception	
Visual Quality	**Selected Abilities**	**Approximate Age**
VISUAL ACUITY		
The ability to distinguish detail in static and	Rapid improvement	5–7
dynamic settings	Plateau	7–8
	Rapid improvement	9–10
	Mature (static)	10–11
	Plateau (dynamic)	10–11
	Mature (dynamic)	11–12
FIGURE-GROUND PERCEPTION		
The ability to separate an object from	Slow improvement	3–4
its surroundings	Rapid improvement	4–6
	Slight spurt	7–8
	Mature	8–12
DEPTH PERCEPTION		
The ability to judge distance relative	Frequent judgment errors	3–4
to oneself	Few judgment errors	5–6
	Rapid improvement	7–11
	Mature	By age 12
VISUAL-MOTOR COORDINATION		
The ability to integrate use of eyes and hands	Rapid improvement	3–7
in object tracking and interruption	Slow slight improvement	7–9
	Mature	10–12

visual regard are stationary. Static visual acuity is most commonly measured by use of a Snellen eye chart. A Snellen assessment is expressed in fractions. An individual with a 20/20 rating is able to distinguish objects at a distance of 20 feet (6.1 m) in the same manner as others with normal vision at the same distance of 20 feet. An individual with a 20/200 rating is able to distinguish at 20 feet what others with normal vision could distinguish at 200 feet (60.9 m).

Dynamic visual acuity is the ability to distinguish detail in moving objects. It is less frequently assessed than static visual acuity for various reasons, but it is of interest to anyone required to make precise judgments based on visually guided tracking. The baseball player preparing to strike or catch a ball needs to have good dynamic visual acuity, as does the volleyball player or skeet shooter. Dynamic visual acuity is measured by flashing checkerboard targets with varying levels of grid precision on a screen. These targets travel horizontally at varying speeds, and the individual indicates when the "small checks" can be seen in the moving object.

Williams (1983) reported that static visual acuity is mature by age 10 and, in general, is less well developed in 5- and 6-year-olds. Rapid improvement occurs between 5 and 7 years of age, with little change seen from ages 7 to 9, followed by rapid improvement between ages 9 and 10. By age 12 static visual acuity is generally adultlike.

Dynamic visual acuity appears to mature somewhat later than static visual acuity. Morris (1977) found improvement in individuals up to 20 years of age. Williams (1983) reported that dynamic visual acuity becomes increasingly refined during three separate periods: 5 to 7 years, 9 to 10 years, and 11 to 12 years of age. Furthermore, boys display better visual acuity (both dynamic and static) than girls at all ages. This information may help us better understand why it is essential to adjust the skill requirements in a sport such as baseball if we expect children to sustain their interest over time. That girls often lag behind their male counterparts can probably be attributed to socialization factors (historically fewer opportunities for practice and less active encouragement). This may also explain why girls tend to do less well on object interception tasks and tend to drop out of these sports earlier. Adult leaders must modify the rules to enhance the potential for success and sustained participation for both boys and girls at various developmental levels.

CONCEPT 13.3

Vision is the primary sensory modality and plays an important role in the process of motor development.

Figure-Ground Perception

Figure-ground perception is the ability to separate an object of visual regard from its surroundings. Gallahue (1968) demonstrated that various combinations of blending and/or distracting backgrounds influenced the abilities of 6-year-olds to distinguish objects of visual regard from their surroundings. Combinations that caused a maximum amount of blending and distraction were most disruptive of the children's abilities to distinguish a figure from its background in the performance of a simple stepping test. Conditions in which only color blending or visual distractors were present were less disruptive. With regard to the developmental nature of visual figure-ground perception, Williams (1983), interpreting data from Frostig et al. (1966), reported stable figure-ground perception between 8 and 10 years of age. Prior to that, however, slow improvement occurs between 3 and 4 years, with large improvement seen from 4 through 6 years. Smaller changes were reported from ages 6 to 7 followed by a slight spurt between 7 and 8 years. Williams further suggested that figure-ground perception becomes increasingly

refined from 8 to 13 years and may even continue to improve to 17 or 18 years of age. One may conclude that mature figure-ground perception involves elements of attention as well as visual-motor maturation.

Along with good dynamic visual acuity, figure-ground perception enables the performer not only to clearly distinguish an object but also to separate it from its background. Such a highly refined skill is essential to the batter or outfielder in baseball, the wide receiver or quarterback in football, or the performer on the uneven bars in gymnastics. The ability to clearly extract the object of regard (*figure*) from its background (*ground*) is essential for success. It is important to recognize that this perceptual quality is still developing in children. Modifications of the task requirements or manipulating the background against which certain movement tasks are performed may do much to enhance motor performance.

Depth Perception

Depth perception is one of the most intriguing aspects of visual perception. Depth perception allows us to see three-dimensionally, an astonishing feat when you consider that separately our retinas function two-dimensionally but when combined provide a visual image complete with minute depth cues. These cues to depth are both monocular and binocular.

Monocular depth cues are those that can be picked up by one eye. Such things as size, texture gradient, shading, convergence, overlap, proportionality, and linear perspective are common monocular cues to depth. Each of these are used by the artist to give the "illusion" of depth on canvas. They also give us important three-dimensional visual cues to depth.

Binocular depth cues require both eyes to work in concert. *Retinal disparity,* an important component of depth perception, refers to an object of visual regard being viewed from a slightly different angle by each eye. Therefore, the image projected on each retina is slightly different, and the information passed on to the visual area of the cortex results in binocular disparity. Hence, the images that we receive have depth.

Little is known about the developmental aspects of depth perception. Williams (1983) reported, however, that binocularity and depth perception improve from 2 through 5 years of age. She also indicated that by age 7 children can accurately judge depth with monocular cues. Based on this and the extensive literature on infant depth perception, it is probably safe to conclude that depth perception begins developing in a basic way during the first months of infancy, but that it continues to improve throughout early childhood. It is doubtful whether depth perception in general can be improved through special training. It is possible, however, that depth perception in specific situations can be improved (Sage, 1984).

Teachers, parents, and coaches need to consider the visual perceptions of depth when teaching new ball skills. Ball size, color, and texture as well as distance, trajectory, and speed play important roles in providing depth cues for successful object interceptions (Isaacs, 1980; Payne, 1985; Payne and Isaacs, 2002). One need only observe the child who turns his or her head to avoid an approaching ball to see why depth cues are important to successful catching. Turning the head to one side eliminates binocular vision and forces the child to depend on monocular cues. Too often these monocular cues are insufficient to make the accurate and refined adjustments required for mature catching. As a result the child reverts to a less mature scooping catching pattern, or the ball hits the child's face or chest before it is stopped or dropped. Successful object interception requires making use of all the depth cues available, especially during the early stages of skill development.

Visual-Motor Coordination

Visual-motor coordination refers to the ability to track and make interception judgments about a moving object. The development of visual abilities begins early in infancy and continues to improve with age. Morris (1980) indicated that by age 5 or 6 children can accurately track moving objects in a

horizontal plane, and that by age 8 or 9 they can track balls moving in an arc. Payne and Isaacs (2002) noted that

> as dynamic visual acuity improves, so does the ability to track fast-moving objects because whenever an object is moving at an angular velocity at which smooth eye movements are no longer possible, the pursuit task becomes a function of dynamic visual acuity. (p. 193)

Williams (1983) reported that accurate perception of movement continues to develop to about 10 to 12 years of age.

Object interception is the second aspect of visual-motor coordination. Object interception, or *coincidence-anticipation timing* as it is frequently referred to in motor learning literature, involves the ability to match estimates of an object's location with a specific motor response. For example, the batter in baseball must estimate where the ball will be at a certain time and simultaneously activate the motor system to bring the bat into contact with the ball at the right moment. Object interception abilities improve greatly with age and practice (Dorfman, 1977). At this point it is difficult to propose a developmental model for object interception ability because of the vast number of confounding variables. However, observation of numerous children attempting to hit pitched balls leads us to conclude that younger children and less-experienced individuals make numerous judgment errors, but older children and more-experienced persons make fewer errors. Experience clearly appears to be an essential element in making accurate estimates of object interception. The question of whether experience alone or maturation of the visual-motor apparatus in conjunction with experience is responsible for improved judgments awaits further study.

PERCEPTUAL TRAINING

An individual's visual perceptual sophistication is intricately related to success in the performance of numerous movement skills, so it is essential for the teacher or coach to be aware of the developmental nature of children's visual abilities. The perceptual requirements of fundamental manipulative skills that involve imparting force to an object or receiving force from an object are especially great. When working with young children, we must make appropriate adjustments in the equipment to accommodate the developmental levels of their perceptual abilities. Changing the weight or size of balls by using foam, fleece, plastic, or soft rubber is likely to have a dramatic influence on the degree of success experienced. Making modifications in the color and size of the objects will also have an impact.

Modifying the rules of play to permit greater clarity and consistency of perception, time to react, or ease of tracking is also recommended. For example, in baseball, using a pitching machine set at a predetermined speed and trajectory will help children develop their tracking skills. Hitting a ball off a tee will enable younger children to experience greater success and to focus on developing a level swing without compounding the complexity of the task with object-tracking.

A third consideration in perceptual training is to recognize that the mechanics of the movement are influenced by the perception levels required for successful performance. If the visual requirements are great, the mechanics are more likely to be complicated. The mechanics of a tennis serve are more difficult than those for swimming or skipping.

Finally, individuals who work with children must recognize that a child's perceptual development *and* motor development are crucial to successful movement performance. We must adjust our level of expectations to the perceptual as well as the physical maturity of each individual.

PERCEPTUAL-MOTOR DEVELOPMENT IN CHILDREN

The visual perceptual abilities of young children are not the same as those of adults. The child's visual world is in the developmental stages and is therefore restricted. The development of perceptual abilities significantly inhibits or enhances a child's movement performance. From the previous section we have seen that the converse of this may

be true; that is, movement performance may significantly inhibit or enhance the development of children's perceptual abilities. The child restricted in perceptual development often encounters difficulties in performing perceptual-motor tasks.

The realization that the process of perception is not entirely innate prompts one to hypothesize that the quality and quantity of movement experiences afforded young children are related to some extent to the development of their perceptual abilities. The initial responses of young children are motor responses, and all future perceptual and conceptual data are based, in part, on these initial responses. Young children must establish a broad base of motor experiences for higher learning to develop properly. Meaning is imposed on perceptual stimulation through movement. The matching of perceptual and motor data is thought by many to be necessary for the child to establish a stable spatial world (Barsch, 1965; Kephart, 1971). The more motor and perceptual learning experiences that children have, the greater the opportunity to make this "perceptual-motor match" and to develop a plasticity of response to various movement situations.

CONCEPT 13.4

Practice in perceptual-motor activities may enhance perceptual-motor abilities, but there is insufficient evidence to claim that improved perceptual-motor abilities will enhance academic achievement.

Unfortunately, the complexity of our modern society often deters the development of many perceptual-motor abilities. The environment in which today's children are raised is so complicated and dangerous that they are constantly being warned not to touch or to avoid situations that offer great amounts of motor and perceptual information. The environment of today's children is also often passive and sedentary. Many children grow up in large cities, apartment buildings, cramped day-care centers, and school environments that do not encourage or promote learning through movement. Too few children in contemporary society climb trees, walk fences, jump streams, or ride horses. They miss many of the experiences that children ought to have to develop their movement abilities. Children who spend time watching television or playing computer games develop sedentary, passive habits. The absence of varied movement experiences and the adaptations that come with practice and repetition can stifle motor development.

CONCEPT 13.5

Children frequently lag in their perceptual-motor learning because of environmental restrictions.

Artificial means must be devised to give children additional experiences and practice in the perceptual-motor activities that modern society cannot provide naturally. Substitute experiences may have positive effects on the development of visual perceptual abilities in children. The physical education teacher should be an essential person in the educational curriculum. A sound, developmentally based physical education program will encourage children's perceptual-motor skills and promote many of the basic readiness skills required for success in school.

What Is "Perceptual-Motor"?

The hyphen in **perceptual-motor** is there for two reasons. First, it signifies the dependency of voluntary movement activity on some forms of perceptual information. All voluntary movement involves an element of perceptual awareness resulting from some sort of sensory stimulation. Second, the hyphen indicates that the development of one's perceptual abilities depends, in part, on motor activity. Perceptual-motor abilities are learned. As such, they use movement as an important medium in which learning occurs. The quality of movement performance depends on the accuracy of an individual's perceptions and his or her ability to interpret these perceptions into a series of coordinated movement acts. *Eye-hand coordination* and *eye-foot coordination* have been used for years to express the dependency of efficient movement on the accuracy of sensory information. The individual on the free throw line has numerous forms of sensory input that must be sorted out and expressed in the final perceptual-motor act of shooting the basketball. If the perceptions are accurate, and if they are blended into a coordinated sequence, the basket is made. If not, the player misses the shot. All voluntary movements involve the use of one or more sensory modalities to greater or lesser degrees. Until recently we did not fully appreciate the important contributions movement experiences make toward the development of perceptual-motor abilities.

Perception means "to know" or "to interpret information." Perception is the process of organizing incoming information with stored information, which leads to a modified response pattern. Perceptual-motor development may be described as a process of attaining increased skill and functional ability by using sensory input, sensory integration, motor interpretation, movement activation, and feedback. These elements are described as follows:

1. Sensory Input: receiving various forms of stimulation by way of specialized sensory receptors (visual, auditory, tactile, and kinesthetic receptors) and transmitting this stimulation to the brain in the form of a pattern of neural energy.
2. Sensory Integration: organizing incoming sensory stimuli and integrating it with past or stored information (memory).
3. Motor Interpretation: making internal motor decisions (recalibration) based on the combination of sensory (present) and long-term memory (past) information.
4. Movement Activation: executing the movement (observable act).
5. Feedback: evaluating the movement by way of the various sensory modalities (visual, auditory, tactile, and/or kinesthetic), which in turn feed information back into the sensory input aspect of the process, thus beginning the cycle again.

The Perceptual-Motor Components

Although movement experiences in regular physical education programs are by general definition perceptual-motor activities, programs that focus on reinforcing perceptual-motor quality are significantly different in emphasis from those that focus on gross motor quality. In remedial and readiness programs, emphasis is on improving specific perceptual-motor components, so movement activities are grouped according to the perceptual-motor qualities they enhance, namely, body awareness, spatial awareness, directional awareness, and temporal awareness. Activities designed to enhance these abilities are used in regular physical education programs, but the primary objective is movement skill acquisition and increased physical activity rather than perceptual-motor acquisition.

The development and refinement of children's *spatial worlds* and *temporal worlds* are two of the primary contributions of perceptual-motor training programs. The jargon used in programs across North America varies greatly. There seems to be general agreement, however, that the following perceptual-motor qualities are among the most important to be developed and reinforced in children.

CONCEPT 13.6

Developmentally based physical education programs have the potential to enhance perceptual-motor functioning.

Body Awareness

Body awareness is often used in conjunction with *body image* and *body schema*. Each term refers to the developing capacity of a child to accurately discriminate among her body parts. The ability to differentiate among body parts and to gain a greater understanding of the nature of the body occurs in three areas. The first is knowledge of the body parts—being able to accurately locate the parts of the body on oneself and on others. Second is knowledge of what the body parts can do. This refers to the child's developing recognition of how the body performs a specific act. Third is knowledge of how to make the body parts move efficiently. This refers to the ability to reorganize the body parts for a particular motor act and to perform a movement task.

Body image has to do with the internalized picture that a child has of his or her body and the extent to which that image matches reality. Self-perceptions of height, weight, shape, and individual features affect how we compare ourselves with others. Establishing a realistic body image is important in childhood and thereafter. Anorexia and bulimia have been clearly linked to unrealistic body images and are now concerns for children. In addition, there appears to be a close link between body image and self-esteem (Marsh and Peart, 1988; Marsh et al., 1991).

Spatial Awareness

Spatial awareness is a basic component of perceptual-motor development that may be divided into two subcategories: (1) knowledge of how much space the body occupies and (2) the ability to project the body effectively into external space. Knowledge of how much space the body occupies and the body's relationship to external objects may be developed through a variety of movement activities. With practice and experience, the child progresses from his egocentric world of locating everything in external space relative to himself (*subjective localization*) to establishing an objective frame of reference (*objective localization*). The child also learns to deal with the concepts of self-space and general space. *Self-space* refers to the area immediately surrounding an individual bounded by how far one can extend his or her body from a fixed point on the ground. *General space* refers to that which is beyond a person's self-space. For example, preschoolers tend to determine the locations of objects relative to where they are standing (subjective localization in one's self-space). Older children are able, however, to locate objects relative to their proximity to other nearby objects without regard to the location of their bodies (i.e., objective localization in general space). The concepts of subjective localization and self-space are closely akin to Piaget's preoperational thought phase of development. The concepts of objective localization and general space are identified with higher cognitive structures in his concrete operations phase. Refer to chapter 2 for a discussion of Jean Piaget's phases and stages of cognitive development and the role that movement plays in each of his developmental phases.

The spatial awareness of adults is generally adequate, despite occasional difficulties in locating the relative positions of various objects. For example, when reading a road map while traveling through unfamiliar territory, many people become confused as to whether they are traveling north, south, east, or west. It can be difficult to turn either way while looking at a map, without almost literally placing oneself on the map. The absence of familiar landmarks and the impersonality of the road map make it difficult to objectively localize oneself in space relative to this particular task. Young children encounter much the same difficulty but on a broader scale. They must first learn to orient themselves subjectively in space and then proceed carefully to venture into unfamiliar surroundings in which subjective clues are useless. Providing children with opportunities to develop spatial awareness is an important attribute of a good, developmentally based physical education program that recognizes the importance of perceptual-motor development.

Directional Awareness

An area of great concern to many classroom teachers is that of **directional awareness.** Through directional awareness children are able to give dimension to objects in external space. The concepts of left–right, up–down, top–bottom, in–out, and front–back are enhanced through movement activities that place emphasis on direction. Directional awareness is commonly divided into two subcategories: laterality and directionality.

Laterality refers to an internal awareness or feel for the various dimensions of the body with regard to their location and direction. A child who has adequately developed the concept of laterality

does not need to rely on external cues for determining direction. She does not need, for example, to have a ribbon tied to her wrist as a reminder about which is left and which is right. She does not need to rely on cues such as the location of a watch or a ring to provide information about direction. The concept seems so basic to most adults that it is difficult to conceive how anyone could fail to develop laterality. However, we need only look into the rearview mirror of a car to have directions reversed and sometimes confused. Backing up a trailer hitched to a car or parallel parking are experiences that most of us avoid because it is difficult to decide whether to turn the wheel to the left or right. The pilot, astronaut, and deep-sea diver must possess a high degree of laterality or "feel" for determining up from down and left from right.

Directionality is the external projection of laterality. It gives dimension to objects in space. True directionality depends on adequately established laterality. Directionality is important to parents and teachers because it is a basic component of learning how to read. Children who do not have fully established directionality will often encounter difficulties in discriminating among various letters of the alphabet. For example, the letters *b, d, p,* and *q* are all similar. The only difference lies in the direction of the "ball" and the "stick" that make up the letters. The child without fully established directionality encounters considerable difficulty in discriminating among several letters of the alphabet. Entire words may even be reversed. The word *cat* may be read as *tac,* or *bad* may be read as *dab* because of the child's inability to project direction into external space. Some children encounter difficulty in the top–bottom dimension, which is more basic than the left–right dimension. They may write and see words upside down and are totally confused when it comes to reading.

Establishing directional awareness is a developmental process that relies on both maturation and experience. It is normal for the 4- and 5-year-old to experience confusion in direction. We should, however, be concerned for the 6- and 7-year-old child who consistently experiences these problems because this is the time when most schools traditionally begin instruction in reading. Adequately developed directional awareness is one important readiness skill necessary for success in reading, and movement is one way in which this important perceptual-motor concept may be developed.

Temporal Awareness

The preceding discussion of the various aspects of perceptual-motor development dealt with the child's spatial world. Body awareness, spatial awareness, and directional awareness are closely interrelated and combine to help children make sense of their spatial dimensions. **Temporal awareness,** on the other hand, concerns the acquisition of an adequate time structure in children. It is evoked and refined at the same time the child's spatial world is developing.

Temporal awareness is intricately related to the coordinated interaction of various muscular systems and sensory modalities. *Eye-hand coordination* and *eye-foot coordination* reflect the interrelationship of these processes. We refer to an individual with a well-developed time dimension as coordinated. One who has not fully established this dimension is often regarded as clumsy or awkward. Everything that we do possesses an element of time. There is a beginning and an end, and no matter how minute, there is a measurable span of time between the two. It is important that children learn how to function efficiently in this time dimension as well as in the space dimension. Without one, the other cannot develop to its fullest potential.

Rhythm is the basic and most important aspect of developing a stable temporal world. The term has many meanings but is described here as the synchronous recurrence of events related in such a manner that they form recognizable patterns. Rhythmic movement involves the synchronous sequencing of events in time. Rhythm is crucial in the performance of any act in a coordinated manner. Cooper (1982) tape-recorded the sounds of outstanding performers completing the movement patterns of selected sport skills. The sounds were transcribed into musical notations, illustrating that recordable rhythmical elements

were present. The recorded rhythms of these outstanding athletes were beaten out on a drum in several teaching situations with beginners, who learned the movements of the champions more rapidly than they did when standard teaching techniques were used. Cooper and Andrews (1975) concluded that "it appears that beginning performers can profit by listening to and emulating certain elements of the rhythmic pattern of the good performers. Teachers should take full advantage of this phenomenon" (p. 66). Surely this statement applies to children as well as athletes. We must recognize the rhythmic elements in all efficient movements.

H. Smith (1970) indicated that children begin to make temporal discriminations through the auditory modality before the visual and that there is transfer from the auditory to the visual but not the reverse. Activities that require children to perform movement tasks to auditory rhythmic patterns should begin when they are young and remain a part of their daily lives. The activity possibilities are endless. Moving to various forms of musical accompaniment, ranging from drumbeats to instrumental selections, contributes to temporal awareness. Table 13.2 provides a summary of the

TABLE 13.2 Factors Associated with Perceptual-Motor Components

- Body Awareness
  - Knowledge of body parts
  - Knowledge of what body parts can do
  - Knowledge of how to make body parts move efficiently
- Spatial Awareness
  - Subjective localization
  - Objective localization
  - Self-space
  - General space
- Directional Awareness
  - Laterality
  - Directionality
- Temporal Awareness
  - Synchronization
  - Sequence
  - Rhythm

various aspects related to the perceptual-motor components.

PERCEPTUAL-MOTOR TRAINING

During the 1960s and 1970s several **perceptual-motor training** programs were established throughout North America. These programs were given considerable exposure in the popular press. Based on these articles and the claims of some, many people formed the impression that perceptual-motor programs were panaceas for the development of cognitive and motor abilities. Considerable confusion and speculation developed over the values and purposes of perceptual-motor training programs. Programs adhering to one technique or another emerged almost overnight. Too often, people were inadequately trained, ill informed, and not clear on what they were trying to accomplish. The smoke has now cleared, and concerned educators have taken a closer, more objective look at perceptual-motor training programs and their role in the total educational spectrum. Instead of claiming they are panaceas or adhering to one training technique or another, many are viewing perceptual-motor programs as important facilitators of *readiness development.* Perceptual-motor activities are being recognized as important contributors to the general readiness of children for learning. The contribution of perceptual-motor activities to specific perceptual readiness skills needs to be closely reexamined.

CONCEPT 13.7

Perceptual-motor training programs can be effective when viewed as readiness programs that assist young children in learning to learn.

Readiness programs may be classified as concept developing and concept reinforcing. *Concept development programs* are generally designed for children who have been limited or restricted in their experiential backgrounds (e.g., socioeconomic class, prolonged illness, ethnic background, or development delays). Programs such as Head Start, Smart Start (Wessel and Zittel, 1995), and I Can (Wessel and Zittel, 1998) are examples of concept-developing programs in which a variety of multisensory experiences including perceptual-motor activities are used to develop fundamental readiness skills.

Concept reinforcement programs are those in which movement is used in conjunction with traditional classroom techniques to develop basic cognitive understandings. In this type of program, movement is used as an aid or vehicle for reinforcing cognitive concepts presented in the nursery school or primary grade classroom. Some recent examples of resources that focus on concept reinforcement include those developed by Cheatum and Hammond (2000) and Cone, Werner, Cone, and Woods (1998).

CONCEPT 13.8

Insufficient evidence exists to support the efficacy of perceptual-motor training programs designed to remediate childhood learning disabilities.

Remedial training programs are the third and most controversial type of perceptual-motor training program. They have been established as a means of alleviating perceptual inadequacies and increasing academic achievement. Programs have been developed by Delacato (1959), Getman (1952), Kephart (1971), and others to aid cognitive development through perceptual-motor remediation techniques. The avowed purpose of these programs is to enhance academic achievement. Little solid support for this claim exists, however, although abundant testimony and opinions are available. A meta-analysis of more than 180 research studies designed to measure the efficacy of perceptual-motor training on academic achievement and cognition clearly reveals that such programs make little or no "direct" contribution to these areas (Kavale and Mattson, 1983). These findings were supported by position statements from the Council for Learning Disabilities (1987) and the American Academy of Pediatrics

(1999). The American Academy of Pediatrics stated that the treatment methods advocated by Delacato are "based on an outmoded and oversimplified theory of brain development. Current information does not support the claims of proponents that this treatment is efficacious" (p. 1149).

Having stated the concerns regarding remedial training programs, it is worth noting that some recent research investigations have resulted in specific brain growth in laboratory animals as a result of complex movement experiences (Ivanco and Greenough, 2000; Jones and Greenough, 1996; Jones, Klintsova, Kilman, Sirevaag, and Greenough, 1997; Kleim, Pipitone, Czerlanis, and Greenough, 1998). How these findings will establish the groundwork for human subjects and subsequent applications in programming remains to be seen.

Readiness and Remediation

Research indicates that as children pass through the normal developmental stages, their perceptual abilities become more acute and refined. This is due partly to the increasing complexity of the neuromuscular apparatus and sensory receptors and partly to children's increasing ability to explore and move through the environment. Piaget's (1954) work has traced the gradual development of perception from crude, meaningless sensations to impressions of a stable spatial world. His stages of development rely heavily on motor information as a primary information-gathering device. As the perceptual world unfolds, children seek stability and reduce variability as far as possible. They learn to differentiate among things that can be ignored, things that are easily predictable, or things that are wholly unforeseen and must be observed and examined to be understood, according to Piaget and others. Movement plays an important role in this process of developing perceptual readiness for cognitive tasks. Table 13.3 compares Piaget's (1952) stages of development with those proposed by Kephart (1971) and by these authors.

The majority of our perceptions, visual perceptions in particular, result from the elaboration and modification of these basic reactions by experience and learning. When we speak of children being perceptually ready to learn, we are referring to a time in which they have sufficiently developed their basic perceptual and conceptual learning capacities. Achieving perceptual readiness for learning is a developmental process in which perceptual-motor activities play an important part. Specific perceptual readiness skills, such as visual perceptual readiness for reading, may be affected by the quality and quantity of a child's perceptual-motor experiences, but this has not been conclusively demonstrated in controlled research studies.

The process of being able to read (and accomplish other important tasks) involves a number of abilities including visual perceptual ability. The reading process may be considered three basic areas: language, skill, and perception. Considerable research has been conducted in the first two areas, but scholars are just beginning to explore the third. The perceptual phase of reading involves the identification and recognition of words on a printed page. Form and shape perception may be enhanced through movement as well as directional awareness of up, down, left, and right. All are important factors associated with word identification and recognition. The greatest amount of perceptual-motor development takes place between ages 3 and 7. These are the crucial years preceding and during the time that most children begin to learn to read. A child is perceptually ready to read when he or she has acquired a sufficient backlog of information to encode and decode sensory impressions at a given time. Ideally, the child's previous learning experiences were numerous and of high quality. A sufficient number of children enter first grade lagging in their perceptual abilities to warrant programs in readiness training that use perceptual-motor development activities as one of many avenues for intervention. The physical activity portion of the school day can play an important role in helping many of these children catch up with their peers.

Perceptual-Motor Activities

Many of today's perceptual-motor programs and curricula incorporate an ecological approach. Specified movement activities or skills are intentionally

TABLE 13.3   Comparison of Piaget's, Kephart's, and Gallahue's Phases and Stages of Development

Approximate Chronological Age	Piaget's Cognitive Phases and Stages	Kephart's Developmental Sequences	Gallahue's Phases and Stages of Motor Development
0 to 6 months	*Sensorimotor Phase* Use of reflexes Primary circular reactions Coordination of prehension and vision, secondary circular reactions	*Reflexive Stage* *Motor Stage* Rudimentary motor pattern development	*Reflexive Phase* Encoding stage Decoding stage
6 to 12 months	Secondary schemata Discovery of new means, tertiary circular reactions	Balance Receipt and propulsion Globular form	*Rudimentary Phase* Reflex inhibition stage
1 to 2 years	Beginnings of insight and cause/effect relationships Egocentric organization Perceptive movement	*Motor-Perceptual Stage* Laterality Hand-eye coordination Gross motor pattern development Syncretic form Form recognition	Precontrol stage
2 to 4 years	*Preoperational Thought Phase* Perceptually oriented, period from self-satisfying behavior to rudimentary social behavior Awareness of a conceptual hierarchy, beginnings of cognition		*Fundamental Movement Phase* Initial stage Elementary stage
4 to 6 years	Beginning abstractions	*Perceptual-Motor Stage* Directionality Eye-hand coordination *Perceptual Stage* Form perception Constructive form Form reproduction	Mature stage
7 to 10 years	*Concrete Operations Phase* Additive composition, reversibility, associativity, identity, deductive reasoning Relationships Classification	*Perceptual-Cognitive Stage*	*Specialized Movement Phase* Transition stage
11 years and over	*Formal Operations Phase* Intellectual maturity Symbolic operations Abstract thinking Propositional thinking	*Cognitive-Perceptual Stage* *Cognitive Stage*	Application stage Lifelong utilization stage

TABLE 13.4 Suggested Perceptual-Motor Activities

Deficit Area—Body, directional, spatial, and temporal awareness
- Play follow the leader with movement
- Construct obstacle courses with narrow openings, over and under barriers, and uneven surfaces
- Use blindfolds with locomotor and manipulative activities
- Scatter parts of dismembered dolls around the room/gym and have child retrieve parts to make a complete doll
- Perform locomotor skills at different tempos to follow the tempo of a musical instrument

Deficit Area—Using multiple sources of sensory information
- Perform movement activities in and out of water; compare movements
- Perform body rolling on various surfaces and angles
- Use barefoot movement on different types of surfaces
- Play games where two bodies or body parts must be touching and moving in unison
- Perform movements wrapped in blankets, oversized clothing, or sacks of various textures

Deficit Area—Crosslateral and midline problems
- Play games that incorporate agility (changing directions rapidly and accurately)
- Perform exercises such as sit-ups with trunk twists (allows the right hand to touch the left foot, and vice versa)
- Use beanbag exploration that requires placing a beanbag held in the right hand on a part of the body located on the left side
- Reinforce midline crossing with throwing and striking activities
- Play a nonelimination Simon Says game emphasizing midline and opposition movements

Deficit Area—Balance and coordination
- Incorporate equipment such as tiltboards, balance boards, and balance beams
- Perform static balance positions with eyes open, eyes closed, and eyes focused on a target (stationary and moving)
- Perform static and dynamic balance activities while holding a weighted object in only one hand
- Teach students to say verbal cues that coincide with their movements
- Have students perform particular movement under varying environmental and task conditions

Data from Sherrill, C. (1998). *Adapted Physical Activity, Recreation and Sport: Crossdisciplinary and Lifespan.* 5th ed., St. Louis: McGraw-Hill.

practiced under a variety of environmental and task conditions. In that way, perception is specific to an individual child and the environment is perceived in the context of what affordances it provides (Winnick, 2000). Regular and adapted physical education teachers and pediatric physical and occupational therapists tend to serve as the primary program developers and deliverers for children with perceptual-motor difficulties. Teachers and therapists require activities that focus on the specific delays demonstrated in their students or clients and incorporate an ecological approach. Claudine Sherrill, one of the leading contributors to the field of adapted physical activity, suggests some of the activities and instructional strategies in table 13.4.

ASSESSING PERCEPTUAL-MOTOR DEVELOPMENT

During the past several years numerous measures of perceptual-motor development have been constructed. Generally, these tests were developed as measures for children who had been classified as "slow learners," "neurologically impaired," or as having a condition such as "attention deficit hyperactivity disorder (ADHD)." They have been used with varying degrees of success. The classroom teacher and physical education teacher are often the first to pick up "subjective" cues of possible perceptual-motor difficulties in preschool and primary grade children. The validity of these subjective observations must not be discounted or minimized. On the contrary, the careful daily observation of a child's behavior can be valuable and reliable in detecting potential lags in development. A child who shows signs of possible developmental problems should be referred to the school psychologist for

testing. The results of the testing should be shared with parents and the teachers with whom the child comes in contact. The adults can form an effective team to eliminate or diminish the difficulty. The checklist of cues in table 13.5 may aid the teacher in assessing children with potential perceptual-motor

TABLE 13.5   Checklist of Possible Perceptual-Motor Dysfunctions

1. Has trouble holding or maintaining balance. _____
2. Appears clumsy. _____
3. Cannot carry body well in motion. _____
4. Appears to be generally awkward in activities requiring coordination. _____
5. Does not readily distinguish left from right. _____
6. In locomotor skills, performs movements with more efficiency on one side than the other. _____
7. Reverses letters and numbers with regularity. _____
8. Is unable to hop or skip rhythmically. _____
9. Has difficulty making changes in movement. _____
10. Has difficulty performing combinations of simple movements. _____
11. Has difficulty in gauging space with respect to the body and collides with objects and other children. _____
12. Tends to be accident-prone. _____
13. Has poor hand-eye coordination. _____
14. Has difficulty handling the simple tools of physical activity (beanbags, balls, and other objects that involve a visual-motor relationship). _____
15. Has persistent poor general appearance. _____
    (a) Shirttail always out. _____
    (b) Shoes constantly untied. _____
    (c) Fly constantly unzipped. _____
    (d) Socks bagged around ankles. _____
    (e) Hair uncombed. _____
16. Is inattentive. _____
17. Does not follow directions; is able to follow verbal but not written directions, or vice versa. _____
18. Has speech difficulties. _____
    (a) Talks too loudly. _____
    (b) Talks too softly. _____
    (c) Slurs words. _____
    (d) Leaves off ends of words. _____
    (e) Uses immature sentence structure. _____
19. Poor body posture. _____
20. Has hearing difficulties. _____
    (a) Frequently turns head to one side. _____
    (b) Holds or prefers one ear over the other. _____
21. Has difficulty negotiating stairs. _____
22. Daydreams excessively. _____
23. Is excessively messy in work. _____
    (a) Goes out of the lines. _____
    (b) Inconsistency of letter size, etc. _____
    (c) General sloppiness. _____
24. Is unable to copy objects (words, numbers, letters, etc.). _____

problems. The checklist is designed to serve only as a subjective indicator of possible perceptual-motor difficulties. There is little interrelationship among these variables, and there is no predictable pattern for determining difficulties. A teacher who observes a child's weaknesses in several of these items should seek further information through more objective evaluation procedures.

CONCEPT 13.9

Both formal and informal devices for assessing perceptual-motor functioning are available to provide important cues to developmental difficulties in children.

SUMMARY

Perceptual-motor training programs possess many of the same elements as reputable developmentally based physical education programs. Many of the movement skills taught in a perceptual-motor curriculum, either readiness or remedial, parallel those taught in regular developmental physical education classes. The goals of each program are different. A primary goal of the developmental physical activity program is to enhance movement control through practice and instruction in a variety of movement skills, while the goal of the perceptual-motor program is to enhance perceptual-motor qualities through practice and instruction in a variety of movement activities. Perceptual-motor training programs that purport to enhance academic achievement or to promote specific readiness for schoolwork do so amid considerable controversy and a lack of research support. Public testimony and opinion have served for years as the basis of support for perceptual-motor training programs. This is not adequate. However, the value of perceptual-motor experiences to a general state of

readiness should not be dismissed. Enhancement of body, spatial, directional, and temporal awareness as a means of guiding the child toward improved movement control and efficiency in fundamental movement is worthwhile. Practice in perceptual-motor activities may, under certain conditions, enhance perceptual-motor abilities. Whether these abilities have a direct effect on academic performance is highly questionable. One can be assured, however, that they do play an important role in developing and refining the child's movement abilities.

A comparison of Gallahue's phases of motor development to Kephart's developmental sequence and Piaget's cognitive phases of development was presented in table 13.3. Careful review of these models reveals the interrelated nature of the perceptual, motor, and cognitive processes. The magnitude of this relationship and the conditions necessary for improved functioning in each area await further well-controlled scientific research.

CRITICAL READINGS

Burton, A. W. (1990). Assessing the perceptual-motor interaction in developmentally disabled and handicapped children. *Adapted Physical Activity Quarterly, 7,* 325–337.

Burton, A. W., & Davis, W. E. (1996). Ecological task analysis: Theoretical and empirical foundations. *Human Movement Science, 15,* 285–314.

Council on Learning Disabilities. (1987). The CLD position statements: Measurement and training of perceptual and perceptual-motor functions. *Journal of Learning Disabilities, 20* (6), 347–350.

Magill, R. A. (2001). *Motor Learning: Concepts and Applications* (Chapter 6). 6th ed. St. Louis: McGraw-Hill.

Rose, D. J. (1997). *A Multilevel Approach to the Study of Motor Control and Learning* (Chapters 4 & 5). Boston: Allyn and Bacon.

Sherrill, C. (1998). *Adapted Physical Activity, Recreation and Sport: Crossdisciplinary and Lifespan* (Chapter 12). 5th ed. St. Louis: McGraw-Hill.

Winnick, J. P. (2000). Perceptual-motor development. In J. P. Winnick (Ed.), *Adapted Physical Education and Sport* (Chapter 18). 3rd ed. Champaign, IL: Human Kinetics.

 WEB RESOURCES

A unique Web book on vision
www.yorku.ca/dept/psych/yorkvis

Discussion on ecological approach and perceptual-motor understanding
http://ione.psy.uconn.edu/~cespaweb/info.html

Information from PE Central on perceptual-motor activities
www.pecentral.org/adapted/adaptedmenu.html

North American Society for the Psychology of Sport and Physical Activity
www.naspspa.org

CHILDHOOD SELF-CONCEPT DEVELOPMENT

KEY TERMS

Self-concept
Self-esteem
Self-confidence
Self-efficacy
Competence
Perceived competence
Movement competence

CHAPTER COMPETENCIES

Upon completion of this chapter you should be able to:

- List and describe sociocultural correlates that may affect motor development
- Distinguish similarities, differences, and relationships among various terms used in the study of self-concept
- Describe the developmental aspects of self-concept
- Demonstrate how movement competence is related to self-esteem
- Analyze similarities and differences of movement competence on social status in males and females
- List the consequences of a negative self-concept
- Propose means of enhancing self-esteem through movement
- Describe problems associated with assessing self-concept

KEY CONCEPT

Self-concept is a multidimensional construct linked to perceived physical competence throughout childhood and beyond.

Do you remember when you were a child with nothing to do but play for hours each day? Do you remember the excitement of that first struggle to the top of the climbing wall, your first successful ride on a two-wheeler, or your first swim all the way across a pool? We can all remember how good it felt to succeed and can probably even remember how it felt to fail. The successes and failures of childhood may seem remote and meaningless to us now, but they were important events that influenced what and who we are today. Many of these events centered around early play experiences. The feelings children have about themselves are greatly determined by their play experiences, both successful and unsuccessful.

Children are active, energetic, and emerging beings. Many of their lives are spent in play and active exploration of an ever-expanding world. The so-called play world of children occupies large portions of their days and is of central importance. It is a primary means by which children learn more about themselves, their bodies, and their potential for movement. Many basic affective concepts have their roots in the carefree, exhilarating world of play.

Self-concept is an important aspect of a child's affective behavior influenced through the world of games, play, and vigorous movement. A stable, positive self-concept is so crucial to a child's ability to function effectively that its development cannot be left to chance. The important contributions that movement and vigorous physical activity can make to forming a positive self-concept should not be overlooked. As adults we should be genuinely interested in the development of good self-concepts in our children. In this chapter we will examine self-concept development and the potential of physical activity for enhancing self-esteem.

WHAT IS SELF-CONCEPT?

The topic of "self" has been a central focus of the psychosocial literature for more than a hundred years. The now classic work of William James (1890) undergirds much of the current work on the developing self. A variety of terms have been used with "self" as a hyphenated prefix (figure 14.1). As a result considerable confusion has existed over meanings, similarities, and differences. We will attempt to clarify these often subtle differences before examining the role of movement in the establishment of a positive view of self. There is considerable overlap and cross-use among these terms as they are commonly used in the literature today.

Self-concept, as used here, is the umbrella term under which several other variations of self are categorized. Self-concept is generally viewed as one's awareness of personal characteristics, attributes, and limitations and the ways in which these qualities are both like and unlike those of others. Self-concept is how one views herself or himself without passing personal judgment or comparison with others. On the other hand, **self-esteem** is the value that one attaches to his or her unique characteristics, attributes, and limitations. Santrock (2001) describes self-esteem as "the global evaluative dimension of the self" (p. 380). In other words, it refers to the feelings and judgments a person perceives as a representative description of himself or herself. Whereas self-concept is merely one's perceptions of self, self-esteem is the value one places on those perceptions.

James (1890) was the first modern scholar to attempt to decipher the elusive meaning of self-esteem. His now famous formula concluded that one's feelings of self-worth (self-esteem) are equal to the ratio of one's accomplishments to one's potential for achievement. The closer the success to potential ratio is to 1.0, the nearer one is to his or her ideal self. Perhaps Coopersmith (1967) defined self-esteem best when he stated that "self-esteem is a personal judgment of worthiness that is expressed in the attitudes the individual holds toward himself" (p. 5). Although the terms are linked, self-esteem is not the same as self-confidence.

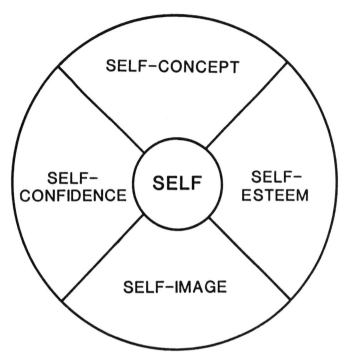

Figure 14.1
Terms commonly used to describe one's perception of self.

Self-confidence denotes one's belief in his or her ability to carry out a mental, physical, or emotional task. It is one's anticipated ability to master particular challenges and to overcome obstacles or difficulties. Self-confident persons believe that they can cause things to happen in accordance with their desires. Self-confidence as used here means the same as Bandura's (1982) term **self-efficacy,** which he defines as "the conviction that one can successfully execute the behavior required to produce the [desired] outcome" (p. 39).

Self-confidence may be unrelated to self-esteem in some situations. For example, a child may not have a sufficient level of self-confidence to attempt a difficult gymnastics movement, but may still possess a high level of self-esteem. In support of this notion Dickstein (1977) stated that "self-confidence involves carrying off a particular task or fostering a role. Level of self-confidence at any one moment may be unrelated to an overall level of self-esteem" (p. 136). One must conclude, however,

that the perceived importance of the activity or task by the individual or significant others (peer, parents, teachers, coaches) may forge a link between self-confidence and self-esteem. If the task is viewed as important, then competence in executing the task will have an impact on self-esteem. Therefore, *competence* becomes an important construct in the development of self-esteem.

The notion of **competence** as related to self-concept was first introduced by White (1959) and later expanded by Coopersmith (1977) and Harter (1978, 1999). Competence may be viewed as one's ability to meet particular achievement demands. Competence refers to one's level of mastery, which may range from poor to adequate to superior. Competence is an important factor in the development of one's self-concept (Ebbeck and Stuart, 1996). More specifically, the perception of one's competence (i.e., **perceived competence**) in a given situation and its perceived importance may have a significant impact on one's actual competence,

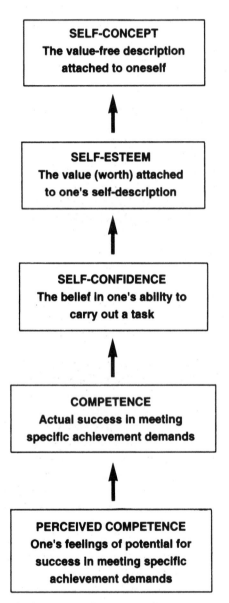

A HIERARCHICAL VIEW OF SELF-CONCEPT DEVELOPMENT

Figure 14.2
A hierarchical view of self-concept development.

self-confidence, self-esteem, and self-concept (figure 14.2). Estimates of perceived physical competence (i.e., ability) have been shown to contribute to children's achievement motivation (Weiss and Horn, 1990) and degree of sport participation (Weiss and Chaumeton, 1992). In other words, low estimates of physical ability are likely to lead to attrition in youth sport participation, whereas high levels of perceived ability are likely to motivate children to continue sports participation.

SELF-CONCEPT: GLOBAL OR MULTIDIMENSIONAL?

A question that has intrigued theorists and researchers for decades involves the general nature or specificity of one's self-concept; that is, is self-concept a global trait, or can it be differentiated into various components? Weinberg and Gould (1999) suggest that it is best to view self-concept not only on global terms but also segmented into components such as social self-concept, academic self-concept, and physical self-concept.

It follows then that one possesses both a differentiated concept of self and a global self-concept. In support of this, Rosenberg (1979) insisted that the two are not identical, stating, "Both exist within the individual's phenomenal field as separate and distinguishable entities and each can and should be studied in its own right" (p. 20). Rosenberg (1982) in a later paper makes the telling point that: "Although widely overlooked in self-esteem studies, it is fairly obvious that a person's global self-esteem is not based solely on his assessment of his constituent qualities. His self-esteem is based on his self-assessments of qualities that count" (p. 536). In other words, global self-concept is the product of one's perception of his or her competence in areas that have personal meaning. It is unaffected by one's self-assessment of competence in areas that have little or no personal significance. It follows, therefore, that if being good at games, play activities, and sports is important to a child, then success in these areas will have an impact on his global self-concept. If, however, these attributes are not perceived as being personally meaningful, then they will have little impact (Harter, 1987; Marsh, 1994).

CONCEPT 14.1

Global self-concept is the product of one's perceptions of competence in areas that have personal meaning.

In modern North American society, being good in games, play activities, and sports is of high positive value to both boys and girls. Competence in these areas is important for social acceptance and status within the peer group. Moreover, adults frequently give children the impression that their competence in physical endeavors is closely linked to their acceptance and value within the family or team unit. In a society that places high positive value on success in games and sport, it is reasonable to assume that one of the important components of global self-concept is **movement competence** and that movement competence plays a crucial role in positive self-esteem development.

Harter (1978, 1982a, 1999) and Harter and Connell (1984), studying the developmental aspects of self-concept, attempted to isolate three self-evaluative dimensions of competence. The Self-Perception Profile for Children (Harter, 1985) and the Pictorial Scale of Perceived Competence and Social Acceptance for Young Children (Harter and Pike, 1984) subdivide perceived competence into cognitive and physical (movement) domains, along with measures of social acceptance and general self-worth. Harter (1982a, 1982b) found that children in grades 3 through 9 make clear distinctions among categories. However, Harter and Pike (1984) did not find the same to be true with younger children (ages 4 to 7). These children tended to lump cognitive and physical competence together into a category of "general competence," and to view social acceptance (by the peer group and mother) as important. Also, they did not possess concepts of general self-worth. It appears, therefore, that the notion of movement competence has significant implications for children

from about the third grade onward. Prior to that time children tend to view themselves as either competent or incompetent with little distinction between the physical and cognitive domains. More recently, however, Marsh et al. (1991) investigated the multidimensional structure of self-concept in children 5 to 8 years of age. The results of this study, which used the Self-Description Questionnaire (Marsh, 1990), revealed that when appropriately measured, self-concepts are better differentiated by young children than previously assumed. Therefore, we can conclude that when properly measured, self-concept is multidimensional in young children as well as older children, adolescents, and adults.

CONCEPT 14.2

Movement competence plays an important role in self-concept development, because children generally value being good in games, sports, and play activities.

A person is unique because of his or her self-concept and view of the world. The sum of life experiences and the person's feelings about these experiences contribute to this mental model. We find out about ourselves in many ways. By choosing, trying things, experimenting, and exploring, we discover who we are, what we can do, and what we cannot do. Not only do we discover who we are, but through our experiences we contribute to the making or formation of our unique identities.

DEVELOPMENTAL ASPECTS OF SELF-CONCEPT

A person's self-concept is learned, and it begins to develop at least at birth. Some authorities argue that the emotional state of the expectant mother, ranging from relaxed and happy to tense and unhappy, may have a dramatic effect on the unborn child.

The early months of infancy mark the first tangible beginnings of self-concept development.

The tenderness, warmth, and love from the parent to the child convey the first feelings of value and affection. The infant's sense of well-being is affected by the parent's emotional state and attention to his or her physical needs. The fulfillment of psychological needs is as important, for the infant needs to establish a sense of trust, security, recognition, and love. Trust is a basic issue to be resolved in the early parent-infant relationship. Mothers and fathers create a sense of trust in their children by combining sensitive care with a firm sense of personal reliability.

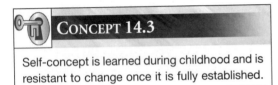

CONCEPT 14.3

Self-concept is learned during childhood and is resistant to change once it is fully established.

Self-concept is established in the infant and young child through the affirmation of others. Children increase their competence under the care of loving, capable, and nurturing adults. Werner (1989a; 1989b), in her thirty-year longitudinal study of 698 "high-risk" individuals from infancy onward, clearly identified the importance of the presence of at least one consistent, nurturing, unconditionally accepting adult in a child's life for successful adaptation to occur. Erik Erikson (1963, 1980) was among the first to recognize the importance of establishing a sense of trust during a child's early years. His stage of "trust versus mistrust" (discussed in greater detail in chapter 2) is rooted in the child's developing sense of being loved and valued in a world that has constancy and permanence.

CONCEPT 14.4

Parents, teachers, and coaches are significant others in the lives of children and as such play important roles in the development of their self-concepts.

The toddler experiences the satisfaction of mastering the art of walking successfully or solving a problem with a new toy. The development of a sense of autonomy is an important facilitator of a positive self-concept, influenced greatly by central adults in the life of the child. The dependency of children on significant others is temporary, and the temporary nature of dependence leads children to the exploratory behaviors and mastery attempts of early childhood and beyond. Adults have unique opportunities to reinforce the ways in which children learn about themselves by providing opportunities for self-discovery and by consistently accepting the individuality of each child. During this period caretakers should respect a child's need for freedom and independence within carefully defined limits.

Much of what the young child learns is imitative, and this learning is not restricted to overt action. Feelings and attitudes can also be learned through imitation. As a result, the moods and emotions of a central adult affect many of the attitudes and feelings that the child develops.

As a child's social world and the influence of others expands, he or she develops a greater sense of independence. Upon entering school, children begin to shift their frame of reference from the home and family to the school and the teacher. The number of significant others that affect the child's developing self increase as teachers and peers begin to exert greater influence. The teacher becomes a primary model for the child, and there is a great desire to please. Schempp et al. (1983) found that an atmosphere in which children were encouraged to make decisions promoted the development of positive self-concepts, attitudes, creativity, and motor skills. Those who were expected to do well and were involved in decision making had higher self-concept scores than those who were expected to do poorly or were not involved in decision making. The implications of these findings are enormous when applied to the teacher/learner or coach/athlete dyads.

Peer relationships also become a greater factor in the development of a child's self-concept and self-esteem. Maureen Weiss, one of the leading experts in developmental sport psychology, has conducted

TABLE 14.1 Self-Concept Related Factors of Peer Relationships in Youth Sports

Positive Factors

- Self-esteem enhancement
- Prosocial behavior
- Loyalty
- Things in common
- Emotional support
- Absence of conflicts

- Help and guidance
- Intimacy
- Pleasant play/association
- Attractive personal qualities
- Companionship
- Conflict resolution

Negative Factors

- Conflict
- Betrayal

- Unattractive personal qualities
- Inaccessible

Data from Weiss, M. R., Smith, A. L., & Theeboom, M. (1996). "That's what friends are for": Children's and teenagers' perceptions of peer relationships in the sport domain. *Journal of Sport & Exercise Psychology, 18,* 347–379.

numerous investigations in the area of psychological aspects of youth sport participation. She and her colleagues found several positive and negative dimensions of peer relationships in youth sport settings that relate to self-concept development (Weiss, Smith, and Theeboom, 1996). A summary of these factors can be found in table 14.1.

Older children feel good about accomplishing new and difficult tasks, establishing independence, and performing meaningful work to earn money. The thoughtful parent recognizes the importance of the peer group at this level and gradually helps the child develop a sense of mature independence. A person's sense of worth and effectiveness develops chiefly through successful experiences in coping. Coping skills are essential for confidence. One must be willing to accept oneself as well as others who are different. Children and adults who can cope are adaptable rather than rigid in their behavior. They are diligent, can concentrate on a task, and can work through difficulties. Self-confidence is developed through the joy of finding what one does well—of doing anything really well. Movement skill and fitness acquisition are important avenues by which self-confidence may be enhanced. They are especially important for most children, because many of their daily life experiences are centered around the need for efficient and effective movement.

The work of Damon and Hart (1986) argues strongly for the developmental nature of self-concept, as revealed in a three-year longitudinal study of self-understanding in children 4 through 18. Their results also lend support to the basic assumption that an individual's sense of self tends to be stable over time.

MOVEMENT COMPETENCE AND SELF-ESTEEM

The perception of competence is one of the most important variables underlying motivation (Crawford, 1989; Duda, 1986; Harter, 1978; White, 1959). Harter's expansion on White's theory of competence motivation argues that the quality of one's experiences is the critical determinant for the developing of competence. Competence is a facilitator of confidence, and confidence fosters a positive view of self. Demonstrating competence leads to pride and joy, but failing to demonstrate competence leads to shame and self-doubt. A child's perceived competence affects her continued interest in an activity and in further mastery attempts. When applied to physical activity, Harter's theory of competence motivation means that if an individual perceives himself as physically competent, he will continue to participate in physical activities.

If, however, he perceives himself to be physically incompetent, he will limit participation and suspend mastery attempts.

 CONCEPT 14.5

Perceived competence and actual competence promote self-confidence, which has the potential for enhancing dimensional aspects of one's self-esteem and self-concept.

The development of perceived competence is a primary goal of youth sport participation (Knoppers, 1992; Weinberg and Gould, 1999). Several studies have demonstrated the importance of perceived competence for continued participation in sport (Crawford, 1989; Gould and Horn, 1984; Marsh, 1985; Weiss and Chaumeton, 1992). Physical activity can enhance or limit self-concept development in children, because it is a central focus in their lives. Both boys and girls place great value on competence in physical activities, and this is an essential factor in global self-esteem (Harter, 1983; Weiss, 1987).

Zaharopoulos and Hodge (1991) examined differences between adolescent athletes and nonathletes and gender. The results of their cross-sectional study indicated that athletes differed significantly from nonathletes in physical ability self-concept, but not in global self-concept. Additionally, females did not differ from males in physical ability self-concept. These findings support the concept of multidimensionality in self-concept, but refute the notion that sport participation enhances self-concept in general. These results confirmed the results of an earlier investigation by Marsh and Peart (1988).

The relationship between a child's social status and his or her movement competence has been a subject of interest to researchers for many years. Numerous studies point out that there is a link between high positive peer group acceptance and ability in games and sports, especially for boys. Athletic skill is paramount for many boys,

predicated upon motor coordination, strength, size, and physical maturity (Tuddenham, 1951). Recently, however, several investigations have pointed out that girls have less positive perceptions of their physical competence than boys (Fox, Corbin, and Couldry, 1985; Granleese, Trew, and Turner, 1988; Marsh, 1985; van Wersch, Trew, and Turner, 1990).

Skill level is often controlled by factors outside the child's influence. Such things as physical stature, health-related conditions, experience, and the quality of instruction make it impossible for many children to meet the values of their peer groups. As a result, they feel inferior and rejected and develop poor self-images. Personal insecurity and social maladjustment often have their roots in this area.

Schoolyards, gymnasiums, and play environments provide excellent opportunities for positive self-concept development. A child's perceived competence as well as her actual competence in the physical, cognitive, and affective domains are important facilitators of positive self-concept development. With regard to the physical domain, Roberts, Kleiber, and Duda (1981) tested fourth and fifth graders, and Harter (1982b) tested sixth graders who were either nonparticipants or participants in organized youth sport programs. The results of their independent investigations indicated that participants perceive themselves as more competent in games and sports than nonparticipants. Ulrich (1987), however, found somewhat different results in her study of younger children in grades K through 4. She compared children's perceptions of physical competence, their actual motor competencies, and their participation in youth sport programs. Her results revealed that the perceived physical competencies of young children were not significantly related to their participation in organized sports. However, their actual motor competencies were significantly related to sport participation. It seems that whereas older children are clearly influenced by their perceptions of physical competence and participation, younger children may not be.

CONSEQUENCES OF A POOR SELF-CONCEPT

A poor self-concept is reflected in the feelings of "I can't," "I'm always wrong," or, "I'm worthless." Children who feel bad about themselves and the world they know are not likely to feel better about parts of the world they do not know. As a result, they are often indifferent or fearful about exploring new territory. It does not look inviting and appears hostile and full of possibilities for humiliation and defeat. This threatening new world does not lure the child out but thrusts in on her, invading those few places in which she feels secure. A child with a negative self-concept regards unfamiliar experiences with fear.

CONCEPT 14.6

A negative self-concept can have devastating effects on all aspects of a child's life.

A child who feels worthless due to repeated failures often falls back on the strategy of deliberate failure, which serves as a self-protective device. Children who view themselves as failures will not even be tempted to try new tasks.

Children with poor self-concepts are also negatively affected by what they think others think of them. Children, as well as adults, tend to live up to the expectations of others or at least to what these expectations are perceived to be. Teachers are of tremendous importance in shaping children's basic attitudes toward themselves in relation to school. During the elementary years significant correlations exist between children's perceptions of their teachers' feelings toward them and their own self-images. Teachers who emphasize positive self-concepts tend to be associated with students who hold positive views of themselves. Using such terms as *stupid, dumb, always wrong, bad boy* or *bad girl, troublemaker,* and *lousy* is harmful to children. These spoken words, as well as our unspoken indications of disapproval, dismay, disgust, anger,

and surprise, influence what children think others think of them. Given enough negative information, a child soon adapts to a negative role. A cycle of failure and perceived expectation of failure is established.

Children with poor self-images are rarely cheered when they succeed. Their perceptions of themselves as nonachievers, combined with their convictions that others perceive them in the same manner, are difficult to change when success is infrequent. Even when normal patterns of failure are broken occasionally with success, children with poor self-images regard the successes as temporary and believe that things will certainly go wrong soon.

The influence of a poor self-concept on the learning process can be tremendous. High anxiety, underachievement, behavior problems, learning difficulties, and delinquency are among the problems. Students' perceptions of themselves as "learners" or "nonlearners" affect academic achievement levels. Low achievement is often due to a child's definition of himself as a nonlearner. He resists learning because it is inconsistent for him, in his view, to learn. A child who feels that he cannot achieve may negate or reduce his actual ability, which may be average, above average, or even higher. Conversely, a child with a success-oriented outlook plunges into a project or takes on a new challenge with every expectation of achievement.

The role of physical activity in self-concept development must not be minimized, but questions remain. Does increased movement competence lead to improved self-esteem? Does one's level of self-esteem influence achievement? Parents, teachers, therapists, and coaches, for the most part, have adopted the behavioristic point of view that improved levels of movement competence lead to enhanced self-esteem. On the other hand, those who emphasize competitiveness and reward the more skillful athletes may do little to enhance perceptions of physical competence among those who are less skillful (van Wersch et al., 1990). Other educators have adopted a cognitive view of learning that promotes student self-discovery and perceived competence through developmentally appropriate activities (Bigge and Shermis, 1999). Teachers and coaches who adopt a developmental model of education and adapt their instruction to the individual needs of children may be enhancing perceived competence and promoting further mastery attempts in all students (Gallahue, 1996). Self-concept enhancement has been an established goal for most teachers and coaches who subscribe to a developmental skill and fitness model of instruction. One's level of self-esteem can be a factor in influencing achievement, and achievement can be an important factor in influencing self-esteem.

CONCEPT 14.7

Perceived physical competence can be enhanced through success-oriented, developmentally based movement programs.

MOVEMENT TECHNIQUES FOR ENHANCING SELF-ESTEEM

Children who have difficulty performing many fundamental skills basic to proficient performance in games and sports encounter repeated failures in their everyday play experiences. As a result, they often have trouble seeing themselves as worthy beings. Taylor (1980) stated that "one of the best and easiest pathways to a strong self-concept is through play. Play offers opportunities to assist the child in all areas of development. Its importance can be found in how he [the child] perceives himself, his body, his abilities and his relationships with others" (p. 133). Educators and parents need to determine how to use the movement activities of children to encourage the formation of stable, positive self-concepts. Formulated from research findings and decades of professional observations and experiences, in the following paragraphs the authors offer commonsense' principles regarding self-concept enhancement through movement.

CONCEPT 14.8

Success-oriented movement experiences play an important role in self-concept enhancement.

Success

The most important thing that we can do is to help children develop proper perspectives on success and failure in their daily lives. Because of the egocentric nature of children, it is very difficult for them to accept both success and failure. Success is that feeling of "I can," "I did it," or "Look at me" that we love to see in children. It is the sense of accomplishment that accompanies mastering a new skill or executing a good move. Failure is that feeling of "I can't," "I don't know how," or "I am always wrong." It is the feeling of frustration and hopelessness that often follows failure to master a skill or execution of a poor move.

We need to help children develop a balance between success and failure. We need to bolster self-worth so that when they fail to achieve something, they will not be completely defeated. A backlog of successful experiences will help develop that "I can" attitude. Success is important, particularly at the initial stages of learning. We need only look at ourselves and our tendencies to continue activities at which we are successful. This basic principle of learning theory is applicable to both children and adults. We need to take the importance of success into consideration when working with young children by using teaching methods that emphasize success.

The use of problem solving or guided discovery in teaching new movement skills enables all children to experiment and explore their movement potentials. Children become involved in the process of learning instead of being solely concerned with the product. This child-centered, success-oriented approach allows for a variety of solutions or "correct" answers. The teacher and the children are more concerned about individual solutions to a problem than finding the one best way. The astute teacher of young children recognizes that there is no *best* way of performing at this level of development. The wise teacher instead focuses on helping children learn more about their bodies and how they move and fostering more mature patterns of movement. For example, the teacher may structure a challenge such as, "How can you balance on three body parts?" or "Who can balance on three body parts?" The number of possible solutions is great and so is the range of difficulty. All children gain increased knowledge of how to move and balance their bodies. The teacher, through questioning or movement challenges, also avoids imposing predetermined models of what performances should be and how they should look.

Individualizing instruction is another way of emphasizing success for each child. Individualized instruction takes into account the uniqueness of each learner and provides every child with opportunities to achieve at his or her particular level of ability. Although it is often difficult because of large classes and limited staff, time, and facilities, teachers should try to individualize whenever possible. The typical preschool program does a tremendous job of individualizing instruction by employing an open classroom approach with a variety of interest centers. Too often, however, children entering elementary school are faced with the rigid structure of traditional classroom and gymnasium programs that assume that all children are at the same level in their interests, abilities, and motivation for learning. Not all children are "typical" first graders. Within any given class, children exhibit a wide range of cognitive, affective, and motor abilities. Greater attention to individual needs, interests, and abilities will do much to strengthen the success potential of each child.

Traditional methods of teaching movement are valuable, especially at higher skill levels, but teachers often dominate and require all students to perform at certain levels or emulate particular models. Some children may have considerable difficulty achieving desired standards of performance. Teacher-dominated methods rarely provide success-oriented experiences for everyone. Although these methods should be included in the movement activity program, they should not be stressed too early in the learning process. Teachers

of young children should allow for individual differences in readiness rates and abilities to learn new movement skills.

Movement programs that make use of problem-solving approaches and individualized instruction whenever possible make positive contributions to self-concept development. But what is involved in using these success-oriented approaches?

Developmentally appropriate movement experiences that are challenging and properly sequenced are very beneficial for children. As educators and parents, we help children form good self-images by encouraging them to establish reasonable expectations of themselves and by clearly outlining our intentions (figure 14.3).

Developmentally Appropriate Activities

Children are not miniature adults ready to be programmed for the whims and wishes of adults. They are growing and developing beings with needs, interests, and capabilities different from those of adults. Too often, we fall into the trap of trying to create miniature athletes out of 6- and 7-year-olds without first developing the children's fundamental movement abilities. Too often, we force children to specialize in the development of their movement abilities at early ages. They become involved in competitive athletics before they are ready to handle the physical and emotional demands. Competition is not evil or something to be removed from the lives of children, but it must be kept within the proper perspective. Parents and coaches should not be preoccupied with winning games. Instead, they should focus on the balanced, wholesome, and healthful development of children under wise guidance. The needs, interests, and capabilities of each child must be carefully considered.

CONCEPT 14.9

Developmentally appropriate and properly sequenced movement activities can contribute to self-concept enhancement.

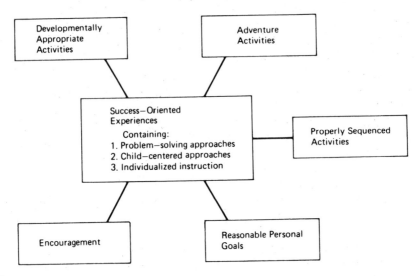

Figure 14.3
Five important factors to consider when using success-oriented experiences to enhance self-concept development.

Sequencing of Tasks

A third factor involved in using a success-oriented approach to enhancing self-concepts is understanding the sequencing and difficulty of a movement task. The proper sequencing of movement activities is crucial in determining a child's sense of success or failure. For example, a child should learn to do a handstand by first mastering, in order, a tripod, a frogstand, and a headstand. Too often, parents and teachers neglect to develop fundamental movement abilities before proceeding to higher level skills. Instead of looking at the development of movement skills from the point of view of the child, we look at movement from the perspective of a mature athlete. It is much better to begin at a lower level where a child's chances for experiencing success are greater, and then proceed to develop skill upon skill in a logical sequential progression. Success at the initial stages of learning will not only encourage continued performance but also will promote continued mastery attempts and generate success at later stages. Children who attempt difficult tasks without the proper basic skills may not succeed and may give up entirely. It is important that we analyze movement activities in which children engage and determine logical sequences for accomplishing them. Competition should not be

introduced too early in the learning process. Because competition determines winners and losers, it may be prematurely discouraging or overly encouraging. It is also a distraction from sound skill development. Postpone competitive situations until each child can make a sound appraisal of his or her ability and equate success with effort and skill rather than with winning or losing.

Reasonable Expectations

A fourth area in which we can influence a child's developing self is in helping him or her establish reasonable expectations of his or her abilities. Young children see the world in extremes: black or white, good or bad, right or wrong. It is important to help children develop attitudes about success based on personal goals rather than absolute scores. Children need to establish reasonable expectations for themselves. We help by offering goals that are challenging but commensurate with their skill levels and interests. For example, lowering the basket or reducing the size of the basketball will provide children with more opportunities for success than insisting on the use of a regulation ball and putting the standard at the regulation 10-foot height. When success is achieved, new goals need to be established to keep the activity challenging.

Adventure Activities

We can also have an impact on the self-concepts of children in the area of adventure challenge activities. Children need to experience the thrill of climbing, hanging, balancing, riding, and crawling through objects. They need the feeling of mastery that comes from succeeding at activities that require courage and imagination.

The teacher, by using voice inflection and stimulating the young child's imagination, can create an atmosphere of challenge and adventure. Imaginary obstacles may be put in the path of an activity. The balance beam can be transformed into a "narrow log" across a "shark-infested pond." Through adventure activities, both real and imagined, children learn more about their bodies and overcome challenges.

Encouragement

We influence a child's developing self-concept through communication of our expectations and support. We must describe how we feel about the child's accomplishments and potential. Praise and positive encouragement must be used judiciously because children will regard them as meaningless if overdone. We can communicate our feelings to children by praise for a job well done, with a pat on the back or a smile. We need to convey messages that "you are loved" and "you are worthwhile." Remember that it is often not so much what we say to children that influences their feelings about themselves as how we treat them. Children tend to value themselves to the degree that they are valued. The way we feel about children builds in (or builds out) self-confidence and a sense of self-worth. Children build their pictures of themselves from the words, attitudes, body language, and judgments of the significant others around them.

By providing children with a nurturing climate of acceptance and experiences of success, negative attitudes can be changed to high self-esteem. When we make a specific statement regarding inappropriate behavior, we should restrict our comments to the behavior instead of making generalized criticisms of the child as a person. For example, it is much better to say "I am concerned about your difficulties with sharing" rather than "nobody likes a stingy person." Similarly, it is dangerous to label children as "stupid," "bad," or "clumsy." They often believe the labels attached to them and inadvertently act out their expected roles. We should not link undesirable behavior with a personal lack of worth. We should not make children feel that they are personally worthless because their academic achievements or sports performances do not meet our expectations.

Devastating remarks have no place in teacher-child communication. The teacher's role is not to injure but to prevent injury and to heal. Encouragement in the development of one's movement skills and level of physical fitness plays an important role in helping children develop stable, positive self-concepts.

ASSESSING SELF-CONCEPT IN CHILDREN

Problems in accurately assessing self-concept have plagued psychologists for years. The validity of a vast majority of measures of self is questionable, and the reliability of the information is often subject to criticism. Despite these obvious limitations, a number of self-report measures have become available in recent years. The basic assumption underlying any self-report measure is that the respondent is the only individual qualified to reveal his or her feelings and that these responses provide an accurate and truthful indication of how that person feels.

CONCEPT 14.10

Encouragement, not unbridled praise, is an important facilitator of self-esteem enhancement as well as increased competence.

CONCEPT 14.11

A child's self-concept is difficult to measure or assess with scientific accuracy.

Numerous professionals have developed instruments that purport to measure self-concept in children. Most noteworthy are those assessments developed by Susan Harter and her colleagues (Harter, 1982b; Harter, 1985; Harter and Pike, 1984). Harter's instruments, in particular her "Self-Perception Profile for Children," attempt to measure not only a sense of a child's general self-worth but also specific domains such as scholastic competence, social acceptance, physical appearance, behavioral conduct, and athletic competence.

SUMMARY

Self-concept is an important aspect of the affective development of children. The concepts that children have of themselves are based on their self-perceptions and their perceptions of what others think of them. Their self-concepts are in the developmental stages and are profoundly influenced by their daily life experiences. Adults must encourage the development of positive and stable self-concepts in children, because once they are firmly established, they are difficult to change.

Because of the importance of vigorous play in the lives of children and the high value placed on physical ability by children and adults, movement serves as an important facilitator of a positive self-concept. Sound principles of growth and development must be adopted and followed to provide children with success-oriented experiences that minimize the failure potential. We must employ developmentally appropriate movement experiences that are within the ability level of the individual. We must be sure that new movement tasks are learned in the proper sequence, based on sound teaching progressions. We must also help children establish reasonable goals for performance within the limits of their abilities. We must be sure also to provide encouragement and to incorporate adventure activities into their lives. Although movement is only one avenue by which a positive self-concept may be fostered, we must recognize that it is important for most children.

CRITICAL READINGS

Ebbeck, V., & Weiss, M. R. (1998). Determinants of children's self-esteem: An examination of perceived competence and affect in sport. *Pediatric Exercise Science, 10,* 285–298.

Harter, S. (1999). *The Construction of the Self.* New York: Guilford.

Santrock, J. W. (2001). *Child Development* (Chapter 12). 9th ed. St. Louis: McGraw-Hill.

Weinberg, R. S., & Gould, D. (1999). *Foundations of Sport and Exercise Psychology* (Chapter 22). 2nd ed. Champaign, IL: Human Kinetics.

Weiss, M. R., Smith, A. L., & Theeboom, M. (1996). "That's what friends are for": Children's and teenagers' perceptions of peer relationships in the sport domain. *Journal of Sport & Exercise Psychology, 18,* 347–379.

WEB RESOURCES

A study of Erik Erikson's stages of psychosocial development
http://childstudy.net/erikson.html

Homepage for the journal *Development Psychology*
www.apa.org/journals/dev.html

North American Society for the Psychology of Sport and Physical Activity
www.naspspa.org

Society for Research in Child Development
www.srcd.org

Adolescence

Youth comes but once in a lifetime.
—Henry Wadsworth Longfellow

ADOLESCENCE

Peter A. Lee

Peter A. Lee, M.D., Ph.D., is professor of pediatrics and chief of the Division of Pediatric Endocrinology at Penn State University College of Medicine, Milton S. Hershey Medical Center, Hershey, Pennsylvania. He has held academic appointments at Johns Hopkins University and the University of Pittsburgh and served as the director for the clinical research centers at Johns Hopkins Hospital and Children's Hospital of Pittsburgh. Dr. Lee's primary research interests involve problems of human sexual and pubertal development.

What are the underlying changes of pubertal development that affect motor development?

These changes relate to an increase in body mass and to body composition changes, primarily skeletal and muscle growth. Boys have significantly greater skeletal muscle mass throughout childhood than girls do, but there is no difference between the sexes in muscle strength during early pubertal years, even though boys have higher testosterone levels and girls have progressed farther into pubertal development. Differences arise by the late teen years.

During puberty, with maturation of the reproductive-sexual system, there is dramatic somatic growth. Relative quantities of sex hormones impact overall growth. Estrogens, classically considered female hormones, have a major impact on bone growth, whereas androgens, traditional male hormones, have a greater impact on muscle development. Both sexes secrete and need both types of hormones, sex differences being one of relative quantity. While puberty among girls is primarily a consequence of estradiol (the most potent estrogen) stimulation, females also secrete androgens, which stimulate muscle growth. Conversely, while testosterone (the most potent androgen) stimulates male pubertal development, estrogen, present in relatively much smaller quantities, is necessary to complete skeletal maturation. Staging of puberty, categorizing a continuous process, allows categorization of estrogen effect (breast staging in girls) and androgen effect (genital staging in boys and pubic hair staging in both sexes).

Girls begin puberty (stage 2) earlier than boys. Because of this, with estrogen as the potent stimulator of skeletal growth, girls experience the pubertal growth spurt earlier than boys. An increase in muscle strength occurs after the growth spurt in height, while flexibility and speed peak before growth spurts. Greater flexibility during puberty is retained into adult life. This is not true for strength, which depends upon other factors, including exercise and fitness.

Somatic changes involve actual and relative increase in lean body mass (for example, muscle and bone). An increase in strength with age and pubertal development occurs for both sexes. Throughout childhood and thereafter, there is a relationship between cortical area of bone and muscle area. This relationship is similar before puberty for boys and girls. With puberty, muscle area becomes relatively great among boys. This is consistent with a greater relative influence of estrogen upon bone growth and androgen upon muscle development.

Childhood weight is predictive of adult bone mineral content, but not density. Hence, the determinants of growth are also determinants of skeletal size, but density of bone is related to other factors. Direct relationships exist between bone mineral density, body size, weight, fat mass, lean body mass, muscle strength, physical activity, and nutrition.

Recent studies suggest that puberty is beginning earlier among children than in past years. How does this affect motor development?

Although puberty is beginning earlier among some girls, it has not yet been determined that puberty is being completed at a younger age. In fact, current evidence suggests that the age of menarche and the attainment of full pubertal growth and development have not changed. Adequate data are not available to determine if the age of puberty is different among males. Thus, any changes in motor development would be a consequence of earlier sex hormone secretion.

An earlier onset of puberty would suggest changes in both agility and strength since earlier-maturing girls perform better at comparable ages than late-maturing girls. In terms of speed of movement, explosive strength, and static strength, early maturers perform better than late maturers during adolescence, but that difference is lost in early adulthood. In fact, explosive strength and functional strength becomes greater for late maturers.

ADOLESCENT GROWTH, PUBERTY, AND REPRODUCTIVE MATURITY

KEY TERMS

Puberty

Genotype

Phenotype

Adolescent growth spurt (circumpubertal period)

Peak height velocity

Pace of sexual maturation

Menarche

Ejaculation

Timing of puberty

Gonadotropic (GnRH) hormones

Estrogens

Tanner stages

Relative sterility of puberty

Secondary sex characteristics

Maturity assessment

CHAPTER COMPETENCIES

Upon completion of this chapter you should be able to:

- Describe and interpret the normal curve and displacement and velocity graphs of human growth
- Describe variations in biological maturity within and across genders
- Discuss characteristics of the adolescent growth spurt
- List and discuss factors associated with the onset of puberty
- Describe hormonal factors associated with the onset of puberty
- Distinguish between "puberty" and "reproductive maturity"
- Chart the sequence of events leading to reproductive maturation
- Discuss the concept of adolescent reproductive sterility
- List and describe how the stages of sexual maturation are used as a maturity assessment technique

KEY CONCEPT

The transition from childhood to adolescence is marked by a number of significant physical and cultural events that, in combination, contribute markedly to growth and motor development.

The period that makes up what we know as "adolescence" is affected by both biology and culture. It is affected by biology in that the end of childhood and the onset of adolescence are marked by the beginnings of sexual maturation. It is affected by culture in that the end of adolescence and the beginning of adulthood are marked by financial and emotional independence from one's family. As a result, the adolescent years have been reshuffled over time. In North American society today the period of adolescence is significantly longer than it was a hundred or even fifty years ago. The earlier onset of **puberty** (the start of sexual maturation) coupled with a longer period of dependence on family has caused us to view adolescence in a much broader perspective.

Secular trends in biological maturation over the past hundred years have dramatically lowered the average age of puberty. However, economic and sociocultural trends over that same period have dramatically extended the average age of adolescence beyond the "teen" years. Whereas adolescence used to span the years from about 13 to 18, sexual maturation now begins as early as age 8 and economic dependency may extend until age 20 or beyond.

CONCEPT 15.1

The period of adolescence has lengthened due to the combined effects of biology and culture.

Tremendous changes are occurring during adolescence. The adolescent growth spurt, the onset of puberty, and sexual maturation are the primary biological markers of adolescence. Each of these will be discussed in the sections that follow.

ADOLESCENT GROWTH

The onset of adolescence is marked by a period of accelerated somatic increases in both height and weight. The age of onset, duration, and intensity of this growth spurt is genetically based and will vary considerably from individual to individual. One's **genotype** (growth potential) establishes the boundaries for individual growth. However, an individual's **phenotype** (environmental conditions) will have a marked influence on the achievement of this growth potential.

CONCEPT 15.2

One's genotype controls the onset, duration, and intensity of the growth spurt, whereas one's phenotype influences growth potential.

An adolescent's genotype will play the determining role in linear body measures, skeletal maturation, sexual maturation, and body type. Final adult standing height, trunk, arm, and leg length are ultimately determined by genetic factors. Similarly, bone ossification, the onset of puberty, and how fat is distributed around the body are products of genotype. Each of these may be modified to a certain extent, but an individual cannot go beyond his or her inherited potential. On the other hand, the environment will influence how close one comes to his or her genetic potential. Such things as body weight, skinfolds, and circumferences are subject to significant modification.

CONCEPT 15.3

Secular trends in biological maturation have lowered the average age of puberty in North America.

Height

Because of the interaction of genotype with the environment, considerable variability in the growth process occurs among individuals during the adolescent period. However, a definite period of accelerated growth takes place at the end of childhood; this period is known by a variety of terms, including *adolescent growth spurt, period of preadolescent acceleration,* and *circumpubertal period.* This period of "growing like a weed" begins prior to sexual maturation; therefore, for our purposes, we will refer to it as the *adolescent growth spurt.*

CONCEPT 15.4

The adolescent growth spurt marks the first visual indicator of the onset of puberty.

The **adolescent growth spurt (circumpubertal period)** is a period that lasts about four and a half years. Males, on the average, begin their growth spurts around age 11, reach their **peak height velocity** by age 13, and taper off by age 15. Peak height velocity refers to the maximum annual rate of growth in height during the adolescent growth spurt. Females are about two years advanced, beginning their spurts around age 9, peaking in velocity at age 11, and tapering off by age 13 (Malina and Bouchard, 1991). It is not uncommon to show a one-year incremental gain in height during the period of peak velocity of 6 to 8 inches (15.2–20.3 cm) or more. Further growth continues at the end of the adolescent growth spurt but at a much slower rate. Males appear to reach their mature adult heights at around age 18. Females are reported to attain their maximum heights at around age 16 (Malina and Bouchard). These ages, however, are only approximate indicators of when maximum heights are attained. There is considerable variation among individuals in the attainment of maximum statures, and most growth studies cease when the research participants leave high school, preventing follow-up beyond the school years. Growth in stature frequently continues at a modest rate for both males and females several years beyond high school.

CONCEPT 15.5

The adolescent growth spurt lasts about four years, beginning in females about two years earlier than in males.

The adolescent growth spurt is highly variable from individual to individual. Some will have completed the process before others have begun. The results are clearly evident in the typical youth sport setting where "men" and "boys" are frequently grouped together with little or no accommodation for maturation variations. Remember, development is age-influenced but it is not age-dependent. Overreliance on chronological age as a guide for youth sport team selection is unwise and inconsistent with what we know about motor development and quality education. We must, therefore, use standards other than age for team selection.

Figure 15.1 provides a longitudinal view of the growth patterns of two individuals (the Gallahue children, David Lee and Jennifer). Annual height, weight, and girth measurements were taken from childhood through adolescence. Although a longitudinal view of only two individuals does not provide a complete picture of the growth process, figure 15.1 does provide us with a typical height distance curve of two individuals. Notice how at age 9, Jennifer, an average maturer, was taller than her brother was at that age, but how by age 10 David Lee was a full 4 inches (10.2 cm) taller than his sister at that age. Notice also that between age 9 and 11, David Lee (an early maturer) grew a full 10 inches (25.4 cm) in height, whereas his sister grew only by about 3 inches (7.6 cm) during the same period. Jennifer's adolescent growth spurt was at its greatest velocity between 11 and 12 years of age when she grew 3 inches (7.6 cm) before slowing down at menarche and plateauing by age 16. Similarly David Lee's velocity curve slowed down although he continued to make small annual incremental height gains to age 19.

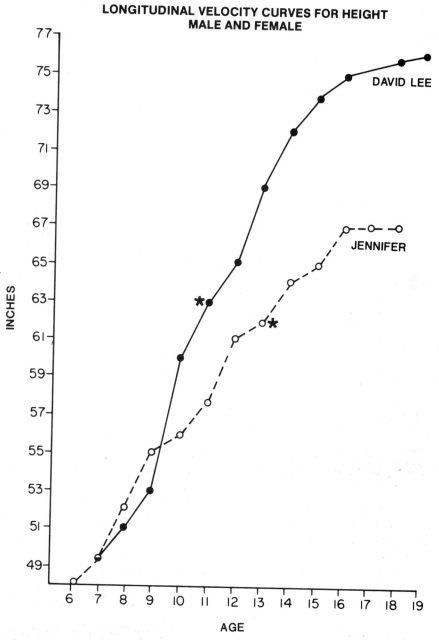

Figure 15.1

Longitudinal velocity curves for height for a single male and a single female from childhood through adolescence. (* = date of menarche for Jennifer, onset of axillary hair development for David Lee)

Events within the adolescent growth spurt are interdependent. For males the period of most rapid growth coincides with the appearance of secondary sex characteristics such as axillary and pubic hair. For females the peak velocity in growth tends to occur prior to menarche. Females with an early growth spurt tend to reach menarche earlier than those with a later growth spurt (Tanner, 1989). Furthermore, early-maturing girls and late-maturing boys are frequently thought to have more adjustment problems than their age-mates.

CONCEPT 15.6

Adult height can be predicted from adolescent growth data with reasonable accuracy.

The attainment of maximal adult height is of interest to most adolescents. Males are frequently concerned about being too short, and females often fret about being too tall. A number of prediction formulas are available, and mature adult height is correlated with height prior to the preadolescent growth spurt. Therefore, if a child was in the 50th percentile prior to puberty, he or she is likely to continue to be at the same percentile after puberty. Attainment of adult height is dominated by one's genotype, and under normal circumstances, only minimally influenced by the environment. (On the other hand, environmental factors strongly influence one's attained adult weight.)

Table 15.1 provides a percentile equivalent chart for height in inches/centimeters for males and females 12 to 17 years of age. This chart may be used to predict adult height and to determine an individual's percentile equivalent in comparison with other youth from the United States. For example, a male at the 25th percentile at age 12 (57.8 in./146.8 cm) will probably remain within that percentile and can expect to attain a height of about 67 inches (170 cm) by age 17. This would make him about 2 inches (5 cm) shorter than the average 17-year-old North American male (69.2 in./175.8 cm) and about 3 inches (7.6 cm) taller than the average North American female

TABLE 15.1 Height in Inches/Centimeters of Youths Aged 12–17 Years by Gender and Age at Last Birthday[1]

Gender and Age	Mean	Percentile						
		5th	10th	25th	50th	75th	90th	95th
MALES								
12 years	60.0/152.4	54.6/138.7	55.7/141.5	57.8/146.8	60.0/152.4	61.9/157.2	64.0/162.6	65.2/165.6
13 years	62.9/159.8	57.2/145.3	58.3/148.1	60.4/153.4	62.8/159.5	65.4/166.1	68.0/172.7	68.7/174.5
14 years	65.6/166.6	59.9/152.1	60.9/154.7	63.2/160.5	66.1/167.9	68.1/173.0	69.8/177.3	70.7/179.6
15 years	67.5/171.5	62.4/158.5	63.7/161.8	65.7/166.9	67.8/172.2	69.3/176.0	71.0/180.3	72.1/183.1
16 years	68.6/174.2	64.1/162.8	65.2/165.6	67.0/170.2	68.7/174.5	70.4/178.8	72.1/183.1	73.1/185.7
17 years	69.1/175.5	64.1/162.8	65.7/166.9	67.2/170.7	69.2/175.8	70.9/180.1	72.6/184.4	73.7/187.2
FEMALES								
12 years	61.1/155.2	55.8/141.7	57.4/145.8	59.5/151.1	61.2/155.4	63.0/160.0	64.6/164.1	65.9/167.4
13 years	62.5/158.8	57.8/146.8	58.9/149.6	60.7/154.2	62.6/159.0	64.4/163.6	66.0/167.6	66.9/169.9
14 years	63.5/161.3	59.6/151.4	60.5/153.7	61.9/157.2	63.5/161.3	65.2/165.6	66.7/169.4	67.4/171.2
15 years	63.9/162.3	59.6/151.4	60.3/153.2	62.0/157.5	63.9/162.3	65.8/167.1	67.2/170.7	68.1/173.0
16 years	64.0/162.6	59.7/151.6	60.7/154.2	62.4/158.5	64.2/163.1	65.6/166.6	67.2/170.7	68.1/173.0
17 years	64.1/162.8	60.0/152.4	60.9/154.7	62.3/158.2	64.3/163.3	65.9/167.4	67.4/171.2	68.1/173.0

[1]Source: Data from Height and Weight of Youths, 12-17 in *Vital and Health Statistics, 11,* No. 124 Series U.S. Public Health Service.

(64.3 in./163.3 cm). Conger and Peterson (1984) indicate that once an early maturer and a late-maturing age-mate pass the period of accelerated adolescent growth that "their comparative standings in height are most likely to return to those of preadolescence" (p. 94). The genetic influence on stature is strong and unless significant long-term changes are made in diet and lifestyle during the growing years there will be little variability from the predicted growth channel. Figures 10.1 and 10.3 (pp. 166 and 168) depict mean height for age scores for males and females from 2 to 20 years old using the latest data from the National Center for Health Statistics [NCHS] (2000).

Steroid use by adolescents during the growing years may have permanent effects on stature. Steroid use by prepubertal children may cause the epiphyses of the long bones to fuse prematurely (American College of Sports Medicine Position Statement on the Use and Abuse of Anabolic-Androgenic Steroids in Sports, 1987). Certain steroid products, however, have been safely prescribed by physicians for years to stimulate growth in males with uncomplicated short statures. Growth retardation, however, is seen in asthmatic children due to heavy usage of corticosteroid drugs to expand the bronchial passages. Further research is necessary to determine the long-term effects of steroid use on adolescent stature. The dosage, duration, and types of steroids used must be investigated before conclusions can be drawn.

CONCEPT 15.7

Steroid use for therapeutic and growth-enhancing purposes can affect the growth potential of the adolescent in as yet unexplained ways.

Weight

Weight changes during adolescence are great. For both males and females, increases in weight tend to follow the same general curves as for increases in height. Peak weight velocity, the period during the adolescent growth spurt when weight gain is the greatest, is generally greater in boys than in girls. Also, it appears that peak weight velocity occurs closer to peak height velocity in boys than in girls (Malina and Bouchard, 1991). Weight gain in adolescent males is primarily due to increases in height and muscle mass. Fat mass tends to remain relatively stable at this time. In females, however, adolescent weight gain is due largely to increases in fat mass and height, and to a lesser degree to increases in muscle mass. Skeletal maturation, increases in both muscle and fat tissue, and organ growth contribute to the weight gains of adolescence for both males and females.

CONCEPT 15.8

Weight gains during adolescence roughly approximate the curves for height, but weight is much more affected by environmental factors.

Overreliance on adolescent weight curves is unwise because weight reflects a combination of developmental events and as a result is limited in its information value. For example, failure to gain weight or actual loss of weight may be a reflection of an adolescent's increased attention to diet and exercise and not a cause for alarm. Failure to make incremental gains in height, however, would be a cause for concern. Weight gain throughout adolescence will be affected by diet, exercise, gastric motility, and general lifestyle factors as well as by hereditary factors. We know that youth in the United States have greater percentages of body fat than their counterparts of twenty years ago. This average higher body fat percentage has been attributed to the sedentary lifestyle and unhealthy eating patterns of many members of our society. Approximately 11 percent of adolescents (12 to 17 years) are reported to be overweight (85th percentile of weight for height), up from 5 percent in the 1960s and 1970s (Kipke, 1999).

By the age of 10, males have attained approximately 55 percent of their final adult weights, and females have attained 60 percent (National Center for Health Statistics [NCHS], 2000). Prior to age 10 the average weights of both males and females are almost identical, with males being only slightly heavier. However, during the adolescent growth spurt, females are frequently heavier than their male age-mates. Females tend to weigh more than males until about age 14 whereupon their weight gains begin to level off. Males, however, continue to make significant gains in weight until about age 22. Figures 10.2 and 10.4 (pp. 167 and 169) depict a definite secular trend in weight from childhood through adolescence for both males and females (NCHS, 2000).

The reasons for this include changes in the health and nutritional status of youth, socioeconomic factors, genetic factors, and changes in activity patterns. Whatever the case, weight is of considerable importance to the adolescent. The constant bombardment from the media and our obsession with the "perfect body" has raised the weight consciousness of the typical adolescent to the point of obsession. Care must be taken to help the adolescent understand the changing nature of his or her body and not to overstep the fine line between a healthy regard for weight control and an obsessive preoccupation with weight gain.

Heart and Lungs

The remarkable changes in height and weight are easily observed during adolescence, but what about other less apparent but equally important changes? Growth of the heart and lungs is dramatic and is a primary factor in the increased functional capacity of the adolescent.

The heart increases by about one-half in size and almost doubles in weight during adolescence (Malina and Bouchard, 1991). Females have slightly smaller hearts than males during childhood, begin accelerated growth of the heart earlier, and attain significantly smaller total growth by the end of adolescence. Although heart rate is related to overall body size, we see a gradual lowering of heart rate throughout the entire growth process. By age 10, male resting heart rates are on the average 3 to 5 beats per minute slower than those for females. By late adolescence, males have an average resting heart rate of 57 to 60 beats per minute, com-

pared with females at 62 to 63 beats per minute (Malina and Bouchard). Systolic blood pressure rises steadily throughout childhood and accelerates rapidly during puberty before settling down to its adult value by the later period of adolescence (Katchadourian, 1977).

Growth of the lungs parallels heart growth during adolescence. Both the size of the lungs and their respiratory capacity increase rapidly during puberty after a period of gradual growth during childhood. Respiration rates decrease throughout childhood and puberty for both males and females. However, *vital capacity* (the amount of air that can be inhaled with a single breath) increases much more rapidly in boys from about age 12 onward even though males and females are almost identical in this measure prior to puberty (Katchadourian, 1977). Dramatic gender differences may be attributed to the larger heart size and traditionally more aerobically active lifestyles of males.

Physical differences between males and females are just that—differences, and nothing else. For one to ascribe "superiority" or "inferiority" to one gender over the other on the basis of biological differences is absurd. On the other hand, those who deny the relevance of basic physical gender differences apart from reproductive functions are naive. Fundamental genetic differences between males and females are irrevocably established at conception and heightened during the adolescent period. Significant differences in height, weight, body proportions, and functional capacity of the heart and lungs can be expressed only in terms of population averages, and there is considerable overlap between the sexes. The only way in which males and females are truly unique is in reproductive functions. To understand this uniqueness we must understand the process of puberty and reproductive maturity.

PUBERTY

The onset of puberty is generally termed *pubescence.* Pubescence is the earliest period of adolescence, generally about two years in advance of sexual maturity. During pubescence secondary sex characteristics begin to appear, sex organs mature, changes in the endocrine system begin to occur, and the adolescent growth spurt begins. Adolescent females are considered to have delayed puberty when breast development (tanner stage 2) has not started by 13.3 years of age (Sperling, 1996). Medical texts have traditionally reported that only about 1 percent of girls show signs of puberty before age 8 (Kaplowitz and Oberfield, 1999). Recent research, however, has raised speculation that the onset of puberty is occurring earlier in girls than previous studies have shown. Based on examination of 17,000 girls (not randomly selected) by Herman-Giddens and colleagues (1997), it was concluded that

> In the United States the onset of puberty in girls is occurring earlier than previous studies have documented, with breast and pubic hair development appearing on average 1 year earlier in white girls and 2 years earlier in African-American girls. (Kaplowitz and Oberfield, p. 940)

Caution is advised in concluding that the normal age of puberty is earlier today than a generation ago (Rosenfield, 2000; Lee, Kulin, and Guo, 2001), primarily because the **pace of sexual maturation** leading to menarche has not changed since the 1960s in the United States.

CONCEPT 15.9

Menarche is the primary event of female puberty, but it does not mark reproductive maturity, which may be delayed by as much as two years.

The highlight of puberty in females is marked by a clearly distinguishable event, menarche. On the average, in the United States **menarche,** or the first menstrual flow, occurs at 12.1 and 12.9 in black and white girls, respectively (Brown et al., 1998). The reasons for this discrepancy are largely unknown. Black girls begin pubertal development (i.e., breast and pubic hair development) almost fifteen months earlier than their white peers, an interesting observation when one realizes that the

average age of menarche in the mid-1800s was age 15 (Malina, 1991). The development of mature ova follows menarche by as much as two years; therefore, puberty is not complete in females until sexual maturity has been attained.

The potential for delayed menarche and the hypothesized causes has been a topic of intense debate. Historically, it has been observed that as the intensity of physical training increases the age of menarche also increases, with the latest age of menarche found in the most elite performers (Stager, Robertshaw, and Miescher, 1984). This view is supported by retrospective data comparing the age of menarche of athletic and nonathletic samples, in which it has been found that the mean age of menarche in athletes is later than in their nonathletic counterparts (Malina, 1994).

Malina (1994) offers several explanations for the possibility of the later age of menarche in athletic samples. He suggests that late maturers are taller and leaner than early maturers and many sports select for these body build characteristics. Leanness in certain sports is often viewed as a desirable performance-related quality. Dietary practices incorporated to reduce body fat may be associated with delayed onset of menarche. Socialization factors, psychological and emotional stresses, family history, even the number of siblings in one's family (Malina et al., 1997) are possible factors in later onset of menarche.

Malina, however, is quick to point out most investigations in this area are subject to error due to their retrospective nature. Research participants in these studies must rely on their memories in reporting when they began menstruating. For some, those memories may be accurate. Others may be more vague in remembering when this event occurred. Malina also states that due to the standard deviations of a year or more in these investigations, they do not show that all female athletes experience late menarche.

The highlight of puberty in males is less distinct than it is for females. In a clinical sense, it is marked by the first **ejaculation** (the sudden discharge or ejection of semen), but, as with menarche, this milestone does not truly mark reproductive maturity. Only when live sperm are produced is reproductive maturity attained. Live sperm generally appear in boys between 13 and 16 years of age.

Sequence of Puberty

During the period of infancy and childhood, both boys and girls develop at highly similar rates. They have few differences in height, weight, and heart and lung size, and body composition is essentially the same. By age 10 children have attained about 80 percent of their adult height and a little over half of their adult weight. But as children begin their second decade, dramatic changes occur not only in measures of growth but in sexual maturation as well. The onset of puberty marks the transition from childhood to sexual adulthood. Exactly when this process begins and what starts the process is not clearly understood. We do know, however, that the timing of the process is highly variable and may begin as early as age 8 or earlier in females and age 9 in males, or as late as ages 13 and 15, respectively (Kipke, 1999). The general sequence of events that mark puberty is much more predictable than the specific dates on which they will occur.

Sequentially, for the male adolescent, growth spurt is preceded by testicular growth and coincides with enlargement of the penis. This is generally followed by the first appearance of pubic hair. *Axillary hair* (hair under the arms) formation soon follows, along with a deepening of the voice. Mature sperm formation and sexual maturation occur shortly after, followed by the appearance of facial hair and increased body hair.

The sequence of puberty for females is also predictable. There is a close correlation between the female growth spurt and breast development (Herman-Giddens et al., 1997). Budding of the nipples occurs prior to budding of the breasts. Breast bud development coincides with the beginning of pubic hair formation, followed by growth of the genitalia. Axillary hair formation and menarche soon occur, followed by the development of mature ova and the capacity for becoming pregnant. A tendency toward acne and slight deepening of the voice are the final events of female sexual maturation. Table 15.2 provides a visual representation of the sequence of events marking puberty and an approximate timetable. Many of the events of puberty overlap and should not be expected to occur in specific time frames.

Hormonal Influences

The onset of puberty may be influenced by a variety of factors, but genetics plays a dominant role. For example, southern Chinese females tend to achieve menarche earlier than females of European origin (Huen et al., 1997), and black females are ahead of whites (Brown et al., 1998). Furthermore, the events of puberty are much more closely related between identical twins than among nonidentical twins and nonrelated age-mates (Tanner, 1989). Factors within the environment may also have a dramatic impact on puberty. Although incompletely understood, stress, nutritional status, general health, and metabolism all appear to affect the onset and duration of puberty in some as yet unexplained manner. It is now clear that stress does not trigger puberty, but it does play an important role in modulating the **timing of puberty** (Susman et al., 1989; Susman, 1997).

CONCEPT 15.10

The onset of puberty is regulated by heredity and may be influenced by nutrition, illness, climate, and emotional stress.

The endocrine system plays a critical role in the growth and maturation process. Malina (1986) reports that "endocrine secretions are themselves strongly influenced by genetic mechanisms.... The nervous system, in turn, is intimately involved in regulating endocrine secretions" (p. 24). There appears to be a complex interaction among the endocrine system, the nervous system, and the gonads leading to puberty.

The pituitary gland, located below the brain, appears to be of critical importance. When the *hypothalamus* (a central regulating nerve center in the brain) matures, it secretes hormones that in

TABLE 15.2 **Sequence of Events Marking Puberty**

Males	Females	Approximate Age of Onset
First testicular growth	Beginning of growth spurt	9–10
	Budding of nipples	10–11
Beginning of growth spurt	Budding of breasts	11–12
Start of pubic hair growth	Start of pubic hair growth	
	Growth of genitalia	
	Peak of growth spurt	12–13
	Axillary hair formation	
	Menarche	
Penile and testicular peak of growth spurt		13–14
Axillary hair formation	Mature ova production	14–15
Deepened voice	(End of puberty)	
Mature sperm production	Acne	15–16
(End of puberty)	Deeper voice	
	Mature pubic hair & breast development	
Facial hair	Cessation of skeletal growth	16–17
Body hair		
Mature pubic hair development		
Cessation of skeletal growth		18–19

turn stimulate the anterior pituitary gland to begin releasing **gonadotropic (GnRH) hormones**. The hormones released by the anterior pituitary gland have a stimulating effect on other endocrine glands, resulting in the release of other growth and sex hormones. The release of sex-related hormones initiates maturation of the gonads. **Estrogens** (female hormones) account for initiation of the events of female puberty. In summary, multiple factors influence the onset and duration (i.e., pace) of puberty including: (1) genetic and biological influences, (2) stress, (3) nutrition, (4) diet, (5) exercise, (6) percent body fat, (7) chronic illness, (8) socioeconomic status, and (9) environmental toxins. To date, however, the precise triggers are still unknown (Kipke, 1999; American Academy of Pediatrics, 2000), but the outcome is clearly modulated by secretion of GnRH. In a recently revised policy statement by the American Academy of Pediatrics (2000, p. 612) it was concluded that: "Amenorrhea should not be considered a normal response to exercise." Furthermore, menstrual dysfunction may be associated with decreased bone mineral density.

REPRODUCTIVE MATURITY

The onset of the preadolescent growth spurt and puberty marks the transition from childhood to reproductive maturity. The physical changes and appearance of secondary sex characteristics are frequently a cause for heightened interest in one's body and a dramatically increased level of self-consciousness. If young adolescents appear preoccupied with matters of sex, it is because a whole host of dramatic and rapid changes are occurring right before their eyes. The young adolescent frequently feels like a spectator in his or her growth process. Each day seems to bring about changes that are whispered about, giggled over, and closely scrutinized. The wise adult will be sensitive to these physical changes and the impact that they have on the social and emotional development of the individual. The journey from childhood to reproductive maturity follows a predictable pattern for both males and females. The student of motor development will want to be knowledgeable about these events and will learn to recognize physical changes that offer cues to physical maturity. Many of these have been discussed in the previous sections on growth and puberty. This section will, therefore, focus on a brief overview of sexual maturation in females and males, and a reliable technique for maturational assessment.

In the paragraphs that follow, we will repeatedly refer to the work of J. M. Tanner. Although over forty years old, the **Tanner stages** are still used as the universal standard for classifying sexual maturity.

Females

Breast growth marks the first visible sign of the female journey to sexual maturity. *Breast development* begins around age 11 and is completed around age 15, although it may begin as early as age 8 and not end until age 18 (Katchadourian, 1977; Sperling, 1996). Breast development has been described by Tanner (1962) and is outlined in table 15.3, along with female pubic hair development. These stages can be useful as reliable developmental landmarks of sexual maturity.

Pubic hair is usually the second sign of progress toward sexual maturity. On the average, hair growth begins between 11 and 12 years of age, and the triangular adult pattern of growth is established by about age 14. The stages of pubic hair development developed by Tanner (1962) provide useful indices of sexual development.

Changes in the *female genitalia* are usually the third step in progress toward reproductive maturity. The external sex organs (i.e., the vulva, mons, labia, and clitoris) increase in size and become sensitive to stimulation. Changes in a female's exterior genitalia are not as useful for clinically assessing maturity as indices of pubic hair growth and breast development. The internal sex organs of the female also undergo considerable change. The uterus and ovaries increase in weight. The uterus makes dramatic weight gains, becomes larger, and "develops an intricate and powerful musculature" (Katchadourian, 1977, p. 59). The vagina increases in size, and the ovaries, although structurally complete at birth, continue to moderately gain weight throughout adolescence.

Menarche occurs after the peak of the growth spurt and about two years after the start of breast development, but it does not mark the beginning of reproductive maturity. Generally, up to 1.5 years may pass from the first menstrual cycle until the young female is physiologically capable of

TABLE 15.3	Stages in Female Breast and Pubic Hair Development	
Breast Development		**Pubic Hair Development**
STAGE		
1. Prepubertal—Flat appearance like that of a child		Prepubertal—Absence of pubic hair
2. Small raised breast bud		Sparse amount of downy hair mainly at sides of the labia
3. Enlargement and raising of the breast and areola		Increased amount of hair with pigmentation, coarsening, and curling
4. Areola and nipple form a contour separate from the breast		Adult hair, but limited in area
5. Adult breast—areola is in the same contour as the breast		Adult hair with horizontal upper border

Source: Adapted from photographs in J. M. Tanner, *Growth at Adolescence* (Oxford, England: Blackwell Scientific, 1962).

conception. This lag is known as the period of **relative sterility of puberty.** It is, however, unwise to assume that this is a "safe" period from conception. Individual differences between menarche and reproductive maturity are great, and no safe period can be guaranteed.

Males

Puberty begins in males with growth of the testes. Increased testicular growth begins around 11.5 years of age and may range from ages 10 to 14 (Tanner, 1962). Growth continues until somewhere between ages 14 and 18 (Katchadourian, 1977). As the male reproductive gland, the testes produce *sperm* and male sex hormones. The ability of the male to ejaculate seminal fluid is largely a function of the prostate gland, which becomes much larger during puberty. Ejaculation is a psychological as well as a physiological event and occurs most frequently in the young male through nocturnal seminal emissions and masturbation beginning at about age 12. Clearly this increase in sexual behavior is associated with rising levels of testosterone. Mature sperm are not contained in the ejaculate until approximately ages 15 to 17.

CONCEPT 15.11

The ability to ejaculate seminal fluid is a primary event of male puberty, but reproductive maturity requires mature sperm production.

Pubic hair growth begins as early as age 10 or as late as 15. As with female sexual maturation, Tanner (1962) developed a five-stage scale for males (table 15.4). Mature, stage 5, pubic hair distribution continues into the mid-20s in males, and the area is less clearly defined than in females. It has been noted that the use of pubic hair alone for Tanner staging may lead to inaccurate classification of some males in the earliest phase of pubertal maturation. There may be testicular development without the presence of pubic hair (Biro et al., 1995).

The *external male genitalia,* the penis and scrotum, change little in appearance throughout childhood. Penis growth begins about a year after the first onset of testicular and pubic hair growth. The scrotum first becomes larger, followed by lengthening and then thickening of the penis. See table 15.4 for the stages of male genital development described by Tanner (1962). The size and

TABLE 15.4 Stages in Male Genital and Pubic Hair Development

Genital Development	Pubic Hair Development
STAGE	
1. Prepubertal—Size of testes and penis like that in early childhood	Prepubertal—Absence of pubic hair
2. Testes enlarge and scrotal skin darkens and becomes coarse	Sparse amount of downy hair mainly at the base of the penis
3. Continuation of stage 2, along with increase in penis length	Increased amount of hair with pigmentation, coarsening, and curling
4. General enlargement in penis size and scrotal skin pigmentation	Adult hair, but limited in area
5. Adult genitalia	Adult hair with spread to the thighs and horizontal upper border

Source: Adapted from photographs in J. M. Tanner, *Growth at Adolescence* (Oxford, England: Blackwell Scientific, 1962).

shape of a male's penis is unrelated to physique, race, and virility (Masters and Johnson, 1970).

Secondary sex characteristics such as axillary hair, facial hair, and deepening of the voice are all associated with progress toward reproductive maturity. Axillary and facial hair usually begin to appear about two years after the growth of pubic hair. Facial hair, an important "badge" of manhood, first appears on the upper lip. It then starts to grow on the upper cheek in an area parallel with the lower ear, and then under the lower lip. In the final stage, facial hair growth spreads to the lower face and chin, creating a full beard (Katchadourian, 1977). Axillary hair appears in concert with facial hair, and body hair continues to spread until well after puberty.

Maturity Assessment

A **maturity assessment** is a means of determining how far one has progressed toward physical maturation. A variety of techniques, including circumpubertal, skeletal, and dental assessments, measure the progress of a particular body part or system toward maturity. Unfortunately, these maturity assessments are seldom used in routine preparticipation physical examinations of young athletes. The omission is unfortunate because young athletes could be more fairly equated for competition. Chronological age is the most frequently used measure of maturity. Throughout this text we have continually referred to the individuality and extreme variability of the growth process, particularly during later childhood and early adolescence. Although existing maturity assessments are expensive, time consuming, and inconvenient, developmental standards based on factors other than chronological age should be used to assess and place young athletes. Some process of equating youth for participation and competition should be

devised to reduce the incidence of athletic injuries by equalizing competition (Malina, 2000).

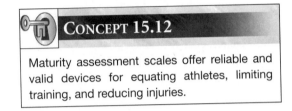

CONCEPT 15.12

Maturity assessment scales offer reliable and valid devices for equating athletes, limiting training, and reducing injuries.

Caine and Broekhoff (1987) presented a convincing argument for including a standardized maturity assessment in the preparticipation physical examination that every youth should undergo prior to sports participation. They argued that maturity assessments can be used to match adolescents for contact sports, and to determine when youth are experiencing growth spurts, which make them more susceptible to injury. They further argued that the stages of circumpubertal maturation proposed by Tanner (1962) can be easily and effectively used. To accommodate social-cultural mores and avoid embarrassment, parents can be asked to assess the circumpubertal maturity of their children or young athletes can rank their maturity levels with reference to the pubic hair scales. Duke et al. (1980) and Kreipe and Gewanter (1983) reported moderate to high correlations between self-assessed stages and physician-assessed stages of pubic hair development.

The benefits of maturity assessment are obvious. First, it can aid in injury reduction, serving as a basis for matching athletes for contact sports. Second, it can serve as a means of limiting or disqualifying individuals for participation in contact sports. Third, it can be used to identify rapid growth periods and to justify reductions in training regimens in long-term, high-intensity sports such as cross-country, swimming, gymnastics, and ballet.

SUMMARY

The period of adolescence has gradually expanded due to biological and cultural factors to the point where it now encompasses the child's second decade. Dramatic growth increments, the onset of puberty, and

reproductive maturation are highlights of the adolescent period.

Adolescent growth in height and weight follows a predictable pattern, although there is considerable variability in the onset and duration of the preadolescent growth spurt. Wide variations in stature are typical among preadolescents and have many ramifications for athletic participation and social acceptance.

The onset of puberty is generally considered to coincide with the start of the growth spurt. Puberty is influenced by a variety of genetic factors operating in concert with environmental circumstances.

Puberty and reproductive maturity are not the same thing. Reproductive maturity occurs somewhat after the onset of puberty. Menarche in females and ejaculation in males do not indicate the arrival of reproductive maturity. The development of mature ova and the production of sperm are the hallmarks of reproductive maturity.

Maturity assessments can be used as an effective aid for equating young athletes for competition and reducing the risk of injury. Circumpubertal assessment measures, although not without difficulties, are reliable and valid means of determining maturity levels.

CRITICAL READINGS

American Academy of Pediatrics (2000). Medical concerns in the female athelete. *Pediatrics, 106,* 610–613. (revised policy statement).

Katchadourian, H. (1977). *The Biology of Adolescence.* San Francisco: W. H. Freeman.

Kipke, M. (Ed.). (1999). *Adolescent Development and the Biology of Puberty: A Summary of a Workshop on New Research.* Washington, DC: National Academy of Sciences.

Malina, R. M. (1984). Menarche in athletes: A synthesis and hypothesis. *Annals of Human Biology, 10,* 1–24.

Malina, R. (2000). Matching youth in sport by maturity status. *Spotlight on Youth Sports, 22*(4), 1–4.

Malina, R. M., & Bouchard, C. (1991). *Growth Maturation and Physical Activity* (Chapters 16 & 17). Champaign, IL: Human Kinetics.

Rosenfield, R. V. (2000). Current age of onset of puberty. *Pediatrics, 106,* 622–623.

Spurling, M. A. (Ed.). (1996). *Pediatric Endocrinology.* Philadelphia: W. B. Saunders.

WEB RESOURCES

Centers for Disease Control and Prevention: National growth charts
www.cdc.gov/growthcharts/

Information on puberty from the American Academy of Pediatrics
www.aap.org/family/puberty.htm

Various topics related to puberty
www.keepkidshealthy.com/adolescent/puberty.html

CHAPTER 16

SPECIALIZED MOVEMENT ABILITIES

KEY TERMS

Specialized movement skills
Proficiency barrier
Transition stage
Application stage
Lifelong utilization stage
Cognitive stage
Associative stage
Autonomous stage
Getting the idea stage
Fixation/diversification stage
Beginning/novice level
Awareness stage
Exploratory stage
Discovery stage
Intermediate/practice level
Combination stage
Advanced/fine-tuning level
Performance stage
Individualized stage

CHAPTER COMPETENCIES

Upon completion of this chapter you should be able to:

- Discuss the relationship between fundamental movement skills and specialized movement skills
- Describe the steps in changing a well-learned but improperly performed movement technique
- Demonstrate knowledge of important characteristics of the learner that will affect your interaction as an instructor
- Discuss the effects of athletic competition on growth and development of children and adolescents
- Describe knowledge about the developmental sequence of specialized movement skills
- Describe the process of learning a new movement skill based on both the cognitive state of the learner and the goals of the learner
- Demonstrate knowledge of how to intervene effectively in the learning process based on one's level of movement skill learning
- Demonstrate knowledge of the concept of fostering improvement through movement control, emotional control, and learning enjoyment

KEY CONCEPT

The development of specialized movement skills is highly dependent upon opportunities for practice, encouragement, quality instruction, and the ecological context of the environment.

Specialized movement skills are mature fundamental movement patterns that have been refined and combined to form sport skills and other specific and complex movement skills. Specialized movement skills are task specific, but fundamental movements are not.

Most children have the potential by about age 6 to perform at the mature stage of most fundamental movement patterns and to begin the transition to the specialized movement phase. Neurological makeup, anatomical and physiological characteristics, and visual perceptual abilities are sufficiently developed to function at the mature stage in most fundamental movement skills. There are a few exceptions to this generalization—striking a moving object and volleying, because of the sophisticated perceptual-motor requirements of these tasks. However, many adolescents lag in their movement capabilities because of limited opportunities for regular practice, poor or absent instruction, and little or no encouragement. We are all familiar with teens and adults who throw balls at the elementary stage or jump for distance using movement patterns characteristic of a typical 2- or 3-year-old child. Older children, adolescents, and adults should be able to perform fundamental movements at the mature stage. Failure to develop mature forms of fundamental movements has direct consequences on an individual's ability to perform task-specific skills at the specialized movement phase. Successful progression through the transition, application, and lifelong utilization stages in a particular movement task depends on mature levels of performance at the fundamental movement phase (figure 16.1). A person could hardly expect to be successful at softball if his or her fundamental striking, throwing, catching, or running abilities were not at mature levels. There is a hypothesized **proficiency barrier** (Seefeldt, 1980) between the fundamental movement phase and the specialized movement phase of development. The transition from one phase to another depends on the application of mature patterns of movement to a wide variety of movement skills. If the patterns are less than mature, ability will be impaired.

CONCEPT 16.1

Mature fundamental movement development is prerequisite to successfully incorporating corresponding specialized movement skills into one's movement repertoire.

This chapter focuses on the specialized movement skill phase of development. Two important points should be kept in mind. First, even though a person may be cognitively and affectively ready to advance to this phase, progression depends on successful completion of specific aspects of the previous phase. Second, progress from one phase to another is not an all-or-none proposition. One is not required to be at the mature stage in all fundamental movements before advancing to subsequent stages. Although a 14-year-old who specialized early in gymnastics may be performing at highly sophisticated levels in several locomotor and stability movements, she may not be able to throw, catch, or kick a ball with the proficiency expected for her age and developmental level. So too, a high school football player may be an adept lineman or running back, but unable to enjoy the aerobic benefits of swimming, basketball, or soccer because of failure to develop the requisite fundamental movement skills.

DEVELOPMENTAL SEQUENCE OF SPECIALIZED MOVEMENTS

After the child has achieved the mature stage in a particular fundamental movement pattern, little change occurs in the "form" of that movement

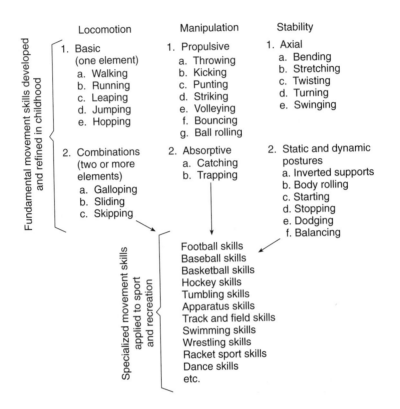

Figure 16.1

Mature fundamental movement skills should be mastered prior to the introduction of specialized movement skills.

ability during the specialized movement phase. Refinement of the pattern and stylistic variations in form occur as greater skill (precision, accuracy, and control) is achieved, but the basic pattern remains unchanged. However, dramatic improvements in performance based on increased physical abilities may be seen from year to year. As the adolescent improves in strength, endurance, reaction time, speed of movement, coordination, and so forth, we can expect to see improved performance scores. Chapters 12 and 17 provide detailed discussions of the physical abilities of children and adolescents, respectively. One is led to the conclusion that there is a link between skillful movement and physical activity levels. It has been documented that there is steady decline in vigorous physical activity among males and females from age 12 onward (CDC, 1992). Certainly, some of this decline

is due to the lack of physical education programs, in quantity and quality. A recent CDC report (CDC, 2000) indicates that only 19 percent of high school students are physically active for 20 minutes or more, five days a week, in physical education classes.

Within the specialized phase, there are three separate but often overlapping stages. The onset of stages during this phase of development depends on neuromuscular, cognitive, and affective factors within the individual. Specific factors within the task and the individual as well as conditions within the environment stimulate movement from one stage to another.

A person's fundamental movement patterns are little changed after they reach the mature stage, and physical capabilities influence only the extent to which specialized movement skills are acted out in sport, recreational, or daily living situations. Therefore, specialized movement skills are mature fundamental movements that have been adapted to the specific requirements of a sport, recreational, or daily living activity. The extent to which these abilities are developed depends on a combination of conditions within the task, the individual, and the environment.

A key to successful teaching at the specialized movement skill phase, whether the students are skilled adolescents or unskilled adults, is recognizing conditions that may limit or enhance development. Once these conditions have been identified for each individual, teaching becomes more a matter of reducing the constraints (limiting conditions) and maximizing the affordances (enhancing conditions) than simply stressing mechanically "correct" execution of the skill. The three stages within the specialized movement phase are outlined next.

CONCEPT 16.2

Progress through the stages within the specialized movement skill phase depends on the foundation of movement patterns previously established during the fundamental movement phase.

Transition Stage

The **transition stage** is characterized by the individual's first attempts to refine and combine mature movement patterns. With children, there is heightened interest in sport and standards of performance. Children generally enjoy pitting their developing movement skills against those of others. During this stage children are attracted to several different types of sports and do not feel limited by physiological, anatomical, or environmental factors. Leaders begin to emphasize accuracy and skill in the performance of games, lead-up activities, and a wide variety of sport-related movements. During this stage the individual works

at "getting the idea" of how to perform the sport skill. Skill and proficiency are limited.

Application Stage

During the **application stage** the individual becomes more aware of personal physical assets and limitations and, accordingly, focuses on certain types of sports. Emphasis is on improving proficiency. Practice is the key to developing higher degrees of skill. The movement patterns characteristic of the beginner during the transition stage smooth out. More complex skills are refined and are used in official sports and designated recreational activities for both leisure and competition.

Lifelong Utilization Stage

In the **lifelong utilization stage** individuals reduce the scope of their athletic pursuits by choosing a few activities to engage in regularly in competitive, recreational, or daily living settings. Further specialization and skill refinement occur in this "fine-tuning" stage. Lifetime activities are chosen on the basis of personal interests, abilities, ambitions, availability, and past experiences. Opportunities to participate are limited in this stage because of increased responsibilities and time commitments.

Many individuals do not go through the development and refinement of specialized movement skills in the sequence presented. Children are often encouraged to refine their skills in a particular sport at an early age. Early participation in sports is not detrimental, but premature specialization may have a high cost. The development of a broad range of mature fundamental movement patterns could be sacrificed, thereby limiting the potential for participation in a wide variety of activities.

YOUTH SPORT

Under ideal conditions, the transitional movement skill stage begins around ages 7 or 8. With their growing interest in performance capabilities and sport, increasing cognitive sophistication, and improved group interaction children are more attracted to organized competition. The growth in youth sport participation over the past twenty-five years has been phenomenal. An estimated 20 to 35 million children in the United States participate in youth sports (Poinsett, 1996). Nearly every community in the sample group provided some form of competitive activity for youth. It would be hard to find any sizable community in North America today that does not provide competitive sport experiences for its youth outside the school setting as well as school-sponsored programs. Youth sport is big, it is popular, and it is here to stay.

CONCEPT 16.3

Sport participation is important to millions of children and adolescents, who need competent leadership and developmentally appropriate experiences.

Youth sport can have detrimental as well as beneficial effects, all of which have been fully discussed over the years. See the *American Sport Education Program: ASEP* (Human Kinetics, 2002) and the American Academy of Pediatrics position statement on organized sports for children and preadolescents (Washington, et al., 2001) for highly practical sources of information. Sport allows individuals at the transition and application stages to improve their skills and get plenty of vigorous physical activity in competitive situations. Competitive sport, however, should not be regarded as the only skill outlet for children. Noncompetitive and leisure-time activities such as hiking, canoeing, fishing, jogging, and the like, as well as various forms of cooperative recreation and dance, are also beneficial for youth. Tables 16.1 through 16.9 provide an overview of several sport skills and the var-

ious fundamental locomotor, manipulative, and stability movements involved in the performance of these skills.

Knowing the Learner

It is vitally important for you as a parent, teacher, coach, or therapist to know your learners and to recognize that each comes to you with a different set of physical, mental, emotional, and social capabilities. You must accommodate an awesome number of individual differences when planning skill learning and practice sessions. Some of these individual differences are easy to detect, others are not. However, it is to your advantage to be aware of as many factors as possible. The following are important points to remember:

- People learn at different rates.
- Each person's potential for performance excellence is unique.
- Fundamental movement and perceptual-motor abilities should be mastered before the specialized skill is attempted.
- Responses to instructional approaches vary among learners.
- Responses to winning and losing vary among individuals.
- Responses to praise and criticism, reward and punishment, vary among individuals.
- Former experiences vary among individuals.
- Variations in home-life experiences influence people differently.
- Strengths in some areas can compensate for deficiencies in other areas.
- Attention spans and concentration abilities vary among individuals.
- The developmental levels of individuals vary, resulting in dissimilar potential for learning and performance.
- There is no uniformity in the physical potential of individuals (particularly during the preteen and early teenage years).
- Individuals display greater or lesser degrees of both gross and fine motor skills depending on a variety of environmental factors as well as inherited and biological factors.

CONCEPT 16.4

It is essential for the instructor to know the learner in order to make a difference in motor development and movement skill learning.

TABLE 16.1	Basketball Skills		
Fundamental Movements	**Specialized Movement Skills**		
MANIPULATION			
• Passing	—Chest pass		—Shovel pass
	—Overhead pass		—Push pass
	—Baseball pass		
• Shooting	—Lay-up shot		—Jump shot
	—Two-hand set shot		
• Bouncing	—Stationary dribbling		—Bounce pass
	—Moving dribbling		
• Catching	—Pass above the waist		—Rebounding
	—Pass below the waist		—Pass to the side
			—Jump ball reception
• Volleying	—Tipping		
	—Center jump		
LOCOMOTION			
• Running	—In different directions while dribbling		
	—In different directions without ball		
• Sliding	—Guarding while dribbling		
• Leaping	—Lay-up shot		
	—Pass interception		
• Jumping	—Center jump		—Rebounding
	—Tip-in		—Catching a high ball
STABILITY			
• Axial movements	—Pivoting		
	—Bending		
• Dynamic balance	—Compensation for rapid changes in direction, speed, and level of movement		
• Dodging	—Feinting with the ball		

- The ability to analyze, conceptualize, and solve problems varies among individuals.

Cues to Teaching a New Movement Skill

When teaching a new movement skill the instructor will find it beneficial to do the following:

- Identify the type of skill (i.e., open or closed; gross or fine; discrete, serial, or continuous; and stability, locomotor, or manipulative).

- Establish a practice environment consistent with the nature of the skill.
- Introduce externally paced activities under internally paced conditions first (i.e., control the environment and conditions of skill practice first).
- Introduce situations that require responses to sudden and unpredictable cues in externally paced activities as skill develops.
- Strive for greater consistency, duplication, and elimination of environmental

TABLE 16.2 **Contemporary Dance Skills**

Fundamental Movements	Specialized Movement Skills
LOCOMOTION • Walking • Running • Leaping • Jumping • Hopping • Galloping • Sliding • Skipping	—Contemporary dance is a movement form that uses a movement vocabulary specific to the particular creative effort being expressed. The choreographer uses movement as a vehicle of expression. Therefore, fundamental locomotor and stability movements serve as the means for conveying concepts and ideas.
STABILITY • Axial movements • Static and dynamic balance	—Bending, stretching, twisting, turning, reaching, lifting, falling, curling, pushing, pulling —Numerous balance skills requiring synchronizing rhythm and proper sequencing of movement

TABLE 16.3 **Football Skills**

Fundamental Movements	Specialized Movement Skills	
MANIPULATION		
• Throwing	—Forward pass —Centering	—Lateral
• Kicking	—Place kick —Punting	—Field-goal kicking
• Catching	—Pass above the waist —Pass below the waist —Pass at waist level	—Over the shoulder —Across the midline —Hand-off
• Carrying	—Fullback carry —One-arm carry	
LOCOMOTION		
• Running	—Ball carrying —Pursuit of ball carrier	
• Sliding • Leaping and jumping	—Tackling —Pass defense	—Blocking —Pass reception
STABILITY		
• Axial movements	—Blocking —Tackling	
• Static and dynamic balance	—Blocking —Stances —Dodging a tackle	—Rolling —Pushing

TABLE 16.4 Softball/Baseball Skills		
Fundamental Movements	**Specialized Movement Skills**	
MANIPULATION		
• Throwing	—Overhand throw for accuracy	
	—Overhand throw for distance	
	—Underhand toss	
	—Overhand pitch	
	—Underhand pitch	
• Catching	—Above-waist ball	—Grounder
	—Below-waist ball	—Across midline
	—Fly ball	—Line drive
• Striking	—Batting	
	—Bunting	
LOCOMOTION		
• Running	—Base running	
	—Fielding	
• Sliding	—Fielding	
	—Base sliding	
• Leaping	—Base running	—Fielding
• Jumping	—Fielding	
STABILITY		
• Axial movements	—Batting	
	—Fielding	
	—Pitching	
• Dynamic balance	—Compensation for rapid changes in direction, speed, and level of movement	

influences for internally paced activities as skill develops.
- Encourage the learner to "think through" the activity in the early stages of learning.
- Encourage the learner to screen out unnecessary cues as skill develops.
- Know and respect the cognitive state of the learner as well as his or her learning goals.

LEVELS AND STAGES OF MOVEMENT SKILL LEARNING

The sequential progression in the learning of a new movement skill may be classified into general levels or stages. Fitts and Posner (1967) proposed a three-stage model for movement skill learning that centers on the cognitive state of the individual along the learning continuum. Gentile (1972) proposed a

TABLE 16.5   Soccer Skills

Fundamental Movements	Specialized Movement Skills	
MANIPULATION		
• Kicking	—Instep kick	—Inside of foot kick
	—Toe kick	—Outside of foot kick
	—Heel kick	—Dribbling
	—Corner kick	—Passing
	—Goal kick	—Goalie punt
• Striking	—Heading	
	—Juggling	
• Catching	—Goalie skills	
• Throwing	—Throw-in	
	—Goalie throw	
• Trapping	—Sole	
(Collecting)	—Double-knee	
	—Stomach	
	—Single-knee	
	—Chest	
LOCOMOTION		
• Running	—With ball	
	—Without ball	
• Jumping and leaping	—Heading	
• Sliding	—Marking	
STABILITY		
• Axial movements	—Goalie skills	
	—Field play skills	
• Dynamic balance	—Marking	
	—Dodging opponent	
	—Feinting with ball	

two-stage model based on the goals of the learner. Gallahue and colleagues' (1972, 1975) three levels model with accompanying substages incorporates elements from both Fitts and Posner and Gentile, but also proposes specific responsibilities for the instructor (i.e., parent, teacher, coach, therapist) along the learning continuum. The following paragraphs provide a brief look at each model.

CONCEPT 16.5

Movement skill learning is an age-independent process that follows a predictable sequence of stages that identify the cognitive state and the learning goals of the individual along the learning continuum.

TABLE 16.6 Track and Field Skills

Fundamental Movements	Specialized Movement Skills	
MANIPULATION		
• Throwing	—Shot put	Hammer
	—Discus	
	—Javelin	
LOCOMOTION		
• Running	—Dashes	—Pole-vault approach
	—Middle distances	—High-jump approach
	—Long distances	—Long-jump approach
• Leaping takeoff	—Low hurdles	—Running long-jump
	—High hurdles	—Pole-vault takeoff
• Jumping	—High jump	
	—Long jump	
• Vertical jump	—High jump	
STABILITY		
• Axial movements	—Pivoting and twisting (shot put, discus, javelin, and hammer)	
• Dynamic balance	—Compensation for rapid changes in speed, direction, and level of movement	

Fitts and Posner's Three Stages of Skill Learning

Fitts and Posner (1967) were the first to propose that learning a new movement skill occurs in stages. Their three-stage model still forms the basis for research today (Magill, 2001). Fitts and Posner viewed movement skill learning from the standpoint of the cognitive state of the learner and contend that the learner gradually progresses along a continuum of change from the *cognitive stage,* to the *associative stage,* and finally to the *autonomous stage.*

During the **cognitive stage,** the learner tries to form a conscious mental plan for performing the skill. For example, an individual learning how to snowboard down a mountain slope might ask the following questions: "How do I stand on the board without falling?"; "What do I do when my board starts to slide downhill?"; "Where is my balance point?"; "How do I change directions?"; and most importantly, "How do I stop?"

The second stage is called the **associative stage** because at this point the learner is able to make conscious use of environmental cues and associate them to the requirements of the movement task. Our snowboarder, for example, is now able to associate changes in the boards speed and direction with the slope of the hill, the conditions of the snow, and the angle of the board.

During the **autonomous stage** performance of the movement task becomes habitual with little or no conscious attention given to the elements of the task during performance. At this stage our snowboarder streaks down the mountain, deftly

TABLE 16.7 **Racquet Sport Skills**

Fundamental Movements	Specialized Movement Skills	
MANIPULATION		
• Striking	—Forehand shot —Backhand shot —Overhead shot —Sweep	—Lob shot —Smash —Corner shot —Drop shot
LOCOMOTION		
• Running	—Net rush —Ball retrieval	
• Sliding	—Lateral movement to ball	
STABILITY		
• Axial movements	—An aspect of all strokes (twisting, stretching, pivoting)	
• Dynamic balance	—Compensation for rapid changes in direction, level, and speed of movement	

TABLE 16.8 **Volleyball Skills**

Fundamental Movements	Specialized Movement Skills	
MANIPULATION		
• Striking	—Overhand serve —Underhand serve	—Spike —Dink
• Volleying	—Set —Dig	
LOCOMOTION		
• Sliding	—Lateral movement	
• Running	—Forward —Backward —Diagonal	
• Vertical jump	—Spike	
STABILITY		
• Axial movements	—Found in general play (stretching, twisting, turning, falling, reaching)	
• Dynamic balance	—Rapid changes in speed, level, and direction of movement	

TABLE 16.9	Gymnastic Skills	
Fundamental Movements	**Specialized Movement Skills**	
LOCOMOTION		
• Running	—Approach	
• Vertical jumping	—Back flip	
	—Front flip	
• Skipping	—Skip-step	
• Leaping	—Various stunts	
STABILITY		
• Axial movements	—One or more found in numerous stunts and apparatus skills (bending, stretching, twisting, turning, falling, reaching, pivoting)	
• Static balance	—Integral part of all stationary tricks and landing on dismounts	
• Inverted supports	—Tip-up	—Headstand
	—Tripod	—Handstand
• Body rolling	—Forward roll	—Back walkover
	—Backward roll	—Front walkover
• Dynamic balance	—Compensation for changes in direction, level, and speed of movement	

changing speeds and directions with slight changes in body posture and pressure on the snowboard, and without consciously attending to the task.

Gentile's Two Stages of Skill Learning

In 1972 Gentile proposed an alternative two-stage model for learning a new movement skill and has since expended it to view the process from the perspective of the goals of learner (2000). Gentile's two stages are called the *getting the idea stage* and the *fixation/diversification stage.*

At the **getting the idea stage** the primary goal of the learner is to obtain a basic awareness of the essential requirements for successful performance of the skill. During this first stage in learning a new

movement skill, the learner establishes the basic movement patterns for executing the task and begins to make crude discriminations in how it is performed. The learner at this stage learns how to complete the task under highly specific conditions. For example, the goal of our snowboarder in getting the idea of how to move downhill while balancing with both feet strapped to the snowboard is to be able to do so under specific conditions involving the slope of the hill and the surface conditions. Should the snow conditions change from powder to packed snow or to ice, or from a gentle slope to a steep one, the learner will not be able to regulate this new and radically different environment without once again "getting the idea" of how it is done under these new and different conditions.

During Gentile's second stage, the **fixation/ diversification stage,** the goal of the learner is to achieve consistency of performance and the ability to adapt to changing conditions and to the task being an open or closed skill (see chapter 1). If it is a closed movement task, the learner works for consistency from trial to trial (i.e., "fixation") as in shooting free throws in basketball. If the movement is open, the learner strives for fluidity and adaptability (i.e., "diversification") under constantly changing environmental conditions, as in snowboarding.

CONCEPT 16.6

The learning of a new movement skill can be viewed from the perspective of levels and stages that provide the instructor (i.e., parent, teacher, coach, therapist) with specific cues for maximizing learning.

Combining Levels and Stages of Skill Learning

In 1972 the senior author first proposed a model for movement skill learning based on elements of both the Fitts and Posner and the Gentile models (Gallahue, Werner, and Luedke, 1972, 1975), that has since been modified and expanded (Gallahue, 1982, 1996). Gallahue's view of learning a new movement skill adapts elements from the previous two models in that it recognizes both the cognitive state of the learner and the goals of the learner. Additionally, it proposes appropriate actions on the part of the instructor in being a facilitator of learning at the *beginning/novice level, intermediate/ practice level,* and *advanced/fine-tuning level* of learning a new movement skill (see table 16.10).

At the **beginning/novice level** of learning a new movement skill the learner tries to develop a conscious mental plan of the essential requirements of the task. Because of the conscious attention given by the learner to the task, performance is highly variable, generally erratic, and with lots of errors. Fatigue often sets in early because the learner tries to pay attention to all of the elements of the task and is unable to screen out relevant information from that which is unimportant. The beginning level of learning a new movement skill has three accompanying stages: the *awareness stage,* the *exploratory stage,* and the *discovery stage.*

At the **awareness stage** the cognitive state of the learner is one of being naïve and ignorant about the task, its basic requirements, and the appropriate terminology used to describe the task. The goal of the learner is to develop a basic conscious awareness of the general characteristics of the task. This is a "getting the idea" stage. For example, when learning how to do a forward roll the learner first develops an awareness of the essential requirements of the task (i.e., to tuck and forward) and an understanding of how the terms "tuck your chin," "push off with your hands," and "stay in a small ball" are used in performing the task.

At the **exploratory stage** the learner has a conscious awareness of the basic requirements of the task and now experiments with performing the task in a variety of ways. The cognitive state of the learner is typified by knowing what the body is supposed to do, but being unable to do so with consistency. The goal of the learner is to experiment with the varied possibilities of how the task may be performed. This is viewed as a "precontrol" stage in which there is great variability and gross errors in performance. For example, when learning to do a forward roll, our learner may explore the many rolling possibilities by experimenting with the movement concepts of rolling with different amounts of *effort,* occupying various amounts of *space,* and rolling in *relationship* to different objects and people (Gallahue, 1996). At this stage our forward roller explores the movement concepts of how the body *can* move.

At the **discovery stage** of learning a new movement skill the cognitive state of the learner is one of consciously forming a mental plan of how the task should be performed. The goal of the learner is to find more efficient ways of performing the task. This is a "coordinating and controlling" stage in which the learner begins to gain greater motor

TABLE 16.10 The Levels and Stages of Learning a New Movement Skill, with Attention to the Learner's Cognitive State and Goals, and the Role of the Instructor

Levels and Stages of Learning a New Movement Skill	Cognitive State of the Learner	Goals of the Learner	Role of the Instructor
BEGINNING/NOVICE LEVEL	Learner tries to form a conscious mental plan of the movement task:	Learner tries to gain basic awareness of the requirements of the movement task:	Instructor helps the learner with the general framework of the movement task:
• Awareness stage	—Wants to know how the body *should* move	—To get an idea of how the task is performed	—By helping the learner get the general idea of the task
• Exploratory stage	—Knows what to do, but unable to do it with consistency	—To experiment with how the body *can* move	—By helping the learner explore and self-discover how to perform the task
• Discovery stage	—Forms a conscious mental plan for performing the task	—To find more efficient ways of performing the task	—By helping the learner gain greater movement control and motor coordination
INTERMEDIATE/ PRACTICE LEVEL	Learner has a good general understanding of the movement task:	Learner tries to get the "feel" of the movement task:	Instructor helps the learner focus on combining and refining skills:
• Combination stage	—Puts skills together with less conscious attention to their elements	—To integrate multiple skills into a fluid time/space sequence	—By helping the learner integrate and use skill combinations
• Application stage	—Makes efforts to refine the skill	—To use the task in some form of activity	—By helping the learner refine and apply the task
ADVANCED/FINE TUNING LEVEL	Learner has a complete understanding of the movement task:	Learner tries to perform the task with unconscious effort (i.e., "zone"):	Instructor focuses on skill maintenance and refinement:
• Performance stage	—Gives little or no conscious attention to the elements of the task	—To perform with increased accuracy, control, and movement efficiency	—By helping the learner achieve increased precision of movement
• Individualized stage	—Fine-tunes performance based on personal attributes and limitations	—To modify performance to maximize success	—By helping the learner personalize the movement task

control and "discovers" how to perform the task. At this stage our forward roller begins to internalize the skill concepts of how the body *should* move.

For individuals at the beginning/novice level of learning a new movement skill, the instructor needs to be aware of the conscious cognitive requirements of this stage. The intent, at this level, is to provide the learner with the gross general framework of the task. To do so the instructor needs to:

- Provide for visual demonstrations of the skill to promote cognitive awareness.
- Introduce the major aspects of the skill only (be brief).
- Permit the learner to try out the skill early.
- Provide plenty of opportunity for exploration of the skill and self-discovery of its general elements.
- Recognize that this is primarily a cognitive stage and that the learner needs only to get the general idea of the skill.
- Compare the new skill, when possible, to similar skills with which the learner may be familiar.
- Provide immediate, precise, and positive feedback concerning general aspects of the skill.
- Avoid situations that place emphasis on the product of one's performance; focus instead on the process.

The **intermediate/practice level** is the second level of learning a new movement skill. At this level the learner has a general understanding and appreciation for the requirements of the task and is able to perform in a manner approximating the requirement of the final skill. Additionally, the learner now has a better understanding of the requirements of the skill and a mental plan for performing it under both static and dynamic conditions. There is less conscious attention to the elements of the task at this level, but greater attention to the goal of the task. The poorly coordinated movements of the beginning level disappear, and the learner now begins to get the "feel" for the skill as kinesthetic sensitivity becomes more highly attuned. At this level the learner relies more on

muscle sense and less on the verbal and visual cues of the beginning level. The intermediate/practice level of learning a new movement skill has two accompanying stages: the *combination stage,* and the *application stage.*

At the **combination stage** the learner begins to put movement skills together in different combinations, first in pairs then in increasingly complex forms. The cognitive state of the learner is one of trying to combine skills with decreasing conscious attention to the elements of the task. The goal of the learner is to integrate multiple skills into a fluid sequence of events in both time and space. Our forward roller now practices doing a roll from a squat to a squat position, then from progressively more complex forms—from a stand, from a walk, and finally over an object. This is a stage of "integrating" and "using" movement skills in combination with one another.

At the application stage more attention is given to refining the task and applying it as a specialized movement skill to some form of daily living, recreational, or introductory sport-related activity. The cognitive state of the learner is one of refining the skill, and the goal of the learner is to use the skill or combination of skills in some form of activity. Attention is given to smoothing out the task and using it in an applied sense. For example, our forward roller now adapted her rolling skills to introductory forms of various martial arts and gymnastics activities. This is a "refining" and "applying" stage.

The instructor working with learners at the intermediate/practice level of learning a new movement skill needs to focus on greater skill development. Practice conditions should promote skill refinement and maximize feedback. To accomplish this the instructor needs to:

- Provide numerous opportunities for practice.
- Provide opportunities for skill refinement in a supportive, nonthreatening environment.
- Devise practice situations that progressively focus on greater skill refinement.
- Provide short, fast-paced practice sessions with frequent breaks before implementing longer sessions with fewer breaks.

- Help the learner self-analyze the task and then provide constructive feedback to the learner.
- Structure quality practice sessions that focus on quality performance (i.e., "perfect practice makes perfect").
- Accommodate for individual differences in the rate of skill learning.
- Focus attention on the whole skill whenever possible.
- Set up practice sessions that simulate the intensity and demands of the real-life daily living, recreational, or competitive situation.

The **advanced/fine-tuning level** is the third and final level in learning a new movement skill. The cognitive state of the learner at this stage is one of having a complete understanding of the skill. The mental plan for the skill is highly developed and little or no conscious attention is given to the cognitive elements of the task. The individual is able to screen out irrelevant information and is not bothered by distractions. There is excellent timing and anticipation of movements and the action appears almost automatic. The learner at this level is frequently said to be "in the grove" or in a "zone" when performing the task. At the advanced/fine-tuning level there are two stages, the *performance stage* and the *individualized stage*.

At the **performance stage** of learning a new movement skill the learner is further involved in refining and applying the elements of the movement task but with emphasis on using it in specific performance situations. The cognitive state of the learner is one in which little or no conscious attention is given to the task, and the goal of the learner is to perform with increased accuracy, control, and efficiency. This is a "precision" stage. Using our rolling example, the performer in the sport of gymnastics now performs a floor exercise routine using a variety of rolling movements. The attempt at this stage is to do so with considerable precision by pointing the toes, positioning the arms just so, and tucking the body in a manner that exudes power and grace.

The **individualized stage** is the final stage in learning a new movement skill. At this stage the cognitive state of the learner is one of making fine-tuning adjustments in skill performance based on unique strengths or weaknesses and attributes or limitations. The goal of the learner is to modify performance to maximize success based on such things as body size, physical conditioning, emotional control, and the cognitive requirements of the task. This is a "personalizing" stage. Our gymnast, for example, when incorporating rolling moves into her floor exercise routine will take her height, weight, strength, endurance, and injury status into consideration when performing her routine. In short, to be successful she will have to personalize her routine.

Instructors of individuals at the advanced/fine-tuning level of movement skill learning must focus on additional refining, maintenance of the skill, and providing selected feedback. Instructors should not require the learner to consciously attend to the skill as a whole. Therefore, instructors should:

- Structure practice sessions that promote intensity and enthusiasm.
- Be available to provide encouragement, motivation, and positive support.
- Offer suggestions and tips on strategy.
- Structure practice sessions that duplicate real-life situations.
- Help the learner anticipate her or his actions in gamelike situations.
- Know the learner as an individual and be able to adjust methods to meet individual needs.
- Provide feedback that focuses on specific aspects of the skill.
- Avoid asking the learner to think about performance of the skill, which might result in "analysis paralysis."

Changing a Well-Learned Technique

When an individual displays a well-learned but improper technique in performing a skill, you are faced with the dilemma of determining whether to attempt to change the habit or to leave it alone. The individual may be experiencing success with the technique, but you know that proper execution would be more efficient and successful. A well-learned technique is difficult and time-consuming to change because any new learning requires taking an unconscious advanced skill and returning it to a conscious cognitive level. Under stress and in conditions where rapid decisions are required, the individual is likely to revert to the incorrect technique. Only after considerable practice will the incorrect response be consistently replaced by the correct action. In deciding whether to change an individual's technique, the instructor needs to consider the following issues:

- Determine if there is sufficient time to make the change (in weeks and months, not hours and days).
- Determine if the individual wants to make the change.
- Be certain that the individual understands why the change is being made.
- Be certain that the individual realizes that performance will regress prior to improvement.
- Provide a supportive, encouraging environment.
- Structure practice sessions that will gradually bring the learner back to and beyond where she or he was prior to intervention.

FOSTERING IMPROVEMENT

By age 7 most children have the potential to be at the transitional skill stage. Emphasis on skill improvement at this time results from the increase in the child's performance potential. The learner and the instructor (i.e., the parent, teacher, therapist, or coach) are becoming more concerned with the degree of skill, accuracy, and form used in performing a movement task. Our primary purpose is to help learners improve in accordance with their developmental needs and potential. The operational goal of improvement helps us to see all learners (whether they are children, adolescents, or adults) at their actual developmental levels. By assessing current levels of motor behavior and

providing meaningful and enjoyable learning experiences, developmental teachers will foster improvement.

The operational goal of improvement encompasses three other concepts that guide us. The first of these concepts is *movement control* in which we reflect our knowledge of the three categories of movement (stability, locomotion, and manipulation), the phases of motor development (reflexive, rudimentary, fundamental, and specialized), and the levels of movement skill learning (beginning/novice, intermediate/practice, and advanced/fine tuning). Developmental teaching also incorporates variations and presentations that move from the general to the specific in planning. By condensing information into the concept of movement control, we form a basis for analyzing our effectiveness in improving the skills of learners.

The second concept under the goal of improvement is *emotional control*. Instructors are concerned with how learners understand themselves and others. We rely heavily on appropriate communication skills in ourselves and in others. These communication skills include self-discipline as well as experiences through which learners can develop responsibility and self-control. The concept of emotional control provides a guide for evaluating past experiences and designing new experiences.

The third and final concept is *learning enjoyment*. This concept also gives instructors a guide for evaluating their programs with improvement in mind. The objective is to stimulate an eagerness to learn within each individual. Success-oriented experiences and opportunities to receive praise and recognition positively reinforce one's view of learning. By making the learning of new movement skills enjoyable, we promote intrinsic motivation within the individual.

The overall goal of improvement, with its three emphases of (1) movement control, (2) emotional control, and (3) learning enjoyment, provides us with a compact philosophical construct that can serve as an operational guide to teaching action. This construct can and should be modified. Its purpose is not to limit parents, teachers, therapists, and coaches but to empower them by providing operational guidelines to ensure that instruction is meaningful, relevant, and fun. Every instructor must rely on some sort of philosophical construct. Without one, we might impose inappropriate per-

formance expectations on learners. The purpose of the suggested philosophical construct is to provide a basis for keeping instruction realistic, practical, and meaningful.

SUMMARY

The refinement of specialized movement abilities occurs in three stages. In the transitional stage, it is crucial that a smooth shift be made from mature fundamental movement patterns to corresponding specialized movement skills. This transition will be hampered if the individual has not developed mature patterns necessary for performance. Instructors must be alert to the proficiency with which the individual knows the specialized skill and not give in to the temptation of ignoring incorrect form as long as the outcome is satisfactory. Too often focus is on the product rather than on the process. There is no legitimate reason for failing to use the mature, mechanically correct, pattern in the performance of a specialized movement skill. Use of a mature pattern of movement will, in the long run, enhance movement performance. However, once proficiency has been achieved, has become relatively automatic, and has been applied to numerous situations, it is entirely appropriate to encourage unique variations.

At the application stage, attention is focused on greater degrees of precision, accuracy, and control. Performance scores generally improve at a rapid rate, and the individual is keenly aware of the specific advantages and limitations of his or her body. The individual at this level is also influenced by a variety of social, cultural, and

psychological factors in selecting specific activities for regular involvement.

The lifelong utilization stage is a continuation and further refinement of the previous stage. It is the pinnacle of the phases and stages of motor development. This stage encompasses lifetime sport and recreational activities. Failure to develop and refine the fundamental and specialized skill abilities of the previous stages will restrict any person's ability to reach this stage.

The learning of a new movement skill occurs in levels or stages. The models proposed by Fitts and Posner (1967) and Gentile (1972, 2000) can be adapted and expanded into a three-level model with accompanying stages. Paying attention to where the learner is in this skill-learning hierarchy provides the instructor with important clues to successful interaction.

The goal of the instructor concerned with the motor development and movement education of youth is to foster improvement in such a way that there is an orderly and developmentally sound progression through the fundamental movement and specialized skill phases. Improvement in movement control, emotional control, and learning enjoyment serves as a practical philosophical construct around which to plan and implement meaningful learning experiences.

CRITICAL READINGS

American Academy of Pediatrics. (2000). Intensive training and sports participation in young athletes. *Pediatrics, 106*, 154–157.

American Sport Education Program. (2002). Champaign, IL: Human Kinetics.

Gallahue, D. L. (1996). *Developmental Physical Education for Today's Children*. Dubuque, IA: McGraw-Hill.

Gallahue, D. L., Werner, P. H., & Luedke, G. C. (1972). *Moving and Learning: A Conceptual*

Approach to the Physical Education of Young Children. Dubuque, IA: Kendall-Hunt.

Magill, R. A. (2001). *Motor Learning. Concepts and Applications* (Chapters 11 & 12). Boston, MA: McGraw-Hill.

Martens, R. (1997). *Successful Coaching*. Champaign, IL: Human Kinetics.

National Federation Interscholastic Coaches Association. (1997). *Coaching Principles: Course*

Instructor Guide. American Sport Education Program. Champaign, IL: Human Kinetics.

Poinsett, A. (1996). *The Role of Sports in Youth Development.* New York: Carnegie Corp.

Washington, R. L., Bernhardt, D. T., Gomez, J., & Johnson, M. D., et al. (2001). Organized sports for children and preadolescents. *Pediatrics, 107,* 1459–1462.

 WEB RESOURCES

Homepage of the American Sport Education Program
www.asep.com/

The Institute for the Study of Youth Sports
http://ed-web3.educ.msu.edu/ysi/

The National Alliance for Youth Sports
www.nays.org/

Various youth sport skill development resources from the American Alliance for Health, Physical Education, Recreation and Dance
www.aahperd.org/

FITNESS CHANGES DURING ADOLESCENCE

KEY TERMS

Convenience samples
Field test
Interrater reliability
Intrarater reliability
Stratified random sample
Hydrostatic weighing
Electrical impedance
Skinfold calipers
Body mass index (BMI)

CHAPTER COMPETENCIES

Upon completion of this chapter you should be able to:

- Describe adolescent gender differences and similarities in health-related fitness
- Discuss changes in movement dimensions such as balance, timing, or force production/control
- Demonstrate knowledge of major changes in body composition and physiological functioning in adolescent males and females
- List and describe age-related aspects of health-related fitness during adolescence
- List and describe age-related aspects of performance-related fitness during adolescence

KEY CONCEPT

Although differences exist between genders as well as within genders on measures of health-related and performance-related fitness, adolescent males and females have the potential to make significant improvements through regular participation in physical activity.

Health-related fitness and performance-related fitness change rapidly during adolescence. Both males and females are capable of making significant increments in all measures of fitness. This chapter examines these changes. The first section is devoted to the components of health-related fitness. Results of the 1985 National Children and Youth Fitness Study (NCYFS) are the primary source of data because of the validity of the sample and the reliability of the data. The figures presented in this section are based on the mean sample scores for each health-related fitness item tested. There is considerable variability in performance scores on all items at all age levels.

The information presented in the discussion and figures on performance-related fitness is based on a synthesis of post-1960 studies reported by Haubenstricker and Seefeldt (1986). These data were selected because they are considered the best representative sampling available of changes in motor skill performance.

The reader is encouraged to carefully study the figures and tables throughout this chapter. It will be of far more value to you to gain a conceptual grasp of the meaning implied in the slopes of the curves than to memorize specific data points.

HEALTH-RELATED FITNESS

In adolescents, physical activity levels are associated with sex, socioeconomic status, and the activity levels of significant others (Raudsepp and Viira, 2000). There is, however, a distinct lack of reliable data that permits us to make accurate comparisons across generations or across cultures. The problem

exists primarily in sampling and data collection techniques. Prior to the publication of the National Children and Youth Fitness Study (1985, 1987), large-scale, population-based field studies used **convenience samples.** Although thousands of children and youth were tested on a variety of fitness items, little attention was given to sampling procedures. As a result the data tend to be suspect and are not suitable for generalizations across ages and the population as a whole. For example, it is possible that participants in some locations were more highly motivated by the testing than others. As a result, performance scores could be biased in favor of more highly motivated participants. Furthermore, in convenience samples little attention is given to geographical representation, rural versus urban settings, and private versus public school populations, all of which may have dramatic effects.

CONCEPT 17.1

Field assessments of physical fitness are frequently unsuitable for the formulation of generalizations about youth fitness because of questionable underlying assumptions, sampling procedures, and data collection techniques.

Another inherent difficulty with nationally normed **field test** fitness data published prior to the NCYFS is in the test administration. Different examiners, usually trained physical education professionals, collected data at each site. Also, all students in the convenience sample method were receiving physical education, a factor that may have skewed the data upward. It is difficult, if not impossible, to ensure consistency among testers. Therefore, **interrater reliability** (objectivity) and **intrarater reliability** (consistency) tend to be poor.

A third problem in comparing generational scores rests in the test items. Comparison can be made only among items performed and administered in exactly the same manner. Changing the protocol, even slightly, for an assessment item may result in drastically inflated or deflated scores.

With these concerns in mind we have chosen to use the NCYFS data as a basis for our discussion about the health-related fitness of adolescents. To date, the NCYFS data are the most valid and reliable. The NCYFS is based on a **stratified random sample** of 5,140 males and 5,135 females from twenty-five randomly selected counties in the United States. Over 88 percent (4,539) of the randomly selected males completed the test battery, and exactly 83 percent (4,261) females completed the testing (Errecart et al., 1985). The high participation rate and the definitive manner in which the sample was obtained contributed greatly to the validity and generalizability of the results. Reliability of the NCYFS was ensured by a highly trained field staff of ten individuals who "directly" supervised administration of the assessment measures given by trained teachers (Ross et al., 1987). The NCYFS results represent the best field data available in the United States in validity of the sample and reliability of the data.

Each of the sections that follow discuss the various health-related components of fitness in respect to the NCYFS data. Comparisons, where appropriate, are made with norms from the AAHPERD Health-Related Physical Fitness Test (HRPFT, 1980). In general, HRPFT scores are better than NCYFS scores. This may be due to the sampling and test administration issues discussed earlier. When comparing the two tests (HRPFT and NCYFS), carefully observe the slope of the two curves. In most cases, the slopes are remarkably similar, thereby strengthening the validity of the data for both tests in changes over time. Note where age differences in the slopes of the two lines exist. These differences may reflect variations in activity patterns between the two studies due to sociocultural shifts in activity levels over time. Table 17.1 provides a synthesis of findings from the NCYFS.

Aerobic Endurance

Aerobic endurance is related to the functioning of the heart, lungs, and vascular system. One's aerobic capacity may be evaluated in the laboratory through a variety of stress tests that require the subject to exert an all-out effort to go into oxygen debt. These "max" tests, as they are known, are usually performed on a treadmill or bicycle ergometer. The VO_2 max score is obtained as the result of exhaustive exercise. Although measuring VO_2 max is the preferred method of determining aerobic capacity, large longitudinal population studies using treadmill and ergometer tests are nonexistent. Instead, research has focused on *population samples* across ages using field test estimates of aerobic endurance. As a result, the one-mile jog has emerged as the most popular and valid field test item with adolescents (Hunt et al., 2000). In a ten-year retrospective study of various fitness components Updyke (1992) found that aerobic fitness declined annually among a large cross-sectional convenience sample of children and youth.

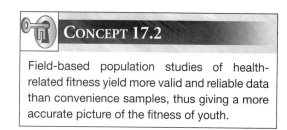

CONCEPT 17.2

Field-based population studies of health-related fitness yield more valid and reliable data than convenience samples, thus giving a more accurate picture of the fitness of youth.

Based on the National Children and Youth Fitness Study (NCYFS) as depicted in figure 17.1, males on the average continue to improve in aerobic endurance until age 16, whereupon they regress slightly through age 18. These results are similar to mean mile walk/run times on the AAHPERD Health-Related Physical Fitness Test (HRPFT). However, the males tested in the HRPFT regressed slightly between ages 10 and 11, followed by steady improvement through age 14. This in turn was followed by a general plateauing of scores through age 17. It is difficult to explain the discrepancy in the slope of the two curves (figure 17.2) at age 11, but this may be a function of the sampling techniques employed. (The HRPFT used a convenience sampling technique, whereas the NCYFS used a stratified random sampling technique.) Nevertheless, the similar slope of the two curves demonstrates that males improve in

TABLE 17.1   Common Field Measures of Adolescent Health-Related Fitness and a Synthesis of Findings

Health-Related Fitness Component	Common Field Measures	Synthesis of Findings
Aerobic endurance	1-mile walk/run	— Males and females both improve at a near parallel rate — Males are faster than females at all ages — Males continue to improve until late adolescence — Females regress and plateau from midadolescence onward — Males show rapid yearly increments until late adolescence
Muscular strength/ endurance	Modified situps Abdominal crunch	— Females improve at a less rapid rate than males — Females tend to plateau in performance during midadolescence — Males outperform females at all ages
	Pull-ups	— Females average less than one pull-up throughout adolescence — Males demonstrate slow gains prior to puberty followed by rapid gains throughout adolescence — Males significantly outperform females at all ages
Joint flexibility	Sit-and-reach	— Females outperform males at all ages — Females make yearly incremental improvements until late adolescence — Males regress during early adolescence followed by rapid improvement
Body composition	Percent body fat using skinfold calipers (calculated from triceps and calf skinfold measurements) Body mass index (calculated from height and weight)	— Females have a higher percent body fat than males at all ages — Female body fat percentages increase rapidly during early and midadolescence followed by a plateau in late adolescence — Males increase in percent body fat during late childhood and the preadolescent period — Males decrease in percent body fat during early adolescence and maintain low fat levels throughout adolescence

their mile walk/run times with age. That the boys in the NCYFS continued to improve until age 16 may be reflective of differences in aerobic activity patterns among boys between those sampled in the HRPFT and those in the NCYFS. Note, however, that for both tests, males, with age, tend to plateau after age 16 in their performance on the mile walk/run test. This should be viewed with concern in that it reflects a tendency toward more sedentary activity patterns of the older adoles-

cent. The dropoff in scores coincides with the age at which most males are eligible to drive and work.

With regard to the performance of females on the mile walk/run test of aerobic endurance, the results are of similar concern. Although we might expect the male to outperform his female counterpart due to a variety of anatomical and physiological variables, we would hope to see a descending slope (i.e., lower times) over a longer

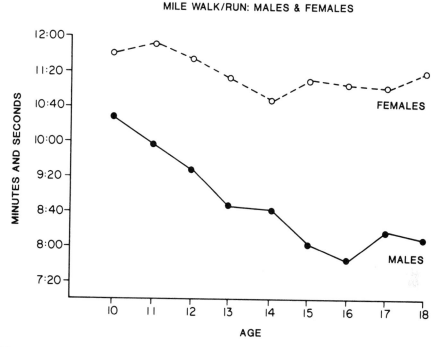

MILE WALK/RUN: MALES & FEMALES

Figure 17.1

One-mile walk/run: mean scores for males and females 10–18 years, in minutes and seconds.
Source: Data from J. G. Ross et al., "The National Children and Youth Fitness Study: New Standards for Fitness Measurement" in *Journal of Physical Education, Recreation and Dance* (1985).

period. Based on the results of the NCYFS, the female is closest to her male counterpart on the mile walk/run at age 10, and the gap between males and females remains roughly parallel until age 14. It widens, however, at a dramatic rate from then on (figure 17.1). Although females performing on both the NCYFS and the HRPFT tended to improve with age until around 13 or 14 years, there was a decided tendency to regress and plateau in performance. The 18-year-old female is at almost the same level as her 12-year-old counterpart.

Data from the HRPFT tend to support that published in the NCYFS. However, females in the HRPFT peaked at an earlier age and regressed at a more rapid rate than those tested in the NCYFS (figure 17.3). In studies where body size has been controlled for, laboratory tests of VO_2 max indicate

that males increase through childhood and adolescence into early adulthood. Females peak VO_2 continues to increase through childhood and puberty but levels off at the end of adolescence (Armstrong and Welsman, 2000). Sex differences become more pronounced, in favor of males, from later childhood through adolescence.

Muscular Strength and Endurance

Modified sit-ups and chin-ups are frequently used as field measures of *abdominal isotonic strength/endurance*. They are isotonic in that the muscles go through a full range of motion while in a contracted state. They are related to strength because a significant force is overcome, and they are related to endurance because a maximum number of repetitions is recorded. From 6 to 9 years of age both

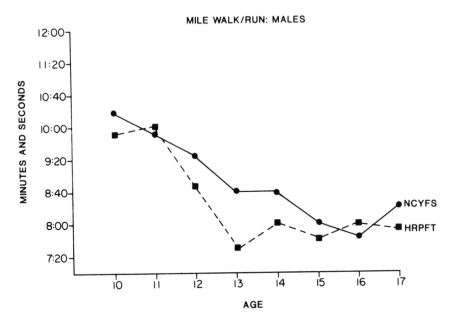

Figure 17.2
Comparison of one-mile walk/run scores between NCYFS and HRPFT: mean scores for males 10–17 years, in minutes and seconds.

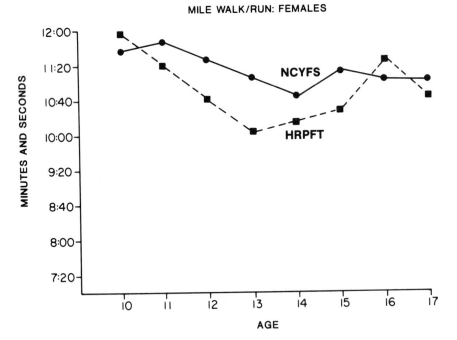

Figure 17.3
Comparison of one-mile walk/run scores between NCYFS and HRPFT: mean scores for females 10–17 years, in minutes and seconds.

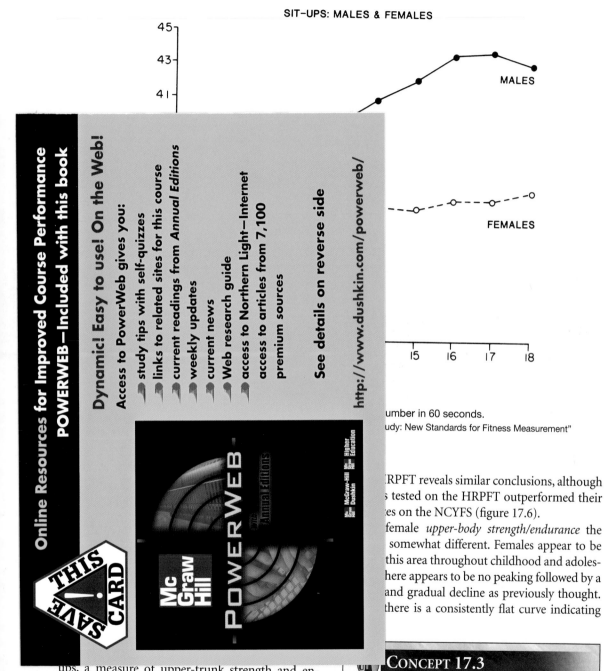

SIT-UPS: MALES & FEMALES

MALES

FEMALES

...umber in 60 seconds.
...udy: New Standards for Fitness Measurement"

...RPFT reveals similar conclusions, although ...s tested on the HRPFT outperformed their ...es on the NCYFS (figure 17.6).

...female *upper-body strength/endurance* the ... somewhat different. Females appear to be ...this area throughout childhood and adoles-...here appears to be no peaking followed by a ...and gradual decline as previously thought. ...there is a consistently flat curve indicating

...ups, a measure of upper-trunk strength and endurance, provides support for the contention that strength increases at a near linear rate for boys from about age 12 (the approximate age of onset of male puberty) through about age 18. Comparing mean scores from published norms on bent-knee sit-ups

CONCEPT 17.3

Females are comparable to males in abdominal strength and endurance prior to puberty, but males make significantly more rapid gains throughout adolescence.

Card overlay text:

Online Resources for Improved Course Performance
POWERWEB—Included with this book

Dynamic! Easy to use! On the Web!

Access to PowerWeb gives you:

- study tips with self-quizzes
- links to related sites for this course
- current readings from *Annual Editions*
- weekly updates
- current news
- Web research guide
- access to Northern Light—Internet access to articles from 7,100 premium sources

See details on reverse side

http://www.dushkin.com/powerweb/

POWERWEB
Annual Editions
McGraw-Hill Dushkin · Higher Education

McGraw Hill

SAVE THIS CARD!

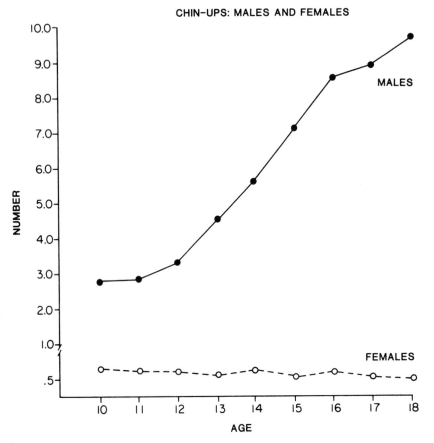

Figure 17.5

Chin-ups: mean scores for males and females 10–18 years, number completed.
Source: Data from J. G. Ross et al., "The National Children and Youth Fitness Study: New Standards for Fitness Measurement" in *Journal of Physical Education, Recreation and Dance* (1985).

low levels of upper-body strength/endurance at all ages. Females, however, seem to fare somewhat better on measures of abdominal endurance as measured by the NCYFS. Mean score values for the bent-knee sit-up test improve slightly with age. In terms of abdominal strength/endurance, older adolescents tend to score slightly higher than their younger counterparts. Mean score values for bent-knee sit-ups on the HRPFT revealed similar results, although females tended to perform at a higher level at all ages on the HRPFT (figure 17.7).

Beunen and Thomis (2000) indicated that strength increases follow a general type of growth curve typically found for most external body dimensions, including height. Furthermore, in males there is a distinct spurt in strength that occurs three months to one year of peak height velocity. For females there is a less dramatic increase in strength. The sudden upsurge by boys may be explained by their increased muscularity brought about by high levels of testosterone. Furthermore, the tendency on the part of males at all ages to "go all out" on measures of fitness may account for the vast discrepancy between males and females. Females do not improve at such a rapid rate perhaps because of greater amounts of fatty tissue in proportion to lean muscle mass. The tendency on the part of females to level off during mid- and later adolescence could also be a matter of motivation and lack of all-out enthusiasm rather than of purely physiological factors. These are

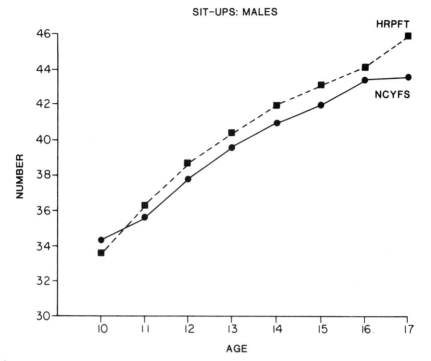

SIT-UPS: MALES

Figure 17.6

Comparison of bent-knee sit-up scores between NCYFS and HRPFT: mean scores for males 10–17 years, number in 60 seconds.

important points to consider. One must be careful to avoid the implication that no matter how hard females try to improve their performances on measures of strength and endurance they will fail. The data using motivated females suggest the opposite.

In fact, although in terms of absolute strength men are usually stronger than women because of their higher quantity of muscle, when compared to relative strength (i.e., muscle cross-sectional area) no significant differences in strength exist between the sexes (Faigenbaum, 2000).

The often dramatic differences exhibited between males and females and the span of years in which improved performances can be expected on measures of muscular strength and endurance should be examined carefully. Although males on the average can be expected to outperform females in measures of strength and endurance due to anatomical, physiological, and biomechanical advantages, there is not an adequate biological ex-

CONCEPT 17.4

Males tend to make rapid gains in muscular strength and endurance throughout adolescence, whereas females tend to peak at the onset of puberty and regress slightly by the end of this period.

planation of differences in the span of years over which relative improvements may be seen. A reasonable explanation may be based on social, cultural, and childrearing differences between males and females (Raudsepp and Viira, 2000).

Flexibility

The sit-and-reach test has become the standard field measurement of *joint flexibility*. Data clearly indicate that on the average females make near

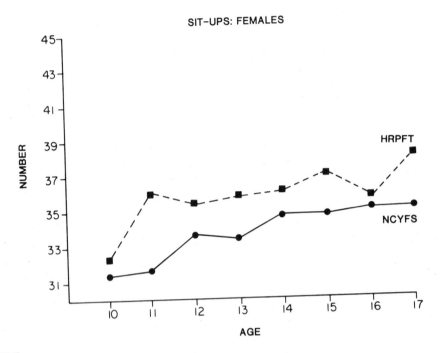

Figure 17.7

Comparison of bent-knee sit-up scores between NCYFS and HRPFT: mean scores for females 10–17 years, number in 60 seconds.

linear improvements in sit-and-reach scores from ages 10 to 16, followed by a slight decline. Females at all ages outperform their male counterparts on this measure (figure 17.8). Reasons for this discrepancy have not been adequately explained but may center around anatomical differences as well as sociocultural variances in activity patterns favoring joint flexibility in females.

There is a slight dropoff in sit-and-reach scores for males around age 12. This may be associated with the prepubescent growth spurt during which

the long bones are growing faster than the muscles and tendons. As a result, performance of the sit-and-reach regresses until the muscles and tendons catch up. Also, both males and females begin to plateau and regress slightly in their flexibility scores around age 17. Decreases in joint flexibility during this period are clearly associated with a general decrease in the activity levels of the older adolescent and with aging. A high level of joint flexibility may be maintained well into adulthood and beyond if appropriate activities are maintained. In other words, the phrase "use it or lose it" applies. Loss of flexibility begin around age 17.

Body Composition

Body composition (percent body fat) is a major marker of health-related fitness. To accurately assess one's body composition, the percentage of body fatness needs to be separated from the other components of one's total body weight.

CONCEPT 17.5

As a population, females display greater joint flexibility throughout adolescence than their male counterparts, but both tend to regress over time due to reduced activity patterns rather than age.

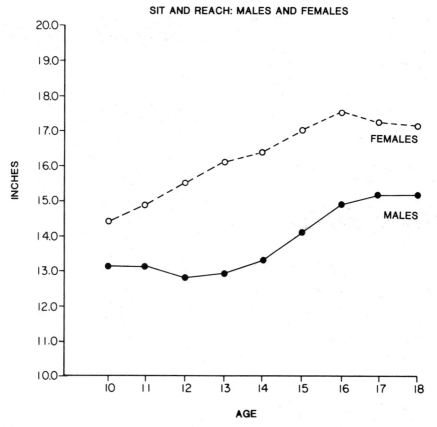

SIT AND REACH: MALES AND FEMALES

Figure 17.8

Sit-and-reach: mean scores for males and females 10–18 years, in inches.

Source: Data from J. G. Ross et al., "The National Children and Youth Fitness Study: New Standards for Fitness Measurement" in *Journal of Physical Education, Recreation and Dance* (1985).

Hydrostatic weighing is an accurate, although inconvenient, method of determining percent body fat. It involves submerging an individual under water and calculating his or her underwater weight from which an accurate estimate of percent body fat can be calculated. Accurate hydrostatic weighing is not a practical measure for field-based assessments of body composition. **Electrical impedance** techniques hold great promise. They are less inconvenient than hydrostatic weighing, but they involve costly equipment not frequently available in field settings.

Despite their limitations, **skinfold calipers** and calculating one's **body mass index (BMI)** have become the preferred methods of estimating per-

cent body fat in the field. The reliability of the caliper technique has been frequently challenged, but when administered by trained personnel, it may yield fairly accurate results. Figure 17.9a and b depict body mass index for boys and girls from age 2 to 20, respectively (CDC, 2000). Although highly similar prior to puberty, there are increasing differences between the sexes throughout adolescence. When comparing BMI scores generationally, on the average, today's adolescents are significantly fatter than their counterparts (CDC, 2000). Eleven percent of all U.S. adolescents are overweight today, almost double the percentage from 1980 (National Center for Health Statistics, 2001). There

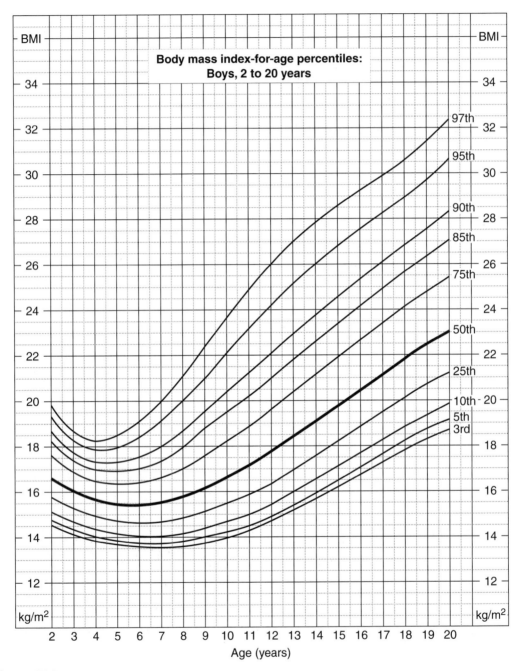

Figure 17.9a

Body mass index-for-age percentiles, boys, 2 to 20 years, CDC growth charts: United States.

Source: Developed by the National Center for Health Statistics in collaboration with the National Center for Chronic Disease Prevention and Health Promotion (2000).

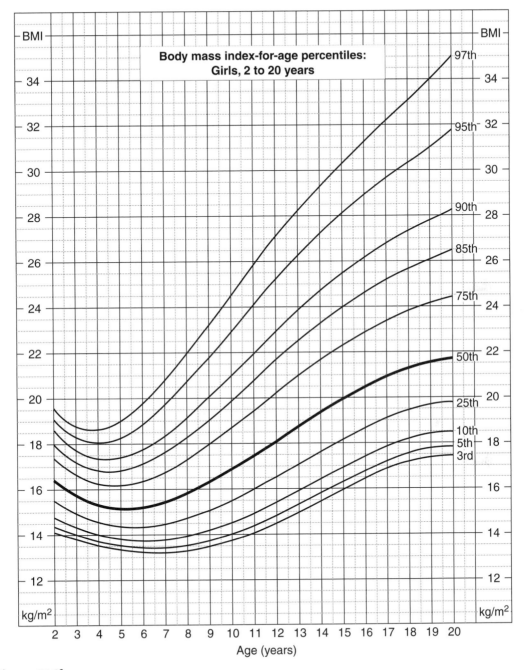

Figure 17.9b

Body mass index-for-age percentiles, girls, 2 to 20 years, CDC growth charts: United States.

Source: Developed by the National Center for Health Statistics in collaboration with the National Center for Chronic Disease Prevention and Health Promotion (2000).

CONCEPT 17.6

As a population, females steadily gain in percent body fat measurements from preadolescence through adolescence.

CONCEPT 17.7

Male body fat percentages increase during the preadolescent period, decline sharply at puberty, and level off throughout adolescence.

is a trend toward increased fatness among different generations of American youth. Moreover, *The United States Youth Risk Behavior Survey* (CDC, 1996) revealed that almost 60 percent of high school females were attempting to lose weight, while only slightly more than 24 percent of their male peers were also attempting weight loss. The same survey also revealed a steady drop in vigorous physical activity by high school students, both female and male, from grades 9 through 12.

Regular vigorous physical activity can alter body composition. Exercise coupled with caloric regulation will result in an increase in lean body mass and a decrease in percent body fat in children, adolescents, and adults. The extent to which body composition can be altered depends on the degree and length of training. Alterations in body composition are not necessarily permanent. As activity levels decrease, body fat percentages increase. Parizkova (1982) demonstrated a significant relationship between physical activity levels and lean body mass percentages. Also, several researchers (Bandini et al., 1990; Bar-Or, 1983; Moore et al., 1991; Pate et al., 1999; Romanella et al., 1991) have noted that intensity of activity is significantly lower in obese children, adolescents, and adults. Lloyd and colleagues (2000) conducted a longitudinal study in which they looked at the cumulative long-term sport histories of eighty-one females with regard to bone mineral density. The results of their study showed that the

amount of physical activity that distinguishes sedentary teenage females from those who are active on a nearly daily basis is related to a significant increase in bone mineral density favoring the active teenagers. Clearly, increased levels of physical activity coupled with moderation in caloric intake are keys to increasing bone mineral density in females, and to reducing the trend toward increased fatness in both males and females. The reader is referred to the policy statement of the American Academy of Pediatrics (2000) on *Medical Concerns in the Female Athlete*, including disordered eating, menstrual dysfunction, and decreased bone mineral density.

CONCEPT 17.8

Differences between males and females on measures of health-related and performance-related fitness are just that, differences, explainable by a variety of anatomical, physiological, and sociocultural factors.

PERFORMANCE-RELATED FITNESS

The *motor fitness* components of speed, power, agility, balance, and coordination are generally considered to be the performance- or skill-related components of fitness. These differ considerably from the health-related components of fitness in that they are genetically dependent, resistant to major environmental (experiential) modifications, and relatively stable. Also, these traits are closely related to skillful performance in a variety of sports.

Quantitative changes in a variety of gross motor skills have been studied by several investigators over the past several decades. As a result we have a wealth of information on the performance capabilities of males and females from childhood to adulthood. It is even possible to compare performance scores between generations and arrive at some tentative conclusions concerning secular trends in motor performance on selected skills. Haubenstricker and Seefeldt (1986) presented data

TABLE 17.2 **Common Field Measures of Adolescent Motor Fitness and a Synthesis of Findings**

Motor Fitness Component	Common Field Measures	Synthesis of Findings
Speed	30- to 60-yard dash	— Boys and girls are similar throughout childhood — Boys outperform girls at all ages — Males make more rapid improvement after puberty than females — Males make significant annual gains throughout childhood and adolescence — Females tend to plateau in midadolescence
Muscular power (Lower trunk)	Jump for distance Jump for height	— Boys and girls are similar throughout childhood — Boys slightly outperform girls during childhood, but the gap widens significantly at male puberty
Muscular power (Upper trunk)	Throw for distance	— Males make significant annual increments throughout adolescence — Females begin to plateau during early adolescence and regress by midadolescence
Balance Static balance	Stabilometer Stick balance 1-foot balance	— Males and females make significant qualitative, as well as quantitative, improvements with age
Dynamic balance	Beam walk	— Males make rapid improvement at all ages but especially after puberty — Females and males improve with age throughout childhood and adolescence — Females tend to outperform males during childhood on both static and dynamic measures — Males and females are similar on both static and dynamic measures throughout adolescence with no clear advantage for either

summaries for four motor performance items assessed by a variety of investigators prior to 1960 and since 1960. Three of these—running for speed, jumping for distance, and throwing for distance using the post-1960 data—are summarized in the following sections and presented in table 17.2.

Running Speed

Running speed may be assessed across studies that use different distances by converting dash times, usually 30- to 60-yard (27.4–54.8 m) dashes, to units of yards covered per second. To further

standardize measurements, Haubenstricker and Seefeldt (1986) reported that only those studies that used a stationary start were included. The results of these comparisons led them to conclude that:

> There is systematic improvement in the running speed of children during the middle and late childhood years. This improvement in running speed continues during the teenage years for males. The running speed of post-1960 females increases until age 15, after which time it appears to plateau. (pp. 67–69)

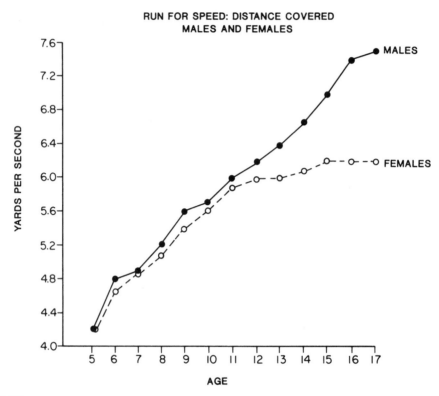

Figure 17.10

Age changes in running speed: mean scores for males and females 5–17 years, from post-1960 studies.

Source: Data from J. Haubenstricker and V. Seefeldt, "Acquisition of Motor Skills During Childhood" in V. Seefeldt (Ed.), *Physical Activity and Well-Being,* 1986 (Reston, VA: AAHPERD).

Figure 17.10 graphically depicts changes in running speed with age from childhood through adolescence. Running speed is similar in boys and girls, only slightly favoring the boys, throughout childhood. However, beginning at about age 12, males begin to make more rapid improvements while their female age-mates begin to plateau. Reasons for the early plateauing on the part of ad-

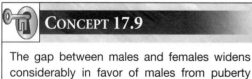

Concept 17.9

The gap between males and females widens considerably in favor of males from puberty onward on measures of speed and power.

olescent females may be explained, in part, by early maturation and lower levels of personal motivation as compared with their late-maturing and often more highly motivated male age-mates. Figure 17.11 illustrates comparable results in actual age changes in running the 100-yard (91.4 m) dash.

Jumping for Distance

Jumping for distance, a purported measure of muscular power, has been assessed in a large number of studies. In summarizing performance scores of children and adolescents 5 to 17 years of age, Haubenstricker and Seefeldt (1986) found that males only slightly outperform females, and that

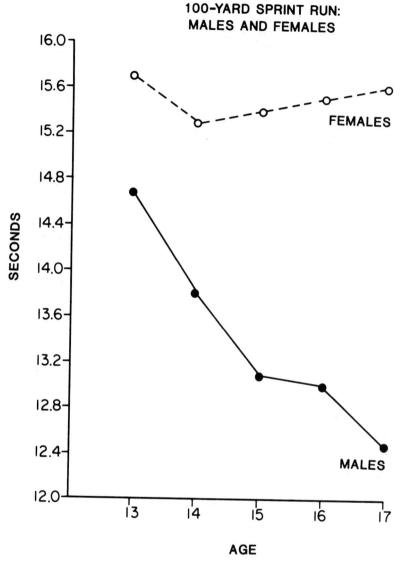

Figure 17.11

100-yard sprint run mean scores for males and females 13–17 years, in seconds

Source: Data from J. G. Ross et al., "The National Children and Youth Fitness Study: New Standards for Fitness Measurement" in *Journal of Physical Education, Recreation and Dance* (1985).

there is steady improvement for both from ages 5 to 14 (figure 17.12). After that females begin to level off and may even decline. Males, however, continue to improve at a linear rate to about age 17 (figure 17.13). The discrepancy between males and females on the standing long jump that begins to appear after age 12 and the widening gap may be explained in a variety of ways.

First, jumping for distance incorporates an element of strength. Males from puberty onward

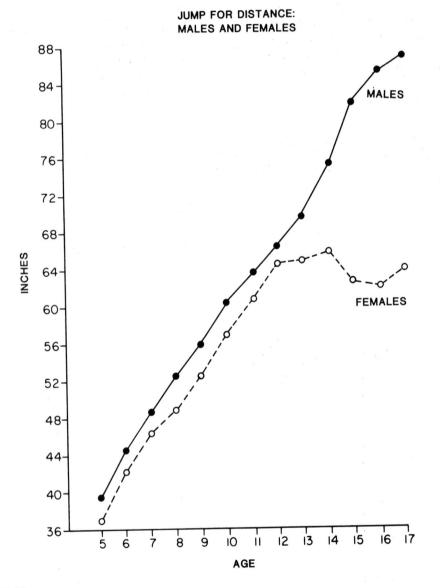

JUMP FOR DISTANCE: MALES AND FEMALES

Figure 17.12
Age changes in standing long jump: mean scores for males and females 5–17 years, from post-1960 studies.
Source: Data from J. Haubenstricker and V. Seefeldt, "Acquisition of Motor Skills During Childhood" in V. Seefeldt (Ed.), *Physical Activity and Well-Being,* 1986 (Reston, VA: AAHPERD).

demonstrate dramatic strength gains, whereas their female counterparts, because of low levels of circulating androgens, tend to level off in their strength. Therefore, a widening of the gap at this time is to be expected. The tendency of females to regress may also be explained by lack of motivation or increasingly sedentary lifestyles. Changes in body proportions and lower centers of gravity may also contribute to these changes.

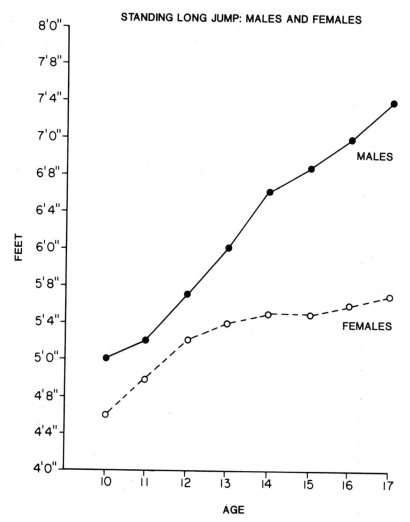

Figure 17.13

Standing long jump mean scores, for males and females 10–17 years, in feet

Source: Data from J. G. Ross et al., "The National Children and Youth Fitness Study: New Standards for Fitness Measurement" in *Journal of Physical Education, Recreation and Dance* (1985).

Throwing for Distance

Throwing for distance is a frequently used measure of muscular power in the upper extremities. As with running for speed and jumping for distance, skill enters into the equation and it may be biased against individuals, both male and female, who have not had sufficient throwing experiences. Those who run, jump, or throw at the

mature stage are likely to score well on performance measures that incorporate these skills. The contribution of a mature pattern is no more evident than in throwing for distance. Immature throwers are at a distinct disadvantage. Therefore, significantly lower mean performance scores for females throughout childhood and adolescence may be due to lower skill levels

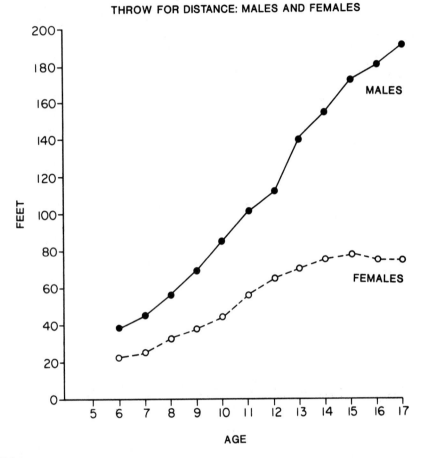

THROW FOR DISTANCE: MALES AND FEMALES

Figure 17.14

Age changes in throwing for distance: mean scores for males and females 6–17 years, from post-1960 studies.

Source: Data from J. Haubenstricker and V. Seefeldt, "Acquisition of Motor Skills During Childhood" in V. Seefeldt (Ed.), *Physical Activity and Well-Being*, 1986 (Reston, VA: AAHPERD)

rather than weakness in the upper arm and shoulder girdle area. Figure 17.14 clearly shows significant differences between males and females at all ages, and the gap only widens with age. Males experience a significant upsurge in performance scores around age 13 corresponding roughly with the onset of puberty. Females, however, demonstrate a much more gradual increase to age 15 followed by a tendency to regress slightly. Reuschlein and Haubenstricker (1985) offered the best explanation for these dramatic differences between genders. In their study of the throwing patterns of fourth, seventh, and tenth graders, 51, 61, and 70 percent of the males, respectively, threw with "good form" at what may be considered the mature stage, but only 15, 19, and 23 percent of the females, respectively, threw at the mature stage.

Balance

Williams (1983) found in her review of age and gender differences in balance performance that, in general, balance improves from ages 3 to 18. Difficulty, however, exists in directly comparing the abundant information that exists on balance. A wide variety of measures have been used over the years to

Activities

The activities that adolescents engage in are important in cultural socialization. Skills of daily living, recreational activities, and competitive sport experiences play a major role in the socialization process. The influence of physical activity on psychosocial development will be examined further in the section that follows.

Ensuring optimal development of adolescents should be a priority commitment of all socializing agents, whether it be the home, community, or school. No one group, however, can be responsible for the successful integration of adolescents into society. All must work in concert to affect a maximum positive transition into adulthood. The following five recommendations have been adapted from the 1995 report of the Carnegie Council on Adolescent Development.

1. *Reengage families with their adolescent children.* Parents need to remain actively involved in their adolescents' education. They need to feel welcome in the school, and school personnel need to assist parents in dealing with their child's transition into adolescence.
2. *Create developmentally appropriate schools for adolescents.* States and school districts should empower middle schools and junior high schools to serve as health-promoting agencies as well as educational institutions. Health education programs that are developmentally appropriate need to be an integral part of the educational program.
3. *Develop health promotion strategies for young adolescents.* To reverse the dramatic increase in behavior-related conditions such as sexually transmitted disease, teen pregnancy, auto accidents, homicides, drug abuse, and teen suicide, proactive steps must be taken to instill in adolescents the knowledges, skills, and values that promote positive mental and physical health.
4. *Strengthen communities with young adolescents.* The community as a socializing agent must provide safe, attractive, positive growth-promoting settings during the out-of-school hours. Youth organizations must expand their reach in offering more activities that teach adolescents about life, responsibility, and respect.
5. *Promote the constructive potential of the media.* The power of the media must be used more constructively, limiting mindless violence and unrestrained sexuality and emphasizing positive role models and responsible behaviors.

PHYSICAL ACTIVITY AND SOCIALIZATION

Motor development does not take place in a vacuum but, rather, in a social setting that includes physical activity. The need for group affiliation is a frequently cited reason for participation in physical activity. Another reason is the enhancement of self-esteem through increased movement competence and confidence (Weiss, 1987). Physical activity as a socializing agent is a powerful influence on attitude formation and moral development (Shields and Bredemeier, 1995).

CONCEPT 18.6

Games, play, and sport offer opportunities for affiliation and group identity formation.

Affiliation

One of the most compelling forces of later childhood and adolescence is the need to belong. An adolescent's need to be identified as a member of a team or club often sparks interest in physical activity. The popularity of peer play and youth sport is in large part attributable to the need for affiliation. When adolescents were asked why they were involved in peer play activity, Coakley (2001) reported that one of the most frequently cited reasons was reaffirmation of friendships. Winning is not often the initial reason for engaging in peer play, but when play is converted to organized sport, winning does become an overriding goal of activity involvement.

The need for affiliation, fun, and success must be fulfilled in any sport program. Based on a survey of 8,000 youths who responded to a sport participation and attrition questionnaire tabulated for age, gender, and race, "to have fun" was reported to be the primary reason for sport participation for all groups (Seefeldt et al., 1992). Athletes must have opportunities to compete and excel, but fun and fellowship must not be ignored in a relentless quest to be "number one." Overemphasis on competition is frequently cited as a reason for dropping out of sport activities, along with burnout induced by overtraining and inadequate instruction. It has been estimated that the annual dropout rate for all youth sports is about 35 percent (Gould, 1987).

Sport offers many benefits to its participants, but a healthy balance between competition and cooperation must be maintained. Recognition of the primary need for affiliation should alert teachers, coaches, and parents to the value of play, games, and sport as socializing agents.

Self-Esteem

The nature of self-esteem development and the influences of physical activity on the developing self were discussed in detail in chapter 14 (Childhood Self-Concept Development). Self-concept is a trait that may be factored into several components representing the psychomotor, cognitive, and affective domains. Terms such as *movement competence, movement confidence,* and *perceived physical competence* refer to dimensional aspects of self-concept related to one's physical sense of self.

CONCEPT 18.7

Self-esteem and achievement are linked, but it is difficult to document a causal relationship between the two.

Physical activity as part of an adolescent's total constellation of behavior provides one important avenue by which self-concept may be reinforced. Weiss (1987) cautioned, however:

> A continuing controversy among educators pertains to the causal relationship between self-esteem and achievement. Specifically, does achievement or gains in competence lead to enhanced self-esteem, or does self-esteem influence achievement? That is, does a high level of self-esteem increase the likelihood for successful accomplishment? (pp. 103–104)

In terms of adolescent socialization, the question posed by Weiss, although interesting and in need of clarification, is moot. Regardless of whether self-esteem influences achievement or achievement influences self-esteem, physical activity plays an important but largely undetermined role in this process. In summary, and by way of introduction to the next section, it has been wisely noted that: "by our commitment to particular values we come to value ourselves" (Shields and Bredemeier, 1995, p. 15).

Values Formation

A major function of socialization is the transference of the beliefs, attitudes, and values of a culture to its citizens. All three have cognitive, affective, and action components of varying strengths. A **belief** is something that one holds to be true based on a strong cognitive component that may or may not be acted upon. On the other hand, an **attitude** is a feeling of like or dislike about something. It is a learned behavior that has placed a worth or judgement on something or someone. An attitude is a strong emotion, based on a cognitive knowledge or belief, that results in a behavior that may be either positive or negative. A **value** has been defined by Rokeach as "an enduring belief that a specific mode of conduct or end-state of existence is personally or socially preferable to an opposite or converse mode of conduct or end-state of existence" (Shields and Bredemeier, 1995, p. 15). Values have a strong cognitive link to what one sees as desirable. One who values something also tends to have a strong affective bond to the value that in turn tends to lead one to action (figure 18.1).

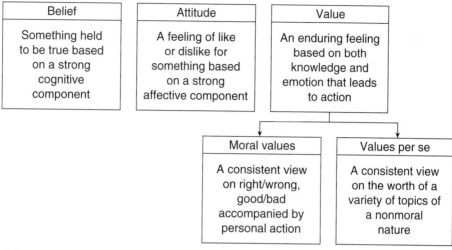

Figure 18.1

Beliefs and attitudes lead to values, which form the basis for character development through sport.

CONCEPT 18.8

Belief, attitude, and value formation are major functions of cultural socialization.

As learned behaviors, beliefs, attitudes, and values are acquired in a social context, and as such they may be taught, modified, and shaped. Their acquisition involves three things: compliance, identification, and internalization. *Compliance* is associated with doing something in the hope of getting a favorable response from someone else. For example, a young athlete, although not inclined to stretch out before a training run does so because the coach is watching. *Identification* requires one to adopt the attitude or behavior of another. The runner stretches out in preparation for her training run even when the coach is not around because she knows the coach wants her to do so. *Internalization* deals with taking on a behavior as part of one's value system. Our runner now stretches out prior to her training run because of her desire to do so.

It is values that when viewed in the moral sense, rather than values per se, as in our jogging example, of right and wrong, or good and bad that

fuels moral growth. It is moral values that are most directly related to character development through moral growth (Hunter, 2000). Physical activity can contribute to the moral growth of the adolescent, when grouped into the often elusive constructs of *character, sportsmanship,* and *fair play.*

Moral Growth

Moral behavior within a sport context is called **sportsmanship.** It is commonly believed that participation in sport develops character and instills the moral ideals of a culture in the young athletes. Sport has great potential for developing moral behavior because of the variety of emotions and unpredictable situations that arise (Coakley, 2001). Sport provides an ideal setting in which to teach the qualities of honesty, loyalty, self-control, and fairness. Participants distinguish between the *social conventional aspects* of sportsmanship and the *moral aspects of sports.* The social conventional aspects of sport are intended to maintain the structure of the social organization such as shaking hands with an opponent after a fierce tennis match, rather than cursing your opponent or belittling her play. The moral aspects of sport are rooted in honesty, loyalty, teamwork, self-control, and fair play. To date, however, no longitudinal studies have investigated moral reasoning development in a sport context. Little is known about character building through sport and if sport promotes, hinders, or has little impact on moral reasoning and behavior on or off the play field (Shields and Bredenkamp, 1995; Arnold, 2001).

 CONCEPT 18.9

Moral growth may be fostered through games, play, and sport.

Therefore, shaking hands and congratulating opponents after a contest are not examples of moral behaviors but of accepted standards of conventional behavior. Moral behaviors are intentional behaviors that benefit others. Refraining from lying, cheating, and intimidating opposing players are moral behaviors governed by respect for the rights of others.

Moral development enhances the strength of the conscience. Kohlberg (1981, 1984), a cognitive developmentalist, proposed a three-level hierarchical model of moral development that can be subdivided into six stages. Although Kohlberg's model has been criticized for its many limitations (Arnold, 2001), it serves as an excellent example of how moral reasoning may occur when viewed from a developmental perspective.

The first level is known as *preconventional morality*. The preconventional level is characteristic of the preschool and primary grade child. At this level the child is egocentric, avoids punishment, and responds to power. In stage 1 of this level, the child operates on a "whatever feels good is okay" philosophy. In stage 2, the concept of "it is okay as long as you don't get caught" predominates. At the *conventional morality level* there is a real desire to win approval and to please others. Being liked and conforming to group norms are important individual goals at stage 3 of this level. At stage 4, the law and order stage, the individual recognizes that behavior is governed by the rules of society and that laws define what is right. Operation at the conventional level is typical of the child-

hood and adolescent period. Some experts suggest that most people do not get beyond stage 4. At the *postconventional morality level* the individual is inner-directed rather than other-directed. At stage 5, the social contract stage, the individual recognizes that what is "right" is what is agreed on by the whole of society, and that some laws are unjust and can be changed. Personal behavior at this level is not regulated by law but by personal decisions about right and wrong. At stage 6, the universal ethical principle stage, the individual exhibits the highest level of **morality,** according to Kohlberg. At this stage the individual determines right and wrong within a logical, consistent, and universal framework. The dignity and worth of all of humankind is recognized (figure 18.2).

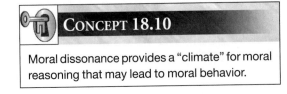 **CONCEPT 18.10**

Moral dissonance provides a "climate" for moral reasoning that may lead to moral behavior.

Moral development is not automatic but requires social settings in which moral dilemmas can be provoked, worked out, and restructured. Play activities, games, and sport offer ideal settings in which all levels of moral behavior can be observed and developed and real moral growth can occur. Unless the thought process is stimulated, dissonance (i.e., incongruity, or lack of agreement between "what is" and "what should be" thought about) will not occur. If dissonance does not occur, it is unlikely that moral growth will take place. For example, sport and physical activity can build character, but only when structured in ways that sportsmanship is developed. Sportsmanship is not an automatic outgrowth of sports participation. It is fostered through cognitive dissonance in a climate of caring coaching and developmentally appropriate experiences. Figure 18.3 provides a schematic representation of the steps leading to moral behavior.

Because moral behavior in sport is too important to be left to chance, the United States Olympic Committee adopted a *Coaching Ethics Code* (1996). This code is intended to serve as a framework for right behaviors on the part of coaches. If these stan-

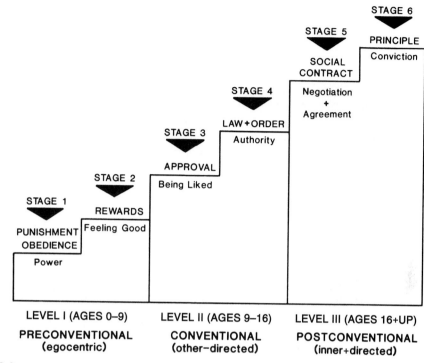

Figure 18.2
Kohlberg's stages of moral development.

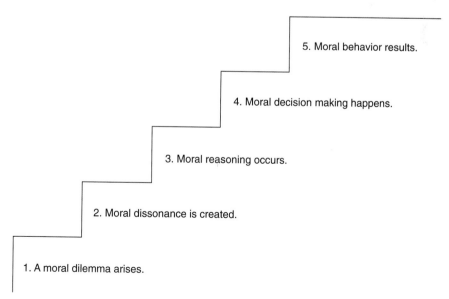

Figure 18.3
The steps leading to moral behavior.

dards are adhered to, the proper treatment of athletes as individuals is ensured. Adolescent athletes need coaches who are not only competent, confident, and highly motivated but also fair and consistent in their coaching behaviors and supportive of athletes as individuals first and athletes second.

SUMMARY

Socialization is a lifelong process that is particularly important during the period of adolescence. Cultural socialization is influenced by social status, social roles, and societal norms of behavior. Adolescents are confronted with changing status and an increasing number of roles to play. Adolescents are shaped by society, and society is shaped by them.

A variety of societal factors affect the process of adolescent socialization. Other people, institutions, and activities serve as primary socializing agents. Physical activity is an important arena of adolescent socialization. The games, play, and sport of one's culture offer opportunities for affiliation, self-esteem enhancement, attitude formation, and moral growth. The process of development is continual and multifaceted. Motor development both influences and is influenced by the process of cultural socialization.

CRITICAL READINGS

Arnold, P.J. (2001). Sport, moral development, and the role of the teacher: Implications for research and moral education. *Quest, 53,* 135–150.

Carnegie Council on Adolescent Development. (1995). *Great Transitions: Preparing Adolescents for the New Century.* Waldorf, MD: Author.

Coakley, J. J. (2001). *Sport in Society: Issues and Controversies.* Boston, MA: Times Mirror/Mosby.

Hunter, J.D. (2000). *The Death of Character, Moral Education in an Age without Good or Evil.* (Chapter 1 & 2) New York: Basic Books.

Lumpkin, A., Stoll, S. K., & Beller, J. M. (1994). *Sport Ethics, Applications for Fair Play* (Chapter 1). St. Louis, MO: Mosby.

Morgan, W., Meier, K., & Schneider, A. (2001). *Ethics in Sport.* Champaign, IL: Human Kinetics.

Shields, D. L. L., & Bredemeier, B. J. L. (1995). *Character Development and Physical Activity.* Champaign, IL: Human Kinetics.

United States Olympic Committee. (1996). *Coaching Ethics Code.* Colorado Springs, CO: Author.

 ## WEB RESOURCES

Bill of Rights for Young Athletes
http://ed-web3.educ.msu.edu/ysi/bill.html

Homepage of the American Academy of Child & Adolescent Psychiatry
www.aacap.org/

Website devoted to sportsmanship and character development through sports participation
www.charactercounts.org/sports/sports.htm

Adulthood

Age does not depend upon years,
but upon temperament and health.
Some men are born old,
and some never grow so.

—Tyron Edwards

ADULTHOOD

Wojtek Chodzko-Zajko

Wojtek Chodzko-Zajko, Ph.D., is head of the Department of Kinesiology at the University of Illinois, Champaign. He has served on the World Health Organization's Scientific Advisory Committee, which issued Guidelines for Physical Activity in Older Adults. *Dr. Chodzko-Zajko has also been editor of the* Journal of Aging and Physical Activity *and president of the International Society on Aging and Physical Activity. In addition, he has participated in the American College of Sports Medicine Strategic Health Initiative on Aging and Exercise.*

Why do you find the study of adult development and aging interesting?

Probably because of the tremendous heterogeneity associated with the aging process. I never cease to be amazed by the remarkable variability exhibited by individuals as they grow older. Some persons exhibit signs of debilitating psychological and physiological decline as early as their fifth or sixth decade of life, while others remain remarkably active and vigorous well into their eighth, ninth, and, sometimes, tenth decades. For many years it was thought that the primary determinant influencing the direction taken by human aging was genetics. However, in recent years we have come to realize that lifestyle characteristics such as nutrition, smoking, alcohol consumption, and physical activity can have a powerful impact on the aging process. In recent years I have found great intellectual satisfaction in examining the extent to which older adults are able to actively participate in the direction taken by their own aging.

What do you anticipate being a notable future research direction in the area of adult development and aging?

As an exercise scientist working in the area of aging, my early work tended to focus on examining the effects of physical activity on various aspects of the aging process. In recent years I have come to realize that while physical activity is tremendously important, physical activity alone is not sufficient for the maintenance of high quality of life in old age. In order to age successfully, older persons will need to be not only physically active, but also socially, intellectually, culturally, and (for many seniors) spiritually active. I believe that a major future research trend in the area of adult development and aging

will be the examination of the impact of integrated activity programs in older adults. For example, the success of the Elder Hostel movement in North America and the University of the Third Age throughout the world suggests that there is a great demand for intellectual, cultural, and artistic programming among the older adult community. Furthermore, there is a growing body of research to suggest that participating in lifelong learning programs is associated with tangible physical and psychological benefits. However, relatively few research studies have examined the impact of such integrated programs in a systematic and controlled manner. I believe that one of the research trends of the future will be to examine how interventions which provide opportunities for physical, intellectual, cultural, and spiritual growth can influence the direction taken by human aging.

How has the study of adult development and aging benefitted the average person?

The study of adult development and aging has done much to alter stereotypic attitudes and values about old age and the aging process. It was once widely accepted that advancing age was associated with inevitable and inescapable physiological and psychological decline. However, it is now recognized that aging need not always be associated with decline and decay, doom and gloom. For many older persons, there is a very real possibility that they will be able to grow old as healthy, independent, productive, respected, and valued members of society. By helping to redefine stereotypic and ageist concepts of aging and old age, research in adult development and aging has done a great deal to benefit the average person as he or she grows older.

CHAPTER

19

PHYSIOLOGICAL CHANGES IN ADULTS

KEY TERMS

Task specificity

Interindividual variability

Intraindividual variability

Free radicals

Homeostasis

Osteoporosis

Antioxidants

Brain plasticity

Age markers

Hypoxia

Arteriosclerosis

Atherosclerosis

Senile miosis

Presbycusis

CHAPTER COMPETENCIES

Upon completion of this chapter you should be able to:

- Discuss the limitations of generalizing about declines during the adult years
- Describe how the interaction among characteristics of the individual, the nature of the task, and the environmental conditions affects the motor performance of adults
- Discuss how the concepts of task specificity, interindividual variability, and intraindividual variability influence the success levels of adult motor performance
- Describe the theories of aging related to cellular changes, the human immune system, and homeostasis
- Identify age-related changes in the musculoskeletal system
- Identify age-related changes in the central nervous system
- Identify age-related changes in the circulatory and respiratory systems
- Identify age-related changes in the sensory systems

> ## KEY CONCEPT
>
> Throughout adulthood, changes in the body's physiological systems may influence motor performance and may represent a mechanism of the aging process.

Decade after decade the average lifespan of human beings has reflected a steady increase. Continual improvements in health care, disease reduction, and lifestyle changes have resulted in steady increases in the average number of years both men and women live. As a result, more older adults are represented in the general population (figure 19.1a). Likewise, with increased medical interventions and improved lifestyle behaviors many more adults are living and will live into their eighties and nineties (figure 19.1b) (U.S. Census Bureau, 2001).

As we enter adulthood, we experience a number of physical and physiological changes that affect our behavior. Likewise, as we continue through the life span, changes in our affective and cognitive abilities alter how we respond to our environment. As discussed in earlier chapters, these domains are not mutually exclusive but are intricately interrelated. These relationships are evident when an older individual compensates for an age-related slowing of reaction time by using different cognitive strategies to accomplish a task. We also see the association between the different domains when older individuals experience declines in self-competency and self-esteem as age-related changes in muscular strength begin to limit their abilities to perform functional daily living skills.

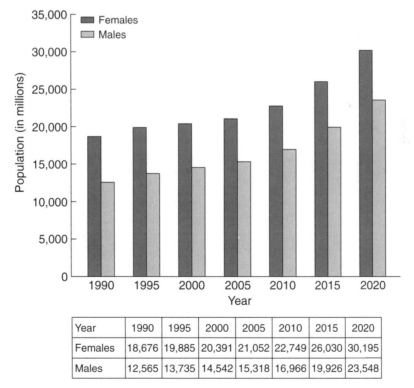

Year	1990	1995	2000	2005	2010	2015	2020
Females	18,676	19,885	20,391	21,052	22,749	26,030	30,195
Males	12,565	13,735	14,542	15,318	16,966	19,926	23,548

Figure 19.1a

Past figures and future projections of the population of adults 65 years of age and older.

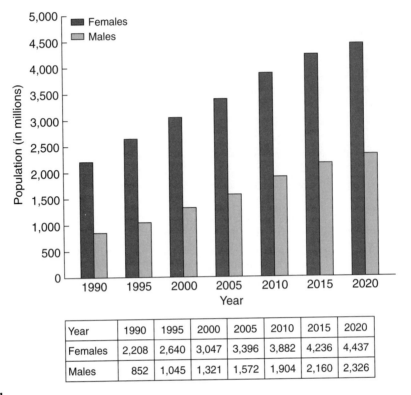

Year	1990	1995	2000	2005	2010	2015	2020
Females	2,208	2,640	3,047	3,396	3,882	4,236	4,437
Males	852	1,045	1,321	1,572	1,904	2,160	2,326

Figure 19.1b

Past figures and future projections of the population of adults 85 years of age and older.

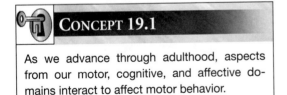

CONCEPT 19.1

As we advance through adulthood, aspects from our motor, cognitive, and affective domains interact to affect motor behavior.

When we generalize about behavior and performance across the life span, we usually make the observation that individuals experience continual improvement from infancy through adolescence, a leveling off during young adulthood, a slow decline during middle adulthood, and a much greater decline during older adulthood. A major problem emerges, however, when we describe a complex event like human development in such simplistic terms. This oversimplified perception of the aging process can place unrealistic expectations on young children and unnecessary limitations on older adults. In adulthood some functions follow the general pattern, but other characteristics show no signs of deterioration, and some show the capacity for continual improvement. Spirduso and MacRae (1990) point out that variability in the motor performance of adults increases with each decade of life. "The descriptions of 'average' behavior for specific age groups grow less and less accurate for an individual's performance as the age of the group increases" (p. 183).

The motor behavior exhibited by an individual depends on the interaction of a number of variables categorized by: (1) the nature of the task; (2) the environmental conditions; and (3) the cognitive, affective, and psychomotor characteristics of the individual. The nature of a task involves such elements as degree of difficulty, duration, and the need for speed or accuracy. An older adult whose vision has weakened may not be able to perform a specific task successfully if it involves speed. If, however, there are no time requirements, the individual may complete the task with a high degree of success.

CONCEPT 19.2

Although many age-related changes reflect general trends, individual characteristics play a major role in determining whether a person follows those trends.

Examples of the environmental conditions that may influence motor behavior include room temperature, lighting, floor surface texture, and degree of familiarity of surroundings. An older individual with an age-related slowing of the circulatory system will likely feel uncomfortable in a cool room. Discomfort and stiffness could limit the person's ability to complete required tasks.

The third category related to motor behavior pertains to the state of the individual. In reference to the cognitive domain, the ability to understand skill instructions is vital to the successful completion of a motor task. An inability to follow verbal instructions may be the result of an age-related loss in hearing, which could prevent or restrict pertinent information from reaching otherwise healthy processing centers of the brain. On the other hand, an older person who appears to have trouble understanding verbal instructions may have Alzheimer's disease (a disease that greatly affects cerebral functioning). Affective domain characteristics that may influence motor behavior include motivation, peer relationships, and self-confidence. An older adult who has recently lost a spouse or a close friend may lack the motivation to be physically active or to try hard in the performance of a motor task he or she regards as unimportant.

Finally, in the motor domain, physiological changes play a crucial role in the performance of a motor task. Older adults usually experience declines in muscular strength, vision, and other systems. These age-related changes are discussed in greater detail later in this chapter.

CONCEPT 19.3

Individual characteristics, demands of the task, and environmental circumstances are major factors in determining the level of success experienced by the adult in performance of a motor task.

In reviewing various aspects of motor performance in the adulthood years, three key principles emerge. The first of these is that the maturity or success of the performance of a motor task is **task specificity**. The generalization that the motor performance of an individual will deteriorate with age may be true for some tasks but certainly not for all. The degree of performance success depends on the specific demands of the task. Does the task require speed of movement, accuracy, or both? Does the task require a specific amount of joint flexibility or cardiovascular endurance? Does the task require a great deal of memorization? As we mentioned earlier in this chapter, certain physiological systems will experience age-related functional decline through adulthood, whereas other physiological systems may remain relatively unchanged. If the demands of a particular task require an individual to use a physiological system in decline, performance may be less than ideal. If, however, the motor task demands require the use of healthy physiological systems, no physiological limitations should prevent the individual from performing the task successfully. Other limiting factors (i.e., constraints) may impair task performance, but these also follow the concept of task specificity. A high degree of room illumination may be necessary for the completion of one task, whereas it may have little or no bearing on whether another task is completed successfully.

CONCEPT 19.4

The aging of different physiological systems varies among adults and within individual adults.

A second principle that emerges from this review is that there is a tremendous amount of **interindividual variability** in how people age. Both genetics and lifestyle play vital roles in determining the life spans of individuals. A person who has a lineage of nonagenarians (persons 90 years of age or older, but less than 100) probably has in her genetic blueprint the makings of a long life. Her lifestyle choices will affect whether her longevity will reach its genetic potential. Level of physical activity, smoking, stress, drug abuse, and diet are important lifestyle variables that impact the number of years we live. Similarly, in the area of motor performance in adults, a certain physiological system may deteriorate more slowly in one individual than in another because of genetic differences. If a motor task requires a high degree of muscular strength, for example, the person who genetically loses muscular strength at a slower rate may have an easier time completing the task than a person whose ancestors tended to experience strength loss more rapidly. An individual's lifestyle choices may affect various physiological systems and, in turn, may influence the performance of a motor task dependent on the healthy functioning of those physiological systems. A number of additional variables affect the outcomes of motor tasks. We cannot isolate a single variable and predict the likelihood of success. We can, however, realize that genetic blueprints and lifestyles vary widely and consequently affect the motor performances of specific tasks in different ways, depending on requirements of the tasks.

This leads to the next principle of **intraindividual variability**. Individual physiological systems do not necessarily experience age-related declines at the same rate. Certain physiological characteristics will begin to decline in early adulthood, and others wait until later. Still other characteristics will not experience declines at all. Generalizing about an individual's overall developmental rate without considering variations among her or his personal characteristics may limit the individual's movement potential.

Combining the three principles of task specificity, interindividual variability, and intraindividual variability with the knowledge that motor performance can vary in accordance with the requirement of the task, the environment, and the biology of the individual provides us with the foundation to evaluate the motor performance of adults from an individual basis rather than a generalistic approach. A percentage of the adult-aged population will face limitations and stereotyping when their performances are evaluated with a generalistic approach. As with children and adolescents, the motor performance of adults should be assessed using individual characteristics following their individual developmental rates.

WHY DO WE AGE?

A number of theories seek to provide the answer to the age-old question "Why do we age?" Many early theorists suggested that the human body simply wears out through the wear and tear of daily living. They compared the human body to a machine that breaks down and wears out parts with continual use (and sometimes abuse). The performance of the machine deteriorates, and it eventually ceases to operate. This analogy suggests that deterioration is a continual process. Although this may be the case with some human characteristics, it is not representative of the total aging process. To the contrary, numerous investigations have demonstrated that the use of the human body (i.e., through exercise and physical activity) can slow, stop, or in some cases reverse aspects of age-related deterioration. Chodzko-Zajko (1999a) points out "it is well established that significant physiological, psychological, social, and societal benefits accrue from participation in physical activity and that the benefits of a physically active lifestyle extend throughout the lifespan" (p. 213).

CONCEPT 19.5

Changes at the cellular level, at the immune system level, and/or in the interaction of the physiological systems may represent the underlying causes of aging.

A number of theories have been presented to address the question of why we age. The level at which these theories approach the aging question range from the cellular to the whole organism.

At the cellular level we are interested in what happens to the integrity of the cells of the human body during aging. Every part of the body is structured of cells. Each cell has a specific function and possesses the genetic material to accomplish that function. Cells divide and increase in number for growth, maturation, and/or maintenance of a particular organ or tissue. What has been demonstrated is that the number of times a cell can divide is limited. Hayflick (1980) observed that connective tissue cells divided approximately fifty times. It is possible that the cells are programmed genetically to shut down after a certain number of replications. Another possibility is that the genetic material that dictates cell function may change or mutate as time passes. As these mutated cells increase, either through ongoing cell mutation and/or replication during cell division, they may cause deterioration in the tissue or organ. Depending on the function of the affected organ or tissue, deficits may appear in motor performance, overall health, or both. The likelihood of such deficits increases when these cellular changes occur in more than one organ or tissue. A third possibility at the cellular level pertains to the free radical theory. Certain molecules within a cell react violently when they come in contact with oxygen. These molecules break away from the cell and become unstable fragments. These highly reactive molecular components are referred to as **free radicals.** Free radicals attempt to bind with other molecules within healthy cells negatively influencing the normal cell function and possibly causing DNA

damage. Aging may be a manifestation of this process (Hoyer, Rybash, and Roodin, 1999).

A second approach to understanding why we age involves the function of the human immune system, which consists of the lymph nodes, spleen, thymus, and lymphoid tissue in the tonsils and intestine. The purpose of the immune system is to protect us from various organisms that enter the body. With age, the human immune system gradually decreases in effectiveness. This increases the vulnerability of older adults to illnesses and extends their recovery times. In addition, the immune system of an older individual may begin to target healthy organ and tissue cells for destruction, as if they were "bad" cells. These immune system malfunctions may represent the process by which we age.

A third possible explanation as to why we age involves the concept of **homeostasis.** Homeostasis refers to the maintenance of stability in the physiological systems and their interrelationships. Homeostasis is the state in which various systems of the body (i.e., sensory, digestive, and cardiovascular) work in harmony to keep the body in normal, healthy condition. The human body is an incredibly complex network of systems that carry out their functions both independently and in combination. Guyton (1991) stated that the cells of the organs and tissues within the interrelated systems benefit from a homeostatic state and contribute to its maintenance. This harmonious state is maintained until a particular system or group of systems malfunctions or cannot contribute to the maintenance of homeostasis. The degree to which negative consequences are manifested depends on the ability of the other systems to adapt and the degree to which the dysfunctional system is unable to contribute to the homeostatic network. A moderate level of dysfunction in a particular system may impair health and the ability to carry out functional daily living skills. A high level of disruption leads to death.

There appears to be a reciprocal relationship between aging and the maintenance of a homeostatic state. With age, the balance among the systems involved in homeostasis is less stable and more vulnerable to disruption. Individual systems appear to experience age-related decreases in their ability to contribute to the homeostatic equilibrium. Subsequently, age-related characteristics begin to emerge. Greater susceptibility to illnesses, longer recovery times from illnesses, and greater limitations in motor performance become more prevalent.

CONCEPT 19.6

Current and potential interventions may result in extending the lifespan by slowing the aging process.

As mentioned earlier, life expectancy of both males and females increases consistently and thus the population of older adults in the United States continues to expand. Much of these increases in life expectancy can be attributed to lifestyle. Well-known behaviors such as not smoking, reducing the intake of high cholesterol foods, and minimizing psychological stress contribute to longer life spans. Certainly a physically active lifestyle can add years to one's life expectancy. For the most part, these factors contribute to the average life span by reducing the potential for contracting life-shortening diseases.

Two interventions that have had a positive life extending influence in laboratory animals relate to the intake of **antioxidants** and dietary restriction. The theory behind antioxidants involves the reduction of the influence of free radicals. Antioxidants (agents that prevent or inhibit oxidation) such as vitamins C and E may prolong life and delay the aging process by binding with free radicals before they have the opportunity to harm healthy body cells.

Research beginning in the 1930s, and replicated many times, has demonstrated an increase in the life span of laboratory rats as a result of moderate to severe dietary restriction. By reducing the animals' caloric intake by 25 to 40 percent but maintaining the proper levels of vitamins and nutrients the rats lived significantly longer than their counterparts who were allowed to eat freely (Hoyer, Rybash, and Roodin, 1999). Although certain successes with these intervention strategies have been

experienced with laboratory animals, their potential with humans has yet to be determined.

PHYSIOLOGICAL CHANGES IN THE ADULT MUSCULOSKELETAL SYSTEM

The human skeleton is multifaceted in its function. It protects internal organs, gives form to the body, acts as levers from which muscles attach, provides a reserve site for calcium, and develops blood cells in the bone marrow. Skeletal muscles excited by the central nervous system move most of the bones of the body. In addition, the muscles, tendons, and ligaments provide stability to the articulating joints throughout the body.

Skeleton

Various changes within the skeletal structure appear as a person ages. Many individuals experience a shortening in stature. This "shrinkage" may be attributed to one or more causes. As we age, the disks that separate the vertebrae of the spinal column undergo various changes. In a healthy state, intervertebral disks possess jellylike nuclei. The vertebral disks of older adults often lose a portion of the water content important for shock absorption, and the disks become more fibrous. This, along with changes in bone mineral density in the vertebrae, results in compression of the disks. Disk compression reduces the length of the vertebral column and causes the subsequent loss of overall height. Other contributors to age-related height loss include spinal misalignment and poor posture. Curving of the spine may result from a reduction of the shock-absorption capacity of the vertebral disks. Postural problems may reflect weakening in the muscles that support the spine and thorax (rib cage). Although these conditions appear in many older adults, they are not inevitable. A certain amount of vertebral water content loss may occur, but the muscles supporting the spine and thorax can maintain strength through physical activity and proper exercises. In addition, the loss of bone mineral content may be prevented or slowed through proper treatment.

CONCEPT 19.7

Osteoporosis represents a potentially debilitating disease that requires the attention of individuals at all stages of adulthood.

The disease **osteoporosis** may contribute to height reduction in older adults, but its other consequences can be much more devastating. Osteoporosis is characterized by a reduction of *bone mineral density* severe enough to increase vulnerability to fractures of the bone (figure 19.2).

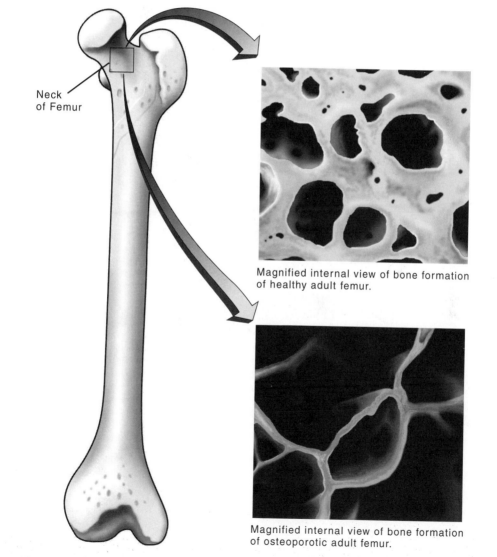

Neck
of Femur

Magnified internal view of bone formation of healthy adult femur.

Magnified internal view of bone formation of osteoporotic adult femur.

Figure 19.2
Bone loss due to osteoporosis.

In healthy bone, the ongoing process of bone mineral production and absorption maintains a balance in calcium metabolism regulated by the endocrine system. With age, that balance between absorption and production becomes less stable, and more bone mineral content is absorbed than is produced. Although this imbalance normally leads to a slight age-related loss in bone density, osteoporosis accelerates the process. As the bone mineral content is reduced, the bones become increasingly porous and fragile. Fractures can occur within a bone, causing that bone to compress. These compression fractures are often seen in the spinal column of older adults with osteoporosis. Normal weight-bearing stress on the spinal column causes tiny fractures in the individual vertebrae. As more fractures occur, the vertebrae become more compressed and the position of the thorax is altered. This positional change can adversely affect the functions of the lungs and other internal organs directly below the thorax region. In addition, postural deviations and spinal deformities are common with osteoporosis (figure 19.3).

Individuals with osteoporosis are more vulnerable to fractures *within* a bone, but fractures *of* the bone also represent a major concern. As the

Progressive Spinal Deformity in Osteoporosis

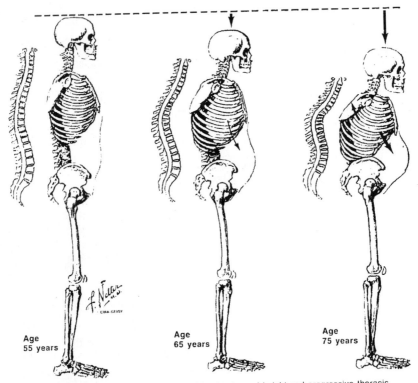

Age
55 years

Age
65 years

Age
75 years

Compression fractures of thoracic vertebrae lead to loss of height and progressive thoracic kyphosis (dowager's hump). Lower ribs eventually rest on iliac crests, and downward pressure on viscera causes abdominal distention

Figure 19.3
Skeletal changes with osteoporosis.
From F. Kaplan, *Clinical Symposia CIBA 35*, No. 5, 1983. © Copyright 1983 CIBA Pharmaceutical Company, Division of CIBA-GEIGY Corporation. Reprinted by permission.

bone mineral content declines and bones become more porous, the individual with osteoporosis is at great risk of bone breakage as a result of minimal trauma. We often hear reports of older adults falling and breaking their hips. Even the force experienced from a fairly mild fall may be sufficient to break a brittle femur ravaged by osteoporosis. Of additional concern is that osteoporotic bones heal at a much slower rate than healthy bones.

Osteoporosis can occur in both men and women, but it is present in a much higher rate in postmenopausal women. Women lose bone at a much faster rate than men due to more drastic hormonal changes with age and because they begin with less bone mass (Spirduso, 1995). Hormonal changes experienced by women following menopause may disrupt bone mineral formation. Other factors that play a role in maintaining bone density are calcium intake and weight-bearing physical activity. Calcium plays an important role in regulating bone metabolism, and weight-bearing stress aids in building and maintaining bone density. Hormonal changes, the reduction of calcium intake, and restrictions in weight-bearing exercises place an individual at risk for significant bone mineral loss.

It has been demonstrated that astronauts in space suffered substantial bone mineral loss after only a few weeks in a weightless environment. Upon arriving back to Earth's gravitational pull and performing various exercises, they recovered most but not all of their preflight bone density. This phenomenon confounds the situation for the older adult recovering from a hip fracture. The weight-bearing restrictions placed on the broken hip for healing purposes can further increase bone mineral loss.

Drinkwater has called osteoporosis the "silent thief of the golden years" (1992). Outward signs of the disease are usually not evident until the vertebrae experience compression fractures. Posture deviations become apparent, or the individual begins to experience back pain from spinal misalignment. However, since the late 1970s diagnostic technology has been able to safely and accurately identify an individual's bone density. Because osteoporosis

is preventable, using such technology to monitor bone density is essential and should begin in early adulthood. Comparing an individual's bone density with a bone density standard for healthy young adults will tell a physician if that person is subject to an accelerated bone loss rate. Treatment can minimize future bone loss. Although osteoporosis is preventable, it is not yet reversible. However, diagnosis and treatment can restrict further bone loss, even in those individuals whose bone mineral stores are depleted.

Treatment for osteoporosis involves hormonal replacement for postmenopausal women; increasing calcium intake; and, of particular interest to the movement specialist, increasing weight-bearing exercises. Additional factors that play a detrimental role in a person's bone density include smoking, alcohol abuse, and high consumption of caffeine (Shephard, 1997). Drinkwater points out a principle of specificity that applies to weight-bearing activities. Weight-bearing stress must be directed to a specific bone area for that bone to be affected. This is valuable information for movement professionals planning physical activities for individuals with osteoporosis. Also, recognize that exercise should be seen as an adjunct to the primary treatment of hormonal replacement (Drinkwater, 1994).

Muscles and Joints

Muscular strength is essential for the performance of motor skills, whether they are related to high-level athletic performance or daily functional living. With age the structure and function of skeletal muscle change. Structurally, muscle mass decreases as the number and size of muscle fibers decline through the late middle and older adulthood years. Functionally, a decrease in muscular strength seems to parallel this loss in muscle tissue. The general adulthood pattern for muscle strength is represented by a peak in strength at about 25 to 30 years, a plateau until approximately 50 years, and a gradual decline until about 70 years, followed by a much sharper strength decline in the succeeding years (figure 19.4). Cross-sectional data indicate an approximate 20 percent loss in strength for males

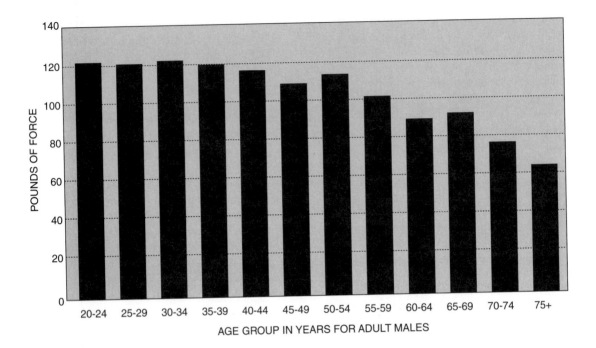

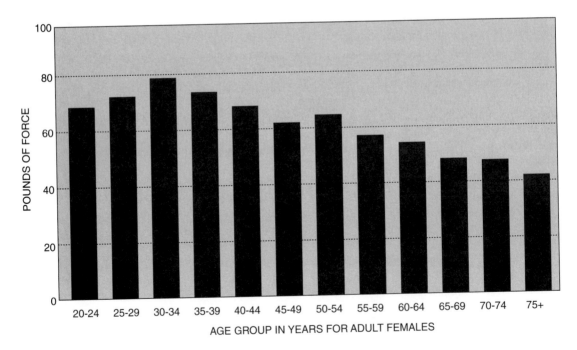

Figure 19.4

Muscular strength across adulthood (adult male and female mean right grip strength measures).

Source: Data graphed from Mathiowetz et al. (1985).

after 55 years of age and a more drastic 35 percent strength decline in women who are 55 years or older (Samson et al., 2000). Longitudinal data appear to support the loss of strength in the older adult years but indicate that significant strength declines are not manifested until the early older adulthood years rather than the late middle adulthood years.

The previous paragraph outlined a general viewpoint regarding age-related muscle performance, but several specific variables should be considered concerning the performance of an individual. Although a loss of muscle mass, or *muscle atrophy*, appears to occur with age, muscle atrophy also occurs as a result of inactivity. Inactivity-induced atrophy can occur at any age and is not only a function of growing old. There is substantial evidence that adults who maintain physically active lifestyles experience much smaller declines in muscular strength than their nonactive peers (Lemmer et al., 2000; O'Neill et al., 2000). In individuals 90 years or older, it has been demonstrated that a strength-training program improves muscular strength and increases muscle mass (Fiatarone et al., 1990). Additional evidence indicates that even frail older adults can gain increases in strength following a low-intensity training program (Westhoff, Stemmerik, and Boshuizen, 2000). Clearly, an individual's lifestyle represents a key variable in determining whether his or her muscular strength capacity will follow or deviate from the general curve.

Another important consideration about strength involves the requirements of a particular task. Although *muscular strength* is often used to describe the muscle functions of a particular movement task, most skills require some combination of muscular strength and *muscular endurance*. It has been demonstrated that muscular endurance is less affected by aging than is muscular strength. Dummer, Vaccaro, and Clarke (1985) found no significant differences between the muscular endurance of young adult swimmers and older adult swimmers. Their findings indicate that it may be possible to offset age-related declines in muscular endurance by engaging in physically active lifestyles. It likewise makes us aware that an older adult may be more likely to complete muscular endurance-related motor tasks than muscular strength-related tasks.

A general trend in age-related changes in muscle function is apparent, but tremendous interindividual variability exists. The loss of muscle mass often seen with increasing years is also affected by the adult's levels of physical activity and muscle use. In addition, the muscle function demands of various tasks influence task performance outcome.

Joints and connective tissues appear to undergo age-related changes. Joints become less flexible. In general terms, joint flexibility peaks for young adults in their twenties and gradually declines thereafter. Much of the reduction of flexibility can be attributed to water loss in the connective tissue resulting in greater stiffness of ligaments and tendons. There is also an age-related loss in the water content of the cartilage tissue. A loss of flexibility, and in some cases a loss of joint stability, can be of significant consequence to the older adult in carrying out everyday functional living tasks. Physically active lifestyles and stretching exercises appear to retard age-related loss in joint flexibility.

At the extreme end, age-related joint diseases such as osteoarthritis not only place limitations on certain movements but can totally restrict them as well. Osteoarthritis is the most prevalent form of arthritis in people 50 years of age or older, and at least half of the population over 60 years of age show some symptoms of the disease. Treatment involves therapy to maintain joint activity and flexibility; increasing strength in muscles associated with affected joints; reducing of body fat to reduce strain on weight-bearing areas; relieving pain with analgesics; and in extreme cases, total joint replacement surgery (Shepard, 1997).

CENTRAL NERVOUS SYSTEM

The components of the central nervous system (CNS) are the brain and spinal cord, with the neuron representing the basic unit by which signals are transmitted. The human brain has approximately 100 billion neurons, requiring an incredibly complex network of neuronal connections. The

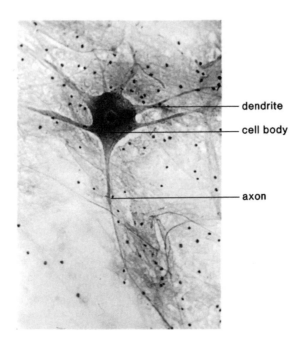

dendrite
cell body
axon

Figure 19.5
Structure of the neuron.

three primary elements of the neuron are the cell body, axon, and dendrite (figure 19.5).

Dendrites carry signals to the cell body, while *axons* carry signals away. Signal transmissions throughout the CNS are both electrical and chemical. Electrical signals travel along dendritic branches to the cell body and then along the axon. The transmission of the signal from one neuron to another involves altering the electrical signal to a chemical signal and then back to an electrical signal. This occurs at the junction between two neurons. The chemical substances released during this event are called *neurotransmitters.*

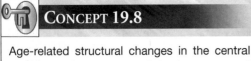

CONCEPT 19.8

Age-related structural changes in the central nervous system may result in decrements of various functions.

A number of age-related changes occur in the CNS. Structurally, the brain experiences a continual loss of neurons that are not replaced. We are born with all of our nerve cells, and when they die they are not replaced. We lose thousands of brain cells each day without generating replacements. Consequently, the brain of the older adult is smaller and weighs less than the brain of a younger adult. In addition, the size of the ventricles or brain cavities increase, particularly during older adulthood. Although this age-related neuronal loss is sufficient to decrease brain size and weight, some sections of the brain are less susceptible to neuron decreases than others. The cerebral cortex experiences a 10 to 20 percent loss of mass between the ages of 20 to 90, whereas other sections of the brain may undergo as much as a 50 percent loss in mass. Therefore, any functional changes that may occur as a result of neuronal loss should be considered specific to certain regions.

Although it should follow that the loss of millions of neurons through adulthood would affect behavior, this assumption ignores the adaptable nature of the brain or what is called **brain plasticity.** Neurons are continually dying, but there is evidence that living neurons develop compensatory dendritic branches to help maintain connections that may otherwise deteriorate. Although the pathway connections may be maintained, the strength of the signal may be reduced or distorted when fewer neurons are involved in the signal transmission. In addition, signals that deviate slightly from their designated courses may not be corrected. The ultimate changes in behavior due to neuron loss remain unclear. While compensation mechanisms may maintain signal pathways, the quality of those signals may be compromised. Some intriguing research in the area of brain plasticity has been conducted recently by William Greenough and his colleagues at the University of Illinois. They have been able to demonstrate structural changes in the brains of laboratory animals who have engaged in complex movement tasks (Ivanco and Greenough, 2000; Jones and Greenough, 1996; Jones, Klintsova, Kilman, Sirevaag, and Greenough, 1997; Kleim, Pipitone, Czerlanis, and Greenough, 1998). While there is a significant leap from laboratory rats to human beings, this line of investigation is worth monitoring.

Other manifestations that appear to be age-related are abnormal formations including *neurofibrillary tangles, senile plaques,* and an accumulation of *lipofuscin.* These formations are often referred to as **age markers** because they appear in the older brain and increase in number as the brain continues to age. Neurofibrillary tangles occur when long, thin fibers that transport chemical substances to all parts of the neuron become twisted and entangled. It is thought that these neurofibrillary tangles may contribute to a slowing of CNS responsiveness and may play a role in the eventual death of the neuron in which they are housed. Senile plaques are spherical formations composed of substances remaining from degenerated neurons. The plaques are located outside of the neuron and may interfere with normal

neuronal transmission by disrupting the synaptic juncture. Experts suggest that senile plaques may play a role in memory loss. Neurofibrillary tangles and senile plaques are also present in large quantities in the brains of individuals with Alzheimer's disease. Lipofuscin is a brownish or yellowish pigment that appears in neurons as the brain ages. The effects of lipofuscin on neuronal function have not been confirmed, but there is a greater concentration of the pigment around less active neurons. Therefore, the presence of lipofuscin may retard or inhibit cell activity.

As mentioned earlier, neurotransmitters are instrumental in the sending and receiving of neuronal signals. They are chemical substances that regulate the passage of signals across the synaptic junction. As the brain ages, this biochemical activity is often affected. The amount of neurotransmitter available as the signal reaches the synapse may be reduced, and the signal may decrease in strength. Extreme deficiencies of the neurotransmitter dopamine is characteristic of Parkinson's disease.

Finally, the aging brain is susceptible to **hypoxia,** a condition in which the brain receives an inadequate amount of oxygen. Nerve cells of the brain are particularly vulnerable to oxygen deficits, which affects their function and longevity. With age, the circulation of oxygen-carrying blood gradually declines due to structural changes in the circulatory system and decreases in physical activity. The movement specialist must remember that increasing the level of physical activity in the older adult can enhance the blood flow to the brain and, in turn, increase the amount of oxygen reaching the nerve cells.

CIRCULATORY AND RESPIRATORY SYSTEMS

The circulatory system involves the heart, blood vessels, and blood delivering nutrients to and removing wastes from the organs and tissues of the body (figure 19.6). The nose, mouth, pharynx, larynx, trachea, bronchi, and lungs comprising the respiratory system serve the body's organs and tissues by

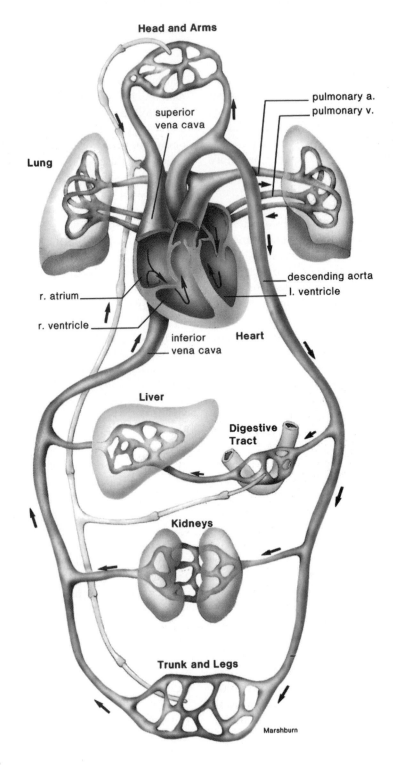

Head and Arms

pulmonary a.
pulmonary v.

superior
vena cava

Lung

descending aorta
l. ventricle

r. atrium

r. ventricle

inferior
vena cava

Heart

Liver

Digestive
Tract

Kidneys

Trunk and Legs

Marshburn

Figure 19.6

Characteristics of the circulatory system.

From Sylvia S. Mader, *Understanding Human Anatomy and Physiology* (Dubuque, IA: Wm. C. Brown, 1991). Reprinted by permission of The McGraw-Hill Companies.

372

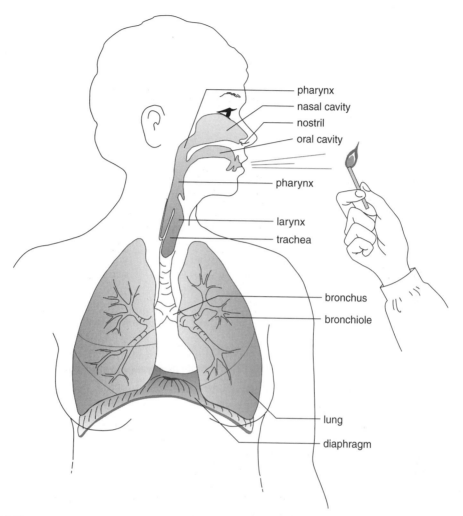

Figure 19.7

Characteristics of the respiratory system.

providing oxygen and eliminating carbon dioxide (figure 19.7). Both systems must function properly to keep the body healthy, and they play important roles in the performance of many tasks. Sufficient oxygen and nutrient delivery and waste transport are necessary for muscle fibers, neurons, and all cells of the body to carry out their appointed functions.

CONCEPT 19.9

Declines in an adult's circulatory and respiratory functions may be the result of age, disease, lifestyle, or combinations of the three.

Although a number of changes take place in the main organs and tissues of the circulatory and respiratory systems as adults age, determining the underlying cause or causes of these changes is extremely difficult. Lifestyle choices, disease, aging, or some combination thereof contribute to changes that occur in these two systems. Separating these variables and delineating their individual effects on the systemic changes represent an arduous and sometimes impossible endeavor, but certain factors are more easily identified as age-related, lifestyle-associated, or disease-initiated. When possible, the origins of these changes will be addressed in the following discussion.

As the adult human body ages, the heart and blood vessels tend to undergo changes that affect their functions. Arteries serve as the primary pathways by which oxygenated blood is pumped to the various organs and tissues throughout the body. The arterial walls contract to keep the blood moving. During the adult years the arterial walls become less elastic and more rigid, representing a condition known as **arteriosclerosis.** An increase in calcification and a buildup of collagen connective tissue in the arteries cause arteriosclerosis, which occurs as a result of aging rather than disease. A second condition, **atherosclerosis,** is also seen in adults as they become older, but it represents a cardiovascular disease rather than the normal aging process. Atherosclerosis occurs when fatty deposits begin to collect within arteries. If the deposits do not completely close off the arterial openings, they create sites on the arterial walls on which blood clots can form. Both arteriosclerosis and atherosclerosis affect the performance of the circulatory system. With both conditions blood pressure increases and the amount of oxygen and nutrients reaching the cells of the body decreases. This may impair the performance efficiency of the organs and tissues.

Other circulatory changes seen in adults as they age include changes in the valves of the heart and vessels. Valves within the circulatory system become thicker and less elastic. As a result, they work less efficiently.

A number of age-related changes are observed in the organs involved in respiration. The function of the lungs tends to increase through adolescence, plateau in the third decade, and gradually decline thereafter. This decline follows an age-related pattern, but the reduction during the fourth and fifth decades tends to be linked to factors such as an increase in body weight rather than to changes in the tissues. Other age-related variables that influence lung function include reduced levels of muscular strength in the muscle groups that aid in respiration. Postural problems often experienced by older adults may anatomically restrict the expansion capabilities of the lungs. Curvatures of the spine can compress the thorax and push the lungs against other internal organs, impairing the work of the lungs and the other crowded organs.

Maximal oxygen uptake (VO_2 max) represents the best physiological measure of total body endurance. It serves to evaluate the greatest amount of oxygen that reaches the tissues during a maximum exercise effort by an individual. The general age-related trend in maximal oxygen uptake levels begins with a continual increase during childhood and adolescence. A plateauing during the twenties is followed by a gradual decline of approximately 1 percent for each subsequent year. Much of this continuous loss during middle adulthood can be attributed to other age-associated conditions such as a decline in the amount of blood pumped by the heart to the tissues and a loss of muscle mass. Many of the previously mentioned declines can be significantly minimized when older adults participate in aerobic-oriented activities. Boileau et al. (1999) points out that for older adults aerobic exercise training has a positive impact on a multitude of factors including mortality, several chronic diseases including coronary heart disease, noninsulin-dependent diabetes, selected cancers, hypertension, body composition, bone mineral density, immune function, and depression. Other investigators have demonstrated that the cognitive functioning of older adults shows improvement when aerobic exercise is part of their lifestyle (Kramer, 2000; Kramer, Hahn, and McAuley, 2000).

SENSORY SYSTEMS

We gain information about the environment through various sensory systems. Different sensory receptors send to the central nervous system information about taste, smell, vision, touch, pain, sound, and other sensations. Some sensory systems—in particular visual, auditory, and proprioception—play crucial roles in motor performance.

 CONCEPT 19.10

Age-related changes in the eyes and ears can result in insufficient or distorted visual, auditory, and proprioceptive transmissions to the brain.

Visual System

For many if not most movement skills, vision represents the dominant sensory system. Vision occurs when the eye receives light rays reflected by objects in the visual field. As the light rays reach the eye, they are refracted as they pass through the cornea, aqueous humor, pupil, lens, and vitreous humor before the image reaches the retina. Refraction involves a process of bending the light rays. The degree to which the rays are bent depends on the transparency of the eye structures and the angles of light rays as they enter the eye. The cornea is the fibrous, transparent covering of the eyeball. The aqueous humor is a watery solution located in a chamber just behind the cornea and in front of the pupil and lens. Muscles attached to the iris contract or relax to determine pupil size. The size of the pupil regulates the amount of light that passes through the crystalline lens and into the vitreous body. The vitreous body holds a jellylike fluid called the vitreous humor. After the light rays have been refracted through the various transparent medium, they form an image on the retina, the inner membrane of the eyeball. The retina transfers the image by way of the optic nerve to the cortex of the brain.

With age, the eye tends to undergo a number of structural and functional changes that affect the quality of vision. Visual quality is generally maintained during the early adulthood years, but anatomical changes that begin to occur during middle adulthood have a gradual but detrimental effect on visual abilities. However, such declines during these middle adulthood years rarely limit the ability to carry out everyday tasks. During the older adulthood years, the visual decrements experienced in middle adulthood become more pronounced and have a greater impact on functional and adaptive abilities.

As the eye ages, the cornea begins to flatten somewhat, increases in thickness, and develops surface waviness and irregularities. These changes in the curvature of the outer eye alter the pathway of the light rays entering the eye and diminish the accuracy of the refractory process. The amount of light that eventually reaches the lens is reduced by the age-related changes in the constricting and dilating properties of the eye muscles regulating pupil size. The eyes of older adults do not respond to changes in light intensity as rapidly as those of young adults. When light is dim, the pupils of older adults do not open as widely as they did in previous years. This condition is known as **senile miosis.** The amount of light received by the lens of an older person with senile miosis can range from one-tenth to one-third that of younger adults. The lens undergoes a variety of changes, particularly in the older adult years. The clear, transparent lens characteristic of young adulthood gradually yellows in older adulthood. This decline in lens transparency results in a filtering effect and a reduction in the amount of light that ultimately reaches the retina. The lenses of the older adult also thicken and decrease in flexibility, which affects how light waves are projected on the retina.

Another problem that occurs with age is cataract formation. *Cataracts* result in a clouding of the lens and can result in complete lens opaqueness. Some cataract formation occurs in an estimated 95 percent of adults over the age of 70. Cataracts are treatable through a corrective or surgically implanted lens. Left untreated, cataracts will result in a reduction or elimination of light rays refracted to the retina.

With age, the clear gelatinous vitreous humor shows signs of becoming more liquid and may develop patches of cloudiness. In addition, the retina loses rods and cones. Rod receptor cells of the retina are particularly important for visually adapting to the dark. Thus, older adults often experience a gradual decline in light and dark adaptation. Cone receptor cells are essential for color vision, so the ability to discriminate colors is often diminished in the older adult. An accumulation of lipofuscin has also been noted in the retinas of older adults.

Structural changes of the eye that begin during middle adulthood and increase in later years often affect the visual function of the eyes. About the age of 40, the ability of an individual to focus at close distances tends to decline. This condition is called *presbyopia*. As an individual ages, this condition worsens. This onset of presbyopia during middle adulthood is generally attributed to age-related changes in the lens, which also cause increased glare sensitivity. In addition, the ability to track moving objects also becomes a problem, generally attributed to weaker eye muscle and focusing abilities. Figure 19.8 depicts various structures of the eye and their age-associated changes.

Auditory System

Although the auditory system does not serve as a primary sensory system for the completion of most motor tasks, auditory information can be extremely valuable in providing feedback in a number of movement situations. Hearing takes place when vibrating sound waves enter the ears and, through a complex process, are transformed into neuronal signals sent to the brain for processing. Audible sound waves travel from their source to the outer ears of a person. The outer ear consists of the pinna (the visible ear structure on both sides of the head) and the external auditory canal. The sound vibrations travel down the external auditory

canal until they come in contact with the tympanic membrane (ear drum). The tympanic membrane begins vibrating in accordance with the vibration characteristics of the sound waves. These vibrations are transferred to three connected middle ear bones and subsequently transmitted to the fluid environment of the inner ear. The vibrations that reach the inner ear stimulate the sound sensitive organ of Corti, which conveys the sensations down the cochlear nerve to the brain.

As adults grow older their ears undergo a number of structural changes that may impair the quality of their hearing. Various membranes and organs throughout the ear tend to become less flexible. This loss of flexibility can dampen the sound vibrations as they move from the external to the inner ear. Hearing loss associated with aging is referred to as **presbycusis.** In addition to membrane changes that may decrease the quality of hearing, presbycusis can result from a loss of cells in the auditory nerve or other organs instrumental in transmitting or interpreting sound waves. A decline in the amount of blood flow to various parts of the ear can contribute to hearing loss as well. In addition to presbycusis, older adults may experience *tinnitus*, a persistent ringing or buzzing noise in the ears. These age-related changes are somewhat permanent, but certain strategies can be explored to improve an older person's hearing. When age-related hearing loss becomes noticeable, a visit to a physician should be scheduled.

The prevalence and consistency of *cerumen* (earwax) changes in older adults. Due to the drying and thinning of tissue in the external auditory canal, a greater amount of cerumen is likely to accumulate. Cerumen also becomes thicker. An accumulation of cerumen can block the external auditory canal, affecting the transmission of sound waves to the middle and inner ears. Such a condition can be treated by a physician, and hearing loss due to cerumen buildup can be restored.

Hearing assistance devices can be beneficial in many cases. It is important, however, to recognize that hearing aids amplify all sounds and may serve

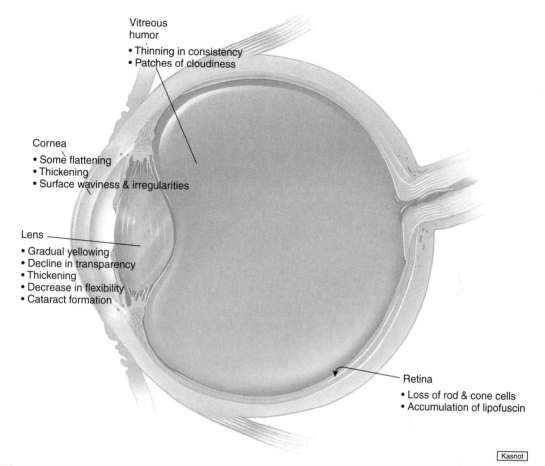

Vitreous humor
- Thinning in consistency
- Patches of cloudiness

Cornea
- Some flattening
- Thickening
- Surface waviness & irregularities

Lens
- Gradual yellowing
- Decline in transparency
- Thickening
- Decrease in flexibility
- Cataract formation

Retina
- Loss of rod & cone cells
- Accumulation of lipofuscin

Kasnot

Figure 19.8

Age-associated changes in the structures of the eye.

From John W. Hole, *Human Anatomy and Physiology* (Dubuque, IA: Wm. C. Brown, 1993). Reprinted by permission of The McGraw-Hill Companies.

to confuse rather than help some individuals. Figure 19.9 depicts various structures of the ear and their age-associated changes.

Proprioception

Proprioception refers to a sense of body awareness and position. One of the primary methods of receiving proprioceptive information is through the vestibular system. The primary function of the vestibular system is to provide information concerning head movement and position. Various components of the vestibular system are located in each inner ear and include the semicircular canals, the utricle, and the saccule (figure 19.10). These three structures are filled with a fluid called *endolymph*. When the head moves, the endolymph moves as well and stimulates sensory receptor

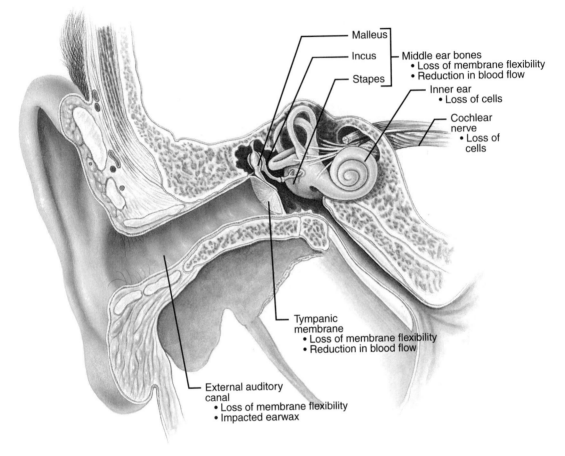

Figure 19.9

Age-associated changes in the structures of the ear.

From John W. Hole, *Human Anatomy and Physiology* (Dubuque, IA: Wm. C. Brown, 1993). Reprinted by permission of The McGraw-Hill Companies.

hair cells located within the vestibular structures. The stimulation of these hair cells initiates the transmission of neural signals by way of the vestibular nerve to various parts of the brain and spinal cord.

In older adults, losses have been noted in the number of sensory cells located within the saccule, utricle, and semicircular canals. In addition, the nerves that transmit messages from the vestibular structures to the brain experience some age-associated degeneration. How these changes influence the motor behavior of an older individual remains subject to speculation. Older adults often experience vertigo and dizziness. Although these conditions may be attributed to age-related changes in the vestibular system, they may likewise occur as a result of certain medications, various diseases, or changes in posture.

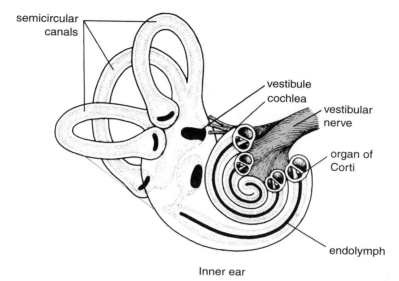

Figure 19.10

Components of the vestibular system.

From Sylvia S. Mader, *Understanding Human Anatomy and Physiology* (Dubuque, IA: Wm. C. Brown, 1991). Reprinted by permission of The McGraw-Hill Companies.

SUMMARY

As adults age, they experience a number of changes, many of them detrimental to motor performance. Many of these declines in performance occur as a result of the aging process; others are related to task demands and environmental conditions. The underlying reasons why we age may include changes in cells and/or in whole physiological systems. Recognize that while aging patterns seem to follow a general trend, individual rates of aging may vary widely. Some of these age-related changes can be observed in the musculoskeletal system, the central nervous system, the circulatory and respiratory systems, and the sensory systems. Although many of these observed changes may be a direct result of the aging process, other causes may include disease and lifestyle habits.

CRITICAL READINGS

Chodzko-Zajko, W. (1999). Successful aging in the new millennium: The role of regular physical activity. *Quest, 52,* 333–343.

Kramer, A. F. (2000). Physical and mental training: Implications for cognitive functioning in old age. *Journal of Aging and Physical Activity, 8,* 363–365.

Malina, R. M. (1996). Tracking of physical activity and physical fitness across the lifespan. *Research Quarterly for Exercise and Sport, 67,* 48–57.

Shephard, R. J. (1997). *Aging, Physical Activity, and Health* (Chapters 3 & 4). Champaign, IL: Human Kinetics.

Spirduso, W. W. (1995). *Physical Dimensions of Aging* (Chapters 1–5). Champaign, IL: Human Kinetics.

WEB RESOURCES

Homepage for the National Institute on Aging
www.nih.gov/nia

Homepage for the Society for Research in Adult
Development
www.norwich.edu/srad/index.html

Population statistics from the U.S. Census Bureau
www.census.gov

The Department of Health and Human Service's
Administration on Aging
www.aoa.dhhs.gov/aoa/pages/welcome.html

MOTOR PERFORMANCE IN ADULTS

KEY TERMS

Reaction time

Fractionated RT

Speed-accuracy trade-off

Balance and postural control

Gait

Daily living activities

CHAPTER COMPETENCIES

Upon completion of this chapter you should be able to:

- Discuss the relationship among aging physiological systems, psychological factors, environmental conditions, and task requirements of motor performance through adulthood
- Describe age-associated changes in reaction time and discuss intervention strategies that may reduce the differences in reaction time observed between older and younger adults
- Discuss balance and postural changes observed in older adults and describe methods that may increase their stability
- Recognize the susceptibility and potential dangers of falls in older adulthood
- Discuss age-related variations in gait patterns and their underlying causes
- Discuss intervention methods to assist older adults in the performance of daily living activities
- Recognize that high-level motor performance can occur at any age

Key Concept

An adult's motor performance depends on the interaction of a wide variety of variables, some of which can be manipulated with ease while others are resistant to change.

When we see an adult throwing a frisbee, typing a letter, rebounding a basketball, walking with the aid of a walker, or going for a run in the park, we are observing motor performance. The movement tasks of adults range from everyday activities to specialized skills. Some tasks require a high level of accuracy, others require a high degree of speed, and still others may dictate a combination of speed and accuracy.

Concept 20.1

Observed declines in motor performance through adulthood may be the result of physiological degeneration, psychological factors, environmental conditions, task requirements, disease, lifestyle, or combinations of these elements.

As we advance in age, we observe a number of changes in the performance of various movement tasks. Most of these changes involve a decline in successful task accomplishment. These detrimental changes in motor performance may be the result of age-related degeneration of physiological systems, age-associated psychological factors, the changing environment, task demands, or some combination of these four variables. It is important, however, to reemphasize the point made by Spirduso and MacRae (1990) that variability in the motor performance of adults can be high. The interaction of several variables, some age-related, will dictate whether an individual will experience a decline in a specific movement task.

As discussed in the previous chapter, the aging process results in a number of physiological changes. Some of those changes may have little or no impact on the behavior of an aging adult. Certain task demands may not place major burdens on physiological systems that have deteriorated, or demands placed on a declining system may be accommodated by one or more of the healthy physiological systems. Other physiological changes, however, may result in an observable decline in the performance of various motor skills. A particular impaired system may play such a primary role in the performance of a certain motor task that other systems cannot provide sufficient compensation. The interaction of two or more declining physiological systems may have a detrimental effect on the performance of specific movements as well.

The environment in which the movement task is performed may play a role in the level of performance success. The amount of light that illuminates a room, the firmness of the floor surface, and the surrounding air temperature represent examples of environmental conditions that could affect performance. Certain environmental circumstances may be detrimental to the execution of a particular movement whether the performer is a child, young adult, or old adult. Other environmental conditions may inhibit performance only when they interact with a declining physiological system or systems. For example, an older adult standing in a dimly lit room may not be able to catch a tossed ball. While his inability to catch the ball may represent an age-associated decline in the skill of catching, it may also be the result of a low level of illumination interacting with age-associated changes in the structure and function of his eyes. Increasing the level of lighting in the room should enable him to catch a tossed ball with little or no difficulty.

The requirements that define how the task is to be performed may interact with certain age-related characteristics to reduce the level of performance efficiency or success. An older adult may have trouble performing a task that requires both speed and accuracy, but no difficulty if the same task requires only accuracy. Changes in the musculoskeletal and central nervous systems may affect the speed at which a task is attempted, but not necessarily its accurate completion.

Although the reasons behind age-related changes in motor performance are many and varied, some behavioral changes are consistently observed. These include decreased reaction times, diminished maintenance of balance and postural control, and alterations in walking patterns.

CONCEPT 20.2

Reaction time is an important component in many motor performance tasks.

REACTION TIME

The study of **reaction time** (RT) has long been a vital aspect in the understanding of motor behavior in humans. RT represents the time delay between the presentation of a stimulus and the initial activation of the appropriate muscle groups to carry out that task. The measurement of RT provides insight into the internal processes taking place during voluntary movement.

CONCEPT 20.3

Reaction time can be separated into different components, each of which may be affected by various age-related changes.

Reaction time can be described by various means. Nonfractionated RT is measured by recording the time between the presentation of a stimulus and the first initiation of the movement. **Fractionated RT** represents an attempt to break the complete RT process into various components. Generally, fractionated RT investigations dissect the total RT process into the two components of premotor RT and motor RT. *Premotor RT* represents the time between the onset of the signal and the first indication of electrical activity (as measured by electromyography) in the muscles used to carry out the task. *Motor RT* follows premotor RT and refers to the time between the first indication of electrical activity and the initiation of the movement (figure 20.1).

Although much more difficult to accomplish, premotor RT may be further sectioned into reception time, motor integration time, and motor overflow time. As a signal travels (via light waves, sound waves, etc.) from its origin through the environment and is picked up by one or more of the body's sensory systems, it reaches part of the brain that will either attach meaning to the signal or discard it as meaningless. The time it takes to execute this phase represents *reception time*. Once meaning has been attached to the signal, it is followed by activity in the motor cortex of the brain that helps determine the movement needed to respond to the signal. This part of the process represents the *motor integration time*. The time difference between this motor cortex activity and the first indication of electrical activity in the muscles used to carry out the task is referred to as the *motor overflow time*. The process involved in RT is amazingly complex, but it is equally amazing that, when the signal and movement task are fairly simple, the time involved in the RT process is generally less than 1 second.

In addition to investigating the various components of RT, researchers have attempted to alter the environmental conditions under which RT is observed. RT may be examined under such circumstances as multiple-choice responses (i.e., responding one way to a green light and a different way to a red light), different sensory systems receiving the signal to begin a task (i.e., vision-light, hearing-bell, etc.), or the intensity of the signal to begin a task (i.e., vision—bright or dim, hearing—loud or soft).

CONCEPT 20.4

Certain intervention strategies can reduce age differences in reaction time.

It has been consistently demonstrated that RT diminishes with age. Early cross-sectional studies indicated that RT reaches its peak somewhere in the early to mid-20s, begins a slow drop through the middle adulthood years, and declines sharply during older adulthood (Hodgkins, 1963; Pierson and Montoye, 1958). However, even these early investigations indicated that the variability in RT is large when people grow older. More recently it has been

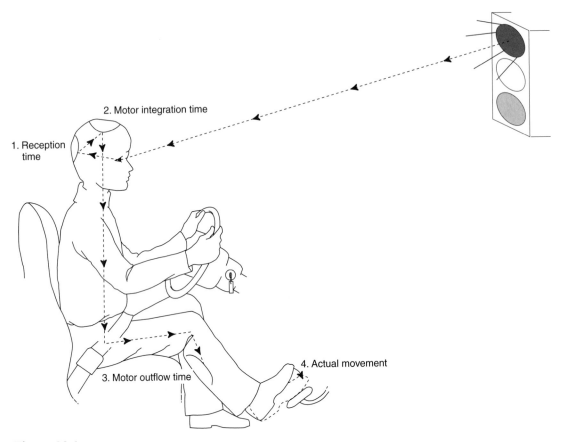

1. Reception time
2. Motor integration time
3. Motor outflow time
4. Actual movement

Figure 20.1
Components of fractionated reaction time.

demonstrated that RT studies placing greater control on certain variables will elicit much smaller age differences than previous studies. Factors such as providing a familiar signal to start the task, allowing sufficient opportunities to practice the specific task involved in the investigation, and enhancing the quality of the starting signal represent ways to greatly reduce age-related differences (Spirduso and MacRae, 1990), particularly in RT studies that deal with a single signal and a single response. Reduction of age-related differences in RT when more complex signals and responses are involved is generally less significant.

Although factors such as practice and the quality and familiarity of the signal help minimize age differences in RT, it remains that younger adults consistently have faster RT than older adults. The breadth of the age-related difference depends on factors associated with each individual's physiological and psychological characteristics, the environment in which the task is performed, and the nature of the task.

Physiologically, several possibilities might contribute to slower responses as a person ages. Spirduso (1986) suggested that "to some extent psychomotor tasks requiring speed may be considered a behavioral window through which the central nervous system's integrity may be viewed" (p. 153). As discussed in the previous chapter, the central nervous system undergoes a number of age-related changes ranging from a loss of brain cells to decreases in blood flow and, subsequently, the amount of oxygen that reaches the brain. These central nervous system changes can be harmful in all aspects, but particularly in the central components of the RT process. The functioning quality of the brain, influenced by the amount of blood and nutrients it receives, has the potential to affect the RT components of reception time, motor integration time, and motor overflow time.

Reception time can be impaired by age-associated changes in the systems that receive sensory information requiring a quick response. Decreases or distortions in the light waves or sound waves received by an aging visual system or auditory system, respectively, could be responsible for an increase in the amount of time it takes to transmit pertinent information to the processing centers of the brain. Additionally, the motor time component of RT may be slowed by a decline in the time required to activate the muscles of an aging muscular system.

Psychologically, a number of factors, either individually or in interaction with other variables, have the potential to slow an older adult's ability to respond quickly. Dacey and Travers (1991) suggest that variables such as motivation, depression, and anxiety may be important factors in RT difference between older and younger adults. The older adult, because of a greater number of lifetime experiences, may not emphasize tasks requiring quick responses. An older adult may be more motivated to perform a task accurately rather than rapidly, whereas a younger adult may emphasize speed and sacrifice accuracy. This involves a phenomenon referred to as the **speed-accuracy trade-off.** The speed-accuracy trade-off is a principle that describes the trend toward a decline in the accuracy of a movement when its speed is increased (Schmidt, 1988). An older adult experiencing a state of depression may be less motivated to perform to her potential on a given task. Older adulthood is a time when factors such as health problems or the death of a spouse or friend create the potential for a psychologically depressed state. Older adults may also experience a sense of anxiety when asked to perform a task with which they may not be familiar.

Altering the environment can, in many cases, aid the older adult in performing a movement task requiring a quick response. As discussed in the previous chapter, many older adults experience a loss in rod cells of the retina causing problems with visually adapting to the dark. An older individual attempting to perform a movement task in a dimly lit room will probably perform the task slowly and with reduced accuracy. However, when the lighting is increased, the amount of light transmitted by the eyes to the processing centers of the brain is heightened and the RT process is enhanced. When movement instructions or signals are auditory, increasing the amplitude or altering the frequency of auditory information increases the possibility that more information will reach the brain and enhance the RT process.

Modifying specific task requirements or conditions enhances the performance speed of older adults. As mentioned earlier in this chapter, providing opportunities to practice a movement task improves the RT of older adults. Practice, likewise, helps reduce any anxiety that an individual may have when attempting an unfamiliar task. Reducing the number of possible movements from which to select following a signal is also a proven means of boosting the RT of older adults.

In addition to environmental conditions and task requirements, many investigators have found that a person's level of physical activity can play a key role in determining RT status (Baylor and Spirduso, 1988; Chodzko-Zajko, 1991; Kroll and Clarkson, 1977; Spirduso, 1975; Spirduso and Clifford, 1978). In an interesting study comparing the RT of young physically active men (YA), young nonphysically active men (YNA), old physically active men (OA), and old nonphysically active men (ONA), Spirduso (1975) found that the RT of the OA men were similar to RT of the YNA men. Of even greater importance, however, was the finding of a marked difference between the OA and ONA men. In a separate study, muscular strength appeared to be inversely related to reaction time in older women (Hunter, Thompson, and Adams, 2001). In other words, older women who were stronger than women of similar age had faster reaction times.

The faster performances of older active adults can be attributed to good central nervous system circulation, necessary for optimal brain cell longevity and processing efficiency, is maintained through exercise. Spirduso (1995) adds that inactivity for both young and old adults may contribute to the wear and tear of the central nervous system due to the accumulated effects of increased blood pressure and higher lipofuscin concentrations. She concludes that exercise can serve as the best protection against senile involution of brain cells in cerebral activity due to its ability to stimulate metabolism, respiration, and blood circulation. Physical activity may, likewise, enhance the functioning of some neurotransmitter systems of older adults. While representing a positive influence on the central RT functions of the brain, exercise appears to promote better functioning of the more peripheral components of RT as well. Physical activity fosters healthy blood circulation to the extremities. Increased circulation provides for adequate extremity temperatures, important for the rapid transmission of nerve signals to the muscles.

BALANCE AND POSTURAL CONTROL

As mentioned earlier in this chapter, the RT process usually involves a time factor of less than 1 second, depending on the complexity of the circumstances. Some motor performance tasks do not require fast RTs for their successful completion, whereas other tasks do. The ability to maintain one's **balance and postural control** efficiently appears to require an adequately functioning RT process. However, RT is only one of many factors that interact for the purposes of maintaining balance and the control of posture. Woollacott and Shumway-Cook (1990) suggest that multiple neural and biomechanical factors work together to achieve the goal of balance. They list the following components that may play an influential role in the control of an individual's balance: (1) postural muscle response synergies; (2) visual, vestibular, and somatosensory systems; (3) adaptive systems; (4) muscle strength; (5) joint range of motion; and (6) body morphology.

 CONCEPT 20.5

Several factors serve as interacting components in the maintenance of balance and posture.

Postural muscle response synergies refer to the timing and sequencing of the activation of muscle groups needed to maintain balance or postural control. Several muscle groups in both the lower body and upper body may be called on to maintain a controlled upright posture or to regulate balance smoothly in a variety of movement situations. The visual system provides valuable information regarding body position in relationship to the environment, and the vestibular and somatosensory systems contribute sensory input regarding body and head position in relation to gravity and joint position awareness.

Adaptive systems allow for the modification of sensory input and motor output when changes take place in the task requirements or in the characteristics of the environment. The strength of the muscles at the ankle, knee, and hip must be adequate to be able to either maintain a specific postural position or to control the restoration of balance when equilibrium is disturbed. The range of motion of the body's various joints determines how restrictive or free a movement can be when that movement requires a high degree of balance. Finally, body morphology elements such as height, center of mass, foot length, and body weight distribution affect the biomechanical function of maintaining stability.

 CONCEPT 20.6

Older adults display different motor patterns than younger adults when attempting to regain stability after their balance has been disturbed.

With age, the process of maintaining postural control and balance becomes less efficient, particularly in the older adult. For many older adults the decrements in controlling posture may represent irreversible changes (Crilly et al., 1989). It has been demonstrated that when the stability of older adults is disturbed, the restoration process is often different and less effective than the process exhibited by younger adults (Woollacott et al., 1986). One difference is the timing of the muscle activation. When a person is standing upright and something causes him to lose his balance and begin to sway backward, the balance recovery procedure generally involves the activation of the ankle dorsiflexors followed by the activation of the knee extensors. The muscle activation response in younger adults tends to be quicker than the muscle response of older adults. Some older adults have even demonstrated a reversal of the muscle activation pattern when attempting to restore balance. They may occasionally activate the knee extensor muscle group first followed by the ankle dorsiflexors. In addition, in an attempt to restore balance, some older adults may incorporate additional muscle groups (i.e., muscles of the hip) not used by younger adults, or activate the agonist muscle group (i.e., knee extensors) and the antagonist muscle group (i.e., knee flexors) at the same time (Manchester et al., 1989), an occurrence observed in very young children (Forssberg and Nashner, 1982).

This cocontraction of the agonist and antagonist muscle groups by older adults may represent a strategy of compensation for the inability to fine-tune the postural control to the same degree as young adults (Woollacott et al., 1988). The proper functioning of the vestibular and visual systems and their interactions appear to be critical in the postural control differences of older and younger adults. As long as these two systems are intact and able to receive and transmit accurate sensory information, the ability of older adults to recover from disturbed balance is similar to that of younger adults. However, when the amount of visual and vestibular input available to both younger and older adults is substantially reduced, the ability of older adults to restore stability following a loss in balance is much weaker than that of younger adults (Teasdale, Stelmach, and Breunig, 1991; Woollacott et al., 1986).

CONCEPT 20.7

Intervention strategies can be incorporated to increase the stability of older adults.

Although many adults experience age-related declines in balance and postural control that may become irreversible (particularly in the older adulthood years), various intervention possibilities may be useful in reducing the magnitude of the decline, promoting compensation strategies, or both. Age-associated changes in the vestibular and visual systems may be difficult or impossible to counter, but alterations in the environment may provide for stronger sensory stimuli. For example, when an older adult is standing or moving on a soft surface, the amount or quality of sensory information sent from the joint, muscle, and vestibular receptors to the processing centers may be decreased. A firmer surface, however, may allow for sharper and more distinct sensory input, particularly for the joint and muscle receptors of the ankles. From a visual standpoint, an increase in room illumination could enhance the number of light waves that reach and are transmitted by the retina.

An increase in muscular strength may moderate the degree of instability of older people. Increases in muscular strength following training programs have been observed at all levels of adulthood. As mentioned in the previous chapter, even adults who were in their nineties experienced muscular strength gains following a strength-training program. Adequate levels of muscular strength in the lower and upper legs are particularly important for both the maintenance of balance and the avoidance of falls resulting from balance disruptions (Whipple, Wolfson, and Amerman, 1987). The consequences of a fall can be substantially more devastating for the older adult than for someone younger (Tinetti, 1990), as will be discussed later in this chapter.

As previously mentioned, a second musculoskeletal-associated factor that may play an influential role in maintaining balance is the range of motion of the body's joints. Although the joint flexibility of older adults tends to be more restricted than that of younger adults (Shephard, Berridge, and Montelpare, 1990), participation in physical activity and exercise has been shown to improve the range of motion of older adults and close the flexibility gap usually observed between young and old adulthood (Dummer, Vaccaro, and Clarke, 1985; Rikli and Edwards, 1991).

There is sufficient evidence to suggest that older adults who participate in exercise programs can experience improvements in their balance and stability. A review of the research indicates that programs designed to enhance balance should incorporate muscular strength, joint flexibility, and aerobic endurance activities along with exercises that stimulate multiple sensory systems and their central integration (Kronhed, Möller, Olsson, and Möller, 2001).

FALLS

Falls represent a major concern for many elderly individuals. Falling is much more common and serious when an adult is older than during early adulthood. Each year approximately 30 percent of adults over the age of 65 experience a fall. Many will endure multiple falls during a one-year period. With age, the likelihood of falling increases. Although the majority of falls experienced by older adults are minor and do not result in injury, more serious falls may result in soft tissue injuries, fractures, the development of psychological fears, or death.

CONCEPT 20.8

Hip fractures resulting from falls are a major concern for older adults.

Soft tissue injuries can range from various degrees of contusions (bruising) to muscle sprains and strains that could reduce an older individual's mobility and restrict her level of independence. Of even greater concern to older adults is the threat of

falls that result in fractures. Fractures may occur at the humerus or wrist when the arm is outstretched in an attempt to cushion or stop a fall. These fractures, however, generally do not decrease mobility. *Hip fractures,* on the other hand, are much more devastating. Fractures of the hip, experienced by more than 200,000 Americans a year (Tinetti, 1990), result in an extensive period of immobility, greater dependency on others for daily living functions, and heightened possibility of institutional care.

Debilitating circumstances such as these may account for a 12 to 20 percent death rate in individuals during the year following hip fractures (Jackson and Lyles, 1990). Many fractures in older adults can be attributed to osteoporosis. The loss of bone mass from *osteoporosis* not only makes bones weaker and more prone to fractures but also lengthens the time required for recovery. Another problem associated with hip fractures includes a susceptibility to instability and deformity of the fracture site (Jackson and Lyles).

A number of physical injuries can occur as a result of falls, but older adults may also develop a sense of fear and/or depression after falling. Approximately half of individuals who have fallen admit to a certain level of fear (Tinetti, 1990). The fear level of these older individuals may lead to overprotectiveness and unnecessary restrictions of mobility and independence. An older adult may begin to avoid even everyday functional tasks such as bathing and dressing. Depression may accompany the sense of fear and compound the psychological effects of a fall.

A number of factors link falls with the death of older adults. As mentioned earlier in this chapter, the majority of falls are not serious. However, falls do kill a small percentage of persons. More common are deaths that occur from fall-related injuries or from circumstances created by a fall. For example, an older adult who fractures her hip in a fall may experience a decline in overall health due to a long-term reduction in mobility and a decreased ability to care for herself. This may eventually lead to death. Finally, multiple falls in an older individual may indicate underlying factors that elevate the risk of death (Dunn et al., 1992). Age-related and disease-related declines in a number of physiological systems may make a person more susceptible to falls. In these instances falling reveals rather than causes more serious health problems. These health problems may be moving an older adult closer to death.

CONCEPT 20.9

A number of circumstances predispose the older adult to falls.

A number of interacting factors appear to predispose older individuals to falling. Many of these factors are physiological; others relate to the environments in which falls take place. Task demands can, likewise, play a role in creating a precarious situation. Physiological factors may include age- or disease-associated changes in various sensory systems, the central nervous system, or the musculoskeletal system. Environmental conditions often involve potentially hazardous circumstances interacting with declining or drug-impaired physiological systems. The demands of certain tasks may require an individual to move beyond a comfort zone of stability making him or her vulnerable to other forces. A list of risk factors for falling and some potential intervention strategies can be found in table 20.1.

As discussed in the previous chapter, declines in the visual, auditory, and vestibular system are common in adults as they age. These declines add to the jeopardy that older adults face in relation to

TABLE 20.1 Risk Factors for Falling and Possible Intervention Strategies	
Possible Risk Factors of the Older Adult	**Possible Intervention Strategies**
• Decrease in muscular strength	—strength training exercises —assistance devices (canes, walkers, handrails)
• Decrease in joint flexibility	—active lifestyles —stretching exercises
• Decrease in visual abilities	—increased room lighting —reduced glare —eyeglasses —surgical treatments
• Decrease in auditory abilities	—removal of cerumen —hearing assistance devices
• Decrease in proprioception	—firm walking surfaces —proper footwear —enhanced visual environment —avoid uneven surfaces —assistance devices (canes, walkers, handrails)
• Slowing of reaction time	—active lifestyles —focused attention on task —allowance for practice of task —increased motivation
• Medication	—awareness of drug side effects —awareness of drug interaction side effects

falling. Falls can occur when an individual trips over a hazardous object because she is unable to see it in a dimly lit room. The inability to distinguish the sounds made by the feet on different types of floor surfaces may reduce or eliminate certain feedback beneficial in maintaining stability. Improper functioning of the vestibular system may result in dizziness and place the person at risk for falling.

A slowing or disruption of the central nervous system can increase an older person's vulnerability to falling. Rapid RT may help a person catch his balance to avoid a fall when stability is lost. Under similar circumstances, a somewhat slower RT may restrict the restoration of balance causing the person to outstretch his arm and break the fall. Although this action may cushion the impact of a fall, it places the person at risk for a fracture of the wrist or humerus. An older adult with an even slower RT may be unable to extend her arms quickly enough to break the fall and may land directly on an unprotected hip (Jackson and Lyles, 1990). Additional central nervous system conditions such as Parkinson's disease and strokes increase the older adult's susceptibility to falls.

Adequate muscular strength (particularly in the lower extremities) is important for maintaining balance and restoring lost stability. Age-related loss in muscle mass and a subsequent loss in strength can be detrimental to maintaining balance and preventing falls (Whipple et al., 1987). Arthritis of lower extremity joints can also decrease fall prevention strategies.

As the health of older adults declines, medication is often prescribed for a variety of conditions. A number of medications predispose the older adult to falling. Certain sedatives and antidepressants can increase the risk of falling, while taking more than one drug at the same time without knowledge of the drug interaction consequences also represents a potential problem.

An older person's home or work environment can present a number of hazards that increase the likelihood of falling. Falls can occur when a person climbs or descends stairs; bathes; moves in and out of a wheelchair; or trips over electrical cords, low

furniture, or small pets. Other falls may occur as a result of shoes that fit poorly. Additional environmental hazards include low levels of room illumination, surfaces that produce glare when light strikes them, and soft, uneven, or unstable floor surfaces. It is possible that the optical patterns on floors and stairs may contribute to falling due to a decline in the older adult's visual perception process (Tinetti, 1990).

The demands of certain tasks can place older adults in situations in which they are at greater risk for falling, particularly when the tasks require intense concentration. Attention to balance may be diverted. Reaching for an object high on a shelf while using a stepladder, bending over and attempting to lift a heavy object, or carrying a full laundry basket down a flight of stairs are potentially hazardous tasks for older adults. Older individuals who participate in more physically active lifestyles appear to have an increased incidence of falls (Tinetti, 1990). Reasons probably include greater exposure to hazardous circumstances and increased intensity in active participation.

GAIT

Walking appears to be a simple, almost automatic task performed without much effort. It is, however, a complex skill requiring the interaction of the central nervous system, the body's muscles and joints, several sensory systems, gravitational forces, and environmental circumstances. Age-related and/or disease-related changes in one or more of the body's systems can interact with physical and/or environmental conditions to cause decrements in the **gait** process. Neurologically, gait uses an intricate combination of voluntary and reflexive action. The muscles and joints of the ankle, knee, pelvis, and to some degree the trunk and shoulder, are vital ingredients in an efficient walking pattern. The gait process makes use of information obtained through the visual, auditory, and vestibular systems, as well as others. The forces related to the earth's gravitational pull are involved with the continual altering of the body's center of gravity and the constant reestablishing of the base of support during the walking cycle. Environmental conditions such as walking surface or objects placed in the path of a walker can alter the gait pattern.

The walking cycle or gait pattern has two phases: the *swing phase* and the *support phase.* Generally speaking, when one leg is in the swing phase, the other leg is in the support phase. The swing phase begins when the toe pushes off the ground surface and ends when the heel strikes the ground surface. During the swing phase, the leg moves through the air in a pendulumlike motion. The support phase begins when the heel first strikes the ground surface and ends when the toe pushes off the ground surface. During the entire support phase, the foot maintains contact with the ground surface. In addition to the support and swing phases, for a brief time in the walking cycle, both feet contact the ground surface at the same time. This is referred to as a *period of double support* and is the major characteristic that differentiates running from walking. Other elements of walking include stride length, stride frequency, stride width, toe-floor clearance during the swing phase, arm swing, and hip and knee rotation.

CONCEPT 20.10

Differences in the gait patterns of older adults and younger adults often originate in different walking speeds.

As individuals move into older adulthood, a variety of gait characteristics undergo changes. Older adults may differ from younger adults in several walking components. Older adults characterized as healthy have displayed decreases in *stride length,* increases in the double support period, reductions in *toe-floor clearance,* alterations of the strategies used when the foot clears obstacles on the floor, and decreases in *gait velocity* (Chen et al., 1991; Elble, Hughes, and Higgins, 1991; Ferrandez, Pailhous,

and Durup, 1990; Hortobágyi and DeVita, 1999; Wall et al., 1991). However, some investigators have reported that many of the declines or reductions observed in the walking patterns of older adults can be attributed to slower paces, rather than to particular physiological problems (Elble et al., 1991; Ferrandez et al., 1990). Although a slower walking speed appears to be characteristic of an older person's gait and may cause a number of other decreases in gait efficiency, intervention strategies such as weight training can improve the gait speed of older adults (Fiatarone et al., 1990). Also, physically active older adults had better gait characteristics when compared with sedentary individuals of similar age (Rosengren et al., 1995).

While it is speculative to state that age alone causes declines in the gait cycle, a number of diseases that often afflict older adults contribute to gait problems. Disorders of the central nervous system such as Parkinson's disease, multiple sclerosis, tumors, or strokes can affect balance control and, in turn, the quality of the gait pattern (Koller and Glatt, 1990). Orthopedic conditions such as arthritis and bunions, often experienced by older adults, may also alter an individual's gait pattern.

ACTIVITIES OF DAILY LIVING

CONCEPT 20.11

Older adults may have difficulty carrying out daily living activities without some environmental modifications.

A multitude of movement-oriented tasks that individuals carry out throughout their lives are required for basic everyday needs. **Daily living activities** such as getting out of bed, getting dressed, bathing, and preparing meals are a few of the many tasks that require the attention of adults. Whereas most young- and middle-aged adults take for granted the ease with which these tasks are performed, many older adults find them difficult. Older adults demonstrate less efficient movement patterns when attempting to rise from the floor to a standing position (VanSant, 1990). When attempting to stand from a horizontal position, an older adult may break down the process into discrete segments (i.e., sit up, get onto all fours, move to a kneeling or a squatting position, then pull up to a standing position). Younger adults tend to move from a horizontal position to a standing position in one fluid motion. This *segmental approach* demonstrated by an older adult may be evident when he rises to a standing position from a bed or a chair.

While some age-related movement patterns in certain daily living activities have been noted, it has also been observed that greater efficiency in those movement patterns can be achieved when the task conditions are modified. VanSant (1990) pointed out that altering environmental conditions, such as varying the height of objects (chair, bed, etc.), can enhance an older person's motor performance. In addition, Hart et al. (1990) found that by providing assistance modifications to various household items, older adults were able to put on their shoes, get on and off the toilet, pour from a teapot, and turn on the tap with less difficulty and greater speed.

Community and societal awareness can add significantly to the independence of older adults and assist them in carrying out daily living activities outside of the home often by making modest environmental changes. For example, crosswalk timer settings are often based upon gait studies performed in indoor laboratory settings. Additional outdoor environmental factors that can significantly slow the pace of an older adult crossing the street include negotiating curbs; adjusting to weather conditions such as wind; and dealing with visual distractions such as traffic or sun glare, which decreases the ability to see the crosswalk sign (Carmeli, Coleman, Omar, and Brown-Cross, 2000). Adjusting the crosswalk timer setting to allow additional time to cross a street safely can increase the comfort and independence levels of older adults and keep them engaged in their community.

Elite Performance

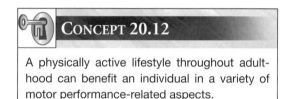

Concept 20.12

A physically active lifestyle throughout adulthood can benefit an individual in a variety of motor performance-related aspects.

The quantity of motor performance activity observed at all levels of adulthood is extremely variable. The health status of various physiological systems, past and present lifestyles, genetic characteristics, environmental conditions, and task demands interact to generate a range of movement outcomes (performed extremely well, performed adequately, or performed poorly). Upon examining cross-sectional and longitudinal track and field accomplishments of masters-level athletes Stones and Kozma (1982) suggested that non-age-related factors such as amount and quality of training, frequency and quality of competitive experience, motivation, and injury proneness may affect the performance trends through adulthood. It has also been suggested that the level of age-associated performance declines may be activity-specific (Salthouse, 1976; Stones and Kozma, 1980, 1981, 1986). Salthouse stated that "when one refers to slowing with age it is necessary to be quite specific about the activity to which one is referring because different activities decline at different rates" (p. 349). Ericsson (2000) found that healthy older adults can attain high levels of performance in specific task domains by regularly engaging in deliberate practice with suitably designed training activities. Fisk and Rogers (2000) examined the skill acquisition characteristics of older adults and developed a list of guidelines for assisting them in learning new skills. These guidelines include providing active rather than passive learning, teaching procedures not just concepts, and providing extended practice opportunities. These guidelines, and others, are summarized in table 20.2.

Many of the age-related changes discussed in this chapter and the previous chapter can cause motor performance declines. However, evidence

TABLE 20.2 **Guidelines for Assisting Older Adults in Acquiring New Skills**

- Provide active rather than passive learning
- Teach procedures not only concepts
- Provide opportunities for modeling requisite behavior
- Train in small groups
- Provide extended practice opportunities
- Provide environmental supports

Data from Fisk, A. D., and Rogers, W. A. (2000). Influence of training and experience on skill acquisition and maintenance in older adults. *Journal of Aging and Physical Activity, 8,* 373–378.

continues to mount that many adults who remain physically active and adapt and compensate for changing environmental and task demands inhibit the typical age-related declines much more effectively than their sedentary peers.

CONCEPT 20.13

Certain individuals may be able to perform motor tasks at elite levels regardless of their age.

TABLE 20.3 **Selected Master Track and Field Age World Records (Indoor)**

Event	Men			Women		
	Age (Years)	Record	Year	Age (Years)	Record	Year
60 meters (sec.)	Open	6.39	1998	Open	6.92	1993
	40	6.97	1990	40	8.01	1997
	50	7.34	2000	50	8.05	1997
	60	7.70	1978	60	9.01	1994
	70	8.39	1994	70	10.12	1998
	80	9.39	1999	80	11.52	2000
	90	13.64	1999			
1 mile (min.)	Open	3:48.45	1997	Open	4:17.14	1990
	40	3:58.13	1994	40	4:57.71	1999
	50	4:35.51	2000	50	5:40.10	1983
	60	5:01.76	1998	60	6:35.55	1999
	70	5:32.40	1987	70	7:29.22	1987
	80	7:04.20	1979	80	12:05.93	1996
High jump (meters)	Open	2.43	1989	Open	2.07	1992
	40	2.10	1994	40	1.72	1995
	50	2.00	1997	50	1.53	1997
	60	1.65	1990	60	1.32	1999
	70	1.49	1997	70	1.19	1998
	80	1.27	1995	80	0.90	2000
	90	0.89	1999			
Long jump (meters)	Open	8.79	1984	Open	7.37	1988
	40	7.52	1996	40	5.61	1987
	50	6.50	1997	50	5.00	1997
	60	5.58	1997	60	4.58	1999
	70	5.05	1995	70	3.40	1998
	80	3.63	1998	80	2.49	2000
	90	2.49	1999			

Data from IAAF International Amateur Athletic Federation (1996–2001). Principality of Monaco; National Masters News (2000). Eugene, OR.

There are, also, those older adults who continue to perform certain motor tasks at extraordinarily high levels. Although the records of *master athletes* are consistently poorer than the records of their younger counterparts, their performances are nonetheless noteworthy, and, in many cases, better than the performances of younger nonelite athletes. A few individuals continued to remain competitive in their sports after reaching master athlete status. Two notable examples in the sport of track and field/road racing are Priscilla Welch of Great Britain and Carlos Lopes of Portugal. While in her forties Priscilla Welch recorded times of 32 minutes, 25 seconds for a 10-kilometer race and 2 hours, 31 minutes, 14 seconds for the marathon (USA Track and Field, 1996). Welch's times place her in world class standing in any age group. In his late thirties Carlos Lopes was the winner of the gold medal in the marathon at the 1984 Olympic Games. In addition to his Olympic feat, Lopes has held master age group (35, 36, and 37 years) world records for the 5-kilometer race and the 10-kilometer race (Mundle, Dietderich, and Harvey, 1996). Other notable master track and field age records are listed in table 20.3.

SUMMARY

A number of factors affect how adults perform motor tasks. These factors include the health status of various physiological systems, psychological characteristics, the changing environment, task demands, or some combination thereof. With age we see declines in motor performance. These declines may be attributed to aging, disease, lifestyles, or a combination of these elements. Reaction times tend to slow. Intervention strategies that reduce reaction time decrements include allowing practice of a task, increasing the intensity of the stimulus, using a task already familiar to the individual, and participating in a physically active lifestyle.

The maintenance of balance and posture decreases in efficiency with age, and particularly in older adulthood. Declines in muscle strength and control, the sensory systems, joint flexibility, and physical characteristics interact to alter the balance and posture process. Poorer balance as well as other conditions increase an older person's susceptibility to falling. For the older adult, falling can result in serious consequences, such as hip fractures. The walking pattern of older adults often differs from that of younger adults. However, many of the observed differences result from slower walking speeds. When the walking speed is increased, many differences disappear. Daily living activities are often more challenging for older adults than for their younger counterparts. However, altering environmental conditions can increase the speed and decrease the difficulty level of many daily living activities. Although we note many age-associated declines in motor performance, a number of individuals remain physically active and, in some cases, perform motor tasks at exceptionally high levels.

CRITICAL READINGS

Hoyer, W. J., Rybash, J. M., & Roodin, P. A. (1999). *Adult Development and Aging* (Chapter 3). 4th ed. St. Louis: McGraw-Hill.

Rimmer, J. H. (1994). *Fitness and Rehabilitation Programs for Special Populations* (Chapter 2). St. Louis: McGraw-Hill.

Santrock, J. W. (2001). *Lifespan Development* (Chapters 14, 16, 18). 8th ed. St. Louis: McGraw-Hill.

Shephard, R. J. (1997). *Aging, Physical Activity, and Health* (Chapters 3 & 4). Champaign, IL: Human Kinetics.

Spirduso, W. W. (1995). *Physical Dimensions of Aging* (Chapters 6–9, 12–14). Champaign, IL: Human Kinetics.

WEB RESOURCES

An Internet resource center for seniors
www.go60.com/home.html

Homepage for the Duke University Center for the
Study of Aging and Human Development–
Longitudinal Study
www.geri.duke.edu/aging/aging.html

Homepage for the Institute on Aging and
Environment
www.uwm.edu/Dept/IAE

Multiple topics related to healthy aging
www.healthandage.com/fpatient.htm

CHAPTER 21

PSYCHOSOCIAL DEVELOPMENT IN ADULTS

KEY TERMS

Life structure

Mentors

Activity theory

Disengagement theory

Retirement

Ageism

Successful aging

CHAPTER COMPETENCIES

Upon completion of this chapter you should be able to:

- Discuss the relationship between the motor and psychosocial domains
- Describe Erikson's theory of psychosocial development with regard to the adult
- Describe Levinson's seasons of life theory with regard to the adult
- Discuss the effects of exercise on select psychological factors of middle-aged and old-aged adults
- Discuss the importance of a physically active lifestyle as it is related to activity theory and disengagement theory
- Describe how remaining physically active can enhance the retirement process
- Define ageism and recognize its various forms
- Describe the importance of health and physical activity as important predictors of longevity and successful aging

KEY CONCEPT

The level of physical activity of adults affects their psychological and sociological states; in turn, psychological and sociological factors such as self-concept and peer relationships influence their commitment to a physically active lifestyle.

Various aspects of the motor domain influence the psychological state and the social characteristics of adults. Exercise, a physically active lifestyle, and the ability to carry out daily living skills are movement-oriented factors that can have a positive effect on how adults feel about themselves and how others view them. Progressive declines in motor performance, a decrease in muscular strength, and an inability to accomplish household tasks represent motor domain conditions that can negatively influence the psychological perspectives and social interactions of adults. In numerous situations the motor domain interacts with the psychosocial domain. When an individual elevates her or his self-esteem and body image following several months of weight training or when adults gather for early morning exercise walks at a city mall, we see the positive influences of motor performance on psychosocial behavior. When individuals with impaired motor functions must be admitted to nursing care facilities and are depressed or insecure, we see the negative influences. Experiences encountered throughout adulthood have the potential to affect a number of psychosocial features. Certain psychological factors that may change during the adult years include self-concept, body image, self-esteem, perception of locus of control, moods of depression, and fears. The development, maintenance, and loss of relationships; the concept of retirement; and ageism are socialization experiences often faced by adults as they grow older.

CONCEPT 21.1

In the aging adult, aspects of the motor domain frequently interact with aspects of the psychosocial domain.

THEORIES OF ADULT PSYCHOSOCIAL DEVELOPMENT

As presented earlier in the text, Erik Erikson developed a stage approach to the psychosocial development of human beings, sometimes referred to as "The Eight Ages of Man." Each stage represents a *crisis state* that must be resolved before advancement to the next stage. Movement from stage to stage comes about through individual needs and societal demands. Erikson's theory proposes that inadequate resolution of a stage crisis will hinder future development at higher stages. Although the successful resolution of each stage crisis is the mechanism for developmental change, Dacey and Travers (1999) point out that Erikson's stages are based on the ideal, and individuals rarely if ever complete each stage perfectly. It is, however, an important component of the theory that the closer an individual gets to resolving a *crisis solution* at each stage, the greater the person's progress.

CONCEPT 21.2

Erik Erikson's theory of psychosocial development has important implications for the adult at any age.

The first five stages of Erikson's theory address early infancy through adolescence. The last three stages are focused on the phases of early, middle, and late adulthood. In this section we will attempt to further define Erikson's final stages as outlined in chapter 2. Table 21.1 recaps the three adulthood stages.

TABLE 21.1 **Erik Erikson's Adulthood Stages of Psychosocial Development**

Stage	Adulthood Years	Psychosocial Process
First Adulthood Stage	Young Adulthood (18–25 years)	Acquiring a sense of intimacy vs. isolation
Second Adulthood Stage	Adulthood (25–65 years)	Acquiring a sense of generativity vs. self-absorption
Third Adulthood Stage	Older Adulthood (65 and older)	Acquiring a sense of integrity vs. despair

In early adulthood, which takes place between 18 and 25 years, Erikson identifies the crisis as one of *intimacy versus isolation.* This period of early adulthood life represents a time when adult friendships are established and an intimate relationship with a member of the opposite sex develops. Erikson suggests that if an individual is unable to form friendships and/or establish that one intimate relationship, then feelings of isolation form.

Generativity versus stagnation represents the crisis facing adults during the latter stages of early adulthood through the middle adulthood years. Generativity refers to the usefulness individuals provide to themselves and to society. Achieving generativity provides an individual with a sense of personal fulfillment. Teachers, clergy, and medical professionals are involved in occupations that have inherent generativity attributes. How individuals perceive their levels of usefulness, however, determines whether generativity is achieved. Erikson suggests that stagnation occurs when adults perceive they are unable to contribute to the betterment of society, even in a small way. Feelings of boredom develop, often followed by a self-indulgent time known as a midlife crisis.

The final stage of Erikson's eight stages involves the crisis of *integrity versus despair.* When older adults take a retrospective look at their life, they are likely to experience a sense of integrity or despair. If adults have lived a contributing, productive, and meaningful life, they can rest in the perception that they have achieved personal integrity. If they have regrets over poor choices and realize that opportunities to make amends are minimal, they may feel a sense of despair.

CONCEPT 21.3

Daniel Levinson's life structure theory provides insight into developmental eras and periods of transitions throughout adulthood.

Through a series of interviews with middle-aged men representing a variety of occupations and socioeconomic levels, Daniel Levinson acquired material for the creation of a theory of adult development and a subsequent book entitled *The Seasons of a Man's Life* (1978). Further research by Levinson (1986) led him to expand his theory to include women (1996). Levinson uses as the foundation of his theory the concept of **life structure.** Life structure can be defined as the underlying design or pattern of an individual's life at any given time. The two most important aspects of the life structure are choices made about marriage and family and choices made about career. These choices help define the development of individuals at any particular time in the life structure.

Levinson's theory incorporates four *eras,* or seasons, of an individual's life. Overlapping time frames between the eras are referred to as *transition* periods. The four developmental eras are childhood and adolescence (birth to 22 years), early adulthood (17 to 45 years), middle adulthood (40 to 65 years), and older adulthood (60 years and older). The overlap between the first and the second era is identified as the early adult transition. Overlaps between the second and third era, and the third and final era are called the midlife transition and the late adult transition, respectively. Figure 21.1

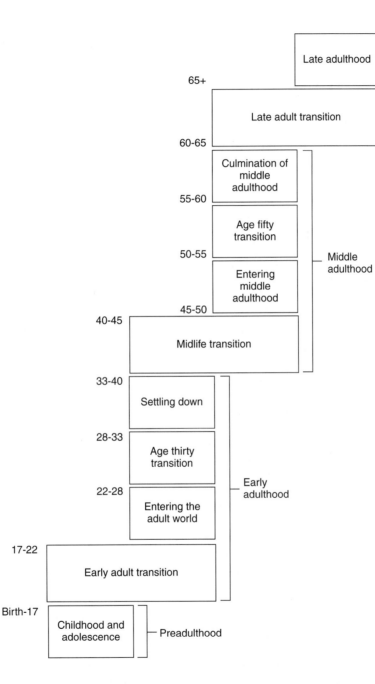

Figure 21.1

Levinson's eras and transitions throughout adulthood.

Reprinted by permission of the publisher from *Themes of Work and Love in Adulthood* by Neil J. Smelser and Erik H. Erikson, Cambridge, Mass.: Harvard University Press. Copyright © 1980 by the President and Fellows of Harvard College.

provides a visual of Levinson's eras and transitions in sequence.

The latter part of the first era represents the onset of adulthood and the origins of independence and responsibility. During the early adult transition period, the relationships between family members and friends change in response to a person's desire for greater individualism and the need to find a niche in the adult world. Upon arrival in the early adulthood era, the individual begins to establish and raise her family, choose an occupation related to her strengths, and pursue ambitions that have been cultivated over the years. While this season of life represents a time of excitement and enthusiasm, it can also depict a time of high stress. Combining the experiences of establishing a new marriage, raising young children, and embarking on a new career can have a cumulative effect on a young adult's stress level. Toward the end of early adulthood, Levinson suggests that the individual attempts to advance in her chosen occupation—an important task during this period.

Upon reaching midlife transition adults begin to face some difficult questions about the past, present, and future. Concerns about slow progress toward the achievement of original goals may arise and doubts about future opportunities may develop. Physical signs of aging begin to appear. Changes in vision develop, and physical fitness levels decline and start to limit the amount of activity in which individuals are involved. During midlife transition Levinson notes that adults will either redefine their goals based on their current situations or begin to experience stagnation.

The realization that progress can be made despite age-related declines makes for a smoother step into the middle adulthood era. During middle adulthood, Levinson states that people recognize the importance of working with younger coworkers and serving as **mentors.** Because a person's professional goals have been achieved or modified, he has a greater sense of security and wants to help others reach their goals. This curtailment of personal ambitions allows for an increase in family involvement.

Levinson's transition into late adulthood can represent a time of trepidation. Many physical characteristics have declined gradually to this point, but sharper drops become apparent during the late adulthood years. Acceptance of the aging process allows older adults to experience this era in a state of contentment. Similar to Erikson's last stage, Levinson's final season involves the advancement toward a sense of integrity.

PSYCHOLOGICAL FACTORS

The experiences in the motor domain interact in many ways with the psychological characteristics of adults. An often used method to explore this motor-psychology relationship is the examination of psychological factors following exercise or association with physical activity. Factors such as a sense of well-being, awareness of body image, perception of locus of control, and states of depression have been improved following participation in an exercise program. Individuals of a middle and/or old adulthood-age group are often targeted as subjects for such interaction investigations.

CONCEPT 21.4

Exercise can have beneficial effects on a number of psychological variables associated with aging.

A *sense of well-being* serves as somewhat of a general term representing some type of positive change in a person's attitude (Hird and Williams, 1989). Following fourteen weeks of an aerobic program Perri and Templer (1985) noted significant improvements in the self-concepts of older adults. In addition, men and women between the ages of 55 and 85 years have demonstrated heightened perceptions of self-concept at the conclusion of an eight-month dance/movement program (Berryman-Miller, 1988). Arent, Landers, and Etnier (2000) examined the results of over thirty studies and found that chronic exercise is associated with improved mood in older adults. Such mood improvements were observed for all types of exercise but were particularly evident with resistance training. McAuley et al. (2000) found that when older adults participate in physical activities such as walking or stretching/toning programs they experience an increase in multidimensional self-esteem. They did suggest that these self-esteem gains may erode once participation in physical activity is reduced or eliminated.

Body image is another psychological factor that has been shown to improve following involvement in an exercise program or higher levels of physical activity. Body image refers to the subjective pictures individuals have of themselves created through their observations and the reactions of others (Thomas, 1989). Loomis and Thomas (1991) examined body attitudes of older women who lived at home and women who resided in nursing facilities. They found that the women living in nursing facilities reported greater dissatisfaction with their body images than did the individuals living at home. The investigators concluded that greater opportunities for participation in physical activity and exercise should be made available to the nursing facility residents.

Locus of control can be defined as a person's perception of her impact on events (Thomas, 1989). An individual with an internal locus of control perceives that she can influence events, whereas a person with an external locus of control believes that events are unaffected by her involvement and happen by chance. The investigation by Perri and Templer (1985) described earlier in this chapter resulted in an enhanced perceived internal locus of control by the adults who participated in the fourteen-week aerobic program.

Depression in adult populations may stem from numerous causes: a decrease in self-esteem due to the loss of employment, hormonal changes following menopause, or a reduction in the ability to carry out daily living skills due to failing health. Valliant and Asu (1985) examined men and women between the ages of 50 and 80 years who participated in different levels of exercise programming. Participants included structured exercisers, self-imposed exercisers, social exercisers, and nonexercisers. The investigators found that the structured group exhibited a reduction in depression following the twelve-week program. Another

investigation examined the effects of exercise on the cognitive functioning of older adults diagnosed with clinical depression (Khatri et al., 2001). The investigators found that physical activity was beneficial to cognitive functioning such as memory for individuals suffering from depression.

SOCIALIZATION FACTORS

For many years social scientists have focused on two approaches, the **activity theory** and the **disengagement theory,** to help describe the optimal process of aging in regard to relationships with other people (Dacey and Travers, 1999). Activity theory suggests that as adults grow older they require interaction with other people and continued physical activity to be happy and satisfied. Disengagement theory is the inverse of activity theory. Disengagement theory suggests that as people age they begin to lose relationships, gradually abandon past interests, and eventually withdraw from society. Disengagement theory argues that the curtailment in social interaction is necessary for older adults to accept society's disengagement of them. Acceptance of this society-individual separation allows older individuals to maintain a sense of integrity in their late adulthood years.

CONCEPT 21.5

Activity theory and disengagement theory provide opposing approaches to successful aging.

Maintaining a physically active lifestyle often requires interaction with individuals of different age groups in a variety of social environments. While these conditions run contrary to disengagement theory, they are consistent with activity theory. Remaining physically active in a social setting represents the activity theory's two primary conditions of sustaining or improving one's health status while preserving or developing relationships. Participation in physical activity encourages older adults to remain attached to society rather than to detach from it.

CONCEPT 21.6

Retirement represents a process rather than a single event.

The theories of activity and disengagement represent a general view of the aging process from a socialization standpoint. An event that represents more of a specific sociological milestone in an older adult's life is **retirement.** Retirement is an interesting phenomenon that some people savor, some tolerate, and some resent. It has been postulated that adults advance through seven phases of retirement (Williamson, Munley, and Evans, 1980) (figure 21.2).

The first step is referred to as the remote phase. The remote phase describes a period when workers put little thought into retirement planning. It often represents a state of denial in that they have no

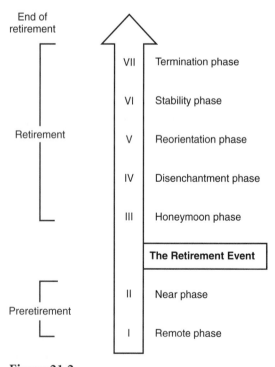

Figure 21.2
Seven phases of retirement.

expectations of not working. As they move to the near phase of retirement, workers begin preretirement planning. Preretirement matters may include financial planning, health maintenance, and leisure activities. Once the designated day of retirement occurs, it is followed by what is termed the honeymoon phase. At this time, retirees receive much gratification from their newly acquired free time. New retirees may be inclined to overcompensate for opportunities they could not pursue earlier in their lives.

The euphoric high experienced during the honeymoon phase is followed by a let-down period called the disenchantment phase. When the day-to-day pattern of retirement living commences, the retiree may experience loss of purpose, reductions in feelings of self-worth, and longings for job-related activities and friends. These feelings may be due to unrealistic expectations about retirement. Making adjustments to counter the disenchantment perspective advances the retiree to the reorientation phase, characterized by a time when options are explored and decisions made regarding realistic expectations of retirement. This is followed by the stability phase in which the retiree makes situational adjustments based on the expectations determined during the previous phase.

A final step is recognized as the termination phase, which represents the development of a time of dependency. The retiree may find it necessary to rely on others due to declines in health, physical abilities, or finances. In the latter case, it may be necessary to return to work, which concludes the retirement period. Time frames or ages are not included in these various phases because of the uniqueness of each individual's physical, emotional, and financial circumstances.

Some experts question the necessity for a phase-type approach, suggesting that retirement reflects a lengthy series of adjustments similar to other life transitions (Hoyer, Rybash, and Roodin, 1999). In either case, aspects of the motor domain can serve beneficial or detrimental roles at various times of the retirement process. Maintaining a physically active lifestyle may reduce the apprehension about the life changes manifested by retirement. The participation in lifelong sports or leisure pursuits such as golf, tennis, cycling, or hiking can make potentially difficult retirement-based transitions somewhat smoother by providing challenge and enjoyment to the retiree within a framework that can be regulated by realistic expectations. In addition, as described in several examples in previous chapters, remaining physically active as long as possible may help delay the onset of health impairment and dependency on others for the performance of daily living skills.

Of concern, however, is that while the vast majority of older adults are aware of the potential health benefits of physical activity many fail to act upon such knowledge. Goggin and Morrow (2001) interviewed 403 adults over the age of 60 years and found that while 89 percent were aware that physical activity resulted in improved health, only about 30 percent were participating in sufficient exercise to realize such benefits. Recognizing this dilemma, Chodzko-Zajko (1999) recommends that a strong focus on programming should be emphasized in future aging-physical activity research.

CONCEPT 21.7

Ageism can be detrimental to an older adult's developmental process.

Another social phenomenon that adults often face as they advance in years is **ageism,** which involves stereotyping (negatively or positively) or discriminating against older adults on the basis of prejudice (Hoyer et al., 1999). A perception that all old people have physical and cognitive deficits and should be treated like children is an example of ageism. It may also involve a dislike for older persons because they are perceived to be of minimal value to society or to represent a drain on societal resources. Ageism is often observed with the prejudicial perceptions of adolescents and adults but can be present in childhood. Behlendorf, MacRae, and Vos Strache (1999) found that even children possess ageism views of older people as less competent than younger adults in physical activities.

Without exploring the underlying bases of such perceptions, suffice it to say that they represent serious misconceptions. Table 21.2 provides several common misperceptions about older populations, many of them related to health status and physical capabilities. Ageism represents, at best, a level of ignorance about the individual value of each person of advanced age, and, at worst, a destructive tool that can damage the opportunities and even lives of older adults.

SUCCESSFUL AGING

It has been proposed that the concept of **successful aging** is multidimensional encompassing the sustained engagement in social and productive activities, the maintenance of high physical and cognitive function, and the avoidance of disease and disability (Rowe and Kahn, 1997) (figure 21.3). In an attempt to determine specific items that may serve as predictors of successful aging, two longitudinal aging studies were initiated at Duke University. The first began in 1955 and observed 276 men and women (aged 60 to 90 years) every two to four years until 1976. The second investigation began in 1968 with 502 men and women (aged 45 to 70 years) and was also completed in 1976 (Shock, 1985). Palmore (1979, 1982) examined the data from the first Duke longitudinal study of aging and identified several significant factors that could be classified as predictors of longevity and of successful aging.

Significant predictors of successful aging for both men and women included the motor domain characteristics of physical functioning and number of physical activities. In regard to the more specific factor of longevity, several components from the motor domain represented significant predicting factors. For both men and women, the physical functioning rating (representing the level of physical function ability in everyday tasks) was a significant predictor. A second significant predictor for men and women was each participant's self-rating of his or her health. For women, a significant longevity predictor was the number of activities involved that required physical mobility.

TABLE 21.2 **Common Misperceptions about Older Adults**

EXAMPLES OF MISPERCEPTIONS BASED ON NEGATIVE STEREOTYPES

1. Most older persons are poor.
2. Most older persons are unable to keep up with inflation.
3. Most older people are ill-housed.
4. Most older people are frail and in poor health.
5. The aged are impotent as a political force and require advocacy.
6. Most older people are inadequate employees; they are less productive, efficient, motivated, innovative, and creative than younger workers. Most older workers are accident-prone.
7. Older people are mentally slower and more forgetful; they are less able to learn new things.
8. Older persons tend to be intellectually rigid and dogmatic. Most old people are set in their ways and unable to change.
9. A majority of older people are socially isolated and lonely. Most are disengaging or disengaged from society.
10. Most older persons are confined to long-term care institutions.

EXAMPLES OF MISPERCEPTIONS BASED ON POSITIVE STEREOTYPES

1. The aged are relatively well off; they are not poor, but in good economic shape. Their benefits are generously provided by working members of society.
2. The aged are a potential political force that votes and participates in unity and in great numbers.
3. Older people make friends very easily. They are kind and smiling.
4. Most older persons are mature, experienced, wise, and interesting.
5. Most older persons are very good listeners and are especially patient with children.
6. A majority of older persons are very kind and generous to their children and grandchildren.

From S. Lubomudrov, "Congressional Perceptions of the Elderly: The Use of Stereotypes in the Legislative Process" in the *Journal of Gerontology,* 27:77–81, 1987.

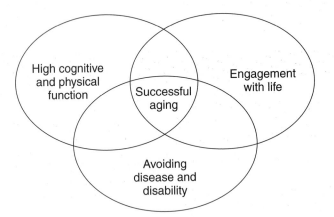

Figure 21.3

Interaction of factors leading to successful aging.

Adapted from Rowe, J. W., and Kahn, R. L. (1997). Successful aging, *The Gerontologist, 37,* 433–440.

CONCEPT 21.8

Lifestyle characteristics can represent important determinants of longevity and successful aging.

One implication that arises from the results of these investigations is that a physically active lifestyle is a key element in the pursuit of successful aging.

Chodzko-Zajko (1999) further states that

> In order to age successfully, older adults need to be not only physically active but also socially, intellectually, culturally, and (for many seniors) spiritually active. . . . One of the challenges for our profession in the new millennium will be to learn how to integrate physical activity into the wider social, cultural, and economic context of active aging as a whole. (p. 214)

SUMMARY

Both Erik Erikson and Daniel Levinson devised theoretical frameworks for the conceptualization of adult psychosocial development. Many aspects of the psychosocial domain interact often and in a number of ways with various characteristics of the motor domain. This is observed in many circumstances in which exercise is involved. Factors such as a sense of well-being, body image, locus of control, and depression may be influenced by an adult's involvement in physical activity. Maintaining a physically active lifestyle may also prove beneficial in the attainment of a sense of integrity during the latter stages of psychosocial development. Older adults, however, will face major decisions about retirement and may encounter ageism that could limit potential opportunities. Older adults who maintain good health and remain physically active can enhance their retirement circumstances while dispelling myths about older adult stereotypes. Health status and levels of physical activity are also recognized as predictors of longevity and successful aging.

CRITICAL READINGS

Hoyer, W. J., Rybash, J. M., & Roodin, P. A. (1999). *Adult Development and Aging* (Chapter 12). 4th ed. St. Louis: McGraw-Hill.

Osness, W. H., & Mulligan, L. (1998). Physical activity and depression among older adults. *Journal of Physical Education, Recreation and Dance, 69,* 16–18, 28.

Rowe, J. W., & Kahn, R. L. (1998). *Successful Aging.* New York: Pantheon Books.

Rowe, J. W., & Kahn, R. L. (1997). Successful aging. *The Gerontologist, 37,* 433–440.

Santrock, J. W. (2001). *Lifespan Development* (Chapters 15, 17, 20). 8th ed. St. Louis: McGraw-Hill.

Spirduso, W. W. (1995). *Physical Dimensions of Aging* (Chapter 10). Champaign, IL: Human Kinetics.

WEB RESOURCES

American Psychological Association section on aging issues
www.apa.org/pi/aging/homepage.html

Homepage for the American Association of Retired Persons
www.aarp.org

Homepage for the American Geriatrics Society
www.americangeriatrics.org

Homepage for the American Society on Aging
www.asaging.org

Homepage for the National Council on Aging
www.ncoa.org

Programming

Natural abilities are like natural plants;
they need pruning by study.

—Francis Bacon

CHAPTER

22 ASSESSING MOTOR BEHAVIOR

KEY TERMS

Reliability
Validity
Objectivity
Norm-referenced tests
Criterion-referenced tests
Product instruments
Process instruments
Screening tests
Ecological task analysis

CHAPTER COMPETENCIES

Upon completion of this chapter you should be able to:

- Describe the various characteristics of a well-developed assessment instrument
- Discuss various ways to categorize and select assessment instruments
- Identify motor assessment instruments that target the age populations of infants, toddlers, and preschoolers
- Identify motor assessment instruments that target the age populations of preschoolers, elementary children, middle school youth, and high school adolescents
- Identify motor assessment instruments that target the age population of adults
- Discuss the concept of naturalistic approaches to assessment

> **KEY CONCEPT**
>
> Motor assessment of developmental levels is essential if developmentally appropriate physical activity programming is to be a reality for infants, children, adolescents, and adults.

Assessment serves an important purpose in the area of motor development. Evaluating various aspects of an individual's motor behavior enables the movement specialist to monitor developmental changes, identify developmental delays, and gain insight into instructional strategies. There is no dearth of assessment instruments that purport to measure motor abilities. Hundreds of formal tests exist, both published and unpublished, designed with the measurement of various motor behavior characteristics in mind. Assessment methods also exist that represent a less formal, more naturalistic approach to the evaluation of an individual's motor characteristics. The challenge for the evaluator is to identify the most appropriate assessment procedures and instruments for the individual or group to be assessed.

CHARACTERISTICS OF ASSESSMENT INSTRUMENTS

A well-designed assessment instrument should have high **reliability, validity,** and **objectivity.** A reliable test will provide consistent scores from one test administration to the next. A valid test is one that measures what it claims to measure. Test validity is determined by experts (content validity), comparison with other tests measuring similar characteristics (criterion validity), or multivariate statistical methods (construct validity). An objective test will yield similar results when it is administered by different testers on the same individual.

> **CONCEPT 22.1**
>
> High values of reliability, validity, and objectivity are important characteristics of assessment instruments.

Assessment instruments can be categorized in various ways. **Norm-referenced tests** are based on a statistical sampling of hundreds or even thousands of individuals. They permit one to compare an individual against a statistical sample intended to be representative of the population at large. Caution, however, should be used when interpreting results from norm-referenced tests. Test norms are generally population-specific; that is, one cannot generalize beyond the population on which the norms were generated.

Criterion-referenced tests, on the other hand, incorporate a preestablished standard to which the individual's scores are compared. The standard represents a performance goal. The individual either achieves the standard or does not. No comparison to other persons is made.

> **CONCEPT 22.2**
>
> Assessment instruments can be categorized as norm-referenced, criterion-referenced, product-oriented, and/or process-oriented.

Assessment tools can also be classified as either **product instruments** or **process instruments.** Product instruments are quantitative and focus on the outcome or result of a particular performance. Examples of product-oriented scores include how far a ball is thrown, how fast a child runs, and how much weight an adult lifts. Mechanics and technique are not considered with product instruments. Process instruments, on the other hand, focus on the form, style, or mechanics used to perform the desired skill. Little attention is directed to the result of the skill performance. Of these two types of assessments the product instruments are by far the most prevalent.

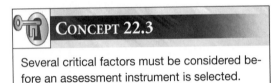

CONCEPT 22.3

Several critical factors must be considered before an assessment instrument is selected.

When selecting an assessment instrument, remember that one category of test is not inherently better than another. A norm-referenced test may address the needs of a particular population more adequately than a criterion-referenced test. Under a different set of conditions, the converse may be true. The same can be said of the process-product comparison. A process instrument may be the better choice for assessing the motor skill patterns of a preschool-aged child who is not disabled, but a product-oriented approach may be more appropriate with an adult who has experienced a stroke. Selecting the most appropriate assessment instrument requires consideration of the reasons why the evaluation is being performed, the instrument's characteristics, the relevance of the procedure to the individual's circumstances, and the capabilities of the evaluator.

FORMAL ASSESSMENT INSTRUMENTS

As previously mentioned in this chapter, numerous assessment instruments are available that attempt to measure motor behavior. As space does not allow a review of all available tests, this section will focus on a select few that represent different assessment approaches with various age groups.

CONCEPT 22.4

A variety of assessment instruments have been developed for the motor performance measurement of infants, toddlers, and preschoolers.

Infancy—Early Childhood

Medical and allied health professionals routinely conduct motor assessments of infants, toddlers, and preschoolers. With the passage of Public Law 99-457 (1986) by the federal government, which amended the 1975 Education of the Handicapped Act by expanding services to children with developmental disabilities from birth to 2 years of age, education professionals began to play a greater role in the assessment of the very young. The following assessment instruments are designed to measure motor behavior aspects of infants, toddlers, and preschoolers. **Screening tests** are often used with the very young child. These tests are designed to provide a relatively quick and simple means of differentiating normal infants or children from those who may not be developing normally. In addition to the following descriptions Zittel (1994) and Burton and Miller (1998) provide an extensive review of many of the following instruments as well as other early childhood assessment devices.

Apgar Assessment

Virginia Apgar (1953) developed the Apgar screening test as a quick and reliable method of assessing the newborn immediately after birth. An Apgar rating is made one minute after birth with subsequent ratings given five or more minutes after delivery. Infants are assigned a value of 0, 1, or 2 for each of the following items: (1) heart rate, (2) respiratory effort, (3) irritability, (4) muscle tone, and (5) color. The maximum total score is 10. Infants with low Apgar ratings generally require immediate attention if they are to survive. Table 22.1 provides a summary of the five items and how they are scored.

Apgar scores appear to be reliable. The test was standardized by Apgar and James (1962) on 27,715 infants. The standardization showed that infants with the lowest Apgar scores had the highest mortality rates and that the device was useful in predicting infant mortality.

Denver Developmental Screening Test–Denver II

The Denver Developmental Screening Test (DDST) constructed by Frankenburg and Dodds

TABLE 22.1 **Scoring the Apgar Screening Test**

	Scoring		
Item Tested	2	1	0
Heart rate	100–140 bpm	Under 100	No heartbeat
Respiratory effort	Regular breathing and lusty crying	Irregular or shallow breathing	No breathing
Reflex irritability (measured by a slap to the soles of the feet)	Lusty crying when soles of feet are slapped	No crying but grimace or movement when soles of feet are slapped	No reaction when soles of feet are slapped
Muscle tone	Spontaneously flexed arms and legs resist attempts at extension	Spontaneously flexed arms and legs offer little resistance from attempts at extension	Completely flaccid
Color[1]	Entirely pink	Some pink	Other than pink

[1]This is the most controversial item in the test. Few infants receive a 2 at one minute, and the item is invalid with dark-skinned babies.

TABLE 22.2 **Sample Items from the Denver II**

Area Tested	Sample Items Measured
Gross motor (32 items measured)	Rudimentary stability abilities: control of head, neck, trunk, rolling over, sitting, standing with support, pulling to stand, cruising, standing alone, walking Fundamental manipulative abilities: kicking, throwing, tricycle riding, catching Fundamental locomotor abilities: jumping in place, long-jumping, hopping Fundamental stability abilities: balancing on one foot, heel-toe walk
Fine motor (30 items measured)	Rudimentary manipulative abilities: reaching, grasping, and releasing, cube stacking, scribbling, copying, draw-a-person
Language (39 items measured)	Vocalizing, laughing, squealing, sound imitation of speech sounds, rudimentary combining words, following directions, recognizing colors, defining words
Personal-social (24 items measured)	Smiling, feeding, drinking from cup, imitating housework, helping in house, removing garment, putting on clothing, washing and drying hands, playing interactive games, separating from mother easily, dressing without supervision

(1967) has long been a helpful device used to screen infants and young children. The *Denver II* (Frankenburg et al., 1990, 1992) replaced the DDST as the latest version of this popular assessment drive. The norms were updated, language items increased, and a subjective test behavior rating scale added. The Denver II is one of the most widely used standardized tests for evaluating the motor development of young children.

Both gross and fine motor skills are assessed along with language and personal-social skills. The 125 items on the test are scaled according to their normal developmental order of appearance in children. Seldom are more than 25 of the 125 items administered in order to provide a profile of the child's developmental level. Table 22.2 provides a brief overview of the test and some of the items assessed.

TABLE 22.3 | **General Description of the Items Measured on the Bayley Scales of Infant Development—Second Edition**

Scale	Items Assessed
Mental scale	Sensory-perceptual acuities Object discrimination Object constancy Memory Learning Problem solving Vocalization Verbal communication Generalizations and classifications
Motor scale	Control of the body Gross motor coordination Fine motor coordination
Infant behavior record	Administered after the mental and motor scales. Assesses the child's social development, interests, emotions, energy, and tendencies to approach or withdraw from situations.

TABLE 22.4 | **General Factors Measured by the Peabody Developmental Motor Scales—Second Edition**

Gross Motor Quotient Factors	Fine Motor Quotient Factors
• Reflexes (8 items) • Stationary (30 items) • Locomotion (89 items) • Object manipulation (24 items)	• Grasping (26 items) • Visual-motor integration (72 items)

The Denver II was developed to serve as an instrument to screen for children with possible problems, monitor children at risk, and to confirm intuitive suspicions.

Bayley Scales of Infant Development—Second Edition

The Bayley Scales of Infant Development—Second Edition (BSID-II) (Bayley, 1993) represents a revision of the 1969 version. Its intent is to identify developmental delays in children and serve as a guide in the development of intervention programs.

The BSID-II is divided into three scales: mental, motor, and behavior rating. Table 22.3 presents a brief overview of these three scales and the general items measured. The mental scale contains 178 items. The motor scale consists of 111 items measuring progressive change in gross motor abilities such as sitting, standing, walking, and stair climbing, and fine motor abilities.

The BSID-II scales have proven to be helpful in determining the developmental status of individual infants at a given age. When administered and interpreted by a trained examiner, they can be a valuable research tool.

The Peabody Developmental Motor Scales—Second Edition

The Peabody Developmental Motor Scales—Second Edition (PDMS-2) (Folio and Fewell, 2000) is designed to assess fine motor and gross motor development of infants and young children. Fine motor characteristics evaluated include manual dexterity, eye-hand coordination, and grasping. Gross motor items include reflexes, locomotor skills, nonlocomotor skills, and balance. The PDMS-2 is both a norm-referenced and a criterion-referenced instrument. Factors purported to be assessed by the PDMS-2 are summarized in Table 22.4.

CONCEPT 22.5

Several assessment instruments have been developed for the motor performance measurement of preschoolers, elementary-aged children, middle school–aged youth, and adolescents.

Early Childhood—Adolescence

Motor assessment can be particularly important during the preschool and school years. Development can be monitored year after year through proper evaluation scheduling. A well-planned assessment schedule can yield valuable information for individualized instructional strategies as students advance through their preschool, elementary, middle school, and high school years. The following assessment instruments were designed with the preschool and school-aged child in mind.

Bruininks-Oseretsky Test of Motor Proficiency

The Bruininks-Oseretsky Test of Motor Proficiency (BOTMP) was developed by Bruininks (1978) as an "individually administered test that assesses the motor functioning of children from 4+ to 14+ years of age" (p. 11). The BOTMP is composed of eight subtests designed to measure important aspects of motor behavior. The gross motor skill and fine motor skill sections of the test may be administered separately and will yield separate composite scores. To arrive at a composite score for the entire battery of tests, a combination gross and fine motor skills test must be taken along with the separate gross motor items and separate fine motor items. A short form of the BOTMP is also available. It has, however, been suggested that the BOTMP short form be used only as a screening device and not for diagnostic or placement purposes (Verderber and Payne, 1987).

The BOTMP has good potential for assessing the motor proficiency of children. It can be of value as a research tool and an aid for identifying children with special needs. A corresponding developmental curriculum package called Body Skills also can be purchased separately from the test. Feasibility with the BOTMP can be a problem, however, as it can be time consuming to administer the test, and children are generally tested individually.

Fundamental Movement Pattern Assessment Instrument

The Fundamental Movement Pattern Assessment Instrument (FMPAI) designed by McClenaghan (1976), later published by McClenaghan and Gallahue (1978), and expanded by Gallahue (Gallahue and Cleland, 2003) is a carefully developed observational assessment instrument. It is used to classify individuals at the "initial," "elementary," or "mature" stage of development

first using a total body configuration approach, followed by an individual segmental analysis approach. The original version assessed five primary fundamental movements (throwing, catching, kicking, running, and jumping). The expanded version is designed to assess more than twenty fundamental movement patterns. The developmental sequence for each of these movements is based on a review of the biomechanical literature on each fundamental movement.

The FMPAI is an easy-to-administer, easy-to-use, subjective motor development test designed to measure the present status of children and to informally assess change over time. It attempts to view the quality of the child's movement and is based on documented and hypothesis developmental sequences for acquiring selected fundamental movement abilities. The FMPAI does not, however, yield a quantitative score, nor can it be used for comparing one child with another. This instrument is intended instead to assess developmental changes over time, using observational assessment as a valid and reliable method of data collection and comparison among individuals. It is not, however, intended to be used as a research device, but rather as a means of informally observing and assessing children for the purpose of effective programming for movement skill enhancement.

Developmental Sequence of Fundamental Motor Skills Inventory

The Developmental Sequence of Fundamental Motor Skills Inventory (DSFMSI) assessment instrument was developed by Seefeldt and Haubenstricker (1976) and Haubenstricker et al. (1981). The DSFMSI categorizes each of ten fundamental motor patterns into four or five stages. The fundamental movements of walking, skipping, hopping, running, striking, kicking, catching, throwing, jumping, and punting have been studied. These developmental sequences are based on combinations of longitudinal and cross-sectional data obtained from film analysis. Children are observed and matched to both visual and verbal descriptions of each stage. Individuals are classified along a continuum from stage 1 (immature) to stage 5 (mature) (Payne and Isaacs, 2002).

Test of Gross Motor Development—Second Edition

The Test of Gross Motor Development—Second Edition (TGMD-2) (Ulrich, 1998) is a revision of an instrument developed by Ulrich (1985) as a means of assessing selected movement skills in children 3 to 10+ years of age. Selected locomotor and manipulative skills comprise the twelve-item test. Locomotor skills include running, galloping, hopping, leaping, horizontal jumping, and sliding. Manipulative skills include two-hand striking, stationary ball bouncing, catching, kicking, overhand throwing, and underhand rolling.

Administration of the TGMD-2 takes approximately fifteen minutes per child. A manual with a clear set of test instructions is available. The TGMD-2 is easy to administer and can be used with a minimum amount of special training. It provides both norm-referenced and criterion-referenced interpretations and places emphasis on the sequence and qualitative aspects of gross motor skill acquisition rather than on the product and quantitative aspects of performance. A set of instructional videos titled *Assessment of Fundamental Motor Skills* (Ignico, 1994) is also available that corresponds with the use of the TGMD-2. These videotapes enable viewers to develop their observational assessment skills.

Ohio State University Scale of Intra Gross Motor Assessment

The Ohio State University Scale of Intra Gross Motor Assessment (O.S.U. SIGMA) was developed to measure basic locomotor and manipulative skills of children ages 2.5 to 14 years. Additional test items include stair and ladder climbing. Accompanying the O.S.U. SIGMA is an instructional program called the Performance Base Curriculum. The Performance Base Curriculum provides activities that correspond to the developmental levels identified in the O.S.U. SIGMA.

Basic Motor Ability Tests–Revised

The Basic Motor Ability Tests-Revised (BMAT-R) developed by Arnheim and Sinclair (1979) consists of a battery of eleven tests designed to measure a variety of motor functions. These include eye-hand coordination, static and dynamic balance, fine and gross motor control, agility, and joint flexibility. Norms are reported for males and females aged 4 to 12 years. The authors of the BMAT-R reported that a group of up to five children can be assessed by a single test administrator in approximately thirty minutes.

Movement Assessment Battery for Children (Movement ABC)

Previously entitled the Test of Motor Impairment-Henderson Revision, the Movement ABC is designed to provide insight into a child's level of motor deficiency (Henderson and Sugden, 1992). It combines both quantitative and qualitative assessment of gross and fine motor tasks and contains standardized norms for ages 4 to 12 years. The previous edition was found to be highly consistent with the BOTMP with regard to motor impairment decisions (Riggen, Ulrich, and Ozmun, 1990). A comparison of age ranges represented by several norm-referenced instruments designed for children and adolescents can be found in figure 22.1.

Adults

The motor performance of adults is variable, and that variability increases with advancing age. Assessing motor characteristics of the adult is a key ingredient in establishing intervention strategies for the maintenance of functional abilities or the perpetuation of an active lifestyle.

CONCEPT 22.6

Several assessment instruments have been developed for the motor performance measurement of adults.

American Alliance for Health, Physical Education, Recreation and Dance (AAHPERD) Field Test for Older Adults

The AAHPERD device is a field test that measures a combination of health-related physical fitness components and motor performance characteristics.

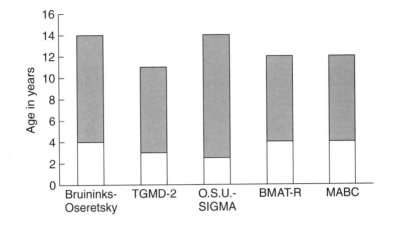

Figure 22.1
Age ranges of norm-referenced tests for children and adolescents.

Areas of investigation include muscular strength and endurance, coordination, flexibility, and aerobic endurance. Test items are designed to relate to the daily functions of the adult over the age of 60 years. In addition, the AAHPERD test can be administered by individuals with limited equipment (Spirduso, 1995).

Scales of Activities of Daily Living

Numerous instruments exist that purport to assess functional ability in activities of daily living (ADL). These activities include basic self-care skills such as eating, dressing, toileting, grooming, and functional mobility. Law and Letts (1989) conducted a critical review of scales of ADL and compared the purpose, clinical utility, reliability, and validity of thirteen instruments. For greater detail on specific scales of ADL, the reader is advised to refer to the Law and Letts study.

Williams-Greene Test of Physical and Motor Function

This instrument was designed to measure the upper-extremity function and mobility capabilities of older adults. Upper-extremity function is measured by tasks that involve simple and repetitive arm and hand movements and various forms of dexterity. Mobility is examined through the measurement of tasks such as balance and gait control (Spirduso, 1995).

NATURALISTIC APPROACHES TO ASSESSMENT

The majority of the previously discussed assessment instruments require formal, structured settings in which to evaluate individuals. Distance to be covered during a run and size of ball to be tossed are examples of how structured tests establish restrictions to the way motor performance is measured. Some assessment instruments are so specific that they dictate what is to be stated when directions are given.

CONCEPT 22.7

Naturalistic approaches to assessment increase the opportunity to evaluate an individual's motor performance from a much broader perspective that encompasses the relationship among the task goal, the environment, and the performer.

By eliminating all but one or two environmental conditions from a particular task, the scope of the individual's ability cannot be truly measured. In addition, an individual's motor performance observed within the structured setting of a test condition may not be indicative of the person's performance in a more natural, realistic situation. Two approaches that attempt to accommodate both the individual being tested and the environmental conditions that may influence motor performance are ecological task analysis and interdisciplinary play-based assessment.

Ecological Task Analysis

Ecological task analysis (ETA) examines performance in light of the relationships among the task goal, the environment, and the performer. Davis and Burton (1991) describe four steps in establishing an ETA. The first step is selecting and presenting the task goal. This involves determining the function(s) of the task or what will be accomplished by the task. The second step is to allow the child or adult being tested the opportunity to choose the skill; the movement pattern; and when the task requires, the implement to complete the task. The third step involves giving the individual guidance by emphasizing the goal of the task and stressing attention to the environmental conditions corresponding to the task. Guidance may also be provided by manipulating certain task dimensions to make the task more difficult without altering the task goal. The fourth step involves providing direct instruction regarding the individual's skill selection and movement form. This incorporates more traditional forms of instruction such as giving a demonstration of the proper skill mechanics.

Ulrich (1988) developed an assessment model that addresses many of the ETA's considerations. His model uses striking an object as the example task. He provides numerous conditions under which an object may be struck. Aspects that may be manipulated include the striking implement, the movement of the ball, the size of the ball, and the conditions under which the individual is observed (formal test, informal play, or structured play). An example of the task conditions and sample score sheet can be seen in tables 22.5 and 22.6.

Ecological task analysis represents a promising approach to the assessment of motor behavior characteristics. It increases the opportunity to

TABLE 22.5	Ulrich's Developmental Task Analysis Model for Striking
Task Conditions	**Proposed Sequence**
A. Striking Implement	$1—A_1 B_1 C_1$
1. Hand	$2—A_1 B_1 C_2$
2. Lightweight racquetball	$3—A_1 B_1 C_3$
racquet	$4—A_1 B_2 C_1$
3. Narrow plastic bat	$5—A_1 B_2 C_2$
B. Ball Movement	$6—A_1 B_2 C_3$
1. Stationary on batting tee	$7—A_1 B_2 C_1$
2. Slow underhand toss	$8—A_1 B_3 C_2$
from 15 feet	$9—A_1 B_3 C_3$
3. Overhand toss from	$10—A_2 B_1 C_1$
15 feet	$11—A_2 B_1 C_2$
C. Ball Size	$12—A_2 B_1 C_3$
1. 12-inch lightweight ball	$13—A_2 B_2 C_1$
2. 8-inch lightweight ball	$14—A_2 B_2 C_2$
3. 4-inch lightweight ball	$15—A_2 B_2 C_3$
	$16—A_2 B_3 C_1$
	$17—A_2 B_3 C_2$
	$18—A_2 B_3 C_3$
	$19—A_3 B_1 C_1$
	$20—A_3 B_1 C_2$
	$21—A_3 B_1 C_3$
	$22—A_3 B_2 C_1$
	$23—A_3 B_2 C_2$
	$24—A_3 B_2 C_3$
	$25—A_3 B_3 C_1$
	$26—A_3 B_3 C_2$
	$27—A_3 B_3 C_3$

From D. A. Ulrich, "Children with Special Needs: Assessing the Quality of Movement Competence" in *Journal of Physical Education, Recreation and Dance* 59:43–47, 1988.

evaluate an individual's motor performance from a broad perspective.

Interdisciplinary Play-Based Assessment

A second assessment approach that attempts to evaluate individuals in a more naturalistic setting is interdisciplinary play-based assessment (IPBA). Used primarily with young children IPBA uses a team of professionals with varying areas of expertise. Team members may represent the areas of psychology, physical therapy, occupational therapy,

TABLE 22.6 Test of Basic Striking Competence (Scoring Example)

OBSERVATIONAL CONTEXTS AND BEHAVIORAL CRITERIA

Name _____ Age _____ Classroom _____

	1 Formal Test				1 Context Score	2 Informal Play				2 Context Score	3 Structured Play				3 Context Score	Total Condition Score
	Eyes focus on ball	Hip and shoulder rotation	Contralateral weight transfer	Contacts ball		Eyes focus on ball	Hip and shoulder rotation	Contralateral weight transfer	Contacts ball		Eyes focus on ball	Hip and shoulder rotation	Contralateral weight transfer	Contacts ball		
Task Conditions	(a)	(b)	(c)	(d)		(a)	(b)	(c)	(d)		(a)	(b)	(c)	(d)		
1. $A_1 B_1 C_1$	2	1	2	2	7	2	1	1	1	5	2	0	1	1	4	16
2. $A_1 B_1 C_2$	2	1	2	1	6	2	1	1	1	5	2	0	1	1	4	15
3. $A_1 B_1 C_3$	2	1	1	1	5	2	1	1	1	5	1	0	1	1	3	13
4. $A_1 B_1 C_1$	1	1	1	1	4	1	1	1	1	4	1	0	1	1	3	11
5. $A_1 B_2 C_2$	1	1	1	0	3	1	1	0	0	2	1	1	0	0	2	7
6. $A_1 B_2 C_3$	1	1	1	0	3	1	1	0	0	2	1	0	0	0	1	5
7. $A_1 B_3 C_1$	1	0	1	0	2	1	0	1	0	2	1	0	0	0	1	5
8. $A_1 B_3 C_2$	1	0	0	0	1	1	0	0	0	1	1	0	0	0	1	3
9. $A_1 B_3 C_3$	1	0	0	0	1	1	0	0	0	1	0	0	0	0	0	2
10. $A_2 B_1 C_1$	2	0	0	1	3	1	0	0	1	2	1	0	0	1	2	7
11. $A_2 B_1 C_2$	1	0	0	1	2	1	0	0	0	1	1	0	0	0	1	4
12. $A_2 B_1 C_3$	1	0	0	0	1	1	0	0	0	1	1	0	0	0	1	3
13. $A_2 B_2 C_1$	0	0	0	0	0	0	0	0	0	0	0	0	0	0	0	0
14. $A_2 B_2 C_2$	0	0	0	0	0	0	0	0	0	0	0	0	0	0	0	0
15. $A_2 B_2 C_3$																
16. $A_2 B_2 C_3$																
17. $A_2 B_2 C_3$																
18. $A_2 B_2 C_3$																
19. $A_2 B_2 C_3$																
20. $A_2 B_2 C_3$																
21. $A_2 B_2 C_3$																
22. $A_2 B_2 C_3$																
23. $A_2 B_2 C_3$																
24. $A_2 B_2 C_3$																
25. $A_2 B_2 C_3$																
26. $A_2 B_2 C_3$																
27. $A_2 B_2 C_3$																
Total Context Score					38/216 18%					31/216 14%					23/216 11%	
Total Striking Competence Score																92/648 14%

Scoring Key
0—Absent
1—Emerging
2—Mastered

417

special education, and adapted physical education. Collectively, the team observes the child interacting with a parent, parents, or family members. Following the interaction session the assessment team discusses their observations and uses an interdisciplinary approach in determining diagnosis and educational planning and placement.

The IPBA approach takes seriously the philosophy that the developmental domains of behavior are interrelated. For a more in-depth discussion on IPBA the reader is urged to read *Transdisciplinary Play-Based Assessment: A Functional Approach to Working with Young Children* (2nd Ed.) by T. W. Linder (1993).

SUMMARY

The process of motor assessment is important in monitoring developmental changes, identifying developmental delays, and providing insight into instructional strategies. A number of assessment instruments exist that purport to measure various aspects of motor behavior. The characteristics of a well-developed test should include strong reliability, validity, and objectivity. Assessment instruments may be classified as norm-referenced, criterion-referenced, process-oriented, and/or product-oriented. Assessment tools exist for individuals from birth to adulthood. Evaluation instruments for infants to preschoolers include the Apgar Assessment, Denver II, Bayley Scales of Infant Development (second ed.), and Peabody Developmental Motor Scales (second ed.). For school-aged children assessments include

the Bruininks-Oseretsky Test of Motor Proficiency, Fundamental Movement Pattern Assessment Instrument, Developmental Sequence of Fundamental Motor Skills Inventory, Test of Gross Motor Development (second ed.), O.S.U. Scale of Intra Gross Motor Assessment, Basic Motor Ability Tests-Revised, and Movement Assessment Battery for Children. Adult assessment instruments include the AAHPERD Field Test for Older Adults and a number of activities of daily living scales.

A more naturalistic approach to assessment attempts to examine an individual's motor performance in light of the relationships among the task goal, the environment, and the performer. Examples of this approach include ecological task analysis and interdisciplinary play-based assessment.

CRITICAL READINGS

Block, M. E., Lieberman, L., & Conner-Kuntz, F. (1998). Authentic assessment in adapted physical education. *Journal of Physical Education, Recreation, and Dance, 69*, 48–57.

Burton, A. W., and Miller, D. E. (1998). *Movement Skill Assessment.* Champaign, IL: Human Kinetics.

Sherrill, C. (1998). *Adapted Physical Activity, Recreation and Sport: Crossdisciplinary and Lifespan* (Chapters 6 & 11). 5th ed. St. Louis: McGraw-Hill.

Spirduso, W. W. (1995). *Physical Dimensions of Aging* (Chapter 12). Champaign, IL: Human Kinetics.

Winnick, J. P. (Ed.) (2000). *Adapted Physical Education and Sport* (Chapter 5). 3rd ed. Champaign, IL: Human Kinetics.

Zittel, L. L. (1994). Gross motor assessment of preschool children with special needs: Instrument selection considerations. *Adapted Physical Activity Quarterly, 11*, 245–260.

 ## WEB RESOURCES

Discussion on movement assessment issues
http://pe.central.vt.edu/assessment/assessment.html

Review of several assessment instruments for adapted physical education
http://pe.central.vt.edu/adapted/adaptedinstruments.html

PROGRAMMING FOR DEVELOPMENTAL PHYSICAL ACTIVITY

KEY TERMS

Skill theme

Content areas

Skill concepts

Movement concepts

Activity concepts

Movement exploration technique

Guided-discovery method

CHAPTER COMPETENCIES

Upon completion of this chapter you should be able to:

- Discuss the interrelatedness among the phases and stages of motor development, the levels and stages of learning a new movement skill, and implementing various styles of teaching
- Individualize physical activity instruction to accommodate the developmental levels of your learners
- Plan physical activity programs for different age groups
- Demonstrate awareness of within-age individual differences in planning physical activity programs for various portions of the life span
- Diagram the conceptual basis for a developmentally based physical activity

> **Key Concept**
>
> The utility of knowledge concerning the process of motor development from infancy through adulthood can be found in developmentally appropriate movement skill learning programs.

Throughout the discussions in the preceding chapters, we have continually focused on the developmental stages that infants, children, adolescents, and adults pass through in their motor development. The thesis of this entire text has centered on the process of motor development and factors that impinge on its normal progression. If the phases and stages of motor development presented in chapter 3 and elaborated on throughout this text have any real meaning, we should be able to construct physical activity programs congruent with these phases. This curricular model should embody the concept that although motor development is age-related it is not age-dependent. It is critically important to know about and be able to apply information about the biology of the individual and the conditions of the learning environment with the requirements of the movement task.

What has been discussed in the preceding chapters is of little value if we cannot apply it to the lives of real people. The value of theory and research that fails to foster models for implementation is limited at best. Intervention programs not based on sound research and theory are equally worthless. This chapter, therefore, proposes a developmentally based, dynamic model for implementing movement experiences for infants, children, adolescents, and adults.

To facilitate presentation of the developmental model at the conclusion of this chapter, we will first review the three categories into which movement may be classified and the appropriate movement skill themes that may be extracted from each

category. Then we will briefly discuss the three major content areas of physical activity and the cognitive core of the developmental program. We will then examine the levels and stages in the process of movement skill learning with particular attention given to the appropriateness of various styles of teaching. Finally, a model will be presented for individuals at the fundamental movement phase, and for those at the specialized movement phase of their movement skill development. But first, please refer to figure 23.1 for a depiction of the dynamic nature of movement skill learning from a pedagogical perspective. The nuenomic LITE should serve as a helpful reminder to all instructors (i.e., therapists, teachers, parents, and coaches) that learning is the primary goal of all developmentally based education.

Categories of Movement and Movement Skill Themes

The three *categories of movement* as they relate to motor development have been discussed extensively. Briefly, a "category of movement" is a classificatory scheme based on common underlying principles of movement. Locomotion, manipulation, and stability are used here to represent these underlying principles. Although others have used the term *nonlocomotor* or *nonmanipulative* rather than *stability* as a category of movement, we have chosen to give recognition to the term *stability* as a movement category. Doing so is not arbitrary or without support. Keough and Sugden (1985) and Gentile (2001) have chosen to classify movement behavior into the categories of locomotion, manipulation, and stability. These three categories serve as the organizing centers of the developmental activity program and as the basis for the formation of movement skill themes.

A **skill theme** is a particular movement skill or cluster of skills around which a specific lesson or series of lessons is organized. In the developmental activity program, a category of movement serves as the organizing center for a group of lessons or

L The instructor (i.e., parent/teacher/coach/therapist) determines what type of *Learning* is desired (i.e., What are the age-appropriate goals or competencies?).

I The instructor assesses, recognizes, and respects the *Individuality* of the learner (i.e., What is developmentally appropriate as determined by some form of assessment?).

T The instructor adjusts the goal of the learning *Task* to suit the needs of the individual (i.e., Task Analysis based on the above needs of the learner).

E The instructor manipulates the conditions of the *Environment* by making specific programming decisions (i.e., To facilitate increased motor control, movement skill learning, and movement competence).

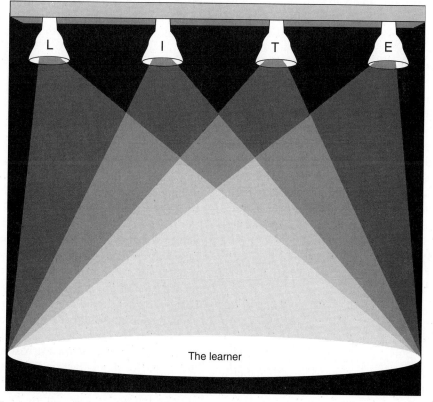

Figure 23.1

The dynamic nature of a developmental program model views learning as a function of interaction among the biology of the individual, the goal of the movement task, and the conditions of the learning environment.

instructional sessions, whereas skill themes serve as the organizing centers of individual lessons. For example, the "organizing center" for a group of lessons may be object manipulation, but the skill theme would be some subset of manipulation such as striking, kicking, or volleying. Each category of movement is briefly reviewed here, and a few examples of possible skill themes are given.

CONCEPT 23.1

Developmental physical activity programs use a movement skill theme approach for the learning of fundamental and specialized movement skills.

Stability

Stability refers to the ability to maintain one's balance in relationship to the force of gravity even though the nature of the application of the force may be altered or parts of the body may be placed in unusual positions. The classification of stability extends beyond the concept of balance and includes various axial movements and postures in which a premium is placed on controlling one's equilibrium. Stability is the most basic form of human movement. It is fundamental to all efficient movement and permeates the categories of locomotion and manipulation. Bending, stretching, pivoting, dodging, and walking on a balance beam are examples of skill themes that may be incorporated into the daily lesson plan at the fundamental or sport skill phase of development.

Locomotion

Locomotion refers to changes in the location of the body relative to fixed points on the ground. To walk, run, hop, jump, slide, or leap is to be involved in locomotion. The movement classification of locomotion develops in conjunction with stability, not apart from it. Fundamental aspects of stability must be mastered before efficient forms of locomotion may occur. Vertical jumping, rebounding, and high jumping are examples of skill themes that may be incorporated into the daily lesson plan at the fundamental or sport skill phase of development.

Manipulation

Gross-motor manipulation is concerned with giving force to objects and absorbing force from objects by the use of the hands or feet. The tasks of throwing, catching, kicking, trapping, and striking are included under the category of manipulation. Object manipulation also refers to the fine motor controls required for tasks such as buttoning, cutting, printing, and writing. The scope of this text, however, has been limited to gross motor aspects of manipulation. Large muscle manipulative abilities tend to develop somewhat later than stability and locomotor abilities. This is partly because most gross-motor manipulative tasks incorporate elements of both stability and locomotion. Throwing a ball, passing a football, and pitching a baseball are examples of skill themes within the manipulative category of movement.

CONTENT AREAS OF PHYSICAL ACTIVITY

Fundamental movement skills and specialized movement skills within the three categories of movement outlined may be developed and refined through the three major **content areas** of physical activity—*educational games, dance,* and *gymnastics activities.* Learning how to participate in particular activities is a means of developing, refining, and reinforcing stability, locomotor, and manipulative abilities appropriate to the developmental level of the individual. Each activity used in the program should be selected on the basis of what it can contribute to movement skill enhancement. Although the primary objective of the learner may be to have fun, the basic objectives of the instructor should be teaching learners how to move and how to learn through movement. Incorporating fun as a motivational tool is an important objective of any good educational program and is critically important to long-term adherence. However, when fun becomes the primary objective, the program ceases to be educational in which learning is the primary objective, and instead becomes recreational in which enjoyment is the primary objective. The ideal is, of course, *learning enjoyment* in which learning and enjoyment *both* occur.

...wing is a common classification

...ies (i.e., muscular strength/ ...robic endurance, joint flexibility) ...mbling (i.e., individual and ...ities, and mat activities) ...ctivities (hand apparatus, large

...a skillful mover at either the funda- ...cialized movement skill phase is the ...on for incorporating educational ...and gymnastic activities in the pro- ...egree to which this is achieved de- ...e particular developmental level of ...nd the instructor's expertise in struc- ...pmentally appropriate movement ex- ...mes, dances, and gymnastic activities ...s the vehicles by which these experi- ...plied.

...NCEPT **23.3**

...epts, movement concepts, and activ- ...pts are taught as a means of learning ...body *should* move and *can* move, and ...should and can move, respectively.

...into the following subcategories:

- Rhythmic fundamentals (i.e., accent, tempo, intensity, and rhythmic pattern)
- Creative dance (dance making)
- Folk dance (i.e., traditional dance)
- Social dance (i.e., partner dance)

Educational Gymnastics

Educational gymnastics is the third major content area of the program representing a wide variety of activities in which individuals work on their own and can improve their performances through their individual efforts. Educational gymnastics is self-testing and may be classified in a variety of

THE CRITICAL THINKING CORE OF THE DEVELOPMENTAL PROGRAM

In our view, the primary focus of the developmentally based physical activity program should be on movement skill acquisition—both fundamental and specialized. Our intent is not to diminish the importance of fitness enhancement, self-concept development, or positive socialization on the part of the learner. All are important strands in the developmental physical activity program. Developmentally appropriate movement skill learning is the core of what the therapist, teacher, and coach do. Developing, maintaining, and refining movement skills makes significant contributions to the

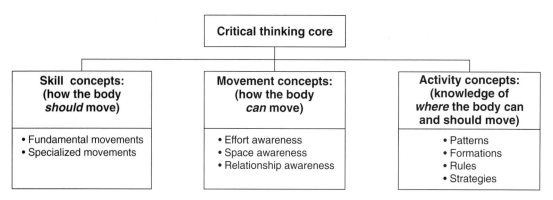

Figure 23.2
The critical thinking core of the developmental movement skill learning program.

learner at all ages and developmental levels. To become a more skillful mover the learner needs to become versed in the *skill concepts, movement concepts,* and *activity concepts* of movement skill learning (figure 23.2).

Skill concepts deal specifically with how the body *should* move. Insufficient instructional time and too many learners at one time are problems for many therapists, teachers, and coaches trying to help their clients, students, or athletes become more skillful movers. If the instructor, however, takes an approach of helping the learner learn about how the body should move, the learner is then provided with the essential tools for self-instruction or instruction in less formal instructional settings. For example, when working with a client in a physical therapy setting after hip-joint replacement surgery, the therapist instructs the client in the proper performance of a series of exercises, with the intent of the client eventually returning to a normal walking gait. Given this initial instruction, and perhaps a printout of exercises to perform at home, the learner has the basic tools to be her own therapist in doing the activities that will lead to a new and improved walking gait. Certainly, it is important for the professional therapist to monitor the client, but by providing her with the skill concepts of how the body should move, she can become an active participant in her rehabilitation.

Movement concepts provide the learner with a framework for how the body *can* move. Seldom

does movement occur under the exact conditions time after time. The environmental context of most movement is open. As you will recall from our discussion in chapter 1, open movement skills occur in an unpredictable and constantly changing environment. Because this environment is fluid, rather than fixed, as in a closed movement skill, the learner needs to develop a movement repertoire that is both flexible and adaptable to changing environmental conditions. The dynamic nature of movement, including its changing context and its situational requirements, make it absolutely essential for the learner to develop an "awareness" of how bodies can move. Rudolph Laban (Laban and Lawrence, 1947) is generally credited with being the first to classify movement into different types of awareness. *Effort awareness* deals with the force, time, and flow of movement. *Space awareness* deals with where the body can move in varying levels, directions, and ranges. *Relationship awareness* focuses on moving with objects and people. Each is depicted in table 23.1.

Activity concepts deal with *where* the body can and should move. Activity concept learning centers on the patterns of movement, formations, rules, and strategies required for effective participation in the daily living, recreational, and sport activities of one's culture. Thus when a teacher helps his students learn the activity concepts of six-a-side soccer, baseball, or contemporary dancing the learner is being provided with important tools for

TABLE 23.1 **The Framework for Movement Concept Learning**

Effort Awareness (How the Body Moves with Varying Amounts of—)	Space Awareness (Where the Body Moves at Different—)	Relationship Awareness (Moving with—)
—**Force** strong light moderate —**Time** fast slow medium sustained sudden —**Flow** free bound	—**Levels** high/medium/low —**Directions** forward/backward diagonally/sideward up/down various pathways (curved, straight, zig-zag, etc.) —**Ranges** body shapes (wide, narrow, curved, straight, etc.) body spaces (self-space and general space) body extensions (near/far, large/small, with and without implements)	—**Objects** (or people) over/under in/out between/among in front/behind lead/follow above/below through/around —**People** mirroring shadowing in unison together/apart alternating simultaneously partner/group

understanding where they should position themselves, how to respond to elements of the activity, and the rules and strategies for successful participation. Activity concepts must be geared to the learner's level of motor and affective development as well as his cognitive development. Remember that in the developmental approach advocated here, activity concepts, although important, are not the primary focus of the movement lesson. The core of the program is movement skill learning.

TEACHING TO FACILITATE LEARNING

The instructor must be aware of and make accommodations for the fact that the learner goes through identifiable levels and stages in learning a new movement skill (chapter 16). These levels are based on two fundamental principles. First, the acquisition of movement abilities progresses from the simple to complex, and second, individuals proceed gradually from general to specific in the development and refinement of their movement skills. Using the levels and stages depicted in figure 23.3,

the following paragraphs discuss how to incorporate various teaching styles in developmentally appropriate ways.

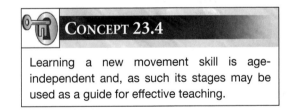

CONCEPT 23.4

Learning a new movement skill is age-independent and, as such its stages may be used as a guide for effective teaching.

This sequential progression is similar for adolescents and adults as well as for children. Because adolescents and adults are frequently at the specialized skill phase, they may spend less time with exploration, discovery, and the combination experiences, and more time in the application and refined performance aspects. Children at the fundamental movement pattern phase of development should spend a great deal of time exploring, discovering, and combining new movements and considerably less time with the application of

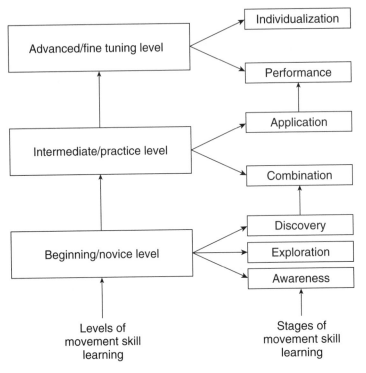

Figure 23.3
Levels and stages of learning a new movement skill.

"best" ways of moving and refined performance. The discussion that follows relies heavily or the Spectrum of Teaching Styles proposed by Mosston and Ashworth (1994).

Facilitating Exploration

After awareness, exploration represents the first stage in the movement skill learning hierarchy. To take advantage of this stage, the instructor focuses on indirect teaching approaches that encourage exploration. The **movement exploration** technique of teaching movement helps enhance awareness of the body and its potential for movement in space. Individuals are encouraged to explore and experiment effort, space, and relationship awareness. Accuracy and precision in performance are not stressed. The instructor refrains from establishing a model of performance for the particular

movement being explored. Instead, participants are presented with a series of movement questions or challenges and given time to solve these problems as they see fit. Any "reasonable" solution to the problem is regarded as correct. At this time, there is no "best" method of performance that the instructor attempts to elicit. More emphasis is placed on creative involvement in the learning process.

Movement exploration experiences are concerned less with the reproduction of the movement act and more with the processes involved in the production of "new" movement sequences (Mosston and Ashworth, 1994). The instructor is not particularly concerned with whether the ball goes in the hoop, how high Noah can jump, or how far Jennifer can throw. The instructor is interested in guiding learners to achieve some degree of success within the levels of their particular abilities.

The instructor also places importance and value on the learner's ability to think and act independently.

This is not to imply that success or goal-directed behavior is not important. On the contrary, movement exploration techniques are particularly appropriate for young children and novice learners of all ages, because they permit experimentation and self-learning and they structure the environment for success. Success and goal-directed behavior are individual standards that do not require emulation of a model or competition with others, but permit achievement within the limits of one's abilities.

> ## CONCEPT 23.5
>
> Developmentally based teaching recognizes the learner's current level of movement skill learning and makes adjustments to facilitate the learning process.

Facilitating Discovery

Discovery represents the second classification of the movement skill learning hierarchy. Movement experiences that incorporate discovery may be included in the lesson by the instructor in an indirect manner similar to the use of movement exploration techniques. The **guided-discovery method** of teaching is often used when the learner is in the process of finding solutions. The use of this technique requires the instructor to avoid establishing a model for "correct" performance at the outset of the experience. Instead, the instructor poses problems in the form of questions or challenges. These questions zero in on movement pattern development rather than on skill development by helping the learner make a series of small but important discoveries.

The movement exploration method uses *problem-solving* techniques as a tactic in developing movement skills.

The method that the individual employs in solving problems posed by the instructor causes exploration and guided discovery to be considered separately here. Whereas movement exploration

considers all solutions correct in the absence of a performance model, the guided-discovery technique incorporates an observation phase into the total experience. The observation phase takes the form of observing the solutions of others in relation to the problem presented. Only after the learners have had an opportunity to solve the problem within the limits of their own understanding and ability is the observation phase used.

Instead of making problems entirely open-ended, as in movement exploration, the instructor gradually narrows the questions to prompt the learners to discover for themselves how to perform the particular movement under consideration. The absence of one best solution at this stage allows for the performance of several "best" ways. After applying solutions to the problem, the learners evaluate their solutions in light of those of others. They are then given an opportunity to reassess their solutions in light of the performance of others (figure 23.4).

Facilitating Combination

Combination represents a transitional category in the hierarchical sequence of movement skill learning. Movement experiences that use a combination of movement skills are incorporated into the lesson through the use of both indirect *and* direct teaching styles.

Indirect combination is a logical extension of the movement exploration and guided-discovery approaches. These experiences differ only in that activities involving stability, locomotion, and manipulation are combined through the problem-solving approaches used at the exploration and discovery stages of learning.

> ## CONCEPT 23.6
>
> Both indirect and direct styles of teaching can be effective, but instructors should adopt teaching styles based on knowledge about the learner as an individual.

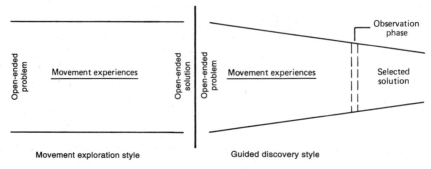

Movement exploration style   **Guided discovery style**

Figure 23.4

Differences between movement exploration and the guided discovery teaching styles; both use indirect (i.e., production) methods.

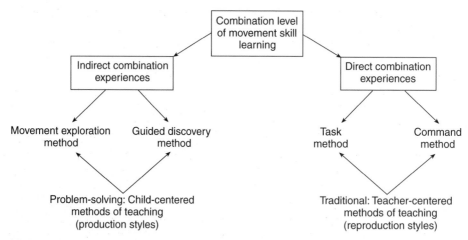

Figure 23.5

At the combination stage of movement skill learning, the instructor often uses both indirect and direct styles of teaching.

Direct combination experiences follow a more traditional approach to developing and refining combinations of stability, locomotor, and manipulative movements. Traditional approaches involve establishing models for correct performance through explanation and demonstrating skills to be learned before they are practiced. The learners then duplicate the movement characteristics of the model as nearly as possible within the limits of their abilities in a short practice session or drill. The instructor then stops the group, and the model is presented again along with general comments concerning problems that the group as a whole may be encountering. The group is next involved in an activity that

incorporates these skills. The instructor circulates among the learners and aids individuals who may be having difficulty executing the skills proficiently. Direct combination experiences require a model for performance to be established before the movement experience begins, whereas indirect combination experiences do not (figure 23.5).

Facilitating Application

Application represents the fourth level of the learning hierarchy. To take advantage of this level of experience, the instructor helps the learner make conscious decisions concerning the best methods of performing the numerous combinations of stability, locomotor, or manipulative skills. Rather than refining combinations of fundamental movements, learners begin to select and apply preferred ways of moving in a wide variety of activities. Application experiences follow the same direct progression as direct combination experiences: explanation, demonstration, and practice, followed by general and specific correction and drill. Application experiences, however, employ more advanced activities than those used in the combination stage. These experiences generally take the form of advanced lead-up activities to dual, team, and individual sports, not low-level games and skill drills. Advanced lead-up activities used during this period incorporate numerous elements of the official sport, modified in time, equipment, and facilities required. The desired combination of specialized movement skills to be performed in the official sport is adopted during this period.

Facilitating Refined Performance

Refined performance is the fifth stage in the movement skill learning hierarchy. Individuals at this stage are ready to test their skills in a variety of real life or contribed sport and recreational activities. As the performance becomes more refined, greater emphasis is placed on accuracy and precision in performing in a single, best way.

CONCEPT 23.7

The highest form of movement skill learning occurs when learners personalize their movement repertoires to reflect individual needs, interests, strengths, and limitations.

Facilitating Individualization

The process of individualization is unique to each performer. Individuals at this stage make fine adjustments in their performance to personalize and maximize performance. Adjustments are made based on body size, weight, limb length, fitness level, motor abilities, disabling conditions, and other factors that may influence the level of performance. The distinctive features of one's golf game, layup shot, or swimming mechanics represent the individualized level of movement skill learning.

Occasional breakthroughs in skill performance come about at this level. The individual critically examines her or his strengths and weaknesses and thoroughly conceptualizes the skill, which enables the person to create entirely new ways of moving. The Fosbury flop method of high jumping pioneered by Olympic gold medalist Dick Fosbury, a once-traditional high jumper in the 1960s; the basketball wizardry of Michael Jordan in the 1990s; and the golf greatness of Tiger Woods are three examples. All were able to individualize skills in their respective sports and, in doing so, vastly improved their performances.

In short, the person at the individualized stage uses both inductive and deductive thought processes in concert with his or her movement capabilities to maximize individual performance potentials. To be able to adapt movements to the demands of the environment and to put a personal stamp on movement skills represents the zenith of the movement skill learning hierarchy. It is the essence of being a *skillful mover*.

A DEVELOPMENTAL PROGRAM MODEL

The developmental model for movement skill learning that we propose is based on the proposition that the development of movement abilities occurs in distinct but often overlapping *phases of motor development* (reflexes, rudimentary movement abilities, fundamental movement patterns, and specialized movement abilities) in each of the *categories of movement* (stability, locomotion, and manipulation). This is achieved through participation in skill themes applied to *content areas* of physical activity (educational games, dance, and gymnastic activities), *components of physical fitness* (health-related and performance-related), and *cognitive concepts* of movement (skill concepts, movement concepts, activity concepts). Concepts are applied at the appropriate *stages of movement skill learning* (exploration, discovery, combination, application, refined performance, individualization) recognized through the implementation of various *teaching styles* (indirect: movement exploration and guided discovery and direct: command and task (figure 23.6)).

CONCEPT 23.8

The developmental curricular model places the learner at the center of the teaching-learning process.

Fundamental Phase

Developmental teaching recognizes that young children are generally involved in developing and refining fundamental movement skills in the three categories of movement. These categories form the organizing centers of the curriculum and subsequent skill themes. The movement skills found under these three categories should, at this point, be treated in relative isolation from the others. These fundamental movements serve as an important basis for specialized movement skills. They are developed and refined at the exploration, discovery, and combination stages of learning movement skills, primarily through indirect styles of teaching

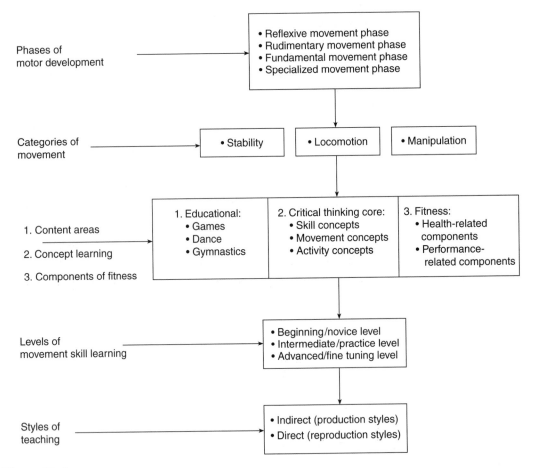

Figure 23.6
Outline of the conceptual framework for a developmentally based program in movement skill acquisition.

that incorporate activities from the three content areas and include instruction in the critical thinking core (figure 23.7).

Specialized Phase

When the developmental model is applied to older children, adolescents, and adults, the focus often changes from the fundamental movement phase to the specialized movement skill phase of development. Remember, however, that learning new movement skills is not the exclusive province of the young. Adolescents, adults, and seniors are persuing new skills such as roller blading, windsurfing, rock climbing, and snow boarding. When doing so, the learning process almost always reverts, at least for

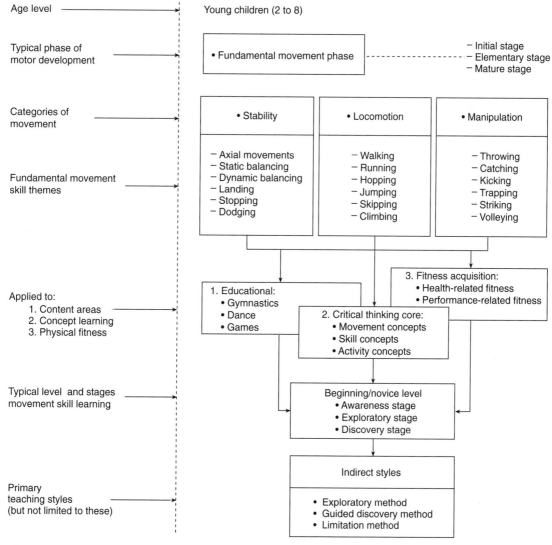

Figure 23.7

Implementing the developmental program model with younger children.

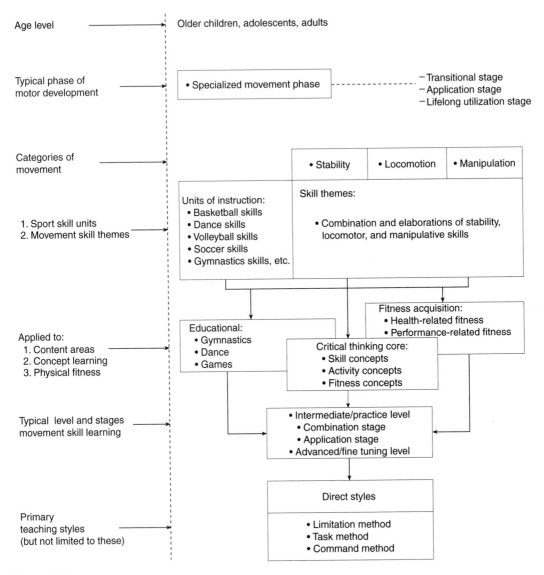

Figure 23.8
Implementing the developmental program model with older children, adolescents, and adults.

a while, to the fundamental movement phase of motor development and the beginning/novice level of movement skill learning. Individuals at the specialized phase are constantly combining various stability, locomotor, and manipulative patterns of movement in a wide variety of sport skills. Because of this, it becomes impossible to implement move-

ment skill themes that focus on only one category of movement. Instead, skill themes at this level are viewed in the context of the daily living, recreational, or sport area to which they are being applied. The game of softball, for example, becomes a "sport skill theme" and involves combinations and elaborations of fundamental manipulative abilities (throwing, catching, striking), locomotor abilities (base running and sliding), and stability abilities (twisting, turning, and stretching).

The instructor, therefore, focuses on skills related to a particular specialized theme. The instructor recognizes that the learner's goals at this level are to combine skills and apply the "best" ways of performing; therefore, the instructor often tends to focus on more direct styles of teaching (figure 23.8).

SUMMARY

For too many years parents, instructors, coaches, and therapists, as well as the general population, have had only a vague notion of the importance of balanced motor development and movement education for infants, children, adolescents, and adults. The developmental model presented here is based on the phases of motor development and stages of movement skill learning. Movement experiences and teaching methodologies that recognize the dynamic developmental level of the individual are used. Educational games, dance, and gymnastic activities as well as movement concepts, skill concepts, and activity concepts, are regarded as the means of achieving increased skill rather than as ends in themselves. Learning to move is too important to be left to chance.

CRITICAL READINGS

Gallahue, D. L., & Cleland, F. (2003). *Developmental Physical Education for Today's Children*. Champaign, IL: Human Kinetics.

Mosston, M., & Ashworth, S. (1994). *Teaching Physical Education*. Columbus, OH: Charles E. Merrill.

 ## WEB RESOURCES

Information website for physical activity programming
www.pecentral.org

Physical activity information website
www.pelinks4u.org

Various resources from the National Association for Sport and Physical Education
www.aahperd.org/naspe/naspe-main.html

Equivalent Measures

APPENDIX A

ENGLISH-METRIC

1 inch = 2.54 centimeters
1 foot = 0.3048 meter
1 yard = 0.9144 meter
1 mile = 1.6093 kilometers

1 ounce = 28.349 grams
1 pound = 0.53 kilogram
1 short ton = 0.907 metric ton

1 fluid ounce = 29.573 milliliters
1 pint = 0.473 liter
1 quart = 0.946 liter
1 gallon = 3.785 liters

METRIC-ENGLISH

1 centimeter = 0.3937 inch
1 meter = 3.281 feet
1 meter = 1.0936 yards
1 kilometer = 0.6214 mile

1 gram = 0.35 ounce
1 kilogram = 2.2046 pounds
1 metric ton = 1.1 short ton

1 milliliter = .06 cubic inch
1 liter = 61.02 cubic inches
1 liter = 0.908 dry quart
1 liter = 1.057 liquid quarts

APPENDIX B

Inches-Centimeters: Conversion Table

IN	CM	IN	CM	IN	CM
1/32	.08	23	58.4	50	127.0
1/16	.16	24	61.0	51	129.5
1/8	.32	25	63.5	52	132.1
1/4	.64	26	66.0	53	134.6
1/2	1.27	27	68.6	54	137.2
1	2.5	28	71.1	55	139.7
2	5.1	29	73.7	56	142.2
3	7.6	30	76.2	57	144.8
4	10.2	31	78.7	58	147.3
5	12.7	32	81.3	59	149.9
6	15.2	33	83.8	60	152.4
7	17.8	34	86.4	61	154.9
8	20.3	35	88.9	62	157.5
9	22.9	36	91.4	63	160.0
10	25.4	37	93.8	64	162.6
11	28.0	38	96.5	65	165.1
12	30.5	39	99.1	66	167.6
13	33.0	40	101.6	67	170.2
14	25.5	41	104.1	68	172.7
15	38.1	42	106.7	69	175.3
16	40.6	43	109.2	70	177.8
17	43.2	44	111.8	71	180.3
18	45.1	45	114.3	72	182.9
19	48.2	46	116.8	73	185.4
20	50.8	47	119.4	74	188.0
21	53.3	48	121.9	75	190.5
22	55.9	49	124.5		

Pounds-Kilograms: Conversion Table

APPENDIX C

LB	KG	LB	KG	LB	KG	LB	KG
1	0.54	26	11.77	51	23.10	76	34.42
2	0.90	27	12.23	52	23.55	77	34.87
3	1.35	28	12.68	53	24.00	78	35.32
4	1.81	29	13.13	54	24.46	79	35.77
5	2.26	30	13.59	55	24.91	80	36.24
6	2.71	31	14.04	56	25.36	81	36.69
7	3.17	32	14.49	57	25.82	82	37.14
8	3.62	33	14.94	58	26.27	83	37.59
9	4.07	34	15.40	59	26.72	84	38.05
10	4.50	35	15.85	60	27.18	85	38.50
11	4.98	36	16.30	61	27.63	86	38.95
12	5.43	37	16.76	62	28.08	87	39.41
13	5.88	38	17.21	63	28.53	88	39.86
14	6.34	39	17.66	64	28.99	89	40.31
15	6.79	40	18.12	65	29.44	90	40.77
16	7.24	41	18.57	66	29.89	91	41.22
17	7.70	42	19.02	67	30.35	92	41.67
18	8.15	43	19.47	68	30.80	93	42.12
19	8.60	44	19.93	69	31.25	94	42.58
20	9.06	45	20.38	70	31.71	95	43.03
21	9.51	46	20.83	71	32.16	96	43.48
22	9.96	47	21.29	72	32.61	97	43.94
23	10.41	48	21.74	73	33.06	98	44.39
24	10.87	49	22.19	74	33.52	99	44.84
25	11.32	50	22.65	75	33.97	100	45.30

BIBLIOGRAPHY

CHAPTER 1
UNDERSTANDING MOTOR DEVELOPMENT: AN OVERVIEW

Bayley, N. (1935). The development of motor abilities during the first three years. *Monographs of the Society for the Research in Child Development, 1,* 1–26.

Bloom, B. S. et al. (1956). *Taxonomy of Educational Objectives: Handbook 1: Cognitive Domain.* New York: David McKay.

Branta, C., Haubenstricker, J., & Seefeldt, V. (1984). Age changes in motor skill during childhood and adolescence. In R. L. Terjung (Ed.), *Exercise and Sport Science Reviews, Vol. 12.* Lexington, MA: Collamore Press.

Clark, J. E., Phillips, S. J., & Petersen, R. (1989). Developmental stability in jumping. *Developmental Psychology, 25,* 929–935.

Clark, J. E., & Whitall, J. (1989). What is motor development? The lessons of history. *Quest, 41,* 183–202.

Clark, J. E., Whitall, J., & Phillips, S. J. (1988). Human interlimb coordination: The first 6 months of independent walking. *Developmental Psychology, 21,* 445–456.

Clarke, H. H. (1971). *Physical Motor Tests in the Medford Boys Growth Study.* Englewood Cliffs, NJ: Prentice-Hall.

Corbin, C., Dale, D., & Pangazi, R. (1999). Promoting physically active lifestyles among youths. *JOPERD, 70*(6), 26–28.

Fagen, R. (1992). *Animal Play Behavior.* London: Oxford University Press.

Gallahue, D. L. (1982). *Understanding Motor Development in Children.* New York: John Wiley.

Gallahue, D. L., Werner, P. H., & Luedke, G. C. (1972). *Moving and Learning: A Conceptual Approach to the Education of Young Children.* Dubuque, IA: Kendall/Hunt.

Gallahue, D. L., Werner, P. H., & Luedke, G. C. (1975). *A Conceptual Approach to Moving and Learning.* New York: John Wiley.

Gentile, H. M. (2000). Skill acquisition: Action, movement, and neuromotor processes. In J. H. Carr & R. B. Shepherd (Eds.), *Movement Science: Foundations for Physical Therapy.* 2d ed. Rockville, MD: Aspen.

Gesell, A. (1928). *Infancy and Human Growth.* New York: Macmillan.

Gesell, A., & Thompson, H. (1934). *Infant Behavior: Its Genesis and Growth.* New York: McGraw-Hill.

Halverson, H. M. (1931). An experimental study of prehension in infants by means of systematic cinema records. *Genetic Psychology Monographs, 10,* 107–286.

———. (1937). Studies of the grasping responses in early infancy. *Journal of Genetic Psychology, 51,* 437–449.

Halverson, L. E. (1966). Development of motor patterns in young children. *Quest, 6,* 44–53.

Halverson, L. E., & Roberton, M. A. (1966). *A study of motor pattern development in young children.* Paper presented at the March 1966 national convention of the AAHPERD, Chicago, IL.

Halverson, L. E., Roberton, M. A., & Harper, C. J. (1973). Current research in motor development. *Journal of Research and Development in Education, 6,* 56–70.

Halverson, L. E., & Williams, H. (1985). Developmental sequences for hopping over distance: A prelongitudinal study. *Research Quarterly for Exercise and Sport, 56,* 37–44.

Keogh, J., & Sugden, D. (1985). *Movement Skill Development.* New York: Macmillan.

Krathwohl, D. R., Bloom, B., & Masia, B. (1964). *Taxonomy of Educational Objectives. Handbook II: Affective Domain.* New York: David McKay.

Kugler, P. N., Kelso, J. A. S., & Turvey, M. T. (1980). On the concept of coordinative structures as dissipative structures: I. Theoretical lines of convergence. In G. E. Stelmach & J. Requin (Eds.), *Tutorials in Motor Behavior.* New York: North Holland.

Lefrancois, G. (1993). *The Lifespan* (Chapter 1). Belmont, CA: Wadsworth.

Magill, R. A. (2001). *Motor Learning-Concepts and Applications.* Boston, MA: McGraw-Hill.

McGraw, M. B. (1935). *Growth: A Study of Johnny and Jimmy.* New York: Appleton-Century.

———. (1940). Neural maturation as exemplified in achievement of bladder control. *The Journal of Pediatrics, 16,* 580–590.

Rarick, G. L. (1981). The emergence of the study of human motor development. In G. A. Brooks (Ed.), *Perspectives on the Academic Discipline of Physical Education.* Champaign, IL: Human Kinetics.

Seefeldt, V. (1972). *Discussion of walking and running.* Unpublished paper, Michigan State University.

Seefeldt, V., & Haubenstricker, J. (1982). Patterns, phases, or stages: An analytical model for the study of developmental movement. In J. A. S. Kelso & J. E. Clark (Eds.), *The Development of Movement Control and Coordination.* New York: Wiley.

Shirley, M. M. (1931). *The First Two Years: A Study of Twenty-Five Babies: Vol. 1: Postural and Locomotor Development.* Minneapolis, MN: University of Minnesota Press.

Smoll, F. L. (1982). Developmental kinesiology: Toward a subdiscipline focusing on motor development. In J. A. S. Kelso & J. E. Clark (Eds.), *The Development of Movement Control and Coordination.* New York: Wiley.

Tanner, J. M. (1962). *Growth at Adolescence.* Oxford, England: Blackwell Scientific Publications.

Thelen, E. (1986a). Development of coordinated movement: Implications for early human development. In M. G. Wade & H. T. A. Whiting (Eds.), *Motor Development in Children: Aspects of Coordination and Control.* Boston, MA: Martinus Nayhoff.

———. (1986b). Treadmill-elicited stepping in seven-month-old infants. *Child Development, 57,* 1498–1506.

Thelen, E., & Cooke, D. W. (1987a). Relationship between newborn stepping and later walking: A new interpretation. *Developmental Medicine and Child Neurology, 29,* 380–393.

Thelen, E., Kelso, J. A. S., & Fogel, A. (1987b). Self-organizing systems and infant motor development. *Developmental Review, 7,* 39–65.

Thelen, E., & Smith, L. B. (1994). *A Dynamic Systems Approach to the Development of Cognition and Action.* Cambridge, MA: The MIT Press.

Thelen, E., & Ulrich, B. D. (1991). Hidden skills: A dynamic systems analysis of treadmill stepping during the first year. *Monographs of the Society for Research in Child Development, 56* (1, Serial No. 223).

Thomas, J. R., & Thomas, K. T. (1989). What is motor development: Where does it belong? *Quest, 41,* 203–212.

Ulrich, B. D., Ulrich, D. A., Collier, D. H., & Cole, E. (1995). Developmental shifts in the ability of infants with Down syndrome to produce treadmill steps. *Physical Therapy, 75,* 14–21.

Wetzel, N. C. (1948). *The Wetzel Grid for Evaluating Physical Fitness.* Cleveland, OH: NEA Services.

Wickstrom, R. L. (1983). *Fundamental Motor Patterns.* Philadelphia, PA: Lea & Febiger.

Wild, M. (1938). The behavior pattern of throwing and some observations concerning its course of development in children. *Research Quarterly, 9,* 20–24.

CHAPTER 2
MODELS OF HUMAN DEVELOPMENT

Alexander, R. et al. (1993). *Normal Development of Functional Motor Skills.* Tucson, AZ: Communication Skill Builders.

Anderson, A. (1997). Learning strategies in physical education: Self-talk, imagery, and goal setting. *JOPERD 68* (1), 30–35.

Barker, R. G. (Ed.) (1978). *Habits, Environments, and Human Behavior.* San Francisco: Jossey-Bass.

Bernstein, N. (1967). *The Co-ordination and Regulation of Movements.* Oxford, England: Pergamon Press.

Bongaart, R., & Meijer, O. G. (2000). Bernstein's theory of motor behavior: Historical development and contemporary relevance. *Journal of Motor Behavior 32,* 57–71.

Bronfenbrenner, U. (1979). *The Ecology of Human Development.* Cambridge, MA: Harvard University Press.

Caldwell, G. E., & Clark, J. E. (1990). The measurement and evaluation of skill within the dynamical systems perspective. In J. E. Clark & J. H. Humphrey (Eds.),

Advances in Motor Development Research. New York: AMS Press.

Delacato, C. (1966). *Neurological Organization and Reading.* Springfield, IL: Charles C. Thomas.

Erikson, E. (1963). *Childhood and Society.* New York: W. W. Norton.

———. (1980). *Identity and the Life Cycle.* New York: W. W. Norton.

Freud, S. (1927). *The Ego and the Id.* New York: W. W. Norton.

Gesell, A. (1928). *Infancy and Human Growth.* New York: Macmillan.

———. (1954). The embryology of behavior. In L. Carmichael (Ed.), *Manual of Child Psychology.* 2d ed. New York: Wiley.

Havighurst, R. (1953). *Human Development and Education.* New York: Longmans Green.

———. (1972). *Developmental Tasks and Education.* New York: David McKay.

Havighurst, R., & Levine, R. (1979). *Society and Education.* Reading, MA: Allyn and Bacon.

Kamii, C. K., & De Vries, R. (1993). *Physical Knowledge in Preschool Education: Implications of Piaget's Theory.* New York: Teachers College Press. (Foreword by Jean Piaget).

Kamm, K. et al. (1990). A dynamical systems approach to motor development. *Physical Therapy, 70,* 763–774.

Kugler, P. N., Kelso, J. A. S., & Turvey, M. T. (1982). On the control and coordination of naturally developing systems. In J. A. S. Kelso & J. E. Clark (Eds.), *The Development of Motor Control and Coordination.* New York: Wiley.

Lefrancois, G. (1993). *The Lifespan.* Belmont, CA: Wadsworth.

Lerner, P. M. (1986). *Concepts and Theories of Human Development.* Reading, MA: Addison-Wesley.

Peterson, R., & Felton-Collins, V. (1986). *The Piaget Handbook for Teachers and Parents.* New York: Teachers College Press.

Piaget, J. (1952). *The Origins of Intelligence in Children.* New York: International Universities Press.

———. (1954). *The Construction of Reality and the Child.* New York: Basic Books.

———. (1969). *The Psychology of the Child.* New York: Basic Books.

———. (1974). Development and learning. In R. E. Riple & V. N. Rockcastle (Eds.), *Piaget Rediscovered.* Ithaca, NY: Cornell University Press.

Roberton, M. A. (1977). Stability of stage categorization across trials: Implications for the stage theory of overarm throw development. *Journal of Human Movement Studies, 3,* 49–59.

Schmidt, R. A., & Lee, T. D. (2000). *Motor Control and Learning. A Behavioral Emphasis.* Champaign IL: Human Kinetics.

Sherman, C. (1999). Integrating mental management skills into the physical education curriculum. *JOPERD 70* (5), 25–30.

Thelen, E. (1989). Dynamical approaches to the development of behavior. In J. A. S. Kelso, A. J. Mandell, & M. E. Schelsinger (Eds.), *Dynamic Patterns in Complex Systems.* Singapore: World Scientific.

Thelen, E., & Ulrich, B. D. (1991). Hidden skills. *Monographs of the Society for Research in Child Development, 65,* no. 223, 1.

Thomas, R. M. (2000). *Comparing Theories of Child Development.* Belmont, CA: Wadsworth Publishing Company.

CHAPTER 3
MOTOR DEVELOPMENT: A THEORETICAL MODEL

Bigge, M. L., & Shermis, S. S. (1999). *Learning Theories for Teachers.* New York: HarperCollins.

Gallahue, D. L. (2000). Motor development. In J. Winnick (Ed.), *Adapted Physical Education and Sports.* Champaign, IL: Human Kinetics.

Haubenstricker, J., & Seefeldt, V. (1986). Acquisition of motor skills during childhood. In V. Seefeldt (Ed.), *Physical Activity and Well-Being.* Reston, VA: AAHPERD.

Kamm, K., Thelen, E., & Jensen, J. (1990). A dynamical systems approach to motor development. *Physical Therapy, 70,* 763–775.

Lerner, R. M. (1986). *Concepts and Theories in Human Development.* New York: Random House.

Seefeldt, V., & Haubenstricker, J. (1982). Patterns, phases, or stages: An analytic model for the study of developmental movement. In J. A. S. Kelso & J. E. Clark (Eds.), *The Development of Movement Control and Coordination.* New York: Wiley.

CHAPTER 4
SELECTED FACTORS AFFECTING MOTOR DEVELOPMENT

American Academy of Pediatrics (AAP). (1988). Policy Statement: Infant Exercise Programs. *Pediatrics 82,* 800.

American Obesity Association (AOA). (2000). *Facts About Obesity.* Washington, DC: Author.

Bar-Or, O., & Baranowski, T. (1994). Physical activity, adiposity, and obesity among adolescents. *Pediatric Exercise Science, 6,* 348–360.

Bayley, N. (1935). The development of motor abilities during the first three years. *Monograph of the Society for Research on Child Development, 1,* 1–26.

Bennett, F. (1997). The LBW, Premature infant. In R. Gross, D. Spiker, & C. Haynes (Eds.), *Helping Low Birth Weight Premature Babies.* Stanford, CA: Standard University Press.

Bergen, D., Reid, R., & Torelli, L. (2001). *Educating and Caring for Very Young Children: The Infant/Toddler Curriculum.* Washington, DC: National Association for the Education of Young Children.

Booth, M. (2000). Assessment of physical activity: An international perspective. *Research Quarterly for Exercise and Sport, 71,* 114–120.

Branta, C. et al. (1987). Gender differences in play patterns and sport participation of North American youth. In D. Gould & M. Weiss (Eds.), *Advances in Pediatric Sport Sciences: Volume 2: Behavioral Issues.* Champaign, IL: Human Kinetics.

Bredenkamp, S., & Rosengrant, T. (Eds.). (1995). *Reaching Potentials: Transforming Early Childhood Curriculum and Assessment.* Washington, DC: National Association for the Education of Young Children.

Bril, B. (1985). Motor development and cultural attitudes. In H. T. A. Whiting & M. G. Wade (Eds.), *Themes in Motor Development.* Dordrecht, The Netherlands: Martinus Nyhoff Publishers.

Bruner, J. S. (1965). *The Process of Education.* Cambridge, MA: Harvard University Press.

D'Agostino, J., & Clifford, P. (1998). Neurodevelopmental Consequences Associated with the Premature Infant. *AACN Clinical Issues: Advanced Practice in Acute and Critical Care, 9*(1), 1–11.

Dennis, W. (1960). Causes of retardation among institutional children: Iran. *Journal of Genetic Psychology, 96,* 47–59.

Dennis, W., & Najarian, P. (1957). Infant development under environmental handicap. *Psychology Monographs, 71,* 7.

Dorgan, C. A. (Ed.) (1995). *Statistical Record of Health and Medicine.* New York: Gale Research Inc.

Eyer, D. E. (1994). *Mother-Infant Bonding: A Scientific Fiction.* New Haven, CT: Yale University Press.

Flegal, K. M., Carroll, M. D., Kuczmarski, R. J., & Johnson, C. L. (1998). Overweight and Obesity in the United States: Prevalence and Trends, 1960–1964. *International Journal of Obstetrics, 22,* 39–47.

Fomon, S. J. et al. (1982). Body composition of reference children from birth to age 10 years. *American Journal of Clinical Nutrition, 35,* 1169–1175.

Gallahue, D. L., & Cleland, F. (2003). *Developmental Physical Education for Today's Children.* Champaign, IL: Human Kinetics.

Gallahue, D. L., Milchrist, P., Morris, H. H., Ozmun, J., & Medalha, J. (1994). *Cross-cultural considerations in the motor performance of young children.* Paper presented at the National Convention of AAHPERD, Denver, CO.

Gallahue, D. L., Morris, H. H., Ma, L., Del Rio, V., Negron, M., Trujillo, H., Ozmun, J. C., McGhie, S., & Mayers, G. (1996). *Variations in motor behavior among young North American (USA) and South American (Chile) children from urban and rural environments.* Paper presented at the 1996 International Pre-Olympic Scientific Congress, Dallas, TX.

Gesell, A. (1954). The ontogenesis of infant behavior. In L. Carmichael (Ed.), *Manual of Child Psychology.* New York: Wiley.

Gesell, A., & Thompson, H. (1929). Learning and growth in identical twins. *Genetic Psychology Monographs, 6,* 1–124.

Hack, M., et al. (1994). School-age outcomes in children with birth weights under 750g. *New England Journal of Medicine 331,* 753–803.

Hess, E. H. (1959). Imprinting. *Science, 130,* 133–141.

Hilgard, J. R. (1932). Learning and maturation in preschool children. *Journal of Genetic Psychology, 41,* 36–56.

Hinton, G. E. (1992). How neural networks learn from experience. *Scientific American, 267,* 144–151.

Kamii, C., & Housman, L. B. (2000). *Young Children Reinvent Arithmetic.* New York: Teachers College Press.

Klebanov, P. K. et al. (1994). Classroom behavior of very low birth weight school children. *Pediatrics, 94,* 700–708.

Kopp, C. B., & Kaler, S. R. (1989). Risk in infancy: Origins and implications. *American Psychologist, 44,* 224–230.

Krebs, R. J. (1995). *Urie Bronfenbrenner E A Ecologia Do Desenvolvimento Humano.* Santa Maria, BRASIL: Casa Editorial. (Urie Bronfenbrenner and the Ecology of Human Development).

Lamb, M. E. et al. (1985). *Infant-Mother Attachment.* Hillsdale, NJ: Lawrence Erlbaum.

Lewis, M. (1998). *Altering Fate: Why the Past Does Not Predict the Future.* New York: Guilford Publications.

Lorenz, K. (1966). *On Aggression.* New York: Harcourt Brace Jovanovich.

Magill, R. (2001). *Motor Learning: Concepts and Applications.* Boston, MA: McGraw-Hill.

Malina, R. M., & Bouchard, C. (1991). *Growth Maturation and Physical Activity.* Champaign, IL: Human Kinetics.

Marcus, M. D. (1993). Binge eating in obesity. In C. G. Fairburn and G. T. Wilson (Eds.), *Binge Eating: Nature, Assessment and Treatment.* New York: Guilford Press.

Mason, J. O. (1991). Reducing infant mortality in the United States through "Healthy Start." *Public Health Reports, 106* (5), 479.

McGraw, M. B. (1935). *Growth: A Study of Johnny and Jimmy.* New York: Appleton-Century.

———. (1939). Later development of children specially trained during infancy. *Child Development, 10,* 1.

Meredith, C. N., & Dwyer, J. T. (1991). Nutrition and exercise: Effects on adolescent health. *Annual Review of Public Health 1991, 12,* 309–333.

National Center for Health Statistics. (2000). *National Vital Statistics Report,* July 24, 48, 94.

National Institute for Mental Health (NIMH). (2000). *Eating Disorders.* Online: athealth.com.

Payne, V. G., & Isaacs, L. D. (2002). *Human Motor Development: A Lifespan Approach.* Boston: McGraw-Hill.

Rickard, K., Gallahue, D. L., Tridle, M., Bewley, N., & Steele, M. (1996). Teaching young children about healthy eating and active play. *Pediatric Basics, 76,* 2–7.

Saigal, S., et al. (1994). Comprehensive assessment of the health status of extremely low birth weight children at eight years of age: Comparison with a reference group. *Pediatrics, 125,* 411–417.

Selkoe, D. J. (1992). Aging brain, aging mind. *Scientific American, 267,* 134–142.

Shirley, M. (1931). *The First Two Years: A Study of Twenty-Five Babies.* Minneapolis, MN: University of Minnesota Press.

Spitzer, R. L. et al. (1993). Binge eating disorder: Its further validation in a multi-site study. *International Journal of Eating Disorders, 13,* 137–153.

Stunkard, A. J. et al. (1986). A twin study of human obesity. *Journal of the American Medical Association, 256,* 51–54.

———. (1990). The body-mass index of twins who have been reared apart. *New England Journal of Medicine, 322,* 1483–1487.

Thomas, J. R. (2000). 1999 C. H. McCloy research lecture: Children's control, learning and performance of motor skills. *Research Quarterly for Exercise and Sport, 71,* 1–9.

Thorndike, E. L. (1913). *The Psychology of Learning.* New York: Teachers College.

Tommiska, V., et al. (2001). A national short-term follow-up study of extremely low birth weight infants born in 1996–1997. *Pediatrics, 104.* Online: www.pediatrics.org/CGI/content/full/107/1/e2.

Troiano, R. P. et al. (1995). Overweight prevalence and trends for children and adolescence. *Archives of Pediatric & Adolescent Medicine, 149,* 1085–1091.

Trost, S. G. (2000). Children's understanding of the concept of physical activity. *Pediatric Exercise Science 12,* 293–299.

Ulrich, B. D. (1984). The effects of stimulation programs on the development of high risk infants: A review of research. *Adapted Physical Activity Quarterly, 1,* 68–80.

Wellman, B. (1937). Motor achievements of preschool. *Childhood Education, 13,* 311–316.

World Health Organization (WHO). (1998). *Obesity: Preventing and Managing a Global Epidemic.* Geneva, Switzerland: Author.

Yanovski Zelitch, S. (1993). Binge eating disorder: Current knowledge and future directions. *Obesity Research, 1,* 306–324.

CHAPTER 5
PRENATAL FACTORS AFFECTING DEVELOPMENT

American Academy of Pediatrics. (1994). Prenatal genetic diagnosis for pediatricians. Policy statement by the Committee on Genetics. *Pediatrics, 93,* 1010–1015.

———. (1996). Newborn screening fact sheets. *Pediatrics, 98,* 473–501.

———. (1997). Environmental tobacco smoke: A hazard to children. Policy statement by the Committee on Environmental Health. *Pediatrics, 99,* 639–642.

———. (1998). Screening for elevated blood lead levels. Policy statement by the Committee on Environmental Health. *Pediatrics, 101,* 1072–1078.

———. (1999). Folic acid for the prevention of neural tube defects. Policy statement by the Committee on Genetics. *Pediatrics, 104,* 325–327.

———. (2000). Fetal alcohol syndrome and alcohol-related neurodevelopmental disorders. Policy statement by the Committee on Substance Abuse and Committee on Children with Disabilities. *Pediatrics, 106,* 358–361.

American College of Obstetricians and Gynecologists. (2000). *Planning your pregnancy and birth.* 3rd ed. Washington DC: The American College of Obstetricians and Gynecologists.

American Diabetes Association (2000). Preconception care of women with diabetes: Clinical practice recommendations 2000. *Diabetes Care, 23,* S65–S68.

Arendt, R., Angelopoulos, J., Salvator, A., & Singer, L. (1999). Motor development of cocaine-exposed children at age two years. *Pediatrics, 103,* 86–92.

Bell, R., & O'Neill, M. (1994). Exercise and pregnancy: A review. *Birth, 21,* 85–95.

Block, M. E. (1991). Motor development in children with Down syndrome: A review of the literature. *Adapted Physical Activity Quarterly, 8,* 179–209.

Brackbill, Y. (1970). Continuous stimulation and arousal level in infants: Additive effects. *Proceedings of the 78th Annual Convention, American Psychological Association, 5,* 271–272.

————. (1979). Obstetrical medication and infant behavior. In J. D. Osofsky (Ed.), *The Handbook of Infant Development.* New York: Wiley.

Centers for Disease Control and Prevention (CDC). (1999). Knowledge and use of folic acid by women of childbearing age—United States, 1995 and 1998. *Morbidity and Mortality Weekly Report, 48,* 325–327.

Centers for Disease Control and Prevention. (2000). Division of STD Prevention. *Sexually Transmitted Disease Surveillance, 1999.* Department of Health and Human Services, Atlanta: Centers for Disease Control and Prevention.

Clapp, J. F. (2000). Exercise during pregnancy: A clinical update. *Clinical Sports Medicine, 19,* 273–286.

Conway, E., & Brackbill, Y. (1970). Delivery medication and infant outcomes. *Monographs of the Society for Research in Child Development, 35,* 24–34.

Division of STD Prevention. (September 2000). *Sexually Transmitted Disease Surveillance, 1999.* Department of Health and Human Services, Atlanta: Centers for Disease Control and Prevention (CDC).

Drews, C. D., Murphy, C. C., Yeargin-Allsopp, M., & Decoufle, P. (1996). The relationship between idiopathic mental retardation and maternal smoking during pregnancy. *Pediatrics, 97,* 547–553.

Gallahue, D. L. (1993). Assessing motor development in young children. In B. Spodek (Ed.), *Studies in Educational Evaluation.* New York: Macmillan.

Gallahue, D. L. (2000). Motor development. In J. Winnick (Ed.), *Adapted Physical Education and Sport.* Champaign, IL: Human Kinetics.

Goldstein, K. M. et al. (1976). The effects of prenatal and perinatal complications on development at one year of age. *Child Development, 47,* 613–621.

Hanson, J. W. (1997). *Testimony for Committee on Genetics.* Presentation to the Public Advisory Committee of the Food and Drug Administration, Dermatologic and Ophthalmic Drugs Advisory Committee. American Academy of Pediatrics.

Henderson, S. E. (1985). Motor skills development. In D. Lane & B. Stratford (Eds.), *Current Approaches to Down Syndrome.* London: Holt, Rinehart and Winston.

Lamaze, F. (1976). *Painless Childbirth.* London: Burke.

Larroque, B., Kaminski, M., Dehaene, P., & Subtil, D. (1995). Moderate prenatal alcohol exposure and psychomotor development at preschool age. *American Journal of Public Health, 85,* 1654–1661.

Lemons, J. A., et al. (2001). Very low birth weight outcomes of the National Institute of Child Health and Human Development Neonatal Research Network. *Pediatrics, 107.* Online: www.pediatrics.org/cgi/content/107/1/e2.

Locksmith, G. J., & Duff, P. (1998). Preventing neural tube defects: The importance of periconceptional folic acid supplements. *Obstetrics and Gynecology, 91,* 1027–1034.

Malina, R. M., & Bouchard, C. (1991). *Growth, Maturation and Physical Activity.* Champaign, IL: Human Kinetics.

March of Dimes. (1997a). Clubfoot and other foot disorders. *March of Dimes Birth Defects Foundation.*

————. (1997b). Fitness for two. *March of Dimes Birth Defects Foundation.*

————. (1997c). National perinatal statistics. *March of Dimes Birth Defects Foundation.*

————. (1999a). Cocaine use during pregnancy. *March of Dimes Birth Defects Foundation.*

————. (2000). Down syndrome. *March of Dimes Birth Defects Foundation.*

————. (1999b). Drinking during pregnancy. *March of Dimes Birth Defects Foundation.*

————. (1999c). Food-borne risks in pregnancy. *March of Dimes Birth Defects Foundation.*

————. (1999d). Genital herpes. *March of Dimes Birth Defects Foundation.*

————. (1999e). HIV and AIDS in pregnancy. *March of Dimes Birth Defects Foundation.*

————. (1999f). Low birthweight. *March of Dimes Birth Defects Foundation.*

————. (1999g). Sickle cell disease. *March of Dimes Birth Defects Foundation.*

———. (1999h). Stress and pregnancy. *March of Dimes Birth Defects Foundation.*

———. (2000a). Smoking during pregnancy. *March of Dimes Birth Defects Foundation.*

———. (2000b). Tay-Sachs disease. *March of Dimes Birth Defects Foundation.*

———. (2000c). Toxoplasmosis. *March of Dimes Birth Defects Foundation.*

Muller, P. F. et al. (1971). Prenatal factors and their relationship to mental retardation and other parameters of development. *American Journal of Obstetrics and Gynecology, 109,* 1205–1210.

Murphy, S. L. (2000). *Deaths: Final data for 1998.* National Vital Statistics Reports, Centers for Disease Control and Prevention, Vol. 48, No. 11, p. 89.

National Center for Health Statistics. (1998). *Health, United States, 1998 With Socioeconomic Status and Health Chartbook.* Hyattsville, MD: Public Health Service, p. 181.

National Down Syndrome Society (2001), New York, NY.

National Institute on Drug Abuse. (1995). NIDA survey provides first national data on drug use during pregnancy. *NIDA Notes, 10,* 6.

Rosett, H. L., & Sander, L. W. (1979). Effects of maternal drinking on neonatal morphology and state. In J. Osofsky, (Ed.), *The Handbook of Infant Development.* New York: Wiley.

Santrock, J. W. (2001). *Child Development.* 9th ed. St. Louis, MO: McGraw-Hill.

Testimony for the Committee on Genetics. (September 1997). Presentation by James W. Hanson, M.D. to the Public Advisory Committee of the Food and Drug Administration Dermatologic and Ophthalmic Drugs Advisory Committee.

Tommiska, V., et al. (2001). A national short-term follow-up study of extremely low birth weight infants born in Finland in 1996–1994. *Pediatrics, 107.* Online: www.pediatrics.org/cgi/content/107/1/e2.

Ulrich, B. D. (1997). Dynamic systems theory and skill development in infants and children. In K. Connolly & H. Forssberg (Eds.), *Neurophysiology and Psychology Motor Development.* London: MacKeigh Press.

Ulrich, B. D. (1998). *Factors contributing to motor rehabilitation in infants with Down syndrome and spina bifida.* Invited paper presented at the III International Congress of Motor Rehabilitation, Aguas de Lindoia, Brazil.

U.S. Bureau of the Census (2000). *Projected Populations.* Population Estimates Program, Population Division, U.S. Bureau of the Census, Washington, D.C.

Ventura, S. J., Martin, J. A., Curtin, S. C., Mathews, T. J., & Park, M. M. (2000). *Births: Final data for 1998.* National Vital Statistics Reports, Centers for Disease Control and Prevention, National Center for Health Statistics, 48, 13.

Witti, F. P. (1978). Alcohol and Birth Defects. *FDA Consumer, 22,* 20–23.

Wolfe, L. A., Brenner, I. K. M., & Mottola, M. F. (1994). Maternal exercise, fetal well-being and pregnancy outcome. In J. O. Holloszy (Ed.), *Exercise and Sport Sciences Reviews, Vol. 22.* Baltimore, MD: Williams & Wilkins.

CHAPTER 6
PRENATAL AND INFANT GROWTH

Crawford, S. M. (1996). Anthropometry. In D. Docherty (Ed.), *Measurement in Pediatric Exercise Science, Canadian Society for Exercise Physiology.* Champaign, IL: Human Kinetics.

Malina, R. M., & Bouchard, C. (1991). *Growth Maturation and Physical Activity.* Champaign, IL: Human Kinetics.

National Center for Health Statistics. (2000). *CDC Growth Charts: United States.* Centers for Disease Control and Prevention.

Pařízková, J. (1996). *Nutrition, Physical Activity, and Health in Early Life.* Boca Raton, FL: CRC Press.

Prechtl, H. F. R. (1986). Prenatal motor development. In M. G. Wade & H. T. A. Whiting (Eds.), *Motor Development in Children: Aspects of Coordination and Control.* Dordrecht, The Netherlands: Martinus Nyhoff.

Rowland, T. W. (1996). *Developmental Exercise Physiology.* Champaign, IL: Human Kinetics.

Santrock, J. W. (2001). *Child Development.* 9th ed. St. Louis: McGraw-Hill.

Tanner, J. M. (1978). *Fetus into Man.* Cambridge, MA: Harvard University Press.

CHAPTER 7
INFANT REFLEXES AND RHYTHMICAL STEREOTYPIES

Ames, I. I. (1937). The sequential patterning of prone progression in the human infant. *Genetic Psychology Monographs, 19,* 409–460.

Bower, T. G. R. (1976). *Development in Infancy.* San Francisco: W. H. Freeman.

Eckert, H. (1987). *Motor Development*. Indianapolis, IN: Benchmark Press.

Kessen, W. et al. (1970). Human infancy: A bibliography and guide. In P. H. Mussen (Ed.), *Manual of Child Psychology*. New York: Wiley.

McGraw, M. B. (1939). Swimming behavior of the human infant. *Journal of Pediatrics, 15,* 485–490.

———. (1954). Maturation of behavior. In L. Carmichael (Ed.), *Manual of Child Psychology*. 2d ed. New York: Wiley.

Pontius, A. A. (1973). Neuro-ethics of walking in the newborn. *Perceptual and Motor Skills, 37,* 235–245.

Prechtl, H. F. R., & Beintema, D. J. (1964). *The Neurological Examination of the Full Term, Newborn Infant*. London: William Heinemann Medical Books.

Sherrill, C. (1998). *Adapted Physical Activity, Recreation and Sport: Crossdisciplinary and Lifespan*. 5th ed. St. Louis, MO: McGraw-Hill.

Shirley, M. (1931). *The First Two Years. A Study of Twenty-Five Babies. 1. Postural and Locomotor Development*. Minneapolis, MN: University of Minnesota Press.

Snow, C. W. (1998). *Infant Development,* 2nd ed. Upper Saddle River, NJ: Prentice-Hall.

Thelen, E. (1979). Rhythmical stereotypies in normal human infants. *Animal Behavior, 27,* 699–715.

———. (1980). Determinants of amount of stereotyped behavior in normal human infants. *Ethology and Sociobiology, 1,* 141–150.

———. (1981). Kicking, rocking, and waving: Contextual analysis of rhythmical stereotypies in normal human infants. *Animal Behavior, 29*(1), 3–11.

———. (1985). Developmental origins of motor coordination: Leg movements in human infants. *Developmental Psychobiology, 18,* 1–22.

———. (1986a). Treadmill-elicited stepping in seven-month-old infants. *Child Development, 57,* 1498–1506.

———. (1986b). Development of coordinated movement. Implications for early motor development. In M. G. Wade and H. T. A. Whiting (Eds.), *Motor Development in Children: Aspects of Coordination and Control*. Dordrecht, The Netherlands: Martinus Nyhoff.

———. (1996). Normal infant stereotypies: A dynamic systems approach. In R. L. Sprague & K. M. Newell (Eds.), *Stereotyped Movements: Brain and Behavior Relationships*. Washington DC: American Psychological Association, pp. 139–165.

Thelen, E. et al. (1985). Rhythmical behavior in infancy: An ethological perspective. *Developmental Psychology, 17,* 237–257.

Thelen, E., Kelso, J. A. S., & Fogel, A. (1987). Self-organizing systems and infant motor development. *Developmental Review, 7,* 39–65.

Thelen, E., & Ulrich, B. D. (1991). Hidden skills: A dynamic systems analysis of treadmill stepping during the first year. *Monographs of the Society for Research in Child Development, 56,* (1, Serial No. 223).

Ulrich, B. D., & Ulrich, D. A. (1995). Spontaneous leg movements of infants with Down syndrome and nondisabled infants. *Child Development, 66,* 1844–1855.

Ulrich, B. D., Ulrich, D. A., Angulo-Kinzler, R. M., & Chapman, D. D. (1997). Sensitivity of infants with Down syndrome to intrinsic dynamics. *Research Quarterly for Exercise and Sport, 68,* 10–19.

Ulrich, B. D., Ulrich, D. A., Collier, D. H., & Cole, E. L. (1995). Developmental shifts in the ability of infants with Down syndrome to produce treadmill steps. *Physical Therapy, 75,* 14–23.

Wyke, B. (1975). The neurological basis of movement: A developmental review. In K. S. Holt (Ed.), *Movement and Child Development*. London: William Heinemann Medical Books.

Zelazo, P. (1976). From reflexive to instrumental behavior. In L. P. Lipsett (Ed.), *Developmental Psychobiology— The Significance of Infancy*. Hillsdale, NJ: Lawrence Erlbaum.

CHAPTER 8
RUDIMENTARY MOVEMENT ABILITIES

Adolph, K. E., Vereijken, B., & Denny, M. A. (1998). Learning to crawl. *Child Development, 69,* 1299–1312.

Alexander, R. et al. (1993). *Normal Development of Functional Motor Skills: The First Year of Life*. Tucson, AZ: Communication Skill Builders.

American Academy of Pediatrics. (1982). The Doman-Delacato treatment of neurologically handicapped children. Policy statement by the Committee on Children with Disabilities. *Pediatrics, 70,* 810–812.

———. (1999). The treatment of neurologically impaired children using patterning. Policy statement by the Committee on Children with Disabilities. *Pediatrics, 104,* 1149–1151.

———. (2000). Swimming programs for infants and toddlers. Policy statement by the Committee on Sports Medicine and Fitness and Committee on Injury and Poison Prevention. *Pediatrics, 105,* 868–870.

Bayley, N. (1935). The development of motor abilities during the first three years. *Monograph of the Society for Research on Child Development, 1,* 1–26.

Case-Smith, J., Bigsby, R., & Clutter, J. (1998). Perceptual-motor coupling in the development of grasp. *American Journal of Occupational Therapy, 52,* 102–110.

Cowden, J. E., Sayers, K. L., & Torrey, C. C. (1998). *Pediatric Adapted Motor Development and Exercise: An Innovative, Multisystem Approach for Professionals and Families.* (1998). Springfield, IL: Charles C. Thomas.

Delacato, C. (1966). *Neurological Organization and Reading.* Springfield, IL: Charles C. Thomas.

Eckert, H. (1973). Age change in motor skills. In G. L. Rarick (Ed.), *Physical Activity: Human Growth and Development.* New York: Academic Press.

———. (1987). *Motor Development.* Indianapolis, IN: Benchmark Press.

Gesell, A. (1945). *The Embryology of Behavior.* New York: Macmillan.

Greenspan, S. I. (1997). *The Growth of the Mind.* Reading, MA: Addison-Wesley.

Halverson, H. M. (1937). Studies of the grasping responses in early infancy. *Journal of Genetic Psychology, 51,* 437–449.

Hellebrandt, F. et al. (1961). Physiological analysis of basic motor skills. *American Journal of Physical Medicine, 40,* 14–25.

Ivanco, T. L., & Greenough, W. T. (2000). Physiological consequences of morphologically detectable synaptic plasticity: Potential uses for examining recovery following damage. *Neuropharmacology, 39,* 765–776.

Jones, T. A., & Greenough, W. T. (1996). Ultrastructural evidence for increased contact between astrocytes and synapses in rats reared in a complex environment. *Neurobiology of Learning and Memory, 65,* 48–56.

Jones, T. A., Klintsova, A. Y., Kilman, V. L., Sirevaag, A. M., & Greenough, W. T. (1997). Induction of multiple synapses by experience in the visual cortex of adult rats. *Neurobiology of Learning and Memory, 68,*13–20.

Kleim, J. A., Pipitone, M. A., Czerlanis, C., & Greenough, W. T. (1998). Structural stability within the lateral cerebellar nucleus of the rat following complex motor learning. *Neurobiology of Learning and Memory, 69,* 290–306.

Landreth, C. (1958). *The Psychology of Early Childhood.* New York: Alfred A. Knopf.

Langendorfer, S. (1987). Separating fact from fiction in preschool aquatics. *National Aquatics Journal, 3*(1), 2–4.

Langendorfer, S. J., & Bruya, L. D. (1995). *Aquatic Readiness.* Champaign, IL: Human Kinetics.

Marsala, G., & VanSant, A. F. (1998). Age-related differences in movement patterns used by toddlers to rise from a supine position to erect stance. *Physical Therapy, 78,* 149–159.

Nash, M. (1997). Fertile minds. *Time, 149*(5), 48–56.

Newell, K. M. (Ed.) (1992). Theme issue on dynamical approaches to motor skill acquisition. *Journal of Motor Behavior, 24,* 2–142.

Ouden, L. D. et al. (1991). Is it correct to correct? Developmental milestones in 555 "normal" preterm infants compared with term infants. *Journal of Pediatrics, 118,* 399–404.

Palmer, F. B. (1992). Effects of physical therapy and infant stimulation. In H. Forssberg & H. Hirschfeld (Eds.), *Movement Disorders in Children, Medicine and Sport Science, vol. 36,* Basel: Karger.

Ramey, C. T., & Ramey, S. L. (1994). Which children benefit the most from early intervention? *Pediatrics, 94,* 1064–1066.

———. (1998). Early intervention and early experiences. *The American Psychologist, 53,* 109–120.

Savelsbergh, G. J., & Kamp, J. (1994). The effect of body orientation to gravity on early infant reaching. *Journal of Experimental Child Psychology, 58,* 510–528.

Shirley, M. (1931). *The First Two Years: A Study of Twenty-Five Babies, 1. Postural and Locomotor Development.* Minneapolis, MN: University of Minnesota Press.

Siddiqui, A. (1995). Object size as a determinant of grasping in infancy. *Journal of Genetic Psychology, 156,* 345–358.

Thelen, E. (1985). Developmental origins of motor coordination: Leg movements in human infants. *Developmental Psychobiology, 18,* 1–22.

———. (1986a). Development of coordinated movement: Implications for early human development. In M. G. Wade & H. T. A. Whiting (Eds.), *Motor Development in Children: Aspects of Coordination and Control.* Dordrecht, The Netherlands: Martinus Nyhoff.

———. (1986b). Treadmill-elicited stepping seven-month-old infants. *Child Development, 57,* 1498–1506.

Thelen, E. (1992). Development of locomotion from a dynamic systems approach. In H. Forssberg & H. Hirschfeld (Eds.), *Movement Disorders in Children, Medicine and Sport Science, vol. 36,* Basel: Karger.

Thelen, E. et al. (1987). Self-organizing systems in infant motor development. *Developmental Review, 7,* 39–65.

Thelen, E., Corbetta, D., & Spencer, J. P. (1996). Development of reaching during the first year: Role of movement speed. *Journal of Experimental Psychology, Human Perception and Performance, 22,* 1059–76.

Ulrich, B. D., & Ulrich, D. A. (1995). Spontaneous leg movements of infants with Down syndrome and nondisabled infants. *Child Development, 66,* 1844–1855.

Ulrich, D. A., & Ulrich, B. D. (1999). Treadmill training facilitates the onset of walking in infants with Down syndrome. Paper presented at the 32nd annual Gatlinburg Conference on Research and Theory in Mental Retardation & Developmental Disabilities, Charleston, SC.

Ulrich, B. D., Ulrich, D. A., & Collier, D. H. (1992). Alternating stepping patterns: Hidden abilities in 11-month-old infants with Down syndrome. *Developmental Medicine and Child Neurology, 34,* 233–239.

Ulrich, B. D., Ulrich, D. A., Collier, D. H., & Cole, E. (1995). Developmental shifts in the ability of infants with Down syndrome to produce treadmill steps. *Physical Therapy, 75,* 14–21.

CHAPTER 9
INFANT PERCEPTION

Aslin, R. N. (1977). Development of binocular fixation in human infants. In D. F. Fisher et al. (Eds.), *Eye Movements: Cognition and Visual Perception.* Hillsdale, NJ: Erlbaum.

———. (1981). Development of smooth pursuit in human infants. In D. F. Fisher et al. (Eds.), *Eye Movements: Cognition and Visual Perception.* Hillsdale, NJ: Erlbaum.

———. (1984). Motor aspects of visual development in infancy. In P. Salapatek & L. B. Cohen (Eds.), *Handbook of Infant Perception.* New York: Academic Press.

Aslin, R. N. et al. (1983). Auditory development and speech perception in infancy. In P. H. Mussan (Ed.), *Handbook of Child Psychology.* New York: Wiley.

Aslin, R. N., & Dumais, S. T. (1980). Binocular vision in infants: A review and a theoretical position. *Advances in Child Development and Behavior, 15,* 53–94.

Aslin, R. N., & Salapatek, P. (1975). Saccadic localization of peripheral targets by the very young human infant. *Perception and Psychophysics, 17,* 292–302.

Atkinson, J., & Braddick, O. (1982). Sensory and perception capacities of the neonate. In P. Stratton (Ed.), *Psychobiology of the Human Newborn,* New York: Wiley.

Banks, M. (1980). The development of visual accommodation during early infancy. *Child Development, 51,* 646–666.

Bernard, J., & Sontag. L. (1947). Fetal reactivity to tonal stimulation: A preliminary report. *Journal of Genetic Psychology, 70,* 205–210.

Bornstein, M. H. et al. (1976). The categories of hue in infancy. *Science, 191,* 201–202.

Cohen, L. B. et al. (1979). Infant visual perception. In J. D. Osofsky (Ed.), *The Handbook of Infant Development.* New York: Wiley.

Dayton, G. O., & Jones, M. H. (1964). Analysis of characteristics of fixation reflexes in infants by use of direct current electroculography. *Neurology, 14,* 1152–1157.

Engen, T., & Lipsett, L. P. (1965). Decrement and recovery of responses of olfactory stimuli in the human neonate. *Journal of Comparative and Physiological Psychology, 59,* 312–316.

Fantz, R. L. (1963). Pattern vision in newborn infants. *Science, 140,* 296–297.

Fantz, R. L. et al. (1975). Early visual selectivity. In L. B. Cohen & P. Salapatek (Eds.), *Infant Perception From Sensation to Cognition.* New York: Academic Press.

Field, J. (1976). The adjustment of reaching behavior to object distance in early infancy. *Child Development, 47,* 304–308.

Fox, R. et al. (1980). Stereopsis in human infants. *Science, 207,* 323–324.

Gibson, E. J., & Walk, R. B. (1960). The visual cliff. *Scientific American, 4,* 67–71.

Haith, M. M. (1966). The response of the human newborn to visual movement. *Journal of Experimental Child Psychology, 3,* 235–243.

———. (1980). *Rules That Babies Look By.* Hillsdale, NJ: Erlbaum.

Haynes, H. et al. (1965). Visual accommodation in human infants. *Science, 148,* 525–530.

Held, R., & Hein, A. (1963). Movement-produced stimulation in the development of visually guided behavior. *Journal of Comparative Physiological Psychology, 56,* 872–876.

Hershenson, M. (1964). Visual discrimination in the human newborn. *Journal of Comparative Physiological Psychology, 158,* 270–276.

Johnson, S. P., & Aslin, R. N. (1996). Perception of object unity in young infants: The roles of motion, depth, and orientation. *Cognitive Development, 11,* 161–180.

Kessen, W. et al. (1972). The visual response of the human newborn to linear contour. *Journal of Experimental Child Psychology, 13,* 9–20.

Krieg, K. (1978). *Tonic Convergence and Facial Growth in Early Infancy.* Unpublished senior honors thesis, Indiana University.

Leventhal, A., & Lipsett, L. P. (1964). Adaption, pitch discrimination and sound vocalization in the neonate. *Child Development, 37,* 331–346.

Lipsett, L. P. et al. (1963). Developmental changes in the olfactory threshold of the neonate. *Child Development, 34,* 371–376.

Magill, R. A. (2001). *Motor Learning: Concepts and Applications.* 6th ed. St. Louis, MO: McGraw-Hill.

McFarlane, A. (1975). Olfaction in the development of social preference in the human neonate. In *Parent-Infant Interaction.* Amsterdam: CIBA Foundation Symposium 33.

Oster, H. S. (1975). *Color perception in ten-week-old infants.* Paper presented at the annual meeting of the Society for Research in Child Development, Denver, CO.

Payne, V. G., & Isaacs, L. D. (2002). *Human Motor Development: A Lifespan Approach.* Boston: McGraw-Hill.

Peeples, D. R., & Teller. D. Y. (1975). Color vision and brightness discrimination in two-month-old human infants. *Science, 789,* 1102–1103.

Pratt, K. C. (1954). The neonate. In L. Carmichael (Ed.), *Manual of Child Psychology.* New York: Wiley.

Salapatek, P. (1975). Pattern vision in early infancy. In L. B. Cohen & P. Salapatek (Eds.), *Infant Perception.* New York: Academic Press.

Santrock, J. W. (2001). *Child Development.* 9th ed. St. Louis, MO: McGraw-Hill.

Schaller, M. J. (1975). *Chromatic vision in human infants: Coordinated fixation to hues of varying intensity.* Paper presented at the meeting of the Society for Research in Child Development, Denver, CO.

Schneider, B. A. et al. (1980). High-frequency sensitivity in infants. *Science, 207,* 1003–1004.

Siqueland, E. R., & DeLucia, C. A. (1969). Visual reinforcement of non-nutritive sucking in human infants. *Science, 165,* 1144–1146.

Snow, C. W. (1998). *Infant Development.* 2nd ed. Upper Saddle River, NJ: Prentice-Hall.

Spears, W. C. (1964). Assessment of visual preference and discrimination in the 4-month-old infant. *Journal of Comparative Physiological Psychology, 57,* 381–386.

Svejda, M., & Schmidt, D. (1979). *The Role of Self-Produced Locomotion on the Onset of Fear of Heights on the Visual Cliff.* Paper presented at the Society for Research in Child Development, San Francisco, CA.

Trehub, S. E. et al. (1980). Infants' perception of melodies: The role of melodic contour. *Child Development, 55,* 821–830.

———. (1991). Observational measures of auditory sensitivity in early infancy. *Developmental Psychology, 27,* 40–49.

Tronick, E. (1972). Stimulus control and the growth of the infants' effective visual field. *Perception and Psychophysics, 11,* 373–375.

von Hofsten, C. (1979). Development of visually guided reaching: The approach phase. *Journal of Human Movement Studies, 5,* 160–178.

———. (1982). Eye-hand coordination in newborns. *Developmental Psychology, 18,* 450–461.

———. (1986). The emergence of manual skills. In M. G. Wade & H. T. A. Whiting (Eds.), *Motor Development in Children: Aspects of Coordination and Control.* Dorbrecht, The Netherlands: Martinus Nyhoff.

Walk, R. D. (1966). The development of depth perception in animal and human infants. *Monograph of the Society for Research in Child Development, 31,* 5.

———. (1978). Depth perception and experience. In R. D. Walk & A. Pick (Eds.), *Perception and Experiences.* New York: Plenum Press.

Williams, H. G. (1983). *Perceptual and Motor Development.* Englewood Cliffs, NJ: Prentice-Hall.

CHAPTER 10
CHILDHOOD GROWTH AND DEVELOPMENT

American Academy of Pediatrics. (2000). Intensive Training and Sports Specialization in Young Athletes. Policy statement by the Committee on Genetics. *Pediatrics, 106,* 154–157.

Barness, L. ed. (1993). *Pediatric Nutrition Handbook.* Elk Grove Village, IL: American Academy of Pediatrics.

Centers for Disease Control (1998). Recommendations to prevent and control iron deficiency in the United States. *Morbidity and Mortality Weekly Report,* April 03, 47 (RR-3);1–36.

Daw, S. F. (1974). Age of boy's puberty in Leipzig, 1727–49, as indicated by voice breaking in J. S. Bach's choir members. *Human Biology, 46,* 381–384.

Eveleth, P. B., & Tanner, J. M. (1976). *Worldwide Variation in Human Growth.* Cambridge, MA: Cambridge University Press.

Gallahue, D. L., & Cleland, F. (2003). *Developmental physical education for today's children.* 4th ed., Champaign, IL: Human Kinetics.

Malina, R. M. (1978). Secular changes in growth and performance. In R. S. Hutton (Ed.), *Exercise and Sport Science Reviews, 6,* 206–235.

Malina, R. M. (1994). Physical growth and biological maturation of young athletes. *Exercise and Sport Sciences Reviews, 22,* 389–434.

Malina, R. M., & Bouchard, C. (1991). *Growth, Maturation and Physical Activity.* Champaign, IL: Human Kinetics.

National Center for Health Statistics. (2000). CDC growth charts: United States. Centers for Disease Control and Prevention. Online: http://www.cdc.gov/growthcharts.

Pařízková, J. (1996). *Nutrition, Physical Activity, and Health in Early Life.* Boca Raton, FL: CRC Press.

Peterson, K. L. (1967). *Atlas for Somatotyping Children.* The Netherlands: Royal Vagorcum Ltd.

Sheldon, W. H. et al. (1940). *The Varieties of Human Physique.* New York: Harper.

———. (1954). *Atlas of Man.* New York: Harper.

Sherrill, C. (1998). *Adapted Physical Activity, Recreation and Sport: Crossdisciplinary and Lifespan.* 5th ed., St. Louis, MO: McGraw-Hill.

CHAPTER 11
FUNDAMENTAL MOVEMENT ABILITIES

Bayley, N. (1935). The development of motor abilities during the first three years. *Monograph of the Society for Research on Child Development, 1,* 1–26.

Bennett, S., Button, C., Kingsbury, D., & Davids, K. (1999). Manipulating visual informational constraints during practice enhances the acquisition of catching skill in children. *Research Quarterly for Exercise and Sport, 70,* 220–232.

Broer, M. R., & Zernicke, R. F. (1979). *Efficiency of Human Movement.* Philadelphia: W. B. Saunders.

Burnett, C. N., & Johnson, E. W. (1971). Development of gait in childhood, Part II. *Developmental Medicine and Child Neurology, 13,* 207–212.

Burton, A. W., Greer, N. L., & Wiese, D. M. (1992). Changes in overhand throwing patterns as a function of ball size. *Pediatric Exercise Science, 4,* 50–67.

Burton, A. W., Greer, N. L., & Wiese-Bjornstal, D. M. (1993). Variations in grasping and throwing patterns as a function of ball size. *Pediatric Exercise Science, 5,* 25–41.

Clark, J. E. (1995). On becoming skillful: Patterns and constraints. *Research Quarterly for Exercise and Sport, 66,* 173–183.

Clark, J. E., & Phillips, S. J. (1985). A developmental sequence of the standing long jump. In J. E. Clark & J. H. Humphrey (Eds.), *Motor Development: Current Selected Research.* Princeton, NJ: Princeton Book Co.

Cratty, B. J. (1986). *Perceptual and Motor Development in Infants and Children.* Englewood Cliffs, NJ: Prentice Hall.

Cratty, B. J., & Martin, M. (1969). *Perceptual-Motor Efficiency in Children.* Philadelphia: Lea & Febiger.

Deach, D. F. (1951). *Genetic Development of Motor Skills in Children Two Through Six Years of Age.* Unpublished doctoral dissertation, University of Michigan.

DeOreo, K. L. (1971). *Dynamic and Static Balance in Preschool Children.* Unpublished doctoral dissertation, University of Illinois.

———. (1980). Performance of fundamental motor tasks. In C. B. Corbin (Ed.), *A Textbook of Motor Development.* Dubuque, IA: Wm. C. Brown.

Eckert, H. (1987). *Motor Development.* Indianapolis, IN: Benchmark Press.

Eckert, H. M., & Rarick, G. L. (1975). Stabliometer performance of educable mentally retarded and normal children. *Research Quarterly, 47,* 619–621.

Fox, J. E., & R. S. Tipps. (1995). Young children's development of swinging behaviors. *Early Childhood Research Quarterly, 10,* 491–504.

Gad-Elmawla, E. K. G. (1980). *Kinematic and Kinetic Analysis of Gain in Children at Different Age Levels in Comparison with Adults.* Unpublished doctoral dissertation, Indiana University.

Gallahue, D. L. (1993). Motor development and movement skill acquisition in early childhood education. In B. Spodek (Ed.), *Handbook on Research on the Education of Young Children.* New York: Macmillan.

Gallahue, D. L., & Cleland, F. (2003). *Developmental Physical Education for Today's Children.* Champaign, IL: Human Kinetics.

Goetzinger, C. P. (1961). Re-evaluation of Heath Rail Walking 1951 to 1967. *Journal of Education Research, 54,* 187–191.

Grieve, D. W., & Gaer, R. J. (1966). The relationship between the length of stride, step, frequency, time of swing and speed of walking for children and adults. *Ergonomics, 9,* 379–399.

Guttridge, M. (1939). A study of motor achievements of young children. *Archives of Psychology, 244,* 1–178.

Halverson, L. E., & Roberton, M. A. (1966). *A Study of Motor Pattern Development in Young Children.* Paper presented at the Annual Convention of the AAHPER Conference, Chicago.

———. (1979). *Motor Development Laboratory Manual.* Madison, WI: American Printing and Publishing.

Halverson, L. E., & Williams, K. (1985). Developmental sequences for hopping over distance: A prelongitudinal study. *Research Quarterly for Exercise and Sport, 56,* 37–44.

Haubenstricker, J. et al. (1983). *Preliminary Validation of Developmental Sequences of Throwing and Catching.* Paper presented at the annual meeting of the North American Society for the Psychology of Sport and Physical Activity, East Lansing, MI.

Johnson, R. (1962). Measurement of achievement in fundamental skills of elementary school children. *Research Quarterly, 33,* 94–103.

Langendorfer, S. (1988). Goal of a motor task as a constraint on developmental status. In J. Clark & J. Humphrey (Eds.), *Advances in Motor Development Research.* New York: AMS Press.

Leudke, G. C. (1980). *Range of Motion as the Focus of Teaching the Overhand Throwing Pattern to Children.* Unpublished doctoral dissertation, Indiana University.

Manoel, E. D., & Oliveira, J. A. (2000). Motor developmental status and task constraint in overarm throwing. *Journal of Human Movement Studies, 39,* 359–378.

Martin, T. P., & Stull, G. A. (1969). Effects of various knee angle and foot spacing combinations on performance in the vertical jump. *Research Quarterly, 40,* 324.

McCaskill, C. L., & Wellman, B. L. (1938). A study of common motor achievements at the preschool ages. *Child Development, 9,* 141.

McClenaghan, B. A. (1976). *Development of an Observational Instrument to Assess Selected Fundamental Movement Patterns of Low Motor Functioning Children.* Unpublished doctoral dissertation, Indiana University.

McClenaghan, B. A., & Gallahue, D. L. (1978a). *Fundamental Movement: A Developmental and Remedial Approach.* Philadelphia: W. B. Saunders.

———. (1978b). *Fundamental Movement: Observation and Assessment.* Philadelphia: W. B. Saunders.

Miller, S. (1978). *The Facilitation of Fundamental Motor Skill Learning in Young Children.* Unpublished doctoral dissertation, Michigan State University.

Myers, C. B. et al. (1977). *Vertical Jumping Movement Patterns of Early Childhood.* Unpublished paper, Indiana University.

Ozmun, J. C., & Robertson, L. D. (1992). *Motor Skill Characteristics of Force Production of Young Children.* Paper presented at the annual convention of the ACSM. Dallas.

Pascual, M. B., & Grimshaw, P. N. (1998). Variability in development of overarm throwing: A longitudinal case study over the first 6 months of throwing. *Perceptual and Motor Skills, 86,* 1403–1418.

Payne, V. G., & Isaacs, L. D. (2002). *Human Motor Development: A Lifespan Approach.* 4th ed. Boston: McGraw-Hill.

Poe, A. (1976). Description of the movement characteristics of two-year-old children performing the jump and reach. *Research Quarterly, 47,* 200.

Raudsepp, L., & Paasuke, M. (1995). Gender differences in fundamental movement patterns, motor performances, and strength measurements of prepubertal children. *Pediatric Exercise Science, 7,* 294–304.

Roberton, M. A. (1978). Stability of stage categorization in motor development. In D. M. Landers & R. W. Christina (Eds.), *Psychology in Motor Behavior and Sport-1977.* Champaign, IL: Human Kinetics.

———. (1985). Changing motor patterns during childhood. In J. K. Thomas (Ed.), *Motor Development During Childhood and Adolescence.* Minneapolis: Burgess.

———. (1987). Developmental level as a function of the immediate environment. In J. E. Clark & J. H. Humphrey (Eds.), *Advances in Motor Development Research.* New York: AMS Press.

Roberton, M. A., & Halverson, L. E. (1984). *Developing Children: Their Changing Movement.* Philadelphia: Lea & Febiger.

Sapp, M. (1980). *Developmental Sequence of Galloping.* Unpublished materials, Michigan State University.

Saunders, J. E. et al. (1953). The major determinants in normal and pathological gait. *Journal of Bone and Joint Surgery, 35,* 543–558.

Savelsbergh, G. J., & van der Kamp, J. (2000). Adaptation in the timing of catching under changing environmental constraints. *Research Quarterly for Exercise and Sport, 71,* 195–200.

Seashore, H. G. (1949). The development of a beam walking test and its use in measuring development of balance in children. *Research Quarterly, 18,* 246–259.

Seefeldt, V. (1972). *Discussion of Walking and Running.* Unpublished research, Michigan State University.

Seefeldt, V., & Haubenstricker, J. (1976). *Developmental Sequences of Fundamental Motor Skills.* Unpublished research, Michigan State University.

———. (1981). *Developmental sequences of kicking: Second revision.* Paper presented at the Midwest AAHPERD Conference, Chicago.

Sinclair, C. (1973). *Movement of the Young Child.* Columbus, OH: Merrill.

Ulrich, B. D. (1997). Dynamic systems theory and skill development in infants and children. In K. Connolly & H. Forssberg (Eds.), *Neurophysiology and Psychology Motor Development.* London: Mac Keigh Press.

Wickstrom, R. L. (1983). *Fundamental Motor Patterns.* Philadelphia: Lea & Febiger.

Wild, M. (1938). The behavioral pattern of throwing and some observations concerning its course of development in children. *Research Quarterly, 3,* 20.

Williams, H. (1970). *A Study of Perceptual-motor Characteristics of Children in Kindergarten Through Sixth Grade.* Unpublished paper, University of Toledo.

Williams, H. G. (1983). *Perceptual and Motor Development.* Englewood Cliffs, NJ: Prentice-Hall.

Williams, K. (1980). Developmental characteristics of a forward roll. *Research Quarterly for Exercise and Sport, 51,* 703.

Yan, J. H., Payne, G., & Thomas, J. R. (2000). Developmental kinematics of young girls' overarm throwing. *Research Quarterly for Exercise and Sport, 71,* 92–98.

CHAPTER 12
PHYSICAL DEVELOPMENT OF CHILDREN

Amateur Athletic Union. (1993). *The Chrysler Fund—Amateur Athletic Union Physical Fitness Program.* Bloomington, IN: Poplars Building.

American Academy of Pediatrics. (2001). Strength training by children and adolescents. *Pediatrics, 107,* 1470–1472.

American Academy of Pediatrics. (1990). Strength training, weight and power lifting, and body building by children and adolescents. *Pediatrics, 85,* 801–803.

American Academy of Pediatrics Committee on Sports Medicine. (1983). Weight training and weight lifting: Information for the pediatrician. *News and Comments, 33,* 7–8.

Armstrong, N., & Welsman, J. R. (2000). Development of aerobic fitness during childhood and adolescence. *Pediatric Exercise Science, 12,* 128–149.

Bandini, L. G. (1987). *Energy expenditure in obese and nonobese adolescents.* Unpublished doctoral dissertation, Massachusetts Institute of Technology.

Baranowski, T. et al. (1992). Assessment, prevalence, and cardiovascular benefits of physical activity and fitness in youth. *Medicine and Science in Sports and Exercise, 24,* 237–247.

Bar-Or, O. (1983). *Pediatric Sports Medicine for the Practitioner.* New York: Springer-Verlag.

———. (1987). A commentary to children and fitness: A public health perspective. *Research Quarterly for Exercise and Sport, 58,* 304–307.

Bernuth, G. A. et al. (1985). Age, exercise, and the endocrine system. In K. Fotherby & S. B. Pal (Eds.), *Exercise Endocrinology.* New York: Walter de Gruyter.

Beunen, G., & Thomis, M. (2000). Muscular strength development in children and adolescents. *Pediatric Exercise Science, 12,* 174–197.

Blair, S. N. (1992). Are American children and youth fit? The need for better data. *Research Quarterly for Exercise and Sport 63,* 120–123.

Blimkie, C. J. R., Ramsay, J., Sale, D., MacDougall, D., Smith, K., & Garner, S. (1989). Effects of 10 weeks of resistance training on strength development in prepubertal boys. In S. Oseid & K. H. Carlsen (Eds.), *International Series on Sport Sciences. Children and Exercise XIII.* Champaign, IL: Human Kinetics.

Clarke, D. (1975). Predicting Certified Weight of Young Wrestlers. *Medicine and Science in Sports, 6,* 52–57.

Clarke, H. H. (1971). *Physical Motor Tests in the Medford Boys Growth Study.* Englewood Cliffs, NJ: Prentice Hall.

Corbin, C. B., & Pangrazi, R. P. (1992). Are American children and youth fit? *Research Quarterly for Exercise and Sport, 63,* 96–106.

Cratty, B. J. (1986). *Perceptual and Motor Development in Infants and Children.* Englewood Cliffs, NJ: Prentice Hall.

Cratty, B. J., & Martin, M. (1969). *Perceptual-Motor Efficiency in Children.* Philadelphia: Lea & Febiger.

Cumming, G. R., & Hantiuk, A. (1980). Establishing of normal values for exercise capacity in a hospital clinic. In K. Berg & B. Erickson (Eds.), *Children and Exercise IX.* Baltimore, MD: Academic Press.

DeOreo, K. L. (1971). *Dynamic and Static Balance in Preschool Children.* Unpublished doctoral dissertation, University of Illinois.

———. (1980). Performance of fundamental motor tasks. In C. B. Corbin (Ed.), *A Textbook of Motor Development.* Dubuque, IA: Wm. C. Brown.

Duda, M. (1986). Prepubescent strength training gains support. *The Physician and Sports Medicine, 14*(2), 157–161.

DuRant, R. H. et al. (1996). The relationship among television watching, physical activity, and body composition of 5- or 6-year-old children. *Pediatric Exercise Science, 8,* 15–26.

Fjortoft, I. (2000). Motor Fitness in Pre-Primary School Children. The Eurofit Motor Fitness Test Explored on 5–7 year-old Children. *Pediatric Exercise Science, 12,* 424–436.

Frederick, S. D. (1977). *Performance of Selected Motor Tasks by Three, Four, and Five Year Old Children.* Unpublished doctoral dissertation, Indiana University.

Glassow, R. L., & Kruse, P. (1960). Motor performance of girls age 6–14 years. *Research Quarterly, 31,* 426–431.

Gumbs, V. L. et al. (1982). Bilateral distal radius and ulnar fractures in adolescent weight lifters. *The American Journal of Sports Medicine, 10,* 375–379.

Gutin, B., Manos, T., & Strong, W. (1992). Defining health and fitness: First steps toward establishing fitness standards. *Research Quarterly for Exercise and Sport, 63,* 128–132.

Katch, V. L. (1983). Physical conditioning of children. *Journal of Adolescent Health Care, 3,* 241–246.

Keogh, J. F. (1965). *Motor Performance of Elementary School Children.* Los Angeles: University of California, Physical Education Department.

Krahenbuhl, G. S., et al. (1985). Developmental aspects of maximal aerobic power in children. In R. L. Terjung (Ed.), *Exercise Science and Sport Research.* New York: Macmillan.

Kuntzleman, C. T., & Reiff, G. G. (1992). The decline in American children's fitness levels. *Research Quarterly for Exercise and Sport, 63,* 107–111.

Lee, P. A., Kulin, H. E., & Guo, S. S. (2001). Age of puberty among girls and the diagnosis of precocious puberty. *Pediatrics, 107,* 1493.

Legwold, G. (1982). Does lifting weights harm a prepubescent athlete? *The Physician and Sportsmedicine, 10*(7) 141–144.

———. (1983). Preadolescents show dramatic strength gains. *The Physician and Sportsmedicine, 11*(10), 25.

Lohman, T. G. (1986). Applicability of body composition techniques and constraints for children and youth. *Exercise and Sports Sciences Review, 14,* 325–357.

Luedke, G. C. (1980). *Range of Motion as the Focus of Teaching the Overhand Throwing Pattern to Children.* Unpublished doctoral dissertation, Indiana University.

Mersch, F., & Stoboy, H. (1989). Strength training and muscle hypertrophy in children. In S. Oseid & K. H. Carlsen (Eds.), *International Series on Sport Sciences.*

Children and Exercise XIII. Champaign, IL: Human Kinetics.

Micheli, L. J., & Micheli, E. R. (1985). Children's running: Special risks? *Annals of Sports Medicine, 2,* 61–63.

Mrzena, B., & Macuek, M. (1978). Uses of treadmill and working capacity assessment in preschool children. In J. Borms & M. Hebbelinck (Eds.), *Medicine and Sports Series, Vol. II, Pediatric Work Physiology.* Basel, Belgium: S. Karger.

National Center for Health Statistics. (2001). Prevalence of Overweight among Children and Adolescents. Online: www.cdc.gov/nchs/products/pubs/pubd/hestats/overweight99.htm.

National Strength and Conditioning Association. (1985). Position paper on prepubescent strength training. *National Strength and Conditioning Association Journal, 7*(4), 27–31.

Ott, A. E., Pate, R. R., Trost, S. G., Ward, D. S., & Saunder, S. R. (2000). The Use of Uniaxial and Triaxial Accelerometers to Measure Children's "Free Play" Physical Activity. *Pediatric Exercise Science, 12,* 360–370.

Ozmun, J. C., Mikesky, A. E., & Surburg, P. R. (1994). Neuromuscular adaptations following prepubescent strength training. *Medicine and Science in Sports and Exercise, 26,* 510–514.

Parizkova, J. (1972). Somatic development and body composition changes in adolescent boys differing in physical activity and fitness: A longitudinal study. *Anthropologie, 70,* 3–36.

———. (1973). Body composition and exercise during growth and development. In G. L. Rarick (Ed.), *Physical Activity: Human Development.* New York: Academic Press.

———. (1977). *Body Fat and Physical Fitness.* The Hague, Netherlands: Martinus Nayhoff B. V. Medical Division.

Pate, R. R., & Blair, S. N. (1978). Exercise and the prevention of atherosclerosis: Pediatric implications. In W. Strong (Ed.), *Pediatric Aspects of Atherosclerosis.* New York: Greene and Stratton.

Payne, G. V., & Morrow, J. R. (1993). Exercise and VO_2max in children: A meta-analysis, *Research Quarterly for Exercise and Sport, 64,* 305–313.

Payne, V. G., Morrow, J. R., Johnson, L., & Dalton, S. N. (1997). Resistaince training in children and youth: A meta analysis. *Research Quarterly for Exercise and Sport, 68,* 80–88.

Peterson, K. L., et al. (1974). *Factor analyses of motor performance for kindergarten, first and second grade children: A tentative solution.* Paper presented at the annual convention of the AAHPERD, Anaheim, CA.

Review and commentary: Children and fitness. (1987). *Research Quarterly for Exercise and Sport, 58,* 295–333.

Rickard, K. et. al. (1995). The play approach in the context of families and schools: An alternative paradigm for nutrition and fitness education for the 21st century. *Journal of the American Dietetic Association, 95,* 1121–1126.

Romanella, N. E., Wakat, D. K., Loyd, B. H., & Kelly, L. F. (1990). Physical activity and attitudes in lean and obese children and their mothers. *International Journal of Obesity, 15,* 407–414.

Ross, J. G., & Gilbert, G. G. (1985). The national children and youth fitness study: A summary of findings. *Journal of Physical Education, Recreation and Dance, 56*(1), 45–50.

Ross, J. G., & Pate, R. R. (1987). The national children and youth fitness study II. *Journal of Physical Education, Recreation and Dance, 58*(9), 49–96.

Rowland, T. W. (1991). Effects of obesity on aerobic fitness in adolescent females. *American Journal of Diseases of Children, 145,* 764–768.

Rowland, T. W. (1997). The "Trigger hypothesis" for aerobic trainability: A 14 year follow-up. *Pediatric Exercise Science, 9,* 1–9.

Rowlands, A. V., Eston, R. G., & Ingledew, D. K. (1997). Measurement of physical activity in children with particular reference to the use of heart rate and pedometry. *Sports Medicine, 24,* 258–272.

Seefeldt, V. (1980). Physical fitness guidelines for preschool children. In *Proceedings of the National Conference on Physical Activity and Sports for All.* Washington, DC: President's Council on Physical Fitness and Sports, pp. 5–19.

Sewell, L., & Micheli, L. (1984). *Strength Development in Children.* Paper presented to the American College of Sports Medicine, San Diego, CA.

Simons-Morton, B. G. et al. (1987). Children and fitness: A public health perspective. *Research Quarterly for Exercise and Sport, 58,* 295–303.

Tolfrey, K., Campbell, I. G., & Batterman, A. M. (1998). Aerobic trainability of prepubertal boys and girls. *Pediatric Exercise Science, 10,* 248–263.

Updyke, W. (1992). In search of relevant and credible physical fitness standards for children. *Research Quarterly for Exercise and Sport, 63,* 112–119.

Van Slooten, P. H. (1973). *Performance of Selected Motor-Coordination Tasks by Young Boys and Girls in Six Socioeconomic Groups.* Unpublished doctoral dissertation, Indiana University.

Vrijens, J. (1978). Muscle strength development in pre- and postpubescent age. In J. Borms & M. Gebbelinck (Eds.), *Pediatric Work Physiology.* New York: Karger.

Ward, D. S., & Bar-Or, O. (1986). Role of the physician and the physical education teacher in the treatment of obesity. *Pediatrician, 13,* 44–51.

Weltman, A., et al. (1986). The effects of hydraulic resistance strength training in pre-pubertal males. *Medicine and Science in Sports and Exercise, 18,* 629–638.

CHAPTER 13
CHILDHOOD PERCEPTION AND PERCEPTUAL-MOTOR DEVELOPMENT

American Academy of Pediatrics (1999). The treatment of neurologically impaired children using patterning. Policy statement by the Committee on Children with Disabilities. *Pediatrics, 104,* 1149–1151.

Barsch, R. (1965). *Achieving Perceptual-Motor Efficiency.* Seattle, WA: Special Child Publications.

Burton, A. W. (1990). Assessing the perceptual-motor interaction in developmentally disabled and handicapped children. *Adapted Physical Activity Quarterly, 7,* 325–337.

Burton, A. W., & Davis, W. E. (1996). Ecological task analysis: Theoretical and empirical foundations. *Human Movement Science, 15,* 285–314.

Cheatum, B. A., & Hammond, A. A. (2000). *Physical Activities for Improving Children's Learning and Behavior: A Guide to Sensory Motor Development.* Champaign, IL: Human Kinetics.

Cone, T. P., Werner, P., Cone, S. L., & Woods, A. M. (1998). *Interdisciplinary Teaching through Physical Education.* Champaign, IL: Human Kinetics.

Cooper, J. M. et al. (1982). *Kinesiology.* St. Louis: Mosby.

Cooper, J. M., & Andrews, W. (1975). Rhythm as a linguistic art. *Quest, 65,* 61–67.

Council on Learning Disabilities. (1987). The CLD position statements: Measurement and training of perceptual and perceptual-motor functions. *Journal of Learning Disabilities, 20,* 347–350.

Delacato, C. (1959). *Treatment and Prevention of Reading Problems.* Springfield, IL: Charles C. Thomas.

Dorfman, P. W. (1977). Timing and anticipation: A developmental perspective. *Journal of Motor Behavior, 9,* 67–79.

Frostig, M. et al. (1966). *Administration and Scoring Manual: Frostig Developmental Test of Visual Perception.* Palo Alto, CA: Consulting Psychologists Press.

Gallahue, D. L. (1968). The relationship between perceptual and motor abilities. *Research Quarterly, 39,* 948–952.

———. (1982). *Developmental Movement Experiences for Children.* New York: Wiley.

Getman, G. N. (1952). *How to Develop Your Child's Intelligence (a research publication).* Lucerne, MN: G. N. Getman.

Hebb, D. O. (1949). *The Organization of Behavior.* New York: Wiley.

Held, R., & Blossom, J. (1961). Neonatal deprivation and adult rearrangement: Complementary techniques for analyzing plastic sensory-motor coordinations. *Journal of Comparative Physiological Psychology, 54,* 33–37.

Held, R., & Mikaelian, H. (1964). Motor sensory feedback versus need in adaptation to rearrangement. *Perceptual Motor Skills, 18,* 685–688.

Hoepner, B. J. (1967). Comparison of motor ability, new motor skill learning and adjustment to a rearranged visual field. *Research Quarterly, 38,* 605–614.

Isaacs, L. D. (1980). Effects of ball size, ball color, and preferred color on catching by young children. *Perceptual and Motor Skills, 51,* 583–586.

Ivanco, T. L., & Greenough, W. T. (2000). Physiological consequences of morphologically detectable synaptic plasticity: Potential uses for examining recovery following damage. *Neuropharmacology, 39,* 765–776.

Jones, T. A., & Greenough, W. T. (1996). Ultrastructural evidence for increased contact between astrocytes and synapses in rats reared in a complex environment. *Neurobiology of Learning and Memory, 65,* 48–56.

Jones, T. A., Klintsova, A. Y., Kilman, V. L., Sirevaag, A. M., & Greenough, W. T. (1997). Induction of multiple synapses by experience in the visual cortex of adult rats. *Neurobiology of Learning and Memory, 68,* 13–20.

Kavale, K., & Mattson, P. D. (1983). One jumped off the balance beam: Meta-analysis of perceptual-motor training. *Journal of Learning Disabilities, 16,* 165–173.

Kephart, N. C. (1971). *The Slow Learner in the Classroom.* Columbus, OH: Merrill.

Kleim, J. A., Pipitone, M. A., Czerlanis, C., & Greenough, W. T. (1998). Structural stability within the lateral cerebellar nucleus of the rat following complex motor learning. *Neurobiology of Learning and Memory, 69,* 290–306.

Magill, R. A. (2001). *Motor Learning: Concepts and Applications.* 6th ed. St. Louis: McGraw-Hill.

Marsh, H. W. et al. (1991). Self-concepts of young children 5 to 8 years of age: Measurement and multidimensional structure. *Journal of Educational Psychology, 83,* 377–392.

Marsh, H. W., & Peart, N. (1988). Competitive and cooperative physical fitness training programs for girls: Effects of physical fitness and multidimensional self concepts. *Journal of Sport and Exercise Psychology, 10,* 390–407.

Morris, G. S. (1977). Dynamic visual acuity: Implications for the physical educator and coach. *Motor Skills: Theory into Practice, 2,* 5–10.

Morris, G. S. (1980). *Elementary Physical Education: Toward Inclusion.* Salt Lake City, UT: Brighton Publishing.

Payne, V. G. (1985). *The Effects of Object Size, Experimental Design and Distance of Projection of Object Reception by Children in the First Grade.* Unpublished doctoral dissertation, Indiana University.

Payne, V. G., & Isaacs, L. D. (2002). *Human Motor Development: A Lifespan Approach.* Boston: McGraw-Hill.

Piaget, J. (1952). *The Origins of Intelligence in Children.* New York: International Universities Press.

———. (1954). *The Construction of Reality and the Child.* New York: Basic Books.

Riesen, A. H., & Aarons, L. (1959). Visual movement and intensity discrimination of pattern vision. *Journal of Comparative Physiological Psychology, 52,* 142–149.

Sage, G. H. (1984). *Motor Learning and Control: A Neuropsychological Approach.* Dubuque, IA: Wm. C. Brown.

Sherrill, C. (1998). *Adapted Physical Activity, Recreation and Sport: Crossdisciplinary and Lifespan.* 5th ed. St. Louis: McGraw-Hill.

Smith, H. (1970). Implications for movement education experience drawn from perceptual motor research. *Journal of Health, Physical Education and Recreation, 4*(3), 30–33.

Smith, O. W., & Smith, P. C. (1966). Developmental studies of spatial judgments by children and adults. *Perceptual Motor Skills* (Monograph Supplement), *22,* 3–73.

Wessel, J. A., & Zittel. L. L. (1995). *Smart Start: Preschool Movement Curriculum for Children of All Abilities.* Austin, TX: Pro•Ed.

Wessel, J. A., & Zittel, L. L. (1998). *I CAN primary skills K-3.* 2nd ed. Austin, TX: Pro•Ed.

Williams, H. G. (1983). *Perceptual and Motor Development.* Englewood Cliffs, NJ: Prentice-Hall.

Winnick, J. P. (2000). Perceptual-motor development. In J. P. Winnick (Ed.) *Adapted Physical Education and Sport.* 3rd ed. Champaign, IL: Human Kinetics.

CHAPTER 14
CHILDHOOD SELF-CONCEPT DEVELOPMENT

Bandura, A. (1982). Self efficacy: Toward a unifying theory of behavioral change. In M. Rosenberg & H. B. Kaplan (Eds.), *Social Psychology of the Self-Concept.* Arlington Heights, IL: Harlan Davidson.

Bigge, M. L., & Shermis, S. S. (1999). *Learning Theories for Teachers.* New York: Harper Collins.

Coopersmith, S. (1967). *The Antecedents of Self-Esteem.* San Francisco: W. H. Freeman.

Coopersmith, S. (1977). A method of determining types of self-esteem. *Journal of Abnormal and Social Psychology, 59,* 87–94.

Crawford, T. A. (1989). *A Developmental Analysis of Competitive Orientation in Team Sports and Individual Sports.* Unpublished doctoral dissertation, Indiana University.

Damon, W., & Hart, D. (1986). Stability and change in children's self-understanding. *Social Cognition, 4*(2), 102–118.

Dickstein, E. (1977). Self and self-esteem: Theoretical foundations and their implications for research. *Human Development, 20,* 129–140.

Duda, J. (1986). Towards a developmental theory of children's motivation in sport. *Journal of Sport and Exercise Psychology, 9,* 130–145.

Ebbeck, V., & Stuart, M. (1996). Predictors of self-esteem with youth basketball players. *Pediatric Exercise Science, 8,* 368–378.

Ebbeck, V., & Weiss, M. R. (1998). Determinants of children's self-esteem: An examination of perceived competence and affect in sport. *Pediatric Exercise Science, 10,* 285–298.

Erikson, E. (1963). *Childhood and Society.* New York: Norton.

———. (1980). *Identity and the Life Cycle.* New York: Norton.

Fox, K., Corbin, C. B., & Couldry, W. H. (1985). Female physical estimation and attraction to physical activity. *Journal of Sport Psychology, 7,* 125–136.

Gallahue, D. L. (1996). *Developmental Physical Education for Today's Children, 3rd ed.* Dubuque, IA: Brown & Benchmark.

Gallahue, D. L. & Cleland, F. (2003). *Developmental Physical Education for Today's Children.* 4th ed. Champaign, IL: Human Kinetics.

Granleese, J., Trew, K., & Turner, I. (1988). Sex differences in perceived competence. *British Journal of Sport Psychology, 27,* 181–184.

Harter, S. (1978). Effectance motivation reconsidered: Toward a developmental model. *Human Development, 21,* 34–64.

Harter, S. (1999). *The Construction of the Self.* New York: Guilford.

———. (1982a). Developmental perspectives on self-esteem. In E. M. Hetherinton (Ed.), *Handbook of Child Psychology, Volume III: Socialization, Personality, and Social Developments.* New York: Wiley.

———. (1982b). The perceived competence scale for children. *Child Development, 53,* 87–97.

———. (1983). Developmental perspectives on the self system. In P. H. Mussen (Ed.), *Handbook of Child Psychology.* New York: Wiley.

———. (1985). *Manual for the Self-Perception Profile for Children.* (Revision of the perceived competence scale for children). Denver, CO: University of Denver.

———. (1987). The determinants and mediational role of global self-worth in children. In N. Eisenberg (Ed.), *Contemporary Topics in Developmental Psychology.* New York: Wiley.

———. (1999). *The Construction of the Self.* New York: Guilford.

Harter, S., & Connell, J. P. (1984). A model of the relationship among children's academic achievement and children's perceptions of competence, control and motivational orientation. In J. Nicholls (Ed.), *The Development of Achievement-Related Cognitions and Behaviors.* Greenwich, CT: J. A. I. Press.

Harter, S., & Pike, R. (1984). The pictorial scale of perceived competence and social acceptance for young children. *Child Development, 55,* 1967–1982.

James, W. (1890). *The Principles of Psychology.* New York: Holt.

Knoppers, A. (1992). Personal and social skills. In V. Seefeldt and E. W. Brown (Eds.), *Program for Athletic Coaches Education.* Dubuque, IA: Brown & Benchmark.

Marsh, H. W. (1985). Age and sex effects in multiple dimensions of preadolescent self-concept: A replication and extension. *Australian Journal of Psychology, 37,* 197–204.

———. (1990). A multidimensional, hierarchical model of self-concept: Theoretical and empirical justification. *Educational Psychology Review, 2,* 77–172.

———. (1994). The importance of being important: Theoretical models in relations between specific and global components of physical self-concept. *Journal of Sport and Exercise Psychology, 16,* 306–325.

Marsh, H. W. et al. (1991). Self-concepts of young children 5 to 8 years of age: Measurement and multidimensional structure. *Journal of Educational Psychology, 83,* 377–392.

Marsh, H. W., & Peart, N. D. (1988). Competitive and cooperative physical fitness training programs for girls: Effects on physical fitness and multidimensional self-concepts. *Journal of Sport and Exercise Psychology, 10,* 390–407.

Roberts, G. C., Kleiber, D. A., & Duda, J. L. (1981). An analysis of motivation in children's sport: The role of perceived competence in motivation. *Journal of Sport Psychology, 3,* 206–216.

Rosenberg, M. (1979). *Conceiving the Self.* New York: Basic Books.

———. (1982). Psychological selectivity in self-esteem formation. In M. Rosenberg & H. B. Kaplan (Eds.), *Social Psychology of the Self-Concept.* Arlington Heights, IL: Harlan Davidson.

Santrock, J. W. (2001). *Child Development.* 9th ed. St. Louis: McGraw-Hill.

Schempp, P. G. et al. (1983). Influence of decision-making on attitudes, creativity, motor skills and self-concept in elementary children. *Research Quarterly, 54,* 183–189.

Taylor, B. J. (1980). Pathways to a healthy self-concept. In T. D. Yaroke (Ed.), *The Self Concept of the Young Child.* Salt Lake City, UT: Brigham Young Press.

Tuddenham, R. S. (1951). Studies in reputation III, Correlates of popularity among elementary school children. *Journal of Educational Psychology, 42,* 1–12.

Ulrich, B. (1987). Perceptions of physical competence, motor competence and participation in organized sports: Their interrelations in young children. *Research Quarterly for Exercise and Sport, 58,* 57–67.

van Wersch, A., Trew, K., & Turner, I. (1990). Pupils' perceived physical competence and its implications for the new PE curriculum. *Research Supplement of the Physical Education Association of Great Britain and Northern Ireland, 7,* 1–5.

Weinberg, R. S., & Gould, D. (1999). *Foundations of Sport and Exercise Psychology.* 2nd ed. Champaign, IL: Human Kinetics.

Weiss, M. R. (1987). Self-esteem and achievement in children's sport and physical activity. In D. Gould & M. R. Weiss (Eds.), *Advances in Pediatric Sport Science: Vol 2, Behavior Issues.* Champaign, IL: Human Kinetics.

Weiss, M. R., & Chaumeton, N. (1992). Motivational orientations in sport. In T. S. Horn (Ed.), *Advances in Sport Psychology.* Champaign, IL: Human Kinetics.

Weiss, M. R., & Horn, T. S. (1990). The relation between children's accuracy estimates of their physical competence and achievement-related characteristics. *Research Quarterly for Exercise and Sport, 61,* 250–258.

Weiss, M. R., Smith, A. L., & Theeboom, M. (1996). "That's what friends are for": Children's and teenagers' perceptions of peer relationships in the sport domain. *Journal of Sport & Exercise Psychology, 18,* 347–379.

Werner, E. E. (1989a). Children of the garden island. *Scientific American, 264,* 106–111.

———. (1989b). High risk children in young adulthood: A longitudinal study from birth to 32 years. *American Journal of Orthopsychiatry, 59,* 72–81.

White, R. (1959). Motivation reconsidered. The concept of competence. *Psychological Review, 66,* 297–323.

Zaharopoulos, E., & Hodge, K. (1991). Self-concept and sport participation. *New Zealand Journal of Psychology, 20,* 12–16.

Zaichkowsky, L. D. et al. (1980). *Growth and Development: The Child and Physical Activity.* St. Louis, MO: C. V. Mosby.

CHAPTER 15
ADOLESCENT GROWTH, PUBERTY, AND REPRODUCTIVE, MATURITY

American Academy of Pediatrics. (2000). Medical concerns in the female athlete. *Pediatrics, 106,* 610–613. (Revised policy statement.)

American College of Sports Medicine Position Statement of the Use and Abuse of Anabolic-Androgenic Steroids in Sports. (1987). *Medicine and Science in Sports, 9,* 11–13.

Biro, F. M., Lucky, A. W., Huster, G. A., & Morrison, J. A. (1995). Pubertal staging in boys. *The Journal of Pediatrics, 127,* 100–102.

Brown, K. M., et al. (1998). Changes in self-esteem in black and white girls between the ages of 9 and 14 years: The NHLBI growth and health study. *Journal of Adolescent Health, 22,* 7–19.

Caine, E. D. J., & Broekhoff, J. (1987). Maturity assessment: A viable preventive measure against physical and psychological insult to the young athlete? *The Physician and Sportsmedicine, 15*(3), 67–69.

Conger, J. J., & Peterson, A. C. (1984). *Adolescence and Youth.* New York: Harper & Row.

Duke, R. M. et al. (1980). Adolescence self-assessment of sexual maturation. *Pediatrics, 66,* 918–920.

Frisch, R. E., & McArthur, J. W. (1974). Menstrual cycles: Fatness as a determinant of minimum weight for height necessary for their maintenance or onset. *Science, 185,* 949–951.

Herman-Giddens, M. E. et al. (1997). Secondary sexual characteristics and menses in young girls seen in office practice: A study from the Pediatric Research in Office Settings Network. *Pediatrics, 99,* 505–512.

Huen, K. F. et al. (1997). Secular trend in the sexual maturation of southern Chinese girls. *ACTA Pediatrics, 86,* 1121–1124.

Kaplowitz, P. B., & Oberfield, S. E. (1999). Reexamination of the age limit for defining when puberty is precocious in girls in the United States. *Pediatrics, 104,* 936–941.

Katchadourian, H. (1977). *The Biology of Adolescence.* San Francisco: W. H. Freeman.

Kipke, M. (Ed.). (1999). *Adolescent Development and the Biology of Puberty.* Washington, DC: National Academy Press.

Kreipe, R. E., & Gewanter, H. L. (1983). Physical maturity screening for participation in sports. *Pediatrics, 75,* 1076–1080.

Lee, P. A., Kulin, H. E., & Guo, S. S. (2001). Age of puberty among girls and the diagnosis of precocious puberty. *Pediatrics, 107,* 1493.

Malina, R. M. (1983). Menarche in athletes: A synthesis and hypothesis. *Annals of Human Biology, 10,* 1–24.

———. (1986). Physical growth and maturation. In V. Seefeldt (Ed.), *Physical Activity and Well-Being.* Reston, VA: AAHPERD.

———. (1994). Physical growth and biological maturation of young athletes. *Exercise and Sport Sciences Review, 22,* 389–433.

———. (2000). Matching Youth in Sport by Maturity Status. *Spotlight on Youth Sports, 22*(4), 1–4.

Malina, R. M., & Bouchard, C. (1991). *Growth, Maturation, and Physical Activity.* Champaign, IL: Human Kinetics.

Malina, R. M., Katzmarzyk, P. T., Bonci, C. M., Ryan, R. C., & Wellens, R. E. (1997). Family size and age at menarche in athletes. *Medicine and Science in Sports and Exercise, 29,* 99–106.

Masters, W. H., & Johnson, V. E. (1970). *Human Sexual Inadequacy.* Boston: Little Brown.

National Center for Health Statistics. (2001). Prevalence of Overweight among Children and Adolescents.

Online: www.cdc.gov/nchs/products/pubs/pubd/hestats/overweight99.htm.

Pathomvanich, A., Merke, O. P., & Chrousos, G. P. (2000). Early Puberty: A Cautionary Tale. *Pediatrics, 105,* 115–116.

Rosenfield, R. L. (2000). Current age of onset of puberty. *Pediatrics, 106,* 622–623.

Sperling, M. A. (Ed.). (1996). *Pediatric Endocrinology.* Philadelphia: W. B. Saunders.

Stager, J. M., Robertshaw, D., & Miescher, E. (1984). Delayed menarche in swimmers in relation to age at onset of training and athletic performance. *Medicine and Science in Sports and Exercise, 16,* 550–555.

Susman, E. J. (1997). Modeling developmental complexity in adolescence: Hormones and behavior in context. *Journal of Research on Adolescence, 7,* 286–306.

Susman, E. J. et al. (1989). The physiology of stress and behavioral development. In O. S. Palermo (Ed.), *Coping With Uncertainty: Behavioral and Developmental Perspectives.* Hillsdale, NJ: Lawrence Erlbaum.

Tanner, J. M. (1962). *Growth at Adolescence.* Oxford, England: Blackwell Scientific Publications.

Tanner, J. M. (1989). *Fetus into Man* (Revised and expanded). Cambridge, MA: Harvard University Press.

Tanner, J. M. et al. (1975). *Assessment of Skeletal Maturity and Prediction of Adult Height.* New York: Academic Press.

CHAPTER 16
SPECIALIZED MOVEMENT ABILITIES

American Academy of Pediatrics. (2000). Intensive training and sports participation in young athletes. *Pediatrics, 106,* 154–157.

American Sport Education Program: ACEP. (2002). Champaign, IL: Human Kinetics.

Centers for Disease Control (1992). *National Health Interview Survey Youth Risk Behavior Survey.* Silver Springs, MD: CDC at Healthy Youth.

Centers for Disease Control (2000). *Promoting Better Health for Young People Through Physical Activity and Sports.* Silver Springs, MD: CDC at Healthy Youth.

Fitts, P. M., & Posner, M. I. (1967). *Human Performance.* Belmont, CA: Brooks/Cole.

Gallahue, D. L. (1982). *Understanding Motor Development.* New York: Wiley.

———. (1996). *Developmental Physical Education for Today's Children.* Dubuque, IA: McGraw-Hill.

Gallahue, D. L., & Cleland, F. (2003). *Developmental Physical Education for Today's Children, 4th Edition.* Champaign, IL: Human Kinetics.

Gallahue, D. L., Werner, P. H., & Luedke, G. C. (1975). *A Conceptual Approach to Moving and Learning.* New York: Wiley.

———. (1992). *Moving and Learning: A Conceptual Approach to the Physical Education of Young Children.* Dubuque, IA: Kendell/Hunt.

Gentile, A. (1972). A working model for skill acquisition with application to teaching. *Quest, 17,* 3–23.

Gentile, A. M. (2000). Skill Acquisition: Action, movement and neuromotor processes. In J. H. Carr and K. B. Shepherd (Eds.). *Movement Science: Foundations for Physical Therapy.* Rockville, MD: Aspen.

Magill, R. (2001). *Motor Learning: Concepts and Application.* Boston, MA: McGraw Hill.

Martens, R. (1997). *Successful Coaching.* Champaign, IL: Human Kinetics.

Poinsett, A. (1996). *The Role of Sports in Youth Development.* New York: Carnegie Corporation.

Seefeldt, V. (1980). Physical fitness guidelines for preschool children. In *Proceedings of the National Conference on Physical Fitness and Sports for All.* Washington, DC: President's Council on Physical Fitness and Sports, pp. 5–19.

Washington, R. L., Bernhardt, D. T., Gomez, J., Johnson, M. D., et al. (2001). Organized sports for children and preadolescents. *Pediatrics, 107,* 1459–1462.

CHAPTER 17
FITNESS CHANGES DURING ADOLESCENCE

AAHPERD. (1980). *Health-Related Physical Fitness Test.* Reston, VA: AAHPERD.

American Academy of Pediatrics. (2000). Medical concerns in the female athlete. *Pediatrics, 106,* 610–613.

Armstrong, N., & Welsman, J. R. (2000). Development of aerobic fitness during childhood and adolescence. *Pediatric Exercise Science, 12,* 128–149.

Bandini, L. G. et al. (1990). Validity of reported energy intake in obese and nonobese adolescents. *American Journal of Clinical Nutrition, 52,* 421–425.

Bar-Or, O. (1983). *Pediatric Sports Medicine for the Practitioner.* New York: Springer-Verlag.

Beunen, G., & Thomis M. (2000). Muscle Strength Development in Childhood and Adolescence. *Pediatric Exercise Science, 12,* 174–197.

Centers for Disease Control. (1996). Youth risk behavior surveillance—United States, 1995. *Morbidity and Mortality Weekly Report, 45,* No. SS-4. Atlanta, GA: CDC.

Centers for Disease Control. (2000). *CDC Growth Charts: United States.* Advance Data #314.

Corbin, C. B., & Pangrazi, R. P. (1992). Are American children and youth fit? *Research Quarterly for Exercise and Sport, 63,* 96–106.

Errecart, M. T. et al. (1985). The National Children and Youth Fitness Study II: Sampling procedures. *Journal of Physical Education, Recreation and Dance, 56,* 54–56.

Faigenbaum, A. (2000). Age- and sex-related differences and their implications for resistance exercise. In T. R. Baechler and R. W. Earle (Eds.). *Essentials of Strength Training and Conditioning.* (Chapter 9, pp. 169–185). Champaign, IL: Human Kinetics.

Haubenstricker, J., & Seefeldt, V. (1986). Acquisition of motor skills during childhood. In V. Seefeldt (Ed.), *Physical Activity and Well-Being.* Reston, VA: AAHPERD.

Health Related Physical Fitness Test. (1980). Reston, VA: AAHPERD Publications.

Hunsicker, P., & Reiff, G. (1977). Youth fitness report, 1958-1965-1975. *Journal of Physical Education and Recreation, 48,* 32–36.

Hunt, B. R. et al. (2000). Validity of a submaximal 1-mile track jog test in predicting VO_2max in fit teenagers. *Pediatric Exercise Science, 12,* 80–90.

Lloyd, T. et al. (2000). Adult female hip bone density reflects teenage sports-exercise patterns. *Pediatrics, 106,* 40–44.

Moore, J. M. et al. (1991). Energy need in childhood and adult-onset obese women before and after a nine month nutrition education and walking program. *International Journal of Obesity, 15,* 337–344.

National Center for Health Statistics. (2001). *Faststats—Overweight Prevalence.* Online: www.dcd.gov/nchs/fastats/overwt.htm.

National Children and Youth Fitness Study I. (1985). *Journal of Physical Education, Recreation and Dance, 56*(1), 43–90.

National Children and Youth Fitness Study II. (1987). *Journal of Physical Education, Recreation and Dance, 58*(9), 49–96.

Parizkova, J. (1982). Physical training in weight reduction of obese adolescents. *Annals of Clinical Research, 34,* 69–73.

Pate, R. R. et al. (1999). Tracking of physical activity, physical inactivity, and health-related physical fitness in rural youth. *Pediatric Exercise Science, 11,* 364–376.

Raudsepp, P., & Viira, R. (2000). Sociocultural correlates of physical activity in adolescents. *Pediatric Exercise Science, 12,* 51–60.

Reuschlein, P., & Haubenstricker, J. (Eds.) (1985). *Physical education interpretive report: Grades 4, 7, and 10.* Michigan Educational Assessment Program. State Board of Education, Michigan Department of Education, Lansing.

Romanella, N. E. et al. (1991). Physical activity and attitudes in lean and obese children and their mothers. *International Journal of Obesity, 15,* 407–414.

Ross, J. G. et al. (1987). Changes in the body composition of children. *Journal of Physical Education, Recreation and Dance, 58*(9), 74–77.

Sallis, J. F., & Patrick, K. (1994). Physical activity guidelines for adolescents: Consensus statement. *Pediatric Exercise Science, 6,* 302–314.

Updyke, W. (1992). In search of relevant and credible physical fitness standards for children. *Research Quarterly for Exercise and Sport, 63,* 112–119.

Williams, H. G. (1983). *Perceptual and Motor Development.* Englewood Cliffs, NJ: Prentice-Hall.

CHAPTER 18
ADOLESCENT SOCIALIZATION

American Academy of Pediatrics. (2001). *Some Things You Should Know About Preventing Teen Suicide.* Online: www.aap.org/advocacy/childhealthmonth/prevteensuicide.htm.

America's Children 2000. (2000). *Part I: Population and Family Characteristics.* Online: http://childstats.gov.

Anderson, N., & Wold, B. (1992). Parental and peer influences on leisure-time physical activity in young adolescents. *Research Quarterly for Exercise and Sport, 63,* 341–348.

Arnold, P. J. (2001). Sport, motor development, and the role of the teacher: Implications for research and moral education. *Quest, 53,* 135–150.

Bungum, T. et al. (2000). Correlates of physical activity in male and female youth. *Pediatric Exercise Science, 12,* 71–79.

Carnegie Council on Adolescent Development. (1995). *Great Transitions: Preparing Adolescents for the New Century.* Waldorf, MD: Author.

Coakley, J. J. (2001). *Sport in Society: Issues and Controversies.* Boston, MA: Times Mirror/Mosby.

Gould, D. (1987). Understanding attrition in children's sports. In D. Gould & M. R. Weiss (Eds.), *Advances in Pediatric Sport Sciences: Vol. 2. Behavioral Issues.* Champaign, IL: Human Kinetics.

Greendorfer, S. L. (1977). Role of socializing agents in female sports involvement. *Research Quarterly, 48,* 304–310.

Greendorfer, S. L., & Lewko, J. H. (1978). Role of family members in sport socialization of children. *Research Quarterly, 49,* 149–152.

Greenspan, (1983). *Little Winners: Inside the World of the Child Sports Star.* Boston: Little, Brown.

Hunter, J. D. (2000). *The Death of Character. Moral Education in an Age without Good or Evil* (Chapter 1–2). New York: Basic Books.

Kohlberg, L. (1981). *The Philosophy of Moral Development: Moral Stages and Idea of Justice.* San Francisco: Harper & Row.

————. (1984). *Essays of Moral Development: Vol. 2. The Psychology of Moral Development.* San Francisco: Harper & Row.

Lumpkin, A., Stoll, S. K., & Beller, J. M. (1994). *Sport Ethics.* St. Louis, MO: Mosby.

Morgan, W., Meier, K., & Schneider, A. (2001). *Ethics in Sport.* Champaign, IL: Human Kinetics.

Raudsepp, L., & Viira, R. (2000). Sociocultural Correlates of Physical Activity in Adolescents. *Pediatric Exercise Science, 12,* 51–60.

Sage, G. H. (1986). Social development. In V. Seefeldt (Ed.), *Physical Activity and Well-Being.* Reston, VA: AAHPERD.

Sallis, J. F., & Nadar, P. R. (1988). Family determinants of health behavior. In G. Roberts (Ed.). *Health Behavior: Emerging Research Perspectives.* New York: Plenum Press.

Seefeldt, V. et al. (1992). *Overview of Youth Sports Programs in the United States.* New York: Carnegie Council on Adolescent Development.

Shields, D. L. L., & Bredemeier, B. J. L. (1995). *Character Development and Physical Activity.* Champaign, IL: Human Kinetics.

U.S. Department of Commerce, Bureau of the Census. (2000). *Statistical Abstract of the United States.* Washington, DC: U.S. Government Printing Office.

U.S. Department of Justice. (1998). National Institute of Justice News: Moore, M. H., & Tonry, M. (1998). *Youth Violence in America.* Chicago: University of Chicago Press. Online: http://www.oip.usdoj.gov/nij/newsletter/0499chapter.html.

U.S. Olympic Committee. (1996). *Coaching Ethics Code.* Colorado Springs, CO: Author.

Weiss, M. R. (1987). Self-esteem and achievement in children's sport and physical activity. In D. Gould &

M. R. Weiss (Eds.), *Advances in Pediatric Sport Sciences, Vol. 2: Behavioral Issues.* Champaign, IL: Human Kinetics.

CHAPTER 19
PHYSIOLOGICAL CHANGES IN ADULTS

Boileau, R. A., et al. (1999). Aerobic exercise training and cardiorespiratory fitness in older adults: A randomized control trial. *Journal of Aging and Physical Activity, 7,* 374–385.

Chodzko-Zajko, W. (1999a). Active aging in the new millennium. *Journal of Aging and Physical Activity, 7,* 213–216.

———. (1999b). Successful aging in the new millennium: The role of regular physical activity. *Quest, 52,* 333–343.

Drinkwater, B. L. (1992). *Osteoporosis: The 'Silent Thief' of the Golden Years.* Presented at the American Alliance for Health, Physical Education, Recreation and Dance National Convention, Indianapolis, IN.

———. (1994). 1994 C. H. McCloy Research Lecture: Does physical activity play a role in preventing osteoporosis? *Research Quarterly for Exercise and Sport, 65,* 197–206.

Dummer, G. M., Vaccaro, P., & Clarke, D. H. (1985). Muscular strength and flexibility of two female masters swimmers in the eighth decade of life. *Journal of Orthopaedic and Sports Physical Therapy, 6,* 235–237.

Fiatarone, M. A., et al. (1990). High-intensity strength training in nonagenarians. *Journal of the American Medical Association, 263,* 3029–3034.

Guyton, A. C. (1991). *Textbook of Medical Physiology.* 8th ed. Philadelphia: W. B. Saunders.

Hayflick, L. (1980). The cell biology of human aging. *Scientific American, 242,* 58–65.

Hoyer, W. J., Rybash, J. M., & Roodin, P. A. (1999). *Adult Development and Aging.* 4th ed. St. Louis: McGraw-Hill.

Ivanco, T. L., & Greenough, W. T. (2000). Physiological consequences of morphologically detectable synaptic plasticity: Potential uses for examining recovery following damage. *Neuropharmacology, 39,* 765–776.

Jones, T. A., & Greenough, W. T. (1996). Ultrastructural evidence for increased contact between astrocytes and synapses in rats reared in a complex environment. *Neurobiology of Learning and Memory, 65,* 48–56.

Jones, T. A., Klintsova, A. Y., Kilman, V. L., Sirevaag, A. M., & Greenough, W. T. (1997). Induction of multiple synapses by experience in the visual cortex of adult rats. *Neurobiology of Learning and Memory, 68,* 13–20.

Kleim, J. A., Pipitone, M. A., Czerlanis, C., & Greenough, W. T. (1998). Structural stability within the lateral cerebellar nucleus of the rat following complex motor learning. *Neurobiology of Learning and Memory, 69,* 290–306.

Kleim, J. A., et al. (1998). Selective synaptic plasticity within the cerebellar cortex following complex motorskill learning, *Neurobiology of Learning and Memory, 69,* 274–289.

Kramer, A. F. (2000). Physical and mental training: Implications for cognitive functioning in old age. *Journal of Aging and Physical Activity, 8,* 363–365.

Kramer, A. F., Hahn, S., & McAuley, E. (2000). Influence of aerobic fitness on the neurocognitive function of older adults. *Journal of Aging and Physical Activity, 8,* 379–385.

Lemmer, J. T., et al. (2000). Age and gender responses to strength training and detraining. *Medicine and Science in Sports and Exercise, 32,* 1505–1512.

Malina, R. M. (1996). Tracking of physical activity and physical fitness across the lifespan. *Research Quarterly for Exercise and Sport, 67,* 48–57.

Mathiowetz, V., et al. (1985). Grip and pinch strength: Normative data for adults. *Archives of Physical Medicine and Rehabilitation, 66,* 69–72.

———. (1995). *Physical Dimensions of Aging.* Champaign, IL: Human Kinetics.

O'Neill, D. E. T., Thayer, R. E., Taylor, A. W., Dzialoszynski, T. M., & Noble, E. G. (2000). Effects of short-term resistance training on muscle strength and morphology in the elderly. *Journal of Aging and Physical Activity, 8,* 312–324.

Samson, M. M., et al. (2000). Relationships between physical performance measures, age, height and body weight in healthy adults. *Age and Aging, 29,* 235–242.

Shephard, R. J. (1997). *Aging, Physical Activity, and Health.* Champaign, IL: Human Kinetics.

Spirduso, W. W. (1995). *Physical Dimensions of Aging.* Champaign, IL: Human Kinetics.

Spirduso, W. W., & MacRae, P. G. (1990). Motor performance and aging. In J. E. Birren & K. W. Schaie (Eds.), *Handbook of the Psychology of Aging.* 3rd ed. San Diego, CA: Academic Press.

U.S. Census Bureau. 2001. *Population Estimates Program and Population Projections Program.* Washington, DC.

Westhoff, M. H., Stemmerik, L., & Boshuizen, H. C. (2000). Effects of a low-intensity strength training program on knee-extensor strength and functional ability of frail older people. *Journal of Aging and Physical Activity, 8,* 325–342.

CHAPTER 20
MOTOR PERFORMANCE IN ADULTS

Baylor, A. M., & Spirduso, W. W. (1988). Systematic aerobic exercise and components of reaction time in older women. *Journal of Gerontology, 43,* 121–126.

Carmeli, E., Coleman, R., Omar, H. L., & Brown-Cross, D. (2000). Do we allow elderly pedestrians sufficient time to cross the street in safety? *Journal of Aging and Physical Activity, 8,* 51–58.

Chen, H. C., Ashton-Miller, J. A., Alexander, N. B., & Schultz, A. B. (1991). Stepping over obstacles: Gait patterns of healthy young and old adults. *Journal of Gerontology, 46,* 196–203.

Chodzko-Zajko, W. J. (1991). Physical fitness, cognitive performance and aging. *Medicine and Science in Sports and Exercise. 23,* 868–872.

Crilly, R. G., Willems, D. A., Trenholm, K. J., Hayes, K. C., & Delaquerriere-Richardson, L. F. (1989). Effect of exercise on postural sway in the elderly. *Gerontology, 35,* 137–143.

Dacey, J., & Travers, J. (1991). *Human Development Across the Lifespan.* Dubuque, IA: Wm. C. Brown.

Dummer, G. M., Vaccaro, P., & Clarke, D. H. (1985). Muscular strength and flexibility of two female masters swimmers in the eighth decade of life. *Journal of Orthopaedic and Sports Physical Therapy, 6,* 235–237.

Dunn, J. E., Rudberg, M. A., Furrier, S. E., & Cassel, C. K. (1992). Mortality, disability, and falls in older persons: The role of underlying disease and disability. *American Journal of Public Health, 82,* 395–400.

Elble, R. J., Hughes, L., & Higgins, C. (1991). The syndrome of senile gait. *Journal of Neurology, 239,* 71–75.

Ericsson, K. A. (2000). How experts attain and maintain superior performance: Implications for the enhancement of skilled performance in older individuals. *Journal of Aging and Physical Activity, 8,* 366–372.

Ferrandez, A. M., Pailhous, J., & Durup, M. (1990). Slowness in elderly gait. *Experimental Aging Research, 16,* 79–89.

Fiatarone, M. A., et al. (1990). High intensity strength training in nonagenarians. *Journal of the American Medical Association, 263,* 3029–3034.

Fisk, A. D., & Rogers, W. A. (2000). Influence of training and experience on skill acquisition and maintenance in older adults. *Journal of Aging and Physical Activity, 8,* 373–378.

Forssberg, H., & Nashner, L. (1982). Ontogenetic development of posture control in man: Adaptation to altered support and visual conditions during stance. *Journal of Neuroscience, 2,* 545–552.

Hart, D., Bowling, A., Ellis, M., & Silman, A. (1990). Locomotor disability in very elderly people: Value of a programme for screening and provision of aids for daily living. *British Medical Journal, 301,* 216–220.

Hodgkins, J. (1963). Reaction time and speed of movement in males and females of various ages. *Research Quarterly, 34,* 335–343.

Hortobágyi, T., & DeVita, P. (1999). Altered movement strategy increases lower extremity stiffness during stepping down in the aged. *Journal of Gerontology: Biological Sciences, 54A,* B63–B70.

Hoyer, W. J., Rybash, J. M., & Roodin, P. A. (1999). *Adult Development and Aging.* 4th ed. St. Louis, MO: McGraw-Hill.

Hunter, S. K., Thompson, M. W., & Adams, R. D. (2001). Reaction time, strength, and physical activity in women aged 20–89 years. *Journal of Aging and Physical Activity, 9,* 32–42.

International Amateur Athletic Federation (IAAF). (1996–2001). *World Records.* Principality of Monaco.

International Amateur Athletic Federation (IAAF). (1997). *World Records.* Principality of Monaco.

Jackson, T. W., & Lyles, K. W. (1990). Hip fractures. In W. R. Hazzard, R. Andres, E. L. Bierman, & J. P. Blass (Eds.), *Principles of Geriatric Medicine and Gerontology* 2nd ed. New York: McGraw-Hill.

Koller, W. C., & Glatt, S. L. (1990). Gait disorders. In W. R. Hazzard, R. Andres, E. L. Bierman, & J. P. Blass (Eds.), *Principles of Geriatric Medicine and Gerontology.* 2nd ed. New York: McGraw-Hill.

Kroll, W., & Clarkson, P. M. (1977). *Fractionated Reflex Time, Resisted and Unresisted Fractionated Reaction Time Under Normal and Fatigued Conditions.* Paper presented at the Annual Conference of the North American Society for the Psychology of Sport and Physical Activity, Ithaca College, Ithaca, NY.

Kronhed, A.G., Möller, C., Olsson, B., & Möller, M. (2001). The effect of short-term balance training on community-dwelling older adults. *Journal of Aging and Physical Activity, 9,* 19–31.

Manchester, D., Woollacott, M., Zederbauer-Hylton, N., & Marin, O. (1989). Visual, vestibular and somatosensory contributions to balance control in the older adult. *Journal of Gerontology, 44,* 118–127.

Mundle, P., Dietderich, S., & Harvey, R. (1996). *Masters Age Records.* North Hollywood, CA: National Masters News.

National Masters News (2000). Eugene, OR.

Pierson, W. R., & Montoye, H. J. (1958). Movement time, reaction time, and age. *Journal of Gerontology, 13,* 418–421.

Rikli, R. E., & Edwards, D. J. (1991). Effects of a three-year exercise program on motor function and cognitive processing speed in older women. *Research Quarterly for Exercise and Sport, 62,* 61–67.

Rimmer, J. H. (1994). *Fitness and Rehabilitation Programs for Special Populations.* St. Louis, MO: McGraw-Hill.

Rosengren, K. S. et al. (1995). Gait adjustments in sedentary and exercising older adults. *Journal of Sport & Exercise Psychology, 17,* S90.

Salthouse, T. A. (1976). Speed and age: Multiple rates of age decline. *Experimental Aging Research, 2,* 349–359.

Santrock, J. W. (1999). *Lifespan Development.* 7th ed. St. Louis: McGraw-Hill.

Schmidt, R. A. (1988). *Motor Control and Learning: A Behavioral Emphasis.* Champaign, IL: Human Kinetics.

Shephard, R. J. (1997). *Aging, Physical Activity, and Health.* Champaign, IL: Human Kinetics.

Shephard, R. J., Berridge, M., & Montelpare, W. (1990). On the generality of the 'sit and reach' test: An analysis of flexibility data for an aging population. *Research Quarterly for Exercise and Sport, 61,* 326–330.

Spirduso, W. W. (1975). Reaction and movement time as a function of age and physical activity level. *Journal of Gerontology, 30,* 435–440.

———. (1986). Physical activity and the prevention of premature aging. In V. Seefeldt (Ed.), *Physical Activity & Well-Being.* Reston, VA: American Alliance for Health, Physical Education, Recreation, and Dance.

———. (1995). *Physical Dimensions of Aging.* Champaign, IL: Human Kinetics.

Spirduso, W. W., & Clifford, P. (1978). Replication of age and physical activity effects on reaction and movement time. *Journal of Gerontology, 33,* 26–30.

Spirduso, W. W., & MacRae, P. G. (1990). Motor performance and aging. In J. E. Birren & K. W. Schaie (Eds.), *Handbook of the Psychology of Aging.* 3rd ed. San Diego, CA: Academic Press.

Stones, M. J., & Kozma, A. (1980). Adult age trends in record running performances. *Experimental Aging Research, 6,* 407–416.

———. (1981). Adult age trends in athletic performance. *Experimental Aging Research, 7,* 269–280.

———. (1982). Cross-sectional, longitudinal, and secular age trends in athletic performances. *Experimental Aging Research, 8,* 185–188.

———. (1986). Age by distance effects in running and swimming records: A note on methodology. *Experimental Aging Research, 12,* 203–206.

Teasdale, N., Stelmach, G. E., & Breunig, A. (1991). Postural sway characteristics of the elderly under normal and altered visual and support surface conditions. *Journal of Gerontology, 46,* 238–244.

Tinetti, M. E. (1990). Falls. In W. R. Hazzard, R. Andres, E. L. Bierman, & J. P. Blass (Eds.), *Principles of Geriatric Medicine and Gerontology.* 2nd ed. New York: McGraw-Hill.

USA Track and Field. (1996). *Masters Records.* Indianapolis, Indiana.

VanSant, A. F. (1990). Life-span development in functional tasks. *Physical Therapy, 70,* 788–798.

Wall, J. C., Hogan, D. B., Turnbull, G. I., & Fox, R. A. (1991). The kinematics of idiopathic gait disorder: A comparison with healthy young and elderly females. *Scandinavian Journal of Rehabilitation Medicine, 23,* 159–164.

Whipple, R. H., Wolfson, L. I., & Amerman, P. M. (1987). The relationship of knee and ankle weakness to falls in nursing home residents: An isokinetic study. *Journal of the American Geriatrics Society, 35,* 13–20.

Woollacott, M., Inglin, B., & Manchester, D. (1988). Response preparation and posture control: Neuromuscular changes in the older adult. *Annals of the New York Academy of Sciences, 515,* 42–53.

Woollacott, M. H., & Shumway-Cook, A. (1990). Changes in posture control across the life span: A systems approach. *Physical Therapy, 70,* 799–807.

Woollacott, M. H., Shumway-Cook, A., & Nashner, L. M. (1986). Aging and posture control: Changes in sensory organization and muscular coordination. *International Journal of Aging and Human Development, 23,* 97–114.

CHAPTER 21
PSYCHOSOCIAL DEVELOPMENT IN ADULTS

Arent, S. M., Landers, D. M., & Etnier, J. L. (2000). The effects of exercise on mood in older adults: A meta-analytic review. *Journal of Aging and Physical Activity, 8,* 407–430.

Behlendorf, B., MacRae, P. G., & Vos Strache, C. (1999). Children's perceptions of physical activity for adults:

Competence and appropriateness, *Journal of Aging and Physical Activity, 7,* 354–373.

Berryman-Miller, S. (1988). Dance movement: Effects on elderly self-concept. *Journal of Physical Education, Recreation, and Dance, 59*(5), 42–46.

Chodzko-Zajko, W. (1999). Active aging in the new millennium. *Journal of Aging and Physical Activity, 7,* 213–216.

Dacey, J., & Travers, J. (1999). *Human Development Across the Lifespan.* 4th ed. St. Louis: McGraw-Hill.

Goggin, N. L., & Morrow, J. R. (2001). Physical activity behaviors of older adults. *Journal of Aging and Physical Activity, 9,* 58–66.

Hird, J. S., & Williams, J. M. (1989). The psychological effects of chronic exercise in the elderly. In A. C. Ostrow (Ed.), *Aging and Motor Behavior.* Indianapolis, IN: Benchmark Press.

Hoyer, W. J., Rybash, J. M., & Roodin, P. A. (1999). *Adult Development and Aging.* 4th ed. St. Louis, MO: McGraw-Hill.

Khatri, P., et al. (2001). Effects of exercise training on cognitive functioning among depressed older men and women. *Journal of Aging and Physical Activity, 9,* 43–57.

Levinson, D. J. (1978). *The Seasons of Man's Life.* New York: Knopf.

———. (1986). A conception of adult development. *American Psychologist, 47,* 3–13.

———. (1996). *Seasons of a Woman's Life.* New York: Alfred Knopf.

Loomis, R. A., & Thomas, C. D. (1991). Elderly women in nursing home and independent residence: Health, body attitudes, self-esteem and life satisfaction. *Canadian Journal on Aging, 70,* 224–231.

McAuley, E., Blissmer, B., Katula, J., Duncan, T. E., & Mihalko, S. L. (2000). Physical activity, self-esteem, and self-efficacy relationships in older adults: A randomized controlled trial. *Annals of Behavioral Medicine, 22,* 131–139.

Osness, W. H., & Mulligan, L. (1998). Physical activity and depression among older adults. *Journal of Physical Education, Recreation and Dance, 69*(9), 16–18, 28.

Palmore, E. (1979). Predictors of successful aging. *The Gerontologist, 19,* 427–431.

———. (1982). Predictors of the longevity difference: A 25-year follow-up. *The Gerontologist, 22,* 513–518.

Perri, S., & Templer, D. (1985). The effects of an aerobic exercise program on psychological variables in older

adults. *International Journal of Aging and Human Development, 20,* 167–172.

Rowe, J. W., & Kahn, R. L. (1997). Successful aging. *The Gerontologist, 37,* 433–440.

———. (1998). *Successful Aging.* New York: Pantheon Books.

Santrock, J. W. (1999). *Lifespan Development.* 7th ed. St. Louis: McGraw-Hill.

Shock, N. W. (1985). Longitudinal studies of aging in humans. In C. E. Finch & E. L. Schneider (Eds.), *Handbook of the Biology of Aging.* 2nd ed. New York: Van Nostrand Reinhold.

Spirduso, W. W. (1995). *Physical Dimensions of Aging.* Champaign, IL: Human Kinetics.

Thomas, C. L. (Ed.) (1989). *Taber's Cyclopedic Medical Dictionary.* Philadelphia: F. A. Davis.

Valliant, P. M., & Asu, M. E. (1985). Exercise and its effects on cognition and physiology in older adults. *Perceptual and Motor Skills, 51,* 499–505.

Williamson, J. B., Munley, A., & Evans, L. (1980). *Aging and Society: An Introduction to Social Gerontology.* New York: Holt, Rinehart & Winston.

CHAPTER 22
ASSESSING MOTOR BEHAVIOR

Apgar, V. (1953). A proposal for a new method of evaluation of the newborn infant. *Current Research in Anesthesia and Analgesia, 32,* 260–267.

Apgar, V., & James, L. S. (1962). Further observations on the newborn scoring system. *American Journal of the Diseases of Children, 704,* 419–428.

Arnheim, D. D., & Sinclair, W. A. (1979). *The Clumsy Child.* St. Louis: C. V. Mosby.

———. (1969). *Manual for the Bayley Scales of Infant Development.* New York: Harper & Row.

Bayley, N. (1993). *Bayley Scales of Infant Development, Second Edition.* San Antonio, TX: The Psychological Corp.

Block, M. E., Lieberman, L. J., & Conner-Kuntz, F. (1998). Authentic assessment in adapted physical education. *Journal of Physical Education, Recreation, and Dance, 69*(3), 48–57.

Bruininks, R. H. (1978). *Bruininks-Oseretsky Test of Motor Proficiency.* Circle Pines, MN: American Guidance Service.

Burton, A. W., & Miller, D. E. (1998). *Movement Skill Assessment.* Champaign, IL: Human Kinetics.

Davis, W. E., & Burton, A. W. (1991). Ecological task analysis: Translating movement behavior theory into practice. *Adapted Physical Activity Quarterly, 8,* 154–177.

Folio, M. R., & Fewell, R. R. (2000). *Peabody Developmental Motor Scales.* 2nd ed. Austin, TX: Pro-Ed.

Frankenburg, W. K. et al. (1990). *Denver II Technical Manual.* Denver, CO: Denver Developmental Materials, Inc.

———. (1992). The Denver II: A major revision and restandardization of the Denver Developmental Screening Test. *Pediatrics, 89,* 91–97.

Frankenburg, W. K., & Dodds, J. B. (1967). The Denver Developmental Screening Test. *Journal of Pediatrics, 71,* 181–191.

Gallahue, D. L., & Cleland, F. (2003). *Developmental Physical Education for Today's Children.* 4th edition. Champaign, IL: Human Kinetics.

Haubenstricker, J. et al. (1981, April). *The efficiency of the Bruininks-Oseretsky Test of Motor Proficiency in discriminating between normal children and those with gross motor dysfunction.* Paper presented at the Motor Development Academy at the AAHPERD Convention, Boston, MA.

Henderson, S. E., & Sugden, D. A. (1992). *Movement Assessment Battery for Children.* Sidcup, Kent, England: Therapy Skill Builders.

Ignico, A. (1994). *Assessment of Fundamental Motor Skills Videotapes.* Dubuque, IA: Brown & Benchmark.

Law, M., & Letts, L. (1989). A critical review of scales of activities of daily living. *The American Journal of Occupational Therapy, 43,* 522–528.

Linder, T. W. (1990). *Transdisciplinary Play-Based Assessment: A Functional Approach to Working with Young Children.* Baltimore, MD: P. H. Brookes.

Linder, T. W. (1993). *Transdisciplinary Play-Based Assessment: A Functional Approach to Working with Young Children.* 2nd ed. Baltimore, MD: Brookes.

McClenaghan, B. A. (1976). *Development of an Observational Instrument to Assess Selected Fundamental Movement Patterns of Low Motor Functioning Children.* Unpublished doctoral dissertation, Indiana University.

McClenaghan, B. A., & Gallahue, D. L. (1978). *Fundamental Movement: Observation and Assessment.* Philadelphia: W. B. Saunders.

Ohio State University Scale of *Intra Gross Motor Assessment.* Loundonville, OH: Mohican Publishing Co.

Palisano, R. J. et al. (1995). Validity of the Peabody Developmental Gross Motor Scale as an evaluative measure of infants receiving physical therapy. *Physical Therapy, 75,* 939–951.

Payne, V. G., & Isaacs, L. D. (2002). *Human Motor Development: A Lifespan Approach.* 5th ed. Boston: McGraw-Hill.

Peabody Developmental Motor Scales. Allen, TX: DLM Teaching Resources Corp.

Riggen, K. J., Ulrich, D. A., & Ozmun, J. C. (1990). Reliability and concurrent validity of the Test of Motor Impairment Henderson Revision. *Adapted Physical Activity Quarterly, 7,* 249–258.

Seefeldt, V., & Haubenstricker, J. (1976). *Developmental sequences of fundamental motor skills.* Unpublished research, Michigan State University.

Sherrill, C. (1998). *Adapted Physical Activity, Recreation and Sport: Crossdisciplinary and Lifespan.* 5th ed. St. Louis: McGraw-Hill.

Spirduso, W. W. (1995). *Physical Dimensions of Aging.* Champaign, IL: Human Kinetics.

Test of Motor Impairment-Henderson Revision. San Antonio, TX: The Psychological Corp.

Ulrich, D. A. (1985). *Test of Gross Motor Development.* Austin, TX: Pro-ED.

———. (1988). Children with special needs: Assessing the quality of movement competence. *Journal of Physical Education, Recreation & Dance, 59*(1), 43–47.

———. (1998). *The Test of Gross Motor Development.* 2nd ed. Austin, TX: Pro-Eds.

Verderber, J. M. S., & Payne, V. G. (1987). A comparison of the long and short forms of the Bruininks-Oseretsky Test of Motor Proficiency. *Adapted Physical Activity Quarterly, 4,* 51–59.

Winnick, J. P. (Ed.) (2000). *Adapted Physical Education and Sport.* 3rd ed. Champaign, IL: Human Kinetics.

Zittel, L. L. (1994). Gross motor assessment of preschool children with special needs: Instrument selection considerations. *Adapted Physical Activity Quarterly, 11,* 245–260.

CHAPTER 23
PROGRAMMING FOR DEVELOPMENTAL PHYSICAL ACTIVITY

Gallahue, D. L. & Cleland, F. (2003). *Developmental Physical Education for Today's Children.* 4th edition. Champaign, IL: Human Kinetics.

Gentile, A. M. (2000). Skill acquisition: Action, movement, and neuromotor processes. In J. H. Carr & R. B. Shepherd (Eds.). *Movement Science, Foundations for Physical Therapy.* 2nd ed. Rockville, MD: Aspen.

Keough, J., & Sugden, D. (1985). *Movement Skill Development.* New York: Macmillan.

Laban, R., & Lawrence, F. (1947). *Effort.* London: Unwin Brothers.

Mosston, M., & Ashworth, S. (1994). *Teaching Physical Education.* Columbus, OH: Charles E. Merrill.

GLOSSARY

A

Accelerometer. An electro-mechanical device worn by the subject that detects and records motion in a single plane or in multiple planes.

Accommodation. Adaptation that the child must make to the environment when new and incongruent information is added to his or her repertoire of possible responses. A process that reaches outward toward reality and results in a visible change in behavior.

Accommodation (Visual). The ability of the lens of each eye to vary its curvature to bring the retinal image into focus.

Activity Concepts. Knowledge of where the body should move in terms of patterns, formations, rules, and strategies.

Activity Theory. A theory of aging that states that as adults grow older they require interaction with other people and continued physical activity to be happy and satisfied.

Adaptation. The process of making adjustments to environmental conditions and intellectualizing these adjustments through the complementary processes of accommodation and assimilation.

Adolescent Growth Spurt (Circumpubertal Period). The adolescent growth spurt that lasts up to four and a half years.

Advanced/Fine-Tuning Level. The third stage of learning a movement skill characterized by the performer gaining a complete understanding of the skill. At this level the skill is performed smoothly, fluidly, and in a highly coordinated manner. The performer places emphasis on refining and fine-tuning the skill.

Aerobic Endurance. The ability to perform numerous repetitions of a stressful activity requiring considerable use of the circulatory and respiratory systems.

Affordances. Factors that tend to promote or encourage developmental change.

Ageism. The stereotyping or discriminating against older adults on the basis of prejudice.

Age Markers. Abnormal formations that appear in the older brain and increase in number as the brain continues to age.

Agility. The ability to change direction of the entire body quickly and accurately while moving from one point to another.

Algorithm. A procedure or set of rules to follow that will lead to the solution of a given problem. From a dynamic systems perspective of development, algorithms are tested to predict and explain motor behavior.

Anabolic Hormones. Muscle-enhancing hormones such as human growth hormone and testosterone.

Anorexia Nervosa. A severe emotional disorder typified by an aversion to food and an obsession with thinness that may result in death.

Antioxidants. A substance that when ingested prevents or inhibits oxidation by binding with free radicals before they harm healthy body cells. Serves as a basis for a theory of aging reversal intervention.

Application Stage. The stage within the specialized movement phase that represents a heightened awareness of personal physical assets and limitations, and more complex skills are refined and used in official sports and designated recreational activities for both leisure and competition.

Arteriosclerosis. An age-related condition in which the arterial walls become less elastic.

Assimilation. Interpretation of new information based on present interpretations by taking in information from the environment and incorporating it into one's existing cognitive structures.

Associative Stage. The movement skill learning stage at which the learner is able to make conscious use of environmental cues and associate them with the requirements of the movement task.

Atherosclerosis. A cardiovascular disease represented by fatty deposits collecting within arteries.

Atrophy. A decrease in the size of muscle fibers.

Attitude. An emotion that results in a feeling of like or dislike about something.

Auditory Perception. The ability to receive and process information that is obtained by the sense of hearing.

Autonomous Stage. The movement skill learning stage at which performance of the movement task becomes habitual, with little or no conscious attention given to the elements of the task.

Awareness Stage. The movement skill learning stage at which the cognitive state of the learner involves being naive and ignorant about the nature of the task, its basic requirements, and its appropriate terminology.

B

Balance. The ability to maintain one's equilibrium in relation to the force of gravity. Balance may be static, dynamic, or rotational.

Balance and Postural Control. The maintenance of a state of equilibrium of the body and its parts in response to the force of gravity. Interaction of the muscles and joints, vision, vestibular and somatosensory systems, and body morphology contribute to the maintenance of balance and postural control.

Beginning/Novice Level. The first level in learning a new movement skill often characterized by slow, uncoordinated, and jerky movements accompanied by conscious attention to every detail of the activity.

Behavior Setting Theory. A branch of ecological psychology that contends that the specific environmental conditions of one's life space account for a large portion of individual variation. Different

settings evoke different responses and hence lead to different patterns of development.

Belief. Something held to be true based on a strong cognitive component.

Between-Child Differences. Variations in the level of skill performance maturity from one child to the next.

Between-Pattern Differences. Variations in the level of skill performance maturity from one fundamental movement skill to the next.

Bifoveal Fixation. Alignment of the fovea of both eyes in such a manner that visual fusion can occur.

Binocular Vision. The working together of both eyes to provide depth perception.

Biological Age. A variable age that corresponds roughly to chronological age, determined by measures of morphological, skeletal, dental, or sexual age.

Body Awareness. The developing capacity to accurately discriminate among body parts and to gain a greater understanding of the nature of the body and its movement in space.

Body Composition. The proportion of lean body mass to fat body mass.

Body Mass Index (BMI). An estimation of percent body fat arrived at by calculating:

$$wt(kg) \div stature(cm) \times 10,000$$
$$or$$
$$wt(lb) \div stature(in) \times 703$$

Bonding. A strong emotional attachment that endures over time, distance, hardship, and desirability.

Bone Mineralization. A process promoted by physical activity that makes bone stronger and less brittle.

Brain Plasticity. The ability of the brain to adapt to trauma through mechanisms such as the establishing of compensatory neuronal pathways when primary pathways have been destroyed.

Bulimia Nervosa. A severe emotional disorder typified by regular bouts of food binging and purging that has serious health consequences.

C

Catabolic Hormones. Muscle-destroying hormones.

Category of Movement. Observable movement classified as either stabilizing, locomotor, or manipulative movements, or a combination of the three.

Chemical Pollutants. A category of environmental substances such as lead and mercury to which exposure by an expectant mother may result in birth defects.

Chromatic Intensity. The brightness or hue of a given color that may be measured across the entire color spectrum.

Chronic Malnutrition. Severe and prolonged undernourishment that may result in growth retardation in young children and a variety of nutrition-related conditions, including rickets, pellagra, scurvy, and kwashiorkor.

Cognitive Stage. The movement skill learning stage during which the learner tries to form a conscious mental plan for performing the skill.

Color Perception. The ability of the eyes to distinguish among different colors.

Combination Stage. The movement skill learning stage at which the learner begins to put movement skills together in different combinations, first in pairs and then in increasingly complex forms.

Competence. One's ability to meet particular achievement demands.

Congenital Malformations. Abnormal conditions with which an infant is born.

Consensual Pupillary Reflex. Pupil dilation in dim light and constriction in bright light.

Content Areas. The major areas of physical activity through which fundamental and specialized movement skills may be developed. They include educational games, dance, and gymnastics activities.

Contralateral Pattern. A movement pattern (generally creeping and walking) in which the arm and leg on the opposite side of the body move in unison.

Convenience Sample. The selection of subjects for research investigations based on availability rather than representation.

Coordination. The ability to integrate separate motor systems with varying sensory modalities into efficient movement.

Crawling. Forward motion from a prone position in which a homolateral pattern is used and the abdomen remains in contact with the supporting surface.

Creeping. Forward motion from a prone position in which a contralateral pattern is generally used and the abdomen is up off the supporting surface.

Criterion-Referenced Tests. Assessment instruments that incorporate a preestablished standard to which the individual's scores are compared.

Cross-Sectional Method. A method of study that looks at age-related differences in behavior by permitting the researcher to collect data on different groups of people at varying age levels at the same point in time, yielding average differences across real time, but not individual changes across developmental time.

Cultural Socialization. A lifelong process by which an infant becomes an adult in a cultural setting, accomplished by modifying one's behavior to conform to the expectations of a group.

D

Daily Living Activities. Movement-oriented tasks that individuals carry out throughout their lives that are required for basic everyday needs.

Decoding Stage. The time during the reflexive movement phase when higher brain centers gain greater control of the sensorimotor apparatus and the infant is able to process information more efficiently.

Deductive Theory Formulation. An approach to theory building based on statistical inference. Deductive theories integrate existing facts, lend themselves to the formulation of testable hypotheses, and yield results that either refute or lend further support to the theory.

Depth Perception. The process by which one sees three-dimensionally through the use of monocular and binocular depth cues, and is accurately able to judge distance from oneself.

Descriptive Theory. Any theoretical framework that views development as occurring within typical age periods across the life span.

Development. Changes in an individual's level of functioning over time.

Developmental Direction. A principle of development used for explaining increased coordination and motor control as a function of the maturing nervous system in a predictable sequence from the head to the feet (cephalocaudal), and from the center of the body to its periphery (proximodistal).

Development Milestone Theory. A theory that focuses on subtle strategic indicators of how far development has progressed and views development as an unfolding and intertwining of developmental processes, not as a neat transition from one stage to another.

Developmental Task Theory.   A predictive theory that contends that there are essential tasks that individuals must accomplish within a specified time if they are to function effectively and meet the demands placed on them by society.

Directional Awareness.   A developing sensitivity to internal (laterality) and external sidedness (directionality).

Discovery Stage.   The movement skill learning stage at which the learner is consciously forming a mental plan of how the task should be performed.

Disengagement Theory.   A theory of aging that states that as people age they begin to lose relationships, gradually abandon past interests, and eventually withdraw from society.

Dishabituation.   Measurable increase in reaction to a stimulus after habituation has occurred.

Down Syndrome.   A condition that results from an extra chromosome and results in motor and mental delays and distinct physical features.

Dynamic Flexibility.   The range of motion achieved when rapidly moving a body part to its limits.

Dynamic Systems Theory.   A branch of ecological psychology that views development as a nonlinear, discontinuous, self-organizing process composed of several factors—the task, the individual, and the environment—operating separately and in concert that determine the rate, sequence, and extent of development.

Dynamometer.   A calibrated device that permits measurement of grip strength, leg strength, and back strength.

E

Early Intervention.   Enrichment strategies implemented with high-risk infants in an effort to counteract conditions that may lead to later developmental impairment.

Ecological Task Analysis.   An approach to examining performance in light of the relationships among the task goal, the environment, and the performer.

Ecological Theory.   Also known as "contextual theory"; a theory that is descriptive and explanatory and views development as a function of the environmental "context" and historical time frame in which one lives. The study of human ecology from this developmental perspective is a matter of studying the relationship of individuals to their environment and to one another.

Ectoderm.   The layer of cells during the embryonic period that represent the origins of the sense organs and nervous system.

Ectomorphic.   A classification of physique characterized by a tall, thin, lean appearance.

Ejaculation.   A male's sudden ejection of seminal fluid.

Electrical Impedance.   A method of determining percent body fat by administering a small electrical current through the body and estimating body composition from the current's velocity through the body.

Embryo.   The human organism that begins at the time when the cells differentiate into three layers and continues until it is firmly implanted in the uterine wall and receiving nourishment through the placenta and umbilical cord.

Encoding Stage.   The time during the reflexive movement phase when reflexes play a role in gathering information for storage in the developing cortex.

Endoderm.   The layer of cells during the embryonic period that represent the origins of the digestive, respiratory, and glandular systems.

Endomorphic.   A classification of physique that represents soft and rounded physical features.

Environmental Context.   The environmental conditions under which a movement task is performed.

Estrogens.   The female hormones that account for the initiation of the events of female puberty.

Experience.   Environmental factors that may alter the appearance of various developmental characteristics through the process of learning.

Explanatory Theory.   Any theoretical framework that proposes explanations for questions about developmental processes.

Exploratory Stage.   The movement skill learning stage at which the learner has a conscious awareness of the basic requirements of the task and begins to experiment with performing the task in a variety of ways.

Externally Paced Skills.   A category of skills in which the performer must make rapid responses to changes in environmental cues.

Evoked Potentials.   A method for studying changes in electrical brain responses that yields useful stimulus response information.

F

Fetal Alcohol Syndrome. A condition that results from maternal alcohol abuse during pregnancy with the potential results of mental retardation and physical defects of the child.

Fetus. The human organism that begins at the time around the third month following conception and ends at birth.

Field Test. An assessment procedure conducted outside of a laboratory setting.

Figure-Ground Perception. The ability to separate an object of regard (visual, tactile, gustatory, etc.) from its background.

Fixation/Diversification Stage. The movement skill learning stage at which the goal of the learner is to achieve consistency of performance and the ability to adapt to changing conditions and to the task being an open or closed skill.

Force. The effort that one mass exerts on another resulting in movement, cessation of movement, or resistance of one body against another.

Form Perception. The ability to distinguish among shapes.

Fractionated RT. A process of breaking the complete reaction time process into various components.

Free Radicals. Unstable oxygen molecules produced through normal cell metabolism that ricochet around inside cells damaging DNA and other cell structures. Serves as a basis for a theory of aging.

Fundamental Movement. An organized series of related movements used to perform basic movement tasks such as running, jumping, throwing, and catching. Fundamental movements may be classified as locomotor, manipulative, or stabilizing.

Fundamental Movement Abilities. Observable patterns of motor behavior classified into initial, elementary, and mature stages and composed of basic locomotor activities such as running and jumping, manipulative activities such as throwing and catching, and stability activities such as balancing on one foot or walking on a narrow beam.

Fundamental Movement Pattern. The observable performance of a basic locomotor, manipulative, or stability movement that involves combining movement patterns of two or more body segments, such as performing an underhand or overhand throw in which developmentally appropriate arm, trunk, and leg actions are integrated.

Fusion. Combining two retinal images into a single visual pattern.

G

Gait. An individual's walking pattern. It consists of the swing phase and support phase.

Genetic Defects. Congenital disabilities of which autosomal recessive traits are frequently associated with developmental delays.

Genotype. An individual's genetic growth potential.

Getting the Idea Stage. The movement skill learning stage at which the primary goal of the learner is to obtain a basic awareness of the essential requirements for successful performance of the skill.

Giardia. A condition resulting in severe diarrhea caused by an intestinal parasite frequently transmitted through unsanitary water conditions.

Gold Standard. The ultimate and universally accepted measure of a particular quality. For example, a treadmill test of maximum aerobic capacity is the "gold standard" for assessing aerobic fitness.

Gonadotrophic (GnRH) Hormones. The male hormones that stimulate the endocrine glands to release growth and sex hormones.

Growth. An increase in the size of the body or its parts.

Growth Plate Injury. Damage to the epiphyseal growth plate of a growing bone that may result in premature growth cessation of that bone.

Growth Plates. Cartilaginous structures between the epiphyses of bone that are susceptible to injury in youth from excessive weight bearing.

Growth Rate. One's unique pattern of growth, resistant to external influence.

Growth Retardation. A condition when a child's height fails to fall within the growth norms for his or her age level.

Growth Spurt. A period during adolescence lasting up to four and a half years in which maximum velocity in height is achieved.

Guided-Discovery Method. A teaching style in which the instructor poses problems in the form of questions movement challenges.

Gustatory Perception. The ability to receive and process information obtained by the sense of taste.

H

Habituation. Measurable decline in reaction to a stimulus.

Health-Related Fitness. The aspect of physical fitness that refers to a relative state of being, not an ability, skill, or capacity. The development and maintenance of health-related fitness is a function of physiological adaptation to increased overload.

Heuristics. Rules of thumb or models that give one guidelines and cues for searching for answers to a given problem.

High-Risk Pregnancy. A pregnancy in which the expectant mother has a condition before or during pregnancy that increases her unborn child's chances of experiencing prenatal or postnatal problems.

Homeostasis. The maintenance of stability in the physiological systems and their interrelationships.

Homolateral Pattern. A movement pattern (generally crawling) in which the arm and leg on the same side of the body move in unison.

Hourglass Heuristic. A visual representation intended to aid in conceptualizing the complex process of human motor development that combines descriptive phases and stages, with an explanatory dynamic systems model.

Hydrostatic Weighing. A gold standard method of determining percent body fat by submerging an individual under water and calculating his or her underwater weight from which an accurate estimate of percent body fat can be calculated.

Hypertrophy. An increase in the size of muscle fibers.

Hyponatremia. Reduction in the body's serum sodium level sometimes induced in infants by swallowing excessive amounts of water.

Hypoxia. A condition in which the brain receives an inadequate amount of oxygen.

I

Illicit Drugs. A category of drugs of which the majority are illegal to use or sell and often contribute to problems with pregnancy and fetal development.

Individualized Stage. The final stage in learning a new movement skill. The learner makes fine-tuning adjustments in skill performance based on unique strengths or weaknesses and attributes or limitations.

Inductive Theory Formulation. A fact-based approach to theory building around which a conceptual framework is formed in an attempt to organize and explain these facts.

Interindividual Variability. The difference between individuals in regard to their rates of aging.

Intermediate/Practice Level. The second stage of learning a new movement skill characterized by the performer comprehending the general aspects of the skill. Conscious attention to the skill details diminishes as the mental image of the skill becomes more fixed.

Internally Paced Skills. A type of movement skills that require fixed responses to a given set of conditions.

Interrater Reliability. The consistency of accurate measurements by different individuals.

Intraindividual Variability. The different aging rates of the various body systems within an individual.

Intrarater Reliability. The consistency of accurate measurements by the same individual at different times.

Intraskill Sequences. Progressive variations of the performance of a variety of fundamental movement tasks establishing a series of descriptive stages.

Isokinetic. The ability of a muscle to go through its full range of motion in a contracted state at a constant velocity.

Isometric. The ability of a muscle to maintain a contracted state while exerting force and undergoing little or no change in its length.

Isotonic. The ability of a muscle to go through its full range of motion in a contracted state.

J

Joint Flexibility. The ability of the various joints of the body to move through their full range of motion.

L

Law of Acceleration. Newton's principle of movement that the change in the velocity of an object is directly proportional to the force producing the velocity and inversely proportional to the object's mass.

Law of Action and Reaction. Newton's principle of counterforce that states for every action there is an equal and opposite reaction.

Law of Inertia. The Newtonian principle that a body at rest will remain at rest, and a body in motion will remain in motion at the same speed in a straight line unless acted upon by an outside force.

Learning. An internal process that results in consistent observable changes in behavior.

Lifelong Utilization Stage. The stage within the specialized movement phase that represents an individual's attempt to reduce the scope of his or her athletic pursuits by choosing a few activities to engage in regularly in competitive, recreational, or daily living settings.

Life Structure. The underlying design or pattern of an individual's life at any given time.

Locomotion. Movement patterns that permit exploration through space (i.e., crawling, creeping, walking, running, jumping, hopping, etc.).

Longitudinal Method. A method of study that attempts to explain change over developmental time and involves charting various aspects of an individual's behavior for several years.

Low Birth Weight. A birth weight ranging from 1,500–2,000 grams.

M

Malnourishment. A state of inadequate nutritional intake or use by the expectant mother, the fetus, and/or the placenta that can result in later developmental difficulties.

Manipulation. Movement patterns that permit gross and fine motor contact with objects (i.e., grasping, throwing, catching, kicking, trapping, printing, cutting, etc.).

Maturation. A process of developmental change characterized by a fixed order of progression in which the pace may vary but the sequence of appearance of characteristics generally does not.

Maturity Assessment. Various approaches used in the determination of how far one has progressed toward physical maturation.

Maximal Oxygen Consumption (VO_2max). The largest quantity of oxygen one can consume during physical work; usually measured using a standardized treadmill or bicycle ergometer.

Menarche. The first menstrual flow of an adolescent female.

Mentors. Those helping others reach their goals.

Mesoderm. The layer of cells during the embryonic period that represent the origins of the muscular, skeletal, reproductive, and circulatory systems.

Mesomorphic. A classification of physique with physical features such as well-muscled, broad shoulders, narrow waist, and thick chest.

Mitosis. The process of cell division throughout the prenatal period.

Mixed-Longitudinal Method. A method in which individuals are selected and studied cross-sectionally and followed longitudinally for several years, thus permitting comparison of results and providing a means for validating age-related change with true developmental change.

Morality. Being in accord with standards of right conduct.

Motor. Underlying biological and mechanical factors that influence movement.

Motor Behavior. Changes in motor learning and development that embody learning factors and maturational processes associated with movement performance.

Motor Control. Study of the underlying mechanisms responsible for movement, with particular emphasis given to what is being controlled and *how* the processes governing control are organized.

Motor Development. Continuous change in motor behavior throughout the life cycle brought about by interaction among the requirements of the task, the biology of the individual, and the conditions of the environment.

Motor Fitness. The aspect of physical fitness that refers to genetically dependent characteristics that are relatively stable and related to athletic skill.

Motor Learning. A change in motor behavior resulting from practice or past experience.

Movement. The observable change in the position of any part of the body.

Movement Competence. One's ability to meet particular achievement demands in a movement situation.

Movement Concepts. Knowledge about how the body can move, using the movement framework of effort, space, and relationship awareness.

Movement Exploration Technique. An indirect teaching approach that encourages exploration.

Movement Pattern. An organized series of related movements used to perform a movement task.

Movement Skill. A fundamental movement pattern performed with accuracy, precision, and control. Accuracy is stressed and extraneous movement is limited, as in throwing a ball at a target.

Muscular Endurance. The ability of a muscle or a group of muscles to perform work repeatedly against moderate resistance.

Muscular Strength. The ability of the body to exert force.

Myelination. The development of myelin around the neurons.

N

Neuromaturational Theory. A theory of motor development that holds as its foundation that as the cortex develops it inhibits some of the functions of the subcortical layers and assumes ever-increasing neuromuscular control.

Neuromuscular Adaptation. Interaction of the central nervous system and the muscles that results in enhanced force production of the muscles.

Norm-Referenced Tests. Assessment instruments based on a statistical sampling of hundreds or even thousands of individuals.

O

Obesity. Excessive increase in the amount of stored body fat, generally considered to be at the 85th to 95th percentile of weight for height.

Objectivity. A condition when a test will yield similar results when it is administered by different testers on the same individual.

Obstetrical Medication. A series of drugs administered to the expectant mother prior to and during delivery for various purposes including pain relief and the augmentation of labor.

Olfactory Perception. The ability to receive and process information that is obtained by the sense of smell.

Ontogenetic Skills. Movement skills dependent on learning and environmental opportunities such as swimming, bicycling, and ice skating.

Osteoporosis. A disease characterized by an accelerated loss of bone mineral density.

P

Pace of Sexual Maturation. The tempo or rate of developmental change during adolescence.

Peak Height Velocity. The time during the adolescent growth spurt during which the rate of growth in height reaches its maximum.

Perceived Competence. An individual's perception of his or her level of competence for a given task.

Perception. The process by which we become aware of our surroundings through the use of one or more of our sensory modalities.

Perceptual-Motor. The process of organizing incoming information with stored information that leads to a movement response.

Perceptual-Motor Training. Remedial and readiness programs designed to promote perceptual-motor development in children.

Performance Stage. The movement skill learning stage at which the learner is further involved in refining and applying the elements of the movement task but with emphasis on using it in a specific performance situation.

Peripheral Vision. The visual field that can be seen without a change in the position of the eye.

Phases of Motor Development. The lifelong process of change in motor control seen in typical patterns of movement behavior brought about by factors within the movement task, the biology of the individual, and the conditions of the environment.

Phase-Stage Theory. A descriptive theory that contends that there are universal age periods characterized by typical behaviors that occur in phases or stages and last for arbitrary lengths of time.

Phenotype. An individual's environmental conditions that may influence his or her growth potential.

Phylogenetic Skills. Movement skills that tend to appear automatically and in a predictable sequence and are resistant to external environmental influences such as reaching, grasping and releasing, and walking, jumping, and running.

Physical Fitness. A state of well-being influenced by nutritional status, genetic makeup, and frequent participation in a variety of intense physical activities over time.

Power. The ability to perform one maximum effort in as short a period as possible; sometimes referred to as explosive strength.

Precontrol Stage. A period between the child's first and second birthday when greater control and precision are gained in movement.

Premature. Any newborn weighing under 4.5 pounds (2 kg) coupled with a gestation period of less than 37 weeks.

Presbycusis. Hearing loss associated with aging.

Primitive Postural Reflexes. A subgroup of primitive reflexes that resemble and may serve as precursors to later voluntary movements.

Primitive Survival Reflexes. A subgroup of primitive reflexes that enable the neonate to gain nourishment through involuntary searching and sucking.

Process Instruments. Assessment instruments that focus on the form, style, or mechanics used to perform the desired skill.

Product Instruments. Assessment instruments that are quantitative and focus on the outcome or result of a performance.

Proficiency Barrier. The impairment of the performance of successful specialized movement skills if mature fundamental movement skills have not been mastered.

Puberty. The developmental period that represents the beginning of sexual maturation.

Q

Qualitative Change. Changes in the process or mechanics of executing a movement pattern.

R

Rate Limiters. Constraints that tend to limit or impede developmental change.

Reaction Time. The time delay between the presentation of a stimulus and initial activation of the appropriate muscle groups to carry out a task.

Readiness. The convergence of conditions within a task, an individual, and the environment that make mastery of a particular task appropriate.

Reciprocal Interweaving. The coordinated and progressive intricate interweaving of neural mechanisms of opposing muscle systems into an increasingly mature relationship. Characteristic of

the developing child's motor behavior through *differentiation* (i.e., progression from the gross movement patterns of infancy to the more refined and functional movements of childhood and adolescence), and *integration* (i.e., bringing various opposing muscle and sensory systems into coordinated interaction with one another).

Reflexes. Involuntary, subcortically controlled movements that form the basis for the remaining three phases of motor development. Frequently classified as "primitive and postural reflexes."

Reflex Inhibition Stage. A period during an infant's first year when many of the reflexes are gradually suppressed.

Relative Sterility of Puberty. The period from the first menstrual cycle until a young female is physiologically capable of conception.

Reliability. A condition when a test will provide consistent scores from one test administration to the next.

Retirement. The cessation of a career usually occurring in middle to later adulthood.

Rhythm. The synchronous recurrence of events related in such a manner that they form recognizable patterns.

Rhythmical Stereotypies. Infant movements performed over and over that demonstrate developmental regularities as well as constancy of form and distribution.

Rudimentary Movement Abilities. The first forms of voluntary movement beginning at birth and continuing to about age 2. Maturationally determined and characterized by a highly predictable sequence of appearance.

S

Saccades. Quick movements of the eyes in which there is redirection of visual focus from one object to another.

Schema. A pattern of physical or motor action.

Screening Tests. Assessment instruments designed to provide a relatively quick and simple means for recognizing the existence of problems.

Secondary Sex Characteristics. Readily observable evidence, such as axillary and facial hair, associated with progress toward reproductive maturity.

Secular Trend. Generational changes in height, weight, and physical maturity at a given age.

Segmental Analysis. The examination of developmental changes in fundamental movement skill stages using an analysis of the separate components of a movement within a given pattern.

Self-Concept. An individual's awareness of personal characteristics, attributes, and limitations, and the ways in which these qualities are both like and unlike those of others.

Self-Confidence. An individual's belief in his or her ability to carry out a mental, physical, or emotional task.

Self-Efficacy. The conviction that one can successfully execute the behavior required to produce the desired outcome.

Self-Esteem. The value that one attaches to his or her unique characteristics, attributes, and limitations.

Senile Miosis. An age-related condition in which the pupils of older adults do not open as widely as they did in previous years, restricting the ability to respond to low levels of illumination.

Sensation. Stimuli received by the various sense modalities.

Sensitive Periods. Broad time frames for development of a specific ability or capacity that go beyond the narrow view of the critical period hypothesis.

Sexually Transmitted Diseases. A category of diseases contracted through sexual activity and that place the developing fetus at risk for a wide range of birth defects.

Skill Concepts. Knowledge of how the body should biomechanically move.

Skill Theme. A single movement skill or cluster of skills around which a specific lesson or series of lessons is grouped.

Skinfold Calipers. An instrument that measures skinfold thicknesses in an effort to determine body fat percentage.

Social Roles. The behaviors employed to fulfill a status in a given situation.

Social Status. One's perceived position within a defined group.

Societal Norms. Standards of behavior expected of all members of a given society.

Spatial Awareness. An understanding of how much space the body occupies and the ability to project the body effectively into external space.

Specialized Movement Abilities. An outgrowth of mature fundamental movement abilities in which movement becomes a tool applied to a variety of complex movement activities for daily living, recreation, and sport pursuits.

Speed. The ability to move from one point to another in the shortest time possible. Speed is the total of reaction time and movement time.

Speed-Accuracy Trade-off. The trend toward a decline in the accuracy of a movement when its speed is increased.

Sport Skill. A movement skill applied to a specific sport activity, as in pitching in softball or baseball.

Sportsmanship. Behaving in a moral fashion within a sport context.

Stability. Movement patterns that place a premium on gaining and maintaining one's equilibrium (i.e., static and dynamic balance abilities).

Static Flexibility. The range of motion achieved by a slow and steady stretch to the limits of the joints involved.

Stereopsis. The process of visually detecting depth brought about by retinal disparity between the eyes.

Stratified Random Sample. A collection of research participants, using probability theory, that attempts to provide a valid representation of a much larger group.

Successful Aging. An older adult's perception of effective and productive living often based on the characteristics of longevity, health, and life satisfaction.

T

Tactile Perception. The ability to receive and process information obtained by the sense of smell.

Tanner Stages. A universally accepted means for classifying sexual maturity.

Temporal Awareness. The acquisition of an adequate time structure within an individual.

Teratogen. Any substance that may cause the unborn child to develop in an abnormal manner.

Testosterone. The primary sex hormone associated with the tremendous gains in muscular strength seen in adolescent males.

Timing of Puberty. When developmental change occurs during the period of adolescence.

Total Body Configuration. The examination of developmental changes in fundamental movement skill stages using an analysis of movement variations incorporating the whole body.

Tracking. The ability of the eyes to attend to a moving object.

Transition Stage. The stage within the specialized movement phase that represents the first attempts to refine and combine mature movement patterns.

V

Validity. A condition when a test measures what it claims to measure.

Value. A view of what is desirable based on strong cognitive and affective components that leads to an action.

Very Low Birth Weight. A birth weight under 1,500 grams.

Visual Acuity. The ability to distinguish detail in objects. Visual acuity is both a static and a dynamic phenomenon.

Visual-Motor Coordination. The ability to visually track and make interception judgments about a moving object.

W

Within-Pattern Differences. Within a given pattern, an individual may exhibit a combination of initial, elementary, and mature elements.

Y

Young-for-Date. An infant born at the expected birth weight for gestational age but before full term (i.e., 37 weeks or less).

Z

Zygote. The human organism represented by the union of the sperm and ovum cell nuclei and its continuous growth through the first week following conception.

INDEX

Phase-stage approach, study of development, 25, 26–27, 32–35
Phenotype, meaning of, 291
Phenylketonuria (PKU), 94, 95
Phylogenetic skills, 63
Physical activity
  child growth/development, 176–178
  muscle response to, 176–177
  and self-concept development, 279–280, 281
  and socialization, 348, 349–354
Physical activity instruction
  activity concepts, 424–425
  application, 428–429
  cognitive concept learning, 423–425
  combination, 427–428
  content areas, 422–423
  critical thinking core, 423–425
  developmental approach, 420, 423–425, 429–433
  developmental skill theme, 420–421
  and effort, 424, 425
  fundamental movement phase, 430–431
  games/sports, 423
  guided-discovery method, 427
  gymnastics, 423
  and individualization, 429
  levels of movement skill learning, 423–425, 426
  movement categories, 420–422
  movement concepts, 424
  movement exploration technique, 426–427
  refined performance, 429
  and relationships, 424, 425
  rhythm/dance, 423
  self-testing, 423
  skill concepts, 424
  skill themes, 420–422
  and space, 424, 425
  specialized movement phase, 431–433
Physical development
  adolescence, 291–296

  early childhood, 170–171
  late childhood, 173–174
Physical fitness
  definition of, 73, 239
  motor fitness, 248–253
  training for. *See* Fitness training
Physical fitness assessment (adolescents)
  aerobic endurance, 325–327, 328
  assessment methods, 325
  assessment problems, 324
  balance, 342–343
  body composition, 326, 332–336
  flexibility, 326, 331–332, 333
  jumping for distance, 338–340, 341
  muscular strength/endurance, 326, 327, 329–331, 332
  running speed, 337–338, 339
  sampling methods, 324, 325
  throwing for distance, 341–342
Physical fitness assessment (children), 238–239
  aerobic endurance, 239–241
  assessment instruments, 238
  assessment problem, 238–239
  body composition, 243–244
  flexibility, 242–243
  muscular endurance, 242
  muscular strength, 241–242
Physique, classification of, 177
Piaget's theory, 24, 25, 27, 32, 35–39, 120
  accommodation, 35–36
  adaptation, 35
  assimilation, 36–37
  chronological age in, 25
  cognitive development, 25, 27, 36, 168, 264, 267, 268
  schema, 37
Pictorial Scale of Perceived Competence and Social Acceptance for Young Children, 277
Plantar grasp reflex, 125, 126
Play
  early childhood, 167–170
  and self-concept, 282

Posture
  postural control and aging, 386–388
  types of postures, 188
  upright, infant development, 137
Power, 252–253
  measurement of, 252
Practice level, movement learning, 317, 318
Precontrol stage, and infant development, 48, 136
Pregnancy. *See also* Prenatal development
  birth process, 102–104
  exercise during, 101–102
  high-risk pregnancies, 83, 85
  prenatal testing, 100–101
  teenage pregnancy, 100
Prematurity, 64, 67–68
  long-term effects of, 68, 69
Prenatal development, 83
  and alcohol use, 90–92
  beginning of, 92
  and chemical pollutants, 96–97
  chromosomal abnormalities, 92–93
  and cigarette smoking, 90, 92
  and cytomegalovirus (CMV), 98
  and diabetes, 88–89, 98
  drug effects, 86–90
  environmental factors, 96–97
  exercise effects, 101–102
  genetic defects, 93–96
  hereditary factors, 92–96
  high-risk pregnancy, factors in, 83, 85
  and hormonal and chemical imbalances, 98
  and malnourishment, 86
  and malnutrition, 83, 85–86
  and maternal infections, 98
  prenatal diagnosis and treatment, 100–101
  and radiation exposure, 96
  Rh incompatibility, 99
  and rubella, 98, 99
  and sexually transmitted diseases, 97–98
  stress effects, 99–100